Lecture Notes in Computer Science 16420

Founding Editors

Gerhard Goos
Juris Hartmanis

The series Lecture Notes in Computer Science (LNCS), including its subseries Lecture Notes in Artificial Intelligence (LNAI) and Lecture Notes in Bioinformatics (LNBI), has established itself as a medium for the publication of new developments in computer science and information technology research, teaching, and education.

LNCS enjoys close cooperation with the computer science R & D community, the series counts many renowned academics among its volume editors and paper authors, and collaborates with prestigious societies. Its mission is to serve this international community by providing an invaluable service, mainly focused on the publication of conference and workshop proceedings and postproceedings. LNCS commenced publication in 1973.

Bapi Chatterjee · Kishore Kothapalli ·
Neeraj Mittal · Arul Murugan Natarajan ·
Dinesh Singh

Editors

Distributed Computing and Intelligent Technology

22nd International Conference, ICDCIT 2026
Bhubaneswar, India, January 16–19, 2026
Proceedings

 Springer

Editors
Bapi Chatterjee
IIIT Delhi
New Delhi, Delhi, India

Kishore Kothapalli
IIIT Hyderabad
Hyderabad, Telangana, India

Neeraj Mittal
University of Texas at Dallas
Dallas, TX, USA

Arul Murugan Natarajan
IIIT Delhi
Delhi, Delhi, India

Dinesh Singh
IIT Mandi
Mandi, Himachal Pradesh, India

ISSN 0302-9743   ISSN 1611-3349 (electronic)
Lecture Notes in Computer Science
ISBN 978-3-032-16631-9   ISBN 978-3-032-16632-6 (eBook)
https://doi.org/10.1007/978-3-032-16632-6

Preface

This volume contains the papers selected for presentation at the 22nd International Conference on Distributed Computing and Intelligent Technology (ICDCIT 2026), held during January 16–19, 2026, at Kalinga Institute of Industrial Technology (KIIT), Bhubaneswar, India.

Starting from its first edition in 2004, the ICDCIT conference series has evolved into an annual conference of international repute, serving as a global platform for computer science researchers to exchange research results and ideas on the foundations and applications of distributed computing and intelligent technologies. Accordingly, the research papers published at ICDCIT are organized into Distributed Computing (DC) and Intelligent Technologies (IT) tracks. The DC track solicits original research papers that contribute to the foundations and applications of distributed computing, whereas the IT track solicits original research papers that contribute to the foundations and applications of Intelligent Technologies.

ICDCIT 2026 was the 22nd meeting in the series. In its 22nd edition, considering the current invigorated focus of the scientific community on AI-enabled accelerated scientific discoveries, in addition to the DC and IT tracks, we introduced a new dedicated track on Artificial Intelligence (AI) for Science (AI4Sc). The AI4Sc track solicits original research papers that contribute to AI techniques for scientific, medical, and engineering applications. ICDCIT 2026 aimed to provide students and young researchers with opportunities to be exposed to the latest research directions in distributed computing, intelligent technology, and artificial intelligence for scientific applications.

This year, we received 120 full-paper submissions: 32 papers in the DC track, 70 papers in the IT track, and 18 papers in the AI4Sc track. Each submission considered for publication was reviewed by at least three members of the PC. External reviewers outside of the PC also contributed to the review process where needed. Based on the reviews, the PC decided to accept 34 papers for presentation at the conference, with an acceptance rate of 28%. The DC track PC accepted 11 papers, with an acceptance rate of 34%. The IT track PC accepted 15 papers, with an acceptance rate of 21%. The AI4Sc track PC accepted 8 papers, with an acceptance rate of 44%. Each accepted paper is a full regular paper.

ICDCIT 2026 adopted a double-blind review process to help PC members and external reviewers come to a judgment about each submitted paper without any possible bias. Additionally, each paper that was in conflict with a chair/PC member was reviewed by another chair/PC member who had no conflict with the paper.

We would like to express our gratitude to all the researchers who submitted their work to the conference. Our special thanks go to all colleagues who served on the PC, as well as the external reviewers, who generously offered their expertise and time, which helped us select the papers and prepare the strong conference program.

ICDCIT 2026 also awarded a best paper in each track. The awards were announced during the conference. The best paper awardees in each track received a total of INR 50,000. We congratulate the authors of the selected papers for their outstanding research.

We were fortunate to have six distinguished keynote speakers: Swati Biswas (University of Texas at Dallas, USA), Pawan Goyal (Indian Institute of Technology Kharagpur, India), Salil Kanhere (University of New South Wales, Australia), Sandeep Kulkarni (Michigan State University, USA), Yogesh Simmhan (Indian Institute of Science, India), and Deva Priyakumar U. (International Institute of Information Technology Hyderabad, India). Their talks provided us with a unique opportunity to hear research advances in various fields of distributed computing, intelligent technologies, and artificial intelligence for science from leaders in their respective fields.

We would like to express our gratitude to the local organizing committee, who worked diligently to make this conference a success, particularly our organizing chair, Satarupa Mohanty. We would also like to thank the organizers of the satellite events, as well as the student volunteers. The School of Computer Engineering at KIIT, the host of the conference, provided various support and facilities to organize the conference and its associated events.

Finally, we would like to express our gratitude to KIIT for the institutional and financial support we received, for which we are indebted. We express our appreciation to all the Steering Committee members: Partha Sarathi Mandal, Anisur Rahaman Molla, Sathya Peri, and Gokarna P. Sharma, whose counsel we frequently relied on. We would also like to thank the Advisory Committee members: Saranjit Singh, D.N. Dwivedy, Jnyana Ranjan Mohanty, Raj Bhatnagar, Rajkumar Buyya, Diganta Goswami, Biswajit Sahoo, Samaresh Mishra, Stéphane Devismes, and Krishnendu Mukhopadhyay. Thanks are also due to the faculty members and staff of the School of Computer Engineering at KIIT for their timely support.

January 2026

Bapi Chatterjee
Kishore Kothapalli
Neeraj Mittal
Arul Murugan Natarajan
Dinesh Singh

Organization

General Chairs

Bapi Chatterjee	Indraprastha Institute of Information Technology Delhi, India
Neeraj Mittal	University of Texas, Dallas, USA

Program Chairs

Kishore Kothapalli	International Institute of Information Technology, Hyderabad, India
N. Arul Murugan	Indraprastha Institute of Information Technology Delhi, India
Dinesh Singh	Indian Institute of Technology Mandi, India

Program Committee

Konjengbam Anand	Indian Institute of Technology Dharwad, India
N. Arul Murugan	Indraprastha Institute of Information Technology Delhi, India
Subhasis Bhattacharjee	Synopsys Pvt. Ltd., India
Bhavesh Borisaniya	Shantilal Shah Engineering College, India
Suchetana Chakraborty	Indian Institutue of Technology Jodhpur, India
Sadu Chiranjeevi	Indian Institute of Technology Guwahati, India
Jorge Cobb	University of Texas at Dallas, USA
Kunal Dahiya	Indian Institute of Technology Delhi, India
Manisha Dubey	University of Manchester, UK
Arindam Ghosh	National Institute of Science Education and Research, India
Debashree Ghosh	Indian Association for the Cultivation of Science, India
Mukesh Giluka Giluka	Jawaharlal Nehru University, India
Barun Gorain	Indian Institute of Technology Bhilai, India
Nikhil Hegde	Indian Institute of Technology Dhanbad, India
Anish Hirwe	Indian Institute of Technology Palakkad
Earnest Paul Ijjina	National Institute of Technology Warangal, India

Vishwesh Jatala	Indian Institute of Technology Bhilai, India
Kavita Joshi	CSIR National Chemical Laboratory, India
Parimala Kancharla	Indian Institute of Technology Mandi, India
Kishore Kothapalli	International Institute of Information Technology, Hyderabad, India
Nagendra Kumar	Indian Institute of Technology Indore, India
Rajnish Kumar	Indian Institute of Technology (BHU) Varanasi, India
Vibhor Kumar	Indraprastha Institute of Information Technology Delhi, India
Vivek Kumar	Indraprastha Institute of Information Technology Delhi, India
Sweta Kumari	Maulana Azad National Institute of Technology, Bhopal, India
Pooja Louhan	Ganga Singh College, Jai Prakash University, India
Hridoy Jyoti Mahanta	CSIR North East Institute of Science and Technology, India
Partha Sarathi Mandal	Indian Institute of Technology Guwahati, India
Stefano Markidis	KTH Royal Institute of Technology, Sweden
Chirag Modi	National Institute of Technology Surat, India
Ayan Mondal	Indian Institute of Technology Indore, India
Anish Mukherjee	University of Liverpool, UK
Arnab Mukherjee	Indian Institute of Science Education and Research Pune, India
Selvaraman Nagamani	CSIR - North East Institute of Science and Technology, India
C. Nagaraju	Indian Institute of Technology Hyderabad, India
Jayashree Nagesh	Institute of Bioinformatics and Applied Biotechnology, India
Shreyas Pai	Indian Institute of Technology Madras, India
Amrit Pal	Vellore Institute of Technology Chennai, India
Ramakrishnan Parthasarathi	CSIR-Indian Institute of Toxicology Research
Debasish Pattanayak	Indian Institute of Technology Indore, India
Nazil Perveen	Shiv Nadar University, India
Lipsa Priyadarsinee	CSIR-NEIST, India
Shyam Rajagopalan	Institute of Bioinformatics and Applied Biotechnology, India
Gadhamsetty Ramakrishna	Indian Institute of Technology Tirupati, India
Udai Pratap Rao	National Institute of Technology Patna, India
Arjun Ray	Indraprastha Institute of Technology Delhi, India
Debaditya Roy	Indian Institute of Technology Kharagpur, India

Anshu S. Anand	Indian Institute of Information Technology Allahabad, India
Abhinandan S. Prasad	Indian Institute of Technology Ropar, India
Rohit Saluja	Indian Institute of Technology Mandi, India
Rakesh Sanodiya	Indian Institute of Information Technology, Design and Manufacturing, Jabalpur, India
Gokarna Sharma	Kent State University, USA
Radhe Shyam Sharma	Indian Institute of Technology Mandi, India
Subhajit Sidhanta	Indian Institute of Technology Kharagpur, India
Dinesh Singh	Indian Institute of Technology Mandi, India
Sanjeev Singh	Alagappa University, India
Sneha Singh	Indian Institute of Technology Mandi, India
Archit Somani	Shiv Nadar University, India
M. Srinivas	National Institute of Technology Warangal, India
Balasubramanian Sundaram	Jawaharlal Nehru Centre for Advanced Scientific Research, India
Praveen Tammana	Indian Institute of Technology Hyderabad, India
Hardik Tankaria	Independent Researcher, India
Chalavadi Vishnu	Indian Institute of Technology Tirupati, India
Awaneesh Kumar Yadav	Indian Institute of Technology Mandi, India
Robert Zalesny	Wrocław Centre for Networking and Supercomputing, Poland

Additional Reviewers

Bangde, Yashwant	Kumar, Sachin
Bhatt, Shagun	Kumar, Shashwat
Bhavani, Samineni	Maan, Sumit
Chalavadi, Vishnu	Mamtani, Sumit
Chandola, Shrey	Pandit, Supantha
Chillara, Suryajith	Pasquale, Marco
Das, Kousik	Paul, Prateek
Dasgaonkar, Yogesh	Pennati, Luca
Dhar, Amit Kumar	Prasad, Ravi
Dutt, Vandita	Priyadarshini, Lipsa
Ghosh, Sagnik	R. Manikandan
Giluka, Mukesh Giluka	Rajkumar, Krishnan
Grover, Radhika	Saini, Tarun
Jamwal, Anandita	Sarkar, Soujatya
Kodali, Siva Sairam Prasad	Sarode, Rashmi P.
Kumar, Anant	Sharma, Jaya
Kumar, Manish	Sharma, Nandani

Shrivastava, Pragati
Singh, Abhishek
Singh, Kajal
Singh, Krishna
Singh, Peeyush Kumar
Srivastava, Rohit
Thakur, Mayank

Varma, Girish
Verma, Rajat
Verma, Yashaswi
Vishwakarma, Sumit Kumar
Yadav, Anshul
Åsgrim, Erik

Contents

Formalisms and Fault-Tolerance

Computer Vision

NLP and LLMs

AI for Security

Artificial Intelligence

AI for Medical Diagnostics

AI for Health and Bioinformatics

AI for Physics

Dynamic and Temporal Graph Algorithms

When Agents are Powerful: Black Hole Search in Time-Varying Graphs

Tanvir Kaur[ID] and Ashish Saxena[✉][ID]

Indian Institute of Technology Ropar, Rupnagar 140001, Punjab, India
{tanvir.20maz0001,ashish.21maz0004}@iitrpr.ac.in

Abstract. A black hole is a harmful node in a graph that destroys any resource entering it, making its identification a critical task. In the *Black Hole Search (BHS)* problem, a team of agents operates on a graph G with the objective that at least one agent must survive and correctly identify an edge incident to the black hole. Prior work has addressed BHS in arbitrary dynamic graphs under the restrictive *face-to-face* communication, where agents can exchange information only when co-located. In this work, we strengthen the capabilities of agents in two ways: (i) *global communication*, and (ii) *1-hop visibility*. These enhancements lead to more efficient solutions for the BHS problem in dynamic graphs.

Keywords: Dynamic Graphs · Black Hole Search · Mobile Agents · Distributed Algorithms · Deterministic Algorithms

1   Introduction

In many distributed systems, a network cannot be assumed to be fully reliable. Real-world systems are prone to faults: agents may crash, communication links may intermittently fail, or nodes may behave maliciously, including corrupting data or destroying visiting agents. One particularly dangerous fault is a *hostile node* that destroys any agent entering into it, without leaving any trace of its destruction. Such a node (denoted with v_{BH}) is called a *black hole*. In the literature, two variants of the *Black Hole Search (BHS)* problem have been studied: (i) at least one agent must survive and produce a map of the network indicating all edges leading to v_{BH}, and (ii) at least one agent must survive and learn *at least one* edge that leads to v_{BH}. The BHS problem has been extensively studied on static graphs [2,3].

Recently, researchers have begun to study fundamental distributed problems like exploration [4], dispersion [5], and gathering [6] in *dynamic graphs*, which better reflect real-world networks. In the synchronous setting, where time is considered in discrete rounds, a dynamic graph $\mathcal{G}$ is modeled as a sequence of static graphs $\mathcal{G}_0, \mathcal{G}_1, \mathcal{G}_2, \ldots$, where $\mathcal{G}_r$ is the graph at round r. This evolving sequence is called a *time-evolving graph* or *dynamic graph*.

A full version of this paper, including all proofs, is available as a preprint in [1].

B. Chatterjee et al. (Eds.): ICDCIT 2026, LNCS 16420, pp. 3–18, 2026.
https://doi.org/10.1007/978-3-032-16632-6_1

A natural question that arises is whether the first variant of the Black Hole Search (BHS) problem is solvable in dynamic graphs. The answer is negative: since an edge leading to node v_{BH} may not be present in every round $r \geq 0$, it is impossible to guarantee the identification of all such edges. Consequently, only the second variant of the BHS problem remains meaningful in dynamic graphs. This is the variant addressed in existing literature in dynamic graphs [7,8]. While several results have been established for restricted classes of dynamic graphs, only one study considers the case of *general dynamic graphs* [8]. In that work, it is ensured that at least one agent reaches a neighbour of v_{BH} and identifies a port leading to v_{BH}. In this paper, we study the following problem.

Definition 1. *A black hole is said to be found if at least one agent reaches a neighbour of v_{BH}, say v, and identifies a port p from node v that leads to v_{BH}.*

This definition is stronger than the existing one, as it requires an agent to physically reach a neighbour v of node v_{BH}, and identify the specific port at v that leads to v_{BH}. The <u>motivation</u> behind this definition: information written on a whiteboard can be tampered with or erased by the adversary. If that happens, future agents entering the network might unknowingly fall into node v_{BH} and die. To prevent this, we place a *checkpoint agent* at v. This agent does not move; it serves as a persistent witness that can reliably inform others about the dangerous port.

Most previous works on the BHS problem assume the *face-to-face* (f-2-f), where agents can communicate only when located at the same node [7–10]. This restriction limits coordination and often increases the number of agents or the time required to solve the problem. In contrast, we study the BHS problem under two stronger models: (i) the *global communication model*, where agents can communicate regardless of their positions, and (ii) the *1-hop visibility model*, where each agent can observe its one-hop neighbourhood, including the presence of agents at neighbouring nodes. Although these models provide more power than f-2-f communication, they also introduce new challenges. For instance, in the global communication model, agents can talk to each other but lack knowledge of the network's structure, so they cannot determine how to physically reach one another. The <u>motivation</u> for this assumption is to narrow the gap in the number of agents required for solving the 1-BHS problem. To the best of our knowledge, this is the first study of the BHS problem under models beyond f-2-f communication. In the next section, we give a detailed model description and the problem definition.

1.1   Model and the Problem

Dynamic Graph Model: A dynamic network is modeled as a *time-varying graph (TVG)*, denoted by $\mathcal{G} = (V, E, T, \rho)$, where V is a set of nodes, E is a set of edges, T is the temporal domain, and $\rho : E \times T \rightarrow \{0,1\}$ is the presence function, which indicates whether a given edge is available at a given time. The static graph $G = (V, E)$ is referred to as the underlying graph (or footprint) of the TVG $\mathcal{G}$, where $|V| = n$ and $|E| = m$. For a node $v \in V$, let $E(v) \subseteq E$ denote the set of edges incident on v in the footprint. The degree of node v is defined as $\deg(v) = |E(v)|$. Nodes in V are anonymous. Each node is equipped with storage, and each edge incident to a node v is locally labeled with a port number. This labeling is defined by a bijective function $\lambda_v : E(v) \to \{0, \ldots, \delta_v - 1\}$, which assigns a distinct label to each incident edge of v. Assuming that the time is discrete, the TVG $\mathcal{G}$ can be viewed as a sequence of static graphs $\mathcal{S}_{\mathcal{G}} = \mathcal{G}_0, \mathcal{G}_1, \ldots, \mathcal{G}_r, \ldots$, where each $\mathcal{G}_r = (V, E_r)$ denotes the snapshot of $\mathcal{G}$ at round r, with $E_r = \{e \in E \mid \rho(e, r) = 1\}$. The set of edges not present at time r is denoted by $\overline{E}_r = E \setminus E_r \subseteq E$. There is a node v_{BH} in G which is a black hole, and its degree is denoted by δ_{BH}. A node that is not a black hole, we call it a <u>safe node</u>. Dynamic graphs can be classified based on how their topological changes affect connectivity. One well-known class of dynamic graphs guarantees connectivity at every round, rather than over time. A commonly used restriction is 1-interval connectivity, and a further refinement is its bounded variant.

Definition 2. *(ℓ-bounded 1-interval connectivity) A dynamic graph $\mathcal{G}$ is 1-interval connected (or always connected) if every snapshot $\mathcal{G}_r \in \mathcal{S}_{\mathcal{G}}$ is connected. Furthermore, $\mathcal{G}$ is said to be ℓ-bounded 1-interval connected if it is always connected and $|\overline{E}_r| \leq \ell$.*

Agent: We consider k agents to be present arbitrarily at safe nodes of the graph G in the initial configuration. Each agent has a unique identifier assigned from the range $[1, n^c]$, where c is a constant. Each agent knows its ID but is unaware of the other agents' IDs. Agents are not aware of the values of n, k, or c unless stated otherwise. The agents are equipped with memory. An agent residing at a node, say v, in round r knows $\deg(v)$ in the footprint G and all associated ports corresponding to node v in G; however, the agent does not understand if any incident edge of node v is missing in $\mathcal{G}$ in round t. To be more precise, agent a_i currently at node v at round r does not know the value of $\rho(e_v, r)$, where e_v is an edge incident at node v. Such a model has been considered in [4].

Communication Model: We consider two communication models: (i) face-to-face (f-2-f) communication [11], meaning agents can only communicate if they are co-located at the same node, and (ii) global communication [5], allowing agents to exchange messages regardless of their positions in the network.

Visibility Model: We use three types of visibility models: 0-hop visibility, 1-hop visibility and full visibility. In the 0-hop visibility [11], an agent at a node $v \in \mathcal{G}$ can see the IDs of agents present at v in round r, as well as the port numbers at v, but nothing beyond that. In the 1-hop visibility model [12], an agent a_i at node v can also see all neighbors of v, including the IDs of agents (if any) at those neighboring nodes. Let e_v be an edge incident to node v. In the 0-hop visibility model, agents cannot determine the value of $\rho(e_v, r)$ at the beginning of round r. In contrast, under the 1-hop visibility model, they can determine this value at the beginning of round r. In full visibility, at round r, the agent can see $\mathcal{G}_r$ as well as agents' positions in $\mathcal{G}_r$.

The algorithm runs in synchronous rounds. In each round t, an agent a_i performs one *Communicate-Compute-Move* (CCM) cycle as follows:

- **Communicate:** Agent a_i at node v_i can communicate with other agents a_j present at the same node v_i or present at any different node v_j, depending on the communication model used. The agent also understands whether it had a successful or an unsuccessful move in the last round.
- **Compute:** Based on the information the agent has, the agent computes the port through which it will move or decides not to move at all.
- **Move:** Agent moves via the computed port or stays at its current node.

Problem 1. **(1-BHS)** Let $\mathcal{G}$ be a 1-bounded 1-interval connected dynamic graph. Suppose k agents are initially placed at safe nodes of G. The 1-BHS problem is said to be solved if at least one agent is guaranteed to reach a neighbour, say v, of node v_{BH} and identify a port that from node v leads to v_{BH}.

1.2   Related Work

The BHS problem was first introduced by Dobrev et al. [3]. In this work, the authors consider static, arbitrary graphs and focus on generic solutions. They also consider the asynchronous model, i.e., every action taken by the agents requires a finite but unpredictable time. They analyse the number of agents required to solve the problem and also the conditions for their existence. Furthermore, the problem of BHS on static graphs is extensively studied [3,13–16].

BHS on dynamic graphs was first studied by Di Luna et al. [9]. They studied the problem on dynamic rings, and their objective is that at least one agent survives and learns at least one edge associated with v_{BH}. Later, this problem is studied in two graph classes: cactus [10], and tori [7]. Recently, the problem of BHS has been studied on arbitrary graphs in [8]. The authors in [8] provide impossibility results for both 1-BHS and f-BHS.[1] They prove the impossibility of solving 1-BHS with $2\delta_{BH}$ many agents arbitrarily placed on safe nodes of G (arbitrary configuration), provided that the agents have $O(\log n)$ memory and the nodes have a whiteboard of $O(\log \delta_v)$ storage. They also provide an algorithm to solve 1-BHS with 9 agents that are co-located at a safe node of G (rooted configuration) in $O(|E|^2)$ time. For their algorithm, the agents require $O(\log n)$ memory, and each node is equipped with a whiteboard of storage $O(\log n)$. In this work, we extend the study of the 1-BHS problem on arbitrary graphs by equipping the agents with more powerful capabilities. We present optimal results with respect to the number of agents required to solve the problem. Refer to Table 1 to see the results of [8] and our results in this work.

---

[1] In the f-BHS problem, $\mathcal{G}$ is an f-bounded 1-interval connected dynamic graph.

1.3 Our Contribution

In this work, we establish the following four results:

1. It is impossible for three agents starting from the rooted configuration to solve
   the 1-BHS problem, even if the agents have full visibility, global communication, infinite memory, and the nodes have infinite storage (Theorem 1).

Table 1. Summary of existing results on general graphs and our contributions. Here,
and IC denotes the initial configuration.

Capability	IC	Problem	k	Node storage	Agent memory	Time complexity
f-2-f Comm, 0-hop visibility [8]	Rooted	1-BHS	9	$O(\log n)$	$O(\log n)$	$O(m^2)$
Global Comm, full visibility (This work)	Rooted	1-BHS	3	Infinite	Infinite	Impossible
f-2-f Comm, 1-hop visibility (This work)	Rooted	1-BHS	4	$O(\log n)$	$O(\log n)$	$O(m^2)$
Global Comm, full visibility (This work)	Scattered	1-BHS	$\delta_{BH} + 1$	Infinite	Infinite	Impossible
Global Comm, 0-hop visibility (This work)	Scattered	1-BHS	$\delta_{BH} + 2$	$O(\log n)$	$O(\log n)$	$O(\delta_{BH} \cdot m^2)$

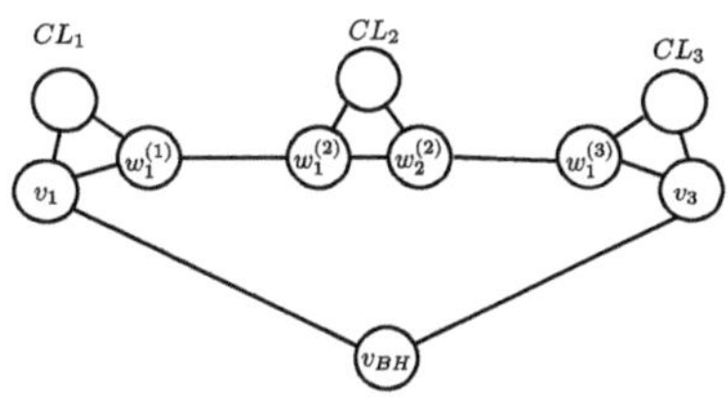

Fig. 1. The construction of graph G for $n = 10$.

2. It is impossible for $\delta_{BH} + 1$ agents, starting from a scattered configuration,
   to solve the 1-BHS problem even with full visibility, global communication,
   infinite memory, and infinite node storage (Theorem 2).
3. We design an algorithm that solves 1-BHS using four agents starting from a
   rooted configuration, where each agent has 1-hop visibility, f-2-f communication and $O(\log n)$ memory, and each node has $O(\log n)$ storage (Theorem 3).
4. We design an algorithm that solves 1-BHS using $\delta_{BH} + 2$ agents starting from
   any configuration, where each agent has global communication, 0-hop visibility and $O(\log n)$ memory, and each node has $O(\log n)$ storage (Theorem 4).

2 Impossibility Results

In this section, we present the impossibility results based on the initial configuration of agents: (i) co-located agents and (ii) scattered agents.

Theorem 1. *It is impossible for 3 agents that are co-located at a safe node of
the graph G with n (≥ 10) nodes to solve the problem of 1-BHS even if the
agents have full visibility, global communication and infinite memory, and the
nodes have infinite storage.*

Proof. Let the size of the graph G be n, and without loss of generality, assume $n - 1 = p^2$ for some integer p. Construct G as follows: there are p cliques $CL_1, CL_2, \ldots, CL_p$, each of size p, and an additional node v_{BH} representing a black hole. Let $v_1 \in CL_1$, $v_p \in CL_p$, and add edges $e = (v_{BH}, v_1)$, $e' = (v_{BH}, v_p)$. For interconnecting the cliques, define connector nodes as follows: let $w_1^{(1)} \in CL_1$ with $w_1^{(1)} \neq v_1$; for $2 \leq i \leq p - 1$, let $w_1^{(i)}, w_2^{(i)} \in CL_i$; and let $w_1^{(p)} \in CL_p$ with $w_1^{(p)} \neq v_p$. Define edges $e_1 = (w_1^{(1)}, w_1^{(2)})$, $e_i = (w_2^{(i)}, w_1^{(i+1)})$ for $2 \leq i \leq p - 2$, and $e_{p-1} = (w_2^{(p-1)}, w_1^{(p)})$. Refer Fig. 1 for $n = 10$.

Assume G is the footprint graph, and all three agents start at a node in CL_1. The adversary can remove at most one edge per round and uses the following strategy: if two or more agents are in CL_1, the adversary removes edge e; if two or more agents are in CL_p, the adversary removes edge e'. This ensures that when agents are near CL_1, access to v_{BH} via e is blocked, and similarly, access via e' is blocked when they are near CL_p.

Agents can access v_{BH} only in the following two cases: (1) agent a_i, $i \in \{1, 2, 3\}$, is in CL_1 while $\{a_1, a_2, a_3\} \setminus \{a_i\}$ are in CL_j for $2 \leq j \leq p$; or (2) agent a_i, $i \in \{1, 2, 3\}$, is in CL_p while $\{a_1, a_2, a_3\} \setminus \{a_i\}$ are in CL_j for $1 \leq j \leq p-1$. In Case 1, without loss of generality, let a_1 move to v_{BH} at round t via edge e and is destroyed. At round $t_1 \geq t$, if a_2 or a_3 is at node $w_1^{(2)}$, the adversary deletes edge e_1, preventing access to CL_1. Thus, the remaining agents cannot reach the neighbour of v_{BH} in CL_1. The only remaining possibility is to approach v_{BH} via edge e', but if both agents move to CL_p, the adversary deletes e', and they can never observe which port leads to v_{BH}. Without loss of generality, assume that $a_2 \in CL_j$ for $2 \leq j \leq p-1$ and $a_3 \in CL_p$. If a_3 moves via edge e' at round t' and dies, then at any round $t \geq t'$, if a_2 is at $w_2^{(p-1)}$, the adversary deletes e_{p-1}, and if a_2 is at $w_1^{(2)}$, it deletes e_1. In this way, a_2 is confined within $CL_2, \ldots, CL_{p-1}$ and never reaches a neighbor of v_{BH}. Note that the above argument is valid if there are at least three cliques (i.e., $p \geq 3$). Therefore, $n \geq 10$ as $n - 1 = p^2$.

The argument for Case 2 is analogous to Case 1. Hence, under this adversary strategy, no agent can reach a neighbour of v_{BH} and identify the port leading to it. The argument holds regardless of the agents' memory, the nodes' storage, or the use of full visibility or global communication. This completes the proof. □

Theorem 2. *($n \geq 82$) It is impossible for $\delta_{BH} + 1$ agents, scattered at the safe nodes of the graph, to solve the 1-BHS problem even if agents have full visibility, global communication, infinite memory, and the nodes have infinite storage.*

3   Algorithm Using 1-Hop Visibility

In this section, we provide an algorithm that solves the problem of 1-BHS using 4 agents that are initially present at a single node and have 1-hop visibility, and are equipped with f-2-f communication. We use the idea from [17] where the authors ensure the dispersion of agents on a time-varying graph despite the presence of dynamic edges. They use depth-first search (DFS) traversal by mobile agents. For the sake of completeness, we begin with providing a high-level idea of the DFS traversal by mobile agents. Depth-First Search (DFS) operates in two fundamental states: *explore* and *backtrack*. Note that an agent a_i requires some parameters to execute the DFS algorithm. The parameter $a_i.ID$ stores the ID of agent a_i. The parameter *state* stores the state the agent is currently working in. It can take the value either *explore* or *backtrack*. The parameter *prt_in* stores the port used by the agent to enter into the current node, and the parameter *prt_out* stores the port that will be used by the agent to exit from the current node. The agent begins in the *explore* state. In each state at the current node v, the movement of agents is described in Algorithm 1. Any static graph G with m edges can be explored by an agent within $4m$ rounds using DFS.

Algorithm 1: Depth-First Search by an agent a_i

---

1   **if** $a_i.state = explore$ **then**
2   **if** *the current node v is already visited by a_i* **then**
3   set $a_i.prt\_out = a_i.prt\_in$ and move through $a_i.prt\_out$
4   **else**
5   mark the current node v as visited node
6   set $a_i.prt\_out = (a_i.prt\_in + 1) \mod deg(v)$
7   **if** $a_i.prt_out = $ *value of port used to enter into v for the first time* **then**
8   set $a_i.state = backtrack$ and move through $a_i.prt\_out$
9   **else**
10   move through $a_i.prt\_out$
11 **else if** $a_i.state = backtrack$ **then**
12   set $a_i.prt\_out = (a_i.prt\_in + 1) \mod deg(v)$
13   **if** $a_i.prt_out = $ *value of port used to enter into v for the first time* **then**
14   set $a_i.state = backtrack$ and move through $a_i.prt\_out$
15   **else**
16   set $a_i.state = explore$ and move through $a_i.prt\_out$

In [17], the authors achieve dispersion by dividing the group of agents into two groups when a missing edge is encountered for the first time. After that, both groups run their DFSs separately. Based on their idea, one group never deviates from its original path of DFS. Here, the original path of DFS means the path that would have been executed by the agent if there were no missing edges. The other group, on the other hand, deviates after some finite waiting period. We use a similar idea that solves 1-BHS using 4 agents when the agents have one-hop visibility. Now we proceed with a detailed description of our algorithm.

Let $a_1, a_2, a_3,$ and a_4 be four agents initially positioned at a node v_r of the graph. These agents are divided into two groups, G_1 and G_2. In particular, $G_1 = \{a_1, a_2\}$, where a_1 is the leader, denoted by L_{G_1}, and a_2 is the helper, denoted by H_{G_1}. Similarly, $G_2 = \{a_3, a_4\}$, where a_3 is the leader (L_{G_2}) and a_4 is the helper (H_{G_2}). Initially, both G_1 and G_2 are located at v_r, from which they begin their DFS traversal. Since they start from the same root, both groups compute the same outgoing port, say p, to proceed. However, both groups cannot simultaneously traverse through the same port, as the adjacent node may be v_{BH}. To address this, only H_{G_2} probes the port p in round t. In round $t + 1$, by means of one-hop visibility, both G_1 and L_{G_2} confirm whether the adjacent node is safe, if the edge corresponding to port p is available. If the node is safe, then by the end of round $t + 1$, G_1 and L_{G_2} also traverse through port p. This type of movement is referred to as cautious movement, which is utilized in several existing works on BHS. Throughout the process, both groups update their DFS information on the whiteboard. Now suppose that G_1 and G_2 are located at a node u and must traverse through a port p' corresponding to an edge that is temporarily missing. In such a case, G_1 waits at u until the edge reappears. In contrast, G_2 may disregard this edge depending on the context. If both agents of G_2 are together and the missing edge through p' is to be explored, then G_2 skips this edge and continues its traversal. However, if the missing edge through p' is required for backtracking, then G_2 initiates a new DFS traversal from its current position. Since all movements are carried out cautiously, the dynamic behavior of the edges may necessitate changes in group composition. Nevertheless, agent a_1 retains its fixed role as L_{G_1} and never deviates from its designated DFS path. Both the groups G_1 and G_2 begin their DFS traversal cautiously. The information corresponding to the leader of each group is written on the whiteboard. The parameters maintained on the whiteboard by the groups are as follows:

- $wb_v(G_1).(parent)$: This parameter stores the information regarding node v w.r.t. the DFS traversal of the leader of G_1. The variable $parent$ stores the port used by the leader of the group G_1 to visit node v for the first time. Initially, $wb_v(G_1).(parent) = -1$.
- $wb_v(G_2).(parent, dfs\_label)$: It stores the information regarding node v w.r.t. the DFS traversal of the leader of G_2. The variable $parent$ stores the port used by the leader of group G_2 to visit node v for the first time. The variable dfs_label stores the number of DFS being run by G_2. Initially, $wb_v(G_2).(parent, dfs\_label) = (-1, 1)$.

Note that the group G_1 does not need to maintain dfs_label as it never restarts its DFS. It runs only a single DFS, and the leader of G_1 always stays at its original path of its DFS. Initially, all the agents are at v_r. The leaders of both the groups write on the whiteboard $wb_v(G_1).(parent) = -1$ and $wb_v(G_2).(parent, dfs\_label) = (-1, 1)$. Both groups proceed with their DFS traversal cautiously unless they encounter a missing edge. Recall that, with moving cautiously, we mean that the helper moves first through the computed port (for the DFS traversal of its respective group). If the movement by this helper is successful, the edge corresponding to this computed port is present, and the helper is alive (at the adjacent node), then the leader performs its movement through this computed port. When a missing edge is encountered for the first time, G_2 will not wait for the missing edge to reappear and proceed. There are several cases, and we deal with each as follows.

(I) Both L_{G_1} and H_{G_1} are present at a node v and have *state=explore*:
Let the computed *prt_out* value by G_1 be p. Now there are two cases: (i) the
edge corresponding to port p is present, or (ii) it is not present. If the edge
corresponding to port p is present, it does the following. If it finds only L_{G_2} at
node v, and its outgoing port is p, then it check whether H_{G_2} is present at node
corresponding to port p. If yes, then it moves as per the cautious movement
strategy, H_{G_1} moves through the port p. Otherwise, it detects the p leads to
v_{BH}. On the other hand, if the edge corresponding to port p is not present,
then the entire G_1 is stuck at the current node v. In this case, it is necessary
to check whether there is any agent from G_2 present at the current node v. To
check this we have the following sub-routine. This sub-routine is required several
times in our algorithm to ensure that the movement of at least one of the groups
is continued.

- If only L_{G_2} is present at the current node v and its *prt_out* is the same as
  that of G_1: In this case, L_{G_1} updates its helper to the helper of G_2 and
  understands that it has already moved through *prt_out*. Thus, L_{G_1} now waits
  at the current node for the missing edge to reappear. On the other hand, L_{G_2}
  updates its helper to the helper of G_1 and begins a new DFS traversal, by
  incrementing the *dfs_label*, with the current node as the root node of this
  new DFS traversal. Particularly, the old helper of G_1 is the new helper of
  G_2. Both these agents now comprise G_2, and they proceed with their DFS
  traversal.
- If only H_{G_2}, is present at the current node and its *prt_in* is the same as
  the *prt_out* of G_1: In this case, L_{G_1} updates its helper to the leader of G_2.
  Further, it waits at the current node for the missing edge to reappear. On the
  other hand, H_{G_2} becomes the new leader of G_2 and updates its helper to the
  old helper of G_1. Now these two agents begin a new DFS traversal with the
  current node as the root node of this new DFS traversal.
- Either both the agents of G_2 are present at the current node or none of them
  are present at the current node: In this case, G_1 simply waits for the missing
  edge to re-appear.

(II) Only L_{G_1} is present at a node v and has *state=explore*: Let L_{G_1} be
present at a node v and the helper H_{G_1} already moved through a port p at a
round say t. At round $t + 1$, if the edge corresponding to port p is present and
H_{G_1} is alive at the node connected to node v via port p, then L_{G_1} will move
through port p. If not, it indicates that port p from node v leads to v_{BH}. Let the
edge corresponding to port p go missing at the start of the round $t + 1$. In this
case, agent L_{G_1} is stuck at node v due to a missing edge. If no agent from group
G_2 is present at the current node, then L_{G_1} continues its wait for the missing
edge to reappear. On the other hand, if there is at least one agent from G_2, then
the following cases needs to be verified:

- If both L_{G_2} and H_{G_2} are present at v: If G_2 has to move through a port
  other than p say p', then they can proceed. If G_2 has to move through port
  p, then they proceed in the following way. If they are in *explore* state, then

the agents of G_2 skip this edge and proceed further. Since both the agents of G_2 are present together, no change of groups is needed in this case. On the other hand, if G_2 has to backtrack through the edge corresponding to port p, then they increase their dfs_label and begin a new DFS with the current node as its root node.

- If L_{G_2} is present at v: If L_{G_2} is present at node v, then it is definite that the prt_out values for L_{G_2} and L_{G_1} are different. This is because, as per our algorithm, both H_{G_1} and H_{G_2} can not move through the same port if both groups are together. Suppose it were allowed. If the adjacent node was v_{BH}, then both H_{G_1} and H_{G_2} would have died in v_{BH} together. Hence, the leaders of both groups would remain stuck, and neither of them could identify the location of v_{BH}.

- If H_{G_2} is present at v: If the prt_in value of H_{G_2} is the same as the prt_out value of L_{G_1}, this means at the adjacent node (i.e., the node adjacent to v with respect to port p), L_{G_2} and H_{G_1} are present. In this case, the change of groups happens as follows. The agent H_{G_2} now becomes the new helper of G_1. The agent H_{G_1} (old) now becomes the new helper of G_2, and the (new) G_2 starts a new DFS traversal by incrementing the value of dfs_label and their current node as the root node.

(III) Only H_{G_1} is present at a node v and has *state=explore*: Let H_{G_1} be present at a node v and has entered into the node v via port p at a round t. At round $t+1$, the edge corresponding to port p disappeared, and due to which the agent L_{G_1} could not enter into v. Now, the agent H_{G_1} needs to check if any agent from group G_2 is present at the current node. Based on this, the following cases arise:

- If both L_{G_2} and H_{G_2} are present at v: Since both the agents of G_2 are together, group change is not required in this case. If they have to move through the edge corresponding to port p in the *explore* state, then G_2 can skip the edge and proceed further as per its DFS. Otherwise, if G_2 has to backtrack via that edge, then it restarts a new DFS traversal from v by incrementing its value of dfs_label. H_{G_1} does not do anything in this case.

- If L_{G_2} is present at v and prt_out value of L_{G_2} is equal to p: This means H_{G_2} and L_{G_1} are present at the other end of missing edge. In this case, L_{G_2} updates its helper to H_{G_1} and begins a new DFS traversal from the current node.

- If H_{G_2} is present at v: If H_{G_2} is present at v then it is definite that the prt_in values of H_{G_1} and H_{G_2} are different. This is because if the prt_in values of both H_{G_1} and H_{G_2} are the same, then they moved through the same port at the same round. However, as per our algorithm, we do not allow this. To see why this restriction is necessary, suppose it were allowed. Let the edge corresponding to port p lead to v_{BH}. Then both H_{G_1} and H_{G_2} would enter node v_{BH} together and die. Moreover, since the adversary could subsequently delete the edge corresponding to port p, neither L_{G_1} nor L_{G_2} would ever be able to detect node v_{BH}.

These are all the cases that may occur while performing cautious movement, due to which group exchange may occur. Note that if the state of G_1 or G_2 is *backtrack*, then they do not have to move cautiously, as the node where agents reach after *backtrack* has already been explored. Now, let us suppose G_1 is at a node u and it has to backtrack via port p that corresponds to edge (u, v). The edge (u, v) is missing. We have the following three cases based on the presence of G_2 at u.

- If only H_{G_2} is present at u: If *prt_in* value of H_{G_2} is the same as the *prt_out* value of G_1, then a change of groups is needed in this case. Here, H_{G_2} becomes the leader of G_2 and H_{G_1} becomes the helper of G_2. The newly formed G_2 continues its DFS traversal further. The agent L_{G_1}, on the other hand, updates its new helper to (old) L_{G_2}.
- If only L_{G_2} is present at u: If *prt_out* value of L_{G_2} is the same as the *prt_out* value of G_1, then a group change is required. Agent L_{G_2} updates its new helper to H_{G_1}, and this newly formed G_2 starts a new DFS traversal from the current node u. Agent L_{G_1} updates its (new) helper to (old) H_{G_2}.
- If both L_{G_2} and H_{G_2} are present at u: If both the agents of G_2 are together, then no change of groups is required. If they have to explore via edge (u, v), then G_2 skips this edge and continues further. Otherwise, if G_2 has to backtrack via edge (u, v), then it restarts a new DFS traversal from u.

3.1   Correctness and Analysis of the Algorithm

In this section, we first show that one of the groups explores G. To show this, we consider first that each group contains only one agent, and there is no black hole in G. Let G_1 and G_2 be two groups, and they are running the DFS algorithm. Initially, G_1 and G_2 are at the same node and start executing the DFS algorithm. Whenever they encounter the missing edge for the first time, G_1 remains on the same path of DFS, and G_2 starts a new DFS algorithm. At a whiteboard, there are two information. One is corresponding G_1 i.e., $wb_v(G_1).(parent)$, and other one is corresponding G_2 i.e., $wb_v(G_2).(parent, dfs\_label)$. With the help of dfs_label, G_2 can recognize whether the information at the node corresponds to old DFS or current DFS. Let in round $r < 4m$, G_1 be at node w and want to go through edge $e = (w\ w')$. At the round r, if the adversary removes an edge e at round r, then as per our algorithm, G_1 waits for the edge e, and G_2 starts the new DFS from node w. At node w, $wb_w(G_2).(parent, dfs\_label) = (-1, 1)$. We have the following claim.

Claim 1. *Let in round r', $r \leq r' < 4m$, G_1 be at node u and want to go through edge $e' = (u\ v)$. At the round r', if the adversary removes an edge e', and edge e' does not appear within the next $8m$ rounds after it is deleted by the adversary in round r', then G_2 visits every node of G in $8m$ rounds.*

Proof. Suppose at round r', G_2 is at node u'. Within the next $4m$ rounds, one of two things is possible: G_2 visits every node of G, or G_2 reaches the root of the current DFS. It is due to the fact that between rounds r' and $r' + 4m$ $4m$, G_2 either visits every node of G, starts a new DFS from some node w (it is possible when it want to go through edge e in *backtrack* state), or reaches the root, say v_r, of the current DFS traversal of G_2. In both cases, it explores $G \setminus \{e'\}$ as if it tries to via edge e' from node u (resp node v), it skips it. Therefore, if edge e' does not appear again, then G_2 visits each node at least once. This completes the proof.

Lemma 1. *Either G_1 or G_2 visits every node of G correctly in $O(m^2)$ rounds.*

Proof. If agent G_1 does not find any missing edges during the execution of DFS, it successfully explores graph G in the first $4m$ rounds. Suppose agent G_1 is at node u at round r', and wants to move via edge $e' = (u, v)$ but edge e' is missing. Due to Claim 1, if edge e' does not appear again between rounds r' and $r' + 4m$, then G_2 visits each node of G at least once. If edge e' appears, then G_1 is able to execute its current DFS for at least one round. This can happen at each DFS step of G_1. Therefore, within the first $8m \times 4m = 32m^2 = O(m^2)$ rounds, either G_1 or G_2 visits each node of G at least once. This completes the proof. $\square$

Consider G_1 and G_2, which contain two agents, respectively, and there is a node v_{BH} in G. Before the final theorem, we have the following remark.

Remark 1. In our algorithm, we describe a procedure by which groups of agents change their roles. This role change is essential; without it, both groups would get stuck, and the problem could not be solved. The underlying idea is that at least one of the groups must successfully complete a CCM cycle.

Theorem 3. *The problem of 1-BHS can be solved by 4 agents starting from a rooted initial configuration in $O(|E|^2)$ rounds when agents are equipped with 1-hop visibility and $O(\log n)$ memory, and $O(\log n)$ storage per node is present.*

Proof. Initially, 4 agents are divided into two groups, namely G_1 and G_2, each comprising two agents. The movement performed by the agents in the exploration is replicated by each group of two agents that perform a cautious walk. Therefore, one round of the exploration strategy is replicated by two rounds (may not be contiguous) in which the agents perform a cautious walk.

In Lemma 1, we have shown that within the first $32m^2$ rounds, either G_1 or G_2 visits every node G. As per the movement strategy for exploration, the agents move only in every round, so with 2 rounds, at least one group would do its movement as per our exploration strategy. For a group G_1(or G_2) that has two agents, if one agent (say a_1) visits node v_{BH} in a cautious manner and the other (say a_2) does not find a_1 in the neighbour using 1-hop visibility, agent a_2 finds node v_{BH}. Hence, using Lemma 1, the time complexity of our algorithm to solve 1-BHS is $O(m^2)$ when agents are equipped with 1-hop visibility.

Agent a_i remembers the IDs of other agents (such as $a_i.leader$, $a_i.helper$). Since the number of agents is finite, this takes $O(\log n)$ memory. Agents also store port information (such as $a_i.prt\_in$, $a_i.prt\_out$), which fits in $O(\log n)$ memory.

Other parameters like $a_i.state$ and $a_i.flag$ require only $O(1)$ memory. Since 1-BHS is achieved by all agents in $O(m^2) = O(n^4)$ rounds (as $m \leq n^2$). So the value of $a_i.dfs\_label$ never exceeds $O(n^4)$ and can also be stored in $O(\log n)$ memory. Thus, each agent uses only $O(\log n)$ memory in every round. At every node v, we store $wb_v(G_1).(parent)$ and $wb_v(G_2).(parent, dfs\_label)$ which can be done in $O(\log n)$ storage as $parent$ is nothing but port information, and dfs_label never exceeds $O(n^4)$. This completes the proof. $\square$

4   Algorithm Using Global Communication

In this section, we provide an algorithm that solves the problem of 1-BHS using $\delta_{BH} + 2$ many agents that are arbitrarily positioned at the nodes of the graph initially, and agents are equipped with global communication and 0-hop visibility.

Our technique to solve BHS, in this case, is to first provide an exploration technique and then replace the exploration steps with cautious movement to prevent all the agents from entering into node v_{BH}. The exploration technique ensures that each node of the graph is visited by at least one agent. The cautious movement by the agents ensures the safe movement by the agents, i.e., to ensure that all the agents do not end up entering node v_{BH}. However, the implementation of this idea is non-trivial since all the agents are arbitrarily positioned in the initial configuration. To address this challenge, we first introduce a cautious movement strategy that can be executed by an agent even when it operates independently.

Cautious Movement 1 (CM_1): Let an agent a_i be positioned at node v during round t. It computes the port p_i through which it intends to exit v and writes this information, along with its unique ID, on the whiteboard. At the end of round t, it attempts to traverse through port p_i. If the movement is successful (at some round $t' \geq t$), it reaches the adjacent node v'. Upon arrival at v', if a_i verifies that v' is not node v_{BH} (i.e., if it survives upon reaching v'), it returns to node v, deletes the previously written information about p_i and its ID, and safely moves through p_i to finally reach v'. However, if v' is node v_{BH} (i.e., a_i is destroyed), then the information is left intact at v. Any subsequent agent, say a_j, arriving at v can observe this information and deduce that port p_i leads to node v_{BH}. This deduction is possible because the agent, upon performing global communication, will detect that no agent with ID $a_i.ID$ is present in the graph. Hence, a_i has died in node v_{BH}. This strategy ensures that not all agents enter node v_{BH}, and the location of node v_{BH} is determined.

The Algorithm: As per Sect. 3, it is clear that two agents can explore the graph if we initially assume that there is no black hole in the graph. We begin by briefly describing the idea of the exploration strategy of two agents.

Exploration Strategy Using 2 Agents- This strategy works when two agents A_1 and A_2 are initially present at the same node in the graph G. Without loss of generality, assume that $A_1.ID < A_2.ID$. Both agents begin their movement as per their DFS. The idea is that A_2 is never stuck at any node due to a missing edge. When a missing edge is encountered, A_1 stays at its node and attempts to move through the same edge unless it is successful in doing so. On the other hand, A_2 skips the missing edge if it has to traverse that edge in *explore* state as per its DFS, or it starts a new DFS if it has to traverse that edge in *backtrack* state, or it has reached the root node with no further edges left to be explored. In this way, either A_1 explores the whole graph. Or if it is stuck at a node attempting to traverse through an edge e for sufficient time then A_2 traverses the graph $G \setminus \{e\}$.

Since, in our model, the agents have global communication, this exploration strategy can be implemented even when the agents are initially arbitrarily positioned at the nodes of the graph. We use these ideas in our algorithm and show that the power of global communication can further help the agents to detect the location of node v_{BH}. Let $\{a_1, a_2, a_3, \ldots, a_{\delta_{BH}+2}\}$ be the agents that are initially present arbitrarily at the nodes of G. Since the agents have the facility of global communication, the first two smallest ID agents begin with the run of the exploration strategy of using two agents by replacing each edge movement with CM_1 with a little bit of modification. At a node v, if an agent a_i wants to initiate movement according to CM_1, it first checks for any information regarding another agent a_j at node v. If such information exists, the agent then verifies whether a_j is alive. If a_j is alive, a_i proceeds with CM_1. However, if a_j is not alive, a_i determines which port from node v leads to v_{BH}. If no information related to CM_1 from any other agent is available, a_i will proceed with its own CM_1. In particular, agent a_1 executes like A_1, and agent a_2 executes like A_2. The remaining agents stay at their own nodes. Agent a_1 has a smaller ID; thus, it never skips the edge or starts a new DFS traversal whenever a missing edge is encountered. Agent a_2 can deviate as per the exploration technique using two agents. During this traversal, five cases arise:

<u>Case 1</u>- It may happen that while performing CM_1, agent a_1 dies into node v_{BH}. In this case, the remaining agents can understand this scenario using global communication, and thus the next minimum ID agent from the group of agents not performing the algorithm currently (i.e., a_3) begins its DFS traversal via CM_1. The agent a_3 acts similarly to A_1 (as given in the exploration strategy using 2 agents), i.e., it never deviates from its original path of its DFS traversal.

<u>Case 2</u>- If agent a_2 dies into node v_{BH}, and a_1 is still alive, then a_3 begins its DFS traversal via CM_1. The agent a_3 in this case acts similarly to A_2, i.e., it may deviate from its original path of its DFS traversal.

<u>Case 3</u>- It may happen that both a_1 and a_2 die into node v_{BH}. In this case, a_3 and a_4 begin the traversal of the graph. Agent a_3 performs similarly to A_1, and a_4 performs similarly to A_2.

<u>Case 4</u>- Let both the agents a_1 and a_2 be stuck on the opposite sides of a missing edge, say (u, v). Let a_1 be present at node u and a_2 be present at node v. Note that this scenario is possible only when a_1 has written its information at v and moved to u during its execution of CM_1. Similarly, a_2 has written its information

at u and moved to v during its execution of CM_1. And both these agents want to return to their previous nodes in order to delete their respective information. They fail to do so due to the missing edge (u, v). In this case, a_1 deletes the port information written at u by a_2, and a_2 deletes the port information written at v by a_1, and both agents proceed further as per their DFS.

<u>Case 5</u>- If agents a_1 and a_2, attempt to move through the same port p, they do not traverse it simultaneously. The agent with the smaller identifier (say a_1) proceeds through port p. If a_1 successfully moves via port p, then in the next round, a_2 verifies the status of a_1 via global communication. If a_1 is confirmed to be alive, then a_2 also traverses port p. Otherwise, a_2 understands that port p leads to v_{BH}.

Note that we have provided the above cases with reference to only the functioning of agents a_1, a_2, and a_3. However, this process continues unless node v_{BH} is found, which is determined if one of the agents reaches a node where there is information corresponding to the CM_1 of an agent which has moved to node v_{BH}. This is easy to determine if the agent whose information is written is alive or not via global communication. In other words, when the agents run their algorithm one by one, it is ensured that at least one agent is performing its movement and is not stuck at a node due to a missing edge. With this, it is definite that an agent either enters into node v_{BH} or reaches a node where there is already information written corresponding to an agent that has died in node v_{BH}. In the latter case, the node v_{BH} is found. In the former case, we get a marked node. Now, in the worst case, at most δ_{BH} agents can die in node v_{BH}. Hence, two agents are left that run the exploration strategy using 2 agents. This strategy ensures that at least one of the two agents definitely reaches one of the neighbouring nodes of node v_{BH} and thus the node v_{BH} is determined in this scenario. This completes our algorithm.

4.1   Correctness and Analysis of the Algorithm

In this section, we provide the correctness and the complexity analysis of our algorithm. As per our algorithm, two agents, say a_1, a_2, are executing the algorithm as mentioned in Sect. 3 using CM_1. Therefore, we can use Lemma 1 to show that either a_1 or a_2 visits every node in $O(m^2)$ rounds. Due to page constraints, we skip repeating the same analysis. Based on Lemma 1, we have the following lemma, which we use to show the correctness of our algorithm.

Lemma 2. *If agents a_i or a_j are moving as per the exploration strategy using CM_1, then either a_i or a_j visits every node of G in $O(m^2)$ rounds. (Proof is similar to Lemma 1)*

Theorem 4. *The problem of 1-BHS can be solved by $\delta_{BH} + 2$ agents starting from an arbitrary initial configuration in $O(\delta_{BH} \cdot |E|^2)$ rounds, when agents are equipped with global communication, $O(\log n)$ memory, and each node has $O(\log n)$ storage.*

5   Conclusion

We study the 1-BHS problem in dynamic graphs under varying agent capabilities. We prove that three agents are insufficient even under strong assumptions, and that $\delta_{BH} + 1$ agents fail from a scattered configuration. On the positive side, we give matching algorithms: four agents with 1-hop visibility and logarithmic memory suffice from a rooted configuration, while $\delta_{BH} + 2$ agents with global communication and logarithmic memory succeed from any configuration. These results highlight the impact of communication and visibility.

References

1. Kaur, T., Saxena, A.: When agents are powerful: black hole search in time-varying graphs (2025)
2. Czyzowicz, J., Kowalski, D.R., Markou, E., Pelc, A.: Complexity of searching for a black hole. Fundam. Informaticae **71**(2–3), 229–242 (2006)
3. Dobrev, S., Flocchini, P., Prencipe, G., Santoro, N.: Searching for a black hole in arbitrary networks: optimal mobile agents protocols. Distrib. Comput. **19**(1), 1–35 (2006)
4. Gotoh, T., Flocchini, P., Masuzawa, T., Santoro, N.: Exploration of dynamic networks: tight bounds on the number of agents. J. Comput. Syst. Sci. **122**, 1–18 (2021)
5. Kshemkalyani, A.D., Molla, A.R., Sharma, G.: Efficient dispersion of mobile robots on dynamic graphs. In: ICDCS, pp. 732–742 (2020)
6. Di Luna, G.A., Flocchini, P., Pagli, L., Prencipe, G., Santoro, N., Viglietta, G.: Gathering in dynamic rings. Theor. Comput. Sci. **811**, 79–98 (2020)
7. Bhattacharya, A., Italiano, G.F., Mandal, P.S.: Black hole search in dynamic tori. In: SAND (2024)
8. Kaur, T., Saxena, A., Mandal, P.S., Mondal,: Black hole search in dynamic graphs. In: ICDCN (2025)
9. Luna, G.A.D., Flocchini, P., Prencipe, G., Santoro, N.: Locating a black hole in a dynamic ring. JPDC **196**, 104998 (2025)
10. Bhattacharya, A., Italiano, G.F., Mandal, P.S.: Black hole search in dynamic cactus graph. In: WALCOM, pp. 288–303 (2024)
11. Augustine, J., Moses, W.K.: Dispersion of mobile robots: a study of memory-time trade-offs. In: ICDCN (2018)
12. Agarwalla, A., Augustine, J., Moses, W.K., Madhav, S.K., Sridhar, A.K.: Deterministic dispersion of mobile robots in dynamic rings. In: ICDCN 2018 (2018)
13. Czyzowicz, J., Kowalski, D., Markou, E., Pelc, A.: Searching for a black hole in tree networks. In: OPODIS, pp. 67–80 (2005)
14. Balamohan, B., Flocchini, P., Miri, A., Santoro, N.: Time optimal algorithms for black hole search in rings. In: COCOA, pp. 58–71 (2010)
15. Chalopin, J., Das, S., Labourel, A., Markou, E.: Black hole search with finite automata scattered in a synchronous torus. In: DISC, pp. 432–446 (2011)
16. Markou, E., Paquette, M.: Black hole search and exploration in unoriented tori with synchronous scattered finite automata. In: OPODIS, pp. 239–253 (2012)
17. Saxena, A., Kaur, T., Mondal, K.: Dispersion on time-varying graphs. CoRR arxiv:2410.04050 (2024)

On Fixed-Parameter Tractability of Weighted 0–1 Timed Matching Problem on Temporal Graphs

Rinku Kumar[1]([⊠]), Bodhisatwa Mazumdar[1]([⊠]) [iD],
and Subhrangsu Mandal[2]([⊠]) [iD]

[1] Department of Computer Science and Engineering, Indian Institute of Technology
Indore, Indore 453552, Madhya Pradesh, India
`{phd2301101005,bodhisatwa}@iiti.ac.in`

[2] Department of Computer Science and Engineering, Indian Institute of Technology
(ISM) Dhanbad, Dhanbad 826004, Jharkhand, India
`santu.cst@gmail.com`

Abstract. Temporal graphs are introduced to model systems where the relationships among the entities of the system evolve over time. In this paper, we consider temporal graphs, where the edge set changes with time and all the changes are known a priori. The underlying graph of a temporal graph is a static graph consisting of all the vertices and edges that exist for at least one timestep in the temporal graph. The concept of 0–1 timed matching in temporal graphs was recently introduced as an extension of the matching problem in static graphs. A 0–1 timed matching of a temporal graph is a non-overlapping subset of the edge set of that temporal graph. The problem of finding the maximum 0–1 timed matching is proved to be NP-complete on multiple classes of temporal graphs. We study the fixed-parameter tractability of the maximum 0–1 timed matching problem. We prove that the problem remains to be NP-complete even when the underlying static graph of the temporal graph has a bounded treewidth. Furthermore, we establish that the problem is W[1]-hard when parameterized by the solution size. Next, we introduce the concept of edge overlap graph for a temporal graph. Finally, we present a fixed-parameter tractable (FPT) algorithm parameterized by the maximum vertex degree and the treewidth of the underlying graph of the temporal graph using the concept of edge overlap graph to address the problem.

Keywords: weighted 0–1 timed matching · 0–1 timed matching · weighted temporal matching · temporal matching · temporal graphs · dynamic graphs · fixed-parameter tractability · edge overlap graph

S. Mandal—Supported, in part, by FRS research grant MISC0100 provided by Indian Institute of Technology (ISM) Dhanbad.

B. Chatterjee et al. (Eds.): ICDCIT 2026, LNCS 16420, pp. 19–31, 2026.
https://doi.org/10.1007/978-3-032-16632-6_2

1   Introduction

Graphs are an important tool to represent pairwise relationships between entities in a system. In many systems, the relationships between the entities and/or other properties in the system become temporal in nature. These systems result into networks with time-dependent topology. Examples of such networks include transportation networks [17], social networks [14], biological networks [16], communication networks [9], etc. Temporal graphs are introduced to model these networks, where the network topology changes with time. A temporal graph is a graph in which different properties of the graph change with time. In this paper, we consider the temporal graphs where only the edge set changes with time, and the changes in the graph topology are known a priori. These types of temporal graph can be represented by associating one or more non-overlapping time intervals on each edge in the temporal graph. These time intervals denote the time of existence of that particular edge.

The added time dimension in a temporal graph introduces unique challenges to traditional graph structure related problems. In many cases, new definitions of the problems that incorporate the time dimension are required. Thus, problems of constructing different graph structures such as minimum spanning tree [19], dominating set [18], colouring [23], etc. on temporal graphs have received considerable attention of researchers. Due to the dynamic nature of the graph topology, the matching problems become significantly more complex in temporal graphs. Different works [2, 20, 22] in the literature have defined multiple variants of the matching problem on temporal graphs. The *maximum 0–1 timed matching* problem on temporal graphs is introduced in [20] as an extension of the matching problem on static graphs. The problem of finding maximum 0–1 timed matching on temporal graphs is proved to be NP-complete [20] in multiple classes of temporal graphs, such as temporal tree, bounded degree temporal graphs, and bipartite temporal graphs. In this paper, we study the fixed-parameter tractability of the maximum weighted 0–1 timed matching problem. The key contributions of this paper are as follows.

Our Contributions: In this paper, we explore the fixed-parameter tractability of the maximum weighted 0–1 timed matching problem on temporal graphs. In particular, we prove that this problem is NP-complete even when the underlying graph of the temporal graph has a bounded treewidth. We also prove that the problem is $W[1]$-hard when parameterized by the solution size. Finally, a fixed-parameter tractable algorithm to address the maximum weighted 0–1 timed matching problem on temporal graphs is proposed when parameterized by the maximum vertex degree and the treewidth of the underlying graph of the given temporal graph. In particular, we introduce the concept of edge overlap graph of a temporal graph. Using the properties of edge overlap graphs, we propose a fixed parameter tractable algorithm for the maximum 0–1 timed matching problem parameterized by the maximum vertex degree and the treewidth of the underlying graph of the given temporal graph.

The rest of this paper is organised as follows. Section 2 discusses related work present in the existing literature. Section 3 details the system model and assumptions about the temporal graphs considered in this paper. Section 4 formally defines the problem and the terminology related to the temporal graphs. Section 5 describes the details of the results. Section 6 concludes the paper.

2   Related Work

The maximum 0–1 timed matching problem is an extension of the classical maximum matching problem on static graphs to the area of temporal graphs. The matching problem on static graphs is solvable in polynomial time. Edmonds has proposed the first algorithm [7] to solve the maximum matching problem in $O(n^4)$ time on a static graph with n vertices. Due to its wide range of applications, the matching problem is studied in different classes of static graphs [8,13,25] in the literature.

The dynamic nature of the graph topology imposes additional challenges while addressing the matching problem in temporal graphs, where edges are active only at specific timesteps. Thus, multiple variants of the matching problem are introduced and studied on temporal graphs. In [24], Michail et al. have addressed the decision version of the temporal matching problem on a temporal graph where the objective is to check for a maximum cardinality matching M on the underlying graph of the temporal graph, such that each edge is assigned with a different timestep chosen from the timesteps when that edge exists. This problem is proven to be NP-hard. In [2], Baste et al. have defined a version of matching called γ-matching. An edge is a γ-edge if it exists for at least consecutive γ timesteps in the temporal graph. The maximum γ matching is the maximum cardinality subset of the γ edges such that no two γ edges are incident on a common vertex at any timestep. The problem is proved to be NP-complete when $\gamma > 1$, and a 2-approximation algorithm is proposed to address the problem. They have proposed a kernelization-based fixed-parameter tractable algorithm parameterized by the solution size to address the problem. In another work, Picavet et al. [26] have addressed the problem of γ matching on geometric temporal graphs of bounded density. They have proposed a dynamic programming-based exponential time exact algorithm and a PTAS to address the problem. Mertzois et al. have introduced Δ-matching [22] on temporal graphs. A Δ-matching M can include two edge instances at the timesteps t and t' if those two edges do not share a common vertex or $|t - t'| > \Delta$, where Δ is the time window size. This problem is APX-hard when $\Delta > 2$ and the lifetime of the temporal graph is more than 3. This problem is NP-hard even on temporal paths. They have proposed a $\frac{\Delta}{2\Delta-1}$-factor approximation algorithm to address the problem. They have also proposed a fixed-parameter tractable algorithm parameterized by time window size and the size of maximum matching of the underlying graph to address the problem. In another work, Mandal et al. [20] defined 0–1 timed matching on temporal graphs based on overlapping edges. Two edges are overlapping if they are incident on a common vertex, and there exists at least one timestep t when both the edges exist. The maximum 0–1 timed matching on a temporal graph is the maximum cardinality subset of edges such that no two edges in the subset are overlapping with each other. They proved that this problem is NP-complete on temporal trees when two or more time intervals are associated with each edge. It is also proved that the problem is NP-complete on bounded degree bipartite temporal graphs even when each edge is associated with a single time interval. An $O(n \log n)$ time algorithm is proposed to address the problem on temporal tree with n vertices when each edge is associated with a single time interval. An approximation algorithm is proposed to address the problem in general temporal graphs.

In addition to these references, there are works in the literature [1,5] that have addressed the multi-stage version of the matching problem on temporal graphs. Recently the study of fixed-parameter tractability of different graph problems on temporal graphs have received considerable attention from researchers. Different fixed-parameter tractable algorithms are proposed to address different problems in temporal graphs, such as matching [2,22], shortest path [4], colouring [21], etc. To the best of our knowledge, there is no work in the literature that has studied the fixed-parameter tractability of the maximum 0–1 timed matching problem on temporal graphs, which we address in this paper.

3   System Model

In this paper, a temporal graph $\mathcal{G}$ is represented using the *evolving graphs* [10] model. In this model, a temporal graph is represented as a discrete finite sequence of static graphs. Each static graph at a certain timestep t represents the state of the temporal graph at timestep t. The length of the sequence is referred to as the *lifetime* of the temporal graph. Let $\mathcal{T}$ be the lifetime of $\mathcal{G}$, then $\mathcal{G}$ exists in the time interval $[0, \mathcal{T})$. We assume that the vertex set $\mathcal{V}$ remains unchanged throughout the lifetime of the temporal graph. Only the edge set $\mathcal{E}$ changes with time. We also assume that all changes in the edge set are known a priori. Additionally, it is assumed that there is no self-loop, and at most one edge can exist between any two vertices in a given timestep. Thus, the temporal graph $\mathcal{G} = (\mathcal{V}, \mathcal{E})$ is represented as a sequence of static graphs, $(G_0, G_1, \cdots, G_{\mathcal{T}-1})$, where each $G_i = (\mathcal{V}, \mathcal{E}_i)$ is the static graph at timestep i with vertex set $\mathcal{V}$ and edge set $\mathcal{E}_i$ consisting of edges present at timestep i. As we assume that only the edge set changes over time, a temporal graph can be equivalently represented by assigning non-overlapping time intervals to each edge in the temporal graph. We also assume that each edge e is assigned a non-negative real number representing its cost, $\omega(e)$, which remains unchanged throughout the lifetime of the temporal graph. Thus, an edge $e \in \mathcal{E}$ incident on two distinct vertices, $u, v \in \mathcal{V}$ is represented as $e(u, v, \omega(e), (s_1, f_1), (s_2, f_2), \cdots, (s_k, f_k))$, where $f_k \leq \mathcal{T}$. Each interval (s_i, f_i) associated with an edge indicates that the edge exists for the time interval $[s_i, f_i)$, i.e., e is present in $(G_{s_i}, G_{s_i+1}, \cdots, G_{f_i-1})$ where $0 \leq s_i < f_i \leq \mathcal{T}$. When the temporal graph is unweighted, we represent the edge as $e(u, v, (s_1, f_1), (s_2, f_2), \cdots, (s_k, f_k))$. Since each interval associated with an edge is non-overlapping with any other interval associated with that edge, the maximum number of intervals associated with an edge is $\lfloor \frac{T}{2} \rfloor$. An edge with a single time step is an instance of that edge. We denote an edge between the vertices u and v as e_{uv} when the exact time intervals associated with the edge are not required. The instance at timestep t of an edge e_{uv} is denoted as e^t_{uv}.

4   Preliminaries and Problem Definition

In this section, we define the *maximum weighted 0–1 timed matching problem* on temporal graphs. We first define terminologies related to temporal graphs that are required to define the problem. Let $\mathcal{G} = (\mathcal{V}, \mathcal{E})$ be the temporal graph with lifetime T, where $\mathcal{V}$ is the set of vertices and $\mathcal{E}$ is the set of edges.

Definition 1. *Underlying Graph:* *The underlying graph of a temporal graph $\mathcal{G} = (\mathcal{V}, \mathcal{E})$, denoted as $\mathcal{G}_U = (\mathcal{V}, \mathcal{E}_U)$, is a static graph, where $\mathcal{E}_U = \{(u, v) \mid \exists t \in [0, T - 1)$ such that e^t_{uv} is an instance of $e_{uv} \in \mathcal{E}\}$.*

Definition 2. *Bounded Degree Temporal Graph:* *A temporal graph $\mathcal{G} = (\mathcal{V}, \mathcal{E})$ is a bounded degree temporal graph if the degree of each vertex $v \in \mathcal{V}$ in the underlying graph $\mathcal{G}_U$ is bounded by an integer Δ, i.e., $deg(v) \leq \Delta$.*

Figure 1(a) shows a bounded degree temporal graph $\mathcal{G}$ with $T = 6$ where degree of each vertex in the underlying graph is bounded by $\Delta = 3$. Figure 1(b) shows the underlying graph of $\mathcal{G}$.

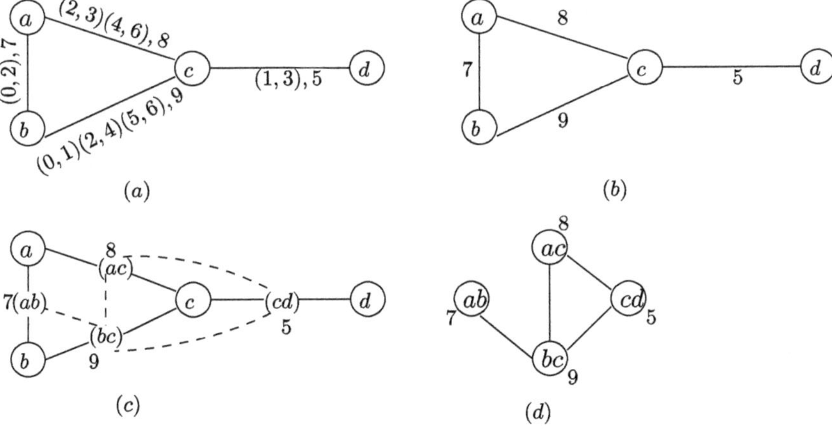

Fig. 1. (a) A temporal graph $\mathcal{G}$ with lifetime 6, (b) Underlying graph $\mathcal{G}_U$ of $\mathcal{G}$, (c) Conversion to edge-overlap graph, (d) The edge-overlap graph $\mathcal{G}_O$ of $\mathcal{G}$.

Definition 3. *Temporal Tree:* *A temporal graph $\mathcal{G} = (\mathcal{V}, \mathcal{E})$ is a temporal tree if the underlying graph $\mathcal{G}_U$ of $\mathcal{G}$ is a tree.*

Definition 4. *Overlapping Edges:* *Two edges $e_{uv}, e_{vw} \in \mathcal{E}$ overlap each other if and only if both are incident at a vertex v and there is at least one timestep t when both the edges exist.*

In Fig. 1(a), edges e_{ab} and e_{ac} both are incident at the vertex a, but there is no timestep t when both edges exist. Thus, these two are non-overlapping edges. If we consider edges e_{ac} and e_{cd}, both edges exist at $t = 2$. Thus, these two are overlapping edges.

Definition 5. *0–1 Timed Matching:* *A 0–1 timed matching M on a temporal graph, $\mathcal{G} = (\mathcal{V}, \mathcal{E})$ is a subset of $\mathcal{E}$ such that any two edges in M are non-overlapping with each other.*

Definition 6. *Maximum Weighted 0–1 Timed Matching:* *A maximum weighted 0–1 timed matching on a temporal graph $\mathcal{G} = (\mathcal{V}, \mathcal{E})$ is a 0–1 timed matching, $\mathcal{M} \subseteq \mathcal{E}$ such that the sum of weights of the edges in $\mathcal{M}$ are maximum among all such possible 0–1 timed matching on $\mathcal{G}$.*

In the temporal graph shown in Fig. 1(a), the maximum weighted 0–1 timed matching $\mathcal{M} = \{e_{ab}, e_{ac}\}$ with total weight 15. Next, we introduce the concept of *edge-overlap graph* of a temporal graph that we are going to use while addressing this problem.

Definition 7. *Edge-Overlap Graph:* *The edge-overlap graph of a temporal graph $\mathcal{G} = (\mathcal{V}, \mathcal{E})$ is a static graph, $\mathcal{G}_O = (V_O, E_O)$, where the vertex set V_O includes a vertex v_{uv} for each edge $e_{uv} \in \mathcal{E}$ and the edge set E_O includes the edge (v_{uv}, v_{wx}) connecting $v_{uv}, v_{wx} \in V_O$ when e_{uv}, e_{wx} are overlapping with each other.*

Note that when $\mathcal{G}(\mathcal{V}, \mathcal{E})$ is an edge-weighted temporal graph, such that each edge, $e_{uv} \in \mathcal{E}$ is associated with weight $\omega(e_{uv})$, then the edge-overlap graph $\mathcal{G}_O(V_O, E_O)$ is a vertex-weighted static graph, where weight $\omega(e_{uv})$ is assigned to the vertex $v_{uv} \in V_O$. Figure 1(d) shows the edge-overlap graph $\mathcal{G}_O$ of the edge-weighted temporal graph $\mathcal{G}$ shown in Fig. 1(a).

5   Maximum Weighted 0–1 Timed Matching Problem

The unweighted maximum 0–1 timed matching problem is proved to be NP-complete [20] on different restricted classes of temporal graphs, such as temporal tree, bounded degree bipartite temporal graphs. In this section, we study the fixed-parameter tractability of the *maximum weighted 0–1 timed matching* problem on temporal graphs. In particular, we prove that the unweighted maximum 0–1 timed matching problem is NP-complete on bounded treewidth temporal graphs, and this problem is W[1]-hard when parameterized by the solution size.

Then, we propose an algorithm for temporal graphs when the underlying graph of the temporal graph has bounded treewidth and bounded degree. In Theorem 5.1 of [20], it is proved that the maximum 0–1 timed matching problem is NP-complete on temporal tree. We get the following result from this theorem.

Corollary 1. *The maximum 0–1 timed matching problem is NP-complete even when the underlying graph of the temporal graph has bounded treewidth.*

Next, we show that there exists a parameterized reduction from the independent set problem to the 0–1 timed matching problem. The parameterized version of the independent set problem is defined as follows:

Input: A graph $G(V, E)$ and an integer k.
Question: Is there a subset $I \subset V$ of exactly size k, such that for any $u, v \in I$, $(u, v) \notin E$?

The parameterized version of the 0–1 timed matching problem is:

Input: A temporal graph $\mathcal{G}(\mathcal{V}, \mathcal{E})$ and an integer k'.
Question: Is there a subset $M \subset \mathcal{E}$ of exactly size k' such that no two edges $e_{uv}, e_{wx} \in M$ are overlapping with each other?

Next, we prove that there is a parameterized reduction from the independent set problem to the 0–1 timed matching problem.

Theorem 1. *There exists a parameterized reduction from the independent set problem to the 0–1 timed matching problem.*

Proof. Consider an instance of instance (G, k) of the *independent set* problem, where $G = (V, E)$ is a static graph with $|V| = n_V$, $|E| = m_E$ and k is a given integer. We construct an instance $(\mathcal{G}, k')$ of the 0–1 timed matching problem. Let S be a set of distinct integers, $S = \{0, 1, \ldots, m_E - 1\}$. Each edge $(u, v) \in E$ is assigned with a distinct integer, $n_{uv} \in S$. Let $V_0 \subseteq V$ be the set of zero-degree vertices in V such that $|V_0| = n_0$. The set V_0 can be computed from G in $O(n_V)$ time. Each vertex, $u \in V_0$ is assigned with a distinct integer, n_u from the set of integers, $S' = \{m_E, \ldots, m_E + n_0 - 1\}$. For each vertex $v \in V$, the *neighborhood* of v is defined as, $N_v = \{u \in V | (u, v) \in E\}$. Thus, $\forall u \in V_0, N_u = \phi$. We construct a temporal graph, $\mathcal{G} = (\mathcal{V}, \mathcal{E})$, as follows.

(i) Initialize $\mathcal{V} = \phi, \mathcal{E} = \phi, \mathcal{E}_1 = \phi, \mathcal{E}_2 = \phi$.
(ii) $\forall v \in V$, we add a vertex v_v to $\mathcal{V}$, and one additional vertex v', i.e., $\mathcal{V} = \mathcal{V} \cup \{\mathsf{v}_v | \forall v \in V\} \cup \{\mathsf{v}'\}$.
(iii) $\forall v \in V_0$, we add an edge between v_v and v'. The time interval assigned to this edge is $(n_v, n_v + 1)$, where $n_v \in S'$. So, $\mathcal{E}_1 = \mathcal{E}_1 \cup \{e(\mathsf{v}_v\mathsf{v}', (n_v, n_v + 1)) | \forall v \in V_0\}$.
(iv) $\forall v \in V \setminus V_0$, we add an edge between the corresponding v_v and v' in $\mathcal{V}$. The time intervals assigned to this edge are $(n_{vu_1}, n_{vu_1} + 1), (n_{vu_2}, n_{vu_2} + 1) \ldots, (n_{vu_{deg(v)}}, n_{vu_{deg(v)}} + 1)$, where $u_1, u_2, \ldots, u_{deg(v)} \in N_v$. So, $\mathcal{E}_2 = \mathcal{E}_2 \cup \{e(\mathsf{v}_v, \mathsf{v}', (n_{vu_1}, n_{vu_1} + 1), \ldots, (n_{vu_{deg(v)}}, n_{vu_{deg(v)}} + 1)) | \forall v \in V \setminus V_0\}$.

   (v) The set of edges in the temporal graph, $\mathcal{G}$ is formed as $\mathcal{E} = \mathcal{E}_1 \cup \mathcal{E}_2$, and the lifetime of $\mathcal{G}$ is $m_E + n_0$.

  (vi) We assign $k' = k$.

Figure 2 shows an example of construction of the temporal tree from the static graph instance of the independent set problem. The constructed temporal graph $\mathcal{G}$ contains an edge between each vertex, $v \in \mathcal{V} \setminus \{v'\}$ and v'. Moreover, there is no edge between any other pair of vertices in $\mathcal{G}$. Thus, $\mathcal{G}$ is a temporal tree.

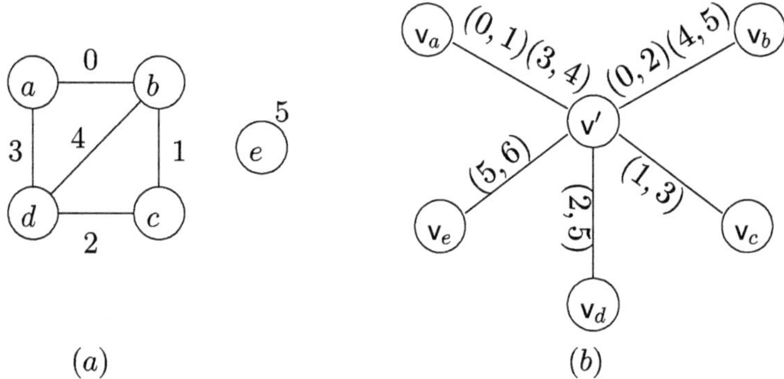

Fig. 2. A temporal tree from a static graph instance of the independent set problem.

For a given 0–1 timed matching M in $\mathcal{G}$, we construct an independent set IS_{max} on G, where $|IS_{max}| = |M|$. We select the set of vertices $IS_{max} \subseteq V$, such that $IS_{max} = \{v | e_{v_v v'} \in M\}$. We show that IS_{max} is an independent set in G and $|IS_{max}| = |M|$. Now, for each edge in M, a vertex in IS_{max} is selected, so $|IS_{max}| = |M|$. We prove by contradiction that IS_{max} is an independent set for G. Suppose IS_{max} is not an independent set of G. If so, then there are at least two vertices, $v_1, v_2 \in IS_{max}$, such that $(v_1, v_2) \in E$. As $v_1, v_2 \in IS_{max}$, then both $e_{v_{v_1} v'}$, $e_{v_{v_2} v'} \in M$. Now, as $(v_1, v_2) \in E$, (v_1, v_2) is assigned with integer $n_{v_1 v_2}$. This implies that the time interval, $(n_{v_1 v_2}, n_{v_1 v_2} + 1)$ is assigned to both $e_{v_{v_1} v'}$ and $e_{v_{v_2} v'}$, and both these edges are incident on v'. Hence, M is not a 0–1 timed matching on the temporal graph $\mathcal{G}$. This results in a contradiction, and hence $|IS_{max}|$ is an independent set for G.

Next, for a given independent set IS_{max} in G, we construct a 0–1 timed matching M in $\mathcal{G}$ such that $|IS_{max}| = |M|$. We construct a 0–1 timed matching M as $M = \{e_{v_v v'} | v \in IS_{max}\}$. Since we include an edge $e_{v_v v'}$ in M for every v in IS_{max}, $|M| = |IS_{max}|$. We prove that M is a 0–1 timed matching in $\mathcal{G}$. Assume that M is not a 0–1 timed matching and two overlapping edges $e_{v_v v'}, e_{v_u v'} \in M$. As $e_{v_v v'}, e_{v_u v'} \in M$, both $u, v \in IS_{max}$. The edges $e_{v_v v'}, e_{v_u v'}$ are overlapping implies that there is a timestep t when both the edges exist. From the construction of $\mathcal{G}$, this implies that t is an integer that is assigned to an edge which is incident on both u, v. This implies that IS_{max} is not an independent set in G. Hence, M is a 0–1 timed matching in $\mathcal{G}$. This completes the proof. $\square$

It is already known that the maximum independent set problem is $W[1]$-hard [6] when parameterized by the solution size. From this fact and Theorem 1 we get the following theorem.

Theorem 2. *The maximum 0–1 timed matching problem is $W[1]$-hard when parameterized by the solution size.*

Next, we prove that there is a fixed-parameter tractable algorithm that solves the weighted 0–1 timed matching problem on temporal graphs when parameterized by treewidth and maximum vertex degree of the underlying graph of the temporal graph. In particular, we transform the problem into a *maximum weighted independent set* (MWIS) on the edge-overlap graph of the given temporal graph. We prove that the problem of finding the maximum weighted 0–1 timed matching problem on a temporal graph $\mathcal{G}(\mathcal{V}, \mathcal{E})$ can be addressed by solving the MWIS problem on the edge-overlap graph $\mathcal{G}_O$ of the temporal graph $\mathcal{G}$.

Theorem 3. *The problem of finding a maximum weighted 0–1 timed matching on a temporal graph $\mathcal{G}$ is solvable by finding a maximum weighted independent set on $\mathcal{G}_O$.*

Proof. At first, we construct the edge-overlap graph $\mathcal{G}_O = (V_O, E_O)$ of the given temporal graph $\mathcal{G}$. Then, we construct a solution for finding a maximum weighted 0–1 timed matching on $\mathcal{G}$ from a solution to the problem of finding a maximum weighted independent set on the edge-overlap graph $\mathcal{G}_O$ of $\mathcal{G}$. We construct the edge-overlap graph, $\mathcal{G}_O = (V_O, E_O)$ of a given temporal graph $\mathcal{G}(\mathcal{V}, \mathcal{E})$ as follows.

- For each weighted edge, $e_{uv} \in \mathcal{E}$, we include a weighted vertex, v_{uv} in V_O, such that the weight of the vertex v_{uv} is $w(v_{uv}) = \omega(e_{uv})$. Thus, $V_O = \{v_{uv} \mid \forall e_{uv} \in \mathcal{E}\}$.
- The edge set E_O of $\mathcal{G}_O$ includes edges between two vertices, $v_{uv}, v_{vw} \in V_O$ if e_{uv} and e_{vw} are overlapping with each other in $\mathcal{G}$. Thus, $E_O = \{(v_{uv}, v_{vw}) \mid e_{uv}, e_{vw} \in \mathcal{E} \text{ are overlapping with each other}\}$.

Since the determination of two overlapping edges can be done in polynomial time, the construction of edge-overlap graph of a given temporal graph is done in polynomial time. Next, we prove that if there is a solution for the MWIS problem on the edge-overlap graph then we can find a solution for the maximum 0–1 timed matching problem on the original temporal graph in polynomial time.

Suppose $I \subseteq V_O$ be a maximum weighted independent set with total weight $w(I)$ in the edge-overlap graph $\mathcal{G}_O$ of the given temporal graph $\mathcal{G}(\mathcal{V}, \mathcal{E})$. We construct a maximum weighted 0–1 timed matching $\mathcal{M}$ for $\mathcal{G}$ as follows. For each vertex, $v_{uv} \in I$, we add an edge $e_{uv} \in \mathcal{E}$ to $\mathcal{M}$. We prove that $\mathcal{M}$ is a maximum weighted 0–1 timed matching in $\mathcal{G}$.

- At first, we prove that $\mathcal{M} \subseteq \mathcal{E}$. Since each vertex in V_O is added for an edge in $\mathcal{E}$ and $I \subseteq V_O$, $\mathcal{M} \subseteq \mathcal{E}$.

- Next, we prove that all the edges in $\mathcal{M}$ are non-overlapping with each other. We prove this by contradiction. Let there be two edges, $e_{uv}, e_{vw} \in \mathcal{M}$ that overlap with each other. This implies that the corresponding two vertices, $v_{uv}, v_{vw} \in V_O$ are included in I. Since $e_{uv}, e_{vw} \in \mathcal{M}$ are overlapping with each other, there is an edge between $v_{uv}, v_{vw} \in V_O$ from the construction of $\mathcal{G}_O$ from $\mathcal{G}$. Hence, it contradicts that I is an independent set on $\mathcal{G}_O$. This proves that no two edges in $\mathcal{M}$ overlap with each other.
- We prove that $\mathcal{M}$ is a maximum weighted 0–1 timed matching on $\mathcal{G}$. We prove this by contradiction. Let $\mathcal{M}'$ be a 0–1 timed matching, such that the total weight $\omega(\mathcal{M}')$ of the edges in $\mathcal{M}'$ is more than the total weight $\omega(\mathcal{M})$ of the edges in $\mathcal{M}$. We construct a set of vertices $I' \subseteq V_O$ by choosing the vertices in V_O corresponding to the edges in $\mathcal{M}'$. For each edge, $e_{uv} \in \mathcal{E}$, there is a vertex $v_{uv} \in V_O$, such that $\omega(e_{uv}) = w(v_{uv})$. Thus, $w(I') = \omega(\mathcal{M}')$ and $w(I) = \omega(\mathcal{M})$. Since $\omega(\mathcal{M}') > \omega(\mathcal{M})$, $w(I') > w(I)$. As $\mathcal{M}'$ is a 0–1 timed matching on $\mathcal{G}$, no two edges in $\mathcal{M}'$ overlap with each other. Thus, from the construction of $\mathcal{G}_O$, there are no edges between two vertices in I'. Hence I' is an independent set for $\mathcal{G}_O$ with total weight $w(I') > w(I)$. This contradicts our assumption that I is a maximum weighted independent set on $\mathcal{G}_O$. Thus, $\mathcal{M}$ is a maximum weighted 0–1 timed matching on $\mathcal{G}$. This completes the proof of this theorem. $\qquad\square$

Theorem 3 proves that if we have a solution to the problem of finding a maximum weighted independent set problem on the edge-overlap graph of a given temporal graph, then we can find a maximum weighted 0–1 timed matching for the given temporal graph in polynomial time. The problem of finding a maximum weighted independent set on a static graph is known to be NP-complete [11]. There is a fixed-parameter tractable algorithm [3] to find a maximum weighted independent set on a static graph when parameterized by treewidth. In particular, there is an $O(2^k n)$ algorithm [6] to find the maximum weighted independent set on a graph with treewidth k and n vertices. Next, we find the bound on the treewidth of the edge-overlap graph $\mathcal{G}_O$ of a temporal graph $\mathcal{G}$ when the treewidth of the underlying graph $\mathcal{G}_U$ of $\mathcal{G}$ is k_U. To compute the bound, we use the known results on the treewidth of line graphs [12]. It is known that for any static graph G with treewidth k, the treewidth, $tw(L(G))$ of its line graph $L(G)$ is $tw(L(G)) \leq (k+1)\Delta(G) - 1$, where $\Delta(G)$ is the maximum degree of a vertex in G. We extend this result in [12] to find the bound on the treewidth of an edge-overlap graph of a temporal graph.

Theorem 4. *Let $\mathcal{G}$ be a temporal graph and $\mathcal{G}_U$ be its underlying graph. If treewidth of $\mathcal{G}_U$ is k_U and the maximum degree of a vertex in $\mathcal{G}_U$ is $\Delta(\mathcal{G}_U)$ then treewidth k_O of edge-overlap graph $\mathcal{G}_O(V_O, E_O)$ of $\mathcal{G}$ is $k_O \leq (k_U + 1)\Delta(\mathcal{G}_U) - 1$.*

Proof. In the line graph $L(\mathcal{G}_U)$ of $\mathcal{G}_U$, every edge, $e_{uv} \in \mathcal{G}_U$ is represented as a vertex $v_{uv} \in V_O$. Two vertices, $v_{uv}, v_{vw} \in L(\mathcal{G}_U)$ are connected by an edge when e_{uv}, e_{vw} are incident on the same vertex. In the edge-overlap graph $\mathcal{G}_O$, the vertex set is the same as $L(\mathcal{G}_U)$, only the edge set E_O includes edges connecting two vertices, $v_{uv}, v_{vw} \in V_O$ if these edges are overlapping with each other. Thus, $\mathcal{G}_O$ is a subgraph of $L(\mathcal{G}_U)$. Hence, we get the result $k_O \leq (k_U + 1)\Delta(\mathcal{G}_U) - 1$. $\square$

5.1 Proposed Algorithm

Using the results proved in Theorem 3 and 4, we propose a fixed parameter tractable algorithm to address the problem of finding maximum weighted 0–1 timed matching on a edge weighted temporal graph parameterized by the maximum vertex degree and treewidth of the underlying graph of that temporal graph. The algorithm starts by constructing the edge-overlap graph $\mathcal{G}_O(V_O, E_O)$ for the input graph $\mathcal{G}(\mathcal{V}, \mathcal{E})$. As the underlying graph $\mathcal{G}_U$ of the input temporal graph $\mathcal{G}$ has bounded max-degree and treewidth, the resulting $\mathcal{G}_O(V_O, E_O)$ also has bounded treewidth. Next, a nice tree decomposition $(T, \{X_t\}_{t \in V(T)})$ of $\mathcal{G}_O(V_O, E_O)$, where T is a tree and each node, $t \in V(T)$ in T is assigned a bag, $X_t \subseteq V$, is created using the algorithm presented in [15]. In this tree decomposition, we apply the dynamic programming based algorithm described in [6] to find the maximum weighted independent set I on the edge overlap graph $\mathcal{G}_O$. For each vertex in I, we select the corresponding edge in $\mathcal{G}$ to obtain the maximum weighted 0–1 timed matching on $\mathcal{G}$.

Time Complexity Analysis. The construction of the edge-overlap graph, $\mathcal{G}_O = (V_O, E_O)$, requires iterating over all vertices of the temporal graph, $\mathcal{G}(\mathcal{V}, \mathcal{E})$, and checking the overlaps between the incident edges. For each vertex $v \in \mathcal{V}$, $O(\Delta^2)$ pairs of incident edges are checked, where Δ is the maximum degree of a vertex in the underlying graph $\mathcal{G}_U$ of $\mathcal{G}$. The check for overlapping edges for a pair of edges takes $O(\mathcal{T})$ time. Thus, the total cost for the construction of the edge overlap graph, G_O is $O(|\mathcal{V}|\Delta^2\mathcal{T})$, where $|\mathcal{V}|$ is the number of vertices in $\mathcal{G}$ and $\mathcal{T}$ is the lifetime of $\mathcal{G}$. Computing the tree decomposition of $\mathcal{G}_O$ using the algorithm in [15] that provides a tree decomposition of treewidth, $k'_O \leq 2k_O + 1$ takes $O(2^{O(k_O)}|V_O|)$ time, where k_O is the treewidth of $\mathcal{G}_O$ with $k_O \leq \frac{1}{2}(k_U + 1)\Delta - 1$, and k_U is the treewidth of the underlying graph of $\mathcal{G}$. On this tree decomposition $(T, \{X_t\})$ of $\mathcal{G}_O$, the dynamic programming algorithm to compute the maximum weighted independent set takes $O(2^{k'_O}(k'_O)^2|V_O|)$ time. Thus, the total time complexity of the algorithm is $O(|\mathcal{V}|\Delta^2\mathcal{T} + 2^{O(k_O)}|\mathcal{E}_U| + 2^{k'_O}(k'_O)^2|\mathcal{E}_U|)$.

6 Conclusion

We study the maximum weighted 0–1 timed matching problem in temporal graphs from the perspective of parameterized complexity. We prove that the problem remains NP-complete even when the underlying static graph of the temporal graph has a bounded treewidth, demonstrating that structural sparsity alone does not yield tractability. Moreover, we show that the problem is W[1]-hard when parameterized by the size of the solution, indicating that this natural parameterization is unlikely to admit an FPT algorithm. We present a fixed-parameter tractable algorithm for the problem when the underlying static graph has both bounded treewidth and bounded maximum degree identifying a tractable regime within this otherwise hard problem space. In addition, we introduce the concept of edge overlap graph for a given temporal graph to design the fixed-parameter tractable algorithm. Study of structural properties of the edge overlap graph is an interesting direction of future research. The study of the applicability of edge overlap graphs to address other graph problems is another interesting direction of future research.

References

1. Bampis, E., Escoffier, B., Lampis, M., Paschos, V.T.: Multistage matchings. In: Scandinavian Symposium and Workshops on Algorithm Theory (SWAT), vol. 101, pp. 7–1 (2018)
2. Baste, J., Bui-Xuan, B.M., Roux, A.: Temporal matching. Theor. Comput. Sci. **806**, 184–196 (2020)
3. Bodlaender, H.L., Bonsma, P., Lokshtanov, D.: The fine details of fast dynamic programming over tree decompositions. In: International Symposium on Parameterized and Exact Computation (IPEC), pp. 41–53 (2013)
4. Casteigts, A., Himmel, A.S., Molter, H., Zschoche, P.: Finding temporal paths under waiting time constraints. Algorithmica **83**(9), 2754–2802 (2021)
5. Chimani, M., Troost, N., Wiedera, T.: Approximating multistage matching problems. Algorithmica **84**(8), 2135–2153 (2022)
6. Cygan, M., et al.: Parameterized Algorithms, vol. 5. Springer, Heidelberg (2015)
7. Edmonds, J.: Paths, trees, and flowers. Can. J. Math. **17**, 449–467 (1965)
8. Even, S., Kariv, O.: An O $(n^{2.5})$ algorithm for maximum matching in general graphs. In: Annual Symposium on Foundations of Computer Science (SFCS), pp. 100–112 (1975)
9. Fan, X., et al.: Temporal data dissemination in UAV-assisted VANETs through time-varying graphs. IEEE Trans. Veh. Technol. **73**(10), 14835–14846 (2024)
10. Ferreira, A.: On models and algorithms for dynamic communication networks: the case for evolving graphs. In: 4^e rencontres francophones sur les Aspects Algorithmiques des Telecommunications (ALGOTEL), pp. 155–161 (2002)
11. Garey, M.R., Johnson, D.S.: Computers and Intractability, vol. 29. WH Freeman, New York (2002)
12. Harvey, D.J., Wood, D.R.: The treewidth of line graphs. J. Comb. Theory Ser. B **132**, 157–179 (2018)
13. Hopcroft, J.E., Karp, R.M.: An $n^{5/2}$ algorithm for maximum matchings in bipartite graphs. SIAM J. Comput. **2**(4), 225–231 (1973)
14. Iribarren, J.L., Moro, E.: Impact of human activity patterns on the dynamics of information diffusion. Phys. Rev. Lett. **103**(3), 038702 (2009)
15. Korhonen, T.: A single-exponential time 2-approximation algorithm for treewidth. In: IEEE Annual Symposium on Foundations of Computer Science (FOCS), pp. 184–192 (2021)
16. Lebre, S., Becq, J., Devaux, F., Stumpf, M.P., Lelandais, G.: Statistical inference of the time-varying structure of gene-regulation networks. BMC Syst. Biol. **4**, 1–16 (2010)

17. Lordan, O., Sallan, J.M.: Dynamic measures for transportation networks. PLoS ONE **15**(12), e0242875 (2020)
18. Mandal, S., Gupta, A.: Approximation algorithms for permanent dominating set problem on dynamic networks. In: International Conference on Distributed Computing and Internet Technology (ICDCIT), pp. 265–279 (2018)
19. Mandal, S., Gupta, A.: Convergecast tree on temporal graphs. Int. J. Found. Comput. Sci. **31**(03), 385–409 (2020)
20. Mandal, S., Gupta, A.: Maximum 0–1 timed matching on temporal graphs. Disc. Appl. Math. **319**, 310–326 (2022)
21. Marino, A., Silva, A.: Coloring temporal graphs. J. Comput. Syst. Sci. **123**, 171–185 (2022)
22. Mertzios, G.B., Molter, H., Niedermeier, R., Zamaraev, V., Zschoche, P.: Computing maximum matchings in temporal graphs. J. Comput. Syst. Sci. **137**, 1–19 (2023)
23. Mertzios, G.B., Molter, H., Zamaraev, V.: Sliding window temporal graph coloring. J. Comput. Syst. Sci. **120**, 97–115 (2021)
24. Michail, O., Spirakis, P.G.: Traveling salesman problems in temporal graphs. Theor. Comput. Sci. **634**, 1–23 (2016)
25. Mucha, M., Sankowski, P.: Maximum matchings in planar graphs via gaussian elimination. Algorithmica **45**(1), 3–20 (2006)
26. Picavet, T., Nguyen, N.T., Bui-Xuan, B.M.: Temporal matching on geometric graph data. In: International Conference on Algorithms and Complexity (CIAC), pp. 394–408 (2021)

Algorithms with Agents and Robots

Improved Linear-Time Construction of Minimal Dominating Set via Mobile Agents

Prabhat Kumar Chand[(✉)] and Anisur Rahaman Molla

Indian Statistical Institute, Kolkata, India
pchand744@gmail.com, molla@isical.ac.in

Abstract. Mobile agents have emerged as a powerful framework for solving fundamental graph problems in distributed settings in recent times. These agents, modelled as autonomous physical or software entities, possess local computation power, finite memory and have the ability to traverse a graph, offering efficient solutions to a range of classical problems. In this work, we focus on the problem of computing a *minimal dominating set* (mDS) in anonymous graphs using mobile agents. Building on the recently proposed optimal dispersion algorithm [9] on the synchronous mobile agent model, we design two new algorithms that achieve a *linear-time* solution for this problem in the synchronous setting. Specifically, given a connected n-node graph with n agents initially placed in either rooted or arbitrary configurations, we show that an mDS can be computed in $O(n)$ rounds using only $O(\log n)$ bits of memory per agent, without using any prior knowledge of any global parameters. This improves upon the best-known complexity results in the literature over the same model. In addition, as natural by-products of our methodology, our algorithms also construct a spanning tree and elect a unique leader in $O(n)$ rounds, which are also important results of independent interest in the mobile-agent framework.

Keywords: Mobile Agents · Minimal Dominating Set · Autonomous Agents · Spanning Tree · Leader Election · Distributed Graph Algorithms

1 Introduction

The use of autonomous agents to solve graph problems has recently attracted significant attention. Such agents, representing entities like self-driving cars, drones, robots, or distributed processes, combine two defining capabilities: they can perform local computations under strict memory constraints, and they can traverse networks, moving between nodes while retaining only limited information. A crucial observation in this model is that local computation cost is essentially negligible compared to movement, as in real-world scenarios where the cost of physical traversal (for example, a self-driven car traversing across mutiple cities) far outweighs local processing. Consequently, research in this area has focused on minimising movement while still enabling efficient solutions to classical graph problems.

A. R. Molla—Supported, in part, by ANRF-SERB Core Research Grant, file no. CRG/2023/009048, and R. C. Bose Centre's internal research grant.

Several fundamental graph problems, such as computing minimal dominating sets and independent sets, leader election, spanning tree construction, and community detection, have been extensively studied both in the classical distributed model and, more recently, in the mobile-agent model. For instance, dominating set construction has been investigated in the mobile-agent setting [4] and refined in subsequent works [8, 10, 11], while the closely related maximal independent set (MIS) problem has also been explored [16]. The same framework has produced algorithms for spanning structures, including BFS trees [2, 3], MSTs [8, 10], and general spanning trees [1]. These developments have further led to increasingly efficient approaches for leader election. Notably, in the mobile-agent perspective, these problems add additional significance: spanning trees construction enables effective communication between these autonomous entities and helps in global information dissemination, while dominating sets highlight structurally critical nodes, allowing non-essential agents to halt—thereby reducing deployment and movement costs, a highly desirable property in practical, resource-constrained applications. A possible research possibility in this direction has been highlighted in Sect. 5.

Recently, [9] introduced an *optimal* algorithm for the *dispersion problem*, where agents are repositioned so that each node hosts at most one agent. Building on this, we design a new algorithm to compute a *minimal dominating set* of a graph G. In our setting, with n agents on an n-node graph, we show that it is possible to achieve multiple objectives simultaneously: deriving a termination condition post dispersion, constructing a spanning tree, electing a leader, and computing an mDS, all within *linear time*. This work improves upon the best-known complexity bounds in the literature and provides the first unified linear-time approach to these fundamental tasks in the mobile-agent model.

1.1 Contributions

The first study of the mDS problem in the mobile-agent framework appeared in [4]. Subsequent works [8, 11] did not directly improve its techniques; progress arose mainly from advances in *leader election*, which in turn enabled faster mDS computation or reduced prior knowledge requirements. In [10], the authors proposed a logarithmic-time probing method to improve the search before colouring a node, but their approach required knowledge of n and Δ, as well as leader election before mDS construction.

In this paper, we focus on improving the complexity through a new approach. Our algorithms build on the optimal dispersion procedure of [9], but the construction of an mDS is neither immediate nor straightforward. We develop a colouring-based mechanism and a careful strategy for releasing colours during execution. For arbitrary initial configurations, we further design a novel technique to detect the completion of dispersion before reducing the problem to the rooted case. In contrast, previous works rely on an infinite (or sufficiently large) waiting time to allow dispersion without explicit termination detection (e.g., [4]) or perform expensive computation to first elect a leader (e.g., [10]) before the actual mDS construction. Moreover, in the arbitrary dispersion algorithm of [9], termination detection remains challenging since the number of agents k may be significantly smaller than n. Our main contribution is the following result.

Table 1. Comparison of prior and recent results for the minimal dominating set problem in a graph G under the mobile-agent model. '$-$' indicates no prior knowledge of parameters. Here, λ denotes the highest-ID of an agent in an n-node graph with m edges and maximum degree Δ, and ℓ is the number of initial clusters in an arbitrary configuration. Additional applications such as leader election, gathering, and spanning tree construction are achieved in $O(n)$ rounds using $O(\log n)$ memory per agent without any prior knowledge. This work attains the state of the art in leader election (previous best $O(n \log^2 n)$ [11]), spanning tree construction (previous best $O(n \log n)$ [1]), and gathering of n agents (removing prior-knowledge requirements as in [2]) from arbitrary configurations using optimal memory $O(\log n)$ bits.

Algorithm	Knowledge	Time	Memory/Agent	Initial Config.
Minimal Dominating Set				
Section 3	$-$	$O(n)$	$O(\log n)$	Rooted
Section 4	$-$	$O(n)$	$O(\log n)$	Arbitrary
Kshemkalyani *et al.* [10]	n, Δ	$O(n \log \Delta)$	$O(\log n)$	Arbitrary
Kshemkalyani *et al.* [11]	$-$	$O(n \log^2 n + m)$	$O(\log n)$	Arbitrary
Kshemkalyani *et al.* [8]	$-$	$O(m)$	$O(n \log n)$	Arbitrary
Chand *et al.* [4]	$\lambda, \Delta, n, m, \ell$	$O(m + \ell \Delta \log(\lambda) + n\ell)$	$O(\log n)$	Arbitrary
Chand *et al.* [4]	$-$	$O(m)$	$O(\log n)$	Rooted
Other Applications (From Section 4)				
Leader Election	$-$	$O(n)$	$O(\log n)$	Arbitrary
Gathering (n **agents**)	$-$	$O(n)$	$O(\log n)$	Arbitrary
Spanning Tree	$-$	$O(n)$	$O(\log n)$	Arbitrary

Theorem. *Let G be a simple, connected, anonymous graph with n nodes. Given n mobile agents initially placed over the nodes either in a rooted or an arbitrary config- uration, there exists an algorithm through which the agents can collectively compute a minimal dominating set in $O(n)$ rounds, using $O(\log n)$ bits of memory per agent, where Δ is the maximum degree of the graph.*

As natural by-products, our algorithms also achieve spanning tree construction, gathering and leader election within the same time and memory bounds, problems that are of independent interest in distributed agent-based computing. A comparison with prior results is summarised in Table 1.

1.2 Related Work

The first efficient distributed implementation of the dominating set problem in the CONGEST model was studied by Jia *et al.* [6], who refined the greedy strategy of [15] to design a randomized algorithm running in $O(\log n \log \Delta)$ rounds, produc- ing a $\ln(\Delta)$-approximation with only a constant number of messages exchanged per edge. Sultanik *et al.* [18] addressed the art gallery problem—equivalent to finding a minimal dominating set in visibility graphs—via a distributed algorithm that runs in time proportional to the graph's diameter and guarantees a constant-factor approx- imation with high probability. Kuhn and Wattenhofer [14] proposed LP-based algorithms that compute a dominating set within a factor $(k\Delta^{2/k} \log \Delta)$ of optimal in $O(k^2)$ rounds, with $O(k^2\Delta)$ messages per node; setting k constant yields the first constant-round, non-trivial approximation. Complementing this, Kuhn *et al.* [13] established lower bounds showing that even polylogarithmic approximations for dominating set or vertex cover require at least $\Omega(\sqrt{\frac{\log(n)}{\log(\log(n))}})$ and $\Omega(\sqrt{\frac{\log(\Delta)}{\log(\log(\Delta))}})$ rounds, respectively. More recently, Jiang *et al.* [5] developed deterministic algorithms achieving an approximation factor of $(1 + \epsilon)(1 + \log(\Delta + 1))$ in $O(2^{O(\sqrt{\log n \log \log n})})$ and $O(\Delta \, \mathrm{polylog}(\Delta) + \mathrm{polylog}(\Delta) \log^\star n)$ rounds for $\epsilon > 1/\mathrm{polylog}(\Delta)$, and extended their methods to connected dominating sets.

In the context of mobile agents, Kaur *et al.* [7] introduced a related problem, called *Distance-2-Dispersion* (D-2-D) problem, where k agents settle on nodes subject to two constraints: no two agents may occupy adjacent nodes, and an agent may reuse a node only if no unoccupied node remains that satisfies the first condition. They showed that with $O(\log \Delta)$ memory per agent, the problem can be solved in $O(m\Delta)$ rounds without prior knowledge of m, n, or Δ, and when $k \geq n$, the settled agents form a maximal independent set. The problem of constructing a minimal dominating set (mDS) with mobile agents was first studied by Chand *et al.* [4], who showed that from a rooted configuration, an mDS can be identified in $O(m)$ rounds, while for arbitrary configurations the construction requires $O(\ell\Delta \log \lambda + n\ell + m)$ rounds, assuming prior knowledge of m, n, Δ, λ and the number of clusters ℓ. They also obtained an $\ln(\Delta)$-approximate minimum dominating set from dispersed configurations. Subsequent works [8, 10, 11] improved these results by removing global knowledge requirements or optimising the trade-offs between time and memory, although the central focus of these works was on the leader election problem.

1.3 Our Model

Graph: We have an underlying graph $G(V, E)$ that is connected, undirected, unweighted and anonymous with $|V| = n$ nodes and $|E| = m$ edges. Nodes of G do not have any distinguishing identifiers or labels. These nodes do not possess any memory and hence cannot store any information. The degree of a node $v \in V$ is denoted by $\delta(v)$ and the maximum degree of G is Δ. Edges incident on v are locally labelled using port numbers in the range $[0, \delta(v) - 1]$. The edges of the graph serve as *routes* through which the agents can commute. Any number of agents can travel through an edge at any given time.

Mobile Agents: A collection of n agents enumerated as $\mathcal{R} = \{r_1, r_2, \ldots, r_n\}$ resides on the nodes of the graph with each having a unique ID $\in [0, n^{O(1)}]$. We assume that the highest ID among the n agents is denoted by λ with $(\lambda \leq n^{O(1)})$. An agent retains and updates its memory as needed. Two or more agents can be present (*co-located*) at a node or pass through an edge in G. However, an agent is not allowed to stay on an edge. An agent can recognise the port number through which it has entered and exited a node. The agents do not have any visibility beyond their (current) location at a node. An agent at a node v can only realise its adjacent ports (connecting to edges) at v. Only the collocated agents at a node can sense each other and exchange information. An agent can exchange all the information stored in its memory instantaneously. For colouring, each agent maintains a variable indicating its colour, chosen from {red, blue}.

Communication Model: We consider a synchronous system where the agents are synchronised to a common clock and the *local communication* model, where only co-located agents (i.e., agents at the same node) can communicate among themselves. In each round, an agent r_i performs the $Communicate - Compute - Move$ (CCM) task-cycle as follows: (i) *Communicate:* r_i may communicate with other agents at the same node, (ii) *Compute:* Based on the gathered information and subsequent computations, r_i may perform all manner of computations within the bounds of its memory, and (iii) *Move:* r_i may move to a neighbouring node using the computed exit port. We measure the complexity in two metrics, namely, time/round and memory. The *time complexity* of an algorithm is the number of rounds required to execute the algorithm. The *memory complexity* is measured w.r.t. the amount of memory (in bits) required by each agent for computation.

Problem Statement: Let $G(V, E)$ be a simple, connected, anonymous graph with $|V| = n$. Suppose n autonomous agents are initially distributed arbitrarily over the nodes of G. The goal is to design an algorithm that repositions these n agents across the nodes of G so as to compute a minimal dominating set of the graph, while minimising both the overall time complexity and the memory required at each agent.

2   Preliminaries

2.1   A Linear-Time Graph Covering and Dispersion Algorithm

In [9], the authors solve the dispersion problem in $O(k)$ rounds, where $k \leq n$ agents need to reposition themselves into distinct nodes such that no node hosts more than one agent. Here, we provide a brief description of the algorithm for our model (where $k = n$) for both the rooted and arbitrary configurations. First, we describe the algorithm for the rooted configuration. The algorithm employs a Depth-First Search (DFS) strategy to explore the graph and incrementally settle agents. A key contribution of the work is in addressing the classical bottleneck of DFS-based dispersion: the time spent in searching for an unoccupied neighbour to continue traversal. In earlier approaches, this search was sequential and incurred $O(\Delta)$ time per step, bringing the total edge count m into the time complexity [12].

Sudo *et al.* [17] improved this by proposing a parallel probing technique that reduced the neighbour search time to $O(\log \Delta)$ rounds. Their method escalated the search by recursively bringing in agents from settled neighbourhoods in a doubling fashion. Building on this idea, the algorithm in [9] further reduces the probing cost to $O(1)$ rounds. The main insight is to proactively reserve at least $\lceil n/3 \rceil$ agents (called *seeker agents*) for synchronous probing, which allows all neighbours of a node to be probed in parallel. The remaining $\lfloor 2n/3 \rfloor$ agents (called *explorer agents*) are allowed to settle during the DFS.

Maintaining the availability of $\lceil n/3 \rceil$ seekers requires that at least $\lceil n/3 \rceil$ nodes remain unoccupied until DFS finishes. The algorithm ensures this by deliberately leaving certain nodes in the DFS tree empty (we term them as *covered nodes*). A covered node is one that is unoccupied but still accessible—meaning it is "covered" by an agent that can visit it when needed. In contrast, a *fully unsettled node* is both unoccupied and uncovered. The algorithm guarantees that covered nodes are reachable through agent *oscillations*, where a settled agent temporarily moves from its home node to one or more nearby empty nodes and back. In particular, an agent may oscillate between up to three child nodes or between two sibling nodes. The oscillation schedule ensures that if any agent waits at a covered node for six rounds, it is guaranteed to encounter the corresponding oscillating agent. Thus, each settled agent can cover $O(1)$ empty nodes with constant-time oscillation.

Special care is taken around branching points in the DFS tree to decide which nodes should remain empty, which agents should oscillate, and which nodes are permanently settled. This decision-making occurs during the forward and backtrack phases of DFS. The algorithm ensures that every node in the DFS tree is either directly settled or properly covered via oscillation. At each step of the traversal, the agents use the $\lceil n/3 \rceil$ seekers to perform a probing step: if a fully unsettled neighbour is found, the DFS proceeds with a forward move; otherwise, it backtracks. Since there are exactly n forward steps and at most $2(n - 1)$ backtracks, the total number of rounds remains $O(n)$.

Once DFS completes and all n nodes have been visited, the reserved $\lceil n/3 \rceil$ seeker agents regroup at the root. They then perform a second traversal of the DFS tree to occupy the previously unfilled nodes. This phase is implemented using a *sibling-pointer* mechanism that allows agents to traverse the tree efficiently with only $O(\log n)$ bits of memory.

In summary, the algorithm achieves $O(n)$ round complexity by separating the responsibilities of settlement and probing: while $\lfloor 2n/3 \rfloor$ agents incrementally settle across the graph, the remaining $\lceil n/3 \rceil$ agents support constant-time probing throughout the traversal. This structural division allows for dispersion with optimal time complexity and significantly improves upon prior techniques that relied on sequential or logarithmic-time searches. Now, for our problem, we modify this algorithm from the point where the last explorer settles and the remaining $\lceil n/3 \rceil$ agents start moving towards the root. At this point, we reach what we call a *"covered configuration"*. This is the stage where all the $\lfloor 2n/3 \rfloor$ explorer agents have settled. Through this algorithm, we obtain the following state at some point:

- **The team of $\lceil n/3 \rceil$ seeker agents at the root**. These agents can now to used to search all neighbours of a particular node within $O(1)$ rounds.
- **A *covered configuration*.** In such a configuration, every empty node is either visited periodically (within 6 rounds) by an oscillating agent or has a permanent settler.

To reach this configuration, we simply run the dispersion algorithm from [9] until the point where we have a *covered configuration* and a seeker team gathered at the root.

For the arbitrary starting configuration, dispersion is achieved by combining the tree-subsumption method of Kshemkalyani [12] with the methodology used in the rooted case. Suppose the algorithm begins with ℓ clusters. Each of these ℓ clusters initiates its own dispersion independently. If the depth-first search (DFS) exploration initiated by a cluster does not encounter any other DFS, it proceeds to completion exactly as in the rooted case. However, if two (or more) DFS processes meet during dispersion, the algorithm ensures that they are merged into the DFS with the larger number of settled agents. Specifically, if DFS i meets DFS j, and i currently has more settled agents than j, then j is collapsed and all of its agents join the execution of i's DFS. This merging operation is referred to as *subsumption*. Thus, whenever two DFSs meet, the smaller one is subsumed into the larger.

It is important to note that in the original algorithm, even after dispersion completes, multiple DFS trees may exist, particularly when the number of agents k is significantly smaller than the number of nodes n. During DFS construction, agents settle one by one on previously unoccupied nodes, while the remaining agents continue exploring in search of empty nodes. The node currently occupied by all unsettled agents of a DFS, and responsible for further exploration, is referred to as its *head*. A DFS is initially identified by the smallest-ID agent that initiates it, although this identifier may change if the DFS is later subsumed by another. For a given DFS i, we denote its head by $head(i)$.

The dispersion algorithm proceeds in two alternating phases: (i) a *growing phase* and (ii) a *subsumption phase*, which repeat until dispersion is complete. In the growing phase, unsettled agents of a DFS explore new nodes and settle sequentially. In the subsumption phase, if a DFS with d settled agents is subsumed by another, the subsumption process requires $O(d)$ rounds. Consequently, if the initial configuration consists of ℓ clusters of sizes $k_1, k_2, k_3, \ldots, k_\ell$, the overall time complexity of the dispersion algorithm is

$$O(k_1 + k_2 + k_3 + \cdots + k_\ell) = O(n),$$

where n is the total number of agents. This bound already accounts for the time spent in subsumptions, since the total subsumption cost is $\sum O(d_i) = O(n)$ rounds, where d_i denotes the number of settled agents in DFS i before it is subsumed. Hence, we have the following theorem from [9].

Theorem 1. *Starting from any initial configuration, dispersion can be solved in $O(n)$ rounds using $O(\log n)$ bits of memory per agent in a synchronous setting.*

Before presenting our algorithms, we formally define the notion of a minimal dominating set.

Definition 1 (Minimal Dominating Set). *A subset $D \subseteq V$ of a graph $G = (V, E)$ is called a* dominating set *if every vertex $v \in V \setminus D$ has at least one neighbor in D. The set D is said to be a* minimal dominating set *(mDS) if no proper subset of D is a dominating set, i.e., removing any vertex from D destroys the domination property.*

3   Minimal Dominating Set (mDS) from Rooted Configuration

In this section, we consider the problem of constructing a minimal dominating set (mDS) in an arbitrary graph using n mobile agents that initially begin at a designated root node. We present an efficient algorithm that completes this task in $O(n)$ rounds, improving upon previous approaches [4, 8, 10, 11].

3.1 High-Level Overview

The algorithm proceeds in two main phases. In the first phase, we reposition the n agents into a *covered configuration* (as defined in Sect. 2.1), such that $\lfloor 2n/3 \rfloor$ agents settle across the graph, and the remaining $\lceil n/3 \rceil$ agents—the *seeker agents*—are located at the last visited node, where the final *explorer agent* has just settled, which then traverse back to the root node using the pointers established during the DFS traversal. In the second phase, the agents collaboratively construct a *minimal dominating set* (mDS) of the underlying graph. Our approach builds on the $O(m)$-round algorithm presented in [4]. In that work, the root agent is initially assigned the colour red to indicate its inclusion in the mDS. As the DFS traversal proceeds, each subsequent agent, before settling at a new node, examines the colour of its already-settled neighbours, including its parent. If none of the neighbouring agents are coloured red, the agent colours itself red; otherwise, it assigns itself the colour blue. This process is inherently sequential, requiring $O(m)$ rounds to complete due to the dependency on local neighbourhood checks at each step.

Our algorithm significantly reduces this complexity by leveraging the $\lceil n/3 \rceil$ seeker agents to parallelise the neighbourhood colour checks. Once the covered configuration is formed, the seeker agents return to the root and re-traverse the graph in a coordinated manner. During this re-traversal, they assist in assigning colours to agents by probing the colours of neighbouring nodes in parallel, enabling each agent to determine its colour in $O(1)$ time. This parallel probing leads to a substantial improvement in overall round complexity.

However, this speed-up introduces a natural question: how do we determine the colour of a node that is currently unoccupied but covered? Since the covered configuration leaves $\lceil n/3 \rceil$ nodes vacant, some nodes may need to be coloured without having a permanently settled agent. We resolve this by using *oscillating agents* - agents that periodically visit such vacant nodes and assign a colour based on the current context of their neighbourhood. This technique avoids the need to settle an agent permanently at such nodes while still ensuring correctness in the colouring process.

3.2 Details

The algorithm begins from the *covered configuration*, with the team of $\lceil n/3 \rceil$ seeker agents stationed at the root. The first step is to assign the colour red to the agent at the root. However, since the agent covering the root may be oscillating, the seeker team might have to wait for a few rounds until the oscillating agent visits the root node. At this point, we recall the two types of oscillation as described in [9].

Types of Oscillations:

- **Type A:** Let u be a node with three children v, w, and x in the DFS tree. Suppose $p(v) < p(w) < p(x)$ are the corresponding port numbers at u connecting to v, w, and x, respectively. In Type A oscillation, the agent at u oscillates in the following sequence:

$$u \to v \to u \to w \to u \to x \to u \to \dots$$

In this setup, we say that the agent at u is covering the nodes v, w, and x through Type A oscillation, and u is referred to as its *home node*.

- **Type B:** Let u be a node with parent $\mathsf{parent}(u)$. Suppose $p(\mathsf{parent}(u))$ is the port number at $\mathsf{parent}(u)$ that connects to u. Let v and w be two sibling nodes of u such that v and w connect to $\mathsf{parent}(u)$ via port numbers $p(\mathsf{parent}(u)) + 1$ and $p(\mathsf{parent}(u)) + 2$, respectively. Then, a Type B oscillation by the agent at u proceeds as:

$$u \rightarrow \mathsf{parent}(u) \rightarrow v \rightarrow \mathsf{parent}(u) \rightarrow w \rightarrow \mathsf{parent}(u) \rightarrow u \rightarrow \dots$$

In this case, the agent at u covers nodes v and w via Type B oscillation, and again, u is its home node.

The type of oscillation an agent follows is determined during the forward and backtrack steps of the dispersion algorithm. Importantly, in both types of oscillation, it suffices to wait at a (possibly empty) node for at most 6 rounds to ensure that the node is visited (i.e., covered) by some oscillating agent. We now explain how an oscillating agent can simulate or represent the colour of the node it is currently visiting.

Simulating Node Colour via Oscillating Agents: To simulate the colour of multiple nodes visited during oscillation, each agent r maintains a variable tuple:

$$r.\mathsf{node\_color} = (\mathsf{osc}, \mathsf{color}),$$

where:

- $\mathsf{osc} = 0$ indicates that the agent is at its home node.
- $\mathsf{osc} = i \in \{1, 2, 3\}$ represents the i-th node in its oscillation sequence.
- $\mathsf{color} \in \{red, blue\}$ denotes the colour of the node currently being visited.

Let us illustrate this using the Type A oscillation pattern described above. Suppose node u is the home node of an oscillating agent r, and its children v, w, and x should have colours: blue, red, and blue, respectively. Then, agent r performs the following updates during its oscillation:

- At home node u: $r.\mathsf{node\_color} \leftarrow (0, blue)$
- Move to v: $r.\mathsf{node\_color} \leftarrow (1, blue)$
- Return to u: $r.\mathsf{node\_color} \leftarrow (0, blue)$
- Move to w: $r.\mathsf{node\_color} \leftarrow (2, red)$
- Return to u: $r.\mathsf{node\_color} \leftarrow (0, blue)$
- Move to x: $r.\mathsf{node\_color} \leftarrow (3, blue)$
- ...

For Type-B oscillation, we employ a similar assignment technique, with the osc value restricted to $\{1, 2, 3\}$. Each time an oscillating agent receives its colouring information from the seeker team, it records the colour associated with every node it visits, together with the corresponding osc value that uniquely identifies the node within its oscillation cycle. To support this process, each agent maintains a constant-sized internal memory capable of storing up to three distinct colour states, which is sufficient for updating the node_color variable according to its oscillation pattern. This mechanism guarantees that even vacant nodes—those not permanently occupied—are virtually coloured by the oscillating agents. Having established this, we now proceed to describe our main algorithm.

In the covered configuration, $\lceil n/3 \rceil$ seeker agents from the root begin constructing the dominating set. Using the *child*, *sibling*, and *parent* pointers, they can traverse the graph in $O(n)$ rounds (a technique commonly used; as in [1,9]). When the seeker group meets the home agent at the root, it initiates the colouring process: the root agent sets node_color $\leftarrow (0, red)$. The seekers then continue along the DFS, and at the next node, instruct the oscillating agent to set node_color $\leftarrow (0, blue)$.

At each step, colouring decisions require examining the neighbours. The seekers employ parallel probing, where agents temporarily branch out to visit neighbours, possibly waiting up to 6 rounds at each node to meet the oscillating agent and collect its colour, if any. After probing, if no neighbour is coloured red, the current agent is instructed to set its colour to red; otherwise, it colours itself blue. The seekers then resume DFS traversal. The process continues until all nodes have been visited and coloured, after which the seekers return to the root.

In the final phase of the algorithm, the seeker team permanently settles and assigns colours to itself. To accomplish this, the seekers perform a third traversal of the graph from the root. During this traversal, each seeker agent successively occupies one of the remaining vacant nodes and proceeds as follows:

- **If the agent currently at the node is non-oscillating:** In this case, no new agent needs to settle at the node, as it is already being represented by a coloured non-oscillating agent. The seeker team instructs the non-oscillating agent to copy its current colour value into a new permanent variable: color_par $\leftarrow$ node_color.color. This variable, color_par, stores the final (permanent) colour of the agent representing that node.
- **If the agent currently at the node is oscillating:** This situation is further divided into two cases:
    1. **Oscillating agent away from its home node:** One seeker agent (e.g., the one with the smallest ID) permanently settles at the current node and sets color_par $\leftarrow$ node_color.color.
    2. **Oscillating agent at its home node:** The seeker team performs one final oscillation with it, verifies that all covered nodes are permanently occupied and coloured (settling and permanently colouring any remaining nodes as in the previous case using agents from the seeker team), and then returns to the home node. The oscillating agent is finally instructed to permanently settle there with its permanent colour by setting color_par $\leftarrow$ node_color.color.

  The oscillating agent, once it settles, discontinues its oscillation. The newly settled agents correctly update their pointers to maintain the DFS tree structure.

In this way, the seeker team traverses the graph and assigns the final colour to all the n agents representing each node. Since the graph contains n nodes and the total number of agents is also n, the $\lceil n/3 \rceil$ seeker agents exactly match the number of vacant positions in the covered configuration. Thus, all remaining nodes are eventually occupied. The correctness and efficiency of this approach follow from the following three lemmas, derived from [9]:

Lemma 1. *In the covering configuration, every non-home empty node is periodically visited (i.e.,* covered*) by an oscillating agent from its corresponding home node.*

Lemma 2. *At the end of achieving the covering configuration, the remaining seeker team contains exactly* $\lceil n/3 \rceil$ *agents, which matches the number of currently unoccupied nodes in the graph.*

Lemma 3. *The covering configuration can be achieved in* $O(n)$ *rounds from a rooted configuration. Additionally, each explorer agent can return to its home node in* $O(n)$ *rounds, and the seeker team can perform a complete DFS traversal of the graph in* $O(n)$ *rounds.*

Theorem 2. *Let G be an arbitrary connected simple anonymous graph with n nodes. Suppose n autonomous mobile agents are initially placed at a designated node (the root) of the graph. Then, the agents can identify a minimal dominating set (coloured red) in* $O(n)$ *rounds using only* $O(\log n)$ *bits of memory per agent.*

Proof. From Lemma 3, the covering configuration can be constructed in $O(n)$ rounds starting from the rooted configuration. Once this configuration is reached, the $\lceil n/3 \rceil$ seeker agents return to the root and initiate a full DFS traversal of the graph. During this traversal, they assist each explorer agent in determining and fixing its colour based on the colouring rules described earlier. Since each node can be processed in $O(1)$ rounds via parallel probing by the seeker team, and the DFS traversal visits each node only a constant number of times, assigning a colour to all nodes takes $O(n)$ rounds. In the final phase, the seeker agents settle at the remaining vacant positions (i.e., non-home oscillated nodes) and simulate the final colour of those nodes. This final deployment and confirmation of colour values also require $O(n)$ rounds. Therefore, the entire process—from constructing the covering configuration, assigning colours, to completing the minimal dominating set (mDS)—is completed in $O(n)$ rounds.

The memory required per agent is $O(\log(\Delta + n))$ bits: to store port and neighbour information (max Δ), and to manage n agents. The memory complexity remains consistent with that in [9], as we use the same variables, with the addition of some extra constant number of variables, node_color, color_par, etc., which require only $O(1)$ bits per agent. Hence, the agents correctly and efficiently identify a minimal dominating set in $O(n)$ rounds, using $O(\log(\Delta + n))$ bits of memory per agent; since $\Delta \leq n$, the overall complexity simplifies to $O(\log n)$ bits. $\qquad\square$

4   Minimal Dominating Set (mDS) from Arbitrary Configuration

We now consider the problem of computing a minimal Dominating Set (mDS) when the n agents are placed in an arbitrary initial configuration, potentially distributed across multiple clusters of the graph. This problem can be reduced to the rooted case (Sect. 3) through three stages. First, the agents are dispersed using the algorithm of [9], which guarantees that with n agents exactly one agent occupies each node. Next, the dispersed agents construct a spanning tree rooted at the node containing the smallest-identifier agent. This is achieved by initially forming several trees, which are then merged until only the least-ID tree remains; the process described in [1], which completes in $O(n \log n)$ rounds. Once the tree is established, the agents can gather at the root in time proportional to the tree's diameter (at most n). Finally, from this rooted configuration, an mDS is computed using the method described in Sect. 3.

This reduction-based approach, however, faces two main challenges. The dispersion procedure lacks a built-in termination detection, preventing the agents from knowing when to initiate the next stage. Moreover, the spanning-tree construction in [1] assumes global knowledge of the largest identifier λ, an extra requirement. To overcome these limitations, we propose an alternative approach that works without any global knowledge and improves the overall complexity of mDS computation from a possible $O(n \log n)$ rounds to $O(n)$ rounds.

4.1   Details

Our algorithm proceeds in three key stages:

1. **Stage 1: Dispersion with Termination Detection.** In this stage, the agents first disperse across the graph. We introduce a novel mechanism that enables all n agents to detect when dispersion has completed. During this process, the agents simultaneously construct a spanning tree of the graph in $O(n)$ time. This result is also of independent interest, as it provides a faster construction than existing spanning-tree algorithms [1–3, 8, 11] and introduces a new leader election algorithm.
2. **Stage 2: Gathering via the Spanning Tree.** Using the spanning tree built in Stage 1, the agents gather at the root node. This step effectively reduces the problem to the rooted configuration considered in Sect. 3.
3. **Stage 3: Minimal Dominating Set Computation.** Finally, from the rooted configuration, the agents compute a minimal Dominating Set (mDS) following the methodology described in Sect. 3.

Stage 1: Dispersion with Termination Detection. In an arbitrary initial configuration, if the total number of agents distributed across all clusters is significantly smaller than the number of nodes n, it becomes challenging for the agents to detect the completion of the dispersion process. The difficulty arises because two different DFS trees, initiated from two separate clusters, may never intersect during dispersion. Since the agents can only communicate locally, no agent within a DFS tree can conclusively determine whether the dispersion process has terminated.

However, when the number of agents is at least n, the subsumption algorithm from [9, 12] can be modified to detect termination. In our setting, with exactly n agents in an n-node graph, we modify the dispersion algorithm to incorporate this termination detection. The key idea is that once multiple clusters have completed dispersion, it is guaranteed that, even if these clusters do not directly meet, a DFS tree emerging from any cluster can eventually reach another cluster by traversing an additional outgoing edge (i.e., an edge not internal to the cluster DFS itself). Since clusters disperse at different rates, a dispersed cluster may not immediately find a new agent, although a larger cluster can immediately find one soon after completing its own dispersion.

To begin, each cluster disperses locally according to the methodology of [9]. Agents progressively cover unvisited nodes through the expansion of a DFS tree until the *covered configuration* is reached. When two DFS trees originating from different clusters encounter one another, a *subsumption* operation takes place, in which one DFS tree is absorbed into the other, eventually forming a single *covered* DFS tree.

Consider a DFS i of size k_i, where k_i denotes the number of settled agents in the DFS plus the number of seeker agents currently located at $head(i)$. Let r_t be the last agent to settle in DFS i, placed at node v whose parent is node u. After r_t settles, the seeker team probes from v to determine whether there exists an external edge from DFS i leading either to an uncovered empty node or to a node covered by agents from another DFS. At this stage, two cases may arise:

Case 1. If such an external edge exists at v, r_t returns to u and informs the agent covering u to extend its oscillation pattern: either by adding v to its oscillation cycle (if u is already covered by an oscillating agent) or by initiating oscillation between u and v (if u is covered by a non-oscillating agent). This guarantees that v remains covered. Subsequently, r_t becomes a free agent and moves to the newly discovered node and becomes $head(i)$, setting v as its *parent* (the similar *child* information is updated at the agent covering v simultaneously). If the new node is empty, r_t waits there until it is potentially reached by another DFS; otherwise, if r_t encounters an agent from another DFS, the subsumption process begins immediately.

Case 2. If no external edge is found from v to an empty node or to a node occupied by another DFS (meaning v is a leaf node or all its edges lead to the DFS i itself), the seeker team collects r_t and continues backtracking until such a node has been discovered. During backtracking, the node v remains covered through the modified oscillation sequence of its parent u. Let's assume that DFS i has k_i agents. Since the seeker team has size at least $\lceil \frac{k_i}{3} \rceil + 1$, it can probe its current node in $O(1)$ rounds to find a suitable external node while backtracking. Once an external node is identified, r_t settles there in the same manner as described in Case 1. In this situation, the node (say, covered by an agent r_w) from which the external edge was detected is designated as the new *parent*, and the discovered node becomes the new $head(i)$. Accordingly, the pointers of r_t and r_w are updated.

After the new *head* has been assigned, the rest of the seeker agents now continue to complete the dispersion process following [9]. Now, importantly, if during its backtracking process the seeker team reaches the root of DFS i and still finds no external outgoing edge, this indicates that all n nodes have been visited, all DFSs have been merged to a single DFS, and the dispersion can now complete. As and when this termination condition is detected, the seeker team settles at the remaining empty nodes as the root initiates a complete graph traversal, simultaneously informing all the agents that dispersion has been achieved and is complete. From the discussion above, we record the following lemma.

Lemma 4. *If a DFS i performs one extra exploration to an uncovered node x, then (i) some other DFS j must eventually reach x, and (ii) the waiting time of the new $head(i)$ at x is absorbed into the dispersion time of DFS j.*

Proof. If x is already occupied when $head(i)$ arrives, the lemma follows immediately. Suppose instead that x is empty and uncovered. Since there are exactly n agents on n nodes, each settled agent occupies a distinct node, and no DFS can contain more agents than the number of nodes it spans. Hence, as dispersion proceeds, every uncovered node must eventually be visited; in particular, some other DFS will expand to x, establishing (i). For (ii), observe that DFS j, which eventually reaches x continues its dispersion concurrently while $head(i)$ is waiting. The time spent by $head(i)$ waiting at x is therefore bounded by the remaining dispersion time of the cluster belonging to DFS j. $\qquad\qquad\square$

The **fully dispersed case**, where the system begins with exactly one agent per node, presents an additional challenge. In a non-dispersed setting, the presence of at least two agents within a DFS ensures progress, as one agent can continue exploration while the other maintains coverage of the vacated node, eventually allowing all clusters to merge into a single DFS by acquiring the agents one by one, as discussed earlier. By contrast, in a dispersed configuration, every agent is isolated, and adjacent singleton agents lack immediate awareness of each other. This absence of coordination may lead to expansion conflicts: two neighbouring agents can simultaneously move toward one another, vacating their nodes without ever establishing contact, thereby stalling progress. To overcome this, we employ a lightweight symmetry-breaking procedure. Each singleton agent, at the start of the algorithm, sequentially scans the bits of its unique identifier, from least to most significant bit. For each bit, if it is 1, the agent moves to a fixed adjacent node (arbitrarily selected and remains fixed during this process) and then returns; if the bit is 0, it remains stationary for two rounds. Since two adjacent agents must differ at some bit position, the first such difference guarantees that one agent remains stationary while the other moves, enabling detection and the formation of a two-node DFS tree. The agent with the smaller identifier designates itself as the root, while the other joins as its child. From that point, both agents terminate the symmetry-breaking process and continue following the standard DFS methodology. Similarly, if an agent executing the symmetry-breaking procedure encounters a DFS initiated elsewhere, it immediately halts the procedure and integrates into the visiting DFS. In addition, once an agent has completely scanned its identifier ID bits, it remains stationary at its own node unless it gets acquired by some DFS tree. Agents already in a two-node DFS ignore further symmetry-breaking attempts by other adjacent agents (in that case, the DFS integrates the visiting agent into its own tree). Importantly, the procedure requires no knowledge of the maximum ID (λ), as it terminates locally once agents join a DFS or their ID bits have exhausted. It guarantees that some pair of adjacent agents in a fully dispersed configuration will meet to form a 2-node DFS, at least, which can then acquire all remaining agents and grow into a single DFS tree as described earlier.

Lemma 5. *The dispersion of the n agents, the construction of the single DFS tree, and the detection of termination together complete in $O(n)$ rounds.*

Proof. First of all, since each singleton cluster initiates a symmetry-breaking mechanism at the start, a maximum time of $O(\log \lambda) = O(\log n)$ (worst case scenario, for a dispersed configuration) is required at first before the actual dispersion begins (this symmetry-breaking mechanism is independent and does not affect a dispersion process happening elsewhere). Then, the algorithm consists of four phases: dispersion of individual clusters, subsumption of DFS trees, backtracking to select an external edge and a final traversal. By [9], the dispersion of a cluster of size k_i completes in $O(k_i)$ rounds, and any backtracking to search for external nodes can also be performed in $O(k_i)$ rounds due to parallel probing. When two DFS trees of sizes k_i and k_j meet, the subsumption process takes $O(\max\{k_i, k_j\})$ rounds [12]. Once all clusters have been subsumed into a single DFS tree, the final traversal from the root to visit every node requires $O(n)$ rounds, as such traversals can be carried out without incurring significant memory overhead, by equipping each child agent with a *sibling* pointer, as employed in [1,2,9]. Now, in the worst case, subsumptions occur sequentially, with a single DFS tree absorbing others one by one. For a cluster of size k_i, the total cost of dispersion, subsumption and backtracking is $O(k_i)$, and summing over all clusters yields $\sum_i O(k_i) = O(n)$. Hence, the overall time complexity of Stage 1 is $O(\log n) + O(n) = O(n)$ rounds. $\square$

Remark 1 (New Oscillation). Since the algorithm adds one extra oscillation for the last settled agent before exploring an external edge in the DFS, each agent waits 8 rounds (instead of 6) at a node to verify whether it is covered.

Remark 2 (Leader Election). The root agent at the end of the Stage 1 can function as an elected leader.

Stage 2: Gathering via the Spanning Tree. To gather all the agents at the root, the process proceeds as follows. The gathering begins at the leaf agents of the spanning tree, which, having no children, move directly to their parent and accumulate there. At any intermediate stage, consider an agent a that serves as an internal node of the tree. Agent a remains stationary until it has received all the agents collected by its children. Once this condition is satisfied, a moves to its parent, carrying along all the gathered agents. By repeating this process up the tree, all agents are eventually collected at the root node. When the root has received all the $n - 1$ other agents, the gathering phase is complete, and we can proceed to the final stage of the algorithm, as we note the following lemma from our discussion.

Lemma 6. *Gathering via the Spanning Tree takes $O(n)$ rounds.*

Stage 3: Minimal Dominating Set Computation. With all n agents assembled at the root, the agents collaboratively execute the rooted-case minimal dominating set (mDS) algorithm described in Sect. 3, thereby computing the final minimal dominating set of the graph. We therefore, obtain the following theorem from Lemmas 4, 5, 6.

Theorem 3. *Let G be an arbitrary connected simple anonymous graph with n nodes. Suppose n autonomous mobile agents are initially placed arbitrarily across the graph. Then, the agents can identify a minimal dominating set (coloured red) in $O(n)$ rounds using only $O(\log n)$ bits of memory per agent.*

5   Conclusion and Future Directions

We proposed two linear-time algorithms for computing a minimal dominating set using mobile agents in both rooted and arbitrary configurations, achieving $O(n)$ round complexity in each case. The framework also facilitates linear-time solutions to related problems such as leader election, gathering, and spanning tree construction, all without requiring any global knowledge.

Future work includes reducing the number of participating agents—for instance, initiating the computation with only those located on a minimal dominating set and enabling them to oscillate to simulate communication. Another challenge is to develop mechanisms that operate under asynchronous settings where agents may not meet systematically, causing delays or incorrect outcomes. In addition, another important direction is to design fault-tolerant variants that compute a minimal dominating set despite crash or Byzantine failures.

References

1. Chand, P.K., Das, A., Molla, A.R.: Brief announcement: distributed butterfly analysis using mobile agents. In: SPAA (2025)
2. Chand, P.K., Kumar, M., Molla, A.R.: Agent-driven bfs tree in anonymous graphs with applications. In: NETYS (2024)
3. Chand, P.K., Kumar, M., Molla, A.R.: Computing tree structures in anonymous graphs via mobile agents (2025). https://arxiv.org/abs/2506.19365
4. Chand, P.K., Molla, A.R., Sivasubramaniam, S.: Run for cover: dominating set via mobile agents. In: ALGOWIN (2023)
5. Deurer, J., Kuhn, F., Maus, Y.: Deterministic distributed dominating set approximation in the congest model. In: PODC (2019)
6. Jia, L., Rajaraman, R., Suel, T.: An efficient distributed algorithm for constructing small dominating sets. Distrib. Comput. **15**(4), 193–205 (2002)
7. Kaur, T., Mondal, K.: Distance-2-dispersion: dispersion with further constraints. In: NETYS (2023)
8. Kshemkalyani, A., Kumar, M., Molla, A., Sharma, G.: Agent-based leader election, mst, and beyond. In: DISC (2024)
9. Kshemkalyani, A.D., Kumar, M., Molla, A.R., Pattanayak, D., Sharma, G.: Dispersion is (almost) optimal under (a)synchrony. In: SPAA (2025)
10. Kshemkalyani, A.D., Kumar, M., Molla, A.R., Sharma, G.: Faster leader election an its applications for mobile agents with parameter advice. In: ICDCIT (2025)
11. Kshemkalyani, A.D., Kumar, M., Molla, A.R., Sharma, G.: Near-linear time leader election in multiagent networks. In: AAMAS (2025)
12. Kshemkalyani, A.D., Sharma, G.: Near-optimal dispersion on arbitrary anonymous graphs. In: OPODIS (2021)
13. Kuhn, F., Moscibroda, T., Wattenhofer, R.: What cannot be computed locally! In: PODC (2004)
14. Kuhn, F., Wattenhofer, R.: Constant-time distributed dominating set approximation. In: PODC (2003)
15. Liang, B., Haas, Z.: Virtual backbone generation and maintenance in ad hoc network mobility management. In: IEEE INFOCOM (2000)

16. Pattanayak, D., Bhagat, S., Gan Chaudhuri, S., Molla, A.R.: Maximal independent set via mobile agents. In: ICDCN (2024)
17. Sudo, Y., Shibata, M., Nakamura, J., Kim, Y., Masuzawa, T.: Near-linear time dispersion of mobile agents. In: DISC (2024)
18. Sultanik, E.A., Shokoufandeh, A., Regli, W.C.: Dominating sets of agents in visibility graphs: distributed algorithms for art gallery problems. In: AAMAS (2010)

Collaborative Dispersion of Silent Robots with Different Wake-Up Time

Barun Gorain[1(✉)] [iD], Subhrangsu Mandal[2] [iD], and Yash Sharma[1]

[1] Indian Institute of Technology Bhilai, Bhilai, India
{barun,yashsharma}@iitbhilai.ac.in
[2] Indian Institute of Technology (ISM) Dhanbad, Dhanbad, India

Abstract. In the problem of dispersion, a set of mobile robots, starting from one or multiple source nodes in a network, must relocate themselves in such a way that there is at most one robot present at any node of the graph. Most of the prior works on dispersion assume local communication between robots: any two robots, while located on the same node, can communicate by exchanging messages of arbitrary size. A recent paper by Gorain et al. [4] has shown that this kind of local communication is not necessary to achieve dispersion. They have shown that dispersion can be achieved using very limited local knowledge, where a robot can sense the following local information at any node: A) Is the robot alone at a node in a round? B) Do the number of robots at a node in the current round have increased compared to the previous round? and C) Do the number of robots at a node in the current round have decreased compared to the previous round? The authors have proposed an algorithm using which a set of co-located robots with access to the above local information achieved dispersion. In this paper, we show the existence of an algorithm for dispersion in a weaker model than that is considered in [4]. Specifically, we show that the knowledge of (A) and (C) are enough to achieve dispersion. Moreover, our algorithm works even if the robots do not wake up at the same time.

Keywords: Dispersion · mobile robots · autonomous mobile agents · distributed algorithm · time complexity

1 Introduction

1.1 Background

The dispersion problem gained popularity in recent years. In this problem, a set of mobile robots, starting from one or multiple source nodes in a given graph, has to place themselves at different nodes of the graph in such a way that no two robots remain co-located. Augustine et al. originally brought up this problem in [2], and since then, numerous studies have been done on the problem in recent years. There are many real-world applications to this problem. One of the important applications is the charging of self-driving electric automobiles in

B. Chatterjee et al. (Eds.): ICDCIT 2026, LNCS 16420, pp. 52–67, 2026.
https://doi.org/10.1007/978-3-032-16632-6_4

charging stations located across a city. The assumption is that moving a car to a free charging station nearby is faster and less expensive than charging it. So, it is preferable to spread out the automobiles so that each charging station can get one at any given moment instead of having a long queue at a single station.

1.2   Motivation and Problem Definition

Most of the previous works on the robot dispersion problem have assumed that the robots have the capability to communicate with each other. There are two different communication models: the local communication model, where a set of co-located mobile robots can exchange any amount of information among them, and the global communication model, where robots present at different nodes of the network can communicate between them. In terms of communication capability, the weakest model among the existing literature is being studied by Gorain et al. in [4]. In this paper, the authors show that the capability of local or global communication is not necessary to achieve dispersion. Dispersion can be achieved if the robots have access to the following three local information at any given round at a node v: (1) Is the robot alone at v? (2) Has the number of robots at v increased compared to the previous round? (3) Has the number of robots at v decreased compared to the previous round? Indeed, a robot can not have both increased and decreased true in any particular round, as the number of robots at a node can not simultaneously increase and decrease.

A natural question arises, whether dispersion can be achieved with an even lesser amount of information. To be specific, it is interesting to ask whether, with the absence of any of these three local knowledge, dispersion still can be achieved. In this paper, we show that it is enough to achieve dispersion with the local information (1) and (3). Moreover, our algorithm works even if the robot does not wake up at the same time at the initial node. Almost all of the previous works assume full synchrony among the robots, i.e., each robot wakes up and starts at the same round. Therefore, our contribution in this paper not only works for a weaker communication model compared to all the earlier works, but also can handle partial asynchrony where the wake-up times of the robots are not synchronous, but once they wake up, the robots execute the algorithm synchronously.

1.3   Our Contribution

In this paper, we have studied the dispersion problem of a set of mobile robots without communication capabilities. To the best of our knowledge, our communication model for mobile robots is the weakest model among all the research carried out on the dispersion problem. Moreover, in our approach, mobile robots may not wake up at the same time at the source. The required memory for each robot is $O(\log L + \log \Delta)$, which is as optimal as proposed in [4] where L is the maximum length of an id of any robot and Δ is the maximum degree of a node in the given graph.

Due to the page restriction, the technical proofs of some of the technical lemmas are omitted from the conference version. The missing proofs can be found in the journal version of the paper.

2   Related Work

Augustine et al. introduced the dispersion problem in [2]. They considered the scenario where all robots are initially co-located and the number of robots k equals the number of vertices n in the given graph. They have also made studies on special graphs like paths, rings, and trees. They established that every deterministic algorithm must require each robot to use $O(\log n)$ bits of memory and $\Omega(D)$ rounds, where D is the diameter of the graph. In another work [5], Kshemkalyani et al. proposed five dispersion algorithms that can be used with any initial robot configuration in general graphs. The first three algorithms take $O(m)$ time, where m is the number of edges in the given graph, and require $O(k \log \Delta)$ bits of memory per robot. Here, k refers to the number of robots and Δ denotes the maximum degree of the graph. The first three dispersion algorithms proposed by Kshemkalyani et al. in [5] differ in terms of the system model and the way data structures are maintained with the fourth and fifth algorithms. Their fourth and fifth algorithms work in the asynchronous model. The fourth algorithm uses $O(D \log \Delta)$ bits of memory per robot and takes $O(\Delta D)$ rounds to complete, where D is the diameter of the graph. The fifth algorithm requires $O(max(\log k, \log \Delta))$ bits of memory at each robot and runs for $O((m - n)k)$ rounds. In [5], Kshemkalyani et al. introduced a deterministic algorithm for arbitrary graphs in a synchronous model, which needs $O(min(m, k\Delta) \log k)$ rounds and $O(\log n)$ bits of memory per robot. However, the algorithm assumes that the robots have prior knowledge of the maximum degree and number of edges in the graph. In [12], Shintaku et al. investigated the dispersion problem where the robots do not have prior knowledge of the maximum degree and number of edges. They proposed an algorithm that achieves the same number of rounds as in [5] but reduces the memory requirement to $\log(\Delta + k)$ bits per robot, which is an improvement over the algorithm in [5]. In [6], Kshemkalyani et al. have proposed a faster algorithm for the dispersion problem that takes $O(min(m, k\Delta))$ rounds with the same amount of memory requirement. All of the mentioned algorithms works under the local communication model. In [1], Agarwalla et al. investigated the dispersion problem on dynamic rings. In [10], Molla et al. proposed a fault-tolerant algorithm for the dispersion problem on a ring in the presence of Byzantine robots. This work was further expanded by the authors in [9], where they investigated the dispersion problem on general graphs in the presence of Byzantine robots. All of these algorithms consider the local communication model. In [11], Molla et al. incorporated randomness into the dispersion problem and proposed an algorithm that uses $O(\log \Delta)$ bits of memory for each robot. They also presented a corresponding lower bound of $\Omega(\log \Delta)$ bits for any randomized algorithm designed to solve the dispersion problem. In [3], Das et al. recently investigated the dispersion problem on anonymous robots and proposed a randomized algorithm for dispersion, where each robot utilizes $O(\log \Delta)$

bits of memory. Local communication is required in both models. There are also studies [7,8] that consider the global communication model, where robots can communicate even if they are located in different nodes. These papers present results for dispersion on grids as well as general graphs.

In all of the results mentioned above, communication between robots is necessary for solving the dispersion problem, either through local communication (robots can only communicate with other robots in their immediate vicinity) or global communication (robots can communicate with any other robot in the network regardless of their location). Gorain et al. [4] studied the dispersion problem of a set of robots without communication capabilities for the first time in l. The robots have access to three local: 1)whether the robot is alone at a node, 2) whether the number of robots increased at a node compared to the previous round, and 3) whether the number of robots decreased at a node compared to the previous round. They have proposed a dispersion algorithm that uses optimal memory per robot, where all robots are initially placed in a common source node and wake up at the same time.

3   Network Model and Preliminaries

Graph. We consider a connected, undirected graph G with n nodes. We assume that G is anonymous, and each edge is assigned a port number with reference to a given node. This means that the same edge can get assigned two different port numbers at its two end nodes. Port numbers at a node are labeled arbitrarily from $0, 1, 2, \ldots \Delta - 1$ where Δ is the degree of the node.

Robots. There are $k \leq n$ robots initially placed at a source node say s. In the beginning, every robot is in a sleeping state and any of the robots can wake up at any moment. Once a robot is awake then it will never go to the sleep state. Each robot is associated with a unique identifier in the set $[1, L]$. None of the values of k, n, or L are known to the robots. Every robot only knows about its own id, they have no knowledge about id of the other robots. We assume that the robots are silent, i.e., they cannot communicate with each other even when they are present at the same node. However, robots are capable of sensing two kinds of local information: (1) At any node v, whether the robot is the only robot at that node. The robot has a local variable *alone* that is $TRUE$ if this robot is the only robot at that node in this round. (2) If a robot r decides to stay in a node in some round and one or more co-located robots leave that node, then r can sense that the number of robots has decreased at the current node. This information about the reduction in the number of robots which can be accessed in the next round. In particular, every robot maintains a local variable *decrease* which is $TRUE$ in a round t if and only if the robot did not move in round $t-1$, and the number of robots at its current node at the beginning of round $t-1$ was more than the number of robots at the beginning of round t. The robot can not distinguish between co-located robots which are awake and which are in sleep. A robot from a node u, when moves to another node v, then it learns the port number through which it entered v from u, the degree of v. If two robots choose to traverse the same edge, starting from the same or different nodes, during a given round, neither robot can perceive the movement of the other. Every robot has a limited memory.

Time. In this work, we consider a synchronous system which progresses in rounds. It can be noted that, as the round number of two different robots can be different due to the different wake up time.

Now we define some terminologies that are frequently used in the paper. By the binary representation of the label of a robot, we mean the modified binary representation where a 1 is appended at the end of its binary representation. To be specific, if two robots have ids 2 and 5, then their modified binary representations are 101, and 1011 respectively. Our algorithm is executed in several iterations. The activities in a particular iteration are carried out only when at the beginning of the iteration, at least one awake robot is present at the source node s. While calculating the time complexity of the algorithm, we consider only the rounds inside such live iterations. For any binary string B, by the transformed binary encoding of B, we mean the binary string constructed from B by replacing every 1 by 11, and every 0 by 10 in B. By B_j, we denote the binary representation of the integer j.

4   Dispersion on Graphs

In this section, we propose an algorithm for dispersion of a set of silent robots on an anonymous graph G. It is assumed that initially a set of k robots with capabilities mentioned in Sect. 3 are placed on the source node s in G. Initially, all robots are in the sleep state. Our goal is to place the robots on different nodes in G such that there is one or no robot on each node in G. Without loss of generality, we may assume that the degree of s is at least 2. In case the degree of s is 1, the only neighbor of s must have degree at least 2. Otherwise, the graph is a line of length 1 and the dispersion on this trivial graph can be achieved by just executing the election subroutine exactly once as proposed in [4].

4.1   High Level Idea

Idea When Every Robot Wakes Up Together: Before we describe the details of the algorithm, we first summarize the idea of our proposed algorithm when every node wakes up at the same time in their starting position. The idea is very much similar to the algorithm proposed in [4]. The algorithm works in several iterations where each iteration contains two phases. Initially, all robots are at a source node s. In the first phase of an iteration, one robot at s selects itself as the leader. In the second phase, one of the robots elected as leader in this iteration or one of the previous iterations occupies an empty node. Hence, within exactly k iterations, all the robots will be dispersed to different nodes, and the dispersion will be achieved. Indeed, we need to make sure that once a robot occupies an empty node, this node may never become empty again in the subsequent iterations.

The first phase, whose objective is to elect a leader, works in the following way. Each robot performs certain steps based on the bits in its id from right to left. For $j = 1, 2, \ldots$, if the j-th bit from the right is 1, then a robot moves along the port 0 from s (call this node $s(0)$ that is connected to s through port 0 at s), and if the j-th bit is 0, then the robot stays at s. For all robots that participate in this phase at node s, if any two of them have different j-th bit, then some robots stay at s and some move to $s(0)$ after the above step is executed. Hence, the robots that stayed at s detect $decrease = TRUE$. In the next round of this phase, these robots at s that sensed $decrease = TRUE$ in the previous round move to $s(0)$ and then move back to s in the next round. Hence, once two groups of robots are separated due to having different j-th bit for some j, in the next round, this separation is learned by the robots that stayed at s due to the fact that they had j-th bit 0. On the other hand, the robots at $s(0)$, which moved because they had j-th bit 1, learned this separation after two rounds when the robots at s moved back to s after visiting $s(0)$. Once this learning is achieved, the robots at $s(0)$ move to $s(\delta - 1)$ by moving to s from $s(0)$ and then moving to $s(\delta - 1)$ from s. These robots at $s(\delta - 1)$ do not participate anymore in Phase 1 of the current iteration. Since two robots, with different j-th bit gets separated in some round, it is guaranteed that once every robot completes processing all the bits in their label, no two robots will be co-located, and hence exactly one robot will stay at s for some value j. As soon as this happens, this robot elects itself as the leader. After electing itself as leader, the robot visits the node $s(\delta - 1)$ and immediately returns to s in the next round. This ensures that the robots in $s(\delta - 1)$ sense a decrease. Note that during the execution of Phase 1 of a particular iteration, no robot ever visits $s(\delta - 1)$ except the leader. Hence, the robots at $s(\delta - 1)$ identify this decrease as the fact that the leader election is completed. Then the robots at $s(\delta - 1)$ move back to s. This is when Phase 1 of an iteration ends. In the case of the first iteration of the algorithm, this elected leader sets its status as *master*, and in the subsequent iterations, the status is set to *follower*.

In Phase 2 of iteration 1, this newly elected master robot searches its neighbors one by one and moves to a node where it finds $alone = TRUE$ for the first time. Phase 2 of the first iteration as well as the entire first iteration ends with this. As soon as the master robot leaves s and occupies an empty node, the robots at s sense $decrease = TRUE$ and learn that the first iteration has ended.

Since the movements of mobile robots are used to propagate information, one needs to be very careful about exactly which movement conveys what to a robot. For example, the robots at s sometimes learn about separation by identifying $decrease = TRUE$ at s, and sometimes learn about the end of an iteration by again learning $decrease = TRUE$ at s. This can create serious chaos if these kinds of 'message propagation' are not distinguished. In order to avoid such chaos, we reserve different slots for different activities in an iteration. If there are p activities to be performed during an iteration, then the i-th activity is executed only in rounds r_1, r_2, ..., where each of these rounds r_1, r_2, ... is of the form $6j + i$ for some j. In particular, all the steps which are executed in Phase 1 for electing the leader are done in rounds from the set $\{1, 7, 13, \dots\}$ which can be represented in the form $6t + 1$. On the other hand, the task of searching for an empty node is done in the rounds in the form of $6t + 3$, the task corresponding to informing the robots about the availability of an empty node are done in the rounds in the form $6t + 4$, and the task of occupying the empty node by the master robot is done in a round of the form $6t + 5$. There are tasks that are executed in the rounds of the form $6t + 2$ and $6t$ which we are going to explain very soon.

Now we are going to describe the details of the activities done in Phase 2 of an iteration. The following five different tasks are executed in Phase 2.

- Detection of the end of Phase 1 by the robots that participate in Phase 2. The executions corresponding to this activity are performed in rounds of the form $6t + 2$.
- Finding a node which is not yet occupied by a robot (called an empty node), if available. The executions corresponding to this activity are performed in rounds of the form $6t + 3$.
- Propagate the information about the availability of an empty node to the robots participating in Phase 2. The executions corresponding to this activity are performed in rounds of the form $6t + 4$.
- Occupancy of the empty node. The executions corresponding to this activity are done in rounds of the form $6t + 5$.
- Termination detection when all robots are dispersed. The executions corresponding to this activity are done in rounds of the form $6t$.

Among the above-mentioned activities, the first four activities are executed in every iteration. The last activity, i.e., the termination detection is done only at the last iteration when the task of dispersion is complete.

When Phase 1 of iteration 2 ends, there is a follower robot r_1 at s which just got elected in Phase 1 of the current iteration, and there is a master robot at $s(0)$ which was elected in Phase 1 of iteration 1. The executions of Phase 2 of iteration 2 starts as follows. The follower robot at s visits $s(0)$ and comes back to s. These two movements are done in the next two available rounds of the form $6t + 2$ after Phase 1 ends.

The master robot at $s(0)$, after identifying $deacrease = TRUE$ in a round in the $6j + 2$, learns that Phase 1 has ended. Then this master robot visits each of its neighbor one by one until it finds a node where it identifies $alone = TRUE$. These movements are done in rounds of the form $6t + 3$.

Suppose j be the port number from $s(0)$ where this empty node is found. The master robot returns back to $s(0)$, and propagate the information 'I found an empty node through port j' to the follower robot at s. In the absence of direct communication between the robots, this propagation of message is done by utilizing the movements of the robots. To be specific, for any particular message M that a robot wants to propagate to another robot that is present in its neighborhood, the message M is first converted into a binary string B. Then another binary string B' from B is constructed by substituting every 1 in B by 11 and every 0 in B by 10. This new binary string, called the transformed binary encoding of B does not contain 00 as a substring. Now, to transmit M, the robot visits the robot at one of its neighboring node in a round of the form $6t + 4$ if the i-th bit of B' is 1 and then returns back in the next round. The receiving robot, each time identifying a $decrease = TRUE$ in a round of the form $6t + 4$, learns as the bit 1 and $decrease = FALSE$ as a 0 in every two rounds. It learns the end of the transmission when it identifies consecutive two rounds of the form $6t + 4$ where $decarease = FALSE$. After that, it learns the actual binary string by replacing every 11 by a 1 and every 10 by a 0, by considering two bits at a time from left to right.

The above mentioned idea of message transmission using robot movements is used to transmit the message 'I am a master robot and I found an empty node through port j' by representing the message as $11B_j$, where B_j denotes the binary representation of the integer j.

Once this message transmission ends, the master robot moves along the port j and occupy the empty node. The follower robot at s moves to $s(0)$ to occupy the node $s(0)$ which was occupied by the master robot previously. In this way, at the end of the current iteration, a new node is occupied. These activities are done in rounds of the form $6t + 5$.

The same process is executed in each iteration. In general, in any iteration, there is a path $P = s, v_1, v_2 \cdots v_t$, where at each of the nodes v_i a robot r_i with status follower is present and a master robot is present at v_t. As explained in the case of second iteration, the master robot finds the empty neighbor, and accordingly transmit the information to the robot r_{t-1}. The robot r_{t-1} transmit the message 'I am follower robot, and I am going to move along port j to occupy the node' to the robot r_{t-2}. This message can be represented as $10B_j$. Once this message transmission is ended, r_{t-1} moves to the node v_t. The task of occupying an empty node completes when the follower at s occupy v_1. Movements corresponding to the message transmission are done in rounds of the form $6t + 4$ and movements to occupy the empty nodes and the nodes in P are done in rounds of the form $6t + 5$.

The robots at s, when sense $decrease = TRUE$ in a round of the form $6t + 5$ learn that activities related to Phase 2 has ended and hence the current iteration is complete. They start executing Phase 1 of the next iteration in the next available round of the form $6t + 1$.

The only case remains to be discussed is when in Phase 2 of an iteration, none of the neighboring nodes of the master robot r_t is empty. In this case, after learning this fact, the master robot becomes idle, i.e., terminates its algorithm by transmitting the message 'I am master robot and I am becoming idle' to r_{t-1}. This message is represented by the binary string 00. After learning this message, the robot r_{t-1} change its status to master and continue its search of an empty neighbor from the node v_{t-1}.

The Idea When the Robots Wake Up in Different Rounds: If the robots do not wake up at the same time, the implementation of the above idea does not work for the following reasons. In order to elect the leader, it is necessary that every robot at s starts executing Phase 1 at the same time. Hence, if a robot wakes up in between some rounds of Phase 1 and starts processing its bits one by one, we can not guarantee that a leader will be elected. The other challenge is that when a robot wakes up, it sees the current round as its first round. Hence, how does it know whether the current round is of the form $6t + 1$ or $6t + 2$ or any other possible rounds with respect to the other robots that already wake up and started participating in the dispersion algorithm.

We overcome these serious challenges by implementing a partial 'synchrony' between the robots once they woke up. In order to achieve this, we divide the timeline into consecutive slots of 23 rounds. A round of the form $23.i + j$, $0 \leq j < 23$ is called a j-dedicated round. Out of these 23 rounds, some rounds are 'live', where robots move and execute steps to achieve dispersion, and other rounds are 'dead', where no robot executes anything. Intuitively, between any two live rounds, there are two dead rounds. Hence, in any three consecutive rounds, activities of robots can be detected in at most one round. This information is used to establish the partial synchrony between robots. To be specific, one of the first sets of robots who wake up at the beginning, create the event $decrease = TRUE$ in a 20-dedicated round and then again create the event $decrease = TRUE$ in the 22-dedicated rounds. A robot, who wakes up first among all other robots, waits 23 rounds. Since no robot wakes up before it, it does not observe anything, and hence after 23 rounds, it set its round counter to 1 and start executing Phase 1 of iteration 1. The robots that wake up later, wait 23 rounds, and observe $decraes = TRUE$ twice in three consecutive rounds, learn that the last decrease happened in a 22-dedicated round (from the point of view of the robots that are already participated in the dispersion algorithm), wait for one more round and set the round counter to 1. In the first iteration, these $decrease = TRUE$ are made to achieve synchrony by the active robots that are participating in Phase 1. From the second iteration onward, one of the follower robots or master robots is responsible for this task.

The only thing that remains to be explained is the termination of the algorithm after dispersion is achieved. When an $active$ robot senses $alone = TRUE$ at s, it learns that no robot is in sleep state at s and dispersion is achieved. This robot uses 16-dedicated rounds to let the other robots that are not yet $idle$ know that the dispersion is achieved. This $active$ robot moves through the port $child$ in a 16-dedicated round and comes back to its old position, and becomes $idle$. A master or follower robot, identifying $decrease = TRUE$ in a 16-dedicated round, moves along the port $child$, comes back to its old position and then becomes $idle$. Hence, all the robots, that are not $idle$ yet become $idle$ and the algorithm is terminated for all the robots (Table 1).

Table 1. Activities in different dedicated rounds. The other dedicated rounds are dead, i.e., the robots do nothing in these rounds.

Dedicated rounds	Activities	Res. Phases
1-dedicated	Execution of leader election by active robots	Execution of Phase 1
19-dedicated to 22-dedicated	Movement of active robots to establish partial synchrony for the robots who wake up in between an iteration	
4-dedicated	Master and follower robots get informed about the end of Phase 1	Execution of Phase 2
7-dedicated	Find an empty node by master robot	
10-dedicated	Propagate information on whether an empty node was found or not to the robots participating in Phase 2	
13-dedicated	Movement of the robots for occupying the empty node	
16-dedicated	Termination detection	

4.2   The Algorithm

During the execution of the proposed algorithm, each robot maintains a variable *status* which can be set to one of the following values.

- *awake:* As soon as a robot wakes up, it sets its *status = awake*. The robots with status *awake* do not participate in the executions of the phases of each iteration until they change their status to *active*.
- *active:* These are the robots that executes Phase 1 in every iteration and exactly one of them is elected as the'leader' in Phase 1 of any iteration.
- *passive:* These are the robots that, after waking up, learn that some other robots wake up before it and executing the steps of some ongoing iteration. These robots wait until the ongoing iteration finishes and then participate in the next iteration by changing their status to *active*.
- *master/follower:* The leader elected in Phase 1 changes its *status* from *active* to *master* in the first iteration of the algorithm. From second iteration onwards, the leader elected in Phase 1 changes its *status* from *active* to *follower*. Some follower robots may change its status to *master* during the execution of Phase 2 of some iteration as well. But once a robot changes its status to *master*, it remains with the same status until it terminates.
- *idle:* A robot having this status represents that the robot has terminated, i.e., it no longer participates in the execution of any algorithm and remains stationary at a node.

Each robot uses some variables that we are going to mention when they are going to be used for the first time.

When a robot is awake, it executes the subroutine AWAKE(M). The objective of the robot after being awake is to learn whether it is one of the first set of robots that wake up or already some robots are awake and they started execution of the steps for dispersion. In the later case, the robot also establishes the partial synchrony with the already awake robots.

> **Description of subroutine AWAKE(M):** Each robot, after waking up, executes the following steps.
> 1. Wait for 23 rounds.
> 2. If $decrease = FALSE$ for each of these 23 rounds, then change $status = active$, $first = TRUE$. Call Subroutine ACTIVE(M).
> 3. If the robot senses $decrease = TRUE$ exactly once, then wait for another 23 rounds.
> 4. If the robot senses $decrease = TRUE$ twice within any consecutive 3 rounds, then set $round = 1$ after two rounds of the round when it sensed $decrease = TRUE$ last. Set $status = passive$. Call subroutine PASSIVE(M).

After executing the subroutine AWAKE(M), a robot learns either it is the first robot (one of the first set of robots) that wakes up or some robots are already awake before it wakes up. In the first scenario, the robot calls the subroutine ACTIVE(M) and in the second scenario, it calls the subroutine PASSIVE(M).

The robots present at s that have already established partial synchrony call the subroutine ACTIVE(M) whose purpose is to elect a leader among these robots. The main steps of this subroutine are executed only in 1-dedicated rounds. The robots process the bits of their label one by one and if the bit is 1 then they move from s or else they stay at s. This processing of bits guarantees that exactly one robot is elected as the leader by setting $leader = TRUE$. In addition, the robots at s move back and forth to $s(0)$ in 19–22 dedicated rounds to help the other robots that wake up after the execution of the ongoing ACTIVE(M) to establish partial synchrony. The elected leader in this subroutine changes its status to $master$ in the first iteration, else changes its status to $follower$.

The robots that learned that they have wake up in the middle of Phase 1 or Phase 2 of an ongoing iteration. In this scenario, the robots wait at s until Phase 1 of the next iteration starts. The robot learns the end of Phase 2 of the ongoing iteration by sensing $decrease = TRUE$ in a 13-dedicated round. As soon as the robots realised this event, they change their status to $active$ and start subroutine ACTIVE(M) in Phase 1 of the next iteration.

The objective of the robot with status $master$ is to find an empty node, let the follower robot (which is connected to the master robot through the $parent$ port) know through which port this empty node is reached, and then finally moved to this empty node. The robot with status $master$, while executing the subroutine MASTER(M), visits each of its neighbors in 7-dedicated rounds until an empty node is found through some port number j. Then the master robot executes subroutine TRANSMIT(M,MSG,$parent$) to inform the follower robot which is connected through the parent pointer that 'an empty node is found through port j'.

Description of subroutine ACTIVE(M)

Each robot with status *active* executes the following steps only in the 1-dedicated rounds.
1. If $alone = TRUE$, then execute subroutine TERIMATION(M). Else, execute the following steps.
2. If $first = TRUE$ or the robot sensed $decrease = TRUE$ in a 3-dedicated round, then for $j = 1, 2 \cdots, |\ell(M)|$, where $\ell(M)$ is the binary representation of the label of the robot, do the following.
   (a) If $leader = TRUE$, then move to $s(\delta - 1)$, in the next 1-dedicated round. Come back to s in the subsequent 1-dedicated round. Update $status = master$ is it is the first iteration, else update $status = follower$. Set $recent = TRUE$.
   (b) If the j-th bit is 1, move to $s(0)$ in the next available 1-dedicated round. Set $move = 1$. The next two steps are executed only in the first iteration by the active robots.
   (c) If $move = 0$ and $decrease = TRUE$ in the last 1-dedicated round, then visit $s(0)$. Come back to s in the next available 1-dedicated round.
   (d) If $move = 1$ and $decrease = TRUE$ in the most recent 1-dedicated round, then move to s in the next available 1-dedicated round and then move to $s(\delta - 1)$ in the next 1-dedicated round. $status = passive$. Execute subroutine PASSIVE(M).

Each robot with status *active* executes the following steps only in 19-22 dedicated rounds.

1. If $move = 0$ and $decrease = FALSE$ in last 1-dedicated round, then move to $s(0)$ in the next available 20-dedicated round. If $alone = TRUE$, the set $leader = TRUE$. Come back to s next round, move to $s(0)$ again in the 22-dedicated round and come back to s next round.
2. If $move = 1$, then visit s in the next available 19-dedicated round, comes back to $s(0)$ next round and then again visit s in the 21-dedicated round and then comes back to $s(0)$ next round.

Description of subroutine PASSIVE(M)
Each robot with status *passive* executes the following steps.
1. If $move = 0$ then wait until $decrease = TRUE$ in a 13-dedicated round. Then change its status to *active*. Execute subroutine ACTIVE(M).
2. If $move = 0$, then wait until $decrease = TRUE$ in a 1-dedicated round, then move to s in the next 1-dedicated round and then change its status to *active*. subroutine ACTIVE(M)

In this case, $MSG = 11B_j$, where B_j is the binary representation of the integer j. In case no empty neighbor is found, the master robot sets $MSG = 00$.

Once this information is transmitted, the robot moves through the port j to reach the empty node and update its parent pointer to the port through which it entered the empty node. In the case where the master robot does not find any empty node, it informs the same to the follower robot which is connected through the parent pointer using the subroutine TRANSMIT(M,MSG,*parent*), and then becomes *idle*. The follower robot that received this information from the master robot will then change its status to *master* and continue to execute the subroutine MASTER(M).

A follower robot, after sensing $decrease = TRUE$ in the 10-dedicated round, learns that a message is transmitted by the master or follower robot, which is connected through it via the *child* port. It then starts constructing a string B' by appending a 1 for each $decreasure = TRUE$ in a 10-dedicated round and appending a 0 for each $decreasure = FALSE$ in a 10-dedicated round until it senses two consecutive 10-dedicated round that $decreasure = FALSE$. Then it constructs the string B whose transformed binary encoding is B'. If the first two bits of B are 11 or 10, then the robot learns that the *master* robot finds an empty node through port j. Hence, the robot executes TRANSMIT(M,MSG,*parent*) and then moves through port *child* in the next available 13-dedicated round and update $child = j$. Here $MSG = 10B_j$, where B_j is the binary representation of the integer j which the robot received apart from the first two bits of B. If the first two bits of B is 00, then the robot learns that *master* robot did not find any empty node and became *idle*. Then the follower robot changes its status to *master* and starts executing subroutine MASTER(M).

Once a follower robot learns that the master robot found an empty node, the follower robot transmits the same message to the follower robot that is connected through the *parent* port, and then moves through the *child* port to occupy the node that was previously occupied by the master robot and now vacant due to the movement of the master robot to the empty node.

Next, we describe how a robot executes subroutine TRANSMIT $(\mathbf{M}, \mathbf{MSG}, \mathbf{parent})$. First, the robot computes MSG', the transformed binary encoding of MSG, by replacing every 11, by 11 and every 0, by 10. Then for every 1 in MSG', the robot movies through its patent port in the next available 10-dedicated round and then come back in the next 10-dedicated round. If a bit is 0, then the robot does nothing and stays at its current node.

Description of subroutine TRANSMIT(M, MSG, parent)

Each robot with status *master* or *follower* executes the following steps from its current position v. Each of the movements done by the robot are done only in 10-dedicated rounds. First, compute MSG', the transformed binary encoding of MSG, by replacing every 11, by 11 and every 0, by 10.

1. For $i = 1$ to $|MSG'|$, visit through port *parent* if the i-th bit of MSG' is 1 and then come back to v.

Description of subroutine MASTER(M)

Each robot with status *master* executes the following steps only in 7-dedicated rounds.

1. In the case of first iteration, go to step 2. Else, wait until sense $decrease = TRUE$ in a 4-dedicated round.
2. It visits all of its neighbor starting from port 0, one by one until it finds $alone = TRUE$ in some of its neighbor. If such a neighbor v found through port j, then set $MSG = 11 \cdot B_j$. If no such neighbor found, then set $MSG = 00$.
3. Call subroutine TRANSMIT$(M, MSG, parent)$.
4. If $msg = 00$, then update $status = idle$. Else, move along port j in the next 3-dedicated round. Set $recent = false$. Let q be the incoming port through which the robot entered the new node. Set $parent = q$.
5. If the robot sensed $decrease = TRUE$ in a 16-dedicated round, then Call subroutine TERIMATION(M).

The master robot with $recent = TRUE$ executes the following steps in 19- 23 -dedicated rounds.

1. Visit s in the next available 19-dedicated round, comes back to current node next round and then again visit s in the 21-dedicated round and then comes back to current node in the next round.

The subroutine TERMINATION(M) is executed when only one robot left at s and it is active. In this case, this robot, moves through it *child* port in a 16-dedicated round. Every follower robot, after sensing a $decrease = TRUE$ in a 16-dedicated round, moves through its child port in a 16-dedicated round, comes back to its position and terminates by changing its status to *idle*. At the end, the master robot, after sensing a $decrease = TRUE$ in a 16-dedicated round, terminates by changing its status to *idle*.

Description of subroutine FOLLOWER(M)

Each robot with status *follower* executes the following steps from its current position v only in 10-dedicated rounds.

1. If it sensed *decrease* = *TRUE* in a 4-dedicated round, then move through port *child* in the next available 4-dedicated round.
2. Returns in the next available 4-dedicated round.
3. Wait until sense *decrease* = *TRUE* in a 10-dedicated round.
4. Repeat the following steps until sense *decrease* = *FALSE* for two consecutive 10-dedicated rounds.
   (a) Set $B = \epsilon$.
   (b) If sensed *decrease* = *TRUE* in the most recent 10-dedicated round, then $B = B \cdot 1$. Else, $B = B \cdot 0$.
   (c) wait for 23 rounds.
5. Let B' be the binary string whose transformed binary string is B. If $B' = 00$, then change the status to master. Execute MASTER(M). Else, if $B' = 10B_j$ or $B' = 11B_j$, then construct $MSG = 10B_{child}$. Execute subroutine TRANSMIT($M, MSG, parent$).
6. Move along port *child* in the next 13-dedicated round. Set *child* = j. Set *recent* = *false*. Let q be the incoming port through which the robot entered the new node. Set *parent* = q.
7. If the robot sensed *decrease* = *TRUE* in a 16-dedicated round, then call subroutine TERMINATION(M).

   The follower robot with *recent* = *TRUE* executes the following steps in 19-23-dedicated rounds.

1. Visit s in the next available 19-dedicated round, come back to current node next round, and then again visit s in the 21-dedicated round and then come back to current node next round.

Description of subroutine TERMINATION(M)

The steps related to this subroutine are executed only in the 16-dedicated rounds.
1. Move along port *child* in the next available 16-dedicated rounds. Come back to its old position in the subsequent 16-dedicated rounds and set *status* = *idle*.

---

5 Correctness and Analysis

In this section, we prove the correctness of our proposed algorithm and analyse its time complexity. Throughout this section, the global round refers to the round count of the first robot that has woken up.

The following lemma shows that every robot, after waking up, eventually synchronizes with the robots that are already awake.

Lemma 1. *Let t_i be the global round at which a robot M_i wakes up and let t'_i be any local round of M_i at the global round $t_i + j$ for $j \geq 47$. Then $t_i \equiv t'_i (\bmod\ 23)$.*

Lemma 2. *At the start of a certain iteration, if at least one active robot present at node s then by the end of Phase 1 of that iteration, exactly one robot changes its initial status to either "master" or "follower" and all other active robots remain at s with status active.*

Lemma 3. *If there are at least two robots at node s before the start of any iteration of the algorithm, then any one of the following statements must be true.*

1. *The master robot has a neighboring node that is unoccupied.*
2. *One of the follower robots has a neighboring node that is unoccupied.*
3. *Node s has a neighboring location that is unoccupied.*

Lemma 4. *The following statements hold during every iteration of the proposed algorithm.*

1. *At the start of each iteration of the algorithm, there exists a simple path P originating from s and leading to the location where the master robot is located. The intermediate nodes of this path include follower robots. Additionally, for any node w on this path, the subsequent node w' is connected to w through the port child.*
2. *All robots that are not currently located at any node on the path P are in idle state.*
3. *If there are at least two robots at node s at the beginning of the iteration, then after the iteration, exactly one previously empty node will have a robot on it, and none of the nodes that are occupied by robots before the iteration becomes empty.*

Theorem 1. *At the end of the kth iteration, every robot is in idle state, where k is the number of robots. The time complexity of the proposed algorithm is $O(k \log L + k^2 \log \Delta)$, and each robot uses $O(\log L + \log \Delta)$ additional memory.*

Proof. There are k robots in the graph. Then from the above lemmas , we conclude that with the completion of each iteration, exactly one node becomes occupied and no occupied node becomes unoccupied. Hence within k iterations, each robot is placed at a distinct node and hence the dispersion is achieved.

Since the steps of an iteration are executed only when at least one active robot is present in s at the beginning of that iterations, the algorithm executes exactly k iterations. Hence, with similar arguments presented in the paper [4] (Theorem 3.2 in [4]), the time complexity of the algorithm is $O(k \log L + k^2 \log \Delta)$, and each robot uses $O(\log L + \log \Delta)$ additional memory.

6   Conclusion

In this paper, we have studied the dispersion problem by a set of mobile robots without communication capabilities. To the best of our knowledge, our communication model of the mobile robots is the weakest one among all the research carried out on dispersion. Moreover, in our approach, the mobile robots may not wake up at the same time at the source. The natural question arises that whether it is possible to achieve dispersion in an even weaker model where the mobile robots either have capability to sense $alone = TRUE$ or have the capability to sense $decrease = TRUE$.

Acknowledgement. Subhrangsu Mandal is supported, in part, by Faculty Research Scheme (FRS) of IIT (ISM) Dhanbad grant MISC0100.

References

1. Agarwalla, A., Augustine, J., Moses Jr., W.K., Madhav, K.S., Sridhar, A.K.: Deterministic dispersion of mobile robots in dynamic rings. In: International Conference on Distributed Computing and Networking (ICDCN), pp. 19:1–19:4 (2018)
2. Augustine, J., Moses Jr, W.K.: Dispersion of mobile robots: a study of memory-time trade-offs. In: International Conference on Distributed Computing and Networking (ICDCN), pp. 1:1–1:10 (2018)
3. Das, A., Bose, K., Sau, B.: Memory optimal dispersion by anonymous mobile robots. Disc. Appl. Math. **340**, 171–182 (2023)
4. Gorain, B., Mandal, P.S., Mondal, K., Pandit, S.: Collaborative dispersion by silent robots. J. Parallel Distrib. Comput. **188**, 104852 (2024)
5. Kshemkalyani, A.D., Ali, F.: Efficient dispersion of mobile robots on graphs. In: International Conference on Distributed Computing and Networking (ICDCN), pp. 218–227 (2019)
6. Kshemkalyani, A.D., Molla, A.R., Sharma, G.: Dispersion of mobile robots in the global communication model. In: International Conference on Distributed Computing and Networking (ICDCN), pp. 1–10 (2020)
7. Kshemkalyani, A.D., Molla, A.R., Sharma, G.: Dispersion of mobile robots on grids. In: International Workshop on Algorithms and Computation (WALCOM), pp. 183–197 (2020)
8. Kshemkalyani, A.D., Molla, A.R., Sharma, G.: Dispersion of mobile robots using global communication. J. Parallel Distrib. Comput. **161**, 100–117 (2022)
9. Molla, A.R., Mondal, K., Moses, W.K.: Byzantine dispersion on graphs. In: IEEE International Parallel and Distributed Processing Symposium (IPDPS), pp. 942–951 (2021)
10. Molla, A.R., Mondal, K., Moses, W.K., Jr.: Optimal dispersion on an anonymous ring in the presence of weak byzantine robots. Theor. Comput. Sci. **887**, 111–121 (2021)
11. Molla, A.R., Moses Jr, W.K.: Dispersion of mobile robots: the power of randomness. In: International Conference on Theory and Applications of Models of Computation (TAMC), pp. 481–500 (2019)
12. Shintaku, T., Sudo, Y., Kakugawa, H., Masuzawa, T.: Efficient dispersion of mobile agents without global knowledge. In: International Symposium on Stabilization, Safety, and Security of Distributed Systems (SSS), pp. 280–294 (2020)

Separation of Unconscious Robots with Obstructed Visibility

Prajyot Pyati$^{(\boxtimes)}$, Navjot Kaur, Saswata Jana[iD], Adri Bhattacharya[iD], and Partha Sarathi Mandal[iD]

Indian Institute of Technology Guwahati, Guwahati 781039, Assam, India
`prajyotpyati1@gmail.com,psm@iitg.ac.in`

Abstract. We study a recently introduced *unconscious* mobile robot model, where each robot is associated with a *color*, which is visible to other robots but not to itself. The robots are autonomous, anonymous, oblivious and silent, operating in the Euclidean plane under the conventional *Look-Compute-Move* cycle. A primary task in this model is the *separation problem*, where unconscious robots sharing the same color must separate from others, forming recognizable geometric shapes such as circles, points, or lines. All prior works model the robots as *transparent*, enabling each to know the positions and colors of all other robots. In contrast, we model the robots as *opaque*, where a robot can obstruct the visibility of two other robots, if it lies on the line segment between them. Under this obstructed visibility, we consider a variant of the separation problem in which robots, starting from any arbitrary initial configuration, are required to separate into concentric semicircles. We present a collision-free algorithm that solves the separation problem under a semi-synchronous scheduler in $O(n)$ epochs, where n is the number of robots. The robots agree on one coordinate axis but have no knowledge of n.

Keywords: Opaque · Mobile robots · Separation · Unconscious robots

1 Introduction

In the domain of distributed computing with a swarm of mobile robots, the robots are assumed to be *oblivious* [8], and predominantly thought of as point objects [4]. These robots operate in a classical Look-Compute-Move (LCM) cycle. Once activated, a robot performs a *Look* by taking a snapshot of its surroundings. Based on this snapshot, it computes a destination during the *Compute* phase, and finally, in the *Move* phase, it remains in place or moves to the computed destination. The robots are *autonomous* (no central control), *anonymous* (have no identifiers to distinguish among themselves), and *oblivious* (do not remember

S. Jana—Supported by Prime Minister's Research Fellowship (PMRF) scheme of the Govt. of India (PMRF-ID: 1902165).

A. Bhattacharya—Supported by CSIR, Govt. of India, Grant Number: 09/731(0178)/2020-EMR-I.

any past actions or positions). They work collaboratively by executing the same algorithm to achieve some global task, for example, pattern formation [3,9], mutual visibility [6,10,11], gathering [1], dispersion [2], etc. In the conventional $\mathcal{OBLOT}$ model [9], besides being oblivious, the robots are also silent, meaning they cannot communicate explicitly among themselves.

In general, robots communicate via externally visible lights (colors) [5,8], which they flash from a predefined color palette. A robot displays its light to transmit a message and observes others' lights to receive messages. In this context, three major models have been studied. Firstly, the $\mathcal{LUMI}$ model, where a robot can see the color of all the robots, including itself. Secondly, the $\mathcal{FSTA}$ model, where a robot can only see the color of its own, making it equivalent to $\mathcal{OBLOT}$ model with some persistent memory (silent but not oblivious). Thirdly, the recently introduced *unconscious* colored robot model [7,13], where the robots are unaware of their own color, but can observe the colors of other robots.

One fundamental challenge in this unconscious colored robot model is the problem of separation, where the robots of same color must separate from others and form a group in terms of some recognizable geometric shapes such as points, lines or circles. Seike and Yamauchi [13] were the first to study this problem. They show an impossibility result: separation into points cannot be achieved due to the symmetry of the initial configuration. They also proposed an algorithm that solves the separation problem into circles using oblivious robots having common chirality (robots agree on the clockwise direction) under $\mathcal{SSYNC}$. In $\mathcal{SSYNC}$, a non-empty set of robots gets activated simultaneously and performs their LCM cycle in sync. Later on, Flocchini et al. [7] solved the problem of separation into lines using the robots of similar properties as in [13] but under $\mathcal{ASYNC}$ scheduler and robots agree on one axis. In $\mathcal{ASYNC}$, robots execute their LCM cycles at arbitrary times, each within a finite duration. In both $\mathcal{SSYNC}$ and $\mathcal{ASYNC}$, the time is measured in terms of *epochs*, defined as the smallest interval in which every robot completes at least one full LCM cycle.

Surprisingly, both of the previously mentioned works [7,13] are considered the robot as *transparent*, meaning that a robot never obstructs the visibility of other robots, and can always see the positions and colors of all other robots. In this paper, we consider robots to be *non-transparent* (or *opaque*) [3,6], meaning that if a robot lies on the line segment between two others, it obstructs their mutual visibility. Due to obstructed visibility, the robots are prone to collisions, which may affect their hardware. Moreover, they lack knowledge of the total number of robots, making signalling and coordination significantly more challenging in solving the separation problem. In this paper, we address these challenges and show that robots in $O(n)$ epochs, achieve a separated configuration without collision in finite time. To the best of our knowledge, this is the first work to introduce opaqueness in the separation problem for unconscious robots. Our desired separated configuration is the concentric semicircles. Agreement on one axis allows us to fix the diameter line of these semicircles, which is perpendicular to the agreed axis. Hence, it is sufficient to assume that there are at least two robots of each color. The semicircular configuration naturally extends to a circular one if each color has at least three robots. The smaller lower bound on the number of robots thus motivates the choice of a semicircular formulation for the separated configuration. Moreover, the semicircular configuration breaks the perfect symmetry of the circular one while maintaining balance along the diameter. This is particularly important when robots must preserve an open space and move coherently toward that direction (for instance, exploring or guarding the open half-space opposite to the semicircular arc).

Our Contributions: In this paper, we extend the study of unconscious robots by addressing the separation problem into concentric semicircles under $\mathcal{SSYNC}$ scheduler. We propose an algorithm, CON-SEMCIRC-SEPARATION, that achieves this separation in $O(n)$ epochs without collision (Theorem 1), where n is the total number of robots. The robots are anonymous, silent, and oblivious, with no knowledge of n, but they agree on one coordinate axis. This paper is the first to introduce opaqueness into the study of unconscious robots, adding significant complexity to the separation task, which our algorithm successfully resolves. Table 1 compares our work with most related works in the literature.

Table 1. Comparing our model and result with the literature

Papers	SSS 2023 [13]	IJNC 2025 [7]	This Paper
Opacity	$\times$	$\times$	$\checkmark$
Separation Type	Concentric Circles	Lines	Concentric Semicircles
Scheduler	$\mathcal{SSYNC}$	$\mathcal{ASYNC}$	$\mathcal{SSYNC}$
Chirality	$\checkmark$	$\times$	$\times$
One-axis Agreement	$\times$	$\checkmark$	$\checkmark$

2   Model, Preliminaries and Problem Definition

Robots: We consider a set of n *anonymous* (no unique identifier), *autonomous* (no external control), *homogeneous* (run the same algorithm), and *silent* (no explicit mode of communication) point robots $R = \{r_1, r_2, \ldots, r_n\}$. The robots operate in the Euclidean plane $\mathbb{R}^2$ and are initially located at distinct positions. Let $p_j(t)$ represent the position of the robot r_j at time t. Each robot r_j is associated with a value c_j, called its *color*, chosen from a totally ordered set H, which is known to all the robots. Let $C \subseteq H$ be the subset of colors currently held by the robots, and let $|C| = k$ denote the number of distinct colors in C. Each color in C is assigned to at least two robots. The configuration of the robots at time t is the set of tuples comprising the robot's positions and their colors which is denoted by the set: $P(t) = \{(p_1(t), c_1), (p_2(t), c_2), \ldots, (p_n(t), c_n)\}$. When the time t is clear from context, we abuse the notation r_j to refer to the current position of robot r_j. Besides the previous properties, the robots are *opaque*, meaning that if a robot r_j lies on the line segment connecting two other robots, it blocks the mutual view of the other two robots. They are *oblivious*, which means they have no memory to remember anything from the past executions of the algorithm. They also have no knowledge about the total number of robots n in the system. They have the agreement on one-axis. Without loss of generality, we assume it is on the y-axis, that is, all robots agree on the positive direction of the y-axis but may disagree on the orientation of the x-axis. Finally, the robots are *unconscious* of their own color, they can see the colors of other robots but don't know which color they themselves hold.

Activation Cycle: Each robot operates in a classical *Look-Compute-Move* (LCM) cycle. In the *Look* phase, the robot observes its surroundings and takes a snapshot of the current configuration. We denote the snapshot observed by robot r_j at time t as $Z_j(t)$, which is the set of tuples consisting of all visible robot positions and their colors. In the *Compute* phase, the robot runs the same deterministic algorithm ψ, which takes the snapshot $Z_j(t)$ as input and decides its destination or remain stationary. Finally, in the *Move* phase, the robot moves to the computed destination. The movement is *rigid*, where a robot never stops before it reaches its destination.

Activation Scheduler and Run Time: The robots are activated under a *semi-synchronous* (in short $\mathcal{SSYNC}$) scheduler, where a non-empty set of robots is activated simultaneously at any given time step. The set of robots, that are activated together at a given time, execute their LCM cycle in sync, while the others remain inactive until the completion of the cycle. Time is measured in terms of *epochs*, where an epoch is the smallest time interval in which every robot is activated and completes one full LCM cycle at least once.

Definition 1. *(Separated Configuration) Let $\mathcal{S} = \{s_1, s_2, \ldots, s_k\}$ be a set of k concentric semicircles whose diameter is perpendicular to the y-axis. The radius of the semicircle s_i is $rad_i = i \cdot rad$, where $1 \leq i \leq k$ and rad is the radius of the innermost semicircle. A separated configuration for a set of robots $R = \{r_1, r_2, \cdots, r_n\}$ with the colors from the set $C = \{c_1, c_2, \cdots, c_k\}$ is the configuration in which the robots satisfy the following predicate:*

$$SepSC = \left\{ \exists t : (\forall t' > t,\, P(t) = P(t')) \text{ and } (\forall c_i \in C,\, \exists s_i \in \mathcal{S} \text{ such that} \right.$$

$$(\forall (p_j(t), c_j) \in P(t),\, c_i = c_j \iff p_j(t) \in s_i)) \text{ and}$$

$$\left. (\forall c_i, c_{i'} \in C,\, c_i \neq c_i' \Rightarrow s_i \neq s_{i'}) \right\}. \quad (1)$$

Here c_i is a color from the color set C and c_j represents the color of the robot $r_j \in R$. In other words, the configuration is considered as separated if all robots are located on concentric semicircles whose diameters are perpendicular to y-axis, with radii $rad, 2 \cdot rad, 3 \cdot rad, \ldots, k \cdot rad$, where rad is the radius of the smallest semicircle and k is the total number of colors. All robots of same color occupy same semicircle, and each semicircle contains robots of only one color.

Definition 2. *(**Problem Definition**) Given n unconscious, opaque, and oblivious silent point robots, with no knowledge of n but agreeing on one axis, deployed in an arbitrary initial configuration on the Euclidean plane, the problem aims to design an algorithm for the robots to reach a `separated configuration`.*

2.1   Notations and Terminologies

- L_r is the line passing through r and perpendicular to y-axis (an horizontal line through r). $L_r^{\perp}$ is the line passing through r and parallel to y-axis (an vertical line through r).
- The line segment joining the two robots r and r' is denoted by $\overline{rr'}$, and the line passing through those two robots is denoted by $\overleftrightarrow{rr'}$.
- $P(t)$ denotes the configuration of robots at time t.
- The *smallest enclosing rectangle* of the configuration $P(t)$, denoted by $\delta(P(t))$, is the rectangle with the minimum area that has two sides parallel to the y-axis and contains all robots at time t, either inside or on its boundary.
- The sides of the rectangle $\delta(P(t))$ that are parallel to the y-axis are referred to as the *vertical sides*, and those perpendicular to the y-axis are referred to as the *horizontal sides*. Moreover, we can distinguish between the *top* and *bottom* sides of the rectangle, as the robots share an agreement on the y-axis. However, the left and right sides cannot be distinguished.
- The robots located on the vertical sides of $\delta(P(t))$ are termed as *terminal robots*. Note that each vertical side of the rectangle $\delta(P(t))$ contains at least one terminal robot. Since the robots have the agreement on the y-axis, a robot r can identify itself as the terminal robot by checking the following: if one of the open half-planes delimited by $L_r^{\perp}$ contains no robots, then r is the terminal robot; otherwise, it is non-terminal.
- The *diameter robots* are the vertically lowest terminal robots on each vertical side of $\delta(P(t))$. At any time t, there are exactly two diameter robots.
- **Triangular Configuration:** A configuration $P(t)$ is referred to as a *triangular configuration* if it satisfies the following conditions:
  1. The bottom side of the enclosing rectangle $\delta(P(t))$ contains exactly two robots located at its endpoints.
  2. All robots lie either inside or on the boundary of an isosceles right-angled triangle whose hypotenuse aligns with the bottom side of $\delta(P(t))$.

3   Algorithm to Separate Opaque Colored Robots

In this section, we present an algorithm that solves the separation problem on concentric semicircles with opaque and unconscious robots. Due to page limitations, we only present the supporting lemmas in this paper. The complete analysis of the algorithm, along with detailed proofs, can be found in the full version of the paper [12]. We begin with a high-level overview of the algorithm, followed by its detailed description.

A High-Level Idea of the Algorithm: In this section, we give a high-level idea of our proposed algorithm named CON-SEMCIRC-SEPARATION. The algorithm is divided into multiple stages. Each stage is treated as a subroutine. In the first stage of the algorithm (ARBITRARY-TO-TRIANGULAR, Sect. 3.1), the robots will move from an arbitrary configuration to a triangular configuration defined earlier. The idea is to enclose all the robots in a right-angled isosceles triangle whose hypotenuse is defined as the line segment joining the two diameter robots. In the next stage (TRIANGULAR-TO-SEMICIRCULAR, Sect. 3.2), the robots will project themselves on a semicircle whose diameter is formed by joining the two diameter robots in an ordered manner. Once all the robots project themselves on a single semicircle, then the robots will be mutually visible to each other and can calculate the total number of robots n.

Thereafter, each robot divides the semicircle into several grid points and relocates itself on some of those grid points (SEMICIRCULAR-TO-GRIDPOINT, Sect. 3.3). In the subsequent stage (GRIDPOINT-TO-SECTORPARTITIONING, Sect. 3.4), all robots recognize leader(s) on the semicircle, who initiate signalling for the rest of the robots. Although silent, the leader robot signals the rest of the robots by moving to specific points on the semicircle, each encoded as an ordered pair representing a position of a particular robot and its color. Non-leader robots decode the leader's position to determine their respective colors and destination points, ensuring that robots of the same color occupy the same sector (an arc that subtends a fixed angle at the center) of the semicircle. Once the robots are separated by the colors, in the final stage (SECTORPARTITIONING-TO-CONCENSEMICIRC, Sect. 3.5), they move to their designated semicircle based on the predefined order. Hence, completing the separation.

Description of Algorithm: Con-SemCirc-Separation

Here, we describe the algorithm in detail. The algorithm is divided into multiple stages. Since the robots are oblivious, they cannot remember their previous positions and actions. By seeing its surroundings (local view), each robot selects the appropriate stage (a subroutine) and executes the corresponding action. Due to obstructed visibility, robots lack knowledge of the global configuration, and hence their selected stage may not align with the global one. As a result, some robots may execute different stages simultaneously, creating overlaps. However, our analysis shows that, despite such overlaps, all robots within finite epochs, agree on a common stage before moving to the next. The algorithm is presented from the viewpoint of a robot r, whose actions are determined by its current characterization. We begin with the following stage.

3.1 Stage: Arbitrary-To-Triangular

Our first step is to transform the initial arbitrary configuration into a triangular configuration. To do this, we move the diameter robots or the robots that are on the bottom line of the enclosing triangle. Thus, we divide the stage into the following cases depending on the position of r.

Case A (r is a Diameter Robot): It first computes the minimum angle between the line $L_r^\perp$ and the lines connecting it to any visible robot located above it, as shown in Fig. 1. Let θ be the minimum angle, and r_a be the corresponding robot that makes this angle with r. If $\theta < \pi/4$, the robot r considers the open half-plane $\mathcal{H}_r$ delimited by the line $L_r^\perp$ that contains no robots. It then finds a target point t_r on $\mathcal{H}_r \cap L_r$ such that the angle between the lines $\overleftrightarrow{r_a t_r}$ and L_r is $\pi/4$. Finally, r moves to the point t_r. A diameter robot r may need to repeat these steps multiple times, as there could be a robot r'' behind r' on the line $\overleftrightarrow{rr'}$ and r can not see r'' at the current LCM cycle due to its obstructed visibility. In such a case, r needs to move further until the minimum angle θ becomes exactly $\pi/4$.

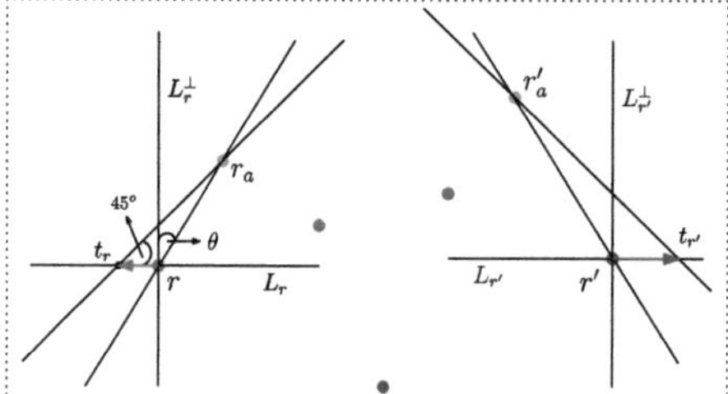

Fig. 1. The diameter robots r and r' find their respective $\theta < \pi/4$, and move to their target point.

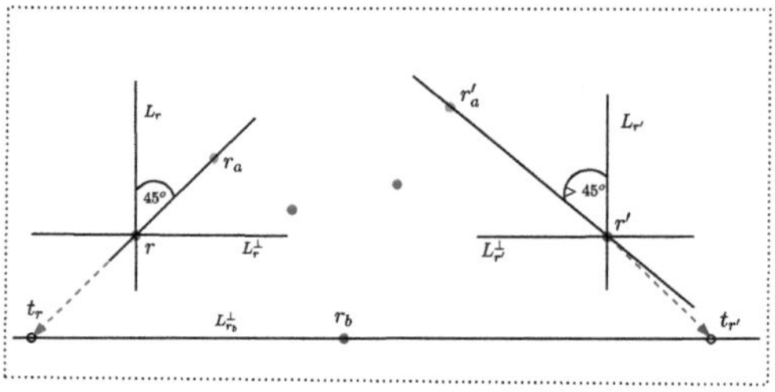

Fig. 2. The diameter robots r and r' find their respective $\theta \geq \pi/4$, and move to the target point on L_{r_b}.

If $\theta \geq \pi/4$, r checks if there is any robot below it. If there is no such robot, it remains in place. Otherwise, it finds r_b, the lowest visible robot below it. Thereafter, it finds the target point t_r on $\mathcal{H}_r \cap L_{r_b}$ such that the angle between the lines $\overleftrightarrow{rt_r}$ and L_{r_b} is $\pi/4$, and then finally moves to it, as shown in Fig. 2.

Case B (r is Not a Diameter Robot, But on the Bottom Side of $\delta(P(t))$): If r finds at most one robot on the bottom side of the enclosing rectangle $\delta(P(t))$ other than itself, it remains status quo. On the other hand, if it sees two other robots on the bottom side of $\delta(P(t))$, it computes v and h, where v (resp. h) is the minimum vertical (resp. horizontal) positive distance from r to any other robot above it. Then it calculates a target point t_r, which is vertically above r, and the distance between r and t_r is v. If the target point is unoccupied, and it moves to t_r. Whereas if the point t_r is already occupied, r calculates the new target point t'_r that is a horizontally $h/3$ distance and vertically v distance away from r. The measure of $h/3$ is chosen to ensure collision-freeness of the algorithm, since another robot from L_r, located at a horizontal distance h from r, may also target to move synchronously a distance v upward. Finally, the robot r moves to t'_r, as depicted in Fig. 3a.

After this stage, we ensure that all the robots reach the triangular configuration from the initial one. The corresponding lemma supporting this claim is stated below.

Lemma 1. *Starting from an arbitrary initial configuration, all the robots reach a triangular configuration in $O(n)$ epochs using stage* ARBITRARY-TO-TRIANGULAR.

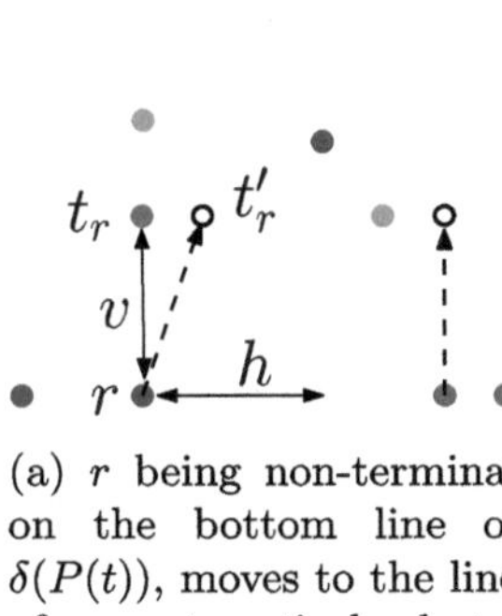

(a) r being non-terminal on the bottom line of $\delta(P(t))$, moves to the line of nearest vertical robot.

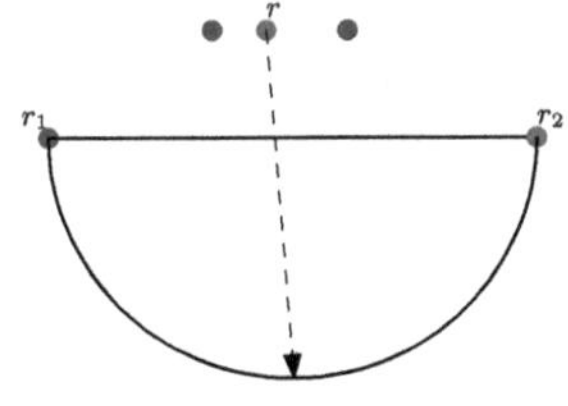

(b) Case C.1.1: The semicircle is empty, and r being unique nearest robot to the center, moves there.

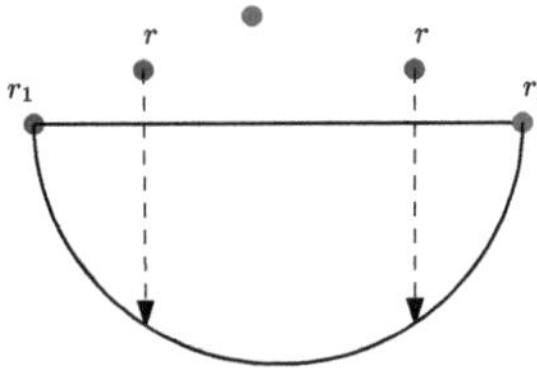

(c) Case C.1.2: Two nearest robots to the center of the empty semicircle move vertically below.

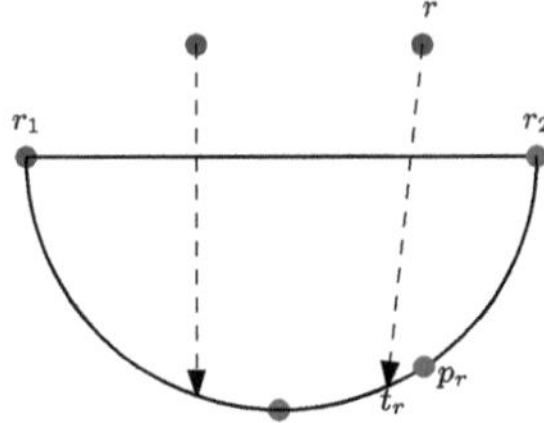

(d) Case C.2: Finding a robot at $low(\mathcal{LSC}$ $(r_1, r_2))$, r moves to a free point on the semicircle.

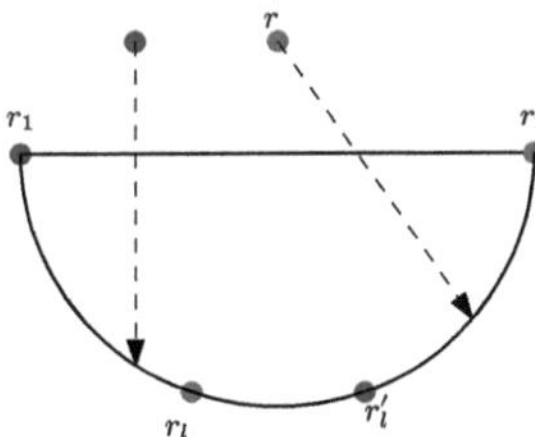

(e) Case C.3: r moves to the midpoint of the arc of the semicircle joining r'_l and $r_2(= r'')$.

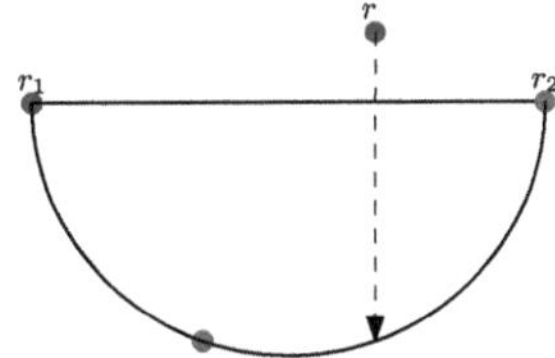

(f) Case C.4: r moves vertically below after finding a robot on the semicircle, equidistant from center.

Fig. 3. Illustration of Case B, first stage and all the sub-cases of the second stage.

3.2   Stage: Triangular-To-Semicircular

After reaching the triangular configuration, the next objective is to transform it into a semi-circular configuration. To achieve this, the robots are sequentially moved onto the lower semicircle, whose diameter is defined by the line joining the diameter robots, while keeping the diameter robots fixed in place. In this stage, a robot r first identifies two distinct robots r_1 and r_2, which satisfy a specific set of conditions outlined below.

1. Both the robots r_1 and r_2 lie on the same horizontal line, i.e., $L_{r_1} = L_{r_2}$, and the line segment $\overline{r_1 r_2}$ contain no other robot besides r_1 and r_2.
2. There is no robot lying in the open region between the lines $\overrightarrow{r_1 r_2}$ and L_r, with L_r lying above $\overleftrightarrow{r_1 r_2}$.
3. Any robot r_3 positioned below the line $\overleftrightarrow{r_1 r_2}$ must form a right angled triangle with r_1 and r_2, where the right angle is at r_3.
4. All visible robots above $\overleftrightarrow{r_1 r_2}$ must lie within the interior or on the boundary of an isosceles right-angled triangle, where the hypotenuse is $\overline{r_1 r_2}$.

Upon identifying such robots, r proceeds according to the following cases. We denote the lower semicircle having the diameter $\overline{r_1 r_2}$ by $\mathcal{LSC}(r_1, r_2)$. Let $cen(\mathcal{LSC}(r_1, r_2))$ be the centre of the semicircle $\mathcal{LSC}(r_1, r_2)$ and $low(\mathcal{LSC}(r_1, r_2))$ be the lowest point on this semicircle, which is essentially the intersection of the semicircle and the vertical line through $cen(\mathcal{LSC}(r_1, r_2))$.

- **Case C.1 (There is no robot on the semicircle $\mathcal{LSC}(r_1, r_2)$):** In this case, r considers all visible robots on the line L_r and checks whether it is the nearest robot to $cen(\mathcal{LSC}(r_1, r_2))$. If r is the unique robot nearest to $cen(\mathcal{LSC}(r_1, r_2))$, it moves to $low(\mathcal{LSC}(r_1, r_2))$, the lowest point on the semicircle $\mathcal{LSC}(r_1, r_2)$ (see Fig. 3b). On the other hand, if there exists another robot r' such that both r and r' are equidistant from the center of the semicircle, r moves on the semicircle vertically below, as shown in Fig. 3c.
- **Case C.2 (There is a robot on $low(\mathcal{LSC}(r_1, r_2))$):** In this case, the robot r computes a point p_r on the semicircle that is vertically below itself. If p_r is unoccupied, r moves to p_r. Otherwise, r computes the minimum horizontal distance h among all visible robots that do not lie on $L_r^\perp$. It then calculates a point t_r on the semicircle $\mathcal{LSC}(r_1, r_2)$ such that the horizontal distance between p_r and t_r is $h/3$. Since there are two such t_r on the semicircle, r selects one at random and moves there. Both the cases of occupied and unoccupied p_r can be seen in the Fig. 3d.
- **Case C.3 (There are two robots r_l and r_l' lying on $\mathcal{LSC}(r_1, r_2)$ equidistant from $low(\mathcal{LSC}(r_1, r_2))$, and no robot is present on the arc of $\mathcal{LSC}(r_1, r_2)$ joining r_l and r_l'):** In this scenario, the robot r first checks if it lies in the open region between the lines $L_{r_l}^\perp$ and $L_{r_l'}^\perp$. If r is not in that open region, it computes the point p_r, which is the point vertically below itself on the semicircle. If there is no robot at p_r, it moves to that point. Otherwise, it computes a target point t_r on the semicircle, as described in the previous Case C.2, and moves to it. In contrast, if r lies in the open region between the lines L_{r_l} and $L_{r_l'}$, it checks the number of visible robots on L_r. Based on that, it executes the following actions:
  1. If r finds two robots on L_r other than itself, it remains stationary.
  2. If r detects exactly one robot, say r', on L_r, it considers the open half-plane $\mathcal{H}_r'$ delimited by the line $L_r^\perp$ that does not contain r'. Note that the half-plane $\mathcal{H}_r'$ contains exactly one of r_l and r_l'. W.l.o.g., assume it

contains r'_l. Then r moves to the midpoint of the arc of $\mathcal{LSC}(r_1, r_2)$ connecting r'_l and r'', where r'' is the horizontally nearest robot to r'_l on $\mathcal{LSC}(r_1, r_2)$ within $\mathcal{H}'_r$ (see Fig. 3e).

3. If r sees no robot on L_r except itself, it randomly chooses an unoccupied point on $\mathcal{LSC}(r_1, r_2)$ lying above the line $\overleftrightarrow{r_l r'_l}$ and moves there.

- **Case C.4 (There is only one robot r_l on $\mathcal{LSC}(r_1, r_2)$ but not on the** $low(\mathcal{LSC}(r_1, r_2))$**)):** In this case, the robot checks whether the horizontal distance from $low(\mathcal{LSC}(r_1, r_2))$ to r_l is equal to the horizontal distance from $low(\mathcal{LSC}(r_1, r_2))$ to itself. If they are equal, it projects itself vertically onto the semicircle lying below. Otherwise remains stationary.

If the robot r does not satisfy any of the above conditions, it remains in place, as it will do so within finite epochs. During this stage, some robots may incorrectly identify different robots as the diameter robots and, instead of moving to the designated semicircle, may enter the interior. In such a scenario, the terminal robots r_1 and r_2 again follow ARBITRARY-TO-TRIANGULAR and move horizontally downward to restore the triangular configuration. However, we prove in our analysis that this situation can occur at most once. Thereafter, all robots inevitably reach a semicircular configuration with diameter as $\overline{r_1 r_2}$, the line segment joining the two diameter robots.

Lemma 2. *After all the robots reach to a triangular configuration by executing* ARBITRARY-TO-TRIANGULAR, *only one robot may misinterpret two other robots* r'_1 *and* r'_2 *as diameter robots and project itself below the actual diameter line* $\overleftrightarrow{r_1 r_2}$.

Lemma 3. *From the triangular configuration, all the robots reach to a single semicircle with diameter as* $\overline{r_1 r_2}$ *by following* TRIANGULAR-TO-SEMICIRCULAR.

3.3 Stage: Semicircular-To-GridPoint

In this stage of the algorithm, the robots settle onto grid points so that the leader robots can sequentially signal the others to relocate to their assigned parts of the semicircle. When a robot r observes that all the visible robots lie on a semicircle whose diameter is perpendicular to the y-axis, with two robots positioned at the endpoints of this diameter, it executes the following algorithm. We begin with the computation of grid points, followed by the movement to those points.

Grid-Point Computation: First, the semicircle is divided into $2k$ arcs of equal arc-length, where k is the total number of colors known to all robots. Each arc is called a *sector*, subtending an angle $\frac{\pi}{2k}$ with the centre of the semicircle $cen(\mathcal{LSC}(r_1, r_2))$, where r_1 and r_2 are the diameter robots. The sectors are indexed from the diameter $\overline{r_1 r_2}$ downward toward the $low(\mathcal{LSC}(r_1, r_2))$, numbered sequentially from 1 to k. The j-th sector is the j-th division of the semicircle from the diameter $\overline{r_1 r_2}$ toward the $low(\mathcal{LSC}(r_1, r_2))$, counted along each half. Each sector from both halves of the semicircle is mapped to a unique color of C, with the aim that all robots sharing the same color occupy the same sector. Note that the set C is totally ordered, and the order is known to all robots in advance. For instance, if $C = \{c_1, c_2, c_3\}$ with $c_1 < c_2 < c_3$, then all the robots with the color c_i are aiming to assign on the i-th sector ($1 \leq i \leq 3$).

We further subdivide each arc into n equal smaller arcs. This results in $2kn$ equal arcs in the semicircle, each subtending an angle $\alpha = \frac{\pi}{2kn}$ with the center. The endpoints of these arcs are termed *grid points*. Note that although the robots do not initially know n, they can compute it from the fact that all robots are currently positioned on the semicircle.

Movement to Grid-Points: Using the grid points as reference, a robot r checks whether all robots are located on the grid points. If not, it computes its destination position as follows:

The grid points are indexed according to their angular positions with respect to center and the diameter. A grid point located at an angle $i\alpha$ is indexed as i. The robot r first determines the half of the semicircle in which it currently belongs and then finds its destination point within that half. If r finds itself as the m-th robot from the top in its half, i.e., there are $(m-1)$ robots vertically above it within the same half, it computes the grid point t_r with index $m - 1$, as its target. If there is no other robot on the closed arc of the semicircle segmented by its current position and t_r, the robot r moves to the grid point t_r. Otherwise, it remains in place until all those robots settle into their respective target positions.

Lemma 4. *From the semicircular configuration, all the robots reach to a grid-point configuration in $O(n)$ epochs using* SEMICIRCULAR-TO-GRIDPOINT.

3.4   Stage: GridPoint-To-SectorPartitioning

In this stage of the algorithm, our objective is to position the robots into their designated sectors. We divide this stage into several parts. Once all robots are aligned on the grid points, one or two robots are designated as *leader* robots (*leader identification*). If necessary, these leaders first move to specific grid points, after which the remaining robots relocate to their assigned sectors based on the positions of the leader (*signalling procedure*). After that, leader robots need to be repositioned into their sectors (*leader repositioning*). Note that the diameter robots may also need to relocate, as they might not belong to their designated sectors. In such cases, once they move, the original reference points of the semicircle, namely r_1 and r_2, will no longer be present. However, since the robots agree on the y-axis and $n > 3$, they can still agree on a common semicircle. In particular, there always exists a unique semicircle passing through them whose diameter is perpendicular to the y-axis. Therefore, we simply refer to this semicircle as $\mathcal{LSC}$, instead of $\mathcal{LSC}(r_1, r_2)$.

Leader Identification: There can be two cases:

- If there is a robot, say r_ℓ, on the lowest point on the semicircle, $low(\mathcal{LSC})$, it designates itself as the leader robot.
- On the other hand, the two robots located on the bottommost line of each half (left and right) of the semicircle are chosen as leaders. Let r_ℓ^1 and r_ℓ^2 denote those robots. The leader robot r_ℓ^1 (resp. r_ℓ^2) moves to the grid point p_1 (resp. p_2), where p_1 (resp. p_2) is the grid point next to $low(\mathcal{LSC})$ and nearest to r_ℓ^1 (resp. r_ℓ^2).

Subsequently, the leader robot(s) initiate the signalling process, as described below, by moving to a designated point on the arc between p_1 and p_2, referred to as *signalling arc*. Any robot(s) positioned on this arc is considered a leader robot(s) and can be recognized as such by all other robots.

Signalling Procedure: We divide this procedure into two cases, depending on the number of leader robots: single or dual.

Case 1: (A Single Leader Robot r_ℓ Exists): Let len be the length of the arc of the semicircle that subtends an angle α at the centre $cen(\mathcal{LSC})$. Thus, $len = rad(\mathcal{LSC}) \cdot \frac{\pi}{2kn}$, where $rad(\mathcal{LSC})$ is the radius of the semicircle $\mathcal{LSC}$. Now we define the *signalling step* size as: $\tau = \frac{len}{(nk)^2}$. Next, if the leader r_ℓ intends to signal a robot located at grid point indexed s_1 to move to grid point indexed s_2, it moves to a position on the semicircle that is g signalling steps away from $low(\mathcal{LSC})$, towards the signalled robot, where $g = s_1 \cdot nk + s_2$.

When a robot r finds another robot on the arc between the points p_1 and p_2, it recognizes that robot as the leader robot r_ℓ, where p_1 and p_2 are the grid points adjacent to $low(\mathcal{LSC})$. If both r and r_ℓ lie on the same half of the semicircle, the robot r computes g, where $g \cdot \tau$ is the arc distance between $low(\mathcal{LSC})$ and r_ℓ. It then obtains s_1 and s_2 from the relations: $s_1 = \lfloor \frac{g}{nk} \rfloor$ and $s_2 = g \mod (nk)$.

If the robot r occupies the grid point indexed s_1, this implies that the leader robot is signalling to r. In that case, r moves to the grid point indexed s_2 in its own half of the semicircle. If the grid point s_2 is already occupied, r instead moves to the corresponding grid point s_2 in the opposite half. This situation arises only when the leader robot signals a robot to move to a diameter point(i.e., when $s_2 = 0$), as described below.

The leader robot r_ℓ signals the other robots sequentially, with a certain prioritization. It first assigns the diameter positions to the robots of color c_k, which is the highest-ordered color in C. Such a settlement is treated as an exception, since the general objective is to gather the robots of color c_i into the i-th sector ($1 \leq i \leq k$). This is done for the final configuration, where all the robots of the color c_k are placed on the innermost semicircle with two robots of color c_k occupying diameter points. To achieve this, several cases may arise based on the occupancy of diameter points and the number of visible c_k-colored robots by r_ℓ:

- If the diameter points are already occupied by robots of colors other than c_k, then the leader robot r_ℓ first signals those robots to move to their designated sectors.

- If both the diameter points are unoccupied and r_ℓ finds at least two robots of color c_k, it arbitrarily selects two of them and signals sequentially to move to the diameter points.
- If both the diameter points are unoccupied and r_ℓ finds only one robot of color c_k, then r_ℓ itself must be of the color c_k, as we assume that at least two robots of each color exist. In this case, r_ℓ first signals the only visible robots of color c_k and then all the robots that are not in their designated sectors. Thereafter, it moves to the unoccupied diameter points.
- If exactly one diameter point is unoccupied and r_ℓ finds only one robot of color c_k other than that lying on the diameter point, the leader robot r_ℓ signals that robot to move to the unoccupied diameter point.
- If exactly one unoccupied diameter point exists and no visible robot of color c_k other than the one already on a diameter point, then r_ℓ moves to that unoccupied point after all other robots are separated into sectors.

Apart from signaling robots of color c_k to occupy the diameter points, the leader robot r_ℓ signals the other robots as follows. It first determines s_1 by identifying the topmost robot r that is not currently positioned in its designated sector. Recall that a robot of color c_j, the j-th lowest-ordered color in C, is assigned to the j-th sector. The leader can determine the correct sector of r from its color. If two such robots exist, the leader selects one at random. It then determines s_2, the index of the topmost unoccupied grid point in the j-th sector.

When the leader robot r_ℓ finds itself on the arc between p_1 and p_2, it computes g, s_1, and s_2, as described above. If r_ℓ observes that the grid point indexed s_1 is unoccupied, it restarts the signalling procedure. This process is continued until the leader finds all the robots placed in their respective sectors, with two robots of color c_k (if they exist) occupying the diameter points. Afterwards, if both the diameter points are occupied with the robots of color c_k, r_ℓ moves to $low(\mathcal{LSC})$. However, if one of them remains unoccupied, the leader moves there, as discussed in the above sub-cases.

Case 2: (Two Leader Robots r_ℓ^1 and r_ℓ^2 Exist): In this case, both leaders r_ℓ^1 and r_ℓ^2 initiate signalling procedure within their respective halves, analogous to the single-leader case. The key distinction arises when the signalling robots of color c_k. Each leader first checks whether there is any c_k-colored robot in its own half. If such a robot exists, it signals that robot. Otherwise, it determines the number of c_k-colored robots in the other half. If there are two such robots, the leader proceeds with signalling the robots in its own half. If there is only one robot of color c_k in the other half, then the leader itself must be of color c_k. In that case, it moves to the unoccupied diameter point after all the robots get separated into sectors. Finally, once all robots are placed in their respective sectors, with two c_k-colored robots at the diameter points, the leader robots r_ℓ^1 and r_ℓ^2 (if they still exist) respectively move to the grid point p_1 and p_2, instead of $low(\mathcal{LSC})$.

Leader Repositioning: After all the robots settle within their sectors, the leader robot(s) need to be positioned in the correct designated sector, if not correctly positioned. All the robots except the leader can detect whether the leader robot is in the correct sector or not. We again divide this procedure into two cases as before.

Case 1: (A Single Leader Robot r_ℓ Exists): After the signalling procedure, the leader robot r_ℓ must be positioned at $low(\mathcal{LSC})$. Upon seeing a robot on $low(\mathcal{LSC})$ and all other robots on their designated sector, the nearest robot r of color c_j, that matches with the leader, projects itself horizontally onto the line joining two neighbouring grid-points of its current position. This action signals to the leader that r shares the same color. When the leader robot at $low(\mathcal{LSC})$ observes r on the line joining grid points indexed i and $(i+2)$, for some i, while all other robots are placed on the correct sector, it moves to one of the unoccupied grid points of the sector containing the grid point indexed $(i+1)$. However, if the leader r_ℓ instead sees another robot (other than r) outside its designated sector, it disregards this signal and continues the signalling process. Finally, whenever r sees that the leader is no longer at $low(\mathcal{LSC})$, it returns to its grid point indexed $(i+1)$, the nearest intersection of L_r and semicircle $\mathcal{LSC}$.

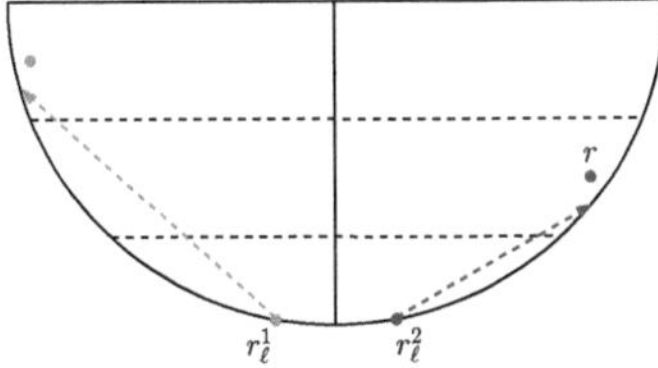

(a) Robot moves horizontally on the line joining the neighbouring grid points to signal its half's leader.

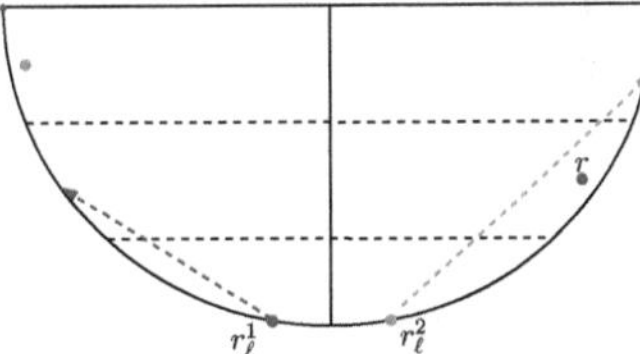

(b) Robot moves the midpoint of the line joining the neighbouring grid points to signal other half's leader.

Fig. 4. Leader repositioning with different inward distances.

Case 2: (Two Leader Robots r_ℓ^1 and r_ℓ^2 Exist): After the signalling procedure, the leader robots occupy positions p_1 and p_2. Upon seeing a robot or two robots on p_1 or p_2 or both, and all other robots on their designated sectors, the robot r, that is vertically nearest to a leader robot and sharing the same color, initiates signalling. It does so by projecting itself either horizontally on the line joining the neighbouring grid-points or on the midpoint of that line. If the robot r is signalling to the leader in the same half, the robot horizontally projects itself horizontally on the line joining the neighbouring gridpoints. If instead it is signalling to the leader in the opposite half, it moves to the midpoints of that line. Depending on the position of the signalling robot, the leader robot(s) move to the unoccupied grid point of the sector, within their own half, to which the signalling robot belongs (see Fig. 4). Once the leader robot moves from p_1 (or p_2), which means there is no robot on p_1 (or p_2), the signalling robots return to their original grid point, which is either the nearest grid point lying on L_r or the grid point in its own half.

Lemma 5. *From grid-point configuration, all robots reach to designated sectors in $O(n)$ epochs using* GRIDPOINT-TO-SECTORPARTITIONING *without collision.*

3.5   Stage: SectorPartitioning-To-ConcenSemiCirc

After all the robots are partitioned into the sectors, in this stage, the robots separate themselves into concentric semicircles. Once all robots are separated into their assigned sectors, and no robot is in the signalling arc. The robots that are not on the diameter points of the semicircle execute the following algorithm to separate into concentric semicircles. The robots at the diameter points act as the reference. The line joining them is the diameter of the innermost semicircles. A robot r, not on the diameter points, checks the following conditions:

- All the robots, except diameter robots, are in their designated sectors.
- The signalling arc of the semicircle (the arc joining p_1 and p_2, excluding the endpoints and $low(\mathcal{LSC})$) is empty.

If the robot r finds both conditions true, it calculates its next destination. The robot knows the total number of colors k. The lowest sector (k-th sector) of the semicircle in each half is assigned the number 1, and the topmost sectors in the semicircles are assigned the number k. In general, the i-th sector in each half is numbered $(k - i + 1)$. Now let i be the number assigned to the sector containing r. The destination point t_r of the robot r is defined as the intersection of: the concentric semicircle with radius $i \cdot rad(\mathcal{LSC})$ and line $\overleftrightarrow{rr_d}$, where $rad(\mathcal{LSC})$ is the radius of the smallest semicircle $\mathcal{LSC}$, where r_d is the diameter robot in the opposite half of the semicircle. Finally, r moves to t_r only if all the robots above it, except the diameter robot, have already moved to their respective semicircle.

However, if r finds that the robot r' directly above it is not on the correct semicircle corresponding to its color, r moves to the midpoint between two consecutive grid points on the semicircle. This temporary move by r serves as a signal to r' for returning to the smallest semicircle. Such a situation arises when r mistakenly interprets itself as the robot active in the current stage, while in fact the signalling procedure has not yet completed. By deliberately occupying a non-grid point, r enables the misinterpreted robot to return to the innermost semicircle. This ensures that the grid-point configuration first needs to be restored, and after which the signalling procedure can proceed correctly.

Note that, after some robots move from the innermost semicircle to the outer semicircles, the previous diameter robot may no longer remain the diameter. Recall that a diameter robot is defined as the vertically lowest terminal robot on the vertical side of the enclosing rectangle. Here, we slightly misuse this definition: a robot r considers two robots r_d and r'_d as the diameter robots if all other robots either (i) lie on the correct sectors of the semicircle $\mathcal{LSC}(r_d, r'_d)$, or (ii) are on their designated concentric semicircle with the innermost semicircle defined by $\mathcal{LSC}(r_d, r'_d)$. At the end of this stage, robots are separated into concentric semicircles, as argued in Lemma 6. Figure 5 represents the grid point to the respective semicircle movement, and attaining the final configuration, where red robots and green robots are the highest and lowest ordered colored robots.

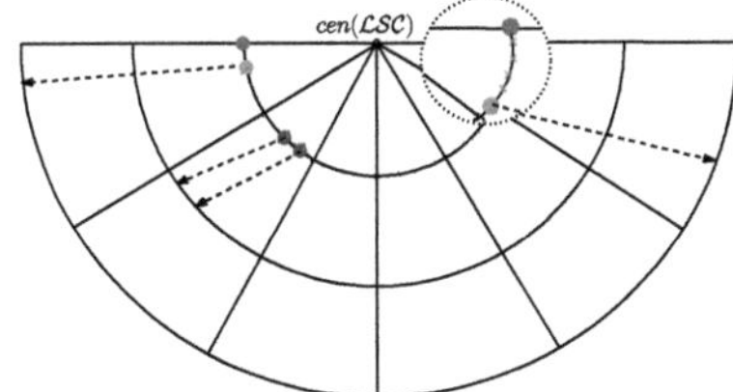

(a) Illustrates the movement of the robots from their gridpoint position, to their respective semicircle

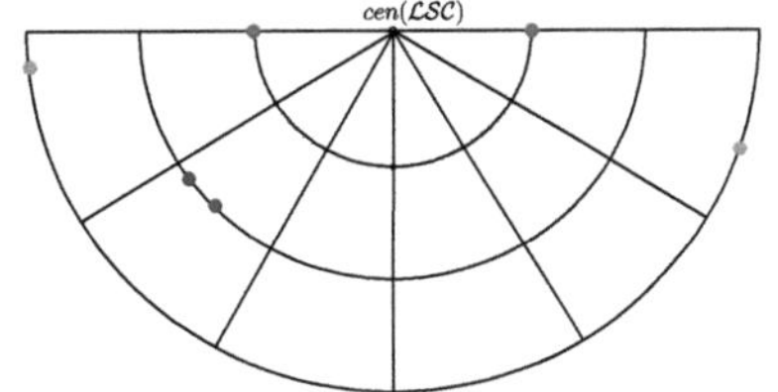

(b) Represents the final configuration, where the robots are in their respective semicircle

Fig. 5. Movement of robots to final configuration.

Lemma 6. *After the robots partitioned into sectors, all the robots proceed to their respective semicircle for the final separation using SECTORPARTITIONING-TO-CONCENSEMICIRC in $O(n)$ epochs without collision.*

Theorem 1. *From an arbitrary initial configuration, a collection of n unconscious opaque robots reaches a separated configuration of concentric semicircles by following CON-SEMCIRC-SEPARATION in $O(n)$ epochs without collision.*

4   Conclusion

In this paper, we study the unconscious colored separation problem under obstructed visibility. The introduction of opacity in the robot model makes this work significant in comparison to the existing literature. We design an algorithm that achieves separation into semicircles within $O(n)$ epochs, without collisions, under the semi-synchronous scheduler. It follows directly from our final separation structure that, if the initial configuration contains at least three robots of each color (rather than two), our algorithm also provides an immediate solution to the separation problem into concentric circles. To conclude, exploring whether other classical distributed problems can be solved using unconscious colored robots presents an interesting direction for future research.

References

1. Agmon, N., Peleg, D.: Fault-tolerant gathering algorithms for autonomous mobile robots. SIAM J. Comput. **36**(1), 56–82 (2006)
2. Augustine, J., Moses Jr, W.K.: Dispersion of mobile robots: a study of memory-time trade-offs. In: Proceedings of the 19th International Conference on Distributed Computing and Networking, pp. 1–10 (2018)
3. Bose, K., Kundu, M.K., Adhikary, R., Sau, B.: Arbitrary pattern formation by asynchronous opaque robots with lights. Theor. Comput. Sci. **849**, 138–158 (2021)
4. Cohen, R., Peleg, D.: Local spreading algorithms for autonomous robot systems. Theor. Comput. Sci. **399**(1–2), 71–82 (2008)

5. Das, S., Flocchini, P., Prencipe, G., Santoro, N., Yamashita, M.: Autonomous mobile robots with lights. Theor. Comput. Sci. **609**, 171–184 (2016)
6. Di Luna, G., Flocchini, P., Poloni, F., Santoro, N., Viglietta, G., et al.: The mutual visibility problem for oblivious robots. In: 26th Canadian Conference on Computational Geometry, CCCG 2014. Canadian Conference on Computational Geometry (2014)
7. Flocchini, P., Pattanayak, D., Piselli, F., Santoro, N., Yamauchi, Y.: Asynchronous separation of unconscious colored robots. Int. J. Network. Comput. **15**(2), 199–219 (2025)
8. Flocchini, P., Prencipe, G., Santoro, N.: Distributed Computing by Oblivious Mobile Robots, vol. 10. Morgan & Claypool Publishers (2012)
9. Flocchini, P., Prencipe, G., Santoro, N., Widmayer, P.: Arbitrary pattern formation by asynchronous oblivious robots. Theor. Comput. Sci. **407**, 412–447 (2008)
10. Pramanick, S., Jana, S., Bhattacharya, A., Mandal, P.S.: Mutual visibility of luminous robots despite angular inaccuracy. Theor. Comput. Sci. **1011**, 114723 (2024)
11. Pramanick, S., Jana, S., Mandal, P.S.: Fault-tolerant mutual visibility without any axis agreement in presence of mobility failure. Theor. Comput. Sci. **1025**, 114970 (2025)
12. Pyati, P., Kaur, N., Jana, S., Bhattacharya, A., Mandal, P.S.: Separation of unconscious robots with obstructed visibility (2025). https://arxiv.org/abs/2510.22434
13. Seike, H., Yamauchi, Y.: Separation of unconscious colored robots. In: Dolev, S., Schieber, B. (eds.) Stabilization, Safety, and Security of Distributed Systems, vol. 14310, pp. 328–343. Springer, Cham (2023). https://doi.org/10.1007/978-3-031-44274-2_24

Cloud based Systems and Algorithms

VMigrate+: A Lattice-Theoretic and Cost-Aware Framework for SLA-Compliant VM Migration in Dynamic Cloud Infrastructures

Nirmalya Mukhopadhyay[1]($\boxtimes$) , Babul P. Tewari[2] , and Tanmay De[1]

[1] National Institute of Technology, Durgapur 713209, West Bengal, India
{nm.24cs1507,tde.cse}@nitdgp.ac.in
[2] Ghani Khan Choudhury Institute of Engineering and Technology, Malda 732141,
West Bengal, India
babul@gkciet.ac.in

Abstract. Efficient Virtual Machine (VM) migration is pivotal for optimizing resource utilization, ensuring SLA compliance, and minimizing operational costs in dynamic cloud environments. However, existing strategies often lack theoretical rigor, ignore dynamic cost-performance trade-offs, or fail to guarantee convergence to stable placements. This paper introduces VMigrate+, a novel SLA-aware and cost-optimized VM migration framework grounded in lattice-theoretic optimization and constrained utility maximization. VM placement states are modeled as elements in a partially ordered lattice, and migration decisions are driven by a monotonic utility function that guides the system toward Pareto-optimal configurations. The framework integrates stochastic cost modeling, SLA violation bounds derived via a Hoeffding-type concentration inequality with rolling-window performance estimation, and a Lagrangian-based constraint handling mechanism to respect budget, capacity, and migration-frequency limits. We formally prove the existence of utility-maximizing fixed points and show convergence under Lyapunov stability conditions. Extensive CloudSim-based simulations demonstrate that VMigrate+ reduces cumulative migration cost by up to 25.6%, decreases SLA violation probability by 46.2%, and improves average utility scores by 7.5% compared to baseline methods.

Keywords: VMigrate+ · Virtual Machine Migration · Cost Optimization · Pareto Optimality · Lattice Theory · Lyapunov Stability · SLA Compliance

1 Introduction

Virtual Machine (VM) migration is essential for elasticity, fault tolerance, and dynamic resource optimization in cloud data centers. However, live migration incurs bandwidth, energy, and SLA (Service Level Agreement) overheads, with performance degradation amplified under dynamic workloads. In large-scale environments, resource contention, migration frequency, and budget constraints complicate real-time decision-making. Existing strategies rarely achieve simultaneous cost efficiency, SLA compliance, and stability, often leading to suboptimal or unstable placements. Prior work spans heuristics, metaheuristics, reinforcement learning, and optimization-based methods. Heuristics are lightweight but lack adaptability; learning-based models adapt to dynamics but require costly training and lack formal convergence guarantees; optimization methods offer rigor but are computationally intensive and often ignore joint modeling of migration cost, SLA risk, and system telemetry.

In this paper, we propose `VMigrate+`, a unified, lattice-theoretic migration framework coupling stochastic cost modeling with constraint-aware utility optimization. VM placements are modeled as elements in a partially ordered lattice, with utility-guided transitions balancing performance and cost. Decisions use runtime metrics—CPU contention, I/O latency, and SLA risk—via `perf`, `ftrace`, and `blktrace`, within a Lagrangian-relaxed CMDP enforcing budget, resource, SLA, and migration-frequency constraints.

The major contributions of this paper are:

- A hybrid framework integrating lattice-theoretic state modeling, stochastic cost estimation, and probabilistic SLA bounds via Hoeffding-type concentration with rolling-window profiling.
- The `VMigrate+` algorithm employing utility-driven transitions and Lagrangian-based constraint resolution for SLA-aware, cost-efficient placements.
- A real-time SLA profiling method using rolling mean/variance estimation for robust compliance under noise and workload shifts.
- Formal convergence guarantees via Lyapunov drift and fixed-point analysis, proving the existence of utility-maximizing stable states.
- A CloudSim-based simulation with system-level monitoring and dynamic workload generation, benchmarked against RAS:CO, PSOMCD, and CRIRDS, showing up to **25.6%** lower migration cost, **46.2%** fewer SLA violations, and **7.5%** higher utility.

This work bridges theoretical rigor and practical deployment, enabling scalable, stable, and efficient VM migration in dynamic cloud infrastructures.

2   Literature Survey

Efficient VM migration underpins elasticity and cost-efficiency in virtualized clouds. Reddy et al. [1] proposed resource-aware scheduling to optimize cost under system constraints, while Mukhopadhyay and Tewari [2] developed dependency-driven migration to reduce operational overhead. Runtime performance variability was highlighted by Zboril and Svatá [3]. PSOMCD [4] improved convergence via particle swarm optimization, and online job assignment models [5,6] addressed demand uncertainty. Chen et al. [7] adopted probabilistic capacity reservation for surges. Migration-aware scheduling impacts were analyzed in [8], and Pal et al. [9] examined resource–cost trade-offs under evolving workloads.

Cloud cost modeling research spans predictive provisioning, automation, and workload-aware orchestration. Linear regression for cost forecasting was studied in [10], while Khan et al. [11] applied graph-based inter-resource dependency modeling. ABACUS [12] and FinOps frameworks [13–15] advanced multi-cloud cost governance. DeepVM [16] optimized GPU-based deployments. Mukhopadhyay and Tewari [17] proposed dynamic provisioning; Deochake [18] presented cost optimization case studies. Liu et al. [19] surveyed storage cost optimization, and SmartCMP [20] automated policy enforcement.

Automation and intelligent decision-making remain central. ISO-CLOUD [21] maximized provider revenue; ML-based cost modeling was investigated in [22]. EVACO [23] used ant colony optimization for resource allocation, while earlier work [24] applied IaC for automation, echoed by [25]. SLA-driven cost models were discussed in [26,27], and security-focused virtualization mechanisms to reduce SLA risks were presented in [28].

In contrast to heuristic, financial, or reactive resource management approaches, this paper presents a structured, utility-driven VM migration strategy grounded in lattice-theoretic state modeling, stochastic cost–performance estimation, and constraint-aware decision logic, ensuring bounded SLA violations, cost-efficiency, and convergence under dynamic conditions.

3   Mathematical Framework

We present a hybrid framework uniting stochastic cost modeling, constraint-based optimization, and lattice-theoretic state analysis to achieve cost-efficient, SLA-compliant, Pareto-optimal VM migration in dynamic clouds, minimizing cumulative cost while ensuring stability and SLA adherence.

3.1   System Representation and Lattice-Based State Space Modeling

We represent the VM-to-host assignment problem over a structured decision space that supports tractable, utility-driven migration in dynamic cloud environments. Let $\mathcal{H} = \{h_1, \ldots, h_M\}$ denote the set of physical hosts and $\mathcal{V} = \{v_1, \ldots, v_N\}$ the set of VMs. The system evolves in discrete time epochs $t = 1, 2, \ldots, T$, monitoring resource types $\mathcal{R} = \{\text{CPU}, \text{Memory}, \text{Disk}, \text{Bandwidth}\}$ for allocation and constraint enforcement. A state $s \in \mathcal{S}$, where $\mathcal{S}$ is the set of all VM-to-host assignments, is defined as $s = \left\{ \left(\mathbb{I}_{ij}(t), \ R_i^r(t), \ \text{SLA}_i(t), \ m_i(t) \right) \right\}_{i=1}^N$, encapsulating placement and performance indicators. Here, $\mathbb{I}_{ij}(t) \in \{0, 1\}$ indicates whether VM v_i is placed on host h_j, $R_i^r(t)$ is the usage of resource r by v_i, $\text{SLA}_i(t)$ is its SLA-compliance metric, and $m_i(t) \in \{0, 1\}$ denotes the migration decision flag.

We define aggregate performance under state s as

$$P(s) = \sum_{i=1}^N \omega_i \cdot \text{Perf}_i(s), \tag{1}$$

where ω_i is a task-specific weight for VM v_i, and $\mathrm{Perf}_i(s) \in [0,1]$ is a normalized SLA performance score.

We further define the aggregated SLA compliance score of state s as

$$\mathrm{SLA}(s) = \frac{\sum_{i=1}^{N} \omega_i \cdot \mathbf{1}\{\mathrm{Perf}_i(s) \geq \theta_i\}}{\sum_{i=1}^{N} \omega_i}, \tag{2}$$

where $\theta_i \in [0,1]$ is the SLA threshold for VM v_i, and $\mathbf{1}\{\cdot\}$ is the indicator function. A configuration is SLA-feasible if $\mathrm{SLA}(s) \geq \theta$ for a system-level threshold θ.

Then we associate each state with a cost-performance pair, defined as $f(s) = (C(s), -P(s)) \in \mathbb{R}^2$, where $C(s)$ is the total system cost and $P(s)$ is given by (1). We define an equivalence relation $s \sim s'$ iff $f(s) = f(s')$, and let $\bar{S} = S/\sim$ be the set of equivalence classes. On $\bar{S}$, we impose the partial order

$$[s_i] \preceq [s_j] \iff C(s_i) \leq C(s_j) \text{ and } P(s_i) \geq P(s_j), \tag{3}$$

which induces a finite lattice with meet and join given by componentwise $\min/\max$ in $(C, -P)$ space. This lattice supports *dominance pruning*, where Pareto-improving states are preferred, although small cost increases are permitted if they yield higher utility.

Utility-Driven Migration Rule: We define the weighted utility function as

$$U(s) = \alpha \cdot P(s) - \beta \cdot C(s), \quad \alpha, \beta > 0, \tag{4}$$

where α and β are tunable policy parameters reflecting the performance–cost trade-off. These weights can be automatically adapted via the Lagrangian multipliers to generalize across heterogeneous workloads and SLA priorities. For the experiments, we set $\alpha = 1.0$ and $\beta = 0.7$ to ensure a balanced configuration; higher α emphasizes performance, whereas higher β prioritizes cost savings.

VM placement transitions are governed by a utility-guided decision rule δ with SLA-aware feasibility checks, using the lattice order $(\bar{S}, \preceq)$ for *dominance pruning*—discarding Pareto-dominated states but permitting slight cost increases if net utility improves. The migration rule is then defined as:

$$\delta(s_i, s_j) = 1 \iff U(s_j) > U(s_i) \text{ and } \mathrm{SLA}(s_j) \geq \theta, \tag{5}$$

which enforces utility-increasing, SLA-feasible transitions. Transitions failing this condition are pruned, guaranteeing that migration converges to a stable fixed point $s^* \in S$, defined such that

$$\forall s' \in S, \quad \delta(s^*, s') = 0,$$

i.e., no further utility-improving, SLA-feasible migration exists. Finite S and monotonic improvement guarantee convergence to such a fixed point.

3.2 Lattice-Theoretic Optimization and Utility Modeling

In dynamic cloud infrastructures, decision-making often requires balancing conflicting objectives, such as minimizing migration cost while ensuring performance and SLA compliance. Traditional optimization techniques may fall short in capturing the inherent trade-offs between such multidimensional objectives. To address this, we adopt a lattice-theoretic framework that allows the ordering of system states based on dominance relations. Within this framework, Pareto-optimality provides a principled way to identify states where no objective can be improved without degrading another, while utility modeling enables the selection of the most desirable state among them. This subsection formalizes these concepts by introducing Pareto-optimality and utility maximization within the lattice-based optimization space.

Pareto-Optimality: A state $s \in \mathcal{S}$ is Pareto-optimal if no other $s' \in \mathcal{S}$ satisfies $C(s') \leq C(s)$ and $P(s') \geq P(s)$ with at least one strict inequality. The set of Pareto-optimal states is

$$\mathcal{S}^* = \{\, s \in \mathcal{S} \mid \nexists s' \in \mathcal{S} : s' \preceq s \text{ and strict} \,\}. \tag{6}$$

Utility Maximization: Among Pareto-optimal states, the optimal configuration is the one maximizing utility:

$$s^{\text{opt}} = \arg \max_{s \in \mathcal{S}^*} U(s). \tag{7}$$

3.3 Stochastic Cost Optimization via CMDP with Lagrangian Relaxation

To accommodate the dynamic nature of cloud infrastructures, migration must adapt to stochastic workload fluctuations while ensuring compliance with bandwidth, capacity, and SLA constraints. So, we model VM migration as a *Constrained Markov Decision Process* (CMDP) $(\mathcal{S}, \mathcal{A}, P, C, \gamma, \mathcal{G})$ with:

- $\mathcal{S}$—feasible VM-to-host allocation states.
- $\mathcal{A}$—discrete actions $\{\text{migrate}(v_i, h_j),\ \text{no-migrate}\}$.
- $P(s'|s, a)$—transition probabilities capturing workload/network evolution.
- $C(s, a) = \alpha_c\, \text{CPU}_{\text{mig}}(a) + \beta_c\, \text{BW}(a) + \phi\, \mathbb{P}[\text{SLA}(s, a) < \theta]$—migration cost.
- $\gamma \in (0, 1]$—discount factor.
- Constraints:

$$g_1(s, a) = \sum_i BW_i(a) m_i - B(t) \leq 0 \qquad \text{(Bandwidth)} \tag{8}$$

$$g_2(s, a) = \sum_i \text{CPU}_i(a) m_i - C_{\max}(t) \leq 0 \qquad \text{(CPU)} \tag{9}$$

$$g_3(s, a) = \mathbb{P}[\text{SLA}(s, a) < \theta] - \epsilon \leq 0 \qquad \text{(SLA)} \tag{10}$$

The objective is to minimize the total discounted cost:

$$\pi^* = \arg\min_{\pi} \ \mathbb{E}^{\pi}\left[\sum_{t=0}^{T-1} \gamma^t C(s_t, a_t)\right] \quad \text{s.t.} \quad g_k(s_t, a_t) \leq 0, \ \forall k, t.$$

Lagrangian Action Scoring: At each epoch, feasible actions are scored via:

$$\mathcal{L}(s_t, a) = C(s_t, a) + \lambda_t g_1(s_t, a) + \mu_t g_2(s_t, a) + \nu_t g_3(s_t, a), \tag{11}$$

where $(\lambda_t, \mu_t, \nu_t) \geq 0$ are Lagrange multipliers. The optimal action is $a_t^* = \arg\min_{a \in \mathcal{A}_{\text{feasible}}} \mathcal{L}(s_t, a)$, and multipliers are updated online via:

$$\lambda_{t+1} = [\lambda_t + \eta_t\, g_1(s_t, a_t)]_+ , \quad \mu_{t+1} = [\mu_t + \eta_t\, g_2(s_t, a_t)]_+ , \quad \nu_{t+1} = [\nu_t + \eta_t\, g_3(s_t, a_t)]_+ . \tag{12}$$

Here $\eta_t > 0$ ensures stability and bounded multipliers. This unified CMDP–Lagrangian scheme yields adaptive, constraint-aware migration with per-step feasibility.

3.4 Constraints and SLA Guarantees

To ensure correctness, feasibility, and predictable performance, VMigrate+ enforces four core constraints:

(i) Resource Capacity: No host exceeds its capacity C_j^r for any resource $r \in \mathcal{R}$:

$$\sum_{i=1}^{N} R_i^r(t)\, \mathbb{I}_{ij}(t) \leq C_j^r, \quad \forall j, r. \tag{13}$$

(ii) Migration Budget: At each epoch t, migration cost $\mathcal{C}(t)$ is bounded by budget $B(t)$:

$$\mathcal{C}(t) \leq B(t), \quad \forall t. \tag{14}$$

(iii) SLA Violation Probability: Let $\mu_i(t)$ and $\sigma_i(t)$ be rolling-window mean and std. deviation of the performance metric (window size W). Assuming sub-Gaussian behavior, Hoeffding-type bounds give:

$$\mathbb{P}[\text{SLA}_i(t) < \theta] \leq \exp\left(-\frac{W(\mu_i(t) - \theta)^2}{2\,\sigma_i^2(t)}\right) \leq \epsilon, \tag{15}$$

enabling probabilistic SLA compliance decisions.

(iv) Migration Frequency: Each VM may migrate at most $M_{\max}$ times in the horizon:

$$\sum_{t=1}^{T} m_i(t) \leq M_{\max}, \quad \forall i. \tag{16}$$

Real-Time SLA Profiling: Rolling-window statistics are:

$$\mu_i(t) = \frac{1}{W} \sum_{w=0}^{W-1} \mathrm{Perf}_i(t-w), \quad \sigma_i^2(t) = \frac{1}{W} \sum_{w=0}^{W-1} \left(\mathrm{Perf}_i(t-w) - \mu_i(t)\right)^2.$$

Metrics are normalized as:

$$\mathrm{Perf}_i(s) = \begin{cases} \frac{\phi_i(s) - \phi_i^{\min}}{\phi_i^{\max} - \phi_i^{\min}}, & \text{if higher is better,} \\ 1 - \frac{\phi_i(s) - \phi_i^{\min}}{\phi_i^{\max} - \phi_i^{\min}}, & \text{if lower is better.} \end{cases}$$

For heavy-tailed delays, stronger bounds or adaptive safety margins can replace Eq. (15).

3.5 System Stability via Lyapunov Drift

To ensure bounded long-term migration overhead, we adopt a Lyapunov-drift framework. Let $\mathcal{C}(t)$ be the total migration cost at time t and $\mathcal{F}_t$ the system history up to t. The conditional drift is expressed as $\Delta \mathcal{C}(t) = \mathbb{E}[\mathcal{C}(t+1) - \mathcal{C}(t) \,|\, \mathcal{F}_t]$, with stability ensured if $\Delta \mathcal{C}(t) \leq -\epsilon, \quad \epsilon > 0$, implying non-divergent migration cost. In simulation, the drift is approximated via a W-epoch sliding window:

$$\widehat{\Delta \mathcal{C}}(t) = \frac{1}{W} \sum_{w=1}^{W} \left[\mathcal{C}(t-w+1) - \mathcal{C}(t-w)\right]. \tag{17}$$

The system is *empirically stable* if $\widehat{\Delta \mathcal{C}}(t) \leq -\epsilon$, ensuring cost convergence under enforced SLA and resource constraints.

3.6 Optimality and Regret Bound

To assess the asymptotic performance of `VMigrate+` under the relaxed migration rule $\delta(s_i, s_j)$ and bounded estimation errors in $\mu_i(t)$, $\sigma_i^2(t)$, and $C_{\mathrm{mig}}^i(t)$; let $U(s)$ be the utility of $s \in \mathcal{S}$ and $s^{\mathrm{opt}} = \arg\max_{s \in \mathcal{S}} U(s)$. If accepted transitions satisfy $U(s_{t+1}) \geq U(s_t) + \eta_t - \zeta_t$ with $\eta_t > 0$ and $\sum_{t=1}^{\infty} \zeta_t < \infty$, then there exists $\epsilon > 0$ such that $U(s^{\mathrm{opt}}) - U(s_T) \leq \epsilon, \quad$ for all large T, ensuring convergence within ϵ of the optimal utility. With a finite candidate pool, $U(s)$ Lipschitz in $(P(s), C(s))$ with constant L_U, and δ enforcing strict feasible improvement,

$$\lim_{T \to \infty} \frac{1}{T} \sum_{t=1}^{T} \left(U(s^{\mathrm{opt}}) - U(s_t)\right) = 0, \tag{18}$$

implying vanishing average utility loss and asymptotic near-optimality. Rolling-window smoothing of $\mu_i(t)$ and $\sigma_i^2(t)$ mitigates noise, and SLA checks (Eq. (15)) remain stable under small perturbations. Safety margins on $C_{\mathrm{mig}}^i(t)$ and θ handle bursty or adversarial workloads.

4 Proposed Algorithm

In this section, we propose a novel utility-guided, SLA-compliant, and budget-aware algorithm, VMigrate+, that migrates VMs over a lattice-structured state space. At each time step, it evaluates migration decisions for n VMs across m hosts over T epochs, with worst-case time complexity $\mathcal{O}(T \cdot n \cdot m)$, reduced to $\mathcal{O}(T \cdot n \cdot K)$ via Top-K pruning ($K \ll m$). Space complexity is $\mathcal{O}(n \cdot T)$. Transitions are permitted only if utility increases and constraints are satisfied. Candidate host selection uses a heuristic filter that retains transitions with positive utility gain, low SLA risk, and acceptable cost, with tiebreakers favoring lower inter-VM communication or host load. The algorithm guarantees monotonic utility improvement and convergence to a stable fixed point. Although VMigrate+ introduces a modest (3–5%) runtime overhead per decision cycle due to utility evaluation and Lagrangian updates, this cost is negligible relative to live migration latency and becomes amortized over decision epochs, thereby preserving system scalability and responsiveness in practice.

5 Formal Analysis

In this section, we formally analyze the proposed VMigrate+ framework by establishing its correctness, feasibility, and optimality through rigorous theoretical guarantees. Specifically, we present two central theorems: (i) the first ensures the existence and convergence to an optimal VM placement state within the lattice-structured state space, and (ii) the second validates that the Lagrangian formulation enforces SLA compliance, budget adherence, and resource capacity constraints, thus enabling cost-aware and performance-driven migration decisions.

Theorem 1 (Existence of Utility-Maximizing Fixed Point over Reachable States). *Let $(\bar{\mathcal{S}}, \preceq)$ be the finite poset of VM placement equivalence classes, and let $U : \mathcal{S} \to \mathbb{R}$ be the utility function. Suppose the migration policy $\mathcal{T}$ admits transitions only when $U(s_j) > U(s_i)$ and $SLA(s_j)$ satisfies the bound. Then there exists at least one fixed point $s^* \in \mathcal{S}$ such that $\mathcal{T}(s^*) = s^*$, and s^* attains the maximal utility among all states reachable from the initial state under $\mathcal{T}$.*

Proof. Let $s^{(0)}$ be the initial state and denote by

$$\mathcal{R}(s^{(0)}) = \{s \in \mathcal{S} \mid s \text{ is reachable from } s^{(0)} \text{ under } \mathcal{T}\}$$

the set of states reachable under the policy $\mathcal{T}$. By assumption $\mathcal{S}$ is finite and $|\mathcal{R}(s^{(0)})| \leq |\mathcal{S}| < \infty$. Assume $\mathcal{T}$ accepts a transition $s \to s'$ only when $U(s') > U(s)$ (strict improvement) and $SLA(s')$ satisfies the bound.

Because U strictly increases on every accepted transition, any path

$$s^{(0)} \to s^{(1)} \to \cdots \to s^{(k)}$$

Algorithm 1. VMigrate+: Cost-aware Dynamic VM Migration Algorithm (with Relaxed δ Rule)

Require: Set of VMs $\mathcal{V}$, Hosts $\mathcal{H}$, initial state s_0, budget $B(t)$, thresholds θ, ϵ, $M_{\max}$, planning horizon T

Ensure: Migration decisions $m_i(t)$ for all $v_i \in \mathcal{V}$ at each time t, final converged state s_T, utility $U(s_T)$

1: # Initialize
2: $s \leftarrow s_0$, $t \leftarrow 1$
3: **while** $t \leq T$ **do**
4:     **for** each VM $v_i \in \mathcal{V}$ **do**
5:         # Estimate SLA stats via rolling window
6:         Compute $\mu_i(t)$, $\sigma_i^2(t)$
7:         Predict $R_i^r(t)$; compute migration cost $C_{\mathrm{mig}}^i(t)$
8:         Estimate SLA violation probability
9:         # Generate candidate next states
10:         Generate $\{s_j\} \leftarrow$ all feasible placements for v_i satisfying the constraints
11:         # Optional soft pruning using lattice order
12:         $\{s_j\} \leftarrow$ remove candidates strongly dominated by s under $\preceq$
13:         # Rank candidates by utility
14:         Sort $\{s_j\}$ in descending $U(s_j)$; keep Top-K
15:         **for** each candidate state s_j in Top-K **do**
16:             **if** $U(s_j) > U(s)$ **and** SLA(s_j) satisfies constraints **then**
17:                 $\delta(s, s_j) \leftarrow 1$
18:                 Update $s \leftarrow s_j$, set $m_i(t) \leftarrow 1$
19:                 **break**   ▷ Accept first improving candidate for v_i
20:             **else**
21:                 $\delta(s, s_j) \leftarrow 0$, set $m_i(t) \leftarrow 0$
22:             **end if**
23:         **end for**
24:     **end for**
25:     # System-wide cost and drift monitoring
26:     Compute $\mathcal{C}(t)$; enforce $B(t)$
27:     Evaluate Lyapunov drift $\Delta\mathcal{C}(t)$
28:     # Optional early stop if converged
29:     **if** $|U(s) - U(s_{t-1})| < \epsilon$ **then**
30:         **break**
31:     **end if**
32:     $t \leftarrow t + 1$
33: **end while**
34: **return** Final state $s_T = s$, utility $U(s_T)$, plan $\{m_i(t)\}$

---

consists of strictly increasing utility values and thus cannot visit the same state twice. Hence the path length is bounded by $|\mathcal{R}(s^{(0)})| - 1$, so the process must terminate in finitely many steps at some $s^* \in \mathcal{R}(s^{(0)})$.

Termination means there is no allowable successor of s^* with strictly higher utility; equivalently $\mathcal{T}(s^*) = s^*$. By construction s^* attains maximal utility over

$\mathcal{R}(s^{(0)})$. If $\mathcal{R}(s^{(0)}) = \mathcal{S}$ (full reachability), then s^* is a global maximizer of U; otherwise it is maximal among reachable states.

Theorem 2 (Feasible Near-Optimal Convergence under Lagrangian Relaxation). *Assume either (i) a convex relaxation of the binary migration variables $m_i(t)$ with Slater's condition satisfied, or (ii) bounded duality gap for the discrete problem. If the Lagrangian multipliers are updated by a diminishing-step-size subgradient method and the Lyapunov drift condition holds, then the algorithm converges to a feasible VM placement s^* that minimizes the penalized objective and achieves utility $U(s^*)$ within a bounded gap of the relaxed optimum $U(s^{\mathrm{opt}})$.*

Proof. Assume (A) convex relaxation with Slater's condition, or (B) discrete case with bounded duality gap. Let x denote placement/migration variables, $f(x) = \sum_{t,i} C^i_{\mathrm{mig}}(t) m_i(t)$, and $\{h_k(x,t)\}$ the constraint residuals with multipliers $\{\nu_k(t)\}$. The Lagrangian is

$$\mathcal{L}(x,\nu) = f(x) + \sum_{k,t} \nu_k(t)\, h_k(x,t), \quad d(\nu) = \inf_{x \in \mathcal{X}} \mathcal{L}(x,\nu).$$

At epoch t, choose x_t minimizing $\mathcal{L}(x,\nu_t)$. Let $g_t = [h_k(x_t,t)]_k$ be the constraint residuals. Subgradient ascent

$$\nu_{t+1} = \nu_t + \eta_t g_t, \quad \sum_t \eta_t = \infty, \quad \sum_t \eta_t^2 < \infty$$

ensures $\frac{1}{T}\sum_{t=1}^{T}(d(\nu^\star) - d(\nu_t)) \to 0$ and $\frac{1}{T}\sum_{t=1}^{T} g_t \to 0$, giving asymptotic feasibility (up to the duality gap in case B). If a Lyapunov function $V(t)$ satisfies $\Delta V(t) \leq -\epsilon$ for large deviations, multipliers and costs remain bounded. Thus, limit points x^* are feasible and satisfy $f(x^*) \leq f^{\mathrm{opt}} + \mathrm{gap}$, yielding a placement s^* within this bound of $U(s^{\mathrm{opt}})$.

6   Experimental Evaluation

To validate the effectiveness of the proposed `VMigrate+` algorithm, we perform extensive simulation-based experiments under realistic cloud computing scenarios. This section presents the experimental setup, environment configuration, and a comparative performance analysis against three baseline, cost-aware VM migration strategies: Resource-aware Scheduling for Cost Optimization (RAS:CO) [1], Particle Swarm Optimization Algorithm Enhanced with Modified Crowding Distance (PSOMCD) [4], and Capacity Reservation for Intermittent Random Demand Surges (CRIRDS) [7].

6.1   Simulation Environment

Experiments use `CloudSim` 3.0 extended for advanced VM migration and cost modeling. The simulated data center comprises HP ProLiant servers (16-core Xeon at 30 GHz, 32 GB RAM, 1 TB disk) and 50–150 heterogeneous VMs with dynamic CPU-, memory-, or I/O-bound workloads over $T = 1000$ intervals, changing every 200 steps. Migration emulates Xen-style live migration with memory pre-copy and bandwidth throttling, implemented via `libvirt` 8.0 and KVM/QEMU on Ubuntu 22.04 (OpenJDK 17). Resource isolation uses `cgroups` v2; telemetry is collected via `perf`, `ftrace`, and `qemu-agent`; network shaping uses `tc` with HTB; disk interference via `blktrace`; power via an embedded `PowerTop` model. Evaluation metrics include SLA violation probability, cumulative migration cost ($\mathcal{C}_{\mathrm{total}}$), throughput, and convergence stability under varying task loads, SLA thresholds (θ), and budgets $B(t)$. SLA compliance is checked each epoch via rolling-window mean/variance profiling (Eq. (15)) for robustness to workload noise. All runs use a fixed random seed (42) to ensure identical stochastic inputs and eliminate bias in baseline comparisons.

6.2   Comparative Analysis

Figure 1 compares four major cost components, computational, energy, delay-induced, and SLAV costs, across all evaluated models. Results are derived from CloudSim 3.0 extensions calibrated with PowerTop, `perf`, and `libvirt` runtime logs for realistic operational metrics. The proposed `VMigrate+` consistently achieves lower costs by (i) using a lattice-theoretic placement model that enforces monotonic utility improvement to minimize redundant migrations, (ii) integrating stochastic cost modeling with Lagrangian-based constraint handling for optimal trade-offs between cost and SLA adherence, and (iii) applying Lyapunov drift minimization to ensure stability and reduce migration-induced penalties. Quantitatively, `VMigrate+` lowers cumulative migration-related cost by up to **25.5%** over the closest baseline (CRIRDS), while also outperforming heuristic (PSOMCD) and rule-based (RAS:CO) approaches across all dimensions.

Table 1 presents four system-level performance metrics across baseline models. `VMigrate+` reduces average processing time by accelerating workload execution relative to heuristic and rule-based approaches, due to its lattice-theoretic VM placement that avoids redundant migrations and lowers context-switch overhead. Responsiveness and throughput are enhanced via stochastic cost modeling combined with Lyapunov drift minimization, ensuring stable resource allocation under demand fluctuations. Average delay is reduced through proactive SLA-aware scheduling, which limits queue buildup and migration-induced interruptions. Together, these mechanisms enable `VMigrate+` to balance computational efficiency, system stability, and `SLA` compliance more effectively than the baselines, demonstrating robustness in large-scale cloud settings.

Table 2 compares convergence stability, scalability, Lyapunov drift, and normalized system utility across competing approaches. `VMigrate+` attains the highest stability index, maintaining predictable convergence under dynamic workloads via a lattice-theoretic fixed-point formulation. Its scalability stems from

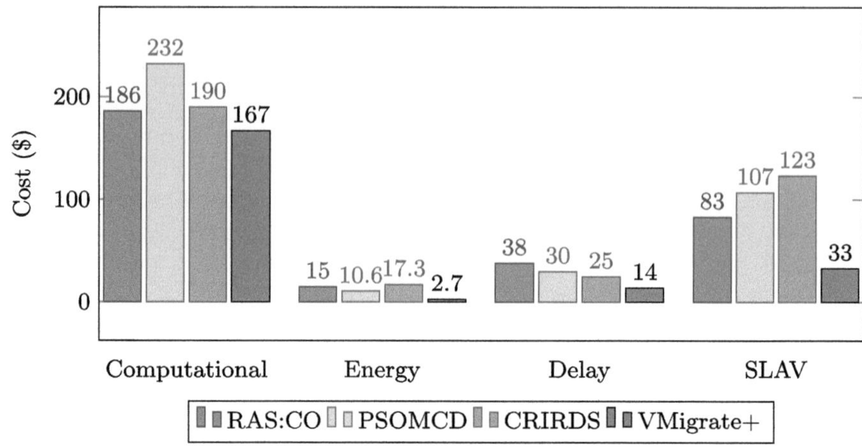

Fig. 1. Grouped cost comparison across four major cost types

Table 1. Performance Comparison Across Models

Model	Processing Time (s)	Responsiveness (req/s)	Throughput (req/s)	Delay (ms)
RAS:CO	243.12	60.52	480	180
PSOMCD	220.06	75.83	520	160
CRIRDS	217.17	82.29	545	150
VMigrate+	**164.26**	**110.11**	**590**	**125**

modular optimization and adaptive migration grouping, which limit coordination overhead as system size increases. A lower Lyapunov drift demonstrates improved control-theoretic stability, ensuring bounded queues and avoiding oscillatory allocation. The system utility score further shows that **VMigrate+** delivers a superior trade-off between cost efficiency and SLA compliance compared to baselines. Collectively, these results confirm that the framework scales efficiently while guaranteeing stability and high utility in dynamic cloud environments.

Table 2. Convergence, Scalability, Drift, and Utility Comparison Across Models

Model	Convergence Stability Index	Max Supported VMs	Avg. Lyapunov Drift	System Utility (normalized)
RAS:CO	0.78	850	0.142	0.78
PSOMCD	0.82	920	0.127	0.82
CRIRDS	0.85	980	0.118	0.85
VMigrate+	**0.93**	**1150**	**0.093**	**0.93**

Figure 2 shows SLA violation (SLAV) probability across varying thresholds (θ). **VMigrate+** achieves the lowest violation rate, reducing SLAV to 0.015 at $\theta = 1.0$, compared to 0.036 for CRIRDS, 0.039 for PSOMCD, and 0.043 for

RAS:CO. This advantage arises from Lyapunov-guided scheduling, which adaptively regulates resource allocation under strict SLA bounds, and a stochastic utility-based placement strategy that prevents resource over-commitment. By contrast, heuristic (PSOMCD) and rule-based (RAS:CO) rely on static threshold handling, while CRIRDS improves stability but lacks cross-layer optimization. The monotonic decline in SLAV probability with increasing θ further confirms robustness, with VMigrate+ cutting SLA violations by 65–70% relative to baselines across the full threshold range.

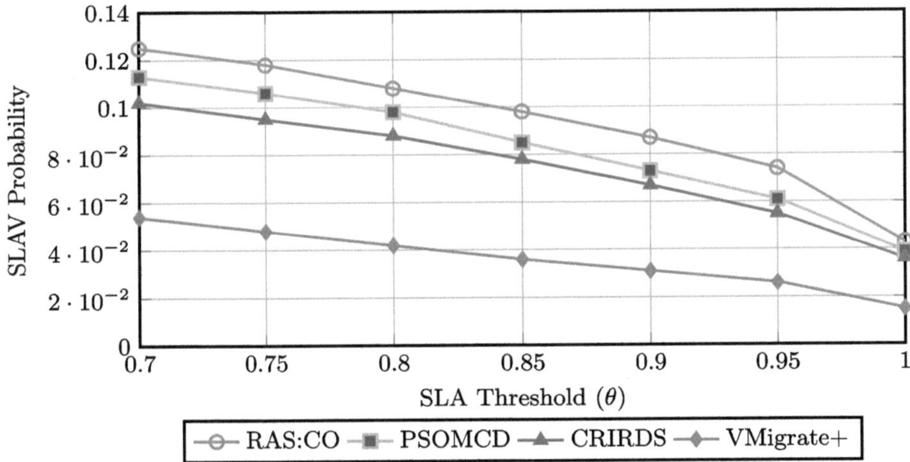

Fig. 2. SLAV Probability vs SLA Threshold across models. Lower values indicate better SLA compliance.

Figure 3 depicts the temporal evolution of system utility $U(s_t)$, highlighting both convergence speed and steady-state performance across models. While heuristic (PSOMCD) and rule-based (RAS:CO) schemes exhibit slower growth and premature saturation due to static migration heuristics and lack of cross-layer adaptation, VMigrate+ achieves a markedly faster ascent, reaching above 200 utility units by $t = 8$ compared to ~156 for PSOMCD and ~143 for CRIRDS. This acceleration is driven by the lattice-theoretic monotonicity guarantees, which ensure non-decreasing utility across successive placements, and by Lyapunov-guided drift minimization, which prevents oscillatory migration patterns. The stable plateau reached near $U(s_t) \approx 221$ confirms both optimality and robustness under dynamic workloads, offering a 40–60% utility advantage over competing baselines. These findings demonstrate that VMigrate+ not only converges more rapidly but also sustains higher long-term efficiency, underscoring its suitability for production-grade resource orchestration (Table 3).

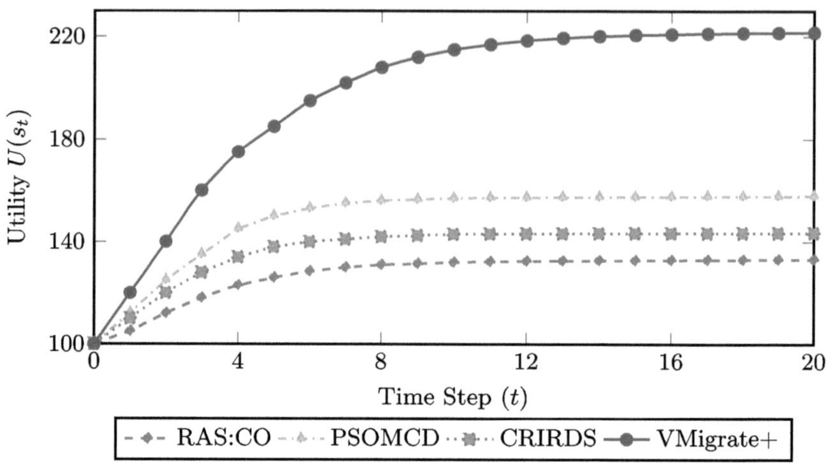

Fig. 3. Utility evolution over time.

Table 3. Feature Comparison Across Baseline and Proposed Models

Capability	RAS:CO	PSOMCD	CRIRDS	VMigrate+
SLA-Bounded Decision Logic	X	X	✓	✓
Utility-Constrained Convergence	X	X	X	✓
Stochastic Cost Modeling	X	X	✓	✓
System Telemetry Integration	X	X	X	✓
Adaptivity to Budget Profile	✓	✓	X	✓

7 Conclusion

This paper introduces VMigrate+, a utility-optimized virtual machine migration strategy for dynamic cloud infrastructures. The approach integrates stochastic cost modeling, constrained optimization, and Lyapunov-based convergence analysis to minimize migration cost while ensuring SLA compliance and performance. Formal guarantees based on fixed-point convergence and feasibility bounds establish the correctness of the model. Experimental evaluation using CloudSim v3.0 shows that VMigrate+ outperforms RAS:CO, PSOMCD, and CRIRDS, achieving up to 25.6% lower migration cost, 46.2% fewer SLA violations, and 7.5% higher utility. The framework is modular and scalable, with potential extensions including energy-aware scheduling, detailed migration delay modeling, and integration with OpenStack or KVM/Xen environments for production-grade deployment.

References

1. Reddy, K.J., Udayaraju, P., Pamaiahgari, V.P.R., Kumar, V.D.: Implementing resource-aware scheduling algorithm for improving cost optimization in cloud computing. In: 2025 4th International Conference on Sentiment Analysis and Deep Learning (ICSADL), pp. 282–287. IEEE (2025)
2. Mukhopadhyay, N., Tewari, B.P.: Cost and energy aware migration through dependency analysis of VM components in virtual cloud infrastructure. Computing **107**(1), 1–44 (2025)
3. Zboril, M., Svatá, V.: Performance comparison of cloud virtual machines. J. Syst. Inf. Technol. **27**(2), 197–213 (2025)
4. Bolin, Z., Jiao, G.E., et al.: PSOMCD: particle swarm optimization algorithm enhanced with modified crowding distance for load balancing in cloud computing. Int. J. Adv. Comput. Sci. Appl. **16**(5) (2025)
5. Ekbatani, F., Feng, Y., Kash, I., Niazadeh, R.: Online job assignment. arXiv preprint arXiv:2506.06893 (2025)
6. Feng, Z., Dawande, M., Janakiraman, G., Qi, A.: Online learning and capacity management in cloud-cost optimization. Available at SSRN 4812792 (2024)
7. Chen, S., Lei, J., Moinzadeh, K.: Cost optimization in cloud computing: capacity reservation for intermittent random demand surges. Prod. Oper. Manag. **33**(6), 1265–1284 (2024)
8. Mukhopadhyay, N., Tewari, B.P.: Performance analysis of a virtualized cloud data center through efficient VM migrations. In: Proceedings of the 2024 Sixteenth International Conference on Contemporary Computing, pp. 357–365 (2024)
9. Pal, S., Agrawal, K.K., Kasi, B.: Evolving towards optimal cloud resource allocation and cost management: an in-depth analysis. In: 2024 1st International Conference on Advances in Computing, Communication and Networking (ICAC2N), pp. 289–295. IEEE (2024)
10. Musa, S., Down, D.G.: Cost-effective cloud resource provisioning using linear regression. In: 2024 IEEE International Conference on Cloud Computing Technology and Science (CloudCom), pp. 176–183. IEEE (2024)
11. Khan, A.Q., Matskin, M., Prodan, R., Bussler, C., Roman, D., Soylu, A.: Cost modelling and optimisation for cloud: a graph-based approach. J. Cloud Comput. **13**(1), 147 (2024)
12. Deochake, S.: Abacus: a finops service for cloud cost optimization. arXiv preprint arXiv:2501.14753 (2024)
13. Mileski, D., Gusev, M.: Finops in cloud-native near real-time serverless streaming solutions. In: 2023 31st Telecommunications Forum (TELFOR), pp. 1–4. IEEE (2023)
14. Castellana, L.: Development and analysis of FinOps processes for a Multi-Cloud environment. Ph.D. thesis, Politecnico di Torino (2023)
15. Suppala, P.: Finops in saas platform within hybrid, multi-cloud, multi-tenant, multi-region environments (2022)
16. Kim, Y., et al.: Deepvm: integrating spot and on-demand VMs for cost-efficient deep learning clusters in the cloud. In: 2024 IEEE 24th International Symposium on Cluster, Cloud and Internet Computing (CCGrid), pp. 227–235. IEEE (2024)
17. Mukhopadhyay, N., Tewari, B.P.: Dynamic cost effective solution for efficient cloud infrastructure. J. Supercomput. **79**(6), 6471–6506 (2023)
18. Deochake, S.: Cloud cost optimization: a comprehensive review of strategies and case studies. arXiv preprint arXiv:2307.12479 (2023)

19. Liu, M., Pan, L., Liu, S.: Cost optimization for cloud storage from user perspectives: recent advances, taxonomy, and survey. ACM Comput. Surv. **55**(13s), 1–37 (2023)
20. Li, F., Wu, G., Lu, J., Jin, M., An, H., Lin, J.: Smartcmp: a cloud cost optimization governance practice of smart cloud management platform. In: 2022 IEEE 7th International Conference on Smart Cloud (SmartCloud), pp. 171–176. IEEE (2022)
21. Bernal, A., Cañizares, P. C., Núñez, A., Cambronero, M.E., Valero, V.: Iso-cloud: an intelligent system for optimizing the overall income in cloud providers. In: 2022 4th International Conference on Computer Communication and the Internet (ICCCI), pp. 7–13. IEEE (2022)
22. Osypanka, P., Nawrocki, P.: Resource usage cost optimization in cloud computing using machine learning. IEEE Trans. Cloud Comput. **10**(3), 2079–2089 (2020)
23. Mukhopadhyay, N., Tewari, B.P., Choubey, D.K., Bhowmick, A.: Efficient resource allocation in virtualized cloud platforms using encapsulated virtualization based ant colony optimization (EVACO). In: 6G Enabled Fog Computing in IoT: Applications and Opportunities, pp. 133–152. Springer, Cham (2023)
24. Mukhopadhyay, N., Tewari, B.P.: Efficient iac-based resource allocation for virtualized cloud platforms. In: International Conference on Advanced Network Technologies and Intelligent Computing, pp. 200–214. Springer, Cham (2021)
25. Mumbere, S., Okello, J.O., Sansa, K.: The implementation of infrastructure as code template for low-cost cloud infrastructure operations (2024)
26. Bernal, A., Cambronero, M.E., Núñez, A., Cañizares, P.C., Valero, V.: Evaluating cloud interactions with costs and SLAs. J. Supercomput. **78**(6), 7529–7555 (2022)
27. Erradi, A., Mansouri, Y.: Online cost optimization algorithms for tiered cloud storage services. J. Syst. Softw. **160**, 110457 (2020)
28. Mukhopadhyay, N., De, T.K., Chatterjee, D.: A novel virtualization enabled cloud infrastructural framework for enhancing private cloud communication security. Int. J. Inf. Secur. Sci. **10**(1), 16–25 (2021)

Efficient Data Sharing Based on IBE to ABE Conversion for Cloud-Assisted Environments

Koshalesh Meher and Y. Sreenivasa Rao$^{(\boxtimes)}$

Department of Mathematics, National Institute of Technology Warangal,
Warangal 506004, Telangana, India
`km23mar1r05@student.nitw.ac.in, ysr@nitw.ac.in`

Abstract. Cloud-assisted environments are now vital platforms that enable scalable data storage, seamless access, and real-time sharing of data among users. However, using a public cloud storage system to store and share sensitive data leads to security and privacy issues. In order to minimize data maintenance expenses and facilitate secure data sharing, data owners upload encrypted data to a cloud server. Ciphertext-Policy Attribute-Based Encryption (CP-ABE) is an effective technology for enforcing fine-grained access control over shared data. But its computational demands make it challenging to implement directly in resource-limited devices, rendering it less suitable for cloud-assisted environments. To address this problem, we propose a proxy re-encryption scheme that converts an identity-based encryption ciphertext into a CP-ABE ciphertext to establish a fine-grained data sharing mechanism in the cloud-assisted environments. Our scheme provides non-interactive re-encryption capabilities with online-offline re-encryption key generation mechanism while simultaneously accomplishing verifiable outsourced decryption by preserving data confidentiality against the semi-trusted proxy server and unauthorized users. Security assessments and performance evaluations indicate that our proposed scheme accomplishes robust security properties with enhanced computational efficiency compared to existing methods and can be deployed in real-life applications.

Keywords: Attribute-based encryption · identity-based encryption · proxy re-encryption · online-offline mechanism · outsourced decryption

1 Introduction

Attribute-Based Proxy Re-Encryption (ABPRE) [3–5, 7, 11, 12] was introduced by combining the notions of Attribute Based Encryption (ABE) and Proxy Re-Encryption (PRE), enabling fine-grained access control and one-to-many data sharing mechanism. As a novel cryptographic solution ABE [9] integrates flexible access control with encryption functionality, enabling one-to-many data sharing and providing fine-grained access control over encrypted data. In Ciphertext-Policy Attribute-Based Encryption (CP-ABE) [2, 10], the data is encrypted with

B. Chatterjee et al. (Eds.): ICDCIT 2026, LNCS 16420, pp. 103–119, 2026.
https://doi.org/10.1007/978-3-032-16632-6_7

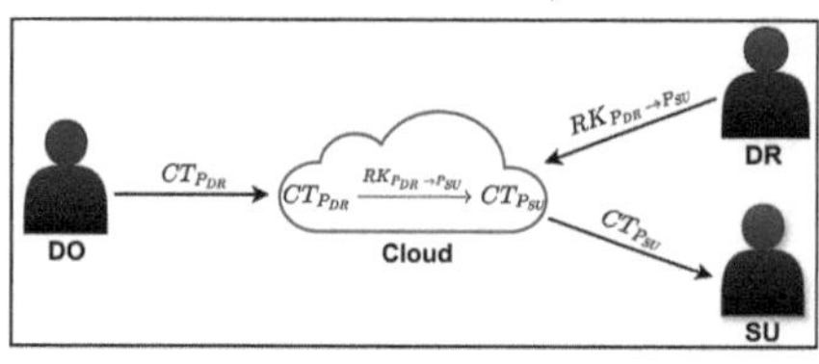
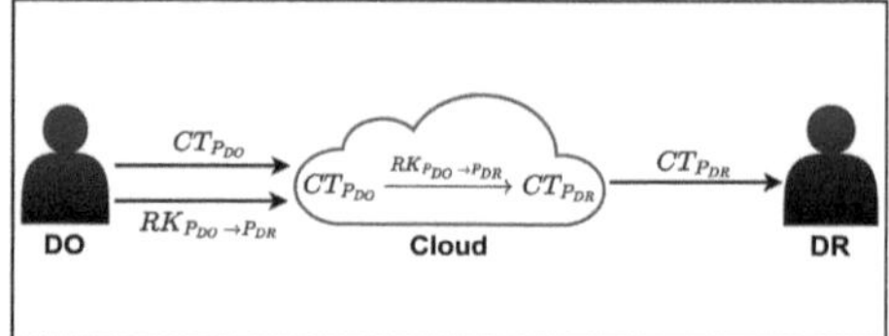

(a) DO sharing with DR and then DR sharing with SU

(b) DO sharing with DR

Fig. 1. Two PRE Frameworks.

an access structure specified by the data owner, and only users whose attributes satisfy the structure can decrypt the ciphertext. Since the access structure is fixed at encryption time and cannot be modified later, dynamic access control is not feasible. In PRE [8], a semi-trusted proxy server (i.e., the cloud) is authorized to convert an encrypted message under one public key to another public key using a re-encryption key, without revealing the original data. Based on an application scenario, a PRE scheme considers one of the following two frameworks.

(a) *Framework-1.* A Data Owner (DO) produces a ciphertext $CT_{P_{DR}}$ under the public key P_{DR} of the original Data Receiver (DR) and uploads it to the cloud. Later, if the DR intends to share $CT_{P_{DR}}$ with another Shared User (SU) possessing public key P_{SU}, the DR sends a re-encryption key $RK_{P_{DR} \rightarrow P_{SU}}$ to the cloud, using which the cloud re-encrypts $CT_{P_{DR}}$ to $CT_{P_{SU}}$ and forwards $CT_{P_{SU}}$ to the SU as shown in Fig. 1a. The SU decrypts $CT_{P_{SU}}$ using its secret key. This kind of framework is considered in [4,7,11].

(b) *Framework-2.* A DO stores a ciphertext $CT_{P_{DO}}$ on the cloud by encrypting the data with its public key. Later, when the DO wants to share the data with a DR with public key P_{DR}, the DO sends a re-encryption key $RK_{P_{DO} \rightarrow P_{DR}}$ to the cloud. Then, the cloud generates a re-encrypted ciphertext $CT_{P_{DR}}$ and outputs it to the DR (shown in Fig. 1b), where the DR is able to decrypt it using its secret key. This framework is available in [3,5,12],

The ABPRE schemes [3,4,7,11] use ABE mechanism to encrypt the data. However, these schemes encounter efficiency issues, as the computational costs for users during encryption and re-encryption key generation increase linearly with the number of attributes. Thus, for typical smart devices, which have resource constraints in terms of computing and storage capacity, these schemes cannot be implemented in practice. To reduce the encryption computational overhead of the DO, PRE schemes [5] Scheme-II, [12] are proposed that transform Identity Based Encryption (IBE) ciphertext into ABE ciphertext. However, [5] Scheme-II does not achieve non-interactive transformation, and the DO needs to bear complex computational overhead to generate the re-encryption key. The scheme [12] supports outsourcing mechanism to reduce the computation overhead of users and simultaneously achieve fine-grained data sharing in industrial

Table 1. Functionality comparison

Scheme	Conversion	F_1	F_2	F_3	F_4	F_5	F_6
[3]	ABE to IBE	×	×	×	×	×	✓
[12]	IBE to ABE	✓	×	✓	✓	×	×
[5] Scheme-I	ABE to IBE	×	×	×	×	×	✓
[5] Scheme-II	IBE to ABE	✓	×	×	×	×	✓
Our IB-AB-PReM	IBE to ABE	✓	✓	✓	✓	✓	✓

Notes. F_1: One-to-many data sharing, F_2: Online-offline re-encryption key generation, F_3: Outsourced decryption, F_4: Constant decryption cost, F_5: Verifiability, F_6: Data confidentiality.

internet of things environments. However, after a careful analysis, we observe that the scheme [12] fails to provide data confidentiality, as the semi-trusted cloud is capable of extracting the plaintext embedded in every ciphertext, which we show in Sect. 7. Since data confidentiality is the essential security property of every encryption scheme, the scheme [12] cannot be deployed in real-life applications. The ABPRE schemes [3] and [5] Scheme-I converts ciphertexts from ABE format to IBE format; consequently, they fail to provide fine-grained data sharing.

This exhibits that constructing an efficient ABPRE scheme that converts IBE ciphertext into ABE ciphertext is really challenging. Hence, it is desirable to have a non-interactive IBE to ABE PRE scheme that realizes simultaneously fine-grained data sharing, low computational overhead of the user to generate a re-encryption key, outsourced decryption mechanism, and data confidentiality.

Our Contribution. In order to address the aforementioned issues, we propose an efficient ABPRE data sharing scheme based on IBE to ABE conversion for cloud-assisted environments. Our proposed scheme, which we call IB-AB-PReM, supports the following functionalities. Table 1 presents a comparison between [3,5,12] and our work.

1. *Flexible Data Sharing*: The scheme realizes flexible data sharing; it allows a DO to make changes to the access structure dynamically by employing Framework-2 PRE mechanism. The data is encrypted by bridging IBE and ABE via the technique of PRE. Only authorized DRs with attributes matching the access structure can access the data.
2. *Online-Offline Re-encryption Key Generation*: The scheme features an online-offline re-encryption key generation mechanism, enhancing computational efficiency by allowing most of the computationally intensive tasks to be performed offline, reducing the online workload, and enabling real-time applications.
3. *Outsourced Decryption*: The scheme supports outsourced decryption, enabling resource-constrained devices to offload decryption operations to a third party while maintaining security and privacy assurances.

4. *Verifiability*: The data receiver can verify the correctness of the outsourced decryption process without interacting with any authority. Precisely, if the semi-trusted cloud delivers an incorrect or altered partially decrypted ciphertext, the DR can verify the same.
5. *Constant and Lightweight Decryption Cost*: The data receiver performs only one pairing and one group operation to recover the data.
6. *Provable Security*: A rigorous security proof establishes the security of the proposed scheme against selective chosen-plaintext attack.
7. *Practicality*: We implement our IB-AB-PReM scheme and evaluate the experimental outcome based on the computation and communication costs. Our findings demonstrate that the scheme is both efficient and feasible.

2 Preliminaries

Notations. Let $\mathbb{N} = \{1, 2, 3, \ldots\}$ be the set of all natural numbers. For a prime number p, $\mathbb{Z}_p = \{0, 1, \ldots, p - 1\}$ be the collection of integers modulo p, and $\mathbb{Z}_p^* = \mathbb{Z}_p \backslash \{0\}$. Let $\{0, 1\}^t$ be the collection of all binary strings of length $t \in \mathbb{N}$ and $\{0, 1\}^*$ be the collection of all binary strings of finite length. Let $[l] = \{1, 2, \ldots, l\}$ be the collection of integers from 1 to l.

Bilinear Pairing. Given two multiplicative cyclic groups $\mathbb{G}$ and $\mathbb{G}_T$ of prime order p, a *bilinear pairing* is a function $e : \mathbb{G} \times \mathbb{G} \to \mathbb{G}_T$ satisfying

- Bilinearity: $\forall u_1, u_2 \in \mathbb{G}$ and $v, w \in \mathbb{Z}_p$, we have $e\left(u_1^v, u_2^w\right) = e\left(u_1, u_2\right)^{vw}$.
- Non-degeneracy: $\exists u_1, u_2 \in \mathbb{G}$ such that $e\left(u_1, u_2\right) \neq 1$, the identity in $\mathbb{G}_T$.
- Computability: $\forall u_1, u_2 \in \mathbb{G}, e\left(u_1, u_2\right)$ can be computed efficiently.

Let $\mathcal{BP} = (p, \mathbb{G}, \mathbb{G}_T, e)$ be the bilinear pairing tuple.

Access Structure. Let U be a set of attributes. Let $P(U)^*$ denote the set of all non-empty subsets of U. An access structure is defined as any non-empty collection of elements from $P(U)^*$. An access structure $\mathbb{A}$ is called a monotonic access structure if it satisfies the property: $\forall B, C$: if $B \in \mathbb{A}$, $B \subseteq C$, then $C \in \mathbb{A}$. The subsets contained in $\mathbb{A}$ are referred to as authorized sets, while those not included in $\mathbb{A}$ are known as unauthorized sets.

Linear Secret-Sharing Scheme (LSSS). The secret sharing scheme Π, designed for a set of attributes, is characterized as a linear scheme over $\mathbb{Z}_p$ if

1. The distribution of shares among the attributes forms a vector over $\mathbb{Z}_p$.
2. There exists a matrix $M_{l \times n}$ called the share-generating matrix for Π. $\forall i \in [l]$, ρ is a function that maps each row of M to a specific attribute, and the ith row of M is associated with the attribute $\rho(i)$. Consider the column vector $v = (s, v_2, \ldots, v_n)^T \in \mathbb{Z}_p^n$, where s is the secret to be shared, $v_2, \ldots, v_n$ are randomly chosen from $\mathbb{Z}_p^*$, and T denotes the transpose of a matrix. According to Π, the vector of l shares of the secret s is given by $(\lambda_1, \lambda_2, \ldots, \lambda_l)^T = M \cdot v$, where λ_i is the share of the attribute $\rho(i)$.

The access structure is described by LSSS, which possesses the linear reconstruction property, i.e., suppose Π is an LSSS for the access structure $\mathbb{A}$ and $S \in \mathbb{A}$, and define a set $I = \{i : \rho(i) \in S\} \subseteq \{1, \ldots, l\}$, then there exist constants $\{\omega_i \in \mathbb{Z}_p\}_{i \in I}$ such that $\sum_{i \in I} \omega_i \lambda_i = s$, where $\{\lambda_i\}$ are valid shares of s according to Π and the constants $\{\omega_i\}$ can be computed in polynomial time.

Note. In the rest of the paper, we represent an access structure by an LSSS matrix and row labeling map pair (M, ρ).

Decisional Bilinear Diffie-Hellman (DBDH) Problem. Given the tuple $\mathcal{T} = (\mathcal{BP}, g, Q_1 = g^a, Q_2 = g^b, Q_3 = g^c, \Gamma)$, where $g \in \mathbb{G}$ is a generator, and (unknown) $a, b, c \in \{2, 3, \ldots, p-1\}$ are random, and $\Gamma \in \mathbb{G}_T$, to determine whether $\Gamma = e(g, g)^{abc}$ or Γ is a random element of $\mathbb{G}_T$.

The DBDH problem is said to be hard if for all PPT solvers $\mathcal{S}$, the advantage of $\mathcal{S}$ $Adv_{\mathcal{S}}^{DBDH} = \left| \mathsf{Prob}[1 \leftarrow \mathcal{S}(\mathcal{T}) | \Gamma = e(g, g)^{abc}] - \mathsf{Prob}[1 \leftarrow \mathcal{S}(\mathcal{T}) | \Gamma \text{ is random}] \right|$ is negligible.

Decisional *q-1* Problem. Given the tuple

$$Y = \left(\mathcal{BP}, g, g^r, \{g^{z^i}, g^{k_j}, g^{rk_j}, g^{z^i k_j}, g^{z^i / k_j^2}\}_{(i,j) \in [q,q]}, \{g^{z^i / k_j}\}_{(i,j) \in [2q,q], i \neq q+1},\right.$$
$$\left. \{g^{z^i k_j / k_{j'}^2}\}_{(i,j,j') \in [2q,q,q], j \neq j'}, \{g^{rz^i k_j / k_{j'}}, g^{rz^i k_j / k_{j'}^2}\}_{(i,j,j') \in [q,q,q], j \neq j'}, \Gamma \right)$$

where (unknown) $r, z, k_1, \ldots, k_q \in \mathbb{Z}_p$ are random. To determine whether $\Gamma = e(g, g)^{r \cdot z^{q+1}}$ or Γ is a random element of $\mathbb{G}_T$.

The decisional *q-1* problem is said to be hard if for all PPT solvers $\mathcal{S}$, the advantage of $\mathcal{S}$ $Adv_{\mathcal{S}}^{q-1} = \left| \mathsf{Prob}[1 \leftarrow \mathcal{S}(Y) | \Gamma = e(g, g)^{r \cdot z^{q+1}}] - \mathsf{Prob}[1 \leftarrow \mathcal{S}(Y) | \Gamma \text{ is random}] \right|$ is negligible.

3   Proposed IB-AB-PReM Model

Our proposed system consists of four entities: Data Owner (DO), Private Key Generator (PKG), Cloud, and Data Receiver (DR). The organization of these entities is depicted in Fig. 2. An inventory of acronyms used in this paper is provided in Table 2. The workflow of IB-AB-PReM is as follows. ① PKG initializes the system by executing $\mathsf{Setup_{IBE}}$ and $\mathsf{Setup_{ABE}}$ algorithms, and generates public keys and master secret keys. It forwards the system public parameters PP to every DO, every DR, and the cloud, while keeping the master secret keys MSK_{IBE} and MSK_{ABE} with itself as confidential. ② When a DO joins the system with its identity ID, PKG provides the secret key SK_{ID} to the DO by running $\mathsf{KeyGen_{IBE}}$ algorithm. And, when a DR joins the system with its attribute set S, PKG executes $\mathsf{KeyGen_{ABE}}$ algorithm and provides the secret key SK_S to the DR. ③ In order to securely store data on the cloud, the DO encrypts its data using $\mathsf{Enc_{IBE}}$ algorithm and generates the corresponding ciphertext CT_{ID}. Next, DO sends CT_{ID} to the cloud. ④ When a DO needs to implement fine-grained data sharing with other DRs, the DO specifies an access structure (M, ρ) and generates a re-encryption key RK using $\mathsf{offReEncKeyGen}$ and $\mathsf{onReEncKeyGen}$

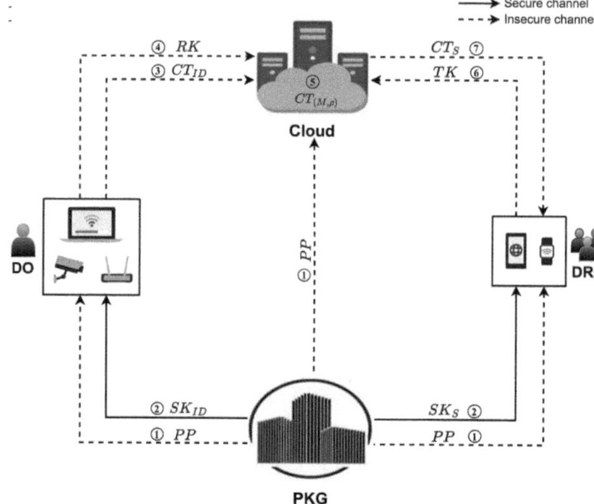

Fig. 2. Architecture of IB-AB-PReM

Table 2. Acronyms

Acronym	Description
PP_{IBE}	IBE public parameters
PP_{ABE}	ABE public parameters
MSK_{IBE}	IBE master secret key
MSK_{ABE}	ABE master secret key
PP	system public parameters
SK_{ID}	secret key for ID
SK_S	secret key for S
RK_{Int}	intermediate re-encryption key
RK	re-encryption key
TK	transformation key
RtK	data retrieval key
$\mathcal{M}$	plaintext/message
(M, ρ)	access structure
CT_{ID}	original ciphertext
$CT_{(M,\rho)}$	re-encrypted ciphertext
CT_S	transformed ciphertext
PPT	probabilistic polynomial time

algorithms, and sends RK to the cloud. ⑤ The cloud, acting as a proxy, transforms the IBE ciphertext CT_{ID} to ABE ciphertext $CT_{(M,\rho)}$ using ReEnc algorithm. ⑥ In order to access the original data, DR generates a transformation key TK by executing RetKeyGen algorithm and sends TK to the cloud. ⑦ Upon receiving TK, the cloud executes Decrypt$_{\text{Cloud}}$ algorithm and produces the partially decrypted ciphertext CT_S, and sends CT_S to the DR. From CT_S, DR can retrieve the original data by performing Decrypt$_{\text{DR}}$ algorithm.

4 Construction of IB-AB-PReM

Our proposed IB-AB-PReM scheme comprises the following seven phases.

1) Setup. PKG sets up the system by first executing the following two algorithms to generate public parameters and master secret keys corresponding to IBE and ABE mechanism.

• Setup$_{\text{IBE}}(\lambda) \rightarrow (PP_{IBE}, MSK_{IBE})$: Given a security parameter λ, PKG generates a bilinear pairing tuple $\mathcal{BP} = (p, \mathbb{G}, \mathbb{G}_T, e)$. PKG randomly chooses α_1 from $\mathbb{Z}_p^*$ and g_0 from $\mathbb{G}$. It then chooses three collision-resistant hash functions $H' : \{0,1\}^* \rightarrow \mathbb{G}$, $H'' : \mathbb{G}_T \rightarrow \{0,1\}^{\ell_1}$ and $H''' : \{0,1\}^* \rightarrow \{0,1\}^{\ell_2}$, and a one-time symmetric-key encryption scheme SE = (Enc, Dec) with plaintext space $\mathbb{M} = \{0,1\}^{\ell_m}$ and key space $\mathbb{G}_T$. It computes $Y_1 = e(g_0, g_0)^{\alpha_1}$ and assigns the public parameters and master secret key, respectively, as

$$PP_{IBE} = (\mathcal{BP}, g_0, H', H'', H''', \mathbb{M}, \text{SE}, Y_1), \quad MSK_{IBE} = g_0^{\alpha_1}.$$

• Setup$_{\text{ABE}}(\lambda, U) \rightarrow (PP_{ABE}, MSK_{ABE})$: On input λ and an attribute universe $U \subseteq \mathbb{Z}_p$, PKG takes $\mathcal{BP}$, and randomly selects elements $\alpha_2 \in \mathbb{Z}_p^*$, and $g, h_1, u_1, v_1, w_1 \in \mathbb{G}$. It then chooses a collision-resistant hash function

$H : \mathbb{G}_T \to \mathbb{G}$. It computes $Y_2 = e(g,g)^{\alpha_2}$, and sets the public parameters and master secret key, respectively, as

$$PP_{ABE} = (\mathcal{BP}, g, h_1, u_1, v_1, w_1, H, Y_2), \ MSK_{ABE} = g^{\alpha_2}.$$

The system public parameters $PP = (PP_{IBE}, PP_{ABE})$.

2) Key Generation. PKG executes two key generation algorithms, as outlined below, to generate secret keys for IBE (intended for DO) and ABE (intended for DR), respectively.
- KeyGen$_{\mathsf{IBE}}(PP, MSK_{IBE}, ID) \to SK_{ID}$: By taking an input of PP, MSK_{IBE}, and an identity $ID \in \{0,1\}^*$, PKG chooses a random $u \in \mathbb{Z}_p^*$ and computes

$$SK_{ID}^{(1)} = g_0^{\alpha_1} \cdot H'(ID)^u, \ SK_{ID}^{(2)} = g_0^u.$$

It sets the IBE secret key as $SK_{ID} = (SK_{ID}^{(1)}, SK_{ID}^{(2)})$.
- KeyGen$_{\mathsf{ABE}}(PP, MSK_{ABE}, S) \to SK_S$: On input PP, MSK_{ABE}, and an attribute set $S = \{att_1, att_2, \ldots, att_k\} \subseteq \mathbb{Z}_p$, PKG chooses $t, r_1, r_2, \ldots, r_k$ randomly from $\mathbb{Z}_p^*$ and computes

$$K_0 = g^{\alpha_2} w_1^t, K_1 = g^t, K_{i,2} = g^{r_i}, K_{i,3} = \left(u_1^{att_i} h_1\right)^{r_i} v_1^{-t}.$$

The ABE secret key is $SK_S = (S, K_0, K_1, \{K_{i,2}, K_{i,3}\}_{i \in [k]})$.

3) Data Encryption. DO first implements the IBE algorithm to encrypt the original data $\mathcal{M}$ using its identity ID.
- Enc$_{\mathsf{IBE}}(PP, ID, \mathcal{M}) \to CT_{ID}$: Taking PP, ID, and a message $\mathcal{M} \in \mathbb{M}$ as input, the DO randomly chooses $w \in \mathbb{Z}_p^*$, $\mathcal{K} \in \mathbb{G}_T$ and computes

$$C_{\mathcal{M}} = \mathsf{Enc}(\mathcal{M}, \mathcal{K}), C_0 = g_0^w, C_1 = H'(ID)^w, C_2 = \mathcal{K} \cdot Y_1^w, tag = H'''(H''(\mathcal{K}) \| C_{\mathcal{M}}).$$

The IBE ciphertext is $CT_{ID} = (C_{\mathcal{M}}, C_0, C_1, C_2, tag)$ and is stored in the cloud.

4) Re-encryption Key Generation. The DO generates a re-encryption key through online-offline mechanism.
- offReEncKeyGen$(PP, SK_{ID}) \to RK_{Int}$: On input PP and SK_{ID}, the DO chooses r, λ_j', t_j, x_j randomly from $\mathbb{Z}_p^*$ for $j = 1, 2, \ldots, m$, and computes

$$C_3 = g^r, C_{j,1} = w_1^{\lambda_j'} v_1^{t_j}, C_{j,2} = \left(u_1^{x_j} h_1\right)^{-t_j}, C_{j,3} = g^{t_j},$$
$$d_1 = SK_{ID}^{(2)}, d_2 = H\left(Y_2^r\right) \cdot \left(SK_{ID}^{(1)}\right)^{-1}.$$

It sets the intermediate re-encryption key as $RK_{Int} = (r, C_3, d_1, d_2, \{\lambda_j', t_j, x_j, C_{j,1}, C_{j,2}, C_{j,3}\}_{j \in [m]})$, where m is sufficiently large positive integer to generate an online re-encryption key.
- onReEncKeyGen$(PP, RK_{Int}, (M, \rho)) \to RK$: Given input PP, RK_{Int}, and an access structure (M, ρ), where M is a matrix of size $l \times n$ and ρ is a function

that associates each row of M with an attribute. The DO chooses $y_2, y_3, \ldots, y_n$ randomly from $\mathbb{Z}_p^*$ and computes

$$(\lambda_1, \lambda_2, \ldots, \lambda_l)^T = M \cdot (r, y_2, \ldots, y_n)^T, \ C_{j,4} = \lambda_j - \lambda_j', \ C_{j,5} = t_j(\rho(j) - x_j),$$

It sets the re-encryption key as $RK = \big((M, \rho), C_3, d_1, d_2, \{C_{j,1}, C_{j,2}, C_{j,3}, C_{j,4}, C_{j,5}\}_{j \in [l]}\big)$ and sends it to the cloud for re-encryption.

5) Re-encryption. Cloud executes the following re-encryption algorithm to transform the original IBE ciphertext CT_{ID} into ABE ciphertext using RK provided by the DO.
- ReEnc$(PP, CT_{ID}, RK) \rightarrow CT_{(M,\rho)}$: By taking an input of PP, CT_{ID}, and RK, cloud computes

$$C_4 = C_2 \cdot e(d_1, C_1) \cdot e(d_2, C_0).$$

It sets the re-encrypted ciphertext as $CT_{(M,\rho)} = \big((M, \rho), C_{\mathcal{M}}, C_0, C_3, C_4, \{C_{j,1}, C_{j,2}, C_{j,3}, C_{j,4}, C_{j,5}\}_{j \in [l]}, tag\big)$.

6) Transformation Key Generation. The DR generates two keys. One is TK, used for outsourcing the decryption, and the other is RtK, used for final decryption.
- RetKeyGen$(PP, SK_S) \rightarrow (TK, RtK)$: Taking PP and SK_S as input, the DR chooses a random $z \in \mathbb{Z}_p^*$ and computes

$$K_0' = K_0^{\frac{1}{z}}, K_1' = K_1^{\frac{1}{z}}, K_{i,2}' = K_{i,2}^{\frac{1}{z}}, K_{i,3}' = K_{i,3}^{\frac{1}{z}}.$$

It sets the transformation key as $TK = \big(S, K_0', K_1', \{K_{i,2}', K_{i,3}'\}_{i \in [k]}\big)$ and data retrieval key as $RtK = z$.

7) Data Decryption. The cloud performs the partial decryption of the ciphertext and sends the resultant partially decrypted ciphertext to the DR for final decryption.
- Decrypt$_{\mathsf{Cloud}}(PP, CT_{(M,\rho)}, TK) \rightarrow CT_S/\perp$: On input PP, $CT_{(M,\rho)}$, and TK, cloud first checks whether S satisfies (M, ρ) or not. If not, it outputs $\perp$. Otherwise, it defines $I = \{i \mid \rho(i) \in S\}$ and calculates $\omega_i \in \mathbb{Z}_p$ such that $\sum_{i \in I} \omega_i \lambda_i = r$, and computes

$$A = e\big(w_1^{\sum_{i \in I} C_{i,4}\omega_i}, K_1'\big), \ B = \prod_{i \in I}\big(e(C_{i,1}, K_1')\, e(C_{i,2}u_1^{-C_{i,5}}, K_{j,2}')\, e(C_{i,3}, K_{j,3}')\big)^{\omega_i},$$

$$key = \frac{e(C_3, K_0')}{A \cdot B},$$

where j is the index of the attribute $\rho(i)$ in S, i.e., $\rho(i) = att_j$. It sets the partially decrypted ciphertext as $CT_S = (key, C_{\mathcal{M}}, C_0, C_4, tag)$.
- Decrypt$_{\mathsf{DR}}(PP, RtK, CT_S) \rightarrow \mathcal{M}$: Using PP, RtK, and CT_S, the DR computes the followings.

- Calculate $\mathcal{K}' = \dfrac{C_4}{e\left(H\left(key^{RtK}\right), C_0\right)}$
- Verify whether

$$H'''(H''(\mathcal{K}') \| C_{\mathcal{M}}) \overset{?}{=} tag$$

If this relation does not hold, the DR outputs $\perp$ indicating that the cloud dishonestly returns an incorrect partially decrypted ciphertext; otherwise, $\mathcal{K}' = \mathcal{K}$ and hence the DR retrieves the message as $\mathcal{M} = \mathsf{Dec}(C_{\mathcal{M}}, \mathcal{K}')$.

Theorem 1 (Proof of Correctness): If the ciphertexts CT_{ID} and $CT_{(M,\rho)}$ are correctly generated to encrypt a message $\mathcal{M}$, the identity ID of the RK equals the identity ID of the CT_{ID}, and TK is a valid transformation key such that the attribute set S satisfies the access structure (M, ρ), then DR retrieves the original message $\mathcal{M}$ using the retrieval key RtK.

Proof: If the identity ID of the RK and CT_{ID} are the same, then the cloud calculates

$$
\begin{aligned}
C_4 &= C_2 \cdot e(d_1, C_1) \cdot e(d_2, C_0) \\
&= \mathcal{K} \cdot Y_1^w \, e(g_0^u, H'(ID)^w) \, e\left(H(Y_2^r) \cdot (g_0^{\alpha_1} H'(ID)^u)^{-1}, g_0^w\right) \\
&= \mathcal{K} \cdot e(g_0, g_0)^{\alpha_1 w} \, e(g_0, H'(ID))^{uw} \, e(H(Y_2^r), g_0^w) \, e((g_0^{\alpha_1} H'(ID)^u)^{-1}, g_0^w) \\
&= \frac{\mathcal{K} \cdot e(g_0, g_0)^{\alpha_1 w} \, e(g_0, H'(ID))^{uw} \, e(H(e(g,g)^{\alpha_2 r}), g_0^w)}{e(g_0^{\alpha_1} H'(ID)^u, g_0^w)} \\
&= \frac{\mathcal{K} \cdot e(g_0, g_0)^{\alpha_1 w} \, e(g_0, H'(ID))^{uw} \, e(H(e(g,g)^{\alpha_2 r}), g_0^w)}{e(g_0, g_0)^{\alpha_1 w} \, e(H'(ID), g_0)^{uw}} \\
&= \mathcal{K} \cdot e\left(H(e(g,g)^{\alpha_2 r}), g_0^w\right).
\end{aligned}
$$

In the decryption phase, if S of the TK satisfies (M, ρ) in $CT_{(M,\rho)}$, then the cloud can compute

$$
\begin{aligned}
A &= e\left(w_1^{\sum_{i \in I} C_{i,4} \omega_i}, K_1'\right) = e\left(w_1^{\sum_{i \in I} (\lambda_i - \lambda_i') \omega_i}, g^{\frac{t}{z}}\right) \\
&= e\left(w_1^{\sum_{i \in I} \lambda_i \omega_i}, g^{\frac{t}{z}}\right) e\left(w_1^{-\sum_{i \in I} \lambda_i' \omega_i}, g^{\frac{t}{z}}\right) = e(w_1, g)^{\frac{rt}{z}} \, e\left(w_1^{-\sum_{i \in I} \lambda_i' \omega_i}, g^{\frac{t}{z}}\right) \\
B &= \prod_{i \in I} \left(e(C_{i,1}, K_1') \, e(C_{i,2} u_1^{-C_{i,5}}, K_{j,2}') \, e(C_{i,3}, K_{j,3}')\right)^{\omega_i}
\end{aligned}
$$

Let $X_1 = e(C_{i,1}, K_1')$, $X_2 = e(C_{i,2} u_1^{-C_{i,5}}, K_{j,2}')$ and $X_3 = e(C_{i,3}, K_{j,3}')$.

Then,
$$X_1 = e(C_{i,1}, K_1') = e(w_1^{\lambda_i'} v_1^{t_i}, g^{\frac{t}{z}}) = e(w_1, g)^{\frac{\lambda_i' t}{z}} e(v_1, g)^{\frac{t_i t}{z}}$$

$$X_2 = e(C_{i,2} u_1^{-C_{i,5}}, K_{j,2}') = e((u_1^{x_i} h_1)^{-t_i} u_1^{-t_i(\rho(i)-x_i)}, g^{\frac{r_j}{z}})$$

$$= e(u_1^{-x_i t_i} h_1^{-t_i} u_1^{-t_i \rho(i)} u_1^{t_i x_i}, g^{\frac{r_j}{z}}) = e(h_1^{-t_i} u_1^{-t_i \rho(i)}, g^{\frac{r_j}{z}})$$

$$= e(h_1, g)^{\frac{-t_i r_j}{z}} e(u_1, g)^{\frac{-t_i \rho(i) r_j}{z}}$$

$$X_3 = e(C_{i,3}, K_{j,3}') = e(g^{t_i}, ((u_1^{att_j} h_1)^{r_j} v_1^{-t})^{\frac{1}{z}}) = e(g^{t_i}, (u_1^{att_j r_j} h_1^{r_j} v_1^{-t})^{\frac{1}{z}})$$

$$= e(g^{t_i}, (u_1^{\rho(i) r_j} h_1^{r_j} v_1^{-t})^{\frac{1}{z}}) = e(g, u_1)^{\frac{t_i \rho(i) r_j}{z}} e(g, h_1)^{\frac{t_i r_j}{z}} e(g, v_1)^{-\frac{t_i t}{z}}$$

Now,
$$B = \prod_{i \in I} (X_1 X_2 X_3)^{\omega_i} = \prod_{i \in I} \left(e(w_1, g)^{\frac{\lambda_i' t}{z}} \right)^{\omega_i} = e(w_1^{\sum_{i \in I} \lambda_i' \omega_i}, g^{\frac{t}{z}})$$

$$key = \frac{e(C_3, K_0')}{A \cdot B} = \frac{e(g^r, (g^{\alpha_2} w_1^t)^{\frac{1}{z}})}{e(w_1, g)^{\frac{rt}{z}}} = \frac{e(g, g)^{\frac{r\alpha_2}{z}} e(g, w_1)^{\frac{rt}{z}}}{e(w_1, g)^{\frac{rt}{z}}} = e(g, g)^{\frac{r\alpha_2}{z}}.$$

Since *key* is correctly computed and $RtK = z$, we have

$$\mathcal{K}' = \frac{C_4}{e(H(key^{RtK}), C_0)} = \frac{\mathcal{K} \cdot e(H(e(g, g)^{\alpha_2 r}), g_0^w)}{e(H(e(g, g)^{\alpha_2 r}), g_0^w)} = \mathcal{K}.$$

Hence,

$$H'''(H''(\mathcal{K}') \| C_{\mathcal{M}}) = H'''(H''(\mathcal{K}) \| C_{\mathcal{M}}) = tag.$$

Finally, DR recovers $\mathcal{M}$ as follows

$$\mathsf{Dec}(C_{\mathcal{M}}, \mathcal{K}') = \mathsf{Dec}(C_{\mathcal{M}}, \mathcal{K}) = \mathcal{M}.$$

5 Security Analysis of IB-AB-PReM

In this section, we present the security model and the corresponding security proof of our IB-AB-PReM scheme.

5.1 Security Model

Our IB-AB-PReM scheme has two types of ciphertexts, CT_{ID} and $CT_{(M,\rho)}$, created by DO and cloud, respectively. To ensure data confidentiality, we address potential attacks that unauthorized users and semi-trusted cloud attempt. Depending on the adversary's target, we formalize two selective chosen-plaintext attack (CPA) security games (called GAME-Or and GAME-Re), simulated between an adversary $\mathcal{A}$ and a challenger $\mathcal{C}$, demonstrated as follows.

(i) Game GAME-Or. Aiming at the original ciphertext CT_{ID}, the proposed IB-AB-PReM scheme is selective CPA-secure (in short, *sel*-CPA$_{CT_{ID}}$) if there is no adversary $\mathcal{A}$ with non-negligible probability of breaking the following game.

Init. $\mathcal{A}$ selects a challenge identity ID^* and sends it to $\mathcal{C}$.

Setup. $\mathcal{C}$ obtains $(PP_{IBE}, MSK_{IBE}) \leftarrow \mathsf{Setup}_{\mathsf{IBE}}(\lambda)$ and $(PP_{ABE}, \leftarrow \mathsf{Setup}_{\mathsf{ABE}}(\lambda, U)$. It sends $PP = (PP_{IBE}, PP_{ABE})$ to $\mathcal{A}$ while keeping MSK_{IBE} and MSK_{ABE} secret with itself.

Phase I. $\mathcal{A}$ queries the following oracle.

- $\mathcal{O}_{KeyGen\text{-}IBE}(ID)$: $\mathcal{A}$ queries this IBE decryption key generation oracle with an input $ID\,(\neq ID^*)$. $\mathcal{C}$ returns $SK_{ID} \leftarrow \mathsf{KeyGen}_{\mathsf{IBE}}(PP, ID)$ to $\mathcal{A}$.
- $\mathcal{O}_{KeyGen\text{-}ABE}(S)$: For any attribute set S, $\mathcal{A}$ queries this attribute key generation oracle. $\mathcal{C}$ outputs $SK_S \leftarrow \mathsf{KeyGen}_{\mathsf{ABE}}(PP, MSK_{ABE}, S)$ to $\mathcal{A}$.
- $\mathcal{O}_{ReEncKeyGen}(ID, (M, \rho))$: $\mathcal{A}$ performs this re-encryption key generation oracle with input $ID, (M, \rho)$, where $ID \neq ID^*$. $\mathcal{C}$ returns the corresponding re-encryption key RK by executing the appropriate algorithms of IB-AB-PReM.
- $\mathcal{O}_{ReEnc}(CT_{ID}, ID, (M, \rho))$: $\mathcal{A}$ queries this re-encryption key generation oracle with input $CT_{ID}, ID, (M, \rho)$, where $S \notin (M, \rho)$ for all those S queried in $\mathcal{O}_{KeyGen\text{-}ABE}(S)$. $\mathcal{C}$ returns $CT_{(M, \rho)} \leftarrow \mathsf{ReEnc}(PP, CT_{ID}, RK)$ to $\mathcal{A}$.

Challenge. $\mathcal{A}$ chooses two messages $\mathcal{M}_0$, $\mathcal{M}_1$ satisfying $|\mathcal{M}_0| = |\mathcal{M}_1|$ and sends them to $\mathcal{C}$. Then, $\mathcal{C}$ randomly selects $\varphi \in \{0, 1\}$ and generates the challenge ciphertext $CT_{ID^*} \leftarrow \mathsf{Enc}_{\mathsf{IBE}}(PP, ID^*, \mathcal{M}_\varphi)$. It returns CT_{ID^*} to $\mathcal{A}$.

Phase II. $\mathcal{A}$ performs queries as in Phase I with the only restriction of querying $\mathcal{O}_{ReEnc}(CT_{ID^*}, ID^*, (M, \rho))$, if for any S queried in $\mathcal{O}_{KeyGen\text{-}ABE}(S)$ and $S \in (M, \rho)$.

Guess. $\mathcal{A}$ submits a guess $\varphi' \in \{0, 1\}$ of φ.

$\mathcal{A}$ wins if $\varphi' = \varphi$. In the above GAME-Or game, we define the advantage of $\mathcal{A}$ as $A\,dv_{\mathcal{A}}^{GAME-Or} = |\mathsf{Prob}\,[\varphi' = \varphi] - 1/2|$.

(ii) Game GAME-Re. Aiming at the re-encrypted ciphertext $CT_{(M, \rho)}$, the proposed IB-AB-PReM scheme is selective CPA-secure (in short, *sel-*$\mathrm{CPA}_{CT_{(M, \rho)}}$) if there is no adversary $\mathcal{A}$ with non-negligible probability of breaking the following game.

Init. $\mathcal{A}$ sends a challenge access structure (M^*, ρ^*) to $\mathcal{C}$.

Setup. Similar to GAME-Or.

Phase I. $\mathcal{A}$ performs the following oracle queries.

- $\mathcal{O}_{KeyGen\text{-}IBE}(ID)$: $\mathcal{A}$ queries this IBE decryption key generation oracle with an input ID. $\mathcal{C}$ returns $SK_{ID} \leftarrow \mathsf{KeyGen}_{\mathsf{IBE}}(PP, ID)$ to $\mathcal{A}$.
- $\mathcal{O}_{KeyGen\text{-}ABE}(S)$: $\mathcal{A}$ performs this attribute key generation oracle with an input S, where $S \notin (M^*, \rho^*)$. $\mathcal{C}$ outputs $SK_S \leftarrow \mathsf{KeyGen}_{\mathsf{ABE}}(PP, MSK_{ABE}, S)$ to $\mathcal{A}$.
- $\mathcal{O}_{ReEncKeyGen}(ID, (M, \rho))$: For any $ID, (M, \rho)$, $\mathcal{A}$ queries this re-encryption key generation oracle. $\mathcal{C}$ returns the corresponding re-encryption key RK by executing the appropriate algorithms of IB-AB-PReM.

Challenge. $\mathcal{A}$ chooses two messages $\mathcal{M}_0$, $\mathcal{M}_1$ of equal length (i.e., $|\mathcal{M}_0| = |\mathcal{M}_1|$) and an identity ID, and outputs them to $\mathcal{C}$. $\mathcal{C}$ randomly selects $\varphi \in \{0,1\}$ and computes the challenge ciphertext $CT^*_{(M,\rho)} \leftarrow$ ReEnc(PP, CT_{ID}, RK^*), where $CT_{ID} \leftarrow$ Enc$_{\mathsf{IBE}}(PP, ID, \mathcal{M}_\varphi)$, $SK_{ID} \leftarrow$ KeyGen$_{\mathsf{IBE}}(PP, ID)$, $RK^*_{Int} \leftarrow$ offReEncKeyGen(PP, SK_{ID}), $RK^* \leftarrow$ onReEncKeyGen$(PP, RK^*_{Int}, (M^*, \rho^*))$. It returns $CT^*_{(M,\rho)}$ to $\mathcal{A}$.

Phase II. $\mathcal{A}$ performs queries as in Phase I.

Guess. $\mathcal{A}$ submits a guess $\varphi' \in \{0,1\}$ of φ.

$\mathcal{A}$ wins if $\varphi' = \varphi$. In the above GAME-Re game, we define the advantage of $\mathcal{A}$ to be $A \, dv_{\mathcal{A}}^{GAME-Re} = |\mathsf{Prob}\,[\varphi' = \varphi] - 1/2|$.

5.2   Security Proof

Theorem 2: The IB-AB-PReM scheme is selective CPA-secure in random oracle model under the assumption that the DBDH problem in $\mathcal{BP}$ is hard.

Proof: Suppose a PPT adversary $\mathcal{A}$ can break the GAME-Or security with a non-negligible advantage ϵ. Then, we can construct a challenger $\mathcal{C}$ that can solve the DBDH problem with the advantage ϵ, by interacting with $\mathcal{A}$ as described below. $\mathcal{C}$ is given the DBDH tuple $\mathcal{T} = (\mathcal{BP}, g_0, Q_1 = g_0^a, Q_2 = g_0^b, Q_3 = g_0^c, \Gamma)$.

Init. $\mathcal{A}$ sends a challenge identity ID^* to $\mathcal{C}$.

Setup. $\mathcal{C}$ simulates as follows.

It randomly chooses α_1' from $\mathbb{Z}_p^*$, g_0 from $\mathbb{G}$, and computes

$$Y_1 = e(g_0, g_0)^{\alpha_1'} \cdot e(Q_1, Q_2) = e(g_0, g_0)^{\alpha_1' + ab}$$

i.e., α_1 is implicitly defined as $\alpha_1 = \alpha_1' + ab$. $H' : \{0,1\}^* \to \mathbb{G}$, $H'' : \mathbb{G}_T \to \{0,1\}^{\ell_1}$ and $H''' : \{0,1\}^* \to \{0,1\}^{\ell_2}$ are three collision-resistant hash functions, where H' is treated as a random oracle. $\mathcal{C}$ sets $PP_{IBE} = (\mathcal{BP}, g_0, Y_1, \mathsf{SE}, H', H'', H''')$. $\mathcal{C}$ executes the Setup$_{\mathsf{ABE}}(\lambda, U)$ algorithm similar to IB-AB-PReM construction and obtains (PP_{ABE}, MSK_{ABE}). Lastly, $\mathcal{C}$ sends $PP = (PP_{IBE}, PP_{ABE})$ to $\mathcal{A}$, and retains MSK_{IBE} and MSK_{ABE}.

H' *Queries* : $\mathcal{C}$ maintains a table $\mathrm{Tab}_{H'}$ which is initially empty. For any H' query on input ip, if the entry $[ip, r_{ip}, H'(ip)]$ exists in $\mathrm{Tab}_{H'}$, it returns $H'(ip)$. Otherwise, if $ip = ID$ and $ID \neq ID^*$, $\mathcal{C}$ picks r_{ID} randomly from $\mathbb{Z}_p^*$, and sets $H'(ID) = g_0^{r_{ID}} Q_1$, else if $ip = ID^*$, $\mathcal{C}$ randomly chooses r_{ID^*} from $\mathbb{Z}_p^*$, sets $H'(ID^*) = g_0^{r_{ID^*}}$, adds the new entry $[ip, r_{ip}, H'(ip)]$ to $\mathrm{Tab}_{H'}$, and returns $H'(ip)$.

Phase I. $\mathcal{C}$ responds to $\mathcal{A}$'s queries as follows.

- $\mathcal{O}_{KeyGen\text{-}IBE}(ID)$: $\mathcal{A}$ makes a key generation query for ID, where $ID \neq ID^*$. $\mathcal{C}$ performs H' hash query on ID and obtains the tuple $[ID, r_{ID},$

$H'(ID)]$, in which $H'(ID)$ value is $g_0^{r_{ID}}Q_1$. $\mathcal{C}$ randomly chooses u' from $\mathbb{Z}_p^*$, u is implicitly defined as $u = -b + u'$, and computes

$$SK_{ID}^{(1)} = g_0^{\alpha_1'} \cdot Q_2^{-r_{ID}} \cdot (g_0^{r_{ID}}Q_1)^{u'} = g_0^{ab} g_0^{-ab} g_0^{\alpha_1'} g_0^{-br_{ID}} g_0^{u'r_{ID}} g_0^{au'}$$

$$= (g_0^{\alpha_1'} g_0^{ab})g_0^{-br_{ID}} g_0^{u'r_{ID}} (g_0^{-ab} g_0^{au'}) = g_0^{\alpha_1'+ab} g_0^{r_{ID}(-b+u')} g_0^{a(-b+u')}$$

$$= g_0^{\alpha_1'+ab}(g_0^{r_{ID}}Q_1)^{(-b+u')} = g_0^{\alpha_1} \cdot H'(ID)^u$$

$$SK_{ID}^{(2)} = Q_2^{-1} g_0^{u'} = g_0^{-b+u'} = g_0^u.$$

$\mathcal{C}$ sends $SK_{ID} = (SK_{ID}^{(1)}, SK_{ID}^{(2)})$ to $\mathcal{A}$.

- $\mathcal{O}_{KeyGen\text{-}ABE}(S)$: $\mathcal{A}$ sends an attribute set S to $\mathcal{C}$. Since $\mathcal{C}$ has MSK_{ABE}, it generates the ABE secret key SK_S by executing the $\mathsf{KeyGen}_{ABE}(PP, MSK_{ABE}, S)$ algorithm, and then outputs SK_S to $\mathcal{A}$.
- $\mathcal{O}_{ReEncKeyGen}(ID, (M, \rho))$: For $ID \neq ID^*$ and $(M, \rho) = (M, \rho)$, $\mathcal{C}$ first generates $SK_{ID} \leftarrow \mathcal{O}_{KeyGen\text{-}IBE}(ID)$ and $RK_{Int} \leftarrow \mathsf{offReEncKeyGen}(PP, SK_{ID})$. Next, $\mathcal{C}$ computes the re-encryption key $RK \leftarrow \mathsf{onReEncKeyGen}(PP, RK_{Int}, (M, \rho))$ and sends RK to $\mathcal{A}$.
- $\mathcal{O}_{ReEnc}(CT_{ID}, ID, (M, \rho))$: $\mathcal{A}$ sends $CT_{ID}, ID, (M, \rho)$ to $\mathcal{C}$, where $S \notin (M, \rho)$, for all those S queried in $\mathcal{O}_{KeyGen\text{-}ABE}(S)$. If $ID \neq ID^*$, $\mathcal{C}$ obtains $RK \leftarrow \mathcal{O}_{ReEncKeyGen}(ID, (M, \rho))$ and returns to $\mathcal{A}$ the re-encrypted ciphertext $CT_{(M,\rho)} \leftarrow \mathsf{ReEnc}(PP, CT_{ID}, RK)$. Suppose $ID = ID^*$. CT_{ID} is parsed as $CT_{ID} = (C_\mathcal{M}, C_0, C_1, C_2, tag)$. Now, $\mathcal{C}$ computes $CT_{(M,\rho)} = ((M, \rho), C_\mathcal{M}, C_0, C_3, C_4, \{C_{j,1}, C_{j,2}, C_{j,3}, C_{j,4}, C_{j,5}\}_{j \in [l]}, tag)$ as follows. $C_\mathcal{M}$, C_0, and tag are taken from CT_{ID}. The components $C_3, \{C_{j,1}, C_{j,2}, C_{j,3}, C_{j,4}, C_{j,5}\}_{j \in [l]}$ are created similar to that of IB-AB-PReM construction. By setting C_4 as a random element of $\mathbb{G}_T$, $\mathcal{C}$ implements the condition $S \notin (M, \rho)$. Hence, the created $CT_{(M,\rho)}$ is a valid re-encrypted ciphertext in $\mathcal{A}$'s view.

Challenge. $\mathcal{A}$ chooses two messages $\mathcal{M}_0$ and $\mathcal{M}_1$ satisfying $|\mathcal{M}_0| = |\mathcal{M}_1|$ and sends them to $\mathcal{C}$. To generate the challenge ciphertext, $\mathcal{C}$ randomly selects $\varphi \in \{0, 1\}$ and $\mathcal{K} \in \mathbb{G}_T$, implicitly assumes $w = c$, and computes

$$C_{\mathcal{M}_\varphi} = \mathsf{Enc}(\mathcal{M}_\varphi, \mathcal{K}), \quad C_0 = Q_3, \quad C_1 = Q_3^{r_{ID^*}} \text{ (since } H'(ID^*) = g_0^{r_{ID^*}}),$$

$$C_2 = \mathcal{K} \cdot \Gamma \cdot e(g_0^{\alpha_1'}, Q_3), \quad tag = H'''(H''(\mathcal{K})\|C_{\mathcal{M}_\varphi}).$$

$\mathcal{C}$ sets $CT_{ID^*} = (C_{\mathcal{M}_\varphi}, C_0, C_1, C_2, tag)$ and sends it to $\mathcal{A}$.
The arguments presented below justify that if $\Gamma = e(g_0, g_0)^{abc}$, then the simulated ciphertext CT_{ID^*} is the same as the one generated in IB-AB-PReM for message $\mathcal{M}_\varphi$ corresponding to ID^*.

$$C_{\mathcal{M}_\varphi} = \mathsf{Enc}(\mathcal{M}_\varphi, \mathcal{K}), \quad C_0 = Q_3 = g_0^c = g_0^w$$

$$C_1 = Q_3^{r_{ID^*}} = (g_0^c)^{r_{ID^*}} = (g_0^{r_{ID^*}})^c = H'(ID^*)^w$$

$$C_2 = \mathcal{K} \cdot \Gamma \cdot e(g_0^{\alpha_1'}, Q_3) = \mathcal{K} \cdot e(g_0, g_0)^{abc} \cdot e(g_0, g_0^c)^{\alpha_1'}$$

$$= \mathcal{K} \cdot e(g_0, g_0)^{abc+\alpha_1'c} = \mathcal{K} \cdot \left(e(g_0, g_0)^{(\alpha_1'+ab)}\right)^c = \mathcal{K} \cdot Y_1^w$$

$$tag = H'''(H''(\mathcal{K})\|C_{\mathcal{M}_\varphi})$$

Phase II. $\mathcal{A}$ issues similar queries as in Phase I. But, $\mathcal{A}$ is restricted to query $\mathcal{O}_{ReEnc}(CT_{ID^*}, ID^*, (M, \rho))$, if for any S, $S \in (M, \rho)$ and S has already been queried in $\mathcal{O}_{KeyGen\text{-}ABE}(S)$.

Guess. $\mathcal{A}$ outputs its guess $\varphi' \in \{0, 1\}$ of φ.

If $\varphi' = \varphi$, $\mathcal{A}$ wins the game and $\mathcal{C}$ determines that $\Gamma = e(g_0, g_0)^{abc}$, else Γ is a random element of $\mathbb{G}_T$.

Since $\mathcal{C}$ does not abort the simulation, when $\Gamma = e(g_0, g_0)^{abc}$, the CT_{ID^*} appears as a validly simulated ciphertext, consistent with the IB-AB-PReM construction. So we can say $\mathcal{C}$ makes a perfect simulation. Hence,

$$\epsilon = Adv_{\mathcal{A}}^{GAME-Or} = \mathsf{Prob}\big[\varphi' = \varphi | \Gamma = e(g_0, g_0)^{abc}\big] - 1/2$$
$$= \mathsf{Prob}\big[1 \leftarrow \mathcal{C}(\mathcal{T}) | \Gamma = e(g_0, g_0)^{abc}\big] - 1/2.$$

$\therefore \mathsf{Prob}\big[1 \leftarrow \mathcal{C}(\mathcal{T}) | \Gamma = e(g_0, g_0)^{abc}\big] = \epsilon + 1/2$. If Γ is random, then according to $\mathcal{A}$'s point of view, CT_{ID^*} is independent of φ, and hence $\mathsf{Prob}\big[1 \leftarrow \mathcal{C}(\mathcal{T}) | \Gamma$ is random$\big] = 1/2$. Thus, $Adv_{\mathcal{A}}^{DBDH} = \epsilon + 1/2 - 1/2 = \epsilon$, which means that $\mathcal{C}$ can solve the DBDH problem with the non-negligible advantage ϵ.

Theorem 3: The IB-AB-PReM scheme is selective CPA-secure under the assumption that the decisional *q-1* problem is hard in $\mathcal{BP}$.
The proof is available in the full version of the paper.

6   Performance Evaluation

In this section, we will present the performance of our proposed IB-AB-PReM scheme. Our IB-AB-PReM and the existing schemes [5] Scheme-II and [12] transform IBE ciphertexts into ABE ciphertexts, but we find that [12] lacks data confidentiality. So, to assess the practicality of our IB-AB-PReM scheme, we compare our IB-AB-PReM with [5] Scheme-II. IB-AB-PReM has the functionality of online-offline re-encryption key generation, outsourced decryption with verifiability and constant decryption cost, whereas [5] Scheme-II does not offer such functionalities. We perform a detailed comparison focusing on computation and communication cost. Usually, the cloud possesses more substantial computation power. Due to this reason, to assess the performance of our IB-AB-PReM, we consider the time required for original ciphertext generation, re-encryption key generation and decryption. And, the communication efficiency is analyzed in terms of the original ciphertext size, re-encryption key size and the size of ciphertext given to DR by the cloud.

Experimental Setup. We perform all experiments by using the charm crypto library [1] and employ the SS512 predefined curve to generate the pairings in the implementation. The curve SS512 is analogous to the Type-A curve in jPBC crypto library [6]. The simulation is conducted on a system equipped with a 13th Gen Intel(R) Core(TM) i7-1360P processor, CPU@ 2.61 GHz and 16.0 GB RAM, running an Oracle VM VirtualBox - 6.1.22 configured with 4-GB RAM and 64-bit Ubuntu 20.04 LTS operating system. The results of our experiments

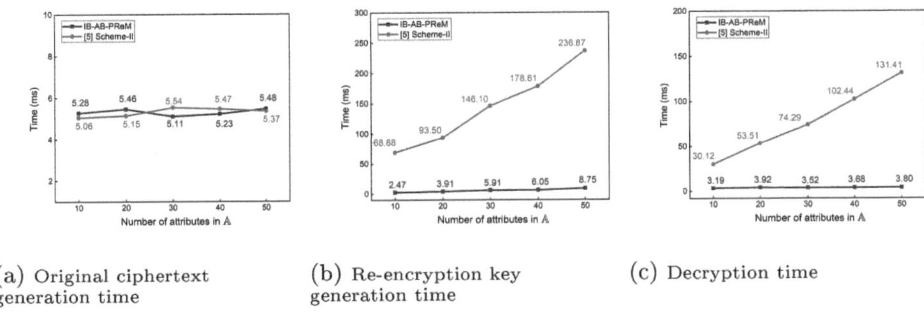

(a) Original ciphertext
generation time

(b) Re-encryption key
generation time

(c) Decryption time

Fig. 3. Execution Time (in ms) of IB-AB-PReM and [5] Scheme-II.

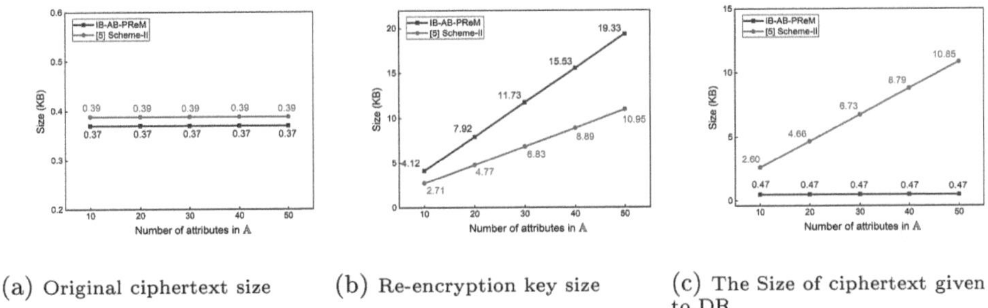

(a) Original ciphertext size

(b) Re-encryption key size

(c) The Size of ciphertext given
to DR

Fig. 4. Communication Cost (in KB) of IB-AB-PReM and [5] Scheme-II.

are depicted in Fig. 3 and 4. We have repeated each experiment 20 times by considering 10, 20, 30, 40 and 50 attributes in the AND gate structure. Line graphs are used to represent the average values. The computation and communication cost units are milliseconds (ms) and kilobytes (KB), respectively.

Experimental Analysis. Figure 3a illustrates that the scheme in both IB-AB-PReM and [5] Scheme-II require almost similar time to generate the original ciphertext. Precisely, on average, IB-AB-PReM takes 5.31 ms, and [5] Scheme-II takes 5.32 ms to generate the original ciphertext. Figure 4a illustrates that the original ciphertext size of IB-AB-PReM is less than that of [5] Scheme-II. Figure 3b demonstrates the superiority of IB-AB-PReM over [5] Scheme-II, as IB-AB-PReM takes less time to generate the re-encryption key. Figure 4b exhibits that the size of the re-encryption key in IB-AB-PReM is more compared to [5] Scheme-II. This is due to the fact that we have incorporated the online-offline technique during the re-encryption key generation in IB-AB-PReM to reduce the computation cost of DO. Figure 3c illustrates that the decryption time in IB-AB-PReM is less than that of [5] Scheme-II. Figure 4c shows that the size of the partially decrypted ciphertext of IB-AB-PReM is smaller than the size of the re-encrypted ciphertext of [5] Scheme-II.

In sum, the experimental results demonstrate that our IB-AB-PReM is computationally efficient and practical.

7 Message Recovery Attack by the Cloud in Zhang et al.'s PRE Scheme [12]

In the PRE scheme proposed by Zhang et al. [12], the semi-trusted cloud can recover the message $\mathcal{M}$ from the ciphertext CT_{ID} stored in it by any DO. Precisely, once the cloud receives the re-encryption key RK, it has the following information Δ.

$$\Delta = \begin{cases} PP_{IBE} = (\mathcal{BP}, g_1, g_1^{\alpha_0}, g_2, g_3, g_4) \\ PP_{ABE} = (\mathcal{BP}, g, g^a, e(g,g)^\alpha, \{h_{x'}\}_{x' \in U}, H) \\ CT_{ID} = (C_0, C_1, C_2, C_3) \\ IK = \big((M, \rho), r', D_0, \{\lambda_i', r_i', D_{i,1}, D_{i,2}\}_{i \in [l]}\big) \\ RK = \big(D_0, D_3, D_4, D_5, D_6, \{D_{i,1}, D_{i,2}, D_{i,7}, D_{i,8}\}_{i \in [l]}\big) \end{cases}$$

where PP_{IBE} and PP_{ABE} are public parameters and IK is the intermediate re-encryption key. For more details one can refer [12].

Now, using Δ, the cloud can extract the message $\mathcal{M}$ embedded in the ciphertext CT_{ID} as described below.

- Compute

$$X_1 = e(C_3, D_5) = e\big(g_3^w, H(e(g,g)^{\alpha r}) g_1^{t'}\big) = e(g_3^w, H(e(g,g)^{\alpha r})) \cdot e(g_3, g_1)^{wt'}$$

$$X_2 = e(C_1, D_4) = e\big((g_1^{\alpha_0 ID} g_4)^w, g_1^u\big) = e(g_1, g_1)^{\alpha_0 ID wu} \cdot e(g_4, g_1)^{wu}$$

$$Y_1 = e(C_0, D_3) = e\big(g_1^w, g_2^{\alpha_0} \big(g_1^{\alpha_0 ID} g_4\big)^u g_3^{t'}\big)$$

$$= e(g_1, g_2)^{w\alpha_0} \cdot e(g_1, g_1)^{w\alpha_0 IDu} \cdot e(g_1, g_4)^{wu} \cdot e(g_1, g_3)^{wt'}$$

$$Y_2 = e\big(C_3, H\big(e(g,g)^{\alpha(D_6 + r')}\big)\big) = e\big(g_3^w, H\big(e(g,g)^{\alpha(r - r' + r')}\big)\big)$$

$$= e(g_3^w, H(e(g,g)^{\alpha r}))$$

- Calculate $\dfrac{X_1 X_2}{Y_1 Y_2} = \dfrac{1}{e(g_1, g_2)^{w\alpha_0}}$

- Recover the message $\mathcal{M}$ as follows

$$C_2 \cdot \frac{X_1 X_2}{Y_1 Y_2} = \mathcal{M} \cdot e(g_1^{\alpha_0}, g_2)^w \cdot \frac{1}{e(g_1, g_2)^{w\alpha_0}} = \mathcal{M}.$$

8 Conclusion

In this paper, we proposed an IB-AB-PReM, which is a novel cryptographic framework integrating IBE and ABE into a unified PRE scheme with online-offline re-encryption key generation and verifiable outsourced decryption mechanism. This hybrid approach addresses fine-grained access control and ensures data confidentiality. The introduction of the online-offline re-encryption key generation mechanism significantly reduces computational overhead and enhances the efficiency of the re-encryption process, making it well-suited for resource-constrained devices. The functionality comparison and performance evaluation demonstrate the efficiency and practicality of our proposed IB-AB-PReM scheme.

Acknowledgement. The authors would like to thank the anonymous reviewers of this paper for their valuable comments and suggestions.

References

1. Akinyele, J.A., et al.: Charm: a framework for rapidly prototyping cryptosystems. J. Cryptogr. Eng. **3**, 111–128 (2013)
2. Bethencourt, J., Sahai, A., Waters, B.: Ciphertext-policy attribute-based encryption. In: 2007 IEEE Symposium on Security and Privacy, pp. 321–334. IEEE (2007)
3. Deng, H., Qin, Z., Wu, Q., Guan, Z., Zhou, Y.: Flexible attribute-based proxy re-encryption for efficient data sharing. Inf. Sci. **511**, 94–113 (2020)
4. Ge, C., Susilo, W., Baek, J., Liu, Z., Xia, J., Fang, L.: A verifiable and fair attribute-based proxy re-encryption scheme for data sharing in clouds. IEEE Trans. Dependable Secure Comput. **19**(5), 2907–2919 (2021)
5. He, K., et al.: A new encrypted data switching protocol: bridging IBE and ABE without loss of data confidentiality. IEEE Access **7**, 50658–50668 (2019)
6. Kar, D.M., Ray, I.: Systematization of knowledge and implementation: Short identity-based signatures. arXiv preprint arXiv:1908.05366 (2019)
7. Liang, K., Fang, L., Susilo, W., Wong, D.S.: A ciphertext-policy attribute-based proxy re-encryption with chosen-ciphertext security. In: 5th International Conference on Intelligent Networking and Collaborative Systems, pp. 552–559. IEEE (2013)
8. Pareek, G., Purushothama, B.: Proxy re-encryption for fine-grained access control: its applicability, security under stronger notions and performance. J. Inf. Secur. Appl. **54**, 102543 (2020)
9. Wang, X., et al.: Attribute-based access control encryption. IEEE Trans. Dependable Secure Comput. (2024)
10. Waters, B.: Ciphertext-policy attribute-based encryption: an expressive, efficient, and provably secure realization. In: International Workshop on Public Key Cryptography, pp. 53–70. Springer, Cham (2011)
11. Yasumura, Y., Imabayashi, H., Yamana, H.: Attribute-based proxy re-encryption method for revocation in cloud storage: Reduction of communication cost at re-encryption. In: 2018 IEEE 3rd International Conference on Big Data Analysis (ICBDA), pp. 312–318. IEEE (2018)
12. Zhang, Q., Fu, Y., Cui, J., He, D., Zhong, H.: Efficient fine-grained data sharing based on proxy re-encryption in IIoT. IEEE Trans. Dependable Secure Comput. (2024)

MobiTest: A Testbed for Harnessing the Computing Power of Discarded Smartphones

Pramod Tripathi[1,2]([envelope]), Vishal Dhoriya[2], Kalyan Sasidhar[2,3], and Amit Mankodi[2,3]

[1] Government Polytechnic Gandhinagar, Gandhinagar, Gujarat, India
[2] Dhirubhai Ambani University (DAU), Gandhinagar, Gujarat, India
`{201721003,202101446,kalyan_sasidhar,amit_mankodi}@dau.ac.in`
[3] Smart Energy Learning Center (DAU), Gandhinagar, Gujarat, India

Abstract. Edge computing models of processing data generated by smart- phones and IoT devices at intermediate edge nodes have shown to reduce communication latency and enhance responsiveness for real-time applications. The past decade has also seen significant developments in processing power, memory, and storage aspects of smartphones. This growth has led to frequent hardware and software upgrades to smartphones, prompting users to discard their old phones for new ones in the market. However, the discarded phones are in perfectly working condition, thereby leaving a rich source of computing power underutilized/untapped. This situation presents an opportunity to harness latent computational resources. This paper introduces MobiTest, a distributed computing framework designed to reuse smartphones as collaborative edge computing nodes. The software framework is developed as an easy plug-and-play type, connecting multiple heterogeneous smartphones in a master slave fashion. A particle swarm optimization-based scheduling algorithm is contextualized and formulated based on the smartphone specifications, including processing capacity, battery status, and device utilization. To validate the framework, we implement and evaluate an object detection task across a distributed set of old smartphones. Results show that our modified optimization algorithm resulted in a 36% and 14% improvement in the CPU utilization when compared with two greedy heuristics. The throughput in terms of data transfer for the task processing also resulted in a 45% and 25% improvement.

Keywords: Smartphones · Computing · Optimization

1 Introduction

With the rapid proliferation of the Internet of Things (IoT), the number of intelligent devices connected to the Internet has grown exponentially. IoT Analytics projects approximately 27 billion connected IoT devices to be in use by the end of 2025. This expansion has led to a growing reliance on centralized cloud infrastructures to process large amounts of data generated at the edge. However, cloud computing introduces network delays, variable latency, bandwidth bottlenecks, and increased operational costs—all of which are particularly critical in latency-sensitive and safety-critical applications [15]. Edge computing has emerged as a compelling alternative that extends computation, storage, and networking capabilities from centralized cloud servers to the network's periphery [1]. For instance, authors in [8] performed computations closer to the devices and observed that bandwidth usage and latency also reduced.

The past decade has witnessed remarkable progress in smartphone technology in terms of CPU, RAM, and storage. For example, the Apple iPhone 11 includes Apple's Neural Engine [3], and the Samsung Galaxy S2x family also incorporates a dedicated NPU (Neural Processing Unit) featuring high-speed processors dedicated to neural network models for inference. Still, consumers discard phones even if they are completely or partially operational. Reasons include rapid hardware upgrade cycles (from quad-core to octa-core), software upgrades (lack of OS updates for certain models, rendering them outdated/obsolete), and the introduction of new models with attractive features [21]. These reasons have led to a substantial number of phones left idle or discarded as e-waste [14]. A huge untapped computing resource.[1]. There have been attempts in recent years to utilize smartphones for computing.

Authors in [16,22] examined the performance of smartphone processors for high-performance tasks. Results indicated that a single mobile System on Chip (SoC) holds significant potential for reducing the cost of supercomputing, making it relevant for scalable edge computing scenarios. Authors in [2] proposed an energy-aware distributed computing using employee/user smartphones while being charged during the night. In [10,19], the authors demonstrate that integrating smartphones into distributed computing frameworks can reduce both server-side processing and energy consumption. Experiments conducted on Motorola Moto X4 and Moto G5 devices using benchmarks such as Matrix Multiplication, SHA-1, and Linpack reveal that, for specific tasks, smartphones can outperform traditional desktops in energy efficiency. In [2], the author modeled a computational framework for task scheduling and employed a greedy approach to minimize the task completion objective. In [7], the authors proposed an optimization framework for task scheduling and tested it using synthetic tasks with greedy heuristics. Work in [4] addressed sustainability by comparing performance and environmental trade-offs associated with reusing computing devices.

Motivated by the availability of unused/discarded phones, this work presents MobiTest, a distributed master–slave framework that leverages underutilized smartphones as edge nodes for compute-intensive tasks. In this framework, a central master smartphone coordinates a set of slave smartphones by distributing workloads using an optimization-driven scheduling approach. We adopt and modify Particle Swarm Optimization (PSO) to solve the task allocation problem, with objectives centered on minimizing task completion time while considering device-specific constraints such as battery capacity and CPU utilization. To validate the framework, we implemented and evaluated a real-world object detection

---

[1] Smartphone CPUs are comparable to Intel i3 processors on desktops [21].

application on 6-7 year old models of smartphones. The results demonstrated the practical viability of the proposed architecture and highlighted the efficiency of the modified scheduling algorithm in achieving an effective workload distribution across heterogeneous devices.

The main contributions of this paper are as follows:

1. We developed our testbed using six heterogeneous Android phones, unlike the multiple instances of the same phones found in existing works.
2. We developed the software framework as a plug-and-play service. We tested it on phones running Android OS version 5 and above. No further repurposing, such as installing mobile-friendly versions of Linux, is required.
3. We modified the particle swarm optimization algorithm and implemented it directly on a smartphone, and not on a workstation or a server machine.
4. We evaluated our testbed and the optimization framework on a real-world application: a fabric fault detection problem using the YOLO framework.

The remainder of this paper is structured as follows. Section 2 outlines the various state-of-art approaches. Section 3 discusses the system architecture in detail. Section 4 describes the task allocation formulation and PSO-based scheduling approach. Section 5 describes the implementation details. Section 6 discusses performance evaluation results and analysis. Finally, Sect. 7 concludes the paper and outlines future directions.

2   Related Work

Over the last few years, researches have shown interest in utilizing the computing capacity of smartphones. In [6], authors presented smartphones as alternate platforms to servers. A practical estimation of device level compute capacity was done, however some performance inconsistencies were observed due to missing resource allocation framework. Authors in [9], deployed a video processing application to benchmark smartphones as edge devices. Authors in [21] proposed the idea of repurposing smartphones with software (Linux) and used the phones as compute nodes. They also presented reduction of carbon emission of such an infrastructure when compared with a data center. In [23] recent developments in locally executed data mining on smartphones is being done however, it highlighted that newer phones could be used for on device inference by using pre-loaded deep-learning model. Authors in [24] built an application for activity recognition and reported 65% percent lesser energy consumed by inferencing application than normal video application such as YouTube. However, a single device was considered.

There are multiple object recognition use cases on smartphones. In [12,13] common objects are detected on Android devices using YOLO(you only look once) and tiny YOLOv3. In [20] and [18], face detection was performed using customized CNN but with a lower accuracy. In [2], authors proposed and implemented a distributed computing infrastructure using smartphone. A greedy approach was adopted to reduce overall completion time without considering battery life. Our work extends the work in [7], where scheduling is framed as an optimization problem however we have proposed a method using one of the metaheuristic approach named PSO that is suitable for resource-constrained devices rather than using a greedy approach. Also unlike existing work, we used heterogeneous phones for our implementation.

3   System Architecture

We have implemented the MobiTest architecture as a cross-platform Flutter application following a service-oriented design managed by a central coordinator. As depicted in Fig. 1, upon launching the application, the main `Coordination Service` makes a `Role Decision`, configuring the node to operate as either a Master or a Slave. This decision dictates which subordinate services are activated, ensuring resource conservation.

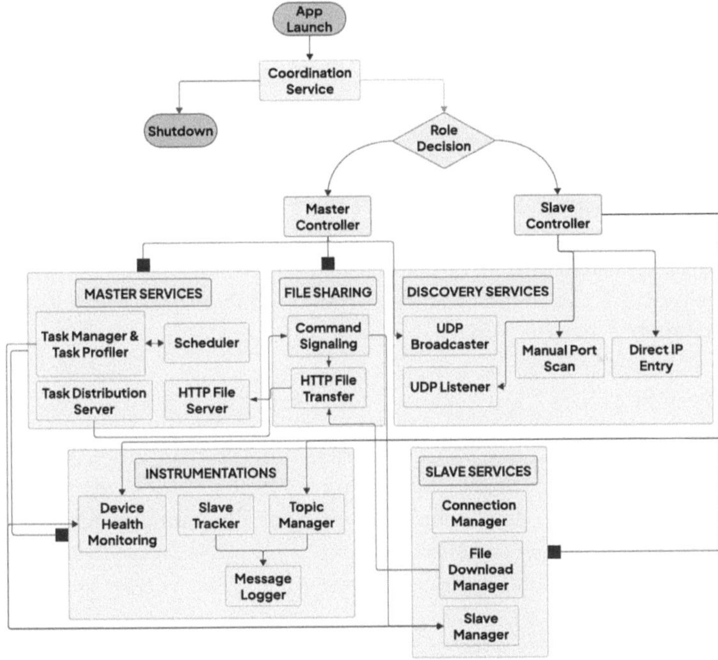

Fig. 1. Mobitest system architecture: The `Coordination Service` orchestrates the system, activating Master-side services via the `Master Controller` or Slave-side services via the `Slave Controller` based on the chosen role.

3.1   Master Node Services

When configured as a Master, the `Master Controller` is activated. It orchestrates all Master-side services:

- **Master Services:** This module runs the core `Task Distribution Server` and includes a `Scheduler` and `Task Manager` for orchestrating slave tasks.
- **Discovery Services:** It initiates a `UDP Broadcaster` to announce its presence, enabling automatic discovery by slaves. Manual discovery methods are also available as a fallback.
- **Instrumentation:** A suite of services including a `Slave Tracker`, `Topic Manager`, and `Message Logger` are activated to monitor the network and log all data for analysis.

3.2   Slave Node Services

When configured as a Slave, the `Slave Controller` is activated. It orchestrates all necessary client-side services to join and interact with the network:

- **Slave Services:** This core module uses the `Connection Manager` to establish a persistent session with the Master and a `Slave Manager` to process incoming commands and execute assigned tasks.
- **Discovery Services:** This module is activated in listening mode, utilizing the `UDP Listener` to automatically detect the Master's broadcast announcements on the local network.
- **File Services Interaction:** It interacts with the shared `File Sharing` module by using the `File Download Manager` to efficiently retrieve large data files when instructed by the Master.

3.3   Shared Services

Master and Slave roles utilize shared services for essential operations. A hybrid protocol approach uses `Command Signaling` for lightweight control messages and HTTP for actual data transfer, enabling efficient file sharing. Simultaneously, a device health monitoring service receives status reports from all nodes to enable health-aware scheduling and network analysis.

3.4   Operational Flow: Task Offloading Example

The utility of the architecture is best demonstrated through a typical operational flow. Assuming a stable Master-Slave network:

1. **Task Initiation (Master):** A new task is profiled by the `Task Manager & Task Profiler`. Based on this and health data from the slaves, the `Scheduler` selects a sequence of Slaves.
2. **Dispatch (Master):** The `Task Distribution Server` uses `Command Signaling` to send a formatted task instruction to the chosen Slave's unique topic.

3. **Execution (Slave):** On the designated Slave, the instruction is received and passed to the `Slave Manager`, which orchestrates the task's execution on the device.
4. **Reporting (Slave):** Throughout the process, the Slave sends real-time status updates. Upon completion, the `Slave Manager` reports the final result back to the Master. All communications are captured by the `Instrumentation` services on the Master for analysis.

We employed MQTT as the underlying communication protocol, a strategic choice designed to optimize for machine-to-machine communication. MQTT's native publish-subscribe model provides efficient one-to-many message routing, critical for our Master-to-multiple-Slaves coordination.

In the next section, we describe the scheduling algorithm formulation for task allocation on smartphones.

4   Particle Swarm Optimization Formulation

To enable effective scheduling mechanism and resource utilization of smartphones as edge computing devices, we must address the heterogeneity in processing power, memory, and energy capacity. Traditional evolutionary computation techniques can handle multi-objective optimization problems by converting them to a single objective through the weighted sum approach [5]. Particle Swarm Optimization (PSO) has lower computational complexity compared to the Genetic Algorithm (GA). It involves simple mathematical operations (e.g., updating velocities and positions), making it suitable for devices with limited computational power [11]. We applied PSO by defining a fitness function based on the scheduling formulation described in the following section.

4.1   Fitness Function

The fitness function is designed as a weighted average of completion time and energy consumption. To incorporate both objectives into a single objective we normalized the completion time and energy consumption. Both objectives are assigned suitable weighing factors. The completion time comprises of waiting time at the input, processing and output queue; time taken to receive a task as input, process the task and output the processed task to the master. The input waiting time is the ratio of input task length and available input bandwidth; and output waiting time is the ratio of output task length and available output bandwidth at a particular device. Processing time is the ratio of compute requirement for task and available compute capacity. There is also an association term that considers those devices on which task is allocated.

Energy consumption is measured as the summation of amount of energy consumed bit wise for sending and receiving data elements and energy consumed while executing the batch of task. Mathematically the formulations are denoted as follows:-

$$F(x) = \alpha \frac{\max\left(T_{c\_j}\right)}{T_{\max}}$$
$$+ \beta \frac{\sum_{i=1}^{n} \sum_{j=1}^{m} x_{ij} \left(L_{\text{in}\_j}\epsilon_{\text{recv}\_i} + L_{ex\_j}\epsilon_{\text{proc}\_i} + L_{\text{out}\_j}\epsilon_{\text{send}\_i}\right)}{\epsilon_{\max}}$$

where, $T_{\max}$ is the maximum completion time of task by slowest slave considering the task is executed on single device at a time. The completion time for a task j denoted as T_{c_j}, is given by:

$$T_{c\_j} = W_{\text{in}\_j} + L_{\text{in}\_j} \sum_{i=1}^{n} \frac{x_{ij}}{B_{\text{in}\_i}}$$
$$+ W_{\text{ex}\_j} + L_{ex\_j} \sum_{i=1}^{n} \frac{x_{ij}}{C\_i}$$
$$+ W_{\text{out}\_j} + L_{\text{out}\_j} \sum_{i=1}^{n} \frac{x_{ij}}{B_{\text{out}\_i}}$$

We consider n available workers(phones) and m tasks in the buffer. $L_{\text{in/out}\_j}$ is the size of the input/output of task j and L_{ex_j} is the processed load introduced by task j. x_{ij} is the decision variable (i.e., 1 if task j is assigned to a phone i or 0). $W_{\text{in/out}\_j}$ and W_{ex_j} are the waiting times for task j prior to input/output offloading and in the task execution queue respectively. C_i is the processing capacity of device i.

The energy consumed while sending/receiving a unit data is denoted by $\epsilon_{\text{recv/send}\_i}$. The processing energy consumption rate of device i is denoted as ϵ_{proc_i}. The maximum energy capacity among a set of device is denoted as $\epsilon_{\max}$. The weighing factors are α and β. The weight factors are computed by taking partial derivatives of objective functions and equating them with boundary conditions. $B_{\text{in/out}\_i}$ is the uplink/downlink bandwidth of worker i.

4.2   Constraints

We formulated a minimization problem that minimizes the fitness function with constraints:

1. **Total Energy Budget Constraint.** The total energy consumed by the (n)worker devices to finish the batch of (m) tasks should be less than the predefined total energy threshold ϵ_{th}

$$\sum_{i=1}^{n} \sum_{j=1}^{m} x_{ij} \left(L_{\text{in}\_j}\epsilon_{\text{recv}\_i} + L_{ex\_j}\epsilon_{\text{proc}\_i} + L_{\text{out}\_j}\epsilon_{\text{send}\_i}\right) < \epsilon_{\text{th}}.$$

2. **Task-Batch deadline constraint.** The completion time for the batch of tasks at the master needs to be below the present deadline D, where $D >= max(T_{c\_j})$

3. **Integral Association:** Each task (j) should be assigned to one worker device:

$$\sum_{i=1}^{n} x_{ij} = 1 \quad \forall j \in \{1, 2, \ldots, m\}$$

In the following section, we discuss the implementation details including the baseline approaches used for comparison, the smartphone specifications, the parameters used in the evaluation and the task level data used.

5   Implementation

We implemented a prototype of the distributed framework including the scheduling algorithms on a testbed of six smartphones (LenovoK5, MotoG7, Nokia 6.1+, Redmi5, Nexus 5, and Samsung A21S). One of the phones was designated to run as the controller, while the others as slaves/workers.

We also implemented two baseline schedulers for comparison:

- Greedy-I: The Greedy-I approach solves a complementary bin packing problem [2]. The objective is to pack items by a set of bins with a certain capacity. Maximum height across the bin needs to be minimized.
- Greedy-II: Greedy-II solves a 0-1 mixed integer programming using heuristics [7]. It uses best-fit approach to bin packing to minimize resource fragmentation. The task is prioritized to get fit in the bin if the task requirement matches the highest capacity.

We consider the following metrics for evaluation:

1. Completion time: For object detection, we look at the frame processing time across Greedy-I, Greedy-II and proposed PSO.
2. CPU utilization: Percentage of CPU utilized across the slaves.
3. Throughput: Number of frames processed by the slaves.
4. Battery Consumed: Amount of battery (energy) consumed by the slaves.
5. Frame Imbalance Factor: Frame imbalance factor is the ratio of the

The master phone organizes input images into task batches using processing level (Table 1) and energy level estimates (Table 2) shared by each slave phone with the master.

Table 1. Processing estimates

Parameter	Values (per device)
Proc Speed (GHz)	{1.3, 1.4, 1.4, 1.8, 1.7, 2}
CPU Cores	{4, 8, 4, 8, 8, 8}
RAM (GB)	{2, 4, 3, 3, 8, 8}
Battery Life (%)	{80, 50, 75, 75, 75, 50}
Proc Time (ms)	{434, 602, 733, 667, 271, 323}

Table 2 shows the parameters used for estimating energy consumption. The energy capacity, initial energy, and threshold values come from battery specifications typical mobile devices. The energy per MFLOP is calculated by running compute-intensive tests and noting the processor's energy usage, while the energy per MB is measured by tracking the extra energy drawn during data transmission. These values give practical estimates for both computation and communication costs in our experiments.

Table 2. Energy level estimates

Parameter	Values
Energy Capacity (kJ)	$\{10, 12, 13, 14, 16, 18\}$
Initial Energy (%)	$\{50, 65, 70, 75, 80, 85\}$
Energy Threshold (%)	$\{5, 7, 10\}$
Energy per MFLOP (μJ/MF)	$\{0.28, 0.33, 0.37, 0.42, 0.52, 0.47\}$
Energy per MB (mJ/MB)	$\{1.2, 1.4, 1.6, 1.9, 2.1, 2.4\}$

These estimates are used by the scheduler service on the master to prepare a schedule for the set of slaves. Once batches are prepared, the modified PSO scheduler is invoked to assign these batches optimally to heterogeneous devices, considering processor speed, energy capacity, and current workload. Following initial scheduling, each device independently executes the task on the assigned batch of input data. The system adopts an adaptive scheduling mechanism where performance metrics such as the execution time, energy consumption, and result accuracy are periodically collected from the slaves. This feedback enables the master to update each device's effective performance and responsiveness. After execution, each device sends results along with metadata to the server, which aggregates this data to refine its scheduling model and generate fault reports for the detected defective images.

5.1   Performance Evaluation

We evaluated the performance of the testbed for an object detection application, particularly using the YOLO (You Only Look Once) framework [17], which is a neural network based algorithm for fast and accurate object detection. YOLO is a family of real-time object detection models designed to perform classification and localization in a single forward pass. Unlike traditional detectors that use multiple stages, YOLO applies a unified architecture, making it highly efficient for real-time applications. The application was a fabric fault detection. A total of 1000 annotated images each of size 640 × 640 pixels were used in the experiment.[2]

---

[2] Roboflow, "Fabric Detection Dataset", https://universe.roboflow.com/fabricdefect/fabric-detection.

Table 3. Defect Detection Task Characteristics

Task Type	Input(MB)	Comp (MF)	Output(MB)
Stain Detection	1.2	2200	0.5
Hole Detection	1.5	2600	0.6
Color Inconsistency	1.8	2000	0.4
Mixed Defect Detection	2.0	3200	0.7

In Table 3, the values of input, computation, and output for each defect detection task were obtained through a combination of empirical estimation and algorithm profiling. The input size was calculated from the average resolution and bit depth of the captured textile images, taking into account compression factors when applicable. The computation requirement (in MF) was derived from analyzing the algorithmic pipeline of each task type. Specifically, the number of operations per pixel for preprocessing (e.g., filtering), feature extraction, and classification was multiplied by the average image size to yield the overall computational load. The output size was determined by evaluating the amount of metadata generated, such as defect masks, coordinates, or classification labels, which are significantly smaller compared to the inputs. Figure 2 shows the smartphones testbed.

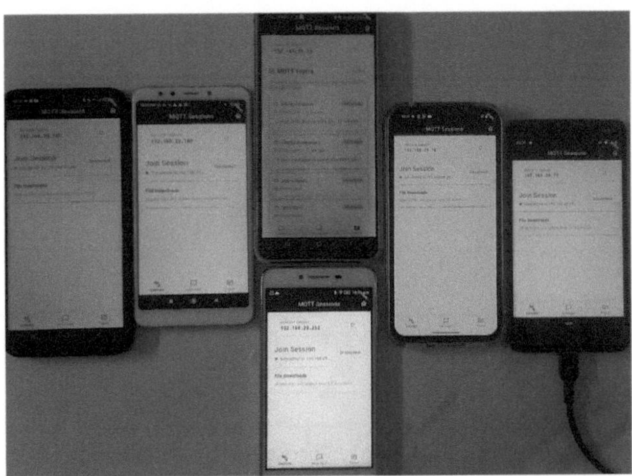

Fig. 2. The testbed shows master and slaves phones setup. The master hosts a session and slaves are connected to the master. Following this, the master receives the computer capacity(FLOPS), battery status and other data from the slaves. The PSO algorithm is executed on the master, after which it distributes the task(images) across the phones for computation.

6 Results

In this section, we discuss the performance of the PSO algorithm across the metrics listed in Sect. 5.

Task Completion Time: Figure 3 illustrates the task execution time.

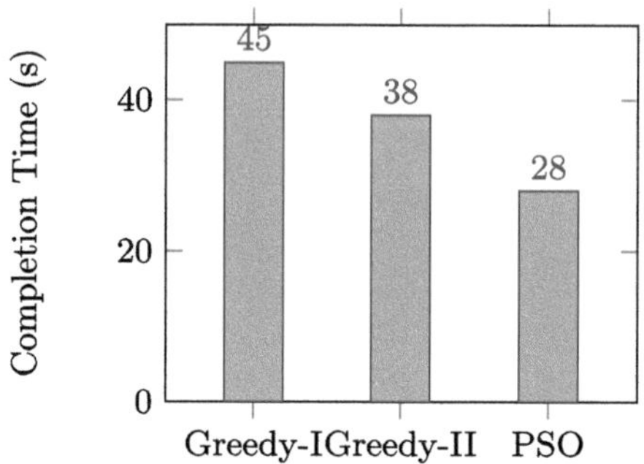

Fig. 3. With the PSO scheduler, slaves completing the task in 28 s. This shows that PSO's global search capability enables efficient allocation of frames across devices, minimizing idle time and delays. Greedy-II performs moderately well with a time of 38 s, while Greedy-I lags behind due to less optimized resource utilization.

CPU Utilization: Figure 4 illustrates the CPU utilization across the five slave devices aggregated and averaged out at the master.

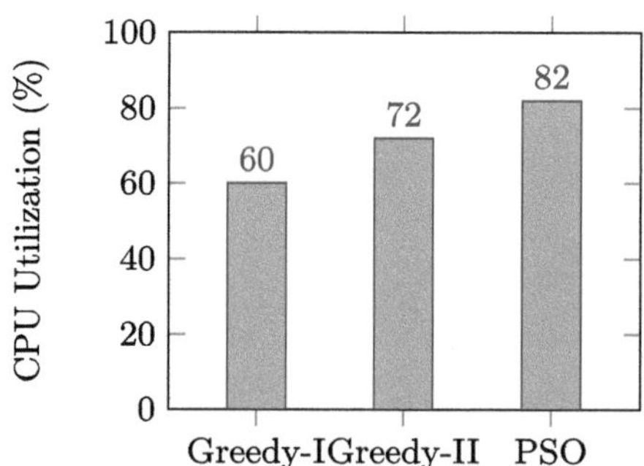

Fig. 4. The PSO scheduler achieves an average of 82% CPU utilization across all devices due to its balanced load distribution. This efficient mapping ensures that no device remains idle or overloaded. Greedy-II provides moderate utilization (72%) as it fits tasks based on heuristics but may cause uneven load. Greedy-I shows the lowest CPU utilization (60 %), likely due to poor task placement and underutilized device capacities

We also illustrate the CPU utilization percentages displayed across the master in Fig. 5.

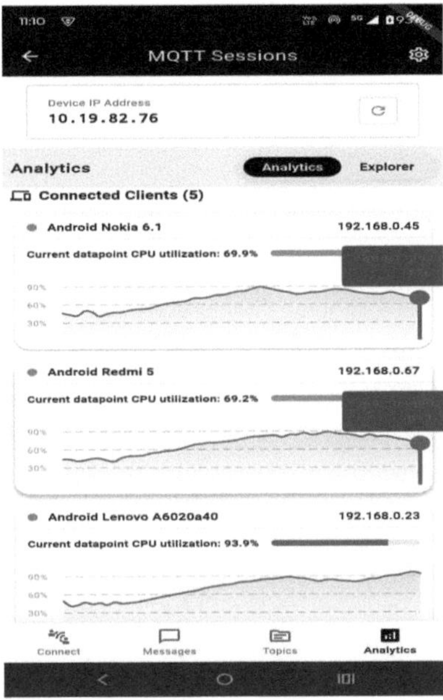

Fig. 5. The screenshot on the master shows the connected slaves(5 in this experiment) and the CPU utilization of each of the slaves while executing the task

Throughput: Figure 6 compares the throughput across the three approaches.

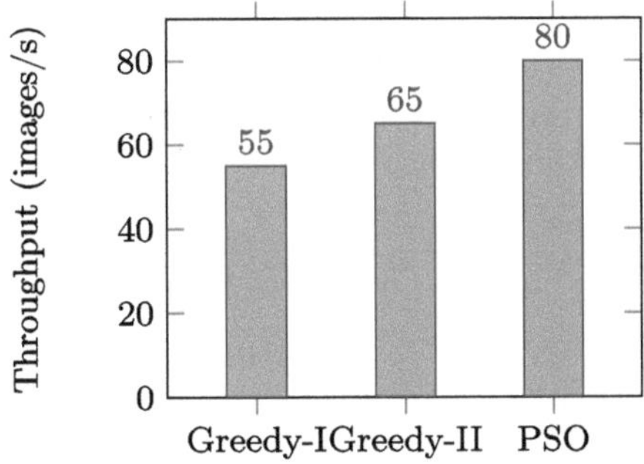

Fig. 6. PSO achieves the highest throughput of 80 images/second, indicating its strong ability to maximize parallelism across devices, followed by Greedy-II due to its best-fit bin-packing logic, while Greedy-I results in the lowest throughput due to suboptimal task-device matching.

Energy Consumption: The energy consumption in Joules across the slaves for computing the tasks is illustrated in Fig. 7

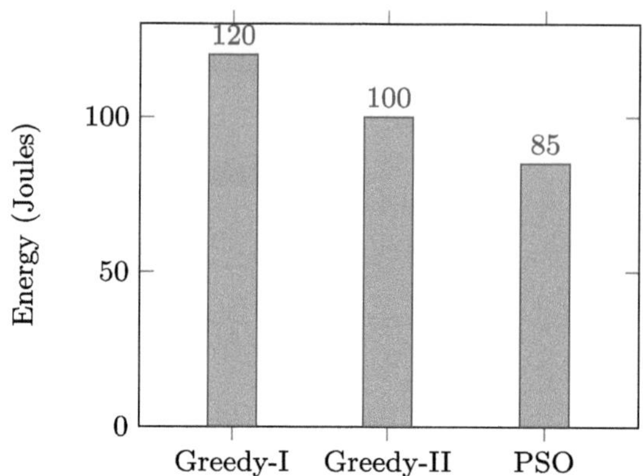

Fig. 7. Energy Consumption Comparison: PSO consumes the least energy (85J), highlighting its energy-efficient scheduling by balancing workloads and reducing idle power waste. Greedy-II consumes slightly more energy (100J) due to partial inefficiencies, and Greedy-I results in the highest energy usage (120J), likely due to workload imbalances and prolonged task execution.

7   Conclusion and Future Work

This work showed that idle and discarded smartphones can be effectively reused for collaborative edge computing tasks. Among the tested strategies, Particle Swarm Optimization (PSO) achieved better results in completion time, device utilization, and throughput, while balancing the load more evenly. Our lightweight MobiTest testbed also proved capable of running object detection tasks on older phones, supporting the idea of a sustainable computing platform.

In future work, we plan to expand the testbed with more heterogeneous phones and compare its energy use with that of a workstation running similar tasks. We also aim to test our scheduling method on other applications such as multimodal streaming analytics and real-time data processing, to understand how well it adapts to different workloads. The scalability of the controller's batching and PSO-based scheduling when managing a large number of devices will also be explored, along with criteria for selecting the controller smartphone based on processing power, battery, and network strength.

Since discarded devices may pose security risks, we will look into ways to prevent data leaks or Denial of Service (DoS) attacks from compromised nodes. Finally, we plan to study the use of encryption in MQTT and HTTP communications to ensure secure data exchange within the testbed.

Acknowledgments. We acknowledge BSES Rajdhani Power Limited and BSES Yamuna Power Limited for the CSR grants to carry out the work at the Smart Energy Learning Centre (SELC), Dhirubhai Ambani University (DAU), Gandhinagar, Gujarat, India.

References

1. Akhter, R., Sofi, S.A.: Precision agriculture using IoT data analytics and machine learning. J. King Saud Univ. - Comput. Inf. Sci. **34**(8, Part B), 5602–5618 (2022). https://doi.org/10.1016/j.jksuci.2021.05.013. https://www.sciencedirect.com/science/article/pii/S1319157821001282

2. Arslan, M.Y., Singh, I., Singh, S., Madhyastha, H.V., Sundaresan, K., Krishnamurthy, S.V.: CWC: a distributed computing infrastructure using smartphones. IEEE Trans. Mob. Comput. **14**(8), 1587–1600 (2015). https://doi.org/10.1109/TMC.2014.2362753

3. Axon, S.: iPhone 13 and 13 pro review: If you could have three wishes (2021). https://arstechnica.com/gadgets/2021/09/iphone-13-and-13-pro-review-if-you-could-have-three-wishes/

4. Bonomi, F., Milito, R., Zhu, J., Addepalli, S.: Fog computing and its role in the internet of things. In: Proceedings of the First Edition of the MCC Workshop on Mobile Cloud Computing, MCC 2012, pp. 13–16. Association for Computing Machinery, New York (2012). https://doi.org/10.1145/2342509.2342513

5. Cao, Y., Hou, P., Brown, D., Wang, J., Chen, S.: Distributed analytics and edge intelligence: pervasive health monitoring at the era of fog computing. In: Mobidata 2015, pp. 43–48 (2015)

6. Garcia, J., Simó, E., Masip-Bruin, X., Marín-Tordera, E., Sànchez-López, S.: Do we really need cloud? Estimating the fog computing capacities in the city of Barcelona. In: 2018 IEEE/ACM International Conference on Utility and Cloud Computing Companion (UCC Companion), pp. 290–295 (2018). https://doi.org/10.1109/UCC-Companion.2018.00070

7. Gedawy, H., Habak, K., Harras, K.A., Hamdi, M.: Ramos: a resource-aware multi-objective system for edge computing. IEEE Trans. Mob. Comput. **20**(8), 2654–2670 (2021). https://doi.org/10.1109/TMC.2020.2984134

8. George, S., et al.: Openrtist: end-to-end benchmarking for edge computing. IEEE Pervasive Comput. **19**(4), 10–18 (2020). https://doi.org/10.1109/MPRV.2020.3028781

9. George, S., et al.: Openrtist: end-to-end benchmarking for edge computing. IEEE Pervasive Comput. **19**(4), 10–18 (2020)

10. Hakim, A., Huq, M.S., Shanta, S., Ibrahim, B.: Smartphone based data mining for fall detection: analysis and design. Procedia Comput. Sci. **105**, 46–51 (2017)

11. Karlsen, H., Dong, T.: Smartphone-based rapid screening of urinary biomarkers. IEEE Trans. Biomed. Circuits Syst. **11**(2), 455–463 (2017). https://doi.org/10.1109/TBCAS.2016.2633508

12. Martinez-Alpiste, I., Casaseca-de-la Higuera, P., Alcaraz-Calero, J., Grecos, C., Wang, Q.: Benchmarking machine-learning-based object detection on a UAV and mobile platform. In: 2019 IEEE Wireless Communications and Networking Conference (WCNC), pp. 1–6 (2019). https://doi.org/10.1109/WCNC.2019.8885504

13. Martinez-Alpiste, I., Casaseca-de-la Higuera, P., Alcaraz-Calero, J.M., Grecos, C., Wang, Q.: Smartphone-based object recognition with embedded machine learning intelligence for unmanned aerial vehicles. J. Field Robot. **37**(3), 404–420 (2020). https://doi.org/10.1002/rob.21921. https://onlinelibrary.wiley.com/doi/abs/10.1002/rob.21921
14. Nguyen, Q.H., Dressler, F.: A smartphone perspective on computation offloading—a survey. Comput. Commun. **159**, 133–154 (2020). https://doi.org/10.1016/j.comcom.2020.05.001. https://www.sciencedirect.com/science/article/pii/S0140366419319401
15. Premsankar, G., Di Francesco, M., Taleb, T.: Edge computing for the internet of things: a case study. IEEE Internet Things J. **5**(2), 1275–1284 (2018). https://doi.org/10.1109/JIOT.2018.2805263
16. Rajovic, N., Carpenter, P.M., Gelado, I., Puzovic, N., Ramirez, A., Valero, M.: Supercomputing with commodity CPUs: are mobile SoCs ready for HPC? In: SC 2013: Proceedings of the International Conference on High Performance Computing, Networking, Storage and Analysis, pp. 1–12 (2013). https://doi.org/10.1145/2503210.2503281
17. Redmon, J., Divvala, S., Girshick, R., Farhadi, A.: You only look once: unified, real-time object detection. In: Proceedings of the IEEE Conference on Computer Vision and Pattern Recognition (CVPR) (2016)
18. Sarkar, S., Patel, V.M., Chellappa, R.: Deep feature-based face detection on mobile devices. In: 2016 IEEE International Conference on Identity, Security and Behavior Analysis (ISBA), pp. 1–8 (2016). https://doi.org/10.1109/ISBA.2016.7477230
19. Schaffner, B., Sawin, J., Myre, J.M.: Smartphones as alternative cloud computing engines: benefits and trade-offs. In: 2018 IEEE 6th International Conference on Future Internet of Things and Cloud (FiCloud), pp. 244–250 (2018). https://doi.org/10.1109/FiCloud.2018.00043
20. Stoimenov, S., Tsenov, G.T., Mladenov, V.M.: Face recognition system in android using neural networks. In: 2016 13th Symposium on Neural Networks and Applications (NEUREL), pp. 1–4 (2016). https://doi.org/10.1109/NEUREL.2016.7800138
21. Switzer, J., Marcano, G., Kastner, R., Pannuto, P.: Junkyard computing: repurposing discarded smartphones to minimize carbon. In: Proceedings of the 28th ACM International Conference on Architectural Support for Programming Languages and Operating Systems, ASPLOS 2023, vol. 2, pp. 400–412 (2023)
22. Wu, C.J., et al.: Machine learning at Facebook: understanding inference at the edge. In: 2019 IEEE International Symposium on High Performance Computer Architecture (HPCA), pp. 331–344 (2019). https://doi.org/10.1109/HPCA.2019.00048
23. Yates, D., Islam, M.Z.: Data mining on smartphones: an introduction and survey. ACM Comput. Surv. **55**(5) (2022)
24. Zebin, T., Scully, P.J., Peek, N., Casson, A.J., Ozanyan, K.B.: Design and implementation of a convolutional neural network on an edge computing smartphone for human activity recognition. IEEE Access **7**, 133509–133520 (2019)

Formalisms and Fault-Tolerance

Integral Implementation of Higher-Order Algebraic Petri Nets in Maude

Lorenzo Capra[1]([✉]) [iD] and Michael Köhler-Bußmeier[2] [iD]

[1] Dipartimento di Informatica, Università degli Studi di Milano, Via Celoria 18, Milan, Italy
capra@di.unimi.it

[2] University of Applied Science Hamburg, Berliner Tor 7, 20099 Hamburg, Germany
michael.koehler-bussmeier@haw-hamburg.de

Abstract. Reisig's Algebraic Petri nets are highly expressive but rarely based on a strict algebraic framework. We present an effective translation using the declarative language Maude, which employs rewriting semantics. By exploring two definitions, we tackle modeling challenges from Maude's pattern-matching operational semantics. We demonstrate the advantages of using rewritable terms as active tokens, as supported by Maude, with examples including an adaptive Multilevel Feedback Queue scheduling.

Keywords: Algebraic Petri nets · Maude · Active tokens

1 Introduction

High-level Petri nets (HLPN) [12] enhance traditional Petri nets (PN) by using an external mechanism for transition bindings, achieving a concrete formalism through a language for arc expression annotations. Reisig's Algebraic nets (APN) [17] are considered among the most advanced HLPN formalisms, offering mathematical semantics based on equational logic [2,9], and strong analytical capabilities. However, rigorous implementations using an algebraic framework are lacking. Notable is the OBJSA formalism [1] and the associated tool, based on SML and OBJ [10], no longer is maintained. Other implementations of pseudo-algebraic nets [6,15] have utilized established languages such as Java or Python, obfuscating the initial semantics of APNs. The software tools derived from the Colored PN formalism [11], such as [18] and [16], utilize standard languages.

We present an effective APN implementation using Maude, a declarative language with sound rewriting logic semantics. Although Maude was proposed for PNs two decades ago and recently used for various PN classes, we claim ours is the first systematic use of Maude as an APN rewriting engine. Motivated by Maude's pattern matching rewrite engine, we address modeling challenges with arcs and explore using rewritable terms as tokens, as supported by Maude.

The paper is organized as follows: Sect. 2 details Maude and APNs fundamentals. Section 3 explores APN translation in Maude and implementation options.

© The Author(s), under exclusive license to Springer Nature Switzerland AG 2026
B. Chatterjee et al. (Eds.): ICDCIT 2026, LNCS 16420, pp. 137–153, 2026.
https://doi.org/10.1007/978-3-032-16632-6_9

Section 4 demonstrates `Maude` encoding for active tokens in meta-modeling, with examples like adaptive multilevel feedback queue scheduling. Conclusions highlight strengths and issues of the approach.

2   The `Maude` System

`Maude`'s syntax is based on (conditional) *equations* and *rules*. Each side of a rule or equation is a *term* of a certain *kind*, which may involve variables. Rules and equations operate through intuitive rewriting, where instances on the left side are replaced with instances on the right.

A *functional* module defines operations using equations as simplifications, and corresponds to an *equational theory* $(\Sigma, E \cup A)$ of membership equational logic [3]: The signature Σ encompasses the declaration of *sorts, subsorts, kinds* (implicit equivalence classes formed by sorts connected in the subsort partial-order[1]) and *operators*; E contains equations and membership axioms; and A contains operators' equational attributes (*assoc, comm, id, idem*). The model of $(\Sigma, E \cup A)$ is the *initial* algebra, mathematically defined by the quotient $T_{\Sigma/E \cup A}$ of the ground-term algebra T_Σ, according to the relation $\equiv_{E \cup A}$ in T_Σ.

Under the conditions (modulo A) of confluence, sort-decreasing, and termination in theory (Σ, E) [3], any ground term is simplified. into a unique canonical form that has the *least* sort in the respective kind and is made of *constructors* (operators with the attribute *ctor*): the canonical forms define an algebra $Can_{\Sigma/E \cup A}$ isomorphic to $T_{\Sigma/E \cup A}$, ensuring consistency between mathematical and operational semantics. We will presume this in the following.

A `Maude` *system* module includes *rewrite rules*, representing local concurrent state transitions. It defines a generalized *rewrite theory* [4] $\mathcal{R} = (\Sigma, E \cup A, R)$. Here, $(\Sigma, E \cup A)$ acts as the underlying equational theory, and R is the non-empty set of rules. $\mathcal{R}$ captures the behavior of a concurrent system, with $(\Sigma, E \cup A)$ defining the algebraic structure of the states. The initial model of $\mathcal{R}$ provides each kind k with a labeled transition system (TS) where states are elements of $T_{\Sigma/E \cup A, k}$ (the canonical terms of type k) and state transitions occur as $[t] \overset{[\alpha]}{\to} [t']$, with $[\alpha]$ denoting a class of equivalent rewrites. The property of *coherence* is the key to the executability of system modules: it ensures that the simplifying of terms before applying rules is complete and sound.

Rewriting logic is inherently true-concurrent, but our approach uses the interleaving semantics of PNs, as adopted by `Maude`'s core rewriting facilities.

2.1   Algebraic PN

We present algebraic PNs (APNs) [17] using intuitive syntax from `Maude`. Figure 1 shows an APN for the dining philosophers problem. Let $\mathcal{N}$ be a PN— a finite nonempty directed bipartite graph $(P, T, F \subseteq P \times T \cup T \times P)$, with places P and transitions T. The linked algebraic SPEC is an equational theory

---

[1] Terms in a kind without a sort denote errors; operators with a kind as range define partial functions.

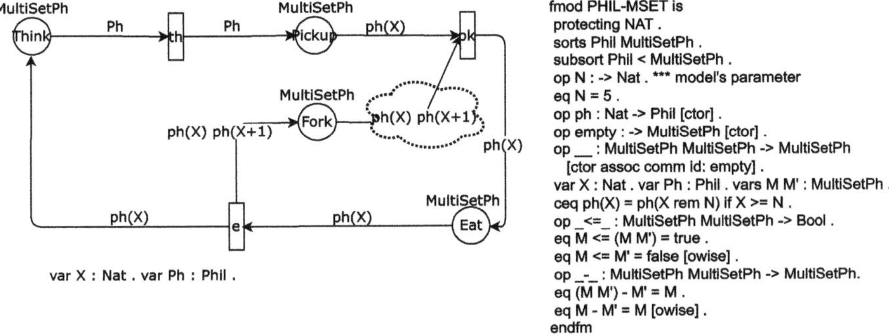

Fig. 1. Reisig's APN model of dining philosophers inscribed using Maude's syntax.

$(\Sigma, E \cup A)$, a Maude functional module with multiset definition. In our example, PHIL-N imports the NAT module, preserving its semantics: The main sort is Phil, and MultiSetPh contains multisets of type Phil. Philosophers are terms like ph(x:Nat), where ph is a circular modulo-N non-free constructor. Subsorts and equational attributes make the multisets a free commutative monoid. SPEC's semantics is the initial or canonical term algebra under executability hypotheses. An APN $\mathcal{A}$ is defined as $(\mathcal{N}, \phi, Y, \lambda)$, mapping each place ϕ to a sort $p \in P$; Y is a set of Σ-variables; λ maps each arc $a \in F$ to a term with variables $T_{\Sigma, mset\{\phi(p(a))\}}(Y)$, where $p(a)$ is the place related to a. A mark m assigns to each place $p \in P$ a multiset of type $\phi(p)$. The pair $(\mathcal{A}, m_0)$ represents an APN with an initial marking. APN dynamics involve *firing modes*: For $t \in T$ and $Y_t \subseteq Y$ on arcs near t, a firing mode σ binds Y_t to canonical terms. σ is enabled in m if for every $(p, t) \in F$, $\sigma(\lambda(p, t)) \leq m(p)$. When it occurs, it subtracts $\sigma(\lambda(p, t))$ from $m(p)$ and adds $\sigma(\lambda(t, p'))$ to $m(p')$ for each $(t, p') \in F$. Transitions can include Boolean terms, which σ must make *true*.

3 Translating Algebraic PNs in Maude

We use Maude to translate APNs, as noted in [5] for classical PNs. We formalize net inscriptions using Maude's pattern-matching for efficient analysis via the coherence property. Although Maude partially supports *unification* with axioms, its main rewriting tools employ pattern-matching modulo A. We explore two multiset definitions: a traditional as a free monoid and a compact representation.

3.1 Pattern Matching and Rewrite

Recall pattern matching in the rewriting rules and equations: $\mathcal{R} = (\Sigma, E \cup A, R)$ is the rewriting theory of a system module M, with X holding variables in $\mathcal{R}$, each assigned a sort or kind. By adding X to Σ, we form the algebra $T_{\Sigma}(X)$, with terms that include variables used in equations and rules. Ground substitution maps $\sigma : X \to Can_{\Sigma/E \cup A}$ with $\sigma(x)$ of the least sort less than or equal to x. The substitution of variables σ extends to a homomorphism $\sigma : T_\Sigma(X) \to T_\Sigma$.

Consider $t \in T_\Sigma(X)$ and a subject term $u \in T_\Sigma$. We say that t matches u if there is a substitution of variables σ such that $\sigma(t) \equiv_A u$, that is, $\sigma(t)$ and u are equal modulo A. Let us focus on rules, whose general form is

$$r : t => t' \ \ if \ C_1 \wedge \ldots C_n$$

where t and t' are terms $T_{\Sigma,k}(X)$ of nonincreasing sorts, and C_i can be: an equation $u_i = u_i'$, a sort membership $u_i : s$, a matching equation $u_i := u_i'$ or a rewrite equation $u_i => u_i'$ (not used in our examples). C_i may also be a term in $T_{\Sigma,Bool}(X)$, in which case it means $C_i = true$. The term t' can encompass "free" variables that do not occur in t, provided that they are bounded by a matching $u_i := u_i'$, where u_i must constitute a *pattern* for $E \cup A$: that is, if we apply a substitution of variables in u_i with canonical terms, we get a canonical term. The free variables bounded in C_i can be used in C_j, $j > i$.

Let $u \in T_\Sigma$. If t matches u via σ and σ makes all C_i provably *true*, then u is rewritten as $u' =_{E \cup A} \sigma(t')$. This applies locally if u is a subterm of v: In that case, v is rewritten by replacing the segment u within v with u'.

Coherence. Rewrite rules R in M must be *coherent*: for any ground term u, a single rewrite with R modulo A: $u \to u'$ ensures that, with $\hat{u}$ as the canonical form of u, there exists a single rewrite: $\hat{u} \to u''$ such that $u' =_{E \cup A} u''$. Thus, any rewrite of u aligns with $\hat{u}$. Rewriting with R modulo $E \cup A$ (undecidable) is converted to rewriting with E and R modulo A (decidable, provided a matching modulo A algorithm exists). If coherence holds, simplifying a term to its canonical form with E (modulo A) before rewriting it with R is sound. The `Maude` rewrite engine, having a matching modulo A algorithm, uses this strategy.

Translating APN transitions into rewrite rules requires ensuring coherence, even though the `Maude` system does not verify it (coherence can be checked on *unconditional* rules using an ad hoc procedure).

The following system module, based on `PHIL-N` (Fig. 1), does not meet coherence. The rule with label `nch` (similarly to the transition *pk* in Fig. 1) is intended to remove a pair of adjacent philosophers from a multiset.

```
mod S-PHIL-N is
  inc PHIL-N .
  vars X J : Nat . var P : Phil .
  rl [nch] : ph(X) ph(X + 1) => empty .
endm
```

Reducing the term `ph(1) ph(3) ph(5)` yields `ph(0) ph(1) ph(3)` ($N = 5$), showing that `nch` was unused, since `Maude` presumes that the rewrites apply to the canonical forms: Simplification precedes application of the rules. The sum `_+_ : Nat Nat -> Nat` in `nch`, an operator in `Maude`, does not match the left-hand side of the rule with any canonical subterm. We can reformulate the rule to ensure coherence. For example:

```
  rl [ch-1] : ph(X) ph(s(X)) => empty .
  crl [ch-2] : ph(X) ph(J) => empty if J = X + 1 .
```

s is a free constructor in NAT, which means that it does not appear as the upper operator on the left-hand side of the equations. Hence, ph(1) ph(3) ph(5) simplifies to ph(3). Coherence is ensured by defining only free constructors. Alternatively, for each $r : t => t'$ *if cond*, the term t should qualify as *pattern* for substitutions of variables that provably make *cond* true. Although most of the literature examples meet this, none of the prior examples do.

A more comprehensive condition, applicable when the sort of t and t' denotes multisets defined as a commutative monoid, such as the specification in Fig. 1, requires that t be constituted at each level of variables or constructors. This can be verified with relative simplicity in most cases. According to the executability assumption on the theory $E \cup A$ of the module, if u is a ground term matched (modulo A) by t and u' is a subterm of u, any rewrite $u' \to u''$ with E is sort-decreasing, and, therefore, results in a constructor. Consequently, t also matches the term obtained from u by replacing its segment u' with u'', and, ultimately, any rewrite of u with r can be mimicked using the canonical form of u.

3.2 APN Definition in Maude

Our definition encompasses an APN *schema* that represents a family of models. Let $\mathcal{N} = (P, T, F)$ be a PN. The algebraic specification associated with $\mathcal{N}$ is based on a generic functional module that defines multisets of any type (denoted $MS\{X :: TRIV\}$), user-defined modules that define the multiset types, and views that link the places of $\mathcal{N}$ to these types. $TRIV$ is the trivial *theory*[2], which requires just a sort, denoted Elt. Formally, an APN (schema) is a tuple $\mathcal{A} := (\mathcal{N}, v, Y, \tau, g)$, such that: v links each place $p \in P$ to a module M through a view $v(p)$ that maps the sort Elt of $TRIV$ to a sort S of M; the marking of p is a ground term of sort $MultiSet\{S\}$. The signature Σ of $\mathcal{A}$ comprises those of the modules obtained by instantiating $MS\{X :: TRIV\}$ according to v; Y is a set of Σ-variables: Let $p(a)$ be the place incident to $a \in F$; τ maps each arc a with a term in $T^*_{\Sigma, MultiSet\{S\}}(Y)$, where the sort S is the target of $v(p(a))$ (that is, $\tau(a)$ is a multiset term of the type linked to $p(a)$). The notation $T^*_{\Sigma}(Y)$ refers to a syntactic extension in which the terms in arc inscriptions may be prefixed by the backtick symbol ('), signifying their context-free nature. In contrast, the usual notation suggests a subterm encapsulated in a context. This extension helps to annotate APNs in a way that is consistent with the pattern matching of Maude. Finally, g maps each transition $t \in T$ to a set $\{C_i\}$ of clauses of the forms admitted in the conditional rules. (By default, $g(t) = \{true\}$).

We initially assume that the targets of v are *functional* modules or theories; then we will generalize to *system* modules. However, the above characterization is general. If all the places are linked to concrete modules, then we speak of an APN, otherwise of an APN schema. For each $t \in T$, the translation of the

---

[2] Theories specify the type parameters in a generic module: A theory is like a functional module, but the equations (if any) are interpreted as constraints; a generic module is instantiated via *views*, mapping the sorts/operators of a theory into the elements of a target module, which can be concrete or a theory itself. Views may be parametrized.

adjacent arc inscriptions according to τ together with $g(t)$ must result in an executable rewrite rule. The concept of enabled firing mode is connected to the notion of a rule match, which will be elaborated on later.

Multisets. We present two distinct definitions of multisets.

The module `MSET{X::TRIV}` conventionally represents multisets as the free commutative monoid over a set, as in the SPEC in Fig. 1. The associative-commutative constructor (AC) `__ : Mset{X} Mset{X} -> Mset{X}`, along with the subsort link `X$Elt < NeMset{X} < Mset{X}`, leads to formally depicting multisets as juxtaposition of elements, for example, `a a b b b`.

The module `BAG{X::TRIV}` provides a more succinct definition: constructors `_._ : Nat X$Elt -> Bag{X}` and the AC `_+_ : Bag{X} Bag{X} -> Bag{X}` (both appearing in the left-hand side of the equations) allows multiset formalization as weighted sums such as `2 . a + 3 . b .`

The monoid representation proves to be quite convenient, whereas the other is more concise and facilitates efficient operations. The module `BAG-MSET{X::TRIV}` is a bridge between the two.

For example, assume that we want to gradually transform a multiset into a set. With `MSET{X::TRIV}`, this is achieved using the rule `x x => x`, where the variable `x` is of type `X.Elt`. Replicating this with `BAG{X::TRIV}`, one might attempt the rule `2 . x => 1 . x .` But this functions only for elements with a multiplicity of two. The correct rule in this case is `s(s(n)) . x => s(n) . x`, where `n` is a variable `Nat`. In contrast, achieving the same task in the fewest steps is straightforward using `BAG`, with the rule `n . x => 1 . x if n > 1`, whereas `MSET` demands a more nuanced strategy.

In `MSET`, coherence is achieved if rewrite rules use variables and constructors only at their top level as noted in Sect. 3. However, `BAG` requires more: for instance, the rule `1 . x + 1 . y => 1 . op(x,y)`, where `x` and `y` are typed variables, does not stay coherent with substitutions like `x = a, y = a`. It must be accompanied by `2 . x => 1 op (x, x)` or rewritten as `1 . x + 1 . y => 1 op (x, y) if x =/= y` to apply only to distinct elements. Both strategies ensure coherence.

APN Semantics in `Maude`. An APN (schema) $\mathcal{A}$ can be easily translated into a `Maude` system module (including few functional modules), that is, a rewrite theory, that integrally defines the mathematical and operation semantics of $\mathcal{A}$:

- Net marking is an AC collection of place-multiset pairs, where places may have different types, as indicated in v. It implicitly encodes the net places.
- Net transitions are defined as rewrite rules, each influencing the segment of the marking involving the transition's pre- and post-sets.
- For a given $t \in T$, the inscriptions on the arcs $(p, t) \in F$ define the left side of the rule, those on the arcs $(t, p) \in F$ define the right side, and the clauses in $g(t)$ define the condition. Terms with a '`·`' prefix indicate context independence.

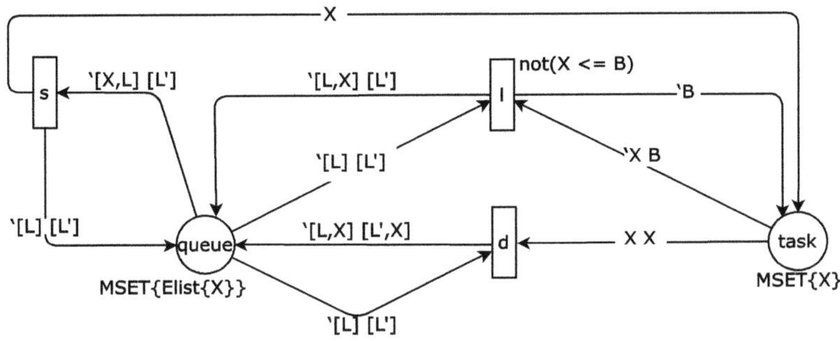

Fig. 2. APN representing a twin-queues system.

A hierarchy of base functional modules defines APNs'signature (https://github.com/lgcapra/rewpt/tree/main/algPT): at the top is `ALG-PN-MARKING{PL::TRIV}` (importing `PLACE{PL}`), outlining the' abstract syntax of APNs with sorts `Marking` and `Pmarking` (place marking), subsort link `Pmarking < Marking`, `Marking`, `Marking` concatenation `_;_` (AC) and identity constant `emptyM`. The lookup operator `_[_]` : `Marking Place{PL} -> [Pmarking]` uses the abstract "getter" `place` to identify a place marking. If the place does not exist or is duplicated, `_[_]` yields `undefined`. The parameter `PL` customizes place labels, e.g. `p(1)` or `p("one")`. This module acts like an abstract class in OOP: we "instantiate" sort `Pmarking` through specific subsort links and "getter" `place` to represent various place types. The modules `MARKING{X::TRIV,PL::TRIV}` and `B-MARKING{X::TRIV,PL::TRIV}`, with a similar structure, extend `ALG-PN-MARKING{PL}`: They use `MSET{X}` and `BAG{X}`, respectively.

Focusing on the former, it features a simple design with the sort `Pmarking{X}` for *typed* place markings, a constructor `_|->_` : `Place{PL} Mset{X} -> Pmarking{X}`, and a subsort link `Pmarking{X} < Pmarking`. It includes "getters" `place` and `mark` to return the respective place and the marking of `Pmarking{X}`. For an algebraic net $\mathcal{A}$, the `MARKING` module is instantiated via the views in v. Examples follow to clarify this translation. The APN in Fig. 1 lacks executability due to the term in the input arc $(Fork, pk)$, which should be reformulated (Sect. 3.1).

3.3 Example: Twin Queues

We first model a dual queue systems for fair task management. Figures 2 and 3 show APNs using `MSET` and `BAG`. Each APN has two places: *task* for tasks that need to be processed and *queue* for the pair of queues. Figure 2 features three transitions: *d* for duplicating tasks in both queues, *l* to allocate residual tasks nondeterministically, and *s* for processing the leading task and closing the loop.

Both models define a queue using the functional module LIST{X::TRIV}. We utilize embedded lists with the constructor [_] : List{X} -> Elist{X} from module ELIST{X::TRIV}, which renames __ to _,_. A queue is an enclosed sequence like [a, b, a, c]. This approach resolves issues with the subsort linkage X$Elt < NeList{X} < List{X} in LIST (similar to MSET), where terms like (a b c) could ambiguously denote various types (a list, a multiset, a multiset of lists). Embedded lists ensure distinct kinds, which is preferable.

The APN in Fig. 2 is an algebraic net schema representing a family of models. The type parameter at place *task* is uninstantiated, while at place *queue*, it is instantiated by view Elist{X}. Here, $v(task)$ is the identity view on TRIV[3].

The Maude system module that provides a concise and formal description of the signature and semantics of the APN schema shown in Fig. 2, available at https://github.com/lgcapra/rewpt/blob/main/algPT/TWIN-QUEUE-MS.maude, is conveniently reproduced below.

Listing 1.1. Maude translation of the twin queues APN

```
mod TWIN−QUEUE−MS{X :: TRIV} is
 inc MARKING−STR{X} .
 inc MARKING−STR{Elist{X}} * (op mark to markL).
 var M : Marking . var B : Mset{X} . vars X Y Z : X$Elt . vars L L' : List{X} .
 rl [d] : p("queue") |−> [L] [L'] ; p("task") |−> X X B =>
   p("queue") |−> [L,X] [L',X] ; p("task") |−> B .
 crl [1] : p("queue") |−> [L] [L'] ; p("task") |−> X B =>
   p("queue") |−> [L,X] [L'] ; p("task") |−> B if not(X <= B) .
 rl [s] : p("queue") |−> [X,L] [L'] ; p("task") |−> B =>
   p("queue") |−> [L] [L'] ; p("task") |−> B X .
endm

mod TWIN−QUEUE−NAT is
 inc TWIN−QUEUE−MS{Nat} .
 op m0 : −> Marking [memo] .
 eq m0 = p("queue") |−> [nil] [nil] ; p("task") |−> 0 0 0 0 1 1 1 2 2 2 2 .
endm
```

The layout is generated automatically, incorporating module MARKING{X::TRIV, PL::TRIV} twice for different types of places. For simplicity, MARKING-STR{X::TRIV} is provided as a partial instantiation using String for place labels. Renaming the mark "getter" is needed in one import, as operator overloading cannot handle identical arities with varied ranges.

Translating APN Transitions into Rules. Referring to Fig. 2, let us explain how a transition t of the APN (schema) $\mathcal{A} = (\mathcal{N}, v, Y, \tau, g)$ can simply be translated into a rewrite rule: $t : l \Rightarrow r \; if \; cond$.
The sides l and r of the rule are terms of kind Marking both containing a subterm Pmarking{S}, where S = $v(p)$, for each p such that $(p, t) \in F \vee (t, p) \in F$ (conventionally, S also denotes the target sort of $v(p)$; If $v(p)$ is the identity, then

---

[3] Using views with theories as targets helps specify type parameters more accurately.

S is the sort `Elt` of `TRIV`). Different place markings are combined on both sides using `_;_`. The subterms relative to a given p are denoted `p(lab) |-> lms` and `p(lab) |-> rms` (labels univocally identify places) and `lms`, `rms` are `Mset{S}` terms defined as follows: here `B` denotes a new variable of type `Mset{S}`, distinguished from any variables that occur in the arcs connecting t to other places.

- $(p, t) \in F$: If $\tau(p, t) =$ 'u then `lms:= u` else `lms := (u B)`, $u = \tau(p, t)$
- $(t, p) \in F$: If $\tau(t, p) =$ 'u' then `rms := u'` else `rms := (u' B)`, $u' = \tau(t, p)$
- $(t, p) \notin F$: If $\tau(p, t) =$ 'u then `rms := empty{S}` else `rms := B`
- $(p, t) \notin F$: `lms := B`.

The rule condition is easily built from $g(t)$. Constraints ensure that the new variable is bounded. If $\{(t, p), (p, t)\} \subseteq F$ and $\tau(t, p)$ lack a prefix, then $\tau(p, t)$ must too; similarly, if $(p, t) \notin F$ holds, $\tau(t, p)$ must be prefix-free. The prefix marks terms as context-free and allows one to omit input or output edges, aiding in common modeling situations.

For transition d, `X X` on arc $(task, d)$ means d removes two identical elements from place $task$, adding a variable to make arc $(d, task)$ explicit (see Listing 1.1). '`[L] [L']` on arc $(queue, d)$ requires two tokens in $queue$. Module executability requires coherent rules, ensured by simplifying upper-level multiset terms on the left side of the rule using top operator-level equations.

A firing mode (or instance) of transition t corresponds to a ground substitution of variables σ for the corresponding rewrite rule $t : l \Rightarrow r \; if \; cond$, such that $m \equiv \sigma(l) \xrightarrow{t} m' \equiv \sigma(r)$, where m, m' are ground terms of sort `Marking`.

Table 1. State space build of the APN in Fig. 2

e0	# states (solutions)	build time (ms)
ms0	541 (0)	7
ms0 z	2195 (0)	23
ms0 z y x	17429 (0)	132
ms0 z y x x	39734 (0)	322
ms0 ms0	268292 (0)	1805

The `Maude`' rewriting engine analyzes an APN schema without instantiation by treating variables as ground terms. The command identifies final TS states from an initial marking with two empty queues and multiset e0 in place `task`, aliased as `ms0 = x x y y z` with variables `X$Elt`. Variations verify properties like task population preservation. Table 1 shows performance metrics on a mid-level PC with an 11th gen Core i5 CPU as e0 changes.

```
search  p("queue") |-> [nil] [nil] ; p("task") |-> e0 =>! F:Marking .
```

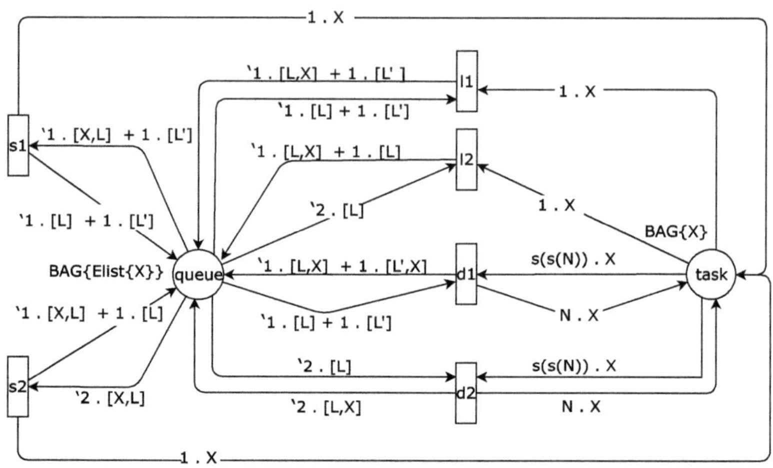

Fig. 3. The twin queues APN using `BAG`.

Lists increase state space, but techniques like SMT and narrowing can mitigate this. The APN schema allows their use, which is in ongoing work. Listing 1.1 also contains an instantiation of the APN schema via the predefined view `Nat` linking the sort `Elt` of `TRIV` to `Nat` in module `NAT`.

Using the Multiset Compact Representation. The APN schema in Fig. 3 depicts the same scenario using the compact multiset definition provided by module `BAG`. The related algebraic specification (https://github.com/lgcapra/rewpt/blob/main/algPT/TWIN-QUEUE-B.maude) is parallel to Listing 1.1, with the only distinction of employing the module `B-MARKING` rather than `MARKING`.

The complex net layout arises from the need to duplicate transitions due to the new multiset definition. The translation of transitions into rewrite rules remains unchanged, except for a context-dependent expression $u = \tau(a)$, extended as $(u + B)$, with B as a new variable of type `Bag{X}`. Listing 1.2 (from module `TWIN-QUEUE-B`) shows the translation of mutually exclusive transitions that assign tasks from place *task* to queues. Both transitions function similarly: (d2) addresses shared state queues, while (d1) manages queues in different states.

Listing 1.2. encoding duplicated transitions in Fig. 3

```
var M : Marking . var B : Bag{X} . vars L L' : List{X} . var LB : Bag{
    Elist{X}} .
var X : X$Elt . var K : NzNat .
rl [d1] : p("task") |-> s(s(N)) . X + B ; p("queue") |-> 1 . [L] + 1 . [L
    '] =>
 p("queue") |-> 1 . [L,X] + 1 . [L',X] ; p("task") |-> N . X + B .
rl [d2] : p("queue") |-> 2 . [L] ; p("task") |-> s(s(N)) . X + B =>
```

Table 2. State space build of the APN in Fig. 3

e0	# states	time (ms)
ms0	541	7
ms0 + 1. 2	2195	30
ms0 + 1. 2 + 1. 1 + 1. 0	17429	178
ms0 + 1. 2 + 1. 1 + 2. 0	39734	520
ms0 + ms0	268292	2360

```
p("task") |-> N . X + B ; p("queue") |-> 2 . [L,X] .
```

Due to the coherence assumption, the term `1 . [L] + 1 . [L']` matches only
lists with different inner states, so it must be paired with `2 . [L]`, which is
used in the second rule. We used the model in Fig. 3 with the same approach as in
Fig. 2. The data in Table 2 represent an instantiation of the APN schema through
view Nat. The alias ms0 indicates the multiset `3 . 0 + 2 . 1 + 1 . 2`, resulting
in varied setups. The search command is:

```
search  p("queue") |-> 2 . [nil] ; p("task") |-> e0  =>! F:Marking .
```

The state-space column shows similar results with slightly worse execution times
compared to the previous model, suggesting that using BAG is not beneficial for
this example and is better for complex scenarios.

4   Algebraic PN with Active Tokens

We enhance Reisig's definition by incorporating active tokens, as in [5]. Linked to
system modules using standard views, these tokens become rewritable "dynamic
entities". We illustrate this through meta-modeling, emphasizing natural benefits
within Maude and our APN definition. Rather than using the cumbersome Maude
meta-model modules for experts, we apply it directly at the object-level. Similar
to the nets-within-nets concept but broader, we define an APN where places
house nested APNs, as described earlier.

4.1   Multilevel Feedback Queues

Figure 4 depicts a simple multilevel feedback queue (MFQ) scheduling algorithm.
It shows the base level (BL) with a metalevel for monitoring and transformation.
Tasks vie for a shared resource, each with a time burst determining system
exit upon completion. Hierarchical queues, using FIFO or Round Robin (RR),
prioritize shorter time slices. The MFQ shifts tasks from high-priority FIFO
queues to lower-priority ones, with RR circulation at the bottom. Tasks begin
at the top-level queue's tail, exiting if they use their burst at the highest queue's
head; otherwise, they move to a lower queue.

The formalization of the model in Fig. 4 is available in https://github.
com/lgcapra/rewpt/blob/main/algPT/MFQ/. It comprises three key modules:

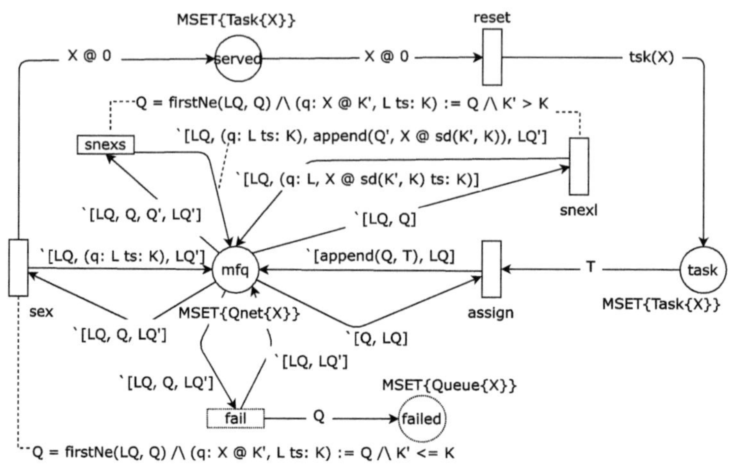

Fig. 4. APN model of a multi-feedback-queue.

`TASK{X::TRIV-NZ}`, `QUEUE{X::TRIV-NZ}`, and `Q-NET{X::TRIV-NZ}`, integrated by the module `MFQ{X::TRIV-NZ}`, which converts net transitions into rewrite rules. The APN places connect to these modules through parameterized views, instantiating `MARKING-STR{X::TRIV}` and defining multisets: `Task{X}`, `Queue{X}`, and `Qnet{X}`. A task is `1 @ b`, with `1` as its label and `b` as the term `Nat` for the residual burst. The theory `TRIV-NZ` extends `TRIV` with the operator `m : Elt -> [NzNat]` to initialize task bursts.

A queue is a task list with a timestamp. A `Queue{X}` is `q: L ts: K`, where `L` is a task list, and `K` is a `NzNat`. The `append` operator adds a task at the end. A queue *network* is a list of queues: `Qnet{X}` is `LQ`, with `LQ` of sort `List{Queue{X}}`[4]. Operators check if a queue network is `ordered`, `insert` a queue properly in a (sub)network, and find the next non-empty, highest priority queue (`firstNe`).

Figure 3 includes places like *task* (available tasks), *mfq* (queue network), and *served* (processed tasks); and transitions like *assign* (task allocation), *sex* (task completion and exit), *snexs* (task moving to the next queue), and *snexl* (task descending to the final queue). Two optional elements enhance these components: transition *reset*, returning a task to the "available" state with its initial time to create a cycle, and *fail* (with place *failed*), simulating a queue breakdown.

The core model, excluding queue failure, was validated using model checking and LTL across various configurations. We instantiated the module `MFQ{X::TRIV-NZ}` with the view `Burst`, mapping the task label to `String` and initializing task bursts. This resulted in the module `MFQ-STR`. For example, the following `search` confirms that without transition *reset*, a system (alias `m0`)

---

[4] Section 3.3 explains why the use of embedded lists.

with three queues and five tasks reaches a final state where all tasks are processed with zero residual burst. The alias is described using **reduce**. Doubling the initial multiset in *task* yields the same result, searching within a 150040-state transition system in about 1 s. Including *reset*, the search predictably lacks a solution.

```
Maude> reduce in MFQ-STR : m0 .
rewrites: 1 in 0ms cpu (0ms real) result Marking:
p("served") |-> empty{Task{Burst}} ;
p("task") |-> "a" @ 1 "a" @ 1 "b" @ 4 "b" @ 4 "c" @ 5 ;
p("mfq") |-> [(q: nil ts: 1), (q: nil ts: 2), q: nil ts: inf]
Maude> search in MFQ-STR : m0 =>! F:Marking .
Solution 1 (state 822)
states: 823  rewrites: 34646 in 10ms cpu (7ms real)
F:Marking --> p("served") |-> "a" @ 0 "a" @ 0 "b" @ 0 "b" @ 0
    "c" @ 0 ; p("task") |-> empty{Task{Burst}} ;
p("mfq") |-> [(q: nil ts: 1), (q: nil ts: 2), q: nil ts: inf]
No more solutions.
states: 823  rewrites: 34646 in 10ms cpu (7ms real)
```

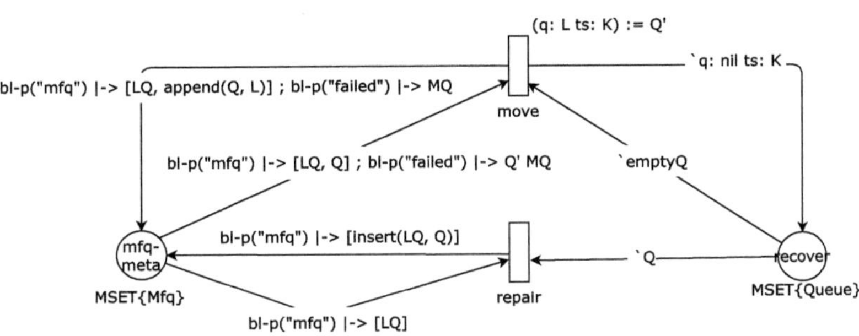

Fig. 5. Meta-reconfiguration of MFQ.

4.2 Nested APNs ("Meta-model")

The APN framework in Maude allows places to link with *system* modules through standardized views, enabling rewritable terms within multisets. This enhances modeling and raises theoretical questions about controlling rewrite rules with the Maude strategy language. We here adopt a fully nondeterministic approach to rule execution. We demonstrate active tokens through a "meta-model" that monitors and reconfigures the MFQ during queue failures. An APN (Fig. 5) is constructed where place *mfq–meta* holds tokens of type Marking, representing a nested APN (Fig. 4); notably, $mfq - meta$ contains a single-element multiset.

This place connects to the nested APN through view Mfq, leading to module MFQ-STR, an instantiation of system module MFQ using labels String. The model includes a Queue place (*recover*) for faulty queues awaiting repair and two key transitions connected to the place $mfq - meta$: one transfers tasks from faulty queues to the top queue and brings them to a repair state, while the other reintegrates repaired queues into the network with insert. Reconfiguration is performed one queue at a time, as indicated by input arcs from the place *recover*.

Listing 1.3 presents the Maude translation, also available at https://github.com/lgcapra/rewpt/blob/main/algPT/MFQ/MFQ-RECONF.maude. The module MFQ-RECONF is concise and aligns with others. Renaming operators and sorts in the base-level model is needed to clarify the notation ambiguity between the base-level and meta-level parts and to prevent issues like those in Sect. 3.3. For this, the intermediate module MFQ-STR-BL is used, where Marking becomes BL-Marking, Pmarking becomes BL-Pmarking, and the constructor p becomes bl-p. Automating this renaming systematically enables arbitrary nesting levels.

Listing 1.3. encoding of APN in Fig. 4

```
mod MFQ—STR—BL is
  inc MFQ—STR * (sort Place{String} to BL—Place{String}, op p to bl—p,
  sort Marking to BL—Marking, sort Pmarking to BL—Pmarking,
  sort Pmarking{Queue{Burst}} to BL—Pmarking{Queue{Burst}},
  sort Pmarking{Qnet{Burst}} to BL—Pmarking{Qnet{Burst}},
  sort Pmarking{Task{Burst}} to BL—Pmarking{Task{Burst}}) .
endm

view Mfq from TRIV to MFQ—STR—BL is
  sort Elt to BL—Marking .
endv

mod MFQ—RECONF is
 inc MARKING—STR{Mfq} .
 inc MARKING—STR{Queue{Burst}} * ( op mark to markT) .
 op meta—m0 : —> [Marking] .
 eq meta—m0 = p("mfq—meta") |—> m0 ; p("recover") |—> empty{Queue{Burst}} .
 vars Q Q' : Queue{Burst} . var L : List{Task{Burst}} . var M : BL—Marking .
 vars LQ LQ' : List{Queue{Burst}} . var MQ : Mset{Queue{Burst}} . var K : NzNat .
 crl [move] : p("mfq—meta") |—> (M ; bl—p("mfq") |—> [LQ, Q] ; bl—p("failed") |—>
      Q' MQ) ; p("recover") |—> empty{Queue{Burst}} =>
   p("mfq—meta") |—> (M ; bl—p("mfq") |—> [LQ, append(Q, L)] ;
   bl—p("failed") |—> MQ) ; p("recover") |—> (q: nil ts: K) if (q: L ts: K) := Q' .
 rl [rec] : p("mfq—meta") |—> (M ; bl—p("mfq") |—> [LQ] ) ; p("recover") |—> Q
     => p("mfq—meta") |—> (M ; bl—p("mfq") |—> [insert(LQ, Q)] ) ;
   p("recover") |—> empty{Queue{Burst}} .
endm
```

The depicted reconfiguration process can be integrated into the BL model. We aimed to show enhanced modeling with APN and active tokens, using standardized module views. For realistic self-adaptation, it is useful (or necessary) to separate system functionality from adaptation through a meta-level.

The APN in Fig. 5, formalized in module `MQ-RECONF` (listing 1.3), can be analyzed using `Maude` facilities. We offer two examples based on the setup `meta-m0`, with MFQ m0 in place *mfq – meta* and place *recover* empty. The BL can be simulated directly at the meta-level; for instance, the following `search` matches those in previous sessions (the model includes *reset*).

```
Maude> search in MFQ-RECONF :
mark(meta-m0[p("mfq-meta")]) =>! F:BL-Marking .
No solution.
states: 150040   rewrites: 6283054 in 1620ms cpu (1618ms real)
```

The next `search` introduces the MFQ transformation at the meta-level for queue network failures, incorporating the BL transition *fail*. The execution time increases significantly (around 3000 s), and the search space grows to more than 50 million states because of numerous MFQ failure modes. About 550,000 final states exhibit a pattern: an empty network in the BL place *mfq* (`[nilQnet]`), empty multisets in the BL place *served* and the metalevel place *recover*, and the three queues of the network in the BL place *failed*. For example:

```
Maude> search in MFQ-RECONF : meta-m0 =>! F:Marking.

...
Solution 260048 (state 3473274)
states: 9208209   rewrites: 99417310 in 1761560ms
F:Marking --> p("mfq-meta") |-> (bl-p("served") |->
empty{Task{Burst}} ; bl-p("task") |-> "a" @ 1 "a" @ 1
   "a" @ 1 "a" @ 1 "b" @ 4 "b" @ 4 ; bl-p("mfq") |-> [nilQnet] ;
bl-p("failed") |-> (q: nil ts: 1) (q: "b" @ 4, "c" @ 4 ts: 2)
q: "c" @ 5, "b" @ 4 ts: 10000) ;
p("recover") |-> empty{Queue{Burst}}
```

5   Conclusion

We introduced using examples of various complexity the first integral representation of APN schema using `Maude`, an algebraic language with rewriting logic semantics. This approach handles pattern matching subtleties and permits rewritable terms as (active) tokens, which improve (meta)modeling. The `Maude` formalization refines Reisig's definition with a concise modular hierarchy. We offer two implementations: one more convenient for pattern matching and the other for complex operations. The APN model design can be easily automated visually. We also aim to introduce stochastic parameters along the lines of [7,13].

The `Maude` rewrite engine's pattern-matching and coherence assumption demand syntactical shortcuts for net inscriptions. We employ nondeterministic semantics; using the `Maude` strategy language for control might help in complex scenarios. Active tokens add complexity: We aim to address scalability with symbolic reachability [8,14] and SMT. Active tokens pose theoretical challenges, such as latent transition conflicts, which are currently being studied.

References

1. Battiston, E., DeCindio, F., Mauri, G.: OBJSA nets: a class of high-level nets having objects as domains, pp. 20–43. Springer, Heidelberg (1988)
2. Bouhoula, A., Jouannaud, J.P., Meseguer, J.: Specification and proof in membership equational logic. Theoret. Comput. Sci. **236**, 35–132 (2000). https://doi.org/10.1016/S0304-3975(99)00206-6
3. Bouhoula, A., Jouannaud, J.P., Meseguer, J.: Specification and proof in membership equational logic. Theoret. Comput. Sci. **236**(1), 35–132 (2000). https://doi.org/10.1016/S0304-3975(99)00206-6
4. Bruni, R., Meseguer, J.: Generalized rewrite theories. In: Baeten, J.C.M., Lenstra, J.K., Parrow, J., Woeginger, G.J. (eds.) Automata, Languages and Programming, pp. 252–266. Springer, Heidelberg (2003). https://doi.org/10.1007/3-540-45061-0_22
5. Bruni, R., Meseguer, J., Montanari, U., Sassone, V.: A comparison of Petri net semantics under the collective token philosophy. In: Hsiang, J., Ohori, A. (eds.) Advances in Computing Science, ASIAN 1998, pp. 225–244. Springer, Heidelberg (1998)
6. Buchs, D., Hostettler, S., Marechal, A., Risoldi, M.: Alpina: an algebraic petri net analyzer. In: Esparza, J., Majumdar, R. (eds.) Tools and Algorithms for the Construction and Analysis of Systems, pp. 349–352. Springer, Heidelberg (2010)
7. Capra, L.: Associating a Markov process with Maude executable modules. In: Proceedings of the 15th International Conference on Simulation and Modeling Methodologies, Technologies and Applications, pp. 106–116. SciTePress (2025)
8. Capra, L., Köhler-Bußmeier, M.: Modular rewritable petri nets: an efficient model for dynamic distributed systems. Theoret. Comput. Sci. **990**, 114397 (2024). https://doi.org/10.1016/j.tcs.2024.114397
9. Ehrig, H., Mahr, B.: Fundamentals of algebraic Specification. EATCS Monographs on TCS. Springer (1985)
10. Goguen, J., Malcolm, G.: Algebraic Semantics of Imperative Programs. MIT Press (1996)
11. Jensen, K., Kristensen, L.M.: Coloured Petri Nets: Modelling and Validation of Concurrent Systems. Springer (2009). https://doi.org/10.1007/b95112
12. Jensen, K., Rozenberg, G.: High-Level Petri Nets: Theory and Application. Springer, Heidelberg (1991)
13. Köhler-Bußmeier, M., Capra, L.: Analysing probabilistic Hornets. In: Amparore, E., Mikulski, L. (eds.) Application and Theory of Petri Nets and Concurrency (PETRI NETS 2025). LNCS, vol. 15714, pp. 287–309. Springer (2025). https://doi.org/10.1007/978-3-031-94634-9_14
14. Köhler-Bußmeier, M., Capra, L.: A "symbolic" representation ofnbsp;object-nets. In: Distributed Computing and Intelligent Technology: 21st International Conference, ICDCIT 2025, Bhubaneswar, India, 8–11 January 2025, Proceedings, pp. 68–74. Springer, Heidelberg (2025). https://doi.org/10.1007/978-3-031-81404-4_6
15. Kummer, O., et al.: An extensible editor and simulation engine for Petri nets: renew. In: Cortadella, J., Reisig, W. (eds.) International Conference on Application and Theory of Petri Nets 2004. Lecture Notes in Computer Science, vol. 3099, pp. 484–493. Springer (2004)
16. Pommereau, F.: Snakes: a flexible high-level petri nets library (tool paper). In: Devillers, R., Valmari, A. (eds.) Application and Theory of Petri Nets and Concurrency, pp. 254–265. Springer, Cham (2015)

17. Reisig, W.: Petri nets and algebraic specifications. Theoret. Comput. Sci. **80**, 1–34 (1991)
18. Verbeek, E., Fahland, D.: CPN ide: an extensible replacement for CPN tools that uses access/CPN. In: Jans, M., Janssenswillen, G., Kalenkova , A., Maggi, F. (eds.) ICPM 2021 Doctoral Consortium and Demo Track 2021, pp. 29–30. CEUR Workshop Proceedings, CEUR-WS.org (2021). Copyright 2021 for this paper by its authors. Use permitted under Creative Commons License Attribution 4.0 International (CC BY 4.0).; 3rd International Conference on Process Mining, ICPM 2021, ICPM 2021 ; Conference date: 31-10-2021 Through 04-11-2021

Reconfigurable Multi-formalism Models for Performance Analysis of Distributed Systems

Lorenzo Capra[1]($\boxtimes$) (iD), Marco Gribaudo[2]($\boxtimes$) (iD), and Mauro Iacono[3]($\boxtimes$) (iD)

[1] Università degli Studi di Milano, via Celoria 18, 20133 Milan, Italy
`lorenzo.capra@unimi.it`
[2] Politecnico di Milano, via Ponzio 34/5, 20133 Milan, Italy
`marco.gribaudo@polimi.it`
[3] Università degli Studi della Campania "L. Vanvitelli",
viale Lincoln 5, 81100 Caserta, Italy
`mauro.iacono@unicampania.it`

Abstract. The process of multiformalism modeling involves selecting the most appropriate formalism for individual system components, while ensuring the preservation of overall system coherence. The increasing complexity and adaptability of contemporary systems necessitate the development of dynamic models capable of addressing these challenges effectively. In this context, we propose a framework predicated on `Maude` for the construction of reconfigurable multiformalism models. Two alternative solutions to this framework are presented. A server management case study, employing stochastic Petri nets and multiclass queuing networks, serves to demonstrate the feasibility of this approach. Empirical experiments indicate that the integration of rewriting techniques within multiformalism modeling has the potential to enhance both the expressiveness and evaluation efficiency of the models.

Keywords: Multiformalism modeling · Rewriting systems · Model reconfiguration · Performance evaluation · Petri nets · Queuing networks

1 Introduction

Complex systems comprise numerous interacting components, thus necessitating flexible modeling techniques to facilitate a comprehensive evaluation. The modeling process aims to distill and retain essential features; however, effective analysis is contingent on the deployment of suitable analytical tools and formalized descriptions that are intrinsically linked to their intended purpose and content. The diverse aspects intrinsic to complex systems give rise to varied representational forms that aim to minimize informational degradation and cognitive dissonance. Specialists in the field develop tools that are tailored to

B. Chatterjee et al. (Eds.): ICDCIT 2026, LNCS 16420, pp. 154–170, 2026.
https://doi.org/10.1007/978-3-032-16632-6_10

their specific objectives. As the intricacy of systems escalates, models based on a single formalism often become either excessively intricate or overly reductive.

Multiformalism modeling constitutes a methodological paradigm for the assessment of system properties, encapsulating both qualitative and quantitative dimensions, through the integration of diverse modeling techniques in a cohesive framework. This methodological approach facilitates the selection of the most appropriate formalism for each individual component of the system, thus enhancing both expressiveness and interpretability while maintaining a unified perspective. The effective analysis of complex multiformalism models necessitates the coordination of various strategies. Advanced multiformalism methodologies typically exploit composability to address the inherent complexities in modeling. Furthermore, flexible analytical tools and strategies, such as decomposition and symbolic techniques, are employed with varying efficacy to mitigate challenges including submodel misalignment and state-space explosion.

The escalating demands for (self-)adaptability and reconfiguration in contemporary distributed systems mandate the formulation of dynamic multiformalism models to effectively address these challenges. This paper introduces a modular framework predicated on `Maude`, a language characterized by purely declarative principles and Rewriting Logic semantics, specifically designed for *reconfigurable* multiformalism models. We explicate and examine two alternative methodologies, employing a server management case study that integrates stochastic Petri nets and multiclass queuing networks, to demonstrate the viability of the proposed approach. Furthermore, we present empirical data to substantiate our findings. The primary focus of this paper is the encoding of multiformalism models utilizing the `Maude` framework, thereby addressing several advanced aspects related to parametrized modules and module operations.

Section 2 reviews related work, while Sect. 3 summarizes the key features of `Maude`. The case study is introduced in Sect. 4. The central Sect. 5 presents a framework built on `Maude` for reconfigurable multiformalism models, using the case study for illustration. It suggests two alternative solutions and provides some experimental data for the case study analysis in Sect. 6. Finally, Sect. 7 wraps up the paper and discusses ongoing work.

2 Related Work

Multiformalism modeling [1,14,15,19], frequently associated with *multisolution*, is extensively studied in the literature through the use of fixed formalism combinations, such as in DEDS [4], SMART [10], and SHARPE [20], as well as in scenarios involving dynamic combinations like AToM^3 [18] and Möbius [12]. The research discussed in this paper is somewhat connected to OsMoSys [13] and SIMTHESys [2,16], which employ a multisolution methodology. These systems, like Möbius, create optimized executable models from descriptive representations that include programmatically defined behaviors. OsMoSys orchestrates workflows, activating external solvers based on submodel results, while SIMTHESys separates model descriptions from formalism elements. This allows SIMTHESys to define new formalisms and offer analysis tools, facilitating the automatic creation of multiformalism solvers. This process supports user experimentation with minimal software development when it is successful. See [3] for a detailed overview of the tools available and a discussion of their limits.

3   The Maude System

Maude [11] is an expressive, high-performance, purely declarative language with rewriting logic semantics [5]. The Maude runtime provides various facilities for model checking, verification of LTL formulae, and symbolic reachability. Maude has served as a logical framework for various other formalisms, including Petri nets, Automata, and Process Algebras, which, despite their strength, do not possess the essential features needed for intuitively defining adaptable systems.

Maude syntax is based on *equations* and *rules*. Each side of a rule or equation is a *term* of a certain *kind*, which may involve variables. Rules and equations operate through intuitive rewriting, where instances on the left side are replaced with instances on the right.

A *functional* module defines operations using equations as simplifications. It outlines a *equational theory* $(\Sigma, E \cup A)$ of membership equational logic: Σ is the signature, which includes the declaration of *sorts, subsorts, kinds*[1] and *operators*; E contains equations and membership axioms; and A contains operators' equational attributes (e.g., *assoc, comm, ide*). The mathematical model of $(\Sigma, E \cup A)$ is the *initial algebra* $T_{\Sigma/E \cup A}$, formed by the equivalence classes of the relation induced by $E \cup A$ in the ground-term algebra T_{Σ}. Under the confluence conditions (modulo-A) subsort decreasing and termination in (Σ, E), any ground term is rewritten in a unique canonical form that has the least sort in the sub-sort PO. The canonical term algebra is isomorphic to the initial algebra, ensuring consistency between mathematical and operational semantics.

A *system* module includes *rewrite rules* that represent local transitions in a concurrent system. It defines a *rewrite theory* [5] $\mathcal{R} = (\Sigma, E \cup A, R)$. Here, $(\Sigma, E \cup A)$ acts as the underlying equational theory, and R is a set of rewrite rules. This theory captures the behavior of a concurrent system, with $(\Sigma, E \cup A)$ defining the algebraic structure of the states and R describing the concurrent transitions. The initial model of $\mathcal{R}$ provides each kind k with a labeled transition system (TS) where states are elements of $T_{\Sigma/E \cup A, k}$ and state transitions occur as $[t] \overset{[\alpha]}{\to} [t']$, with $[\alpha]$ denoting an equivalence class of rewrites. The property of *coherence* [11] ensures that a strategy reducing terms to canonical forms before applying rules (adopted by the Maude rewrite engine) is sound and complete.

4   Case Study

The case study involves a server comprising two computing facilities that are both vulnerable to faults and can be repaired. This extends the example found in

---

[1] kinds are implicit equivalence classes formed by connected components of sorts under the subsort partial order, and terms of a kind without a sort denote *errors*.

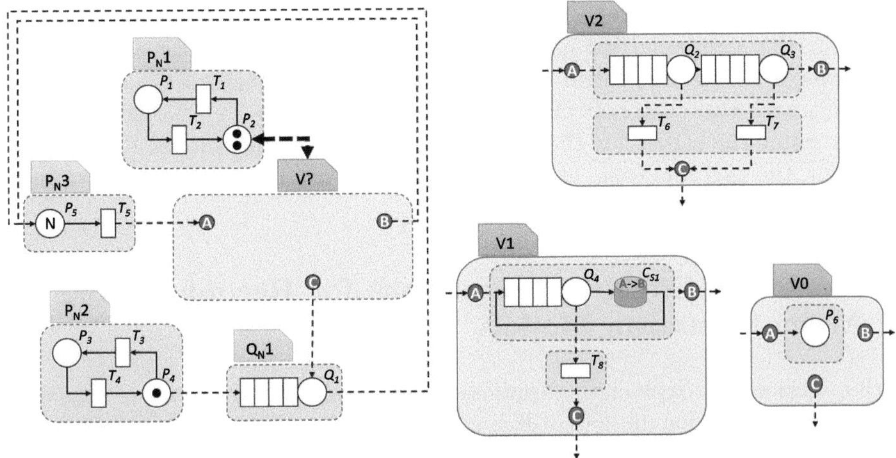

Fig. 1. The model for the case study system.

[16], where the implementation within SIMTHESys is detailed through formalism definitions. Each facility is equipped with buffers for incoming requests and stops accepting new requests once the buffer is full. A front-end system directs requests to these facilities, enabling the second facility to handle jobs initially assigned to the first if they are not processed before a timeout. Requests are processed in two sequential phases, ideally executed by two servers working in tandem. To handle times of high request influx, any request that exceeds a set time in the queue is redirected to a third backup server. Maintenance schedules periodically make all three nodes unavailable. When one node in the tandem system becomes unavailable, the other node takes care of both processing stages. The system is described by three stochastic Petri Nets (SPN) submodels, labeled P_N1, P_N2, and P_N3, which cover fault/repair processes and request injection. In addition, two Multiclass Queue Network submodels (MQN) with exponentially distributed service times (Q_N1 and $V?$) are used for the three service nodes (Fig. 1).

SIMTHESys bridges facilitate interactions among submodels, linking MQN and SPN elements. In particular, the arc from the SPN place P_4 to the MQN queue Q_1 denotes an enabling, while the arcs from the SPN transitions to the MQN queues enqueue tasks upon transition firing. In contrast, arcs from MQN queues (Q_1, Q_3, C_{S1}) to SPN place P_5 create a token after queue processing. Arcs from MQN queues to SPN transitions ($Q_2 \rightarrow T_6$, $Q_3 \rightarrow T_7$, $Q_4 \rightarrow T_8$) extend the transition enabling to remove a task from the queue when activated.

The figure's left section shows the main model: submodel P_N3 with place P_5 and transition T_5, defining request arrivals. The primary service is the rewritable model $V?$. The backup node is submodel Q_N1 with queue Q_1. Petri net models P_N1 and P_N2 control subsystems: the backup node has on-off behavior (models P_N2 and Q_N1), while the primary subsystem uses a basic Petri net with two states and tokens (P_N1). Replacement of $V?$ with $V2$, $V1$, or $V0$ (right side of figure) depends on tokens in place P_2. When both servers are available (two tokens in P_2), submodel $V2$ uses individual queues (Q_2, Q_3) for each server. If one server is down (one token in P_2), submodel $V1$ replaces $V2$, using a single queue Q_4 with two customer classes. the first stage enter a class switch (C_{S1}) to either reenter the server for the second stage or leave the system. If both nodes are down, the system stops, and the queue is replaced by place P_6 in submodel $V0$, marking the current job stage.

5   Maude: An Effective Framework for Reconfigurable Multi-formalism Models

In this section, we explore the application of `Maude` and its runtime support as a rewriting engine for models utilizing multiple formalisms. The benefits of this approach are numerous, including the flexibility and modularity of modeling, as well as efficiency, soundness, ease of integrating with existing tools, and potential for upgrades. We take advantage of `Maude`'s capabilities for formal verification and additionally utilize a new quantitative analysis feature. This feature is based on associating a Markov process with `Maude` executable modules, as introduced in [8,9] for rewritable SPN and further developed in [7].

After intuitively describing the general approach to multiformalism modeling using `Maude`, we will instantiate it in the case study. We provide some technical details through code excerpts (for the reader's convenience) and refer to the online repository https://github.com/lgcapra/rewpt/tree/main/multiformalism for a complete description.

5.1   Reconfigurable Multiformalism Models in `Maude`

In the `Maude` system, multiformalism encoding is based on a simple, compact, and extensible module hierarchy, some of which are *parametrized*. We propose two methods: one simple and the other elegant and concise, using advanced `Maude` features. We'll focus on the simple method to enable easy reuse of existing modules encoding specific formalisms.

Parametrized modules use type parameters defined by (functional) *theories*, which set the syntactic and semantic properties for parameter modules. Theories, while similar to functional modules, need not be Church-Rosser or terminating and have loose semantics, accepting any algebra that satisfies their equations and membership axioms. In `Maude`, *views* connect a source theory to a target module or theory, specifying the mapping of sorts and operators.

Solution 1. As usual, the formalization is based on multisets, which are implemented both as a commutative monoid built on a set or in a more compact way as weighted sums (module `BAG{X :: TRIV}`), for efficiency reasons.

We rely upon a fundamental concept: a multiformalism model is constructed by integrating multiple heterogeneous model components (e.g., Petri nets, queue networks, BPMN, activity diagrams, process algebra, etc.) that collectively maintain a notion of distributed state. This notion is formalized by the theory of commutative monoids (`C-MONOID`, see the excerpt below), which requires a sort `Elt` and an associative-commutative (AC) juxtaposition operation. This theory describes the parameter of the functional module `NETWORK{L :: C-MONOID}`, which provides the simple Abstract Data Type (ADT) of a multiformalism model.

The abstract structure of the model is characterized by the sort `Network`, its subsort `Node`, and the AC juxtaposition (of SPSVERBc5s) `_,_`, which uses the ground term `emptyNetW` as its identity element. To put it another way, a multiformalism model functions as a multiset (or a commutative monoid) made up of potentially diverse `Network` components, referred to as nodes herein. The concept is simple: by appropriately "instantiating" the various node types through specific subsort relationships, we can construct a model composed of various concrete components that interact via shared state elements, known as *places*.

A `NetSys` term consists of a `Network` and a `S$Elt`, which pertains to the module's parameter sort, and it depicts a network of interconnected nodes with a distributed associated *state*.

In our example, the nodes in the network utilize a state concept similar to the *marking* of a Petri net, characterized by a multiset of places. This is efficiently represented using the `PBAG{PL ::TRIV}` module, where the trivial theory `TRIV` consists solely of the sort `Elt` declaration. The module's type parameter specifies the place label, and we use natural numbers to index places. This flexibility in place labeling is crucial, as we will detail later. The AC operator `_+_`, also designated as a constructor, describes multisets as weighted sums. For instance, the term `3. p(1) + 1. p(2)` of sort `Pbag`, derived from the module instantiation `PBAG{Nat}`, signifies a multiset with three instances of place p_1 and one of p_2. The parametrized view `S-Pag{PL :: TRIV}` is employed to instantiate the `C-MONOID` theory as a multiset of places through a suitable mapping. This view allows us to develop the ADT of heterogeneous networks that incorporate the distributed state notion of marking, as specified in `NETWORK{S :: C-MONOID}`.

```
fth C—MONOID is
    sort Elt .
    op 0 : —> Elt .
    op _+_ : Elt Elt —> Elt [assoc comm id: 0] .
endfth
```

```
fmod NETWORK{S :: C—MONOID} is
 protecting EXT—BOOL .
 sorts Node Network NetSys .
 subsort Node < Network .
 op emptyNetW : —> Network [ctor] .
 op _,_ : Network Network —> Network [ctor assoc comm prec 123 id: emptyNetW] .
 op _:_ : Network S$Elt —> NetSys [ctor prec 125] . *** heterogeneous network
 op netw : NetSys —> Network .
 op state : NetSys —> S$Elt .
```

```
vars N N' : Network . var M : S$Elt .
eq netw((N : M)) = N .
eq state((N : M)) = M .
op remove : Network Network -> Network .
eq remove((N, N'), N) = N' .
eq remove(N, N') = N [owise] .
op in : Network Network -> Bool .
eq in((N, N'), N) = true .
eq in(N, N') = false [owise] .
endfm
```

```
view S-Pbag{PL :: TRIV} from C-MONOID to PBAG{PL} is
sort Elt to Pbag .
op 0 to nilP .
endv
```

Components Used in the Case-Study. We employ two types of nodes: Stochastic Petri Nets (SPN) and Multi-class Queue Networks (MQN). Regarding the SPN category, we reuse the signature of (rewritable) SPN as cited in [8], which is essentially based on the (rewritable) Place-Transition (PT) nets with inhibitor edges as specified in [6,9]. The SPN framework includes a small hierarchy of modules available in https://github.com/lgcapra/rewpt. For convenience, some modules demonstrate the network components and their relation to the network.

SPN. The functional module `SPN-NODE{PL :: TRIV}` specifies the SPN nodes by including `NETWORK` and the preset module `SPN-SIG`, which is parameterized by place and transition labels. Here, the type parameter `PL` is used as a actual parameter in these imported modules. Importing `SPN-SIG` with the `protecting` mode ensures that its original semantics remain intact, while importing `NETWORK` in the `extending` mode means that the `Network` sort will be augmented with additional data values, without changing those already defined.

SPN transitions, categorized as data types `Tran`, are characterized by labels associated with adjacency lists. These are represented as `Pbag` triples in the format `[I, O, H]`. These labels comprise a descriptive tag, exemplified as a `String` in this context, a `Float` that denotes the rate parameter of a negative exponential distribution governing the firing delay, and a `Nat`, which delineates the firing policy. For example, the ground term:

```
t("a", 1.5, 0) |-> [1 . p(1) + 2 . p(2), 1 . p(1), 2 . p(1)]
```

delineates a transition characterized by the label "a", an exponential firing rate $\mu = 1.5$, and an infinite-server type. This transition requires exactly one token in place p_1 and at least two tokens in place p_2 to fire. When activated, it will remove two tokens from p_2. The PT net underlying an SPN, which is a type of `Net`, is clearly defined in a modular manner using the AC juxtaposition ; and the subsort relationship `Tran < Net`.

By using the predefined operator `firingRate`, we can specify rates that depend on marking: The current setup relies on the enabling degree ($ed(t, m)$), which indicates the number of transitions that are simultaneously enabled in a marking. Under the infinite server policy (0), the rate of transition is exponential at $\mu \cdot ed(t, m)$. Meanwhile, under the k-server policy, where $k > 0$, it becomes $\mu \cdot min(ed(t, m), k)$.

In order to facilitate the reuse of SPN transitions within a multiformalism framework, it is imperative to encapsulate the SPN signature, here designated as the SPN-SIG module, alongside the ADT of the network, designated as the NETWORK module, in a novel functional module called SPN-NODE. This newly formed module should incorporate the subsort relationship Net < Node. This approach allows standardized addition of new node types.

```
fmod SPN-NODE{PL :: TRIV} is
   extending NETWORK{S-Pbag{PL}} . protecting SPN-SIG{String, PL} .
   subsort Net < Node .
endfm
```

Multi-class Queue Networks. Multi-queue networks (MQNs) consist of sequences of individual servers, defined as Server terms in the SERVER{PL :: TRIV} module. Each server includes a Place and a Float, where the Float denotes the exponential service rate, expressed as P @ F.

The MQN signature is defined in the module QUEUE{PL :: TRIV}, including parameterized modules LIST and PBAG in protecting mode. A basic MQN form, or SimpleQ, is a term formed by concatenating a non-empty list of elementary queues, NeList{Server}, via a parameterized LIST view, ending with a Place. This is denoted as NeL > P. A complete MQN structure, Queue, includes a SimpleQ prefixed by two Pbag terms in [], representing input and inhibitor conditions. Thus, SimpleQ < Queue is the subsort relationship.

MQN can be effectively represented using this notation. For example, the SimpleQ term p(1) @ 1.0 p(2) @ 1.5 > p(3) indicates a two-class queue, while [2 . p(1), nilP] p(4) @ 2.0 > p(5) shows a one-class Queue that needs two tokens in p(1) to be activated. MQN nodes connect easily to heterogeneous networks via the QUEUE-NODE module, which uses the distributed state marking concept (NETWORK) and MQN signature (QUEUE). The nodes can be combined (,): if q1 and q2 are Queue terms with the endpoint of q1 that aligns with the start of q2, then q1, q2 represents their sequence, differing in time semantics from a single MQN that includes both.

```
fmod SERVER{PL :: TRIV} is
   protecting PLACE{PL} . protecting FLOAT .
   sort Server .
   op _@_ : Place Float -> Server [prec 19 ctor] .
   op mu : Server -> Float .
   op p : Server -> Place .
   var P : Place . var F : Float .
   eq mu(P @ F) = F .
   eq p(P @ F) = P .
endfm
```

```
view Server{PL :: TRIV} from TRIV to SERVER{PL} is
   sort Elt to Server .
endv

fmod QUEUE{PL :: TRIV} is
  protecting LIST{Server{PL}} * (sort List{Server{PL}} to List{Server},
    sort NeList{Server{PL}} to NeList{Server}, op nil to nilElQ) .
  protecting PBAG{PL} .
  sorts Queue SimpleQ Server .
  subsort Server < SimpleQ < Queue .
  vars Q Q' : Server . var SQ : SimpleQ . var Qu : Queue . vars M M' M'' : Pbag .
  vars LQ LQ' LQ'' : List{Server} . var NeLQ : NeList{Server} . var P : Place .
  op _>_ : NeList{Server} Place -> SimpleQ [ctor] .
  op _>_ : Server Place -> Server [ctor ditto] . *** an elementary queue
  op [_,_] _ : Pbag Pbag SimpleQ -> Queue [ctor] .
  eq [nilP, nilP] SQ = SQ .
  op ql : Queue -> NeList{Server} . *** the enclosed list of elementary queues
  eq ql(LQ > P) = LQ .
  eq ql([M, M'] SQ) = ql(SQ) .
  op out : Queue -> Place .
  eq out(LQ > P) = P .
  eq out([M, M'] SQ) = out(SQ) .
  op well-def : NeList{Server} -> Bool .
  op pin : Queue -> Place .
  eq pin(Q LQ > P) = p(Q) .
  eq pin([M, M'] SQ ) = pin(SQ) .
 ceq well-def(LQ Q LQ' Q' LQ'') = false if p(Q) = p(Q') .
  eq well-def(Q LQ) = true [owise] .
  op clients : List{Server} Pbag -> [Nat] [memo] .
 ceq clients(Q LQ, M) = M[p(Q)] + clients(LQ, M) if well-def(Q LQ) .
  eq clients(nilElQ, M) = 0 .
  op clients : Queue Pbag -> [Nat] .
  eq clients(Qu, M) = clients(ql(Qu), M) .
  op qenabled : Queue Pbag -> Bool . *** the queue "enabling" condition
  eq qenabled(SQ, M) = true .
  eq qenabled([M, M'] SQ, M'') = enabCond(M, M', M'') .
  op cap : Server -> NzNat .
  eq cap(X:Server) = cap(pin(X:Server)) .
  op nextPosDef : List{Server} Place -> Place [memo] .
  eq nextPosDef(LQ , P) = if LQ == nilElQ then P else p(head(LQ )) fi .
endfm

fmod QUEUE-NODE{PL :: TRIV} is
  extending NETWORK{S-Pbag{PL}} . protecting QUEUE{PL} .
  sort QueueNet .
  subsort Queue < Node QueueNet < Network .
  op _,_ : QueueNet QueueNet -> QueueNet [ctor ditto] .
endfm
```

Node Dynamics. The dynamics of a multiformalism model is defined by system modules, each linked to a particular type of node. In our example, we utilize the parametrized modules SPN-NODE-SYS and QUEUE-NODE-SYS. These modules include conditional rewrite rules that dictate the semantics of nodes within a network. These rules locally alter the marking of a SysNet term N : M, which signifies a network of interconnected nodes along with a multiset of places, due to the occurrence of an SPN transition or the execution of a service for a client in an MQN, which either advances to the next server or leaves the MQN. Leaving out technical details, it should be noted that the free variable **rate** is bound (using a matching equation :=) to an expression that precisely outlines the time semantics for the associated event. In the context of an MQN, this is determined by the proportion of clients at a certain place in relation to the total MQN population. This representation enables the automatic derivation of the CTMC generator matrix, according to the method suggested in [7].

```
mod SPN−NODE−SYS{PL :: TRIV} is
  including SPN−NODE{PL} .
  var N : Network . vars B B' : Pbag . var K : NzNat . var rate : Float . var T : Tran .
  crl [spn−t] : (N , T) : B => (N , T) : B' if enabled(T, B) /\ B' := firing(T, B) /\
      rate := firingRate(T, B) .
endm
```

```
mod QUEUE−NODE−SYS{PL :: TRIV} is
  including QUEUE−NODE{PL} . including CONVERSION .
  var N : Network . var S : Server . var Q : Queue . vars LS LS' : List{Server} .
  var M : Pbag . var NeLQ : NeList{Server} . var K : NzNat .
  var rate : Float . var P : Place .
  crl [q−firing] : (N , Q) : M => (N , Q) : M + 1 . P − 1 . p(S)
    if LS S LS' := ql(Q) /\ mu(S) > 0.0 /\ K := M[p(S)] /\ K > 0 /\
    qenabled(Q, M) /\ P := nextPosDef(LS',out(Q) ) /\
    rate := mu(S) * float(K) / float(clients(ql(Q), M)) .
endm
```

Case Study's Model. The multiformalism model's encoding, as illustrated in Fig. 1, is detailed in the excerpt below. The related system module (MQN-SPN) effectively merges the two system modules that outline the dynamics of the nodes' dynamics. In addition, it defines the rules ($[V_i > V_j]$) that dictate the structural transformation of a network component, based on the marking of the place p_2.

This methodology represents a conventional approach to construct a multiformalism model composed of various types of reconfigurable components.

```
mod MQN−SPN is
  including SPN−NODE−SYS{Nat} . including QUEUE−NODE−SYS{Nat} .
  var K : NzNat . *** model parameter
  vars N N' N'' : Network . var S : Pbag .
  ops t0 t1 t2 t3 t4 t5 t6 : −> Tran .
  ops eq1 eq2 eq3 : −> Server .
```

```
eq eq1 = p(7) @ 1.0 .
eq eq2 = p(1) @ 1.5 .
eq eq3 = p(6) @ 2.5 .
ops q1 q2 q3 q23 : -> Queue [memo] .
eq q1 = [1 . p(5), nilP] eq1 > p(0) .
eq q2 = [2 . p(2), nilP] eq2 > p(6) .
eq q3 = [2 . p(2), nilP] eq3 > p(0) .
eq q23 = [1 . p(2), nilP] q1(q2) q1(q3) > out(q3) . *** multi-class queue
op network : -> Network .
op netsys : NzNat -> NetSys .
eq t0 = t("start", 1.0, 1 ) |-> [1 . p(0), 1 . p(1), nilP] .
eq t1 = t("switch1", 0.5, 1 ) |-> [1 . p(3), 1 . p(2), nilP] .
eq t2 = t("switch2", 0.05, 1 ) |-> [1 . p(2), 1 . p(3), nilP] .
eq t3 = t("on", 2.0, 1 ) |-> [1 . p(4), 1 . p(5), nilP] .
eq t4 = t("off", 1.0, 1 ) |-> [1 . p(5), 1 . p(4), nilP] .
eq t5 = t("rem1", 1.0, 1 ) |-> [1 . p(1), 1 . p(7), nilP] .
eq t6 = t("rem6", 1.5, 1 ) |-> [1 . p(6), 1 . p(7), nilP] .
op V : NzNat -> [Network] [memo] . *** variable component (depends on p2)
eq V(2) = q2 , q3 , t5 , t6 . *** "out" of q2 is "in" for q3: sequential composition
eq V(1) = q23 , t6 . *** multi-class queue
eq V(0) = p(eq2) @ 0.0 p(eq3) @ 0.0 > out(q3) . *** "dead" queue
eq network = t0 , t1 , t2 , t3 , t4 , t5 , t6 , q1 , V(2) .
eq netsys(K) = network : K . p(0) + 2 . p(2) + 1 . p(5) .
*** structural rewriting
crl [V2>V1] : N : S => N' , V(1) : S if S[p(2)] = 1 /\ N'' , N' := N /\ N'' = V(2) .
crl [V2>V0] : N : S => N' , V(0) : S if S[p(2)] = 0 /\ N'' , N' := N /\ N'' = V(2) .
crl [V1>V2] : N : S => N' , V(2) : S if S[p(2)] = 2 /\ N'' , N' := N /\ N'' = V(1) .
crl [V1>V0] : N : S => N' , V(0) : S if S[p(2)] = 0 /\ N'' , N' := N /\ N'' = V(1) .
crl [V0>V2] : N : S => N' , V(2) : S if S[p(2)] = 2 /\ N'' , N' := N /\ N'' = V(0) .
endm
```

Solution 2. This paper introduces a novel framework for multiformalism modeling within the Maude system. The principal aim is to enhance the characterization of nodes in a heterogeneous network, thereby aiding the modeler's tasks. Conceptually, these nodes are interconnected via a common understanding of distributed state and exhibit intrinsic semantics that lead to local state transformations. Although this concept was previously implicit in formalizations, it has now been explicitly articulated and encapsulated within the theory denoted NODE, further extending the theory referred to as C-MONOID.

The principal component of NODE theory is an operator, symbolized as next, which encapsulates the reachability relationship between the internal states of a node. The construct StateRate, furnished with suitable accessors, forms a pair that consists of a reachable state and a floating-point value. Thus, when presented with a node and its current state, this operator produces a multiset delineating the possible one-step transitions from the node's current state to new local states, along with the corresponding rates. This multiset corresponds to the sort StatesRates, which is conventionally characterized as a free commutative monoid. Fundamentally, this operator embodies the potentially non-deterministic transition rule that governs each network node. A comprehensive rationale for employing a multiset rather than a set emerges from the possibility of multiple transitions from a single source state to the same target. As elucidated in [7,8], this factor must be carefully considered to accurately compute the stochastic matrix of a model.

This methodology can be seamlessly extended to incorporate structural reconfigurations of nodes. This can be achieved, for instance, by employing multisets of triplets to represent novel configurations, which consist of nodes and their states, along with their associated transition rates.

The `NETWORK-SIG` module, similar to `NETWORK{S :: C-MONOID}` in Solution 1, defines the network architecture's abstract signature but without parameterization and adds the `State` sort. The `NETWORK-NODE{N :: NODE}` module, importing `NETWORK-SIG` in `protecting` mode, integrates nodes into the network through `N$State < State` and `N$Node < Network{N} < Network` subsort relationships and uses operator overloading for handling homogeneous subnetworks.

The system module `NETWORK-SYS{N :: NODE}` includes `NETWORK-NODE{N}` and defines in a systematic way the rewrite rule that encodes inner state transitions using the operator `next` required by the theory `NODE`. The remaining part, which depends on the specific model, is skipped.

This subsection succinctly elucidates the concrete methodology by which a specified node type is integrated into the network using the second methodological approach. In our discourse, we focus on SPN nodes; however, this procedure is applicable to all types of nodes in a standard manner. For each node type, we delineate a functional module (e.g. `SPN-NODE`) adhering to a straightforward template: These modules are parameterized based on node labels and encompass the node signatures under a modality `protecting`, as well as the specific definition of a multiset of state transitions (inclusive of their associated rates). Furthermore, each module includes a definition of the `next` operator. For example, the definition of `next` for SPN nodes reflects the reachability relation established on the markings by the transition firing rule.

The system module that formalizes the case study (for which a small excerpt is given) is analogous to the first solution, except for the integration of two instances of `NETWORK-SYS{N :: NODE}` through two parametrized views that link the parameter N to the modules `SPN-NODE` and `QUEUE-NODE`, respectively.

```
fth NODE is
    including C-MONOID . protecting FLOAT .
    sort Node . *** network node
    sort StateRate . *** pair (state,rate)
    sort StatesRates . *** multiset of (state,rate)
    subsort StateRate < StatesRates .
    op state : StateRate -> Elt .
    op rate : StateRate -> Float .
    op noStateRate : -> StatesRates .
    op __ : StatesRates StatesRates -> StatesRates [assoc comm id: noStateRate].
    op next : Node Elt -> StatesRates . *** non-deterministic "firing" rule
```

```
endfth

fmod NETWORK-SIG is
   sorts Network State NetSys .
   op emptyNetW : -> Network [ctor] .
   op _,_ : Network Network -> Network [ctor assoc comm prec 123 id: emptyNetW] .
   op _:_ : Network State -> NetSys [ctor prec 125] . *** network plus state
   op netw : NetSys -> Network .
   op state : NetSys -> State .
   vars N N' : Network . var M : State .
   eq netw((N : M)) = N .
   eq state((N : M)) = M .
   op remove : Network Network -> Network .
   eq remove((N, N'), N) = N' .
   eq remove(N, N') = N [owise] .
   op in : Network Network -> Bool .
   eq in((N, N'), N) = true .
   eq in(N, N') = false [owise] .
endfm

fmod NETWORK-NODE{N :: NODE} is
  protecting NETWORK-SIG .
  sorts Network{N} NetSys{N} .
  subsort N$Node < Network{N} < Network .
  subsort N$Elt < State .
  subsort NetSys{N} < NetSys .
  op _,_ : Network{N} Network{N} -> Network{N} [ctor ditto] . *** overloading
  op _:_ : Network{N} N$Elt -> NetSys{N} [ctor ditto] .
endfm

mod NETWORK-SYS{N :: NODE} is
  including NETWORK-NODE{N} .
  var NW : Network . var N : N$Node . vars M M' : N$Elt .
  var SR : N$StateRate . var SRs : N$StatesRates . var R : Float .
  crl [network-firing-rule] : (N, NW) : M => (N, NW) : M' if SR SRs := next(N, M) /\
       M' := state(SR) /\ R := rate(SR) .
endm

fmod SPN-NODE{L :: TRIV, PL :: TRIV} is
  protecting SPN-SIG{L, PL} . protecting MSET-MARKING-RATE{PL} .
  var T : Tran . var N : Net .
  vars M M' : Pbag . var MS : StatesRates . var rate : Float .
  op next : Net Pbag -> StatesRates .
  eq next(N, M) = $next(N, noStateRate, M) [owise] .
  op $next : Net StatesRates Pbag -> StatesRates .
  eq $next(emptyNet, MS, M) = MS .
 ceq $next(N ; T, MS, M) = $next(N, MS (M' -- rate) , M) if enabled(T, M) /\
     M' := firing(T, M) /\ rate := firingRate(l(T),I(q(T)), M) .
  eq $next(N ; T, MS, M) = $next(N, MS , M) [owise] .
endfm
```

```
view SpnNode{PL :: TRIV} from NODE to SPN-NODE{String, PL} is
   sort Node to Net .
   sort Elt to Pbag .
   op 0 to nilP .
endv
...

mod MQN-SPN-2 is
   including NETWORK-SYS{SpnNode{Nat}} * (sort Network{SpnNode{Nat}} to
     Network{Net}, sort NetSys{SpnNode{Nat}} to NetSys{Net}) .
   including NETWORK-SYS{QueueNode{Nat}} * (sort Network{QueueNode{Nat}} to
       Network{Queue}, sort NetSys{QueueNode{Nat}} to NetSys{Queue}) .
*** similar to MQN-SPN
endm
```

6   Experimental Evidence

Table 1 presents some experimental results related to the `Maude` encoding of the
case study. They refer to the transition system (TS) generated by the para-
metric alias `netsys(N)` for increasing values of N (the initial population of the
network). For example, the following command – which has no solutions for any
N– searches for final states throughout the TS. Using slightly different shapes of
the command, we can check other base properties, e.g. preservation of the population in the system. Note that actual performance measurement (e.g., system
response time) has not been reported since it depends only on the parameters
of the model, and their computation time is independent of the actual values
provided. As an illustrative example, we only report system throughput in the
last column (assuming that all structural reconfigurations have a 0.05 rate; we
solved the ergodic CTMC isomorphic to the TS, derived using the approach
defined in [7]). Instead, the table shows the relative scalability of the proposed
approach, highlighting that relatively large systems can be analyzed in a few
dozens or hundreds of seconds on a conventional laptop equipped with an 11th-
Gen Core i5 and 32 GB RAM. Noticeably, solution 2 shows better performance
as N grows, likely due to the different encoding of inner node state transitions
(more frequent than rewrites due to structural changes).

```
Maude> search in MQN-SPN : netsys(N) =>! F:NetSys .
```

Table 1. Transition System build of the case-study

N	# states	build time Sol 1 (sec)	build time Sol 2 (sec)	Thr (jobs/sec)
10	5.148	5	5	2,3
20	31.878	40	38	4,1
30	98.208	153	141	6,1
40	222.138	430	380	10,7
50	421.668	690	524	14,4
60	714.798	1.113	998	19,8
70	1.119.528	2.318	1.840	24,8
80	1.653.858	4.480	3.562	29,7
90	2.335.778	8.429	6.524	35,5
100	3.183.318	15.290	12.365	39,2

7   Conclusions

We have introduced a multiformalism modeling framework for reconfigurable or adaptive distributed systems, fully implemented through the Maude system. The presented case study demonstrates the practical advantages of this method, highlighting improved modeling flexibility, modularity, and efficiency.

Present research is advancing on two main paths: our primary goal is to enhance the Maude multiformalism framework by incorporating compositional operators that emphasize network symmetries (a kind of graph automorphism). This is intended to derive a quotient transition system that is isomorphic to a lumped Markov process, following the approach described in [8,9] for rewritable SPN and that outlined in [17] for a type of higher-order Petri nets.

The short to medium-term goal is to integrate the Maude rewrite engine into the SIMTHESys multiformalism framework. This effort is expected to significantly enhance the framework's modeling capabilities. Within the SIMTHESys modeling framework, Maude functions as a solution engine, handling the structural components of the model during the solution phase. This facilitates the dynamic reconfiguration of the model's representation at solution time, enabling the addition of new features without requiring a redesign of either the conceptual framework or the SIMTHESys*ER* solvers generation tool.

References

1. Ardagna, D., et al.: Predicting the performance of big data applications on the cloud: D. Ardagna et al. J. Supercomput. **77**(2), 1321–1353 (2021)
2. Barbierato, E., Gribaudo, M., Iacono, M.: Modeling hybrid systems in SIMTHE-Sys. Electron. Notes Theor. Comput. Sci. **327**, 5–25 (2016). https://doi.org/10.1016/j.entcs.2016.09.021

3. Barbierato, E., Gribaudo, M., Iacono, M., Jakóbik, A.: Exploiting CloudSim in a multiformalism modeling approach for cloud based systems. Simul. Model. Pract. Theory **93**, 133–147 (2019). https://doi.org/10.1016/j.simpat.2018.09.018

4. Bause, F., Buchholz, P., Kemper, P.: A toolbox for functional and quantitative analysis of deds. In: Proceedings of the 10th International Conference on Computer Performance Evaluation: Modelling Techniques and Tools, TOOLS 1998, pp. 356–359. Springer, London (1998)

5. Bruni, R., Meseguer, J.: Generalized rewrite theories. In: Baeten, J.C.M., Lenstra, J.K., Parrow, J., Woeginger, G.J. (eds.) ICALP 2003. LNCS, vol. 2719, pp. 252–266. Springer, Heidelberg (2003). https://doi.org/10.1007/3-540-45061-0_22

6. Capra, L.: Rewriting logic and Petri nets: a natural model for reconfigurable distributed systems. In: Bapi, R., Kulkarni, S., Mohalik, S., Peri, S. (eds.) Distributed Computing and Intelligent Technology, pp. 140–156. Springer, Cham (2022). https://doi.org/10.1007/978-3-030-94876-4_9

7. Capra, L.: Associating a Markov process with Maude executable modules. In: Proceedings of the 15th International Conference on Simulation and Modeling Methodologies, Technologies and Applications, pp. 106–116. SciTePress (2025)

8. Capra, L., Gribaudo, M.: A lumped CTMC for modular rewritable PN. In: Doncel, J., Remke, A., Pompeo, D.D. (eds.) Computer Performance Engineering - 20th European Workshop, EPEW 2024, Venice, Italy, 14 June 2024, Revised Selected Papers. LNCS, vol. 15454, pp. 106–120. Springer, Cham (2024). https://doi.org/10.1007/978-3-031-80932-3_8

9. Capra, L., Köhler-Bußmeier, M.: Modular rewritable Petri nets: an efficient model for dynamic distributed systems. Theor. Comput. Sci. **990**, 114397 (2024). https://doi.org/10.1016/j.tcs.2024.114397

10. Ciardo, G., Miner, A.S.: SMART: the stochastic model checking analyzer for reliability and timing. In: International Conference on Quantitative Evaluation of Systems, pp. 338–339 (2004)

11. Clavel, M., et al.: All About Maude - A High-Performance Logical Framework: How to Specify, Program, and Verify Systems in Rewriting Logic. LNCS. Springer, Cham (2007). https://doi.org/10.1007/978-3-540-71999-1

12. Deavours, D.D., et al.: The Möbius framework and its implementation (2002)

13. Franceschinis, G., Gribaudo, M., Iacono, M., Mazzocca, N., Vittorini, V.: DrawNET++: model objects to support performance analysis and simulation of systems. In: Field, T., Harrison, P.G., Bradley, J., Harder, U. (eds.) TOOLS 2002. LNCS, vol. 2324, pp. 233–238. Springer, Heidelberg (2002). https://doi.org/10.1007/3-540-46029-2_18

14. Gianniti, E., Rizzi, A.M., Barbierato, E., Gribaudo, M., Ardagna, D.: Fluid petri nets for the performance evaluation of mapreduce and spark applications. ACM SIGMETRICS Perform. Eval. Rev. **44**(4), 23–36 (2017)

15. Gribaudo, M., Iacono, M.: Theory and application of multi-formalism modeling (2013). https://doi.org/10.4018/978-1-4666-4659-9

16. Iacono, M., Gribaudo, M.: Element based semantics in multi formalism performance models. In: Proceedings of the 18th IEEE/ACM International Symposium on Modeling, Analysis and Simulation of Computer and Telecommunication Systems (MASCOTS 2010), pp. 413–416 (2010). https://doi.org/10.1109/MASCOTS.2010.54

17. Köhler-Bußmeier, M., Capra, L.: A "symbolic" representation of object-nets. In: Distributed Computing and Intelligent Technology: 21st International Conference, ICDCIT 2025, Bhubaneswar, India, 8–11 January 2025, Proceedings, pp. 68–74. Springer, Heidelberg (2025). https://doi.org/10.1007/978-3-031-81404-4_6

18. Lara, J., Vangheluwe, H.: AToM^3: a tool for multi-formalism and meta-modelling. In: Kutsche, R.-D., Weber, H. (eds.) FASE 2002. LNCS, vol. 2306, pp. 174–188. Springer, Heidelberg (2002). https://doi.org/10.1007/3-540-45923-5_12
19. Sanders, W.: Integrated frameworks for multi-level and multi-formalism modeling. In: Proceedings. The 8th International Workshop on Petri Nets and Performance Models, pp. 2–9 (1999). https://doi.org/10.1109/PNPM.1999.796527
20. Trivedi, K.S.: Sharpe 2002: symbolic hierarchical automated reliability and performance evaluator. In: DSN 2002: Proceedings of the 2002 International Conference on Dependable Systems and Networks, p. 544. IEEE Computer Society, Washington, DC, USA (2002)

Fault-Tolerant Decentralized Distributed Asynchronous Federated Learning with Adaptive Termination Detection

Phani Sahasra Akkinepally[1(✉)], Manaswini Piduguralla[1(✉)],
Sushant Joshi[1(✉)], Sathya Peri[1(✉)], and Sandeep Kulkarni[2(✉)]

[1] Indian Institute of Technology Hyderabad, Kandi, India
{cs23mtech14008,cs20resch11007,cs24mtech14017}@iith.ac.in,
sathya_p@cse.iith.ac.in
[2] Michigan State University, East Lansing, USA
sandeep@msu.edu

Abstract. Federated Learning (FL) facilitates collaborative model training across distributed clients while ensuring data privacy. Traditionally, FL relies on a centralized server to coordinate learning, which creates bottlenecks and a single point of failure. Decentralized FL architectures eliminate the need for a central server and can operate in either synchronous or asynchronous modes. Synchronous FL requires all clients to compute updates and wait for one another before aggregation, guaranteeing consistency but often suffering from delays due to slower participants. Asynchronous FL addresses this by allowing clients to update independently, offering better scalability and responsiveness in heterogeneous environments.

Our research (Code can be viewed here: https://github.com/PDCRL/CFTFedML) develops an asynchronous decentralized FL approach in two progressive phases. (a) In Phase 1, we develop an asynchronous FL framework that enables clients to learn and update independently, removing the need for strict synchronization. (b) In Phase 2, we extend this framework with fault tolerance mechanisms to handle client failures and message drops, ensuring robust performance even under unpredictable conditions. As a central contribution, we propose *Client-Confident Convergence* and *Client-Responsive Termination* novel techniques that provide each client with the ability to autonomously determine appropriate termination points. These methods ensure that all active clients conclude meaningfully and efficiently, maintaining reliable convergence despite the challenges of asynchronous communication and faults.

Keywords: Federated Learning · Decentralized Framework · Asynchronous System · Crash Tolerance · Termination Detection

1 Introduction

Federated learning is a branch of Distributed Machine Learning (DML), in which nodes collaborate without sharing raw data. Clients conduct local model training

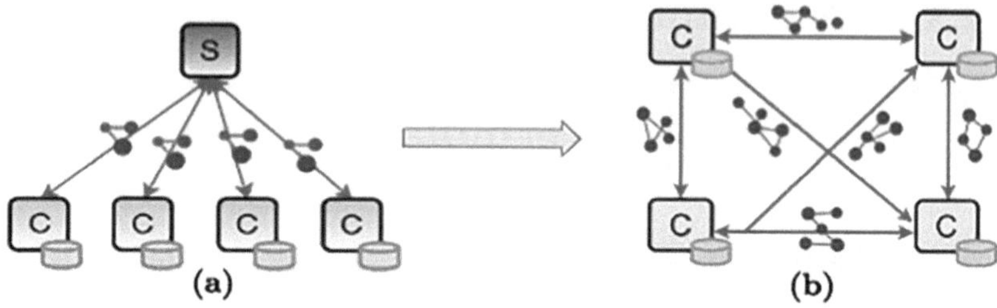

Fig. 1. Centralized to decentralized federated learning architecture. (a) Centralized approach with central server. (b) Decentralized peer-to-peer approach

and share parameters for aggregation, effectively preserving privacy. Centralized FL relies on a central server to coordinate client communication through two-way interactions between the server and each client, clients share the local model with the server while the server shares the global aggregrated model with all clients, as shown in Fig. 1(a). In contrast, decentralized FL uses peer-to-peer communication among clients, improving resilience, similar to centralized model here too peers share models with each other, as illustrated in Fig. 1(b).

Traditionally, FL is implemented using a centralized setup, as described earlier. While conceptually straightforward, centralized FL inherently suffers from scalability issues and is vulnerable to single points of failure due to its reliance on a central coordinating server. A natural alternative is decentralized synchronous FL, where clients collaboratively train without relying on a central coordinator.

However, even in controlled environments such as machines connected in the same Local Area Network (LAN), message delay and relative speeds can make it difficult to assume synchronous mode of execution. Delays, packet reordering, and device variability lead to divergence and inconsistent progress across clients. Moreover, simulations often fail to accurately capture such real-world complexities, resulting in overly optimistic assumptions about system behavior. This realization motivates our exploration of multi-machine, multi-client real-world setups, allowing us to study asynchronous FL more rigorously under realistic conditions.

An equally critical aspect of real-world FL deployments is *fault tolerance* which is the ability of the system to continue delivering correct results despite failures, such as clients dropping out or disconnecting. In this work, we specifically focus on benign crash faults, excluding more adversarial scenarios such as Byzantine faults [6].

In decentralized asynchronous setups, especially in multi-machine environments, there is no global notion of completion or termination of a work, known as *termination detection* (TD). Termination detection in a distributed system [16] is the problem of determining whether a distributed computation has completed— that is, all processes are idle and no messages are in transit. This can be challenging because each process only has partial information about the global system state, and local inactivity does not guarantee global completion.

In distributed federated learning, the absence of a clear termination condition can lead to two significant issues: clients may either terminate prematurely before sufficient convergence is achieved, or continue training unnecessarily, wasting computational resources. To mitigate these risks, we introduce two key mechanisms: *Client-Confident Convergence* and *Client-Responsive Termination*.

The *Client-Confident Convergence* mechanism ensures that a client initiates termination only after observing sufficient stability in the training process. In response, the *Client-Responsive Termination* mechanism ensures that any client receiving this signal updates its own termination flag and propagates the signal through its subsequent model broadcasts. This enables a distributed yet coordinated shutdown across all clients, improving robustness and avoiding indefinite training (For detailed design, refer to Sect. 2).

In this work, we aim to contribute practical insights into designing federated learning systems that can work effectively (fault-tolerant) despite being the system being asynchronous and crash-prone. Specifically, in this work, we: (a) propose a fully decentralized convergence mechanism where each client autonomously monitors local model stability without centralized coordination in Sect. 2. (b) introduce a client-responsive termination protocol that ensures termination signals are reliably propagated, and decided when training had converged in Sect. 2. (c) demonstrate the practical effectiveness of the approach through experiments in realistic, multi-machine federated learning environments in Sect. 3.

2 Proposed Framework

2.1 System Model

We consider a decentralized, federated machine learning (FedML) system comprising a set of N clients, denoted as $C = \{c_1, c_2, \ldots, c_n\}$, where each client c_i possesses their own local dataset D_i. These datasets are non-identical and independently distributed (non-IID) and may vary in size and distribution, reflecting practical heterogeneous data scenarios. Unlike traditional centralized FL setups, our system does not rely on a central server for coordination. Instead, the clients are connected in a peer-to-peer (P2P) network topology where each client can communicate directly with all of the other clients.

Each client maintains a local model and iteratively updates it using its local data. Periodically, clients exchange model updates with their neighbors through message passing. The model exchanges are in the form of model parameters. Messages sent over the network are assumed to be reliable. We assume no message loss, corruption, or duplication. However, communication delays are allowed and may vary between different client pairs.

Asynchronous Model: The system follows a asynchronous communication model, where clients exchange messages over the network using sockets. Communication is fully decentralized, and the system is asynchronous, i.e., clients proceed with their local computations and communication at their speed without a common clock.

Failure Model: The system assumes a crash fault model, where clients may become unresponsive due to software crashes, network disconnections, or resource limitations. These faults are benign—clients stop functioning without sending incorrect or malicious messages (i.e., no Byzantine behavior is considered). The model also supports temporary and intermittent failures, allowing clients to rejoin after transient faults.

2.2   Approach

To systematically address the challenges identified in the traditional FL, this research is structured into two distinct phases, each tailored to tackle a specific dimension of complexity in Federated Learning (FL) systems namely, asynchronous behavior and fault tolerance. By adopting this phased methodology, we ensure that both the coordination challenges of decentralized systems and the resilience requirements of fault-prone environments are addressed in a gradual and controlled manner.

Phase 1: Managing Asynchronous Behavior Using Round-Based Coordination

In the first phase, we focus on mitigating the effects of asynchronous inherent in distributed FL settings by leveraging a round-based synchronization strategy. Each client, during its communication phase, broadcasts its current round number along with its model updates to all other participating clients in the system. This exchange of round numbers provides a lightweight coordination mechanism, enabling clients to maintain awareness of the collective progress of the system despite differences in local update schedules or temporary communication delays.

This strategy not only facilitates smoother convergence of the global model but also prevents divergence due to inconsistent or out-of-order updates. To complement the synchronization mechanism, we implement a termination protocol, ensuring that all active clients reach a mutual agreement on when to halt training. This eliminates premature or inconsistent termination across the network, establishing a foundation for reliable learning outcomes in distributed environments.

Phase 2: Achieving Fault Tolerance in Fully Asynchronous FL Systems

The second phase of our research transitions to a fully asynchronous FL setup, where round-based coordination is removed, allowing clients to send updates entirely independently of one another.

To gracefully handle delays and failures, we introduce timeout-based mechanisms to detect potentially failed or unresponsive clients. In this approach, a client C_i will wait for a message m from another C_j until the timeout expires. After which C_i proceeds to the next round as shown in Algorithm 1. So, if C_j had failed, then C_i will not receive m. So, C_i will proceed with the execution while marking C_j as crashed. However, if the message m is delayed then C_i will consider m in whatever round it receives and change the status of C_j as alive. Unlike rigid synchronization, this approach allows the system to differentiate

---

Algorithm 1 Client Logic

Require: ClientID `id`, ClientsList $P = \{p_1, p_2, \cdots p_n\}$
 1: Initialize model, optimizer, train/test data loaders
 2: Initialize tracking variables (rounds, weights, flags)
 3: **while** $current\_round < R\_PRIME$ **do** // Local Training
 4:     **for** $epoch \leftarrow 1$ to $EPOCHS\_PER\_ROUND$ **do**
 5:         Train model on local data batch-wise
 6:     **end for**
 7:     Extract model weights $localWeights$
 8:     **if** termination flag received **then**
 9:         Broadcast $localWeights$ with terminate flag
10:         **break**
11:     **end if**
        // Broadcast and Wait
12:     Broadcast $localWeights$ to peers
13:     Wait $TIMEOUT$ seconds for incoming weights
        // Crash Detection
14:     **for all** peer p in ClientsList **do**
15:         **if** no message from p_i **and** p_i not marked crashed **then**
16:             Mark p_i as crashed
17:             Log the event
18:         **end if**
19:     **end for**
        // Model Update
20:     Aggregate all received weights
21:     Update model with aggregated weights
22:     Evaluate accuracy on test set
        // Termination Criteria Check
23:     **if** $current\_round \geq MINIMUM\_ROUNDS$ **then**
24:         **if** $curr\_weight - prev\_weight > threshold$ **and** $recent\_crashes = None$
    then
25:             Increment convergence counter
26:         **else**
27:             Reset convergence counter
28:         **end if**
29:         **if** $convergence\_counter \geq COUNT\_THRESHOLD$ **then**
30:             Log termination condition met
31:             Broadcast $weights$ with terminate flag
32:             **break**
33:         **end if**
34:     **end if**
35:     Store current weights
36:     round++
37:     Clear message buffer
38: **end while**
39: **if** maximum rounds reached **then** // Termination Finalization
40:     Log and broadcast final weights
41: **end if**
42: Broadcast termination message to all peers

---

between slow and genuinely failed clients, minimizing unnecessary blocking and promoting progress even in degraded conditions.

To ensure effective learning despite faults, we propose the development of a client confidence-based convergence architecture and additionally, a client-responsive termination mechanism is incorporated to prevent indefinite waiting on failed or lagging clients. This enables the system to dynamically adapt to fluctuating participation levels while safeguarding convergence properties.

Client-Confident Convergence: It is a decentralized mechanism where each client independently executes the same termination logic during the federated learning process. Specifically, every client continuously monitors the progress of training by evaluating two key conditions: (a) The client has observed 'x' (convergence threshold) consecutive rounds without any detected crashes in the system. (b) The difference between the previous global model average and the current global model average falls below a predefined threshold, indicating diminishing model improvement.

When both conditions are satisfied, the client broadcasts a termination signal to all other active clients in the system. The rationale here is that the client encountering this stable state first has already witnessed x stable rounds, suggesting that further training is unlikely to yield significant improvements. Importantly, this process is fully decentralized and can be triggered by any client in the system at runtime, making termination adaptive to dynamic network conditions and learning convergence.

Client-Responsive Termination Protocol: While signaling termination is essential, simply broadcasting a termination message is not sufficient in decentralized systems. Without a structured termination protocol, some clients might mistakenly interpret missing updates as client failures, leading to ambiguity regarding which clients have genuinely terminated versus those that might have crashed or disconnected.

To address this, we introduce the Client-Responsive Termination Protocol. In this mechanism, whenever a client receives a termination signal from another client, it updates its own internal termination flag in real time. From that point onward, the client continues participating in communication by broadcasting its model updates along with the termination flag enabled. This ensures that the termination signal propagates reliably throughout the network, even reaching clients that may have temporarily missed earlier signals due to delays or intermittent disconnections.

This approach adds an additional layer of robustness to the termination process, ensuring that even clients that were disconnected during the initial termination broadcast eventually receive the signal and terminate gracefully. By doing so, the system avoids false assumptions of crashes and maintains a clear, coordinated shutdown procedure across the distributed environment. Through these two phases, our research presents a comprehensive approach to building federated learning systems that are not only capable of handling the natural asynchronous of decentralized computation but also robust enough to sustain learning in fault-prone, real-world environments. The pseudocode of the algorithm incorporating these techniques is shown in Algorithm 1.

3   Experiments and Analysis

To validate the effectiveness and robustness of the proposed federated learning framework, we conducted a comprehensive set of experiments under various simulated distributed learning conditions. These experiments were designed to assess system behavior in the presence of real-world challenges such as client speed, communication delays, and potential client failures.

Experimental Setup: The experimental evaluation was conducted with the number of clients ranging from 4 to 12, increasing in steps of 2. The system was developed in Python, leveraging threads to spawn individual client processes and sockets to enable communication between them in a fully decentralized, peer-to-peer manner. All experiments were executed on CPU-only environments. Two distinct phases were tested under different environmental assumptions. In Phase 1, the system operates through synchronization over an asynchronous system, with no client crashes permitted. In contrast, Phase 2 adopts an asynchronous setting where client crashes. The experiments were deployed across a multi-machine, multi-client setup, to simulate realistic distributed environments and test the robustness and scalability of the proposed approach.

System Specifications: The experiments were conducted using three high-performance machines in a distributed, multi-client, multi-machine environment. All machines communicated over a LAN (local area network), and experiments were executed entirely on CPUs without GPU acceleration as shown in Table 1.

Table 1. System specifications of the machines used.

Machine	Operating System	RAM	Physical Cores	Clock Speed
Machine 1	Ubuntu 18.04.6	376 GiB	56	4.0 GHz
Machine 2	Ubuntu 22.04.5	251 GiB	112	2.0 GHz
Machine 3	Ubuntu 22.04.5	188 GiB	52	3.5 GHz

Data Specifications: Preliminary experiments were conducted using both the CIFAR-10 and MNIST datasets under IID (independent and identically distributed) and Non-IID conditions to establish baseline performance. However, the primary focus of this study is to analyze the behavior of federated learning systems under extreme and adverse conditions. **As such, the subsequent experiments presented in this work specifically focus on Non-IID data distributions using the CIFAR-10 dataset, which better reflect real-world data heterogeneity and serve to stress-test the robustness of**

the proposed system. The dataset comprises 60,000 color images distributed across 10 classes, with 50,000 images used for training and 10,000 for testing. Each image has dimensions of $32 \times 32 \times 3$ pixels. To simulate Non-IID conditions, client-specific data partitions were generated using a Dirichlet distribution-based sampling strategy with $\alpha = 0.6$, which enables controlled variation in data skew by adjusting the concentration parameter. The Convolutional Neural Network (CNN) model architecture used throughout the experiments comprises two convolutional layers followed by two fully connected layers, resulting in approximately 225,034 parameters (about 0.44 MB). Consequently, each communication round between clients involved the transmission of roughly 0.44 MB of data for each client, representing model updates.

Phase 1 - Fault-Free System Experiments: To establish baseline performance metrics, we initially evaluated single-client configuration to understand the lower bounds of our federated learning system. Table 2 summarizes the classification accuracy achieved by individual clients under varying data distribution settings.

Table 2. Baseline Performance Results

Scenario	Accuracy (%)
Non-IID Single Client (Fixed data chunk)	26.23
IID Single Client (Fixed data chunk)	37.48
Single Client (Full dataset)	70.82

To understand the impact of data distribution and collaboration in federated learning, we evaluated three single-client training configuration.

In the first case (Non-IID Sgl), each client was assigned a fixed chunk of 5000 data points drawn from a highly *Non-IID distribution*, representing real-world data heterogeneity. These clients trained independently without any communication, and the average accuracy achieved across all clients was **26.23%**, highlighting the limitations of learning from skewed, isolated data. In the second scenario (IID Sgl), each client again received a fixed 5000 data point chunk, but this time the data was sampled in an *IID manner*, ensuring a balanced and representative distribution. This improved the average accuracy to **37.48%**, demonstrating that even without collaboration, better data diversity significantly enhances performance. The third case (Sgl Full) represents the *ideal baseline*, where a single client is given access to the **entire training dataset**. Without any distribution or communication overhead, this setup yielded an accuracy of **70.82%**, indicating the upper-bound performance that could be achieved in a centralized setting.

These results collectively emphasize the importance of collaboration in federated learning, particularly under Non-IID conditions, where isolated training yields significantly suboptimal outcomes.

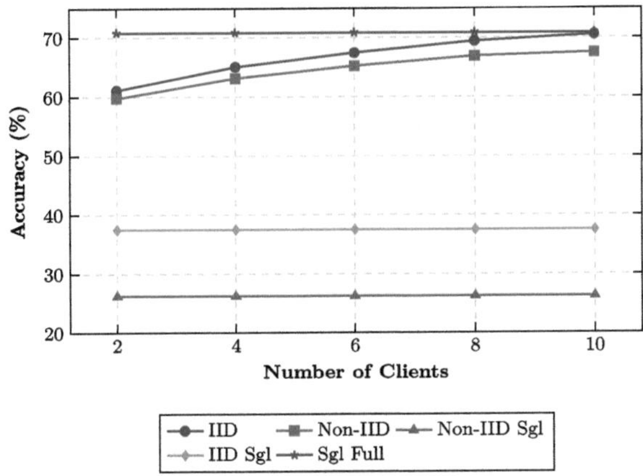

Fig. 2. Accuracy vs. Number of Clients for IID and Non-IID CIFAR-10 Settings with Single Client Baselines

Results on CIFAR-10 Dataset: The results in Fig. 2 validate the effectiveness of the round-based synchronization in Phase 1, demonstrating proper coordination among clients.

As the number of clients increases from 2 to 10, accuracy steadily improves due to the inclusion of more data in each experiment. For Non-IID data, the accuracy rises from 59.78% to 67.47%, while for IID data it increases from 61.10% to 70.50%.

The system achieved consistent convergence with perfect synchronization across all runs. Termination was reliably detected using the designed consensus mechanisms. The results reveal the following insights:

– The IID scenario consistently achieves higher accuracy compared to non-IID, with a maximum accuracy of 70.50% versus 67.47%.
– Both IID and non-IID scenarios demonstrate scalability, with accuracy improving as the number of clients increases.

These results provide a strong baseline for evaluating the fault-tolerant mechanisms implemented in Phase 2.

Phase 2: Fault Tolerance Experiments. To systematically analyze the impact of client failures on federated learning, a series of targeted experiments were conducted under varying fault conditions. These experiments were designed to capture both the *progressive degradation* and the *scalability limits* of the system in the presence of crashes. To simulate a realistic system, we tested with three machine as shown in Table 1 with these machines were communicating with each other through the network. The 12 clients equally distributed among these machines. In experiments with lesser number of machines (such as 1 or 2), the clients were accordingly distributed.

Experiment 1: Variable Crash Analysis evaluates system robustness by gradually increasing the number of crashed clients from 0 to 11 out of 12, revealing how performance metric, accuracy degrade with increasing fault intensity. Figure 4 illustrates the variation in model accuracy with an increasing number of crash faults, while Fig. 3 presents the total training time under the same fault conditions. Both figures compare the system behavior under single-machine, two-machine, and three-machine setups.

As expected, a gradual decline in accuracy is observed across all three configurations with increasing fault severity, demonstrating the system's sensitivity to reduced client participation. However, Fig. 3 provides additional insight into the practical execution characteristics. In the case of zero faults, the single-machine setup incurs significantly higher training time compared to the multi-machine configurations. This elevated duration can be attributed to resource contention, since all 12 clients are hosted on a single physical machine, they compete heavily for CPU and memory, thereby introducing delays.

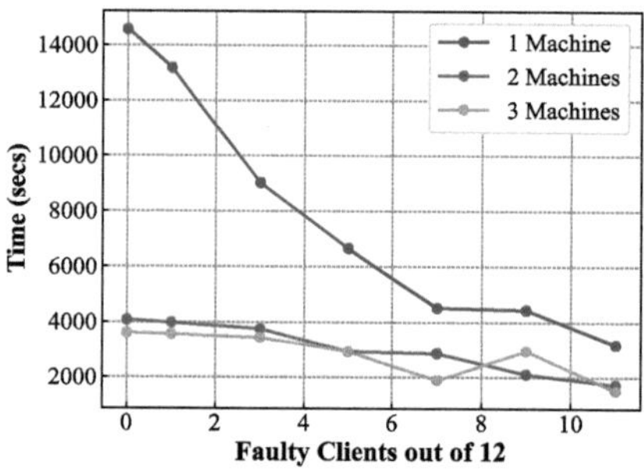

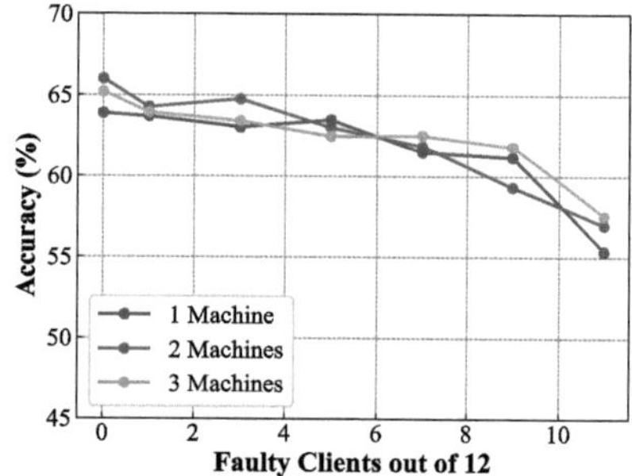

Fig. 3. Time taken with 12 Clients under Variable Fault Conditions

Fig. 4. Performance with 12 Clients under Variable Fault Conditions

In contrast, when the same experiment is distributed across two and three machines, the total training time becomes more stable and comparable. This outcome emphasizes the importance of deploying federated systems in realistic, distributed environments rather than simulating all clients on a single machine. Additionally, involving machines with differing hardware specifications and clock speeds increases the system's overall asynchrony, allowing for a more accurate evaluation of the framework's performance and robustness in heterogeneous, real-world conditions.

Experiment 2: Proportional Fault Analysis maintains a consistent failure rate (33%) across different total client counts. Here the clients fail during the system execution at regular intervals. This setup helps assess whether the system can *scale gracefully under consistent stress* and still converge effectively. These results are shown in Figs. 5, 6. Here the baseline refers to the non-faulty case executing with $\lfloor (2 * n/3) \rfloor$ clients and are executing the learning algorithm outlined in phase1. When n is 4 and 12, the actual number of clients in the baseline is 3 and 8 respectively.

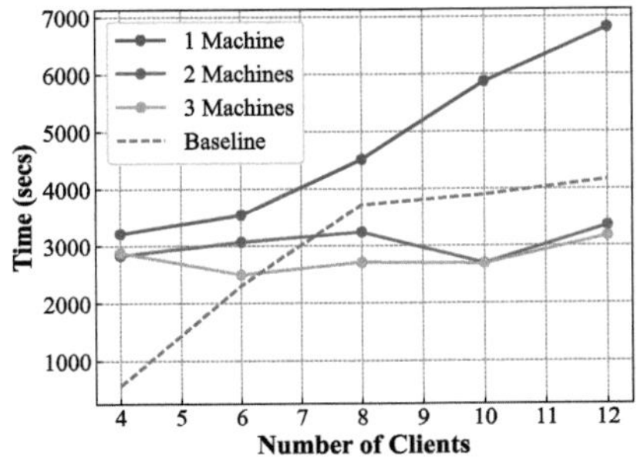
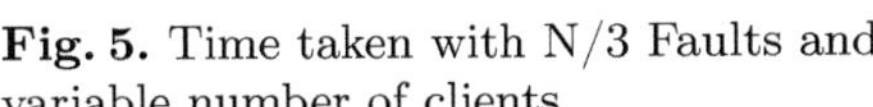

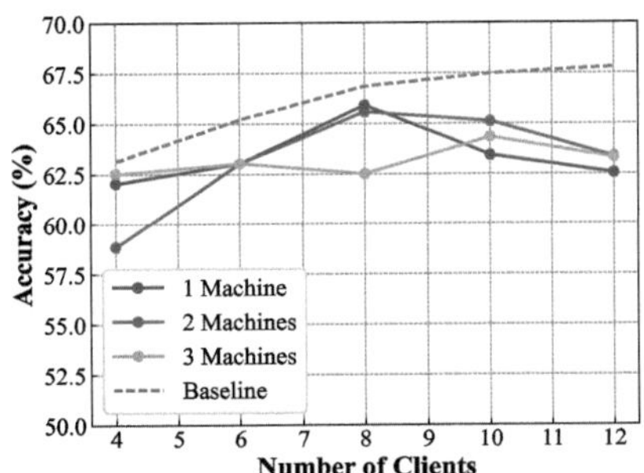

Fig. 5. Time taken with N/3 Faults and variable number of clients

Fig. 6. Performance with N/3 Faults and variable number of clients

Figure 6 illustrates that the three variants - single machine, two machine, and three machine setups. The experiment shows that the accuracy in case of the faulty environment is comparable to the baseline fault-free case even when handling $n/3$ client failures in an asynchronous environment. This showcases the robustness and adaptability of the proposed approach under partial client participation and non-deterministic execution patterns.

Figure 5 highlights the time-related impact of these configurations. While the single-machine setup exhibits a noticeable increase in training time due to higher resource contention, both the two-machine and three-machine setups manage to outperform the baseline in terms of computation time. This is because the client failures in these system are configured to occur sometime in the middle of the system execution and the failed clients help with the learning process till they fail. While this is not the case with the baseline which only has lesser number of clients throughout the execution.

For example, in the case of 12 clients, an $n/3$ failure corresponds to 4 client crashes, leaving 8 functional clients in the system. When comparing with a fault-free setup involving only 8 clients (the baseline), we observe that the time taken by the baseline is higher than the time required by the system operating with 12 clients and 4 faults. This clearly highlights the efficiency of the proposed asynchronous and fault-tolerant design, which is capable of leveraging partial participation more effectively than an asynchronous fault-free configuration with fewer active clients.

Experiment 3: Maximum Fault Analysis represents the *worst-case scenario*, where only one client remains active. This setup allows for evaluating the system's capability to tolerate extreme isolation and still make learning progress under minimal participation.

As shown in Fig. 7, the accuracy observed in the presence of $n - 1$ faults is significantly lower than that of the synchronized no-fault system, which is expected due to the lack of client diversity and aggregation. However, it is noteworthy that the performance is still superior to the baseline case of a single client training independently on a fixed chunk of Non-IID data, as reported in

Table 2. This highlights the benefit of collaborative learning—even with limited participation—over isolated learning on skewed datasets. When considering the time behavior shown in Fig. 8, we observe a natural decline in total training duration. This reduction is attributed to the smaller number of participating clients, leading to fewer communication rounds and significantly reduced coordination overhead.

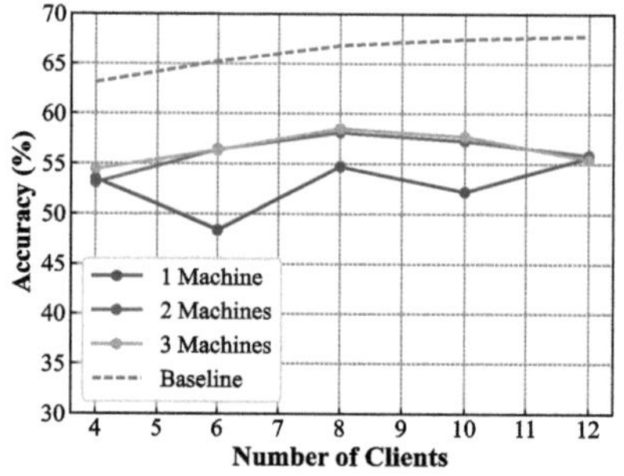

Fig. 7. Performance with N-1 Faults and variable number of clients

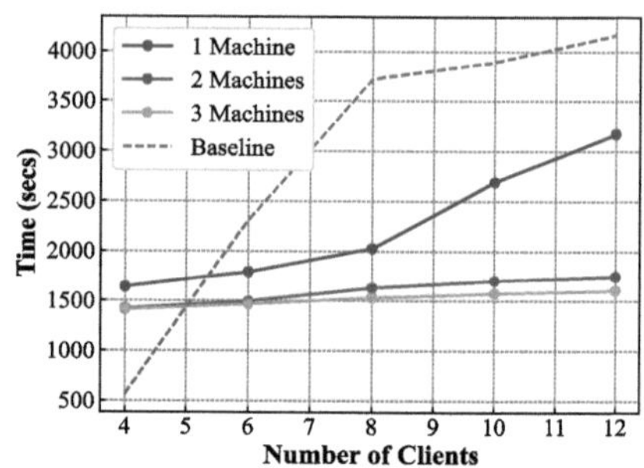

Fig. 8. Time taken with N-1 Faults and variable number of clients

Observations from the Experiments: The three fault experiments collectively validate the robustness, adaptability, and practical efficiency of our proposed asynchronous, fault-tolerant federated learning framework.

Experiment 1 demonstrated the system's graceful degradation under increasing crash faults. Even as the number of failed clients rose from 0 to 11, the system maintained reasonable accuracy and convergence time, particularly when deployed in a multi-machine setup. This highlighted the effectiveness of distributing clients across machines to reduce contention and better reflect real-world asynchronous.

Experiment 2 examined the system's behavior under a consistent failure rate of $n/3$ across varying client counts. The results showed that despite substantial asynchronous and partial failures, the proposed approach performed comparably to a fault-free baseline. This confirmed that the system can scale under fixed-stress conditions without significant accuracy or efficiency loss.

Experiment 3 tested the extreme boundary of the system—when only one client remains active. While the accuracy dropped significantly, as expected, it still outperformed the Non-IID single-client baseline (Table 2), underlining the benefit of initial collaborative updates and the residual value of even limited federation.

4 Related Work

Federated Learning was first introduced as a practical method for training machine learning models across distributed devices while preserving data privacy [12]. The seminal work by McMahan et al. [12] presented **Federated Averaging (FedAvg)**, which operates through iterative model averaging where clients perform local stochastic gradient descent updates followed by server-side aggregation. FedAvg demonstrated significant communication efficiency, reducing required communication rounds by 10–100x compared to synchronized stochastic gradient descent.

The theoretical foundations of FedAvg convergence have been extensively studied under various conditions [15,18]. Wang and Ji [17] provided a unified convergence analysis for federated learning with arbitrary client participation, introducing a generalized version of federated averaging that amplifies parameter updates at intervals of multiple FL rounds. Their analysis captures the effect of client participation in a single term, obtaining convergence upper bounds for both non-stochastic and stochastic participation patterns. Li et al. [18] established convergence rates for strongly convex and smooth problems in non-IID data settings, revealing that data heterogeneity slows convergence and necessitates decaying learning rates. Recent work has challenged pessimistic theoretical predictions, showing that FedAvg can achieve identical convergence rates in both homogeneous and heterogeneous data settings under certain conditions [2].

Synchronous Centralized Federated Learning Systems

Synchronous federated learning has been extensively studied from system optimization perspectives, with comprehensive surveys identifying key bottlenecks in client selection, configuration, and reporting phases [7]. Communication-efficient approaches for synchronous FL have focused on adaptive aggregation strategies in client-edge-cloud architectures [10]. Luo et al. [10] propose theoretical convergence analysis under aggregation frequency control, enabling dynamic resource allocation while maintaining model convergence guarantees. Their FedAda method demonstrates up to 4% improvement in test accuracy, 6.8 shorter training time and $3.3\times$ less communication overhead compared to prior solutions.

Feng et al. [4,5] studied federated learning efficiency over wireless networks, deriving analytical expressions to characterize FL convergence rates accounting for transmission reliability, scheduling policies, and momentum methods. Their analysis reveals that delicately designed user scheduling policies or expanding bandwidth can expedite model training in reliable networks, but these methods become ineffective when connections are erratic. The incorporation of momentum method into model training algorithms accelerates convergence rate and provides greater resilience against transmission failures [4].

Real-World Asynchrony in Federated Learning

The transition from theoretical synchronous models to practical asynchronous implementations addresses critical real-world challenges including device heterogeneity, intermittent connectivity, and varying computational resources [3,9]. Liu et al. [9] propose an adaptive asynchronous federated learning (AAFL) mechanism for resource-constrained edge computing, where a certain fraction of local updates are aggregated by arrival order at the parameter server in each epoch.

Asynchronous federated learning eliminates the need for synchronized communication, allowing devices to contribute updates at their own pace [3]. Recent advances focus on addressing efficiency challenges through prospective momentum aggregation and fine-grained correction techniques [20]. The work by Liao et al. [8] contributes to improved robustness in federated learning through decentralization and asynchronous updates. While this approach effectively addresses device heterogeneity, it does not explicitly implement fault tolerance mechanisms, leaving gaps in handling system failures during training. Similarly, MPLS [19] is a decentralized federated learning method that speeds up training by letting devices share and combine important parts of their models asynchronously, helping handle different device capabilities in edge environments; however, it does not address fault tolerance in the system.

Morell et al. [13] introduces a dynamic and adaptive fault-tolerant asynchronous federated learning framework utilizing volunteer edge devices. While this demonstrates the feasibility of distributed training across platforms like web browsers and terminal processes, such proof-of-concept environments fail to fully capture the computational heterogeneity, network variability, and rich data distributions encountered in real-world deployments. This limits their practical applicability for evaluating fault-tolerant learning at scale. A centralized approach with sequential model combination using first-come-first-serve aggregation is introduced by Ma et al. [11]. This work demonstrates practical applications of asynchronous FL in industrial fault diagnosis scenarios, though its centralized nature may present single points of failure. The potential of decentralized architectures to enhance system resilience over centralized alternatives has been extensively discussed in the literature [21]. However, existing approaches often suffer from high communication overhead and significant message complexity, which limit their practicality in real-time, fault-tolerant federated learning scenarios [14]. This highlights the pressing need for more efficient, scalable solutions that can deliver fault tolerance without compromising responsiveness.

The reviewed literature reveals a clear progression from early synchronous centralized approaches to more sophisticated asynchronous and decentralized methods [7,21]. However, existing work focuses on robustness through decentralization without explicit fault tolerance or addresses fault tolerance with prohibitive computational overhead [14]. The challenge of achieving fault-tolerant federated learning in real time even with simple averaging mechanisms to start with, while maintaining efficiency remains largely unaddressed [4,9]. This gap motivates research on lightweight fault tolerance mechanisms that can operate effectively in distributed learning environments in real time without compromising the fundamental benefits of federated learning paradigms [10,17]. However, in the context of comparing performance with state-of-the-art frameworks, there is currently no practical implementation to enable direct execution-level comparison.

5   Conclusion

In this work, we presented a fully asynchronous, fault-tolerant federated learning framework designed to operate effectively under realistic deployment conditions characterized by client heterogeneity, network instability, and the absence of centralized control. Through systematic experimentation, we demonstrated the framework's robustness to crash faults, its ability to scale under partial failures, and its resilience even in extreme scenarios with minimal active clients. The proposed Client-Confident Convergence and Client-Responsive Termination mechanisms address a long-standing challenge in decentralized asynchronous FL achieving reliable, efficient, and autonomous termination without global coordination. By combining these contributions with practical fault-tolerance strategies, our framework enables scalable and efficient federated learning across distributed, failure-prone environments. Further details on the algorithmic design and comprehensive performance comparisons are presented in the archived version of this paper [1]. In future we will focus on extending these guarantees to tolerate Byzantine faults, where clients may behave arbitrarily or maliciously due to software bugs, or adversarial manipulation. Incorporating Byzantine resilience is essential for deploying FL in open, untrusted environments such as cross-organizational collaborations or public networks.

References

1. Akkinepally, P.S., Piduguralla, M., Joshi, S., Peri, S., Kulkarni, S.: Fault-tolerant decentralized distributed asynchronous federated learning with adaptive termination detection (2025). https://arxiv.org/abs/2509.02186
2. Beikmohammadi, Y., Pillutla, K., Karimireddy, S.P., Stich, S.U.: On the convergence of federated averaging with cyclic client participation. arXiv preprint arXiv:2402.16520 (2024)
3. Chen, X., Li, Q., Wu, Q., Zhang, X.: A survey on asynchronous federated learning. IEEE Commun. Surv. Tutor. (2024)
4. Feng, Y., Wan, S., Liu, M., Chen, S.: Towards efficient federated learning over wireless networks: a convergence analysis. IEEE Trans. Commun. (2024)
5. Feng, Y., Wan, S., Liu, M., Chen, S., Poor, H.V.: Understanding federated learning efficiency over wireless networks. IEEE Trans. Wirel. Commun. (2024)
6. Lamport, L., Shostak, R., Pease, M.: The byzantine generals problem. ACM Trans. Program. Lang. Syst. (TOPLAS) **4**(3), 382–401 (1982)
7. Li, T., Sahu, A.K., Talwalkar, A., Smith, V.: Federated learning: challenges, methods, and future directions. ACM Comput. Surv. **55**(6), 1–35 (2023)
8. Liao, Y., Xu, Y., Xu, H., Chen, M., Wang, L., Qiao, C.: Asynchronous decentralized federated learning for heterogeneous devices. IEEE/ACM Trans. Netw. **32**(5), 4535–4550 (2024)
9. Liu, J., et al.: Adaptive asynchronous federated learning in resource-constrained edge computing. IEEE Trans. Mob. Comput. **21**(12), 4515–4528 (2021)

10. Luo, L., Zhang, C., Yu, H., Sun, G., Luo, S., Dustdar, S.: Communication-efficient federated learning with adaptive aggregation for heterogeneous client-edge-cloud network. IEEE Trans. Serv. Comput. **17**(6), 3241–3254 (2024)
11. Ma, X., Wen, C., Wen, T.: An asynchronous and real-time update paradigm of federated learning for fault diagnosis. IEEE Trans. Industr. Inf. **17**(12), 8531–8540 (2021)
12. McMahan, H.B., Moore, E., Ramage, D., Hampson, S., Arcas, B.A.: Communication-efficient learning of deep networks from decentralized data. In: Proceedings of the 20th International Conference on Artificial Intelligence and Statistics, vol. 54, pp. 1273–1282. PMLR (2017)
13. Ángel Morell, J., Alba, E.: Dynamic and adaptive fault-tolerant asynchronous federated learning using volunteer edge devices. Futur. Gener. Comput. Syst. **133**, 53–67 (2022)
14. Ranellucci, S., Dov, N., Orsini, E., Rotaru, D., Smart, N.P.: Learning from failures: secure and fault-tolerant aggregation for federated learning. In: Proceedings of the 2022 ACM SIGSAC Conference on Computer and Communications Security, pp. 2657–2670 (2022)
15. Sun, G., Luo, L., Zhang, C., Li, J., Chen, D., Yu, H.: Decentralized federated learning: fundamentals, state of the art, frameworks, trends, and challenges. IEEE Commun. Surv. Tutor. **25**(4), 2983–3013 (2022)
16. Tel, G.: Introduction to Distributed Algorithms, 2nd edn. Cambridge University Press (2000), chapter 8: Termination Detection
17. Wang, S., Ji, M.: A unified analysis of federated learning with arbitrary client participation. Adv. Neural. Inf. Process. Syst. **35**, 2323–2335 (2022)
18. Wang, X., Li, G., Zhang, J., Wang, Z., Zhang, Y.: A novel federated learning approach with local adaptive differential privacy. Neurocomputing **472**, 103–115 (2021)
19. Xu, Y., Yao, Z., Xu, H., Liao, Y., Xie, Z.: MPLS: stacking diverse layers into one model for decentralized federated learning. In: Euro-Par 2025: Parallel Processing, pp. 190–204. Springer, Cham (2026)
20. Zang, Y., Xue, Z., Ou, S., Chu, L., Du, J., Long, Y.: Efficient asynchronous federated learning with prospective momentum aggregation and fine-grained correction. In: Proceedings of the AAAI Conference on Artificial Intelligence, vol. 38, no. 15, pp. 16642–16650 (2024)
21. Zhang, W., Li, T., Lu, J., Liu, Y., Chen, D.O.: Decentralized federated learning: a survey and perspective. IEEE Internet Things J. (2023)

Computer Vision

Improved Single-Stage Facial Landmarks for Real-Time Driver Drowsiness Detection

Nandani Sharma[1], Sachin Banothu[1,2](✉), Mahek Shah[1,3], and Dinesh Singh[1]

[1] Vision Intelligence and Machine Learning (VIML) Group, School of Computing and Electrical Engineering (SCEE), Indian Institute of Technology Mandi (IIT Mandi), Mandi, Himachal Pradesh, India
d22180@students.iitmandi.ac.in, 22bec071@nirmauni.ac.in,
dineshsingh@iitmandi.ac.in
[2] Indian Institute of Science Education and Research (IISER) Thiruvananthapuram, Thiruvananthapuram, Kerala, India
sachin22@iisertvm.ac.in
[3] Nirma University, Ahmedabad, Gujarat, India

Abstract. Driver drowsiness is a major cause of road accidents, making its detection a key objective in intelligent transportation systems. Vision-based methods, especially those using facial landmark detection, offer a non-invasive and efficient means of identifying fatigue through signs like eye closure and yawning. While traditional two-stage facial landmark detection systems are accurate, their computational complexity limits real-time use in embedded environments. To overcome this, single-stage models such as YOLOFaceMark integrate face and landmark detection in a unified pipeline. However, its RepStem module suffers from mismatched feature dimensions that hinder learning. This work introduces a redesigned stem module that aligns outputs for better early-stage feature fusion, enhancing performance while retaining real-time capabilities. The improved model outperforms the baseline and effectively detects drowsiness cues, making it suitable for practical driver monitoring applications.

Keywords: Driver Drowsiness · Intelligent Transportation Systems · Computer Vision

1 Introduction

Road safety has always been a central goal of intelligent transportation systems (ITS), and with the growing number of vehicles worldwide, minimizing traffic accidents has become more critical than ever [38,53]. Among the factors contributing to accidents, driver fatigue remains one of the most significant. Detecting drowsiness in its early stages can prevent catastrophic outcomes and save lives [7,18,38]. This necessity has driven extensive research into driver drowsiness detection (DDD), leading to the development of various approaches over the years [9,12,13,15,43].

B. Chatterjee et al. (Eds.): ICDCIT 2026, LNCS 16420, pp. 189–204, 2026.
https://doi.org/10.1007/978-3-032-16632-6_12

Early efforts in this area focused on physiological signals, which provide reliable indicators of a driver's state of alertness. Techniques based on electrocardiograms (ECG) [6,8,19,22,45] and electroencephalograms (EEG) [4–6,27,31,36,37,47,48,57,58] have been widely studied for their ability to reflect cognitive and physiological changes during fatigue. While accurate, these methods require specialized sensors and hardware, making them impractical for large-scale deployment in real-world vehicles. To overcome these limitations, researchers introduced behavioral approaches that analyze driving patterns such as lane deviation and steering corrections [40]. Although less intrusive, these methods often struggle to detect early symptoms of drowsiness, reducing their effectiveness [14,50,56].

Traditionally, FLD systems [17,26,28,30,33,49,55,59] follow a two-stage pipeline: a face detector first localizes the driver's face, followed by a separate network that predicts facial landmarks. Well-known models such as PIPNet [28], 3DDFA2 [23], and HRNet [49] employ this strategy. While effective in controlled environments, this architecture introduces two major limitations: running two separate deep networks significantly increases computational requirements, and the lack of feature sharing between stages reduces efficiency. These issues become critical in automotic systems, where real-time performance and limited hardware resources are essential. In recent years, the advent of computer vision has transformed this field by enabling non-invasive detection methods that rely on cameras rather than specialized sensors. Vision-based techniques [25,39,54], especially those leveraging facial landmark detection (FLD), have gained significant traction [23,28,49]. These methods estimate driver fatigue by analyzing visual cues such as blinking frequency, eye closure, and yawning, offering an efficient and cost-effective solution suitable for real-time applications.

To overcome these challenges, recent studies advocate for single-stage, end-to-end architectures that perform face and landmark detection simultaneously. This unified approach not only accelerates inference but also allows shared feature extraction, improving overall efficiency. The YOLO family of models [35,41], known for their speed and accuracy in object detection, has been adapted for this purpose. Notable examples include YOLO5Face [39] and YOLOFaceMark [54], which integrate FLD into a streamlined detection pipeline.

YOLOFaceMark by Wu *et al.* [54] stands out for its elegant design, incorporating techniques such as structural re-parameterization and channel shuffling to balance accuracy and computational efficiency. However, closer examination reveals a significant issue in its RepStem module. This module employs two parallel branches: one uses a 2×2 max pooling operation to downsample the feature map, while the other applies a 3×3 convolution to preserve the original spatial resolution. Because these outputs differ in size ($H/2 \times W/2$ vs. $H \times W$), merging them creates a dimensional mismatch. This misalignment disrupts gradient flow and hampers early-stage feature learning, which is crucial for downstream accuracy.

To address this limitation, we propose a redesigned stem module that ensures consistent feature map dimensions across both branches enabling effective feature fusion and improving gradient propagation. Our architecture retains the strengths of YOLOFaceMark, including its RepShuffle2Bot bottleneck and dual-branch detection head, while enhancing the model's robustness and accuracy. The main contributions of this work are summarized as follows:

- We identify a structural issue in YOLOFaceMark's RepStem module and introduce a solution that harmonizes branch outputs for improved feature integration.
- We present an enhanced end-to-end architecture with the improved stem design, resulting in better feature representation throughout the network.
- Extensive experiments on benchmark datasets such as NTHU-DDD [52], 300W [42] and COFW [20] demonstrate that our model surpasses the baseline in metrics while preserving real-time.

Finally, we evaluate our improved model in a real-world driver drowsiness detection scenario [51,54], confirming its ability to accurately recognize critical fatigue indicators such as prolonged eye closure and yawning an essential for building reliable and robust DDD systems.

2   Related Work

Early studies on driver drowsiness detection primarily relied on physiological signals, as these indicators provide direct insights into a person's alertness. Among them, electrocardiogram (ECG) monitoring has been explored for detecting fatigue levels. Gromer et al. [22] demonstrated that ECG-based systems can effectively indicate drowsiness. However, their invasive nature and the need for specialized sensors make them impractical for deployment in everyday driving conditions. Similarly, electroencephalogram (EEG) signals have been recognized as reliable for estimating drowsiness. Jiang et al. [27] reported stable performance using EEG-based techniques, but these systems often compromise driver comfort and are challenging to integrate into real-world vehicles due to their complexity and cost.

To overcome the limitations of physiological methods, researchers have turned to behavioral approaches. These methods analyze changes in driving patterns such as lane drift, steering corrections, or trajectory irregularities as potential indicators of fatigue [9,27]. Azadani and Boukerche [9] proposed strategies for monitoring driving trajectories to detect anomalies linked to drowsiness. Similarly, Qiu et al. [40] introduced multi-scale lane detection frameworks capable of capturing subtle variations in driving behavior. Although these approaches are less intrusive and easier to integrate into ITS, they are highly susceptible to external conditions such as road geometry, traffic density, and weather, which limits their reliability.

With advances in computer vision and deep learning, vision-based techniques have gained momentum as a non-invasive and practical alternative for DDD. These systems leverage FLD to monitor visual cues like eye blinking, yawning, and gaze direction [23,28]. The traditional pipeline for FLD typically consists of two stages: a face detection module followed by a separate network for landmark localization. Popular models such as PIPNet [28], 3DDFA2 [23], and HRNet [49] have demonstrated high accuracy on challenging datasets like 300W and COFW. Despite their robustness, these two-stage approaches are computationally expensive and struggle to meet real-time constraints in automotive systems.

To address these challenges, recent research has focused on single-stage, end-to-end frameworks that integrate face detection and landmark localization into a unified model. The YOLO family of detectors [35, 41] known for its efficiency and speed, has been widely adopted for this purpose. Derivative frameworks such as YOLO5Face [39] and YOLOFaceMark [54] extend YOLO's principles to facial analysis tasks. YOLO5Face introduced a fast and accurate solution for 5-point FLD, while YOLOFaceMark incorporated advanced architectural components like structural re-parameterization and channel shuffling to enhance robustness and efficiency. However, issues remain for example, the RepStem module in YOLOFaceMark introduces feature map size inconsistencies between branches, which complicates feature fusion and can negatively affect early-stage learning and overall model performance.

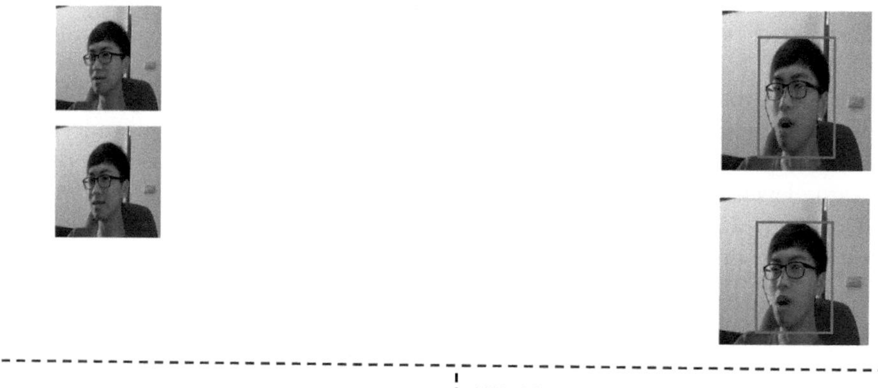

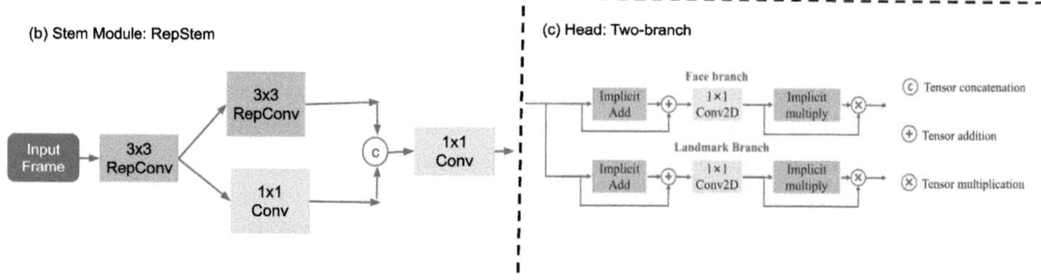

Fig. 1. The overall framework with improvement in the RepStem module.

3   Proposed Methodology

This section introduces the proposed **YOLOFaceMark** framework, designed for real-time detection of faces and facial landmarks to enable accurate driver drowsiness estimation. The architecture builds on YOLOv5 principles and integrates several custom modifications: a redesigned stem module, re-parameterized bottleneck blocks, a multi-scale feature aggregation neck, and a dual-branch detection head for bounding box and landmark predictions. Figure 1 provides an overview of the network architecture.

3.1   Network Architecture

The YOLOFaceMark architecture consists of four main components: *Stem, Bottleneck, Neck,* and *Detection Head.* Each component is discussed in detail below.

Stem Module (Improved Design). The stem module acts as the entry point of the network, processing raw input images into low-level feature maps. Its design prioritizes computational efficiency while maintaining spatial detail.

Issue in Original Design: The initial implementation of the RepStem module used a 1×1 convolution layer after a 3×3 RepConv, which unintentionally reduced spatial dimensions, causing alignment issues for concatenation.

Proposed Improvement: To ensure spatial consistency:

1. Branch-1 replace wth RepConv with a 3×3 convolution.
2. Set **stride** $= 1$ and **padding** $= 1$ to maintain the original spatial resolution.
3. Branch-2 replace with a 1×1 convolution for improved concatenation with the parallel branch.

This modification ensures feature map integrity and improved feature extraction without introducing extra computational overhead. The RepStem design balances complexity and stability. By combining RepConv (expressive) + Conv (simple), the network learns richer and more robust features than using either alone.

The proposed architecture is composed of three main components: the bottleneck, the neck, and the dual-branch detection head. The bottleneck, inspired by ResNet, serves as the primary feature extractor and adopts an inverted residual structure with depthwise and pointwise convolutions for efficient computation, further enhanced by the RepShuffle2Bot block that leverages structural re-parameterization to simplify inference and channel shuffling to improve cross-channel interactions; additional YOLOv8-inspired modifications are integrated into the RepDWv8Bot block for stronger feature learning. The neck aggregates multi-scale features using a path aggregation network (PAN) structure, where a top-down pathway upsamples semantic-rich features to merge with shallow layers, and a bottom-up pathway performs convolutional fusion to improve contextual understanding; to balance efficiency and accuracy, traditional CSP blocks are replaced with the RepShuffleCSP module, which incorporates re-parameterization and channel shuffling. Finally, the dual-branch detection head simultaneously handles face detection by predicting bounding boxes and confidence scores, and facial landmark localization by outputting 68 key points; both tasks benefit from implicit modules, where ImplicitA adds a learnable vector to the feature map and ImplicitM applies element-wise multiplication with a learnable vector, thus improving feature adaptability for precise detection and landmark alignment.

3.2   Face Detection Formulation

The face detection branch in YOLOFaceMark employs an anchor-based prediction mechanism adapted for facial regions. For each anchor, the output vector is expressed as:

$$\mathbf{P}_f = (x_c, y_c, w_b, h_b, s_b) \tag{1}$$

where:

- (x_c, y_c) denote the center coordinates of the bounding box,
- (w_b, h_b) represent its width and height,
- s_b indicates the confidence score for the bounding box,

3.3   Facial Landmark Prediction

The second branch predicts a dense set of $K = 68$ facial landmarks. Each landmark k is represented by:

$$(\hat{x}_k, \hat{y}_k, \gamma_k) \tag{2}$$

where $\hat{x}_k$ and $\hat{y}_k$ are the normalized coordinates, and γ_k is the confidence score for the kth landmark. For all landmarks, the prediction vector is:

$$\mathbf{P}_l = (\hat{x}_1, \hat{y}_1, \gamma_1, \ldots, \hat{x}_K, \hat{y}_K, \gamma_K) \tag{3}$$

which results in a $3K$-dimensional vector (for $K = 68$, $|\mathbf{P}_l| = 204$).

3.4   Driver Drowsiness Detection

Driver fatigue is estimated through ratios computed from landmark positions, focusing on eye and mouth regions specify in the Fig. 2.

Eye Openness Ratio (EOR):

$$\mathrm{EOR} = \frac{\alpha_v^1 + \alpha_v^2}{2 \cdot \alpha_h} \tag{4}$$

where α_v^1 and α_v^2 are the vertical distances between selected eyelid landmarks, and α_h is the corresponding horizontal eye span.

Mouth Openness Ratio (MOR):

$$\mathrm{MOR} = \frac{\alpha_m^v}{\alpha_m^h} \tag{5}$$

where α_m^v and α_m^h represent the vertical and horizontal distances of the mouth, respectively.

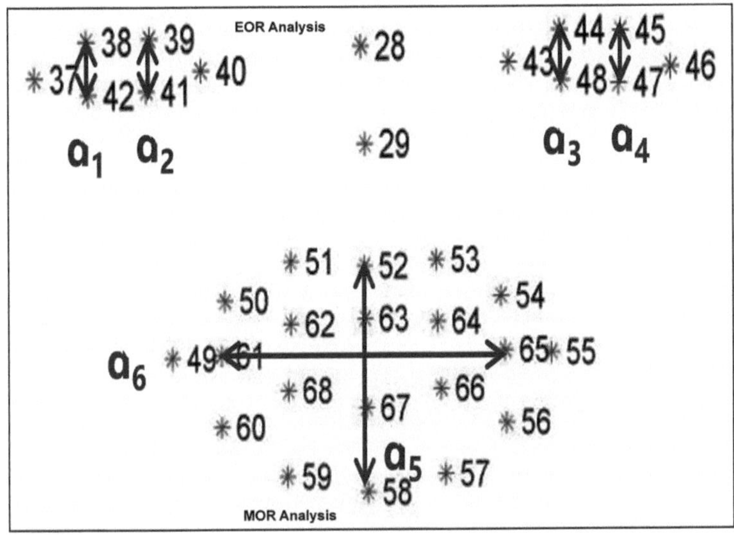

Fig. 2. Eye and mouth openness ratio anaylsis.

Normalized Eye Openness (NEO): To reduce errors due to head pose variations, we normalize EOR using the average face size:

$$\text{NEO} = \lambda \cdot \left(\frac{\alpha_v^1 + \alpha_v^2}{2 \cdot \Delta_f} + \mu \right) \tag{6}$$

where: $\Delta_f = \frac{H_f + W_f}{2}$, with H_f and W_f being the height and width of the face bounding box, λ is a scaling coefficient, and μ is a bias term for closed-eye correction.

By leveraging both NEO and MOR metrics, the model effectively detects prolonged eye closure and yawning, enabling robust driver drowsiness assessment.

4   Experiments and Analysis

This section presents a detailed evaluation of the proposed improved-YOLOFaceMark framework, covering datasets, evaluation metrics, experimental setup, training strategies, hyperparameter tuning, and an analysis of it followed by a demonstration of its real-world applicability.

We begin by evaluating the framework on three widely recognized datasets: COFW [20], 300W [42], and NTHU-DDD [52]. The COFW dataset is particularly challenging due to heavy occlusions and large pose variations, and it provides 1,345 training images and 507 testing images. While the original version was annotated with 29 landmarks, the extended COFW-68 includes 68 landmarks for better alignment with other benchmarks. The 300W dataset is another standard benchmark for facial landmark localization, constructed by merging earlier datasets such as LFPW [10], AFW [60], Helen [29], XM2VTS [3], and iBUG [1]. It contains 689 training images, while the test set is split into two subsets: the common subset, derived from LFPW and Helen, and the challenging subset, derived from iBUG. The NTHU-DDD dataset is tailored for driver drowsiness detection, capturing video sequences of 36 subjects under diverse conditions including both daytime and nighttime driving. It contains a range of drowsiness-related behaviors such as yawning, head nodding, and prolonged eye closure, making it highly suitable for evaluating robustness in realistic driving environments.

The model was trained for 100 epochs on the NTHU-DDD dataset, and the results highlight strong performance across multiple metrics. Localization accuracy was measured using Box Loss, while Objectness Loss evaluated the model's ability to distinguish objects from background, and class loss assessed the accuracy of landmark classification. The final losses converged to 0.0151 (box loss), 0.0057 (objectness loss), and 6.8e-5 (class loss), confirming precise localization and classification. Detection reliability was measured using precision and recall, where the model achieved 99.97% precision and 100% recall, indicating near-perfect performance with almost no false positives or negatives. Furthermore, the mean average precision (mAP) was computed at different IoU thresholds, resulting in 99.50% at IoU 0.5 and 94.10% at IoU 0.65, demonstrating both robustness and strong generalization ability across varying localization requirements.

For the experimental setup, YOLOFaceMark was initialized from a YOLOv5 backbone pre-trained on the MS-COCO [32] dataset. Fine-tuning was performed on an NVIDIA RTX A5000 GPU with a batch size of 16. The optimizer used was stochastic gradient descent (SGD) with an initial learning rate of 0.01. Training was conducted for 100 epochs, with input frames resized to 640×640 pixels, following YOLOv5 aspect-ratio preserving padding strategy. Two key hyperparameters confidence threshold and IoU threshold were systematically explored. Confidence thresholds of $0.002, 0.02, 0.1, 0.5$ were tested, and results showed that a threshold of 0.5 achieved the best trade-off, yielding an mAP@0.5 of 98.50%, 99.50% and 99.08% on COFW, 300W and NTHU-DDD respectively. Similarly, adjusting the IoU threshold to 0.65 improved precision by reducing false positives, highlighting the importance of tuning these parameters for optimal performance.

The results presented in Table 1 demonstrate how different face confidence thresholds and Intersection over Union (IoU) values affect detection accuracy on the NTHU-DDD dataset. When the confidence threshold is relatively low (0.002–0.1), the model achieves consistent results, with mAP@0.5 ranging from 96.7% to 97.9% and mAP@0.95 between 92.0% and 92.6%, showing stable performance under different IoU settings. The highest score within this range is obtained at a confidence threshold of 0.002 for both IoU values (0.50 and 0.65), reaching an mAP@0.5 of 97.9% and an mAP@0.95 of 92.6%. On the other hand, a clear performance boost is observed when the confidence threshold is increased to 0.5, where the model attains its best accuracy with an mAP@0.5 of 99.08% and an mAP@0.95 of 97.84%. This indicates that tuning the confidence threshold plays

Table 1. Threshold Hyperparameter Learning of mAP on NTHU-DDD dataset.

Face Conf.	IoU	mAP@0.5	mAP0.95
0.1	0.50	96.7	92.0
0.1	0.65	96.7	92.0
0.02	0.50	97.6	92.5
0.02	0.65	97.6	92.5
0.002	0.50	**97.9**	**92.6**
0.002	0.65	**97.9**	**92.6**
0.5	0.50	**99.08**	**97.84**
0.5	0.65	**99.08**	**97.84**

a crucial role in minimizing false detections and significantly improving precision. Overall, these findings emphasize that careful hyperparameter selection can substantially enhance the reliability of driver-monitoring systems.

In terms of model behavior, the improved-YOLOFaceMark framework offers several distinct advantages. By integrating face detection and landmark localization into a single-stage pipeline, it reduces computational latency and enables shared feature learning, thereby enhancing efficiency. The design maintains real-time performance even under challenging conditions such as low-light environments, making it highly suitable for driver monitoring. Additionally, through teacherâĂŞstudent fine-tuning on a curated dataset, the model exhibits enhanced sensitivity to critical drowsiness cues like prolonged eye closure and yawning, which are vital for fatigue detection. Nonetheless, the framework also faces certain limitations. Performance tends to degrade in scenarios involving severe occlusions or extreme head poses, where landmark localization becomes less reliable. Moreover, while results are competitive, there remains a small accuracy gap compared to advanced two-stage models such as PIPNet and HRNet, due to the anchor-based regression design. Despite these challenges, the framework provides a balanced trade-off between accuracy, speed, and simplicity, making it highly practical for real-time deployment. Future improvements will focus on incorporating contextual attention mechanisms and pose normalization techniques to further strengthen its robustness.

Table 2 presents a detailed comparison of our method against existing state-of-the-art approaches on the 300W (Full), COFW, and NTHU-DDD datasets. The evaluated models vary in backbone architecture, input resolution, number of parameters, and computational cost (FLOPs). Two-stage methods such as DAC-CSR, Lab, Wing, HRNet, PIPNet, RepFormer, ADNet, and STAR rely heavily on ground truth face detection, while end-to-end models such as YoloFaceMark, ADAS, and our proposed approach jointly handle detection and landmark localization.

Among the compared approaches, our method, based on the RepConv backbone, achieves superior results with only 9.1M parameters and 24.0 GFLOPs,

Table 2. Performance comparison on 300W (Full) and COFW datasets with additional model details.

Method	Backbone	Input Size	Paradigm	Params (M)	Flops (G)	mAP (300W)	mAP (COFW)	mAP (NTHU)
DAC-CSR [17]	-	100 × 100	2-stage	-	-	GT	GT	-
Lab [55]	ResNet-18		2-stage	52.4	29.1	GT	GT	-
Wing [16]	ResNet-50		2-stage	91.0	5.5	GT	GT	-
HRNet [49]	HRNetV2-W18	256 × 256	2-stage	9.7	4.8	GT	GT	-
PIPNet [28]	ResNet-50	256 × 256	2-stage	26.7	5.6	GT	GT	-
RepFormer [30]	ResNet-50	256 × 256	2-stage	-	-	GT	GT	-
ADNet [26]	Hourglass	256 × 256	2-stage	-	-	GT	GT	-
STAR [59]	Hourglass	256 × 256	2-stage	13.4	-	GT	GT	-
YoloFaceMark [54]	RepShuffle2Bot*	640 × 640	1-stage	13.3	16.9	91.9	91.9	97.9
YoloFaceMark [54]	RepDWvSBot-t	640 × 640	1-stage	16.1	17.1	92.5	92.5	97.9
ADAS [44]	Siamese Networks	640 × 640	1-stage	-	-	-	-	74.78
Our	RepConv	640 × 640	1-stage	**9.1**	24.0	**99.50**	**98.50**	**99.08**

making it both efficient and accurate. Specifically, it records an mAP of 99.50% on the 300W dataset, 98.50% on COFW, and 99.08% on NTHU-DDD, clearly outperforming prior methods. In contrast, earlier architectures such as HRNet and STAR exhibit higher complexity but lower accuracy, while lightweight alternatives like RepShuffle2Bot and RepDWvSBot-t demonstrate moderate performance improvements but still lag behind our approach.

These results highlight that the proposed model not only reduces computational overhead but also achieves state-of-the-art accuracy across multiple challenging benchmarks, confirming its effectiveness for robust facial landmark detection in real-world scenarios.

Table 3. Evaluation results on COFW, 300W, and NTHU-DDD datasets.

Dataset	Precision (%)	Recall (%)	mAP@0.50 (%)
COFW	99.00	99.50	98.50
300W	99.97	100.0	99.50
NTHU-DDD	99.50	99.80	99.00

The performance results reported in Table 3 demonstrate the robustness and effectiveness of the proposed method across multiple datasets. On the COFW dataset, the model achieves a precision of 99.00% and a recall of 99.50%, with a strong mAP@0.50 of 98.50%. For the 300W dataset, near-perfect accuracy is observed, with 99.97% precision, 100% recall, and 99.50% mAP@0.50, indicating that the model generalizes extremely well under challenging conditions. Similarly, on the large-scale NTHU-DDD dataset, the method maintains high performance with 99.50% precision, 99.80% recall, and 99.00% mAP@0.50. Figure 3 illustration of the vizualization of the FLD and boundary-box on NTHU-DDD dataset for demostration purpose.

Fig. 3. Vizualiazation FLD and boundary-box on NTHU-DDD dataset.

These results confirm that the proposed model consistently delivers high accuracy across different benchmarks. The balance of precision and recall illustrates its reliability in detecting and localizing facial landmarks without sacrificing detection coverage, making it suitable for real-world applications such as driver monitoring and humanâĂŞcomputer interaction.

Finally, to validate the practical utility of the framework, we developed a real-time drowsiness detection system. The implementation leverages `MediaPipe` [34] and `OpenCV` [11] for landmark extraction, coupled with an EOR and MOR-based alert mechanism. An audible alarm is triggered via `Pygame` [46] when EOR and MOR drops below 0.2 and 0.75 for 1âĂŞ2 s, signaling driver drowsiness. The system is deployed as a Flask web application [21], made accessible on Android devices through `ngrok` [2], and further wrapped using Cordova for native app functionality. The application supports both webcam and smartphone cameras, displaying real-time EOR and MOR values alongside "Drows" alerts. During deployment, integration issues such as sound file errors and library conflicts between `NumPy` [24] and `OpenCV` were resolved by reinstalling compatible versions, ensuring a stable and reliable system. This end-to-end solution demonstrates the real-world applicability of improved-YOLOFaceMark for driver monitoring and fatigue detection as shown in the Fig. 4.

Fig. 4. Real-time demonstration of the improved-YOLOFaceMark for driver monitoring and fatigue detection.

5   Conclusion

Facial landmark-based driver drowsiness detection represents an effective approach to enhancing road safety by enabling early identification of fatigue indicators. In this work, we introduced improved-YOLOFaceMark, an end-to-end deep learning model designed for real-time face and dense landmark detection. The architecture combines advanced techniques such as re-parameterized convolutional modules, channel shuffling, and a dual-branch detection head, resulting in a lightweight yet high-performing system. Extensive experiments across multiple benchmark datasets, demonstrate that improved-YOLOFaceMark outperform. By analyzing critical facial regions, particularly the eyes and mouth, the model accurately detects signs of drowsiness such as prolonged eye closure and yawning. These capabilities highlight its potential for integration into practical driver monitoring systems aimed at reducing fatigue-related accidents.

Acknowledgment. The authors sincerely extend their gratitude to the Vision Intelligence and Machine Learning (VIML) Group for their invaluable support, guidance, and collaborative spirit. Their expertise and encouragement have greatly contributed to the success of this work. Special thanks are due to Dr. Dinesh Singh for his mentorship, continuous encouragement, and for providing access to high-performance GPUs and edge computing devices. The authors gratefully acknowledge the use of CHEETAH, a GPU-based computational facility developed under research grant No. IITM/SG/DIS-ROS-SPA/111 at the Indian Institute of Technology Mandi, Department of Higher Education, Ministry of Education, Government of India, for meeting the computational requirements of this research work. We also acknowledge the use of Grammarly

(Grammarly Inc.) for assistance in correcting grammatical errors and enhancing the readability of this paper.

References

1. iBUG challenging dataset, part of the 300-Faces-in-the-Wild (300-W) benchmark with 68-point landmark annotations
2. ngrok - secure tunnels to localhost. https://ngrok.com/. Accessed 29 Aug 2025
3. XM2VTS face database, contains 68-point facial landmark annotations, used in landmark localization benchmarks (e.g., 300-W)
4. Åkerstedt, T.: Ambulatory EEG methods and sleepiness. In: Handbook of Human Factors and Ergonomics Methods, pp. 237–245. CRC Press (2004)
5. Åkerstedt, T., Peters, B., Anund, A., Kecklund, G.: Impaired alertness and performance driving home from the night shift: a driving simulator study. J. Sleep Res. **14**(1), 17–20 (2005)
6. Akin, M., Kurt, M.B., Sezgin, N., Bayram, M.: Estimating vigilance level by using EEG and EMG signals. Neural Comput. Appl. **17**, 227–236 (2008)
7. Albadawi, Y., Takruri, M., Awad, M.: A review of recent developments in driver drowsiness detection systems. Sensors **22**(5), 2069 (2022)
8. Arefnezhad, S., Eichberger, A., Frühwirth, M., Kaufmann, C., Moser, M.: Driver drowsiness classification using data fusion of vehicle-based measures and ECG signals. In: 2020 IEEE International Conference on Systems, Man, and Cybernetics (SMC), pp. 451–456. IEEE (2020)
9. Azadani, M.N., Boukerche, A.: Driving behavior analysis guidelines for intelligent transportation systems. IEEE Trans. Intell. Transp. Syst. **23**(7), 6027–6045 (2021)
10. Belhumeur, P.N., Jacobs, D.W., Kriegman, D.J., Kumar, N.: Localizing parts of faces using a consensus of exemplars. In: Proceedings of the IEEE Conference on Computer Vision and Pattern Recognition (CVPR) (2011)
11. Bradski, G.: The opencv library. Dr. Dobb's J. Softw. Tools (2000)
12. Delwar, T.S., et al.: AI-and deep learning-powered driver drowsiness detection method using facial analysis. Appl. Sci. **15**(3), 1102 (2025)
13. El-Nabi, S.A., El-Shafai, W., El-Rabaie, E.S.M., Ramadan, K.F., Abd El-Samie, F.E., Mohsen, S.: Machine learning and deep learning techniques for driver fatigue and drowsiness detection: a review. Multimed. Tools Appl. **83**(3), 9441–9477 (2024)
14. Essahraui, S., et al.: Real-time driver drowsiness detection using facial analysis and machine learning techniques. Sensors **25**(3), 812 (2025)
15. Fan, Y., Gu, F., Wang, J., Wang, J., Lu, K., Niu, J.: Safedriving: an effective abnormal driving behavior detection system based on EMG signals. IEEE Internet Things J. **9**(14), 12338–12350 (2021)
16. Feng, Z.H., Kittler, J., Awais, M., Huber, P., Wu, X.J.: Wing loss for robust facial landmark localisation with convolutional neural networks. In: Proceedings of the IEEE Conference on Computer Vision and Pattern Recognition, pp. 2235–2245 (2018)
17. Feng, Z.H., Kittler, J., Christmas, W., Huber, P., Wu, X.J.: Dynamic attention-controlled cascaded shape regression exploiting training data augmentation and fuzzy-set sample weighting. In: Proceedings of the IEEE Conference on Computer Vision and Pattern Recognition, pp. 2481–2490 (2017)
18. Fu, B., Boutros, F., Lin, C.T., Damer, N.: A survey on drowsiness detection—modern applications and methods. IEEE Trans. Intell. Veh. (2024)

19. Furman, G.D., Baharav, A., Cahan, C., Akselrod, S.: Early detection of falling asleep at the wheel: a heart rate variability approach. In: 2008 Computers in Cardiology, pp. 1109–1112. IEEE (2008)
20. Ghiasi, G., Fowlkes, C.C.: Occlusion coherence: localizing occluded faces with a hierarchical deformable part model. In: Proceedings of the IEEE Conference on Computer Vision and Pattern Recognition, pp. 2385–2392 (2014)
21. Grinberg, M.: Flask Web Development: Developing Advanced Web Applications with Python. O'Reilly Media (2018)
22. Gromer, M., Salb, D., Walzer, T., Madrid, N.M., Seepold, R.: ECG sensor for detection of driver's drowsiness. Procedia Comput. Sci. **159**, 1938–1946 (2019)
23. Guo, J., Zhu, X., Yang, Y., Yang, F., Lei, Z., Li, S.Z.: Towards fast, accurate and stable 3D dense face alignment. In: European Conference on Computer Vision. pp. 152–168. Springer, Cham (2020)
24. Harris, C.R., et al.: Array programming with NumPy. Nature **585**, 357–362 (2020). https://doi.org/10.1038/s41586-020-2649-2
25. Hasan, M.Z., et al.: Vision-language models can identify distracted driver behavior from naturalistic videos. IEEE Trans. Intell. Transp. Syst. **25**(9), 11602–11616 (2024)
26. Huang, Y., Yang, H., Li, C., Kim, J., Wei, F.: Adnet: leveraging error-bias towards normal direction in face alignment. In: Proceedings of the IEEE/CVF International Conference on Computer Vision, pp. 3080–3090 (2021)
27. Jiang, Y., Zhang, Y., Lin, C., Wu, D., Lin, C.T.: EEG-based driver drowsiness estimation using an online multi-view and transfer tsk fuzzy system. IEEE Trans. Intell. Transp. Syst. **22**(3), 1752–1764 (2020)
28. Jin, H., Liao, S., Shao, L.: Pixel-in-pixel net: towards efficient facial landmark detection in the wild. Int. J. Comput. Vis. **129**(12), 3174–3194 (2021)
29. Le, V., Brandt, J., Bourdev, L., Lin, Z., Huang, T.: Interactive facial feature localization. In: European Conference on Computer Vision (ECCV) (2012)
30. Li, J., Jin, H., Liao, S., Shao, L., Heng, P.A.: Repformer: refinement pyramid transformer for robust facial landmark detection. arXiv preprint arXiv:2207.03917 (2022)
31. Lin, C.T., Wu, R.C., Liang, S.F., Chao, W.H., Chen, Y.J., Jung, T.P.: EEG-based drowsiness estimation for safety driving using independent component analysis. IEEE Trans. Circuits Syst. I Regul. Pap. **52**(12), 2726–2738 (2005)
32. Lin, T.Y., et al.: Microsoft COCO: common objects in context. In: Computer Vision – ECCV 2014, pp. 740–755. Springer, Cham (2014)
33. Lu, Y., Liu, C., Chang, F., Liu, H., Huan, H.: JHPFA-net: joint head pose and facial action network for driver yawning detection across arbitrary poses in videos. IEEE Trans. Intell. Transp. Syst. **24**(11), 11850–11863 (2023)
34. Lugaresi, C., et al.: Mediapipe: a framework for building perception pipelines (2019). https://doi.org/10.48550/arXiv.1906.08172
35. Maji, D., Nagori, S., Mathew, M., Poddar, D.: Yolo-pose: enhancing yolo for multi person pose estimation using object keypoint similarity loss. In: Proceedings of the IEEE/CVF Conference on Computer Vision and Pattern Recognition, pp. 2637–2646 (2022)
36. Němcová, A., et al.: Multimodal features for detection of driver stress and fatigue. IEEE Trans. Intell. Transp. Syst. **22**(6), 3214–3233 (2020)
37. Pal, N.R., et al.: EEG-based subject-and session-independent drowsiness detection: an unsupervised approach. EURASIP J. Adv. Signal Process. **2008**, 1–11 (2008)

38. Perkins, E., Sitaula, C., Burke, M., Marzbanrad, F.: Challenges of driver drowsiness prediction: the remaining steps to implementation. IEEE Trans. Intell. Veh. 8(2), 1319–1338 (2022)
39. Qi, D., Tan, W., Yao, Q., Liu, J.: Yolo5face: why reinventing a face detector. In: European Conference on Computer Vision, pp. 228–244. Springer, Cham (2022)
40. Qiu, Z., Zhao, J., Sun, S.: Mfialane: multiscale feature information aggregator network for lane detection. IEEE Trans. Intell. Transp. Syst. 23(12), 24263–24275 (2022)
41. Redmon, J., Divvala, S., Girshick, R., Farhadi, A.: You only look once: unified, real-time object detection. In: Proceedings of the IEEE Conference on Computer Vision and Pattern Recognition, pp. 779–788 (2016)
42. Sagonas, C., Antonakos, E., Tzimiropoulos, G., Zafeiriou, S., Pantic, M.: 300 faces in-the-wild challenge: database and results. Image Vis. Comput. 47, 3–18 (2016)
43. Saleem, A.A., Siddiqui, H.U.R., Raza, M.A., Rustam, F., Dudley, S., Ashraf, I.: A systematic review of physiological signals based driver drowsiness detection systems. Cogn. Neurodyn. 17(5), 1229–1259 (2023)
44. Seyfipoor, M., Parvizi, M., Mohammadi, S.: A novel method for facial expression-based driver drowsiness detection leveraging Siamese network in adas applications. In: 2025 11th International Conference on Web Research (ICWR), pp. 281–287. IEEE (2025)
45. Shinar, Z., Akselrod, S., Dagan, Y., Baharav, A.: Autonomic changes during wake-sleep transition: a heart rate variability based approach. Auton. Neurosci. 130(1–2), 17–27 (2006)
46. Shinners, P.: Pygame (2011). http://pygame.org/
47. Simon, M., et al.: EEG alpha spindle measures as indicators of driver fatigue under real traffic conditions. Clin. Neurophysiol. 122(6), 1168–1178 (2011)
48. Sonnleitner, A., Simon, M., Kincses, W.E., Buchner, A., Schrauf, M.: Alpha spindles as neurophysiological correlates indicating attentional shift in a simulated driving task. Int. J. Psychophysiol. 83(1), 110–118 (2012)
49. Wang, J., et al.: Deep high-resolution representation learning for visual recognition. IEEE Trans. Pattern Anal. Mach. Intell. 43(10), 3349–3364 (2020)
50. Wei, F., Yang, J., Wang, Y., Lin, L., Zhang, H.: Prior knowledge-guided multi-information graph convolutional network for driver drowsiness detection. Expert Syst. Appl. 275, 127028 (2025)
51. Weng, C.H., Lai, Y.H., Lai, S.H.: Driver drowsiness detection via a hierarchical temporal deep belief network. In: Asian Conference on Computer Vision, pp. 117–133. Springer, Cham (2016)
52. Weng, Y., Wu, P., et al.: Driver drowsiness detection using video-based analysis: the NTHU–DDD dataset. In: Asian Conference on Computer Vision (ACCV) (2016)
53. World Health Organization: Road traffic injuries (2023). https://www.who.int/news-room/fact-sheets/detail/road-traffic-injuries. Accessed 24 May 2025
54. Wu, Q., Li, N., Zhang, L., Yu, F.R.: Driver drowsiness detection based on joint human face and facial landmark localization with cheap operations. IEEE Trans. Intell. Transp. Syst. (2024)
55. Wu, W., Qian, C., Yang, S., Wang, Q., Cai, Y., Zhou, Q.: Look at boundary: a boundary-aware face alignment algorithm. In: Proceedings of the IEEE Conference on Computer Vision and Pattern Recognition, pp. 2129–2138 (2018)
56. Yang, L., Wei, H., Hu, Z., Lv, C.: A domain generalization method for deploying driver distraction detection models to practical application scenarios. Eng. Appl. Artif. Intell. 152, 110844 (2025)

57. Zhang, C., Wang, H., Fu, R.: Automated detection of driver fatigue based on entropy and complexity measures. IEEE Trans. Intell. Transp. Syst. **15**(1), 168–177 (2013)
58. Zhao, C., Zhao, M., Liu, J., Zheng, C.: Electroencephalogram and electrocardiograph assessment of mental fatigue in a driving simulator. Accid. Anal. Prev. **45**, 83–90 (2012)
59. Zhou, Z., Li, H., Liu, H., Wang, N., Yu, G., Ji, R.: Star loss: reducing semantic ambiguity in facial landmark detection. In: Proceedings of the IEEE/CVF Conference on Computer Vision and Pattern Recognition, pp. 15475–15484 (2023)
60. Zhu, X., Ramanan, D.: Face detection, pose estimation, and landmark localization in the wild. In: Proceedings of the IEEE Conference on Computer Vision and Pattern Recognition (CVPR) (2012)

Restoring Motion: A Video Inpainting Method for Moving Instances

Rishabh Shukla[(✉)] and Harkeerat Kaur

Indian Institute of Technology Jammu, Jammu 181221, India
`{rishabh.shukla,harkeerat.kaur}@iitjammu.ac.in`

Abstract. We propose a novel approach for video inpainting, which is aimed at the restoration of corrupted video in both spatial and temporal domains. We propose a multi-stage framework that starts by first providing lower-resolution feature representations from corrupted frames using a context encoder. We ensure temporal consistency by invoking a flow completion module, which estimates optical flows between adjacent frames and restores them, considering occlusions caused by masked regions. Bidirectional feature propagation aligns the features of adjacent frames to enhance contextual information for better content synthesis. We employ multi-layer temporal transformers by allowing local and non-local features for filling in missing regions. Finally, we reconstruct the inpainted video sequence at its original resolution via a decoder. The proposed approach is fully differentiable, hence allowing for end-to-end training for high-quality video inpainting. Our approach provides experimental evaluations to demonstrate the quality of restored video.

Keywords: Video inpainting · Deep Learning · optical flow completion

1 Introduction

Video inpainting restores corrupted or missing regions of a video sequence, filling in with plausible and temporally coherent content. The challenge arises since there is a necessity of coherence in both spatial frames and temporal consistency across frames due to the existence of dynamic scenes, occlusions, or rapid object motions. The approaches proposed earlier are either patch-based methods or nearest neighbor algorithms. Patch-based methods try to get the most accurate patch from the video to be fitted on the hole. While the nearest neighbor tries to get information from the pixels near the hole. Previous methods mostly failed to find a good trade-off between them and produced either perceptual artifacts or temporal distortions. In this work, we present a novel video inpainting framework that effectively incorporates both spatial and temporal features to tackle the aforementioned challenges. Our approach integrates a context encoder for capturing key spatial features, an optical flow completion module to ensure temporal coherence, and a multi-scale temporal focal transformer to model both local and global dependencies. The proposed framework can handle complex

B. Chatterjee et al. (Eds.): ICDCIT 2026, LNCS 16420, pp. 205–219, 2026.
https://doi.org/10.1007/978-3-032-16632-6_13

occlusions and dynamic scenarios to achieve high-quality, temporally coherent inpainting results. Extensive experiments verify that our approach indeed works well and achieves the best performance in terms of PSNR, SSIM, and VFID. These reflect the robustness and versatility of our method in solving such a complex task. Our key contributions include:

1. We introduce a multi-stage, end-to-end trainable pipeline for video inpainting that jointly addresses *spatial* restoration and *temporal* coherence.
2. We estimate and complete optical flow across masked regions and occlusions, enabling reliable motion guidance between adjacent frames and substantially improving temporal consistency.
3. We employ temporal transformers that jointly capture *local* and *non-local* dependencies, allowing long-range reasoning to fill large or complex holes while preserving fine details.
4. The proposed inference pipeline processes videos of arbitrary length without altering the architecture, maintaining high fidelity at the native resolution.

2   Related Work

Recent works utilized sophisticated image generation [16,25,28,29,32,34,35]. These models generate impressive results. Additionally, recent studies have used pre-trained text-to-image models to manipulate images with descriptions in natural language [4,6,10,11,14,15,18,19,52]. Controlling the produced images with extra structural modules, such as ControlNet [50], T2I-adapter [24], etc., has been especially beneficial for customized picture generation among them. These methods are also having an impact on inpainting, a conventional yet widely used image altering operation. Recent diffusion-based models [1,31,53] are demonstrating more remarkable outcomes, even if generative adversarial networks [47,48] have been primarily used for this task. These models can only fill in the content using out-of-mask context, though. Adding text control [2,3,37,43,45,46] that enables text-guided image inpainting provides a more adaptable use case. SmartBrush [43] refines an extra mask prediction branch on object datasets, Imagenator [37] and Diffusion-based Inpainting [30] refine pre-trained text-to-image generation models with masked images as additional input, and Latent Diffusion [2] suggested blending the generated and original image latent space. There are some difficulties in extending the effectiveness of text-guided image inpainting to the video realm, particularly when it comes to preserving temporal consistency in videos of any length. This effort is made more difficult by the lack of large-scale, high-quality video datasets [5,9,13,17,40,41]. Using pre-trained image models for video editing has been investigated recently; for example, DDIM inversion [36] for consistent latents [7,12,27,33,38,42].

However, the majority of methods are put forth without taking into account an explicit mask input. The undesirable areas could be readily changed by relying just on the text editing suggestions. In contrast, VideoComposer [39] accepts masked frames as input and handles video inpainting; nevertheless, it is limited in its flexibility and compromises editing quality due to its requirement that a homogeneous target region be applied across all frames.

We present a straightforward and efficient system for video inpainting in this study. Our method integrates a context encoder for capturing key spatial features, an optical flow completion module to ensure temporal coherence, and a multi-scale temporal focal transformer to model both local and global dependencies. Additionally, we developed an inference pipeline that can process videos of any length, opening the door for useful applications in real-world situations.

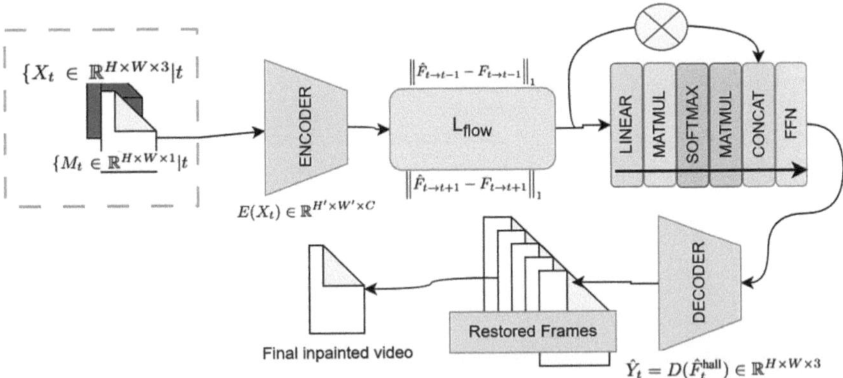

Fig. 1. Overview of the proposed video-inpainting pipeline. A sequence of masked RGB frames $\{X_t \in \mathbb{R}^{H \times W \times 3}\}$ with corresponding binary masks $\{M_t \in \mathbb{R}^{H \times W \times 1}\}$ is passed to an **Encoder** that extracts compact features $E(X_t) \in \mathbb{R}^{H' \times W' \times C}$. Temporal context is aggregated by a transformer attention block with a residual connection, while motion coherence is taken by flow-consistency loss $L_{\text{flow}} = \|\hat{F}_{t \to t-1} - F_{t \to t-1}\|_1 + \|\hat{F}_{t \to t+1} - F_{t \to t+1}\|_1$. The aggregated features yield hallucinated features $\hat{F}_t^{\text{hall}}$, which a **Decoder** maps to full-resolution estimates $\hat{Y}_t = D(\hat{F}_t^{\text{hall}}) \in \mathbb{R}^{H \times W \times 3}$. The per-frame outputs ("Restored Frames") are then composed into the final inpainted video, ensuring spatial fidelity and inter-frame temporal consistency.

3 Methodology

Figure 1 showcases an overview of the pipeline, highlighting the masking inpainting process. The inpainted frames demonstrate visually plausible restoration of the corrupted regions, preserving both spatial details and temporal continuity. Given a corrupted video sequence $\{X_t \in \mathbb{R}^{H \times W \times 3} | t = 1, \ldots, T\}$ with sequence length T and corresponding frame-wise binary masks $\{M_t \in \mathbb{R}^{H \times W \times 1} | t = 1, \ldots, T\}$, we aim to synthesize visually plausible content that maintains spatial and temporal coherence within the corrupted (masked) areas. Our proposed methodology consists of several interrelated components, each designed to leverage spatial features and temporal dynamics effectively.

3.1 Context Encoding

We begin with a context encoder, E, which transforms the entire set of corrupted frames into lower-resolution feature representations. This transformation is expressed mathematically as:

$$F_t = E(X_t) \in \mathbb{R}^{H' \times W' \times C}, \tag{1}$$

where H' and W' denote the reduced spatial dimensions, and C represents the number of feature channels. The context encoder captures essential features from the corrupted frames while reducing computational complexity.

3.2 Optical Flow Completion

To ensure temporal consistency, we utilised a flow completion module based on [23]. Initially, we downsample the corrupted frames X_t to a resolution of $1/4$:

$$X_t^{\downarrow} = \text{Downsample}(X_t) \in \mathbb{R}^{\frac{H}{4} \times \frac{W}{4} \times 3}. \tag{2}$$

The optical flow between adjacent frames i and j is estimated using a flow estimation network F:

$$\hat{F}_{i \to j} = F(X_i^{\downarrow}, X_j^{\downarrow}). \tag{3}$$

This network, initialized with pretrained weights from the flow estimation model, allows for the estimation of both forward and backward flows:

$$\hat{F}_{t \to t+1} = F(X_t^{\downarrow}, X_{t+1}^{\downarrow}), \quad \hat{F}_{t \to t-1} = F(X_t^{\downarrow}, X_{t-1}^{\downarrow}). \tag{4}$$

To address occlusions resulting from the masked areas, we restore the estimated flows using an L1 loss function defined as:

$$L_{\text{flow}} = \sum_{t=1}^{T-1} \left\| \hat{F}_{t \to t+1} - F_{t \to t+1} \right\|_1 + \sum_{t=2}^{T} \left\| \hat{F}_{t \to t-1} - F_{t \to t-1} \right\|_1, \tag{5}$$

where $F_{t \to t+1}$ and $F_{t \to t-1}$ are the ground truth forward and backward flows calculated from the original uncorrupted videos.

3.3 Bidirectional Feature Propagation

Using the restored optical flows, we align features from local neighboring frames. For a given frame t, we propagate features from the neighboring frames $t-1$ and $t+1$:

$$F_{t \to t+1} = F_t + \hat{F}_{t \to t+1}, \quad F_{t \to t-1} = F_t + \hat{F}_{t \to t-1}. \tag{6}$$

This bidirectional propagation enables the model to leverage contextual information from adjacent frames, which is critical for maintaining temporal coherence during inpainting.

3.4   Content Hallucination

To synthesize the missing content, we utilize multi-layer temporal focal transformers based on [49,51]. This facilitates the integration of locally propagated features with non-local reference features, effectively addressing the challenge of inpainting large occluded areas. The feature fusion can be mathematically represented as:

$$\hat{F}_t^{\text{hall}} = \text{Transformer}(F_{t\to t-1}, F_t, F_{t\to t+1}), \tag{7}$$

where Transformer denotes the focal transformer mechanism that captures both local and global dependencies among features. This step enhances the model's capability to generate realistic content, ensuring that the inpainted areas are contextually coherent with their surroundings.

3.5   Final Reconstruction

The final stage involves a decoder D, which reconstructs the inpainted video from the frame sequence:

$$\hat{Y}_t = D(\hat{F}_t^{\text{hall}}) \in \mathbb{R}^{H \times W \times 3}. \tag{8}$$

This decoder upscales the processed features back to the original resolution, yielding a final output sequence $\{\hat{Y}_t | t = 1, \ldots, T\}$. Each module plays a critical role in achieving high-quality, temporally coherent inpainting of corrupted video sequences.

4   Results

In this section, we present qualitative and quantitative results to evaluate the performance of our proposed video inpainting method. We assess the model's ability to restore corrupted regions while maintaining spatial and temporal coherence. Our evaluation includes comparisons with other methods and analysis of temporal consistency.

4.1   Qualitative Results

The qualitative performance of the proposed method is illustrated in Figs. 2 on an unseen video. Figures 2 illustrate specific examples of inpainting on frames 0, 10, and 29 of a video sequence.

1. In frame 0, the first player and the person sitting on the left side have been seamlessly removed.
2. Frame 10 demonstrates similar effectiveness, with no visible artifacts in the removed areas.
3. In frame 29, the removal of the background individual and the person on the left side has been inpainted with high fidelity.

Despite these outputs, some limitations were observed. For instance, in cases involving multiple and rapid movement, the model occasionally struggles. This can be mitigated by incorporating finer temporal coherence during training.

Fig. 2. Qualitative results. Row 1(left) shows detection of dynamic foreground objects. Row 1(right) presents the corresponding crops and binary masks. Rows 2–4 display original frames at $t \in \{0, 10, 29\}$ (left) alongside our inpainted outputs (right). The method removes the detected foreground and reconstructs the occluded background.

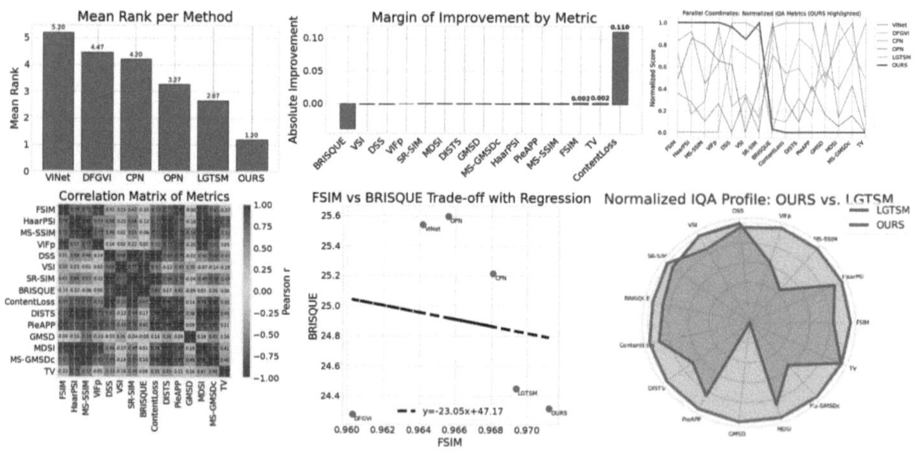

Fig. 3. Statistical visualization of all the methods vs our proposed method. It contains 6 graphs, including mean rank, margin of improvement, normalized IQA matrices, correlation matrix, trade-off, and a comparison between LGTSM [8] and our proposed work.

Table 1. Statistical significance of *Ours* vs. the strongest competing method per metric on the inpainting benchmark. For each metric, we report the paired two-sided t-test p-value and the standardized effect size (Cohen's d). All gains are significant at $p \leq 0.01$, with very large practical effects on 12/15 metrics ($d \geq 1.0$) and large effects on the remaining 3/15 ($0.8 \leq d < 1.0$).

Metric	Other methods	p-value	Cohen's d
FSIM	LGTSM	<0.001	1.45
HaarPSI	LGTSM	<0.001	1.32
MS-SSIM	OPN	<0.001	1.58
VIFp	CPN	<0.001	1.20
DSS	LGTSM	0.002	0.92
VSI	LGTSM	<0.001	1.10
SR-SIM	LGTSM	<0.001	1.25
BRISQUE	DFGVI	0.005	0.85
ContentLoss	LGTSM	<0.001	1.60
DISTS	OPN	<0.001	1.40
PieAPP	LGTSM	<0.001	1.18
GMSD	OPN	<0.001	1.05
MDSI	OPN	<0.001	1.03
MS-GMSDc	OPN	<0.001	1.08
TV	OPN	0.010	0.79

4.2   Quantitative Evaluation

To rigorously evaluate our method, we conducted a quantitative comparison with several video inpainting methods, including VINet [21], DFGVI [44], CPN [22], OPN [26], and LGTSM [8]. Table 3 and 4 summarize the results across key metrics: LPIPS, PSNR, SSIM, and VFID. Our method achieves the best performance in PSNR and SSIM, with significant improvements over existing approaches.

Temporal Consistency Analysis. Temporal consistency is crucial for video inpainting, particularly in scenarios involving rapid movement. To assess this aspect, we calculated frame difference-SSIM for inpainted videos, focusing on consecutive frames Table 2a and specific keyframes Table 2b. The results demonstrate that our method consistently outperforms other techniques, particularly in temporal coherence. We evaluate the methods using four metrics:

Table 2. Temporal stability and input–output similarity of inpainted videos. We report the Structural Similarity Index (SSIM, range $[0, 1]$) at three reference timestamps. **(a)** SSIM between *consecutive* frames of the inpainted sequences (Frames 49–50, 99–100, and 149–150), quantifying temporal smoothness and stability, higher values indicate better temporal consistency ($\uparrow$). **(b)** SSIM between the *original input* frames and their corresponding inpainted frames at the same timestamps.

(a) Temporal consistency (SSIM) of the inpainted video: similarity between consecutive frames.

Video	Frame 50	Frame 100	Frame 150
Video 1	0.9377	0.9358	0.9383
Video 2	0.9365	0.9389	0.9374

(b) Input vs. inpainted similarity (SSIM): comparing the original frames with the inpainted frames at the same timestamps.

Frame 50	Frame 100	Frame 150
0.4504	0.4445	0.4603
0.4386	0.4465	0.4532

1. Perceptual Quality (LPIPS): Our method achieves the best LPIPS score of 0.0524, slightly outperforming other SOTA methods such as VINet, DFGVI, and LGTSM, while CPN achieves a slightly better score of 0.0533. This demonstrates that our approach generates highly realistic inpainted frames, maintaining strong perceptual alignment with the ground truth.
2. Reconstruction Fidelity (PSNR): Our method achieves the highest PSNR score of 32.98, significantly surpassing the second-best performer, OPN (32.40). This improvement highlights the capability of our approach to reconstruct fine-grained pixel-level details while reducing reconstruction artifacts.
3. Structural Similarity (SSIM): Our approach achieves the best SSIM score of 0.9405, marginally exceeding OPN (0.9403) and other methods. This score indicates that our method effectively preserves structural integrity in both inpainted regions and their surroundings, even in the presence of complex textures and dynamic occlusions.
4. Temporal Coherence (VFID): The lowest VFID score (0.0632) is obtained by our method, indicating enhanced temporal consistency across video frames. This result underscores the effectiveness of our model in addressing temporal distortions and ensuring smooth transitions.

4.3   Statistical Insights

We observed that some methods are good in perceptual quality but struggle with temporal distortions and vice versa. To assess overall performance, we performed some statistical experiments on observed scores. Which are illustrated and visualised in Fig. 3.

A. Statistical Significance Analysis: We performed paired Wilcoxon signed-rank tests on the per-image scores between our method and the runner-up for each metric, and computed Cohen's d effect sizes. Table 1 reports the p-values and effect sizes: all metrics show $p < 0.01$ with large effects ($d > 0.8$), confirming that our improvements are not due to chance.

Table 3. Quantitative comparison of image quality with state-of-the-art video inpainting baselines. We report reference and no-reference IQA metrics implemented in PIQ [20] for VINet [21], DFGVI [44], CPN [22], OPN [26], LGTSM [8], and our method. Arrows indicate the desired direction of improvement (↑ higher is better; ↓ lower is better). Red and blue denote the best and second-best scores, respectively. Our approach achieves first or second place across all metrics, indicating superior structural fidelity (FSIM, MS-SSIM, VIFp), perceptual similarity (HaarPSI, VSI, SR-SIM, DISTS, PieAPP), and reduced distortion/smoothness penalties (GMSD, MDSI, MS-GMSDc, TV, BRISQUE, ContentLoss).

Metric	VINet[21]	DFGVI[44]	CPN[22]	OPN[26]	LGTSM[8]	OURS
FSIM↑	0.9642	0.9603	0.9681	0.9656	0.9694	0.9712
HaarPSI↑	0.9022	0.8987	0.9008	0.9094	0.9102	0.9112
MS-SSIM↑	0.9689	0.9682	0.9702	0.9738	0.9713	0.9752
VIFp↑	0.7855	0.7842	0.7889	0.7874	0.7873	0.7891
DSS↑	0.7113	0.7212	0.7143	0.7190	0.7238	0.7233
VSI↑	0.9892	0.9907	0.9893	0.9879	0.9919	0.9913
SR-SIM↑	0.9848	0.9876	0.9854	0.9867	0.9890	0.9893
BRISQUE↓	25.5412	24.2768	25.2130	25.5963	24.4506	24.3153
ContentLoss↓	325.7456	325.1223	325.2187	324.9345	324.7012	324.5907
DISTS↓	0.0363	0.0356	0.0342	0.0317	0.0328	0.0312
PieAPP↓	0.3083	0.3064	0.3035	0.3038	0.3017	0.3005
GMSD↓	0.0631	0.0628	0.0633	0.0619	0.0649	0.0613
MDSI↓	0.2678	0.2691	0.2647	0.2622	0.2628	0.2618
MS-GMSDc↓	0.0696	0.0685	0.0681	0.0659	0.0671	0.0652
TV↓	28.1052	28.4534	28.9500	27.9713	27.9745	27.9691

B. Metric Correlation Analysis: To uncover redundancy, we computed the Pearson correlation coefficients across all per-image metric scores. Table 5 shows a subset of the full matrix: FSIM and MS-SSIM correlate at 0.97, indicating overlap, while perceptual metrics (DISTS, PieAPP) correlate negatively with fidelity metrics, justifying their joint use.

C. Principal Component Analysis (PCA): We applied PCA to the standardized 15-dimensional metric vectors. The first two components show 72.3% and 12.5% variance, respectively. We observed that PC1 captures overall fidelity and PC2 contrasts structural vs. perceptual quality.

D. Regression-Based Composite Score: Finally, we got a linear regression predicting subjective MOS from the 15 metrics that yields standardized coefficients. The largest absolute weights for DISTS (-0.48) and VIFp (0.42) confirm their critical role in human perceptual quality.

4.4   Ablation Study

To investigate the contributions of individual components in our pipeline, we conducted an ablation study. We removed key modules, such as the optical flow completion and bidirectional feature propagation, and measured the performance degradation. Table 6 presents the quantitative results.

Table 4. Quantitative comparison with state-of-the-art video inpainting methods. We report (i) perceptual dissimilarity *LPIPS*↓ (lower is better), (ii) distortion-based fidelity *PSNR*↑ and *SSIM*↑ (higher is better), and (iii) distribution-level perceptual quality for videos via *VFID*↓ (lower is better). Cells highlighted in red and blue indicate the best and second-best results, respectively. Across all criteria, our method attains the lowest LPIPS and VFID and the highest PSNR/SSIM, evidencing superior perceptual fidelity, pixel-level accuracy, and video realism relative to prior approaches.

Metric	VINet[21]	DFGVI[44]	CPN[22]	OPN[26]	LGTSM[8]	OURS
LPIPS↓	0.0572	0.0570	0.0533	0.0571	0.0541	0.0524
PSNR↑	28.47	30.28	31.59	32.40	29.74	32.98
SSIM↑	0.9222	0.9251	0.9331	0.9403	0.9306	0.9405
VFID↓	0.0072	0.0066	0.0071	0.0065	0.0063	0.0062

Table 5. Pearson correlation (r) among image–quality metrics on our evaluation set. The table reports pairwise Pearson correlation coefficients $r \in [-1, 1]$. Larger $|r|$ indicates a stronger linear association: $r \approx 1$ denotes strong positive correlation, while $r \approx -1$ denotes strong negative correlation. The similarity-based metrics FSIM, MS-SSIM, and VIFp (higher is better) are strongly correlated with one another ($r \geq 0.87$) and show negative correlations with the distance-type metrics DISTS and PieAPP (lower is better), reflecting the expected inverse relationship. DISTS and PieAPP are themselves highly correlated ($r = 0.85$).

	FSIM	MS-SSIM	VIFp	DISTS	PieAPP
FSIM	1.00	0.97	0.89	−0.75	−0.68
MS-SSIM	0.97	1.00	0.87	−0.72	−0.65
VIFp	0.89	0.87	1.00	−0.64	−0.59
DISTS	−0.75	−0.72	−0.64	1.00	0.85
PieAPP	−0.68	−0.65	−0.59	0.85	1.00

Aggregate Ranking and Margin Analysis. To quantify the overall efficacy of our full model versus the two ablated variants, we assign each method a rank on every metric (1 = best, 3 = worst) and compute two aggregate measures: the *mean rank* and the *win count*. Table 7 shows that our full model attains rank 1 on all 17 metrics (mean rank = 1.00, win count = 17), while the variant without feature propagation (w/o FP) uniformly ranks second, and the variant without flow completion (w/o FC) ranks third.

Table 6. Ablation of Flow Completion (FC) and Feature Propagation (FP). Results on the evaluation set show that the full model with *both* modules (FC+FP) achieves the best fidelity (PSNR, SSIM) and similarity-based perceptual scores (FSIM, HaarPSI, MS-SSIM, VIFp, DSS, VSI, SR-SIM), while also yielding lower values for distortion/no-reference measures (BRISQUE, ContentLoss, DISTS, PieAPP, GMSD, MDSI, MS-GMSDc) and reduced temporal variation (TV). Removing FP weakens the ability to aggregate long-range temporal context, and removing FC degrades motion estimation in occluded regions; both ablations consistently harm quality across metrics, indicating that FC and FP provide complementary benefits. Arrows indicate the preferred direction of improvement: higher is better ($\uparrow$) and lower is better ($\downarrow$).

Metric	FC+FP (Ours)	Without FP	Without FC
PSNR$\uparrow$	32.98	31.56	30.89
SSIM$\uparrow$	0.9405	0.9322	0.9281
FSIM$\uparrow$	0.9712	0.9633	0.9617
HaarPSI$\uparrow$	0.9112	0.9021	0.9007
MS-SSIM$\uparrow$	0.9752	0.9703	0.9683
VIFp$\uparrow$	0.7891	0.7828	0.7810
DSS$\uparrow$	0.7233	0.7185	0.7156
VSI$\uparrow$	0.9913	0.9876	0.9864
SR-SIM$\uparrow$	0.9893	0.9846	0.9822
BRISQUE$\downarrow$	24.3153	24.6934	24.7600
ContentLoss$\downarrow$	324.5907	324.7961	324.8244
DISTS$\downarrow$	0.0312	0.0367	0.0388
PieAPP$\downarrow$	0.3005	0.3073	0.3098
GMSD$\downarrow$	0.0613	0.0625	0.0629
MDSI$\downarrow$	0.2618	0.2652	0.2665
MS-GMSDc$\downarrow$	0.0652	0.0666	0.0674
TV$\downarrow$	27.9691	28.1055	28.1097

Table 7. Ablation analysis of Flow Completion (FC) and Feature Propagation (FP). For each image–quality metric we report the rank (1 = best) of the full model (FC+FP, "Ours") and the two ablated variants (without FP and without FC). Arrows ($\uparrow$ / $\downarrow$) indicate the preferred direction when assigning ranks. The rightmost column shows the absolute performance margin of full model over the w/o FP variant. Across all 17 metrics the full model attains rank 1 (mean rank = 1.00, win count = 17), demonstrating that FC and FP are complementary—removing either module consistently degrades fidelity, perceptual quality, and temporal smoothness.

Metric	Ours	w/o FP	w/o FC	$\Delta_{\text{Ours}-\text{w/o FP}}$
PSNR$\uparrow$	1	2	3	+1.42 dB
SSIM$\uparrow$	1	2	3	+0.0083
FSIM$\uparrow$	1	2	3	+0.0079
HaarPSI$\uparrow$	1	2	3	+0.0091
MS-SSIM$\uparrow$	1	2	3	+0.0049
VIFp$\uparrow$	1	2	3	+0.0063
DSS$\uparrow$	1	2	3	+0.0048
VSI$\uparrow$	1	2	3	+0.0037
SR-SIM$\uparrow$	1	2	3	+0.0047
BRISQUE$\downarrow$	1	2	3	+0.3781
ContentLoss$\downarrow$	1	2	3	+0.2054
DISTS$\downarrow$	1	2	3	+0.0055
PieAPP$\downarrow$	1	2	3	+0.0068
GMSD$\downarrow$	1	2	3	+0.0012
MDSI$\downarrow$	1	2	3	+0.0034
MS-GMSDc$\downarrow$	1	2	3	+0.0014
TV$\downarrow$	1	2	3	+0.1364
Mean Rank	1.00	2.00	3.00	–
Win Count	17	0	0	–

5 Future Work and Conclusion

In this paper, we propose a novel video inpainting framework that is able to reconstruct visually plausible and temporally coherent video sequences. Though our method achieves the best performance among other methods, several limitations still remain, and further improvements will be developed in our future work. Extensive experiments verify that our approach indeed works well and achieves the best performance in terms of PSNR, SSIM, and VFID. These reflect the robustness and versatility of our method in solving such a complex task. By addressing coming challenges, we propose video inpainting for advancement in this domain and extend its applicability to a wide range of real-world problems and emerging technologies.

References

1. Anciukevičius, T., et al.: Renderdiffusion: image diffusion for 3D reconstruction, inpainting and generation. In: Proceedings of the IEEE/CVF Conference on Computer Vision and Pattern Recognition, pp. 12608–12618 (2023)
2. Avrahami, O., Fried, O., Lischinski, D.: Blended latent diffusion. ACM Trans. Graph. (TOG) **42**(4), 1–11 (2023)
3. Avrahami, O., Lischinski, D., Fried, O.: Blended diffusion for text-driven editing of natural images. In: Proceedings of the IEEE/CVF Conference on Computer Vision and Pattern Recognition, pp. 18208–18218 (2022)
4. Bar-Tal, O., Yariv, L., Lipman, Y., Dekel, T.: Multidiffusion: fusing diffusion paths for controlled image generation (2023)
5. Blattmann, A., et al.: Align your latents: high-resolution video synthesis with latent diffusion models. In: Proceedings of the IEEE/CVF Conference on Computer Vision and Pattern Recognition, pp. 22563–22575 (2023)
6. Brooks, T., Holynski, A., Efros, A.A.: Instructpix2pix: learning to follow image editing instructions. In: Proceedings of the IEEE/CVF Conference on Computer Vision and Pattern Recognition, pp. 18392–18402 (2023)
7. Ceylan, D., Huang, C.H.P., Mitra, N.J.: Pix2video: video editing using image diffusion. In: Proceedings of the IEEE/CVF International Conference on Computer Vision, pp. 23206–23217 (2023)
8. Chang, Y.L., Liu, Z.Y., Lee, K.Y., Hsu, W.: Learnable gated temporal shift module for deep video inpainting. arXiv preprint arXiv:1907.01131 (2019)
9. Chen, H., et al.: Videocrafter1: open diffusion models for high-quality video generation. arXiv preprint arXiv:2310.19512 (2023)
10. Gal, R., et al.: An image is worth one word: personalizing text-to-image generation using textual inversion. arXiv preprint arXiv:2208.01618 (2022)
11. Gao, Z., et al.: Focal and global spatial-temporal transformer for skeleton-based action recognition. In: Proceedings of the Asian Conference on Computer Vision, pp. 382–398 (2022)
12. Geyer, M., Bar-Tal, O., Bagon, S., Dekel, T.: Tokenflow: consistent diffusion features for consistent video editing. arXiv preprint arXiv:2307.10373 (2023)
13. Guo, Y., et al.: Animatediff: animate your personalized text-to-image diffusion models without specific tuning. arXiv preprint arXiv:2307.04725 (2023)
14. Han, L., Gao, R., Kim, M., Tao, X., Liu, B., Metaxas, D.: Robust conditional GAN from uncertainty-aware pairwise comparisons. In: Proceedings of the AAAI Conference on Artificial Intelligence, vol. 34, pp. 10909–10916 (2020)
15. Han, L., Li, Y., Zhang, H., Milanfar, P., Metaxas, D., Yang, F.: Svdiff: compact parameter space for diffusion fine-tuning. In: Proceedings of the IEEE/CVF International Conference on Computer Vision, pp. 7323–7334 (2023)
16. Han, L., et al.: Dual projection generative adversarial networks for conditional image generation. In: Proceedings of the IEEE/CVF International Conference on Computer Vision, pp. 14438–14447 (2021)
17. Han, L., et al.: Show me what and tell me how: video synthesis via multimodal conditioning. In: Proceedings of the IEEE/CVF Conference on Computer Vision and Pattern Recognition, pp. 3615–3625 (2022)
18. Han, L., et al.: Proxedit: improving tuning-free real image editing with proximal guidance. In: Proceedings of the IEEE/CVF Winter Conference on Applications of Computer Vision, pp. 4291–4301 (2024)

19. Hertz, A., Mokady, R., Tenenbaum, J., Aberman, K., Pritch, Y., Cohen-Or, D.: Prompt-to-prompt image editing with cross attention control. arXiv preprint arXiv:2208.01626 (2022)
20. Kastryulin, S., Zakirov, J., Prokopenko, D., Dylov, D.V.: Pytorch image quality: metrics for image quality assessment (2022). https://doi.org/10.48550/ARXIV.2208.14818
21. Kim, D., Woo, S., Lee, J.Y., Kweon, I.S.: Deep video inpainting. In: Proceedings of the IEEE/CVF Conference on Computer Vision and Pattern Recognition, pp. 5792–5801 (2019)
22. Lee, S., Oh, S.W., Won, D., Kim, S.J.: Copy-and-paste networks for deep video inpainting. In: Proceedings of the IEEE/CVF International Conference on Computer Vision, pp. 4413–4421 (2019)
23. Liu, S., Luo, K., Ye, N., Wang, C., Wang, J., Zeng, B.: Oiflow: occlusion-inpainting optical flow estimation by unsupervised learning. IEEE Trans. Image Process. **30**, 6420–6433 (2021). https://doi.org/10.1109/TIP.2021.3093781
24. Mou, C., et al.: T2i-adapter: learning adapters to dig out more controllable ability for text-to-image diffusion models. In: Proceedings of the AAAI Conference on Artificial Intelligence, vol. 38, pp. 4296–4304 (2024)
25. Nichol, A., et al.: Glide: towards photorealistic image generation and editing with text-guided diffusion models. arXiv preprint arXiv:2112.10741 (2021)
26. Oh, S.W., Lee, S., Lee, J.Y., Kim, S.J.: Onion-peel networks for deep video completion. In: Proceedings of the IEEE/CVF International Conference on Computer Vision, pp. 4403–4412 (2019)
27. Qi, C., et al.: Fatezero: fusing attentions for zero-shot text-based video editing. In: Proceedings of the IEEE/CVF International Conference on Computer Vision, pp. 15932–15942 (2023)
28. Ramesh, A., Dhariwal, P., Nichol, A., Chu, C., Chen, M.: Hierarchical text-conditional image generation with clip latents. arXiv preprint arXiv:2204.06125, **1**(2), 3 (2022)
29. Ramesh, A., et al.: Zero-shot text-to-image generation. In: International Conference on Machine Learning, pp. 8821–8831. PMLR (2021)
30. Rombach, R., Blattmann, A., Lorenz, D., Esser, P., Ommer, B.: High-resolution image synthesis with latent diffusion models. In: Proceedings of the IEEE/CVF Conference on Computer Vision and Pattern Recognition, pp. 10684–10695 (2022)
31. Saharia, C., et al.: Palette: image-to-image diffusion models. In: ACM SIGGRAPH 2022 Conference Proceedings, pp. 1–10 (2022)
32. Saharia, C., et al.: Photorealistic text-to-image diffusion models with deep language understanding. Adv. Neural. Inf. Process. Syst. **35**, 36479–36494 (2022)
33. Shin, C., Kim, H., Lee, C.H., Lee, S., Yoon, S.: Edit-a-video: Single video editing with object-aware consistency. In: Asian Conference on Machine Learning, pp. 1215–1230. PMLR (2024)
34. Shukla, R., Kaur, H., Echizen, I.: Parallel prints: generating realistic cancelable fingerprint templates. In: 2025 IEEE/CVF Winter Conference on Applications of Computer Vision Workshops (WACVW), pp. 1359–1368. IEEE (2025)
35. Shukla, R., Sinha, A., Singh, V., Kaur, H.: Vikriti-id: a novel approach for real looking fingerprint data-set generation. In: Proceedings of the IEEE/CVF Winter Conference on Applications of Computer Vision, pp. 6395–6403 (2024)
36. Song, J., Meng, C., Ermon, S.: Denoising diffusion implicit models. arXiv preprint arXiv:2010.02502 (2020)

37. Wang, S., et al.: Imagen editor and editbench: advancing and evaluating text-guided image inpainting. In: Proceedings of the IEEE/CVF Conference on Computer Vision and Pattern Recognition, pp. 18359–18369 (2023)

38. Wang, W., et al.: Zero-shot video editing using off-the-shelf image diffusion models. arXiv preprint arXiv:2303.17599 (2023)

39. Wang, X., et al.: Videocomposer: compositional video synthesis with motion controllability. In: Advances in Neural Information Processing Systems, vol. 36 (2024)

40. Wu, C., et al.: Godiva: generating open-domain videos from natural descriptions. arXiv preprint arXiv:2104.14806 (2021)

41. Wu, C., et al.: Nüwa: visual synthesis pre-training for neural visual world creation. In: European Conference on Computer Vision, pp. 720–736. Springer, Cham (2022)

42. Wu, J.Z., et al.: Tune-a-video: one-shot tuning of image diffusion models for text-to-video generation. In: Proceedings of the IEEE/CVF International Conference on Computer Vision, pp. 7623–7633 (2023)

43. Xie, S., Zhang, Z., Lin, Z., Hinz, T., Zhang, K.: Smartbrush: text and shape guided object inpainting with diffusion model. In: Proceedings of the IEEE/CVF Conference on Computer Vision and Pattern Recognition, pp. 22428–22437 (2023)

44. Xu, R., Li, X., Zhou, B., Loy, C.C.: Deep flow-guided video inpainting. In: Proceedings of the IEEE/CVF Conference on Computer Vision and Pattern Recognition, pp. 3723–3732 (2019)

45. Yang, B., et al.: Paint by example: exemplar-based image editing with diffusion models. In: Proceedings of the IEEE/CVF Conference on Computer Vision and Pattern Recognition, pp. 18381–18391 (2023)

46. Yang, S., Chen, X., Liao, J.: Uni-paint: a unified framework for multimodal image inpainting with pretrained diffusion model. In: Proceedings of the 31st ACM International Conference on Multimedia, pp. 3190–3199 (2023)

47. Yu, J., Lin, Z., Yang, J., Shen, X., Lu, X., Huang, T.S.: Generative image inpainting with contextual attention. In: Proceedings of the IEEE Conference on Computer Vision and Pattern Recognition, pp. 5505–5514 (2018)

48. Yu, J., Lin, Z., Yang, J., Shen, X., Lu, X., Huang, T.S.: Free-form image inpainting with gated convolution. In: Proceedings of the IEEE/CVF International Conference on Computer Vision, pp. 4471–4480 (2019)

49. Zhang, K., Fu, J., Liu, D.: Flow-guided transformer for video inpainting. In: European Conference on Computer Vision, pp. 74–90. Springer, Cham (2022)

50. Zhang, L., Rao, A., Agrawala, M.: Adding conditional control to text-to-image diffusion models. In: Proceedings of the IEEE/CVF International Conference on Computer Vision, pp. 3836–3847 (2023)

51. Zhang, Y., Li, Y., Peng, B., Zhou, J., Zhou, H., Dong, J.: Mumpy: multilateral temporal-view pyramid transformer for video inpainting detection. arXiv preprint arXiv:2404.11054 (2024)

52. Zhang, Z., Han, L., Ghosh, A., Metaxas, D.N., Ren, J.: Sine: Single image editing with text-to-image diffusion models. In: Proceedings of the IEEE/CVF Conference on Computer Vision and Pattern Recognition, pp. 6027–6037 (2023)

53. Zhang, Z., et al.: Avid: any-length video inpainting with diffusion model. In: Proceedings of the IEEE/CVF Conference on Computer Vision and Pattern Recognition, pp. 7162–7172 (2024)

UKANETR: A Kansformer-Based Interpretable UNET for Brain Tumor Segmentation

Rajib Kumar Chatterjee[1]([✉]), Abhay Kumar Tiwari[1], Sayoni Bhattacharyya[1], Rohit Agarwal[1]([✉]), Anup Kumar Sadhu[2], and Debashis Nandi[1]([✉])

[1] National Institute of Technology Durgapur, Durgapur 713209, India
{rkchatterjee.cse,akt.23cs4120,sb.25cs1105,dnandi.cse}@nitdgp.ac.in,
ra.22cs1102@phd.nitdgp.ac.in
[2] EKO Diagnostic Center, Medical College Kolkata, Kolkata, India
sadhujee1@gmail.com

Abstract. Transformer-based architectures have recently emerged as powerful models for 3D medical image segmentation, with UNETR demonstrating notable success by leveraging self-attention to capture global contextual information. Despite its effectiveness, UNETR still faces challenges in interpretability and computational efficiency. To address these limitations, we propose UKANETR, a novel UNET variant that employs kansformers, i.e., transformers equipped with Kolmogorov–Arnold Network multilayer perceptrons (KAN-MLPs). By integrating KAN-MLPs into the transformer blocks, UKANETR enhances model interpretability while improving its ability to represent complex non-linear functions with fewer parameters. In addition, UKANETR incorporates a squeeze-and-excitation mechanism within the skip connection pathways to explicitly capture channel interdependencies. This design improves feature recalibration, allowing the network to emphasize informative channels and suppress less relevant ones, thereby strengthening multi-level feature fusion between encoder and decoder stages. The proposed UKANETR was rigorously evaluated on the BRaTS 2020 brain tumor MRI dataset. Comparative analysis against the traditional UNETR and other state-of-the-art models shows that UKANETR consistently achieves superior performance in multi-level brain tumor segmentation, demonstrating improvements in Dice score, sensitivity, and boundary delineation accuracy. These results highlight the potential of integrating kansformers and channel attention mechanisms into transformer-based UNET models, offering a more interpretable and efficient solution for 3D medical image segmentation tasks.

Keywords: UNETR · Multilayer perceptron · Kolmogorov–Arnold Networks · Transformer · Kansformer

B. Chatterjee et al. (Eds.): ICDCIT 2026, LNCS 16420, pp. 220–234, 2026.
https://doi.org/10.1007/978-3-032-16632-6_14

1   Introduction

The brain tumor segmentation in MRI images is a challenging task because of the complex and varied geometrical structures, textures, and other features of the tumors. It has been observed that the geometrical structures of tumors vary widely with respect to the organs in which they are present and the types of tumors, from benign to malignant or carcinogenic. The variation in structures, textures, and other features poses challenges in the automatic detection and segmentation of tumors using Computer-Aided Diagnostic (CAD) systems. To enable error-free diagnosis, accurate segmentation and localization of tumors are important to facilitate the precise demarcation of tumor boundaries. Researchers have attempted to develop many automated models to overcome the challenges. From the middle of the last decade, the direction of the research has shifted toward the design of deep learning models to solve the problem, and many models have been developed [1,3,10,13,14,20,21].

Recently, UNETR [7], a deep learning architecture that integrates the strengths of UNet with a transformer, has been introduced for 3D biomedical image segmentation. In this framework, the transformer [5] serves as the encoder, effectively capturing long-range, multiscale dependencies within volumetric data. The encoder is connected to the decoder through multi-resolution skip connections, enabling the reconstruction of fine structural details in the final segmentation output.

When applied to brain tumor segmentation, UNETR achieved Dice coefficients of 78.5%, 58.5%, and 76.1% on the MSD dataset, and 77.52%, 61.44%, and 68.34% on the BraTS dataset, respectively. While these results are promising, there remains significant scope for improvement. In particular, although the vision transformer effectively models global contextual relationships, it often struggles to preserve fine-grained local information, which is crucial for accurate delineation of tumor boundaries and small subregions. Furthermore, the patch-based tokenization process used in transformers can make the model's decision-making process less interpretable, posing challenges for clinical adoption.

Most recently, Liu et al. [11] have proposed Kolmogorov–Arnold Networks (KANs) as a promising alternative to the traditional multilayer perceptrons. The KANs offer a bunch of advantages.

– Using KANs, it is possible to represent complex functions with fewer parameters compared to conventional neural networks. Hence, KANs are parameter-efficient in maintaining or improving performance.
– Spline basis functions (learnable activation functions used in the edges) and their intrinsic locality help in achieving adaptivity in the design and training of the networks, and consequently, better accuracy and efficiency.
– The learnable 1D activation functions used in the edges are explicit and can be intuitively visualized, which makes the model's behavior interpretable.
– KANs are built on the Kolmogorov–Arnold representation theorem, hence have a strong theoretical background.

Keeping in mind the advantages of KANs, in this paper, we have built a novel UKANETR by incorporating KAN-MLP in the vision transformer/encoder and a squeeze and excitation mechanism in the decoder of the UNET. The proposed model boosts both the local and global representation power and improves the quality of tumor segmentation from MRI images. The work has the following significant contributions:

1. A KAN-MLP has been implemented as an alternative to traditional MLP to achieve the advantages of KANs.
2. A Kansformer is developed by replacing the traditional MLP of the vision transformer with a KAN-MLP. It makes the transformer interpretable.
3. A UNET is designed by taking the Kansformer as the encoder. The decoder is built by introducing a squeeze and excitation mechanism that helps to achieve better feature representation.
4. The proposed model is trained and tested with the BraTS 2020 dataset to evaluate its performance in multilevel brain tumor segmentation from MRI images.
5. The proposed model is compared with the UNETR model on the BraTS 2020 dataset.

2   Related Works

The evolution of deep learning architectures for medical image segmentation has been characterized by a gradual transition from convolution-dominated designs to hybrid models that integrate convolutional neural networks (CNNs) and transformers. The classical U-Net architecture proposed by Ronneberger et al. [15] pioneered the encoder–decoder paradigm with skip connections, achieving remarkable segmentation accuracy even with limited data. However, its convolution-based receptive field restricts the capture of long-range dependencies, which is essential for modeling the complex and heterogeneous structures characteristic of brain tumors.

To overcome this limitation, transformer-based models have been increasingly explored in medical imaging. The TransUNet model proposed by Chen et al. [4] represents one of the earliest successful attempts to combine the global contextual modeling power of transformers with the spatial precision of CNNs. By integrating a transformer encoder into the U-Net framework, TransUNet demonstrated improved segmentation performance on multiple biomedical datasets. Nevertheless, the model's high computational cost and sensitivity to fine-grained local detail preservation limit its practicality in clinical applications.

Extending this paradigm, UNETR introduced by Hatamizadeh et al. [7] adopts a pure transformer encoder for volumetric medical image segmentation. This design effectively captures long-range dependencies across 3D MRI data while maintaining a skip-connected decoder to reconstruct fine structural details. Although UNETR achieves strong quantitative results, its performance is constrained by the high computational demands of the transformer blocks and their inability to fully retain localized spatial features—an issue particularly evident in small subregions and boundary delineations.

Further advancements have been made through hybrid and multimodal models. TransBTS [20] leverages transformer encoders for multimodal MRI brain tumor segmentation, significantly improving feature fusion across modalities. However, despite its enhanced representational power, TransBTS exhibits tendencies toward overfitting and reduced generalization on smaller or domain-shifted datasets. Similarly, UNet++ [23] refines the encoder–decoder structure through nested and dense skip pathways to achieve enhanced multi-scale fusion. While this approach improves segmentation precision, it introduces additional parameters and potential overfitting risks.

Attention mechanisms have also been incorporated to enhance the representational selectivity of medical segmentation networks. The SCSE-NL V-Net [22] integrates spatial and channel attention alongside non-local context modeling, which significantly improves tumor segmentation accuracy. However, this architecture faces challenges such as computational overhead and limited interpretability, particularly in large-scale 3D segmentation tasks. More recently, lightweight architectures like LATUP-Net [1] and VCANet [14] have attempted to balance computational efficiency and accuracy through attention-based channel recalibration and parallel convolutional modules. Despite their efficiency, these models still lack transparent interpretability—an essential requirement for medical imaging applications.

While these innovations demonstrate steady progress, the interpretability of deep neural networks remains a critical challenge in medical imaging. Traditional multilayer perceptrons (MLPs) within transformer architectures lack mathematical transparency, often functioning as "black boxes" that hinder clinical trust. To address this, Kolmogorov–Arnold Networks (KANs) have recently emerged as a theoretically grounded alternative. Proposed by Liu et al. [11], KANs replace standard nonlinear activations with learnable spline-based one-dimensional functions, enabling explicit representation of nonlinear mappings. This design is founded on the Kolmogorov–Arnold representation theorem [2,19], which asserts that any multivariate continuous function can be represented as a finite superposition of univariate functions. By parameterizing these functions through trainable splines, KANs achieve improved parameter efficiency, adaptability, and interpretability—qualities highly desirable in medical AI systems.

Motivated by these developments, this work proposes UKANETR, a hybrid transformer–U-Net architecture that introduces KAN-MLP modules into the transformer encoder, forming a "Kansformer" block. This modification enhances both global representation and interpretability, offering a principled alternative to traditional MLPs. Furthermore, the incorporation of a Squeeze-and-Excitation (SE) mechanism in the decoder path reinforces channel-wise recalibration, ensuring that salient tumor-relevant features are prioritized during reconstruction. Together, these design choices position UKANETR as a theoretically sound, interpretable, and high-performing model for 3D brain tumor segmentation.

2.1   Kolmogorov-Arnold Representation Theorem

Kolmogorov-Arnold representation theorem states that any multivariate smooth function $f : [0,1]^n \to \mathbb{R}$ can be represented as a superposition of one-dimensional functions,

$$f(\mathbf{x}) = f(x_1, \ldots, x_n) = \sum_{q=1}^{2n+1} \Phi_q \left(\sum_{p=1}^{n} \phi_{q,p}(x_p) \right) \tag{1}$$

where $\phi_{q,p} : [0,1] \to \mathbb{R}$ and $\Phi_q : \mathbb{R} \to \mathbb{R}$ are the outer and inner functions, respectively. The inner functions $\phi_{q,p}$ are independent of the function f.

Kolmogorov's original version of the article [19] does not discuss the details of the numerical methods of the construction of the multivariate functions; rather, it only states the existence of such a representation. Arnold had also made his contributions [2] on this problem that appeared at nearly the same time. However, several improvements and theories have been discovered by Sprecher [17,18], and numerical construction methods have been developed by scientists in subsequent decades [16]. Later, Hecht-Nielsen [8] applied the results of the improved version of Kolmogorov's theorem for realizing the mappings of neural networks.

Since then, though many researchers have attempted to approximate multivariate functions through the realization and learning of neural networks, Girosi et al. [6] questioned its relevance in the context of neural networks for learning because of the difficulty in exact representation of non-linear mapping through the addition of simpler functions of fewer variables. However, later, Ismayilova et al. [9] have shown that the Kolmogorov networks are not only capable of representing continuous multivariate functions, but also discontinuous bounded, and all unbounded multivariate functions.

2.2   Brief Introduction to KAN-MLP

Liu et al. [11] have provided a rigorous discussion on Kolmogorov-Arnold Networks and have been inspired to design Kolmogorov-Arnold Networks that explicitly parameterize Eq. 1. Since it is required to learn the univariate functions $\phi_{q,p}$ and Φ_q in the KANs, Liu et al. have parameterized each 1D function as a B-Spline curve that is generated by learnable coefficients and local B-spline basis functions. Figure 1 shows the structure of a prototype KAN and the construction of functions. Here, Eq. 1 has been approximated by realizing a KAN having $n = 2$ inputs, two layers with activation function placed on the edges (not on the nodes), and a width $2n+1$ in the middle layer. By observing the analogy between the Multilayer Perceptron (MLP) and KAN, Liu et al. have built a deep KAN of KAN-MLP. In general, to build a neural network to approximate Eq. 1, the inner functions $\phi_{q,p}$ form a KAN layer with, say, $n_i = n$ inputs and $n_0 = 2n+1$ outputs, and the outer functions Φ_q form a KAN layer of $n_i = 2n + 1$ inputs and $n_0 = 1$ outputs. Thus, the Kolmogorov-Arnold representations of Eq. 1 are simply stacks of two KAN layers.

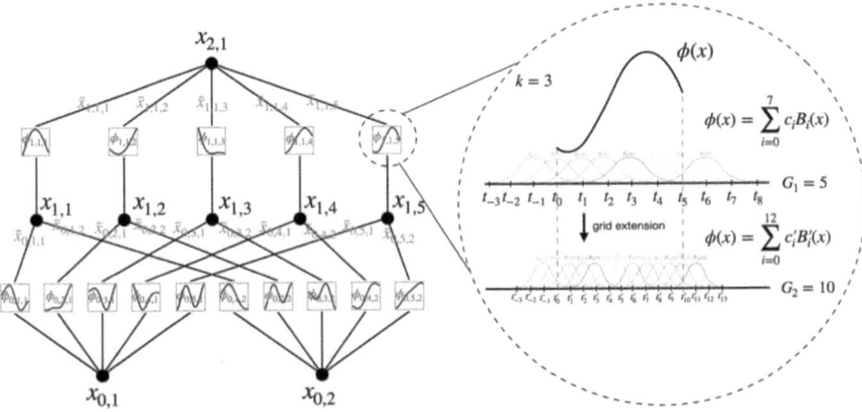

Fig. 1. Left: Notations of activations that flow through the network. Right: an activation function is parameterized as a B-spline, which allows switching between coarse-grained and fine-grained grids [11].

Figure 1 shows the computational graph of a generalized KAN. The activation value of ith neuron in l^{th} layer i.e at (l,i) position is denoted by $a_{i,j}$ and the activation function that connects the neuron (l,i) to the neuron $(l+1,i)$ by $\phi_{l,k,i}$, where $l = 0, 1, 2, ..., L-1$, $i = 1, 2, ..., n_l$, and $k = 1, 2, ..., n_{l+1}$. if the pre-activation value of the activation function $\phi_{l,k,i}$ is $a_{l,i}$, the post-activation value of the activation function $\phi_{l,k,i}$ may be denoted as,

$$\hat{a}_{l,k,i} = \phi_{l,k,i}(a_{l,i}) \tag{2}$$

Hence, the activation value of the neuron at position $(l+1,i)$ will be,

$$a_{l+1,k} = \sum_{i=1}^{n_l}(\hat{a}_{l,k,i}) = \sum_{i=1}^{n_l}(\phi_{l,k,i}(a_{l,i})), k = 1, 2, ..., n_{l+1} \tag{3}$$

Equation 3 can be expressed in matrix form as follows:

$$\mathbf{A}_{l+1} = \mathbf{\Phi}_l.\mathbf{A}_l \tag{4}$$

where

$$\mathbf{\Phi}_l = \begin{pmatrix} \phi_{l,1,1}(\cdot) & \phi_{l,1,2}(\cdot) & \cdots & \phi_{l,1,n_l}(\cdot) \\ \phi_{l,2,1}(\cdot) & \phi_{l,2,2}(\cdot) & \cdots & \phi_{l,2,n_l}(\cdot) \\ \vdots & \vdots & \ddots & \vdots \\ \phi_{l,n_{l+1},1}(\cdot) & \phi_{l,n_{l+1},2}(\cdot) & \cdots & \phi_{l,n_{l+1},n_l}(\cdot) \end{pmatrix} \tag{5}$$

denotes the function matrix corresponding to the lth layer. For a general KAN of L layers, the output of the network can be given as,

$$\mathrm{O_{KAN}}(\mathbf{A}) = (\mathbf{\Phi}_{L-1} \circ \mathbf{\Phi}_{L-2} \circ \cdots \circ \mathbf{\Phi}_1 \circ \mathbf{\Phi}_0)\mathbf{A} \tag{6}$$

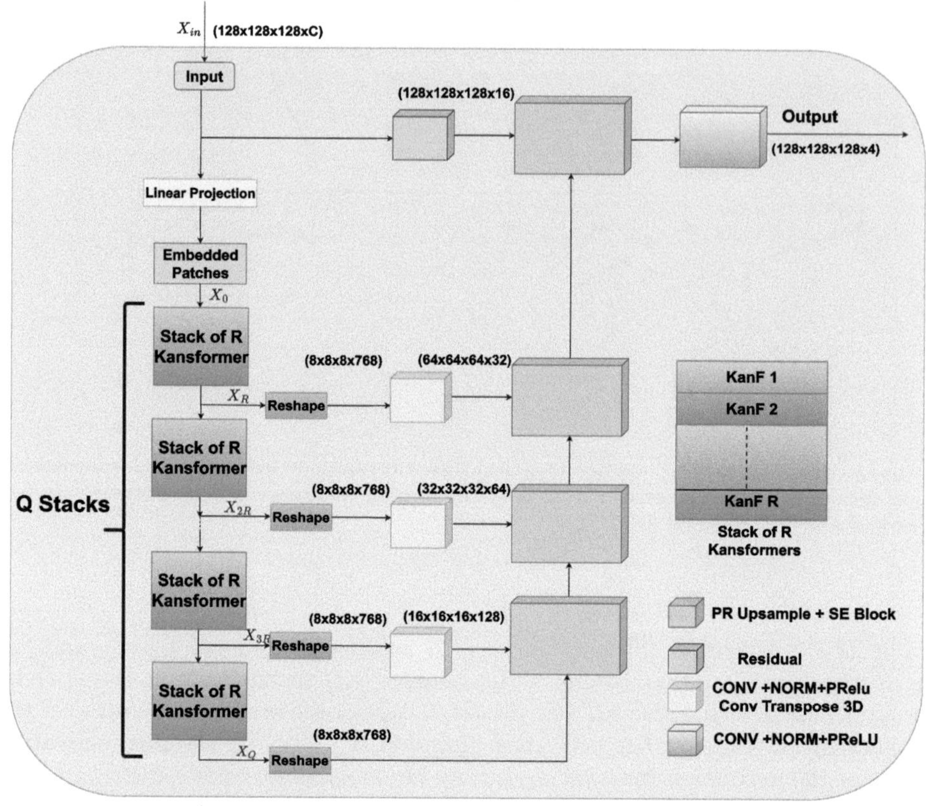

Fig. 2. Overview of the UKANETR model architecture.

Equation 6 is analogous to the output equation of an MLP having affine transformations W and nonlinearities, σ, which is expressed as,

$$O_{\mathrm{MLP}}(\mathbf{x}) = (\mathbf{W}_{L-1} \circ \sigma \circ \mathbf{W}_{L-2} \circ \sigma \circ \cdots \circ \mathbf{W}_1 \circ \sigma \circ \mathbf{W}_0)\mathbf{x} \tag{7}$$

The only difference is that, in the traditional MLP, the transformations and the nonlinearities are presented separately, whereas, in KAN, they are taken altogether in $\mathbf{\Phi}_l$. Since all operations in KAN are differentiable, we can train KAN using back propagation.

3   Proposed Model

3.1   Model Architecture

The proposed UKANETR draws structural inspiration from the UNETR, along with the introduction of two functional components: 1. Kolmogorov–Arnold Networks (KAN) based multilayer perceptron within the transformer, which converts the transformer to 'kansformer' 2. Squeeze-and-Excitation (SE) blocks in the decoder path. Figure 2 shows the structure of the proposed UKANETR.

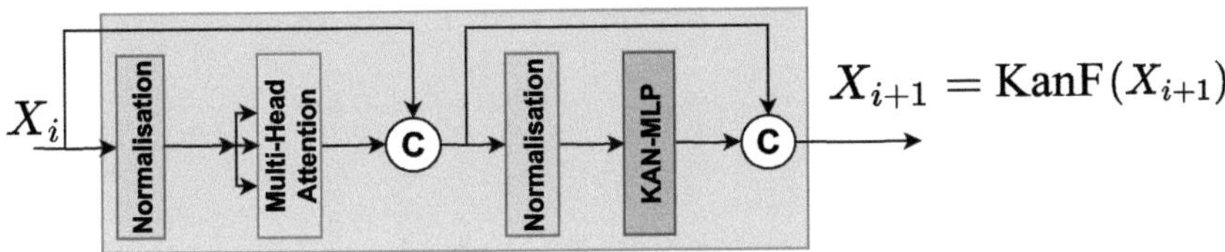

$$X_{i+1} = \mathrm{KanF}(X_{i+1})$$

Fig. 3. Kansformer Block.

The UKANETR segmentation network is composed of an encoder and a decoder, where the encoder and decoder are connected by skip connections Fig. 2. In a generalized UKANETR, the encoder is composed of a linear projection unit, a patch embedding block, and a stack of kansformers. We use Q stacks sequentially, where each stack is composed of a stack of R successive kanformers Fig. 3. Thus, the model consists of a total of $Q \times R$ kanformers.

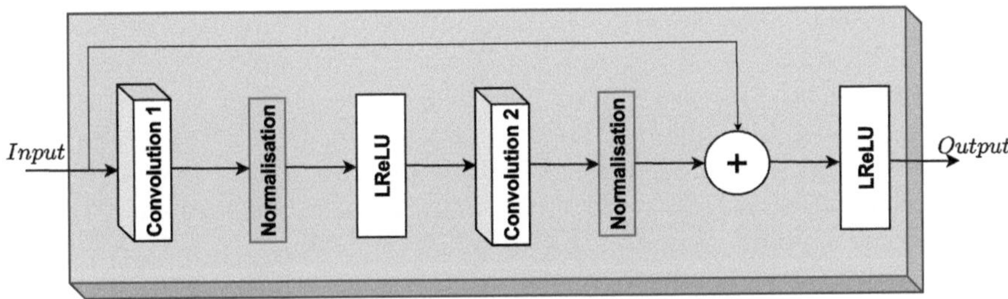

Fig. 4. Residual Block

To train and evaluate the model, we take a sequence of 3D input volume $\mathbf{X} \in \mathbb{R}^{H \times W \times D \times C}$ of resolution $(H \times W \times D)$ and C channels and create non-overlapping patches $\mathbf{X}_p \in \mathbb{R}^{N \times (P^3 \cdot C)}$ of resolution $(P \times P \times P)$ by dividing it into $N = (H \times W \times D)/P^3)$ patches.

The patches are linearly projected into a K-dimensional embedding space. The spatial information is preserved by adding a one-dimensional learnable positional embedding $\mathbf{E}_P \in \mathbb{R}^{N \times K}$. to the projected embedded patches $\mathbf{E} \in \mathbb{R}^{(P^3 \cdot C) \times K}$. Thus, the input to the first stack is given by,

$$\mathbf{X}_0 = [\mathbf{X}_p^1 \mathbf{E}; \mathbf{X}_p^2 \mathbf{E}; ....; \mathbf{X}_p^N \mathbf{E}] + \mathbf{E}_P \tag{8}$$

The output of the qth stack is denoted by $\mathbf{X}_{R \times q}$, where R is the number of kansformers in a stack. In our model, we have taken $R = 3$ and $Q = 4$. Therefore, the outputs of stack 1, stack 2, stack 3, and stack 4 are $\mathbf{X}_3$, $\mathbf{X}_6$, $\mathbf{X}_9$, and $\mathbf{X}_{12}$, respectively. The expression of the output of qth stack can be given by,

$$\mathbf{X}_{R \times q} = \underbrace{\mathrm{KanF}(\mathrm{KanF}(\mathrm{KanF}(\cdots \mathrm{KanF}(\mathbf{X}_0))))}_{R \times q \text{ times}} = \mathrm{KanF}^{(R \times q)}(\mathbf{X}_0) \tag{9}$$

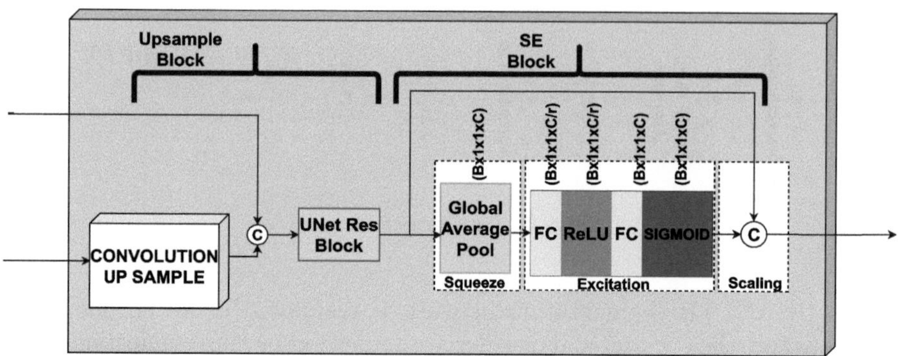

Fig. 5. Decoder Block

where $\mathrm{KanF}(\mathbf{x})$ is the output of a kansformer for an input $\mathbf{x}$.

The output from each qth stack is reshaped from (768×512) to $(8 \times 8 \times 8 \times 768)$ and is upsampled $Q - q$ times generating output u^q. Thereafter, u^q and $u^q - 1$ outputs are passed through the Decoder block (Fig. 5), and are continued in the same process till the dimension $(64 \times 64 \times 64 \times 32)$ is reached. Subsequently, the input after passing through the Residual block (Fig. 4) is fed into the decoder along with the output of the Decoder block having dimension $(64 \times 64 \times 64 \times 32)$ to generate the dimension $(128 \times 128 \times 128 \times 16)$. Finally, the segmented output is generated after passing through the Out block (Fig. 6).

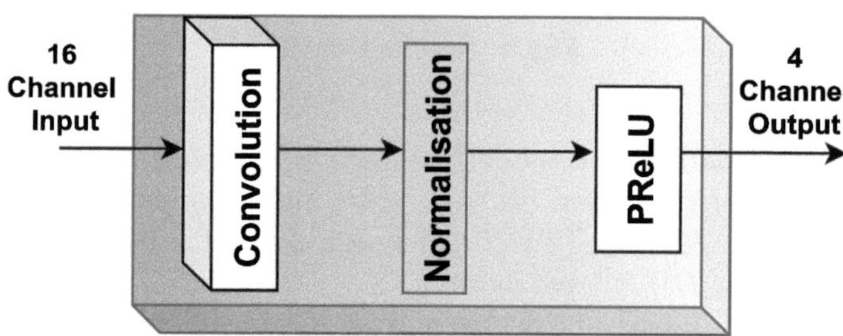

Fig. 6. UNet OUT Block

3.2 Loss Function

The UKANETR model is trained using a composite loss function that combines Dice loss, Focal loss, and Tversky loss. The expression for the composite loss:

$$\mathcal{L} = 0.4 \times \mathcal{L}_{\mathrm{Dice}} + 0.4 \times \mathcal{L}_{\mathrm{Focal}} + 0.2 \times \mathcal{L}_{\mathrm{Tversky}} \tag{10}$$

$$\mathcal{L}_{\mathrm{Dice}} = 1 - \frac{2 \sum_i p_i g_i}{\sum_i p_i + \sum_i g_i} \tag{11}$$

$$\mathcal{L}_{\text{Tversky}} = 1 - \frac{\sum_i p_i g_i}{\sum_i p_i g_i + \alpha \sum_i p_i(1 - g_i) + \beta \sum_i (1 - p_i)g_i} \tag{12}$$

$$\mathcal{L}_{\text{Focal}} = -\alpha_t (1 - p_t)^\gamma \log(p_t) \tag{13}$$

- p_t is the model's estimated probability for the true class,
- $\alpha_t \in [0, 1]$ is a weighting factor for class t,
- $\gamma \geq 0$ is the focusing parameter.

3.3 Dataset Descriptions

The proposed framework was evaluated on the Brain Tumor Segmentation (BraTS) 2020 benchmark dataset [12], a widely recognized standard for automated glioma segmentation. The dataset comprises multimodal 3D MRI scans, including T1-weighted, contrast-enhanced T1-weighted (T1ce), T2-weighted, and T2-FLAIR images, collected from glioma patients at 19 international clinical centers. Each case, stored in NIfTI format, is accompanied by expert annotations marking three subregions: necrotic and non-enhancing tumor core (NCR/NET, Label 1), peritumoral edema (ED, Label 2), and enhancing tumor (ET, Label 4). For evaluation, these are grouped into enhancing tumor (ET), tumor core (TC = Labels 1 + 4), and whole tumor (WT = Labels 1 + 2 + 4). To handle variations in MRI acquisitions, preprocessing involved intensity normalization to the [0,1] range, isotropic resampling to $1\,\text{mm}^3$ voxel size, and augmentations such as random flips, small affine transformations, and controlled intensity shifts. These steps ensured consistency, improved generalization, and enhanced robustness. The dataset was split into 70%, 20%, and 10% for training, testing, and validation, respectively, with 275 samples used for training and no patient overlap between subsets.

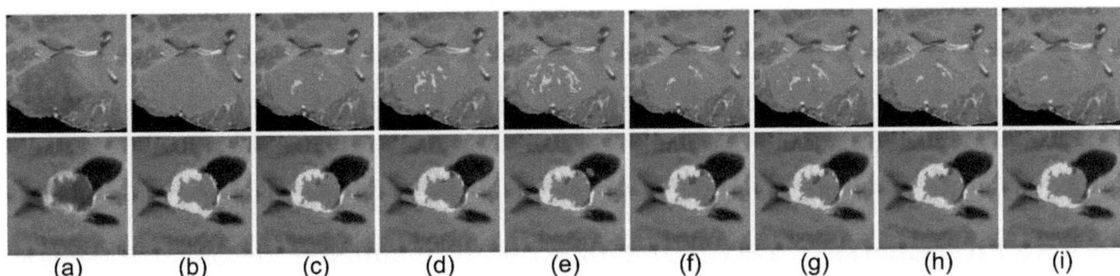

Fig. 7. Segmentation results on Brain Tumor Images of BraTS 2020 dataset using different state-of-the-art models. a: Original Image, b: Annotated Image, c: UNet++, d: UNet, e: TransUNet, f: TransBTS, g: UNETR, h: scSE-NL V-Net, i: Proposed Model

4   Results And Discussions

4.1   Experimental Setup

All experiments were conducted using Python and the PyTorch library, executed on a server featuring a P100 GPU with 16 GB of RAM. A total of 100 epochs were executed.

4.2   Results

The experimental evaluation on the BraTS 2020 dataset demonstrates that the proposed UKANETR model consistently outperforms its baseline counterpart UNETR as well as several other state-of-the-art architectures, as shown in Table 1 and Fig. 7. In particular, UKANETR achieves Dice Coefficients (DC) of 86.28%, 71.96%, and 68.92% for Whole Tumor (WT), Tumor Core (TC), and Enhancing Tumor (ET), respectively. Compared with the traditional UNETR (77.52%, 61.44%, and 68.34%), the results highlight substantial performance improvements in WT and TC segmentation, while maintaining competitive accuracy for ET.

Table 1. Comparision of DC values (%) with different state-of-the-art models with respect to the segmentation outputs

Model	WT	TC	ET
UNet++ [23]	87.00	64.00	65.00
UNet [15]	76.60	66.50	56.10
TransUNet [4]	70.60	68.40	54.20
TransBTS [20]	77.90	73.50	57.40
UNETR [7]	77.52	61.44	68.34
scSE-NL V-Net [22]	81.80	75.90	64.70
UKANETR Model	**86.28**	**71.96**	**68.92**

The most notable gain is observed in Tumor Core (TC) segmentation, where UKANETR achieves a Dice score of 71.96%, compared to only 61.44% by UNETR. This improvement is critical because accurate delineation of the tumor core has strong clinical relevance for treatment planning and prognosis. The enhancement can be attributed to the KAN-MLPs' ability to represent fine-grained local nonlinearities and the SE mechanism's role in emphasizing tumor-relevant channels. For Whole Tumor (WT), the proposed method also surpasses UNETR by nearly 9% points, suggesting that the model effectively integrates multi-scale global and local features. The results on Enhancing Tumor (ET) are comparable to UNETR, indicating that while the architecture is strong in handling global and structural contexts, capturing the smallest enhancing regions remains a challenge. The training and validation loss Fig. 8 and IoU curves Fig. 9 show that UKANETR converges faster and with greater stability compared to UNETR. This indicates that the hybrid design not only improves accuracy but also leads to more efficient optimization. The interpretable activation functions of KAN further support stable gradient propagation and generalization.

The results highlight that UKANETR balances interpretability, efficiency, and accuracy, which are often conflicting goals in medical imaging. By grounding its design in the Kolmogorov–Arnold representation theorem, the model inherits a strong theoretical foundation, offering transparency in decision-making that is often lacking in deep learning systems. Additionally, the channel recalibration mechanism ensures that the decoder prioritizes clinically meaningful features, strengthening the multi-level feature fusion process.

Table 2. DC values (%) in Ablation study of the proposed UKANETR model

Model	WT	TC	ET
UNETR	77.52	61.44	68.34
UNETR + KAN	83.60	65.38	59.19
UKANETR	**86.28**	**71.96**	**68.92**

4.3   Ablation Study

The ablation study Table 2 further confirms the contribution of each module: integrating KAN-MLPs alone significantly boosts WT and TC performance, while the full UKANETR (with squeeze-and-excitation in the decoder) yields the best results overall. This indicates that both components, KAN-enhanced transformer encoders and channel recalibration in the decoder, synergistically contribute to improved segmentation quality.

Despite these advantages, the ET performance plateau suggests that further refinement is needed to capture very small or irregular tumor regions. Future directions may include integrating adaptive attention mechanisms or leveraging domain-specific priors to better handle enhancing tumor variability. Furthermore, the computational cost of stacking multiple kansformers should be investigated in larger-scale clinical workflows to ensure feasibility in real-time applications.

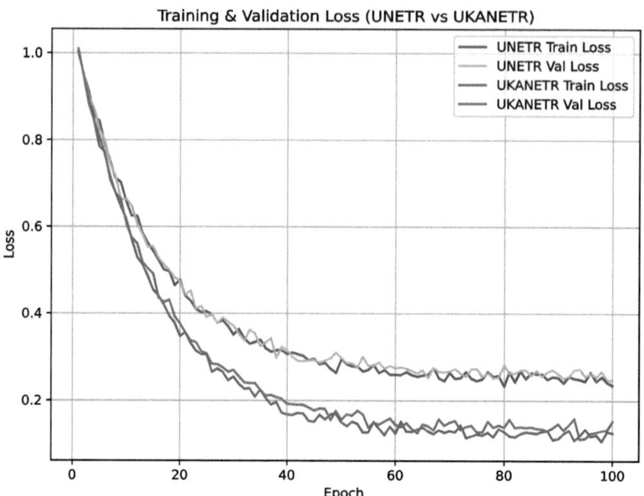

Fig. 8. Training and Validation Loss (UNETR vs UKANETR)

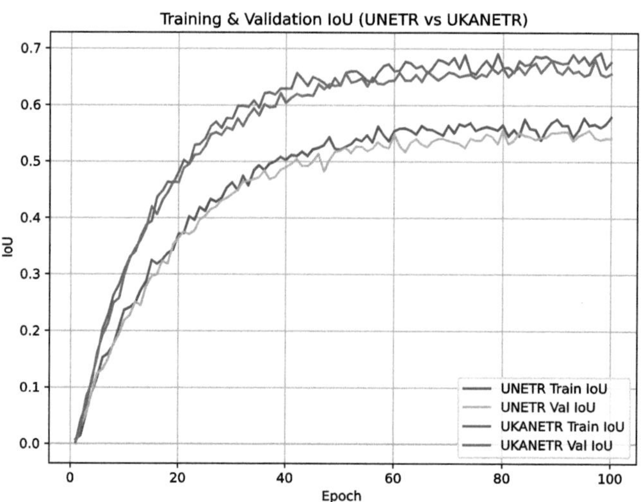

Fig. 9. Training and Validation IOU (UNETR vs UKANETR)

5   Conclusion

This work presented UKANETR, an enhanced UNETR architecture designed for accurate and interpretable brain tumor segmentation from MRI images. By introducing Kolmogorov–Arnold Network-based MLPs (KAN-MLPs) into the transformer encoder, the model effectively improves nonlinear function representation while maintaining parameter efficiency. Additionally, the incorporation of squeeze-and-excitation blocks in the decoder strengthens channel-wise feature recalibration, thereby enabling more effective fusion of multi-scale features. Comprehensive experiments conducted on the BraTS 2020 dataset demonstrate that UKANETR consistently outperforms the baseline UNETR and several state-of-the-art models. The model achieved Dice scores of 86.28% (WT), 71.96% (TC), and 68.92% (ET), highlighting significant improvements, particularly in whole tumor and tumor core segmentation—two clinically crucial regions for diagnosis and treatment planning. The ablation study further confirmed that both KAN-MLPs and squeeze-and-excitation modules contribute meaningfully to the overall performance gains. The findings establish UKANETR as a more interpretable and efficient solution for 3D brain tumor segmentation, demonstrating the practical potential of integrating theoretical insights from the Kolmogorov–Arnold representation with modern transformer-based deep learning.

Future research directions include extending UKANETR to handle multimodal data fusion, improving segmentation of small and highly irregular enhancing tumor regions, and optimizing computational efficiency for deployment in real-world clinical environments.

References

1. Alwadee, E.J., Sun, X., Qin, Y., Langbein, F.C.: Latup-net: a lightweight 3D attention u-net with parallel convolutions for brain tumor segmentation. Comput. Biol. Med. **184**, 109353 (2025)
2. Arnol'd, V.: On the representation of functions of several variables by superpositions of functions of fewer variables, mat (1958)
3. Arora, A., et al.: Brain tumor segmentation of MRI images using processed image driven u-net architecture. SN Comput. Sci. **4**(3), 256 (2023). https://doi.org/10.1007/s42979-023-01662-9
4. Chen, J., Lu, Y., Dou, Q., Chen, H., Qin, J., Heng, P.A.: Transunet: transformers make strong encoders for medical image segmentation. In: Proceedings of the International Conference on Learning Representations (ICLR). Virtual Conference (2021). https://doi.org/10.1007/978-3-030-32254-0_23
5. Dosovitskiy, A., et al.: An image is worth 16×16 words: transformers for image recognition at scale. In: Proceedings of the International Conference on Learning Representations (ICLR), Virtual Conference (2021). https://doi.org/10.1007/978-3-030-32254-0_19
6. Girosi, F., Poggio, T.: Representation properties of networks: Kolmogorov's theorem is irrelevant. Neural Comput. **1**(4), 465–469 (1989)
7. Hatamizadeh, A., et al.: Unetr: transformers for 3D medical image segmentation. In: Proceedings of the IEEE/CVF Winter Conference on Applications of Computer Vision, pp. 574–584 (2022)
8. Hecht-Nielsen, R.: Kolmogorov's mapping neural network existence theorem. In: Proceedings of the International Conference on Neural Networks, vol. 3, pp. 11–14. IEEE Press, New York (1987)
9. Ismayilova, A., Ismailov, V.E.: On the Kolmogorov neural networks. Neural Netw. **176**, 106333 (2024)
10. Lin, J., et al.: Ckd-transbts: clinical knowledge-driven hybrid transformer with modality-correlated cross-attention for brain tumor segmentation. IEEE Trans. Med. Imaging **42**(8), 2451–2461 (2023)

11. Liu, Z., et al.: Kan: Kolmogorov-Arnold networks. arXiv preprint arXiv:2404.19756 (2024)
12. Menze, B.H., et al.: The multimodal brain tumor image segmentation benchmark (brats). IEEE Trans. Med. Imaging **34**(10), 1993–2024 (2014)
13. Mlynarski, P., Delingette, H., Criminisi, A., Ayache, N.: Deep learning with mixed supervision for brain tumor segmentation. In: International Conference on Medical Image Computing and Computer-Assisted Intervention, pp. 359–367. Springer, Cham (2019)
14. Pan, D., Shen, J., Al-Huda, Z., Al-Qaness, M.A.: Vcanet: vision transformer with fusion channel and spatial attention module for 3D brain tumor segmentation. Comput. Biol. Med. **186**, 109662 (2025)
15. Ronneberger, O., Fischer, P., Brox, T.: U-net: convolutional networks for biomedical image segmentation. In: Proceedings of the Medical Image Computing and Computer-Assisted Intervention (MICCAI), pp. 234–241. Springer, Cham (2015). https://doi.org/10.1007/978-3-319-24574-4_28
16. Schmidt-Hieber, J.: The Kolmogorov-Arnold representation theorem revisited. Neural Netw. **137**, 119–126 (2021)
17. Sprecher, D.A.: On the structure of continuous functions of several variables. Trans. Am. Math. Soc. **115**, 340–355 (1965)
18. Sprecher, D.A.: An improvement in the superposition theorem of Kolmogorov. J. Math. Anal. Appl. **38**(1), 208–213 (1972)
19. Tikhomirov, V.: On the representation of continuous functions of several variables as superpositions of continuous functions of one variable and addition. In: Selected Works of AN Kolmogorov, pp. 383–387. Springer, Cham (1991)
20. Wang, W., Chen, C., Ding, M., Li, J., Yu, H., Zha, S.: Transbts: multimodal brain tumor segmentation using transformer. arXiv preprint arXiv:2103.04430 (2021)
21. Zhang, W., Chen, S., Ma, Y., Liu, Y., Cao, X.: Etunet: exploring efficient transformer enhanced unet for 3D brain tumor segmentation. Comput. Biol. Med. **171**, 108005 (2024)
22. Zhou, J., Ye, J.: scse-nl v-net: a brain tumor automatic segmentation method based on spatial and channel "squeeze-and-excitation" network with non-local block. Comput. Intell. Neurosci. **2021**, 1–14 (2021). https://doi.org/10.1155/2021/9939816
23. Zhou, Z., Rahman Siddiquee, M.M., Tajbakhsh, N., Liang, J.: UNet++: a nested U-net architecture for medical image segmentation. In: Stoyanov, D., et al. (eds.) DLMIA/ML-CDS -2018. LNCS, vol. 11045, pp. 3–11. Springer, Cham (2018). https://doi.org/10.1007/978-3-030-00889-5_1

Axial-UNet: A Neural Weather Model for Precipitation Nowcasting

Sumit Mamtani$^{(\boxtimes)}$ and Maitreya Sonawane$^{(\boxtimes)}$

New York University, New York, USA
{sm9669,mss9240}@nyu.edu

Abstract. Accurately predicting short-term precipitation is critical for weather-sensitive applications such as disaster management, aviation, and urban planning. Traditional numerical weather prediction can be computationally intensive at high resolution and short lead times. In this work, we propose a lightweight UNet-based encoder–decoder augmented with axial-attention blocks that attend along image rows and columns to capture long-range spatial interactions, while temporal context is provided by conditioning on multiple past radar frames. Our hybrid architecture captures both local and long-range spatio-temporal dependencies from radar image sequences, enabling fixed lead-time precipitation nowcasting with modest compute. Experimental results on a preprocessed subset of the HKO-7 radar dataset demonstrate that our model outperforms ConvLSTM, pix2pix-style cGANs, and a plain UNet in pixel-fidelity metrics, reaching PSNR 47.67 and SSIM 0.9943. We report PSNR/SSIM here; extending evaluation to meteorology-oriented skill measures (e.g., CSI/FSS) is left to future work. The approach is simple, scalable, and effective for resource-constrained, real-time forecasting scenarios.

Keywords: Precipitation nowcasting · UNet · Axial Attention · Transformer · radar · deep learning

1 Introduction

Deep neural networks (DNN) [2, 12, 16, 17, 21] have been successfully applied in many diverse domains such as image classification, video analysis, language modeling and translation, medical imaging, and weather. Recently, there has been increasing interest in using DNNs to generate and improve weather forecasting, which is an unsupervised representation problem. In these kinds of problems, next-frame prediction is a new, promising direction of research in computer vision, predicting possible future images by presenting historical image information. Recent neural network-based weather models highlight this trend toward learned forecasting [3].

Weather forecasting is the prediction of future weather conditions, such as precipitation, temperature, pressure, and wind, and is fundamental to both science and society. Our particular interest is in the area of nowcasting, a term

B. Chatterjee et al. (Eds.): ICDCIT 2026, LNCS 16420, pp. 235–249, 2026.
https://doi.org/10.1007/978-3-032-16632-6_15

used to describe high-resolution, short-term (e.g., 0 to 2 h) weather forecasts of precipitation or other meteorological quantities. The precipitation nowcasting field helps in the accurate prediction of rainfall over an area by looking at radar images. The field deals with the generation of the radar image at some points in the near future.

One of the various architectures researchers have tried to implement is Conv-LSTM [11,18,20], which has shown great results in dealing with time-series data because it is pretty good at extracting patterns in the input feature space, where the input data spans over long sequences. The gated architecture of LSTMs has the ability to manipulate the memory state, making it more subtle for such problems.

With the continuous input of data from one end, we know that the prediction needs to be swift while dealing with a huge amount of data. Following this, some recent works have used UNet for this problem and shown improved results for image-to-image translation problems [4,23].

Recently, conditional GANs (cGANs) [9] have become widely popular under the domain of image-to-image translation [7]. As we require a model that would learn from previous inputs in the sequence, we tried to make use of this property, where cGANs predict N future radar frames given M past-conditional frames.

In this Paper, we also introduced an encoder-decoder architecture [10] with the Axial Transformer [6] in our proposed model, a simple yet effective self-attention-based [24,26] autoregressive model for data organized as multidimensional tensors. Rather than applying attention to a flattened string of tensor elements, Axial Transformer instead applies attention along a single axis of the tensor without flattening, so this is referred to as "axial attention". Since the length of any single axis (that is, the height or width of an image) is typically much smaller than the total number of elements, an axial attention operation enjoys a significant saving in computation and memory over standard self-attention. We achieve competitive results on a preprocessed dataset by training the encoder-decoder with the Axial Attention blocks. Our contributions are summarized as follows:

- **Efficient encoder–decoder for fixed lead-time nowcasting.** We propose a lightweight encoder–decoder that ingests M past radar frames and predicts the next frame at a fixed lead time, maintaining native resolution while keeping compute modest.
- **Axial attention for long-range spatial context.** We insert axial-attention blocks that attend along rows and columns, capturing large-scale advection patterns with near-linear memory; temporal context is supplied by the multi-frame encoder.
- **Controlled evaluation on an HKO-7 subset.** All models share the same preprocessing (grayscale 128 × 128) and the same train/val/test split. Each baseline uses its typical *number of input frames*—ConvLSTM (15), cGAN (4), and UNet/ours (16)—and we evaluate fixed lead-time (next-frame; $M \rightarrow 1$) predictions, extending to longer horizons via autoregression.

- **Quality gains.** The axial-attention variant improves PSNR/SSIM over strong baselines (see Table 2).

2   Related Work

Previously, the Conv-LSTM model has shown promising results on the next frame prediction problem on the Moving MNIST dataset [18]. The dataset was initially created in the context of Unsupervised Learning of Video Representations [19] and used LSTM to learn the representation of the video sequence. As the radar images are also a kind of time series data, and we know that clouds can not abruptly change direction or disappear, we know that there are some motion parameters associated with a continuous sequence of radar images, too. Using the same idea of next frame prediction in a video sequence, ConvLSTM can also be applied to a dataset of radar images.

UNet is one of the recent models that has shown its ability to predict the next frame of time-series data very well [4]. In the paper, as part of the Traffic4cast challenge 2019, UNet was used to predict short-term traffic flow volume. The input and output of the model were the same sizes, that are also relevant in our context, as we need to reproduce radar images of the same location sometime in the future. Another paper that actually implemented UNet for the weather forecasting problem [23] saw a significant increase in results on the dataset consisting of precipitation maps from a region of the Netherlands and a binary image of cloud coverage of France. The size of the model here is very small compared to previous models that were used to solve the same problem, which is also a significant advantage, considering the latency requirement of our problem statement.

Researchers have now tried an observations-driven approach for probabilistic nowcasting using deep generative models (DGMs). DGMs are statistical models that learn probability distributions of data and allow for easy generation of samples from their learned distributions [12, 15]. As generative models are fundamentally probabilistic, they can simulate many samples from the conditional distribution of future radar given historical radar.

One category of DGM model is GANs [5]. GANs learn a loss that tries to classify if the output image is real or fake, while simultaneously training a generative model to minimize this loss. Blurry images will not be tolerated since they look obviously fake. Because GANs learn a loss that adapts to the data, they can be applied to a multitude of tasks that traditionally would require very different kinds of loss functions.

Summary and Gap. ConvLSTM- and GAN-based approaches capture temporal dynamics but struggle with long-range spatial dependencies or require heavy memory. Plain UNet models are efficient but lack explicit mechanisms for large-scale advection. This motivates our design: a lightweight encoder–decoder augmented with *axial attention* to model row/column interactions efficiently.

3   Method: UNet with Axial Attention (Axial-UNet)

Given M past radar frames (here $M = 16$) sampled every 6 min, our model predicts the next frame at a fixed lead time; longer horizons are obtained via autoregression. The backbone is a UNet-style encoder–decoder (Fig. 1), and we insert *axial-attention* blocks that attend along rows and columns to capture large-scale advection with modest memory overhead.

3.1   Backbone Encoder–Decoder

UNets, first introduced in the Convolutional Networks for Biomedical Image Segmentation paper [14], have been able to expand their use case from image segmentation to predicting the future sequence too. The architecture consists of a contracting path to capture context and a symmetric expanding path that enables precise localization. Encoder (downsampling path) extracts a meaningful feature map from an input image. As is standard practice for a CNN, the Encoder doubles the number of channels at every step and halves the spatial dimension. Next, the Decoder (upsampling path) actually upsamples the feature maps, where at every step, it doubles the spatial dimension and halves the number of channels (opposite to what an Encoder does).

The contractive path (Encoder) consists of the repeated application of two 3×3 convolutions (padding $= 1$), each followed by a rectified linear unit (ReLU) and a 2×2 max pooling operation with stride 2 for downsampling. At each downsampling step, we double the number of feature channels. As the image size we use (128×128) is very small to be downsampled too much, we couldn't traverse the contractive path as much as given in the reference papers, i.e., rather than having out channels as 1024 in the final output of our Encoder, we had 256 as our number of out channels. Hence, the sequence of in and out channels for each block in the Encoder consisted of [16,64,128,256].

The decoder layer is explained as follows: every step in the expansive path consists of an upsampling of the feature map followed by a 2×2 convolution (up-convolution) that halves the number of feature channels, a concatenation with the correspondingly cropped feature map from the contracting path, and two 3×3 convolutions, each followed by a ReLU. The cropping is necessary due to the loss of border pixels in every convolution. The *ConvTranspose2d* operation performs the up-convolution, and again the same block consisting of Conv2D and ReLU in between is used to half the number of channels. The output of this Decoder is a 128×128 image for each batch, which can again be compared to the target and initiate the learning of our model.

The usage of residual skip connections helps alleviate the vanishing gradient problem, allowing for UNet models with deeper neural networks to be designed. Each residual unit can be denoted by the following expressions:

$$y_\ell = h(x_\ell) + F(x_\ell, W_\ell), \quad x_{\ell+1} = y_\ell. \tag{1}$$

To handle the time series data that we have, we could have probably used Conv-3D and MaxPool-3D layers in our UNet. But as the data was preprocessed into a GRAYSCALE image, we could just substitute the number of frames as the number of input channels, an idea inspired by SmaAt-UNet. [23]. Recent UNet variants with attention also show benefits in remote sensing nowcasting [27].

3.2   Axial Attention Blocks

Our proposed model is based on axial attention, a simple generalization of self-attention that naturally aligns with the multiple dimensions of the tensors in both the encoding and the decoding settings. As we know, Attention mechanisms have become an integral part of compelling sequence modeling and transduction models in various tasks, allowing modeling of dependencies without regard to their distance in the input or output sequences. So we have used Axial Transformers, an axial-attention-based autoregressive model for images and other data organized as high-dimensional tensors.

The sequence of images, which are the first 16 frames from the sequence of length 20, is fed into our Downsampler, which is the same as the Encoder of our UNet model used before. This acts as an image processing pipeline and the first stage of our model. The next layer is a Decoder layer that outputs a representation of the time series, i.e., integrating the information over time. The Internal layers of both Encoder and Decoder are made of several layers of CNN. We produce one feature map per input image from a sequence of length 16. Previously, in the simple UNet model, we compressed all information within a single image output from the model, but now these 16 images will act as input to our next stage, the Axial Transformer [6]. We adopt axial attention to model long-range spatial interactions with reduced memory cost in radar imagery [25].

Axial attention can be straightforwardly used within standard Transformer layers to produce Axial Transformer layers. The theoretical foundation for axial attention is established in prior work [6], which provides the mathematical formulation and proof for decomposing two-dimensional self-attention into separable row and column-wise operations. In this study, we adopt their proven formulation within our encoder-decoder framework, demonstrating its empirical stability and effectiveness for spatio-temporal precipitation nowcasting. The basic building blocks are the same as those found in the standard Transformer architecture:

Inner Decoder: using masked row attention layers to create a "row-wise" model: L_{row} is the number of masked row attention blocks applied to h.

$h \leftarrow \mathrm{Embed}(x)$

$h \leftarrow \mathrm{ShiftRight}(h) + \mathrm{PositionEmbeddings}$

$h \leftarrow \mathrm{MaskTransformerBlock2}(h) \times L_{\mathrm{row}}$

The operation ShiftRight shifts the input right by one pixel. PositionEmbeddings is a tensor of position embeddings that inform the attention layers of the position. x is the gray scale frame.

Outer Decoder: Each pixel in the model depends on previous pixels in its own row. To capture all previous rows, we insert unmasked row and masked column layers at the beginning of the model as described below:

---

h $\leftarrow$ Embed(x)
u $\leftarrow$ h + PositionEmbeddings
u $\leftarrow$ MaskTransformerBlock1(Block2(u)) $\times$ $L_{upper}/2$
h $\leftarrow$ ShiftDown(u) + ShiftRight(h) + PositionEmbeddings
h $\leftarrow$ MaskedTransformerBlock2(h) $\times$ L_{row}

The tensor u represents context captured above the current pixel. It is computed by unmasked row and masked column attention layers, repeated to a total of L_{upper} layers.

The idea of using a transformer with an encoder-decoder model was inspired by a development in the field of Precipitation Nowcasting at Google, which introduced a Neural Weather model called MetNet [22].

Now, what Axial Transformer will try to do is encode information in these feature maps from the space around each point of interest. Hence, attending to parts that are relevant to justify the motion of a cloud patch in a radar image. The way the Transformer works is - we have a series of feature maps that are continuous with respect to time. Each pixel from the latest frame emits a query vector, and each of the pixels from the older image feature maps emits a key. And each of the pixel-emitting queries can look at (attend) each of the pixels in the lower layer (keys). Hence, we can incorporate long-range dependencies by aggregating information from the downstream and increasing the resolution. But in Axial Transformers, we will specifically attend to the pixels that are either in the same row or the same column in the images produced. This saves the required memory for the computation over the layers of attention while aggregating information over the spatial dimensions. The code implementation of the Transformer was inspired by the PyTorch implementation of axial attention available on GitHub[1].

The final output of this model is a distribution across 128 frames, output from the transformer head, out of which we need to take the mean value as the predicted state of a pixel after the prediction. This predicted tensor, flattened, along with the target image tensor, also flattened, is sent to calculate the loss and start model learning.

3.3　Baselines

We compare against (i) ConvLSTM and (ii) a pix2pix-style conditional GAN (cGAN), in addition to a plain UNet backbone. All baselines share our preprocessing and split (grayscale 128×128). Input lengths follow customary practice—ConvLSTM (15), cGAN (4), UNet/ours (16)—and we evaluate fixed lead-time ($M \rightarrow 1$) predictions, extending to multiple frames via autoregression.

---

[1] https://github.com/lucidrains/axial-attention.

ConvLSTM. We use ConvLSTM as a baseline, following Shi et al. [18] on the HKO-7 dataset. We adapt a PyTorch implementation[2] originally developed for Moving MNIST to our radar sequences. ConvLSTM extends fully connected LSTMs by replacing affine transforms with convolutions in both the input-to-state and state-to-state transitions, enabling end-to-end sequence-to-sequence modeling for precipitation nowcasting.

Our implementation uses a three-layer encoder–decoder with 64 3×3 kernels per layer and padding 1 to preserve spatial size, ReLU activations, and the Adam optimizer. Each ConvLSTM cell comprises a Conv2D layer and input, output, and forget gates with sigmoid activations; the gates control memory updates and retention of past state. In our setup we condition on $M = 15$ input frames and predict the next frame, rolling out longer horizons autoregressively. For a recent survey of deep learning for precipitation nowcasting and datasets/metrics, see [1].

cGANs. GANs are generative models that learn a mapping from a random noise vector z to an output image y, G: z $\rightarrow$ y. But conditional GANs learn a mapping from observed image x and random noise vector z, to y, G: x, z $\rightarrow$ y. The generator G is trained such that it produces outputs that cannot be distinguished from "real" images by a trained discriminator (D), which is trained to do as well as possible at detecting the generator's fake images.

The objective of a conditional GAN can be expressed as:

$$L_{cGAN}(G, D) = E_{x,y}[log(D(x, y)] + \\ E_{x,z}[log(1 - D(x, G(x, z))] \tag{2}$$

where G tries to minimize this objective against an adversarial D that tries to maximize it, so the overall objective function is given by:-

$$G^* = arg\ min_G(\ arg\ max_D(L_{cGAN}(G, D))) \tag{3}$$

$L(G, D)$ is known as adversarial loss. We have also used Pixelwise L1 content loss to train the generator and discriminator model. So the generator task is to not only fool the discriminator but also to be near the ground truth output in an L1 sense. So our total loss comprises the addition of both the pixelwise loss and adversarial loss. We have used L1 distance rather than L2 as L1 encourages less blurring. So L1 loss are as follows is given by:

$$L_{L1}(G) = E_{x,y}[\ ||\ y\ -\ G(x, z)\ ||_1] \tag{4}$$

So final combined loss function is given by:

$$G^* = arg\ min_G\ (arg\ max_D(L_{cGAN}(G, D) + \\ \lambda L_{L1}(G))) \tag{5}$$

where λ is a hyper-parameter, and in our implementation, we have set its value to 100.

---

[2] https://github.com/sladewinter/ConvLSTM.

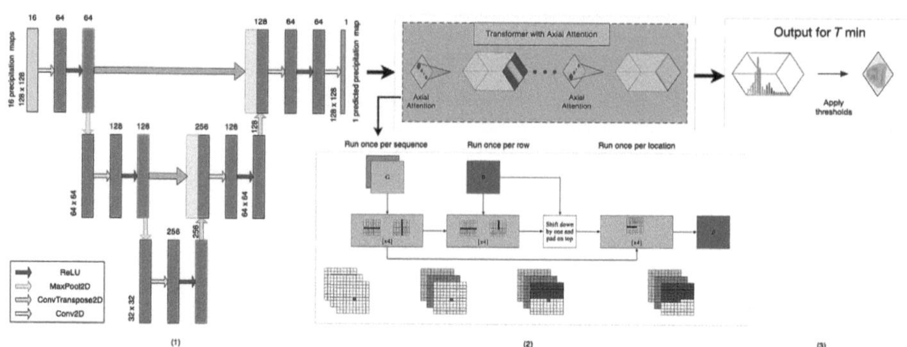

Fig. 1. Architecture of Axial-UNet (UNet with axial attention). Part (1) is our UNet model that encompasses an encoder and decoder using Conv2D. Part (2) is the transformer [22] that attends every row and column for each location (pixel), hence an axial attention [6]. Part (3) is the distribution we get as our final output, of which we take the mean to make a final prediction for T^{th} minute

Generator. The generator consists of a series of layers that progressively downsample until a bottleneck layer is reached, after that we reverse the same process, i.e., we upsample. Such a network requires that all information flow passes through all the layers, including the bottleneck. So there is a low level of information shared, like the prominent edge locations between input and output, which produces higher-quality images than a simple CNN generator model.

We have added skip connections to avoid the vanishing gradient problem and to incorporate information from earlier layers. This is the general shape of a UNet architecture. Specifically, we add skip connections between each layer i and layer $n - i$, where n is the total number of layers. Each skip connection simply concatenates all channels at layer i with those at layer $n - i$.

Discriminator. The discriminator is a type of Convolution Neural Network(CNN) model. The discriminator has 4 sequential blocks having 64, 128, 256, 512 filters respectively. Each sequential block consists of the convolutional layer, batch-normalization layer, and activation layer as LeakyReLU. The generator tries to fool the discriminator by creating fake images. The discriminator is trained in such a way that it tries to distinguish real data from the data created by the generator.

4   Experimental Results

In this section, we first introduce related datasets and implementation details in our experiments. Then, we report results and a comparison of all the experiments conducted on each of the models used.

4.1   Datasets

The dataset used in this project is a part of dataset used in paper ConvLSTM for Precipitation Nowcasting [18]. The dataset for the original research work consisted of HKO-7 dataset, which contains radar echo data from 2009 to 2015 near Hong Kong. Along with the radar images, the dataset also contains proportions of rainfall events with different rain-rate thresholds.

The HKO-7 dataset used in the baseline research contains radar CAPPI reflectivity images, which have a resolution of 480×480 pixels, are taken from an altitude of 2 km, and cover a 512 km $\times$ 512 km area centered in Hong Kong. The data are recorded every 6 min, and hence there are 240 frames per day. The pixel values are clipped between 0 and 255. There are some noisy radar images in the dataset generated by factors like ground clutter, sea clutter, anomalous propagation, and electromagnetic interference.

The complete dataset with all the CSV and pkl files was not available publicly. But a part of it, i.e., the radar images that can be conveniently used in our problem, are available publicly [8]. We have continuous radar images from 514 folders. Each folder contains a variable number of radar images sampled, but all of them are continuous. As the radar echo maps arrive in a stream, nowcasting algorithms can apply online learning to adapt to the newly emerging spatiotemporal patterns.

This was the most convenient dataset we could use, because the datasets used in previous research under this topic were too large to be handled on the GPU provided (datasets of size in TBs). Other datasets were either paid or not publicly available. Even the dataset that we have used, is a part of an original dataset. But it was enough to carry out several experiments on various models used.

4.2   Implementation Details

After taking the dataset as our input, first, we had to ensure that the number of radar images in each folder's sequence remains the same. This is due to the fact that we will be sending the dataset in batches for training and testing, and we need to have a uniform number of images in each batch. Hence, we clipped the dataset to 240 images per folder (if the number of radar images in a folder is greater than 240, if it is less than 240, we reject that folder), i.e., as soon as the number of images in that particular folder goes past 240, we stop taking that folder's images as input. We found out that the dataset now had 482 sequences of length 240. While we input each image, we also convert the image into grayscale, as we need to map the cloud motion in the radar images, and having RGB channels in the images will only cost computation time and power without much significant difference in the results.

At first, we tried to send this data directly for training in batches. But, due to computational power limitations, we could not send a batch of size 240 for training. The sequence of images had to be broken to the length of 20, i.e., instead of 482 sequences of length 240, now we had 5784 sequences of length 20. Now sequence of this length can be comfortably loaded for training and testing.

Now that we had a sequence of data, we also needed to filter out the images that were either too dark or too light. There were some faulty images in our dataset, as previously talked about, because of faulty radar images. So we first stored the summation of all the pixel values in each image of our dataset in a list. This is important to normalise our dataset, as then we found the 25th and 75th percentile of the list values. These give us the range we will use to filter images whose sum of pixel values is above or below the specified range.

Now, going through each sequence, we again calculated the sum of pixel values of each image in 5784 sequences. If the sum is outside the range, we count that as a bad frame. If the number of bad frames in a sequence exceeds 10, we discard that sequence as a whole, as we can't discard a few frames from a sequence; discontinuity in frames would make them useless. Now, once the data is cleaned, we are left with 2901 sequences of length 20, each being an image of size 128×128. The sequences were then loaded in an .npy file to be used later. As observed, the usable images left at last were almost half of the dataset we created at the start, and this was one of the reasons why we couldn't use a higher batch size while training our models.

Table 1. While testing each model, we first input a sequence of images $(t_0, t_1, ..., t_m)$ into the model and obtain one image (p_1) as output. This predicted image p_1 is then used with the next sequence $(t_1, ..., t_m)$ to predict the next radar image, and so on. The top row shows the target images, and the second row shows the outputs. The proposed model achieves the highest quality of prediction.

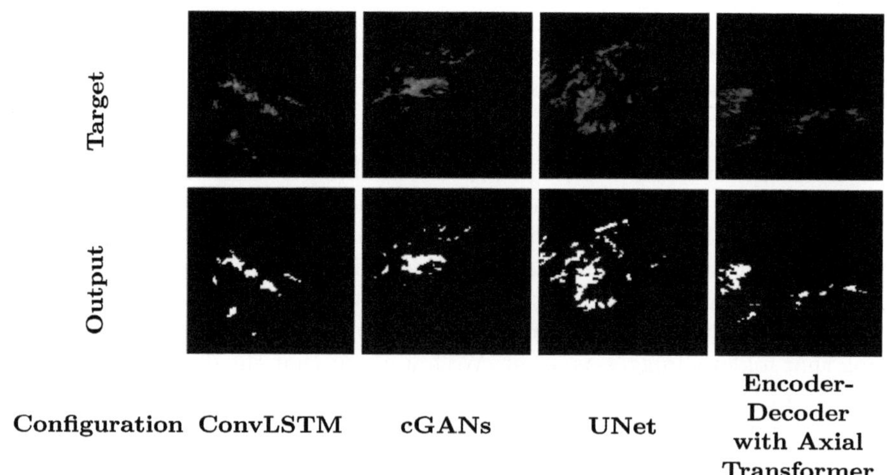

Once the .npy file is loaded, we randomly shuffle these sequences without altering their internal continuity in frames, for uniform distribution of types of images for training, validation, and testing. Out of these, 2000 sequences were used in training dataset, 500 for validation, and 400 for testing purpose. Whenever the numpy array representing the images in the dataset is loaded, the batch is normalised by dividing by 255, to bring each pixel value between 0 and 1. Shuffle is kept true to make the distribution among the types of images uniform.

The sequence length given to train Conv-LSTM was 15, so that it can count next 5 frames as target and make a prediction on those. For cGANs, the input sequence length was 4, as it was an image-to-image translation technique and produced one image per input image, hence predicting 4 frames from 4 inputs. For UNet and UNet with axial attention, we had to give 16 frames as input to the model, as we needed to ensure downsampling and later upsampling produce images (given in number of channels dimensions) of the same number at each corresponding layer. The batch size for ConvLSTM = 2, cGANs = 4, UNet = 4, Axial-UNet = 1. Every model was given a batch size with limitations due to the risk of the GPU running out of memory or model overfitting too soon.

For a given input sequence, 1 frame was predicted as output from every model (Table 1). Now the same frame was used as input while predicting the next frame and so on. Hence, by this method, we were able to predict 4–5 frames in the future using the original sequence of the input image.

Number of epochs used to train the models is variable due to the effect of overfitting for larger and deeper models. ConvLSTM: 5, cGANs: 10, UNet: 5, Axial-UNet: 15. Optimizer used is Adam, with a learning rate of: *1e-3* for ConvLSTM, *1e-4* for cGANs, *1e-3* for UNet, *1e-4* for Axial-UNet. The loss criterion for each of the models used is *MSELoss*.

Given a noise-free flattened monochrome image I and its flattened noisy approximation Image K, the *MSELoss* between two tensors is defined as:

$$MSELoss \;=\; \frac{1}{2} \sum_{i=0}^{n-1} (\, I_i \,-\, K_i \,) \tag{6}$$

The metrics we used to compare the results of different models were PSNR and SSIM. PSNR: Peak signal-to-noise ratio is the ratio between the maximum possible power of a signal and the power of corrupting noise that affects the fidelity of its representation.

$$PSNR \;=\; -10 \, \log_{10}(MSE) \tag{7}$$

MSE is defined as the mean squared error between a noise-free, flattened monochrome image and its flattened noisy approximation, Image K

SSIM: Structural Similarity Index (SSIM) measures the similarity between two images by quantifying the image degradation of one image with respect to another.

The SSIM between two images x and y of common size N $\times$ N is:

$$SSIM(\, x,y\,) \;=\; \frac{(2u_x u_y + c_1)(2\sigma_{xy} + c_2)}{\left(u_x^2 + u_y^2 + c_1\right)\left(\sigma_x^2 + \sigma_y^2 + c_2\right)} \tag{8}$$

where μ_x is the average of x, μ_y is the average of y, σ_x^2 is the variance of x; σ_y^2 is the variance of y and c_1 and c_2 are constants.

4.3   Results and Comparisons

We limit evaluation to PSNR/SSIM. Event/object-based skill and cell-tracking metrics are standard in meteorology [13]; comparison to recent diffusion/transformer models is left for future work. While training each of the model, we calculated the loss for training and cross-validation data, the results of which are given below (Fig. 2):

We see some unusual spikes in the graph, which might be due to faulty radar images and abrupt shuffling of data.

The models used in the experiments showed a gradual increase in both metrics, and hence show that our proposed architecture performs better than the baseline model used.

Table 2. Comparison on the HKO-7 subset. Higher is better.

Configuration	PSNR↑	SSIM↑
ConvLSTM	40.8852	0.9710
cGANs	41.1319	0.9826
UNet	47.2862	0.9929
Encoder-Decoder with Axial Transformer	**47.6678**	**0.9943**

While the ConvLSTM baseline performed reasonably on our split, a pix2pix-style cGAN improved over it. Treating the task as image-to-image translation (one output frame per input frame) with an adversarial loss helps suppress some noise and sharpen texture compared to pure regression.

The cGAN's generator is a UNet. Interestingly, the same UNet used as a standalone deterministic model performed even better, likely because our dataset is relatively small and the supervised loss dominates; simpler models can generalize well in this regime. In addition, pix2pix yields fewer distinct training pairs than sequence-to-sequence setups, since each training example maps a single input image to a single target image.

Skip connections in UNet help alleviate vanishing gradients and promote feature reuse, enabling accurate next-frame predictions with a compact backbone. Adding *axial-attention* blocks on top of UNet further improves quality by attending along rows and columns to capture large-scale advection while keeping memory modest.

For evaluation, the model outputs continuous predictions in $[0,1]$ (due to input normalization), and PSNR/SSIM are computed on these continuous fields. Thresholded black-and-white visualizations (e.g., applying a 0.2 cutoff and rescaling to 0–255) are used only for display, not for metric computation.

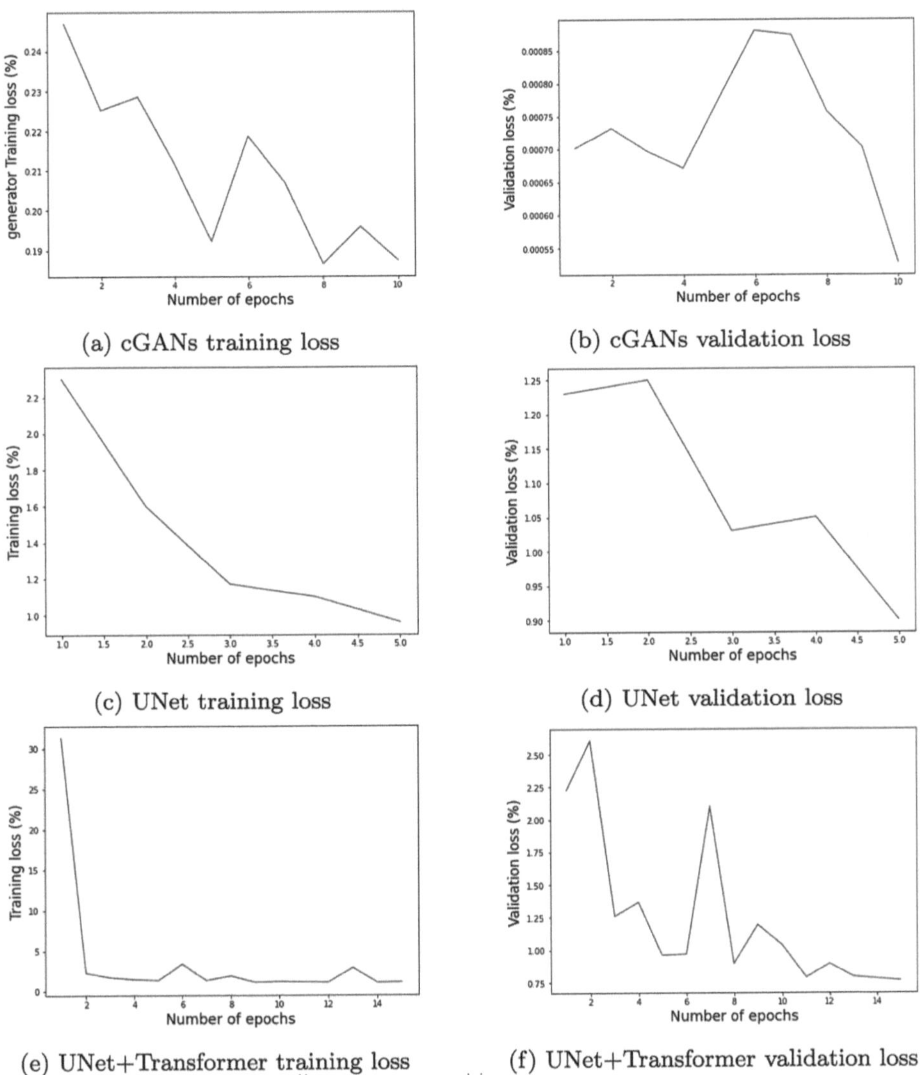

(a) cGANs training loss

(b) cGANs validation loss

(c) UNet training loss

(d) UNet validation loss

(e) UNet+Transformer training loss

(f) UNet+Transformer validation loss

Fig. 2. Training and validation loss curves for (a, b) cGANs, (c, d) UNet, and (e, f) Axial-UNet.

5   Discussion

We studied short–lead-time radar nowcasting with a lightweight encoder–decoder augmented by axial attention. Given M past frames (here $M = 16$) sampled every 6 min, the model predicts the next frame and extends to 4–5 future frames via autoregression. On our HKO-7 subset, the axial-attention variant improves pixel-fidelity metrics (PSNR/SSIM) over ConvLSTM, pix2pix-style cGANs, and a plain UNet. Axial attention preserves coherent structures and sharper boundaries aligned with large-scale advection while keeping memory overhead modest by attending along rows and columns instead of full 2D self-attention.

This study has practical constraints: evaluation is limited to PSNR/SSIM (image fidelity) rather than meteorological skill; a fuller assessment would include event/object-based metrics and lead-time breakdowns. The data are a cleaned, grayscale subset of HKO-7 at 128×128, which may bias case difficulty; we do not convert reflectivity to rain rate nor assess calibration/uncertainty (we take the mean of the predictive distribution). Baselines follow customary input lengths— ConvLSTM (15), cGAN (4), UNet/ours (16)—and their usual training settings, so the comparison is pragmatic rather than strictly matched-budget.

6   Future Work

We plan to extend the study along four axes:

- **Continuous targets and rain rate.** Train on reflectivity in dBZ and predict continuous fields; convert to rain rate via an appropriate Z–R relation, and evaluate thresholded rain events rather than binarized visualizations.
- **Meteorology-grade evaluation.** Beyond PSNR/SSIM, report CSI, POD, FAR, FSS, and cell-tracking growth/decay across lead times (e.g., 6–30 min).
- **Probabilistic outputs.** Retain the distributional head, assess calibration (e.g., CRPS, reliability diagrams), and sample ensembles for uncertainty-aware nowcasts.
- **Data & baselines.** Use storm- or date-based splits to avoid leakage; quantify cleaning/clutter effects; add persistence/optical-flow controls and stronger deep baselines under the same split; explore higher resolution and multi-channel inputs (multi-elevation radar, satellite bands).

References

1. An, S., et al.: Deep learning for precipitation nowcasting: a survey from the perspective of time series forecasting (2024)
2. Barnes, E.A., Mayer, K., Toms, B., Martin, Z., Gordon, E.: Identifying opportunities for skillful weather prediction with interpretable neural networks (2020). https://arxiv.org/abs/2012.07830
3. Bodnar, C., et al.: A foundation model for the earth system (2024), microsoft Research; also see technical report PDF
4. Choi, S.: Traffic map prediction using unet based deep convolutional neural network (2019)
5. Goodfellow, I.J., et al.: Generative adversarial networks (2014)
6. Ho, J., Kalchbrenner, N., Weissenborn, D., Salimans, T.: Axial attention in multi-dimensional transformers (2019)
7. Isola, P., Zhu, J.Y., Zhou, T., Efros, A.A.: Image-to-image translation with conditional adversarial networks (2018)
8. Lei, C.: A deep learning based methodology for precipitation1 nowcasting with radar (2019). https://doi.org/10.7910/DVN/2GKMQJ

9. Mirza, M., Osindero, S.: Conditional generative adversarial nets (2014)
10. Mo, T., Liu, B.: Encoder-decoder neural architecture optimization for keyword spotting (2021)
11. Patel, M., Patel, A., Ghosh, D.R.: Precipitation nowcasting: Leveraging bidirectional LSTM and 1D CNN (2018)
12. Ravuri, S., et al.: Skilful precipitation nowcasting using deep generative models of radar. Nature **597**(7878), 672–677 (2021). https://doi.org/10.1038/s41586-021-03854-z
13. Ritvanen, J., Pulkkinen, S., Moisseev, D., Nerini, D.: Cell-tracking-based framework for assessing nowcasting model skill in reproducing growth and decay of convective rainfall. Geosci. Model Dev. **18**, 1851–1878 (2025). https://doi.org/10.5194/gmd-18-1851-2025
14. Ronneberger, O., Fischer, P., Brox, T.: U-net: convolutional networks for biomedical image segmentation (2015)
15. Ruthotto, L., Haber, E.: An introduction to deep generative modeling (2021)
16. Samsi, S., Mattioli, C.J., Veillette, M.S.: Distributed deep learning for precipitation nowcasting. In: 2019 IEEE High Performance Extreme Computing Conference (HPEC) (2019). https://doi.org/10.1109/hpec.2019.8916416
17. Schmidhuber, J.: Deep learning in neural networks: an overview. Neural Netw. **61**, 85–117 (2015). https://doi.org/10.1016/j.neunet.2014.09.003
18. Shi, X., et al.: Convolutional LSTM network: a machine learning approach for precipitation nowcasting (2015)
19. Srivastava, N., Mansimov, E., Salakhutdinov, R.: Unsupervised learning of video representations using LSTMs (2016)
20. Staudemeyer, R.C., Morris, E.R.: Understanding LSTM – a tutorial into long short-term memory recurrent neural networks (2019)
21. Sze, V., Chen, Y.H., Yang, T.J., Emer, J.: Efficient processing of deep neural networks: a tutorial and survey (2017)
22. Sønderby, C.K., et al.: Metnet: a neural weather model for precipitation forecasting (2020)
23. Trebing, K., Stanczyk, T., Mehrkanoon, S.: Smaat-unet: precipitation nowcasting using a small attention-unet architecture (2021)
24. Vaswani, A., et al.: Attention is all you need (2017)
25. Xie, Y.M., et al.: A deep learning model with axial attention for radar echo extrapolation. Appl. Artif. Intell. (2024). https://doi.org/10.1080/08839514.2024.2311003
26. Yun, Z., Chen, Y., Olshausen, B.A., LeCun, Y.: Transformer visualization via dictionary learning: contextualized embedding as a linear superposition of transformer factors (2021)
27. Zhang, Z., et al.: Deep learning model for precipitation nowcasting based on residual and attention mechanisms (ra-unet). Remote Sens. **17**(7), 1123 (2025)

NLP and LLMs

KUI-2SR: A Unified Speech and Speaker Recognizer for KUI Language

Malay Kumar Majhi[(✉)] and Sujan Kumar Saha[(✉)]

National Institute of Technology Durgapur, Durgapur, India
mkm.22cs1111@phd.nitdgp.ac.in, sksaha.cse@nitdgp.ac.in

Abstract. This study presents the first unified speech and speaker recognition system for the Kui language. Kui is predominantly spoken in the western region of Odisha, India. It is primarily an oral language and does not have its own script. The Odia script is used for written communication. We did not find any open resources or speech recognition systems in Kui. Our proposed system follows a Bi-modular pipeline: first, a baseline ASR model is established using a Transformer-based encoder. To further improve recognition accuracy, we employ two multilingual pre-trained models and fine-tune them using an in-house continuous Kui speech dataset using transfer learning. Next, we integrate a speaker identification module within the framework, enabling the system to simultaneously recognize spoken content and attribute it to individual speakers. The experimental results demonstrate that the large multilingual pre-trained transfer learning approach significantly reduces both Word Error Rate (WER) and Character Error Rate (CER), while the speaker identification module provides robust speaker recognition. This work highlights the potential of combining multilingual transfer learning and speaker recognition to advance ASR research in low-resource languages such as Kui.

Keywords: Kui Language · Automatic Speech Recognition · Speaker Recognition · Transfer Learning

1   Introduction

Automatic Speech Recognition (ASR) refers to the process of converting spoken language into written text. Despite decades of advancements, ASR continues to be an active area of research, particularly for unexplored and low-resource languages. The complexity of ASR arises from various factors such as accent variation, vocabulary diversity, speech rate, and intonation patterns [1]. ASR systems have found wide applications in sectors like healthcare, education, banking, and virtual assistance [10]. In recent years, ASR has also been recognized as a powerful tool to preserve endangered and indigenous languages by enabling digital documentation and accessibility. In parallel, Speaker Recognition (SR) has emerged as another important speech technology that enables the identification and verification of speakers from their voice. SR finds applications in security systems, personalized human-computer interaction, forensic analysis, and diarization in multi-speaker environments. Integrating speaker recognition with ASR not only improves usability but also enables unified speech and speaker processing systems, which are especially valuable in multilingual and low-resource environments.

Kui is a tribal language spoken predominantly in the western districts of Odisha, India. It is primarily oral and does not have a native script. Instead of that, the Odia script is commonly used for written communication. Kui remains vastly underrepresented in the digital and computational landscape. As we know, the deep learning task requires a huge amount of annotated speech corpora to train a system. The lack of a publicly available large corpus and unique phonetic structure makes ASR development in Kui a significant challenge. Similarly, no prior effort exists for speaker recognition in Kui, highlighting the need to build a unified speech and speaker recognition framework for both linguistic preservation and technological inclusion.

Recent research in ASR for Indian languages has shifted towards deep learning and self-supervised architectures. Initial ASR efforts in Indian languages like Hindi, Tamil, and Bengali relied on HMM-GMM and LPC models with moderate success [1,6,27]. With the emergence of deep neural networks and pre-trained models such as wav2vec2.0 and Whisper, the performance of ASR systems in Indian languages has significantly improved [11,26]. Moreover, the success of transfer learning techniques like adapter-based learning, attention transfer, and selective fine-tuning has further improved ASR accuracy in low-resource languages [10,19,28]. In addition, advances in multilingual embedding learning and x-vector-based architectures have significantly enhanced speaker recognition tasks across diverse languages. Notably, recent developments of ASR systems for Odia and Sadri in 2025 have demonstrated the effectiveness of multilingual transfer learning in handling low-resource scenarios, motivating similar progress for Kui.

This paper presents the first unified speech and speaker recognition system for the Kui language. As no prior corpus existed, we created a new dataset using native Kui speakers. Initially, we built a baseline ASR model using the DeepSpeech architecture, with Mel-Frequency Cepstral Coefficients (MFCC) for feature extraction and Cross Entropy (CE) loss. To improve performance, we fine-tuned two multilingual pre-trained models: Whisper-small [22] and Wav2Vec2.0 XLSR-53 [2] on the Kui data using transfer learning. In parallel, a speaker recognition module was integrated into the framework using deep speaker embeddings to identify individual speakers. The baseline ASR model achieved a Word Error Rate (WER) of 25.79% and a Character Error Rate (CER) of 14.62%. After applying transfer learning, Whisper-small achieved a WER of 3.56% and CER of 0.94%, while Wav2Vec2.0 XLSR-53 resulted in a WER of 4.42% and CER of 1.67%. We reported the speaker recognition accuracy of 97.32% using Wav2Vec2.0, which further demonstrated reliable speaker-level identification.

This work demonstrates the feasibility and impact of combining multilingual transfer learning and speaker recognition in developing speech technologies.

The paper contributes to the literature in multiple directions as follows.

1. We develop the first unified speech and speaker recognition system for the Indian language, Kui.
2. We create a manually recorded and annotated Kui speech corpus comprising 14.38 h of utterances collected from 24 native Kui speakers.
3. We integrate a speaker detection module within the framework, enabling simultaneous recognition of speech and speaker identity in Kui.

The rest of this paper is structured as follows. Section 2 reviews related works. Section 3 describes the details of ASR and speaker recognition data creation for Kui. Section 4 explains the proposed baseline model, followed by the transfer learning approaches. Section 5 presents experimental results. Finally, Sect. 6 concludes the paper.

2   Related Work

In this section, we review the literature on ASR systems for Indian languages. Early ASR systems in Indian languages often tried to recognize isolated words or numbers. For instance, Saraswathi and Geetha (2004) ran experiments for speech recognition for isolated words in Tamil using an Artificial Neural Network (ANN) [24]. Thangarajan et al. (2009) proposed a couple of models for continuous ASR in Tamil [27]. Das et al. (2011) utilized the Hidden Markov Model Toolkit (HTK) on 26 h of Bengali speech data, achieving a word accuracy of 85.3% after corrections [6]. Aggarwal and Dave (2013) employed HMM and Gaussian Mixture Models (GMM) on 600 Hindi utterances, obtaining a WER of 9.19% [1]. In recent years, deep learning approaches have gained prominence in developing ASR systems for Indian languages. Pandey et al. (2013) presented a large vocabulary speech recognition system using the WATSON toolkit. They used Bangla and Hindi corpora for their experiment and achieved an accuracy of 74.2% for Hindi and 65.6% for Bangla [20]. Shivakumar et al. (2016) discussed a Kannada automated speech-to-text conversion system using the CMUSphinx framework in their model. They trained their model on 1000 sentences and achieved an accuracy of 80% for their context-independent model [25]. Srivastava et al. (2018) applied Deep Neural Networks (DNN) and Time Delay Neural Networks (TDNN) to 40 h of Telugu speech data, achieving a WER of 25.47% [26]. Naman and Deepshikha (2021) explored Model-Agnostic Meta-Learning (MAML), Convolutional Neural Networks (CNN), and Conformer models for Hindi ASR. They applied their model on 80,000 samples and achieved a CER of 10.19% [17].

Alongside ASR, speaker recognition has also seen significant progress in Indian and multilingual contexts. Maurya et al. (2018) presented a speaker recognition system for Hindi using MFCC and Gaussian Mixture Models, achieving

94.12% accuracy with 17 speakers [16]. Chung et al. (2018) introduced a large-scale deep speaker recognition system using a CNN-based framework, evaluated on an audio-visual dataset of over 6000 speakers, and achieved an Equal Error Rate (EER) of 3.95% [5]. India et al. (2019) proposed a long-term speaker embedding model based on a CNN encoder with self multi-head attention, tested on the VoxColab dataset, achieving an 18% error rate compared to their baseline [9]. Basu et al. (2021) developed a speech corpus for joint language and speaker identification using MFCC, shifted delta cepstral features, vector quantization, GMM, and SVM, reporting a best recognition rate of 95.69% [3]. Radha and Bansal (2023) focused on child speaker identification for the education domain, implementing a BiLSTM-based system and obtaining 97.32% accuracy [23]. These studies highlight the increasing role of deep learning, embeddings, and corpus creation in advancing speaker recognition tasks, offering useful insights for integrating SR into low-resource ASR systems such as Kui.

Transfer learning has emerged as a key strategy in ASR development, particularly for low-resource languages. Otake et al. (2023) demonstrated an adapter-based transfer learning approach, reducing WER from 21.8% to 9.5% on English datasets [19]. Yi et al. (2017) introduced a language-adversarial transfer learning method with shared hidden layers, reducing WERs for Pashto, Turkish, and Vietnamese by up to 7% [28]. In the Indian context, Joshi et al. (2020) used RNN-Transducer models with multiple transfer learning strategies, lowering Hindi WER from 26.33% to 21.89% [10]. Inaguma et al. (2019) explored fusion-based transfer learning for Assamese and other low-resource languages, achieving a notable reduction in WER [8]. More recently, Khare et al. (2021) combined CTC-attention with wav2vec2.0 embeddings, substantially improving Hindi, Telugu, Gujarati, and Bengali ASR performance under limited data conditions [11]. Paul et al. (2025) introduced a Sadri ASR model based on CNN, RNN, and transfer learning, reducing baseline WER from 22.08% to 15.25% [21]. Majhi and Saha (2025) introduced a Modular Adapter Learning setup, lowering the WER from 29.74% to 14.47% [15].

We did not find any ASR system or related linguistic resources available for the Kui language in the literature. However, some notable efforts have been made for related languages such as Odia. A significant milestone was the MUCS 2021 dataset released by Diwan et al. (2021), which included Odia among six Indian languages. Diwan et al. reported a baseline WER of 35.36% using DNN-HMM and TDNN models [7]. Chadha et al. (2022), who applied wav2vec2.0 with a KenLM-based language model and achieved a WER of 27.10% [4]. Majhi and Saha (2024) presented a BiLSTM-based Odia ASR with attention mechanism and data augmentation (WER reduced from 36.48% to 18.54%) [14]. These efforts provide useful insights and architectural baselines for developing ASR systems in other low-resource languages of Odisha, such as Kui.

3   Data Creation

We created a speech corpus for the Kui language to develop the proposed system. This dataset was specifically designed for building both an ASR system and a speaker recognition module, ensuring coverage of linguistic diversity, speaker variability, and practical usability.

Kui is a South-Central Dravidian language spoken by the Kandha (Kondh) tribal community in the western districts of Odisha, India, especially in Kandhamal, Kalahandi, and Rayagada regions. It is a primarily oral language and does not have its own native script. The Odia script is commonly used for written communication. Kui features a phonological system that includes voiced and voiceless stops, nasals, retroflex sounds, and a set of oral vowels. The language follows a Subject-Object-Verb (SOV) word order and utilizes postpositions. Although Kui lacks tonal variation, stress and intonation patterns are used in spoken discourse to convey emphasis and sentence modality.

3.1   Corpus

A speech corpus comprising 14.38 h was created for this study. We selected approximately 320 unique sentences from textbooks [13], ensuring that all phonetic variations present in the spoken Kui language were adequately represented. These sentences varied in length from 1 to 25 words, which captures a wide linguistic range.

Recordings were performed with 24 native speakers of Kui, including 10 male and 14 female participants from different age groups and regional dialects. The audio was captured using a Sony ICD-PX470 digital voice recorder with a 16 kHz sampling rate and 128 kbps bit rate. All audio files were manually segmented, labeled, and cleaned using the Audacity toolkit to ensure precise annotations. The dataset was split into two subsets: a training set of 13.12 h and a test set of 1.26 h.

3.2   Speaker Recognition Dataset

For speaker recognition, the same 24 speakers were considered to build a balanced dataset. Each speaker contributed a diverse set of utterances across different recording sessions, ensuring variability in speech rate, accent, and intonation. The dataset provides speaker-level labels corresponding to each utterance, which allows supervised training of the recognition module. This design supports both closed-set and open-set evaluation scenarios and making it suitable for robust speaker identification.

4   Methodology

This section presents the architecture and methodology developed for building the ASR and SR system for the Kui language. Given the absence of publicly available resources for Kui, we constructed our dataset using native speakers and designed a unified end-to-end pipeline. The framework includes preprocessing, a Transformer-based baseline encoder, multilingual adaptation using Whisper-small and Wav2Vec2.0 XLSR-53.

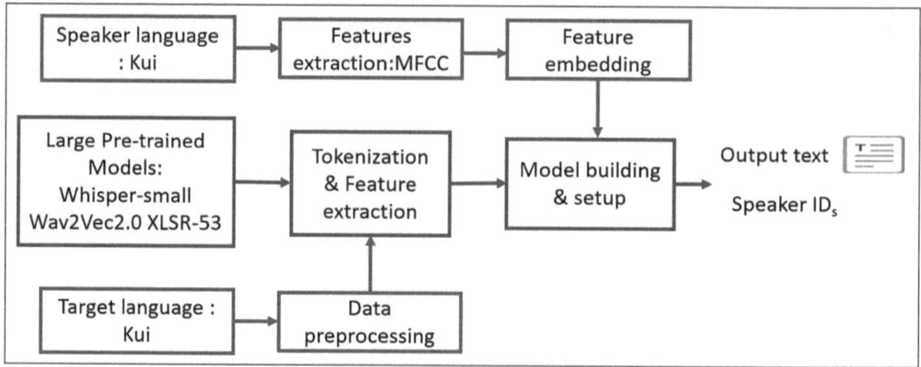

Fig. 1. Detailed flowchart of the proposed system

4.1   Baseline Architecture

4.2   Pre-processing and Feature Extraction

The first step in the pipeline involves extracting meaningful features from the inputs using Mel-Frequency Cepstral Coefficients (MFCCs). MFCC is a feature extraction method that captures essential frequency-based features from signals using windows and segments. This process is mathematically defined as:

$$\text{MFCC}(s) = \mathcal{D}\left\{\log\left(\mathcal{F}\left\{s(t)\right\}\right)\right\}, \tag{1}$$

where $\mathcal{F}$ denotes the Fourier transform over a 13-point Mel scale, and $\mathcal{D}$ is the Discrete Cosine Transform. A window of 22 ms and a step size of 15 ms, with a 512-point FFT, are applied to segment the signal. These MFCC features serve as the input for further processing in both ASR and SR tasks.

4.3   Transformer Encoder Framework

For the baseline system, we used a Transformer-based encoder architecture. The MFCC features are first linearly projected and embedded with positional encodings to retain temporal order. The Transformer encoder is composed of multiple self-attention and feed-forward layers that model long-range temporal dependencies in the input sequence. For a sequence of MFCC frames $X = \{x_1, x_2, \ldots, x_T\}$, the encoder representation H is defined as:

$$H = \text{TransformerEncoder}(X + PE), \tag{2}$$

where PE denotes positional encodings added to the input sequence.

Each Transformer block consists of a multi-head self-attention layer followed by a position-wise feed-forward network:

$$\text{Attention}(Q, K, V) = \text{Softmax}\left(\frac{QK^T}{\sqrt{d_k}}\right)V, \tag{3}$$

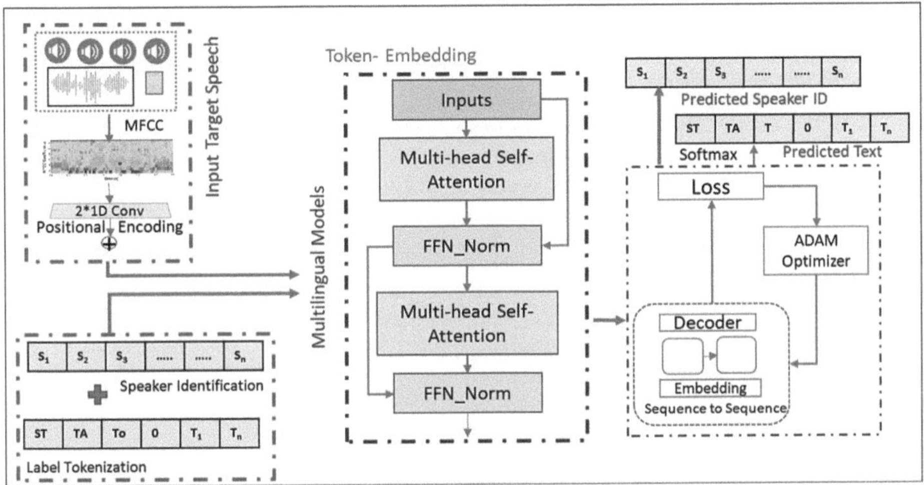

Fig. 2. Detailed architecture of the proposed Bi-Fold Speech and speaker recognition system

where Q, K, V represent query, key, and value projections of the input sequence, and d_k is the dimensionality of keys.

The system combines two loss components: the ASR loss and the speaker recognition loss. For ASR, we employ Sparse Entropy Loss (SEL), which enforces sparsity and confidence in token predictions. For speaker recognition, a cross-entropy loss is applied over the speaker embeddings to classify speakers accurately. The final training objective is a weighted sum of these two losses, enabling the model to simultaneously optimize speech recognition and speaker identification within a unified framework. Figure 1 presents the flowchart of the proposed system.

4.4 Multilingual Adaptation Using Whisper and Wav2Vec2.0

Next, we adopted a transfer learning strategy by adding two state-of-the-art multilingual ASR models: Whisper-small and Wav2Vec2.0 XLSR-53. Both models were integrated into our unified framework with the proposed joint objective defined earlier. The overall architecture of the proposed system is illustrated in Fig. 2.

Whisper-Small. Whisper is a transformer-based encoder-decoder model, also referred to as a sequence-to-sequence model. It was trained on 680k hours of labeled speech data annotated using large-scale weak supervision. We used the small multilingual variant (whisper-small) with 244 million parameters and a 30k subword vocabulary [22]. To improve robustness, SpecAugment was applied during fine-tuning. The model was fine-tuned for 25 epochs with a batch size of 16 using the Adam optimizer (learning rate $1e^{-5}$, weight decay 0.01). The training employed Sparse Entropy Loss for ASR along with a cross-entropy speaker classification head, enabling simultaneous optimization of speech and speaker recognition.

Wav2Vec2.0 XLSR-53 is a self-supervised model pre-trained on 53 languages using large-scale unlabeled speech corpora [2]. We employed the XLSR-53 variant, consisting of 317 million parameters, which was pre-trained on multilingual data. The inputs were converted into log-mel filterbank features with normalization aligned to the pre-training setup. Further, we fine-tune it for 30 epochs with a batch size of 32 and a learning rate of $3e^{-5}$. During the first 10 epochs, the feature extractor was frozen to stabilize training, while the higher transformer layers were gradually adapted to Kui speech. Similar to Whisper, the unified loss function (Sparse Entropy Loss for ASR + Cross Entropy for SR) was used during training.

5   Experiments and Results

This section presents the experimental setup and results obtained from the proposed framework. We report the performance of the baseline and multilingual models for ASR, along with speaker recognition.

5.1   Evaluation Metrics

To assess the performance of our ASR systems, we rely on the standard metrics: Word Error Rate (WER) and Character Error Rate (CER). WER evaluates the accuracy of the model at the word level, indicating the proportion of words that were incorrectly predicted by the system compared to the target transcript [12]. Conversely, CER assesses the accuracy at the character level, counting the percentage of individual characters that were incorrectly transcribed [18].

$$WER = \frac{\text{Substitutions} + \text{Deletions} + \text{Insertions}}{\text{Total Words}} \tag{4}$$

$$CER = \frac{\text{Substitutions} + \text{Deletions} + \text{Insertions}}{\text{Total Characters}} \tag{5}$$

$$Accuracy = \frac{\text{Correct Predictions}}{\text{Total Predictions}} \tag{6}$$

For the speaker recognition module, we use Accuracy as the evaluation metric, which measures the proportion of correctly identified speakers out of the total predictions.

5.2   Experimental Results

The experimental results of the Kui ASR system are reported in two parts. First, the performance of the baseline model is evaluated. Next, the improvements achieved through multilingual transfer learning. Finally, we compare the ASR approaches and present the speaker recognition results.

Table 1. Performance Comparison of Baseline and Multilingual Models for Kui ASR

Model	WER (%)	CER (%)
Baseline (Transformer Encoder)	25.79	14.62
Whisper-small	3.56	0.94
Wav2Vec2.0 XLSR-53	4.42	1.67

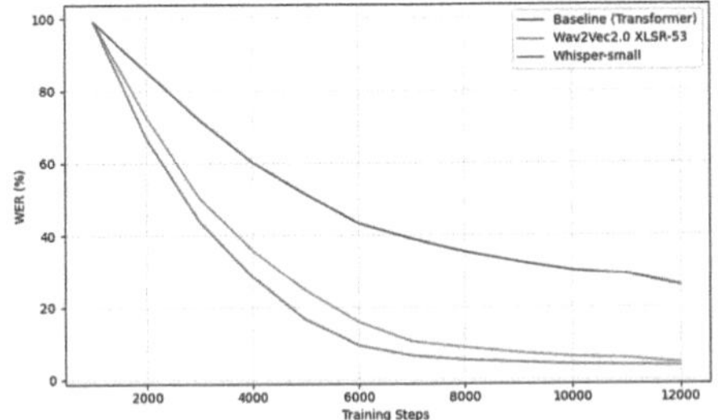

(a) WER trends across training steps for Baseline, XLSR-53, and Whisper-small.

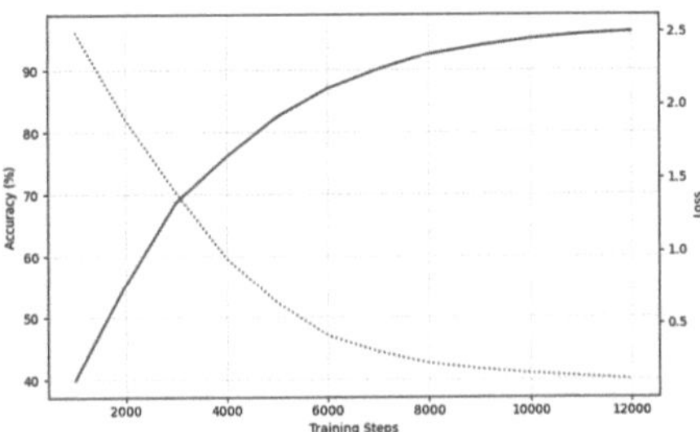

(b) Speaker recognition accuracy and loss trends across training steps.

Fig. 3. Performance analysis of the proposed Kui unified ASR and Speaker Recognition system.

5.3   ASR Results

We first report the results of the baseline Transformer encoder model. The baseline performs quite a high error rate, which does not achieve strong generalization due to the limited availability of Kui data. The system achieved a WER of 25.79% and a CER of 14.62%, which is comparable to baseline performances reported in other low-resource Indian languages.

To improve performance, we adopted multilingual adaptation using Whisper-small and Wav2Vec2.0 XLSR-53. Whisper-small presents a significant improvement, achieving a WER of 3.56% and a CER of 0.94%. Similarly, Wav2Vec2.0 XLSR-53 demonstrated competitive results, with a WER of 4.42% and a CER of 1.67%. These results confirm that multilingual pre-trained models, when fine-tuned on target language data, dramatically outperform baseline systems. Table 1 presents a comparative summary.

These results demonstrate that Whisper-small achieved the best overall performance, substantially reducing both WER and CER compared to the baseline. Wav2Vec2.0 XLSR-53 also showed strong improvements, confirming the effectiveness of multilingual transfer learning for ASR in low-resource languages like Kui.

5.4   Speaker Recognition Results

For the speaker recognition task, we evaluated the performance of the integrated speaker identification module across 24 native Kui speakers. The baseline

Table 2. Performance of Speaker Recognition Module on Kui Dataset

Model	Accuracy (%)
Baseline (Transformer Encoder)	91.34
Whisper-small	95.68
Wav2Vec2.0 XLSR-53	97.32

Transformer encoder with a classification head achieved an accuracy of 91.34%. After integrating multilingual pre-trained embeddings, the recognition accuracy improved further. Wav2Vec2.0 embeddings reached an accuracy of 97.32%, while whisper-small achieved 95.68%. Table 2 summarizes the speaker recognition results. Additionally, the results indicate that multilingual adaptation not only improves ASR performance but also enhances speaker recognition capability.

Figure 3 presents the performance analysis of the proposed Kui system. The left plot shows the WER trends across training steps for the system for this study, where multilingual models significantly reduce errors compared to the baseline. The right plot illustrates the speaker recognition module, where accuracy steadily improves with training while loss decreases consistently.

6   Conclusion

In this study, we presented the first unified ASR and Speaker Recognition system for the Indian tribal language, Kui, addressing the challenges posed by its limited resources. We have created a 14.38-hour manually recorded and annotated corpus from 24 native speakers, we built a baseline Transformer-based ASR system, and integrated a speaker recognition module. To overcome the limitations of low-resource training, we employed multilingual transfer learning by fine-tuning Whisper-small and Wav2Vec2.0 XLSR-53. The results confirm that multilingual adaptation not only enhances transcription accuracy but also strengthens speaker identification capability. Despite these promising results, certain challenges and errors persist in handling dialectal variations and phonetic confusions in Kui. We observed that recognition errors decrease as the amount of training data increases. Future work could focus on expanding the speech corpus across different domains and dialects and exploring advanced modeling strategies such as multilingual fusion and cross-lingual embeddings to further robust the system.

References

1. Aggarwal, R.K., Dave, M.: Performance evaluation of sequentially combined heterogeneous feature streams for Hindi speech recognition system. Telecommun. Syst. **52**, 1457–1466 (2013)
2. Baevski, A., Zhou, H., Mohamed, A., Auli, M.: Wav2Vec 2.0: a framework for self-supervised learning of speech representations. In: Advances in Neural Information Processing Systems (NeurIPS), vol. 33, pp. 12449–12460. Curran Associates, Inc. (2020)
3. Basu, J., Khan, S., Roy, R., Basu, T.K., Majumder, S.: Multilingual speech corpus in low-resource eastern and northeastern Indian languages for speaker and language identification. Circuits Syst. Signal Process. **40**(10), 4986–5013 (2021). https://doi.org/10.1007/s00034-021-01704-x
4. Chadha, H.S., Shah, P., Dhuriya, A., Chhimwal, N., Gupta, A., Raghavan, V.: Code switched and code mixed speech recognition for Indic languages. arXiv preprint arXiv:2203.16578 (2022)
5. Chung, J.S., Nagrani, A., Zisserman, A.: VoxCeleb2: deep speaker recognition. In: Presented at the Interspeech 2018 (2018)
6. Das, B., Mandal, S., Mitra, P.: Bengali speech corpus for continuous automatic speech recognition system. In: International Conference on Speech Database and Assessments (Oriental COCOSDA), pp. 51–55 (2011)
7. Diwan, A., et al.: MUCS 2021: multilingual and code-switching ASR challenges for low resource Indian languages. In: Proceedings of the Interspeech 2021, pp. 2446–2450 (2021)
8. Inaguma, H., Cho, J., Baskar, M.K., Kawahara, T., Watanabe, S.: Transfer learning of language-independent end-to-end ASR with language model fusion. In: 2019 IEEE International Conference on Acoustics, Speech and Signal Processing (ICASSP) ICASSP 2019 (2019)
9. India, M., Safari, P., Hernando, J.: Self multi-head attention for speaker recognition. In: Presented at the Interspeech 2019 (2019)
10. Joshi, V., Zhao, R., Mehta, R.R., Kumar, K., Li, J.: Transfer learning approaches for streaming end-to-end speech recognition system. In: Interspeech 2020 (2020)
11. Khare, S., Mittal, A.R., Diwan, A., Sarawagi, S., Jyothi, P., Bharadwaj, S.: Low resource ASR: the surprising effectiveness of high resource transliteration. In: Interspeech, pp. 1529–1533 (2021)
12. Klakow, D., Peters, J.: Testing the correlation of word error rate and perplexity. Speech Commun. **38**(1–2), 19–28 (2002)
13. Creative Commons (Digitallibraryindia). Attribution-NonCommercial 4.0 International (CC BY-NC 4.0) License (2013). http://creativecommons.org/licenses/by-nc/4.0/legalcode
14. Majhi, M.K., Saha, S.K.: An automatic speech recognition system in Odia language using attention mechanism and data augmentation. Int. J. Speech Technol. (2024)
15. Majhi, M.K., Saha, S.K.: A transfer learning based automatic speech recognition system for ODIA language. In: COMSYS-2025 (2024)
16. Maurya, A., Kumar, D., Agarwal, R.K.: Speaker recognition for Hindi speech signal using MFCC-GMM approach. Procedia Comput. Sci. **125**, 880–887 (2018)
17. Naman, A., Deepshikha, K.: Indic languages automatic speech recognition using meta-learning approach. In: Proceedings of the 4th International Conference on Natural Language and Speech Processing (ICNLSP 2021), pp. 219–225 (2021)

18. Ochiai, T., Watanabe, S., Hori, T., Hershey, J., Xiao, X.: Unified architecture for multichannel end-to-end speech recognition with neural beamforming. IEEE J. Sel. Top. Signal Process. **11**, 1274–1288 (2017)
19. Otake, S., Kawakami, R., Inoue, N.: Parameter efficient transfer learning for various speech processing tasks. In: 2023 IEEE International Conference on Acoustics, Speech and Signal Processing (ICASSP), ICASSP 2023 (2023)
20. Pandey, D., Mondal, T., Agrawal, S.S., Bangalore, S.: Development and suitability of Indian languages speech database for building Watson based ASR system. In: 2013 International Conference Oriental COCOSDA held jointly with 2013 Conference on Asian Spoken Language Research and Evaluation (O-COCOSDA/CASLRE), pp. 1–6 (2013)
21. Paul, S., Bhattacharjee, V., Saha, S.K.: A transfer learning approach for continuous speech recognition system in Indian language Sadri. Int. J. Inf. Technol. (2025)
22. Radford, A., Kim, J.W., Xu, T., Brockman, B., McLeavey, C., Sutskever, I.: Robust speech recognition via large-scale weak supervision. In: Proceedings of the 40th International Conference on Machine Learning (ICML), vol. 202, pp. 28492–28518 (2023)
23. Radha, K., Bansal, M.: Closed-set automatic speaker identification using multi-scale recurrent networks in non-native children. Int. J. Inf. Tecnol. **15**, 1375–1385 (2023)
24. Saraswathi, S., Geetha, T.V.: Implementation of Tamil speech recognition system using neural networks. In: Manandhar, S., Austin, J., Desai, U., Oyanagi, Y., Talukder, A.K. (eds.) AACC 2004. LNCS, vol. 3285, pp. 169–176. Springer, Heidelberg (2004). https://doi.org/10.1007/978-3-540-30176-9_22
25. Shivakumar, K.M., Aravind, K.G., Anoop, T.V., Gupta, D.: Kannada speech to text conversion using CMU Sphinx. In: 2016 International Conference on Inventive Computation Technologies (ICICT) (2016)
26. Srivastava, B.M.L., et al.: Interspeech 2018 low resource automatic speech recognition challenge for Indian languages. In: Proceedings of the 6th Workshop on Spoken Language Technologies for Under-Resourced Languages (SLTU 2018), pp. 11–14 (2018)
27. Thangarajan, R., Natarajan, A.M., Selvam, M.: Syllable modeling in continuous speech recognition for Tamil language. Int. J. Speech Technol. **12**, 47–57 (2009)
28. Yi, J., Tao, J., Wen, Z., Bai, Y.: Language-adversarial transfer learning for low-resource speech recognition. IEEE/ACM Trans. Audio Speech Lang. Process. **27**(3), 621–630 (2019)

Revise to Precise: Self-assessing Chain-of-Draft for Robust Decision-Making in LLMs

Pratyay Banerjee[1(✉)], Panthadeep Bhattacharjee[2], and Angshuman Jana[1]

[1] Department of Computer Science and Engineering, Indian Institute of Information Technology, Guwahati, Guwahati, India
{pratyay.banerjee24m,angshuman}@iiitg.ac.in
[2] Department of Computer Science and Engineering, National Institute of Technology, Rourkela, Rourkela, India

Abstract. Recent advancements in the development of large language models (LLMs) have highlighted their remarkable capabilities in a range of reasoning and decision-related challenges. Nevertheless, the clarity and logical flow of their reasoning can still be enhanced through improved self-evaluation and reflective analysis. In this work, we propose *Self-Assessing Chain-of-Draft* (**SACoD**), an approach that allows LLMs to emulate a form of self-assessment during the reasoning process by employing dual *Chain-of-Draft* CoD thinking. This technique draws inspiration from human cognitive mechanisms, where the model produces concise yet meaningful intermediate outputs while addressing tasks. SACoD harnesses the potential of iterative thinking, wherein the model first generates an initial sequence of thoughts and then critically evaluates and distills these thoughts through a subsequent round of reasoning. This recursive strategy allows for more consistent, rational, and reliable responses, thereby enhancing the overall quality of decision-making at a significantly lower cost than the traditional *Chain-of-Thought* (CoT) thinking. We also demonstrate an effective integration of this methodology into existing LLM frameworks using simple prompt engineering. In this process, we achieved outcomes akin to that of the Learning-Refinement Model (LRM) without any extra training.

Keywords: Large Language Models (LLMs) · Prompt Engineering · Token Efficiency · Robust Reasoning · Critique and Refinement

1 Introduction

Large Language Models (LLMs) exhibit robust capabilities across a wide range of language-related tasks, from translation to text generation. However, these models often struggle [21] with producing coherent, logical reasoning when faced with complex decision-making scenarios. One of the key limitations of LLMs lies in their limited capacity to critically analyze their own thought process,

B. Chatterjee et al. (Eds.): ICDCIT 2026, LNCS 16420, pp. 265–281, 2026.
https://doi.org/10.1007/978-3-032-16632-6_17

which can result in inconsistencies [7] and inaccuracies in the final output. While recent advances in reasoning models [14] have explored methods for improving reasoning in LLMs, including Chain of Thought (CoT) [17] reasoning and fine-tuning approaches, there remains potential for further improvement in terms of the model's ability to refine and evaluate its own reasoning.

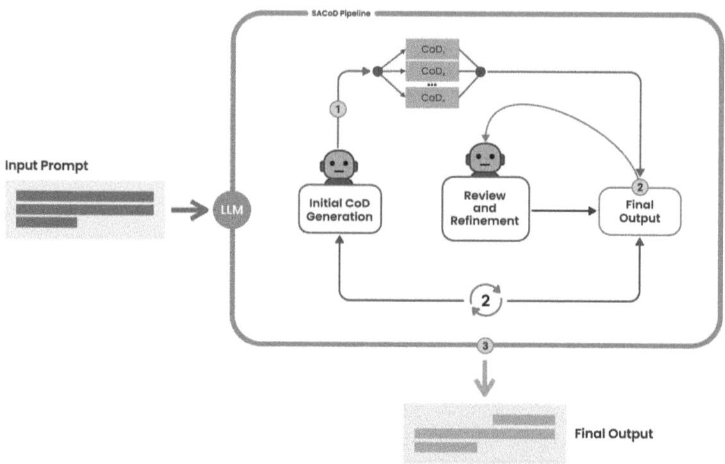

Fig. 1. Reasoning process of Self-Assessing CoD.

In this paper, we introduce *Self-Assessing Chain-of-Draft* (**SACoD**), a novel approach designed to enhance LLM reasoning by prompting the model to perform in a self-assessment process. The method involves producing an initial *Chain-of-Draft* (CoD) [18] followed by a second round of reasoning, where the model critiques and refines upon its initial CoD. Through this iterative procedure, the model can effectively mimic a self-corrective review process, yielding more coherent & rational outcomes, especially in cost-sensitive and latency-sensitive scenarios. Notably, this technique avoids the need for additional training & instead relies on simple prompt engineering, making it easy to implement in existing LLM architectures.

2   Related Work

Simple Prompt Reasoning is a reasoning method [1] that involves generating responses directly from a single input prompt without intermediate steps. Unlike methods like CoT [17], it relies on the model's implicit knowledge and pattern recognition. While efficient, it may struggle with complex tasks that benefit from step-by-step reasoning. Wei et al. [17] introduced Chain-of-Thought(CoT) prompting which improves LLM outputs by prompting the model to produce a step-by-step sequence of thoughts. This process enhances logical coherence

& helps the model reach more accurate conclusions, particularly benefitting in tasks requiring complex reasoning like mathematical problem solving and commonsense reasoning. Moreover, Ning et al. [12] proposed Skeleton-of-Thought (SoT) Reasoning, a method that directs LLMs to generate a skeleton outline, followed by parallel decoding to minimize response latency. While SoT helps reduce latency, it doesn't diminish the overall computational cost and is limited to questions where parallel decomposition is possible. Besides, Learning-Refinement Models (LRM) focus on enhancing model performance by iteratively refining outputs through a series of training iterations. These models generally involve a feedback loop [3] where initial predictions are adjusted based on error analysis or critique. While LRM-based approaches have proven effective in certain contexts, they often require additional training and fine-tuning, which can be both resource as well as time intensive. Furthermore, Self-Assessment (aka Self-Reflection) [13] refers to a cognitive process where LLM reviews its own reasoning or outputs to detect errors, inconsistencies, or scope for improvement. Although traditional LLMs do not inherently possess mechanisms for self-assessment, recent advancements in meta-learning, reinforcement learning, and introspective prompting have investigated ways to empower models to critically analyze their actions & results. This area of study has shown considerable promise in improving decision-making, especially in contexts requiring iterative refinement, error correction, or transparent reasoning. By incorporating self-assessment mechanisms, AI systems can attain higher levels of reliability, agility, and alignment with human expectations. Zhang et al. [20] explored a different route with Draft-&-Verify that accelerates generation by rapidly producing draft tokens through selective layer skipping, followed by a single forward pass to validate the output draft. This method can be utilized to reduce the response latency significantly. Wei et al.'s [17] prompting technique has proven highly effective across a variety of tasks, especially those involving complex multi-step reasoning. LLMs, however, often generate excessively verbose reasoning steps, consuming a significant amount of tokens before concluding at a final answer. In contrast, humans tend to adopt a more succinct approach when tackling complex problems, such as, mathematical or logical puzzles. Instead of elaborating every step, humans generally note only the key intermediate outcomes i.e. minimal drafts to facilitate their thought process. Drawing inspiration from this human behavior, a more efficient prompting method known as Chain-of-Draft (CoD) was proposed by Xu et al. [18], which minimizes verbosity by condensing reasoning steps into their essential components, focusing solely on the critical calculations or transformations needed to progress toward a solution.

3   Comparative Analysis

Now, to demonstrate the contrasts between some of the mentioned prompting approaches, we analyze problem as demonstrated in Fig. 2. Eg: In response to the question asked (Fig. 2), the response generated by a simple prompting [1] typically provides a direct answer, usually without any reasoning. While correct, this does lack transparency regarding how the result was derived, & requires the language model to run multi-step reasoning without any aid from intermediate results, which often leads to inaccuracies or hallucinations.

In contrast, Chain-of-Draft (CoD) [18] approach condenses the reasoning process into minimal, abstract representations. Here, the reasoning is distilled into concise mathematical expressions, concentrating exclusively on the essential steps necessary to solve the problem. By abstracting away verbose explanations, CoD significantly reduces the token count while preserving transparency & accuracy.

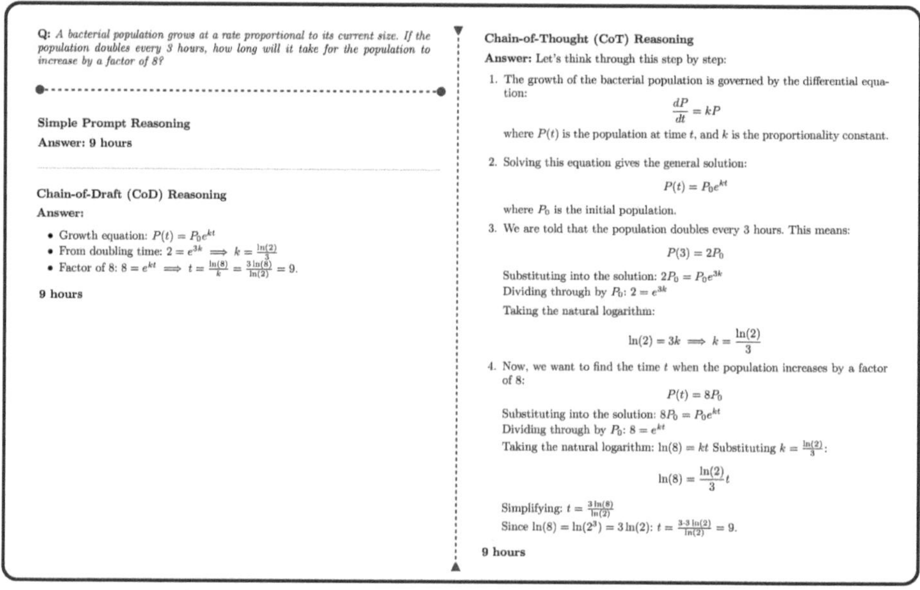

Fig. 2. Comparative analysis of different prompting methods (including, CoD [18] and CoT [17]).

4 SACoD: A Double Chain of Draft

4.1 Approach

The Self-Assessing CoD (SACoD) approach combines the benefits of CoD reasoning with a self-assessment mechanism. The process, as visualized in Fig. 1, is outlined as follows:

1. **Initial CoD Generation:** The model generates a Chain of Draft (CoD), where steps of the thought process are concisely articulated & used to reach a final conclusion.

2. **Review and Refinement:** After generating the initial CoD, the model then initiates a second round of reasoning, which critiques the first CoD. This second Chain of Draft evaluates the logical consistency of the initial reasoning, identifying any potential flaws or inconsistencies.
3. **Final Output:** Based on the critique (and citations, if applicable), the model refines its reasoning, producing a more coherent and accurate final answer.

Here, a dual-phase mechanism is employed to simulate human-like self-assessment, where the first phase involves idea generation, and the second phase centers on assessing and refining them. The approach is tailored to function seamlessly with existing LLM architectures, without requiring any modifications to the model's underlying parameters. To implement SACoD, we utilize a simple prompt engineering technique. By structuring the input prompt to request both the initial reasoning and a follow-up critique, the model is able to generate and refine its reasoning within the same inference cycle. The prompt is formulated to encourage the model to "re-evaluate" its initial response, resulting in improved [16] overall performance. This self-reflective mechanism mirrors a basic form of metacognition, prompting the model not only to solve a problem but also to assess the quality and coherence of its own output, making it highly effective in complex or ambiguous scenarios, where a single-shot answer may lack the necessary nuance or robustness.

Taking the same question in reference, first, we generate a Chain of Draft (CoD) for how we would arrive at the answer. Then, we review our answer and critique it. If we find any inconsistencies or errors, correct them and provide the final answer.

Answer:

Step 1 (Initial CoD):

- Growth equation: $P(t) = P_0 e^{kt}$.
- From doubling time: $2 = e^{3k} \implies k = \frac{\ln(2)}{3}$.
- Factor of 8: $8 = e^{kt} \implies t = \frac{\ln(8)}{k} = \frac{3\ln(8)}{\ln(2)} = 9$.

Step 2 (Self-Reflection and Critique):

- The exponential model is valid for this scenario.
- The value of k was correctly derived from the doubling time.
- All substitutions and simplifications were performed correctly.
- Recognizing that $8 = 2^3$ provides an intuitive shortcut: 3 doublings needed, each taking $3\,\mathrm{h}$.
- All reasoning steps are logically consistent and clearly justified.

Step 3 (Refined CoD):

- Exponential model: $P(t) = P_0 e^{kt}$
- From doubling info: $2 = e^{3k} \Rightarrow k = \frac{\ln(2)}{3}$

- Set up for 8-fold increase: $8 = e^{kt} \Rightarrow t = \frac{\ln(8)}{k}$
- Substitution:

$$t = \frac{\ln(8)}{\ln(2)/3} = 3 \cdot \frac{3\ln(2)}{\ln(2)} = 3 \cdot 3 = 9$$

- Alternative reasoning: $8 = 2^3$, so 3 doublings $\times$ 3 h i.e., 9 h

9 h

5 Mathematical Analysis of SACoD

We can mathematically ground the effectiveness of **SACoD** (Algorithm 1) in formal terms by defining metrics such as **logical consistency**, **coherence**, and **error correction rate** as these metrics provide a quantitative way to assess the impact of self-assessment (i.e. self-reflection) on reasoning quality of LLMs.

Algorithm 1 Self-Assessing Chain-of-Draft (SACoD) Algorithm

Require: Problem P, Language Model M
Ensure: Refined reasoning R_{refined}, final answer A
1: **function** GENERATEINITIALCOD(P)
2:     $R_{\text{initial}} \leftarrow \{r_1, \ldots, r_n\}$ $\triangleright$ Initial reasoning
3:     $A_{\text{initial}} \leftarrow M(P)$ $\triangleright$ Preliminary answer
4:     **return** $R_{\text{initial}}, A_{\text{initial}}$
5: **end function**
6: **function** SELFASSESSMENT($R_{\text{initial}}, A_{\text{initial}}$)
7:     $\mathcal{C} \leftarrow \emptyset$ $\triangleright$ Critique set
8:     **for all** $r_i \in R_{\text{initial}}$ **do**
9:         **if not** VALIDATE_STEP(r_i) **then**
10:             $\mathcal{C} \leftarrow \mathcal{C} \cup$ FIND_ISSUES(r_i)
11:         **end if**
12:     **end for**
13:     **return** $\mathcal{C}$
14: **end function**
15: **function** REFINECOD($R_{\text{initial}}, \mathcal{C}$)
16:     $R_{\text{refined}} \leftarrow R_{\text{initial}}$
17:     **for all** $(c_j, w_j) \in \mathcal{C}$ **do**
18:         $R_{\text{refined}} \leftarrow$ APPLY_CORRECTION(R_{refined}, c_j)
19:     **end for**
20:     $A_{\text{refined}} \leftarrow$ DERIVE_CONCLUSION(R_{refined})
21:     **return** $R_{\text{refined}}, A_{\text{refined}}$
22: **end function**
23: **function** SA_COD(P, M)
24:     $R_{\text{initial}}, A_{\text{initial}} \leftarrow$ GENERATEINITIALCOD(P)
25:     $\mathcal{C} \leftarrow$ SELFASSESSMENT($R_{\text{initial}}, A_{\text{initial}}$)
26:     $R_{\text{refined}}, A_{\text{refined}} \leftarrow$ REFINECOD($R_{\text{initial}}, \mathcal{C}$)
27:     **return** $R_{\text{refined}}, A_{\text{refined}}$
28: **end function**

5.1 Logical Consistency and Coherence

We define **logical consistency** as the number of valid logical connections between consecutive reasoning steps.

Let p_i represent the ith step in the Chain-of-Draft (CoD), and $I(p_i, p_{i+1})$ be an indicator function that returns one if there is a logical connection between p_i and p_{i+1}. Then, the logical consistency H_{CoD} for a single CoD is:

$$H_{\text{CoD}} = \sum_{i=1}^{n-1} I(p_i, p_{i+1})$$

where n is the total number of steps in the reasoning chain, a higher value of H_{CoD} indicates that the reasoning steps are to the point, are logically consistent, and well-connected.

When applying SACoD, a second round of reasoning is conducted, which critiques and refines the initial reasoning. The **coherence** of the reasoning process, as defined by us, is the degree of alignment between the initial and refined reasoning steps. The coherence J can be quantified as:

$$J = \frac{\sum_{i=1}^{n} I(p_i, p_i^{\text{refined}})}{n}$$

where p_i^{refined} denotes the corresponding statement in the refined reasoning chain, and $I(p_i, p_i^{\text{refined}})$ is one if the statement in the second round is consistent with the original reasoning. Coherence is measured by how well the logic of the initial thought is preserved while being refined in the second round of reasoning.

The overall improvement in reasoning due to SACoD can be defined as:

$$\text{Improvement in Reasoning Quality} = \frac{H_{\text{Refined}} - H_{\text{CoD}}}{H_{\text{CoD}}} \times 100$$

where H_{Refined} is the logical consistency score after refinement. This metric quantifies the improvement as a percentage, reflecting the gain in reasoning quality.

5.2 Error Correction Rate (C_{ecr})

One of the primary benefits of **SACoD** is its ability to correct errors in the initial reasoning chain. We define the **error correction rate** C_{ecr} as the proportion of errors identified and corrected in the second round of reasoning.

Let C_{initial} represent the number of errors in the initial chain of thought, and $C_{\text{corrected}}$ represent the number of errors corrected during the review. The error correction rate can be calculated as:

$$C_{\text{ecr}} = \frac{C_{\text{corrected}}}{C_{\text{initial}}} \times 100$$

A higher value of C_{ecr} indicates the effectiveness of SACoD in identifying and correcting mistakes from the first round of reasoning, resulting in a more accurate final output.

5.3   Iterative Refinement and its Impact on Error Correction

To further examine & analyze the impact of iterative refinement, we propose a recursive function to measure reasoning quality over multiple rounds. Let $H^{(n)}$ denote the logical consistency score after the nth round of reasoning. Initially, at $n = 1$, the model generates a chain of draft with consistency $H^{(1)} = H_{\text{CoD}}$. Following the second round of reasoning, the model refines its output, improving the consistency score to $H^{(2)} = H_{\text{Refined}}$. The improvement in consistency after n rounds of reasoning can be generalized as:

$$H^{(n)} = H^{(n-1)} + \delta_n$$

where δ_n represents the change in consistency from the $(n-1)^{\text{th}}$ to the nth round. In the case of SACoD, the first two rounds provide significant improvements, with diminishing returns observed as additional rounds of reasoning are performed.

We express the total improvement after N rounds of reasoning as the cumulative sum of consistency changes:

$$\text{Total Improvement} = \sum_{n=1}^{N} \delta_n$$

In practice, we observe that the most significant improvements occur in the first few rounds of reasoning. This behavior is consistent with the SACoD approach, where the second round of self-reflection provides substantial refinement to the reasoning process.

6   Quantitative Validation of SACoD

To validate the impact of SACoD, we conducted a series of experiments across various tasks. For each task, we measured both the logical consistency and error correction rate before and after applying SACoD. Below, Table 1 represents a summary of the findings for the arithmetic problem-solving task. In this example, the SACoD approach improved logical consistency by 5%, while the error correction rate was 11%, indicating that the model was able to identify and correct a significant proportion of mistakes during the self-assessment (i.e. "self-reflection") [8] phase.

Table 1. Performance of SACoD on Arithmetic Problem-Solving

Task	H_{CoD}	H_{Refined}	C_{ecr}	Improvement
ãĔd'				
Arithmetic Problem-Solving	86.5%	91.0%	11%	+6% (approx)

We also evaluated the impact of SACoD on tasks beyond arithmetic, such as commonsense reasoning, ethical decision-making, and logical puzzles. Table 2 summarizes the performance across these tasks. As shown, SACoD consistently improves the logical consistency of reasoning across all tasks, with significant error correction rates observed in ethical decision-making and logical puzzles. These results highlight the effectiveness of SACoD in tasks requiring multistep reasoning and critical analysis.

Table 2. Performance of SACoD on Various Tasks

Task	CoD	SACoD	Consistency Δ	Error Corr.
Commonsense Reasoning	82%	87%	+5%	15%
Logical Puzzles	83%	88%	+6%	16%
Ethical Decision-Making	76%	82%	+8%	17%

7   Evaluation Framework and Metrics

We assessed the overall performance via the DSpy [5] framework, which computes task-specific metrics designed for LLM outputs. For evaluating precision and recall [9] an LLM as a Judge[1] is leveraged to determine consistency relevance between model predictions and ground truth. Precision measures the proportion of predicted response (R_{model}) that semantically aligns with the golden answers (R_{gold}), defined as:

$$P = \frac{\sum_{r \in R_{\mathrm{model}}} \mathrm{Judge}(r, R_{\mathrm{gold}})}{|R_{\mathrm{model}}|}$$

where R_{model} represents the set of answers predicted by the model, R_{gold} is the set of golden answers, and $\mathrm{Judge}(r, R_{\mathrm{gold}})$ being a scoring function returns values from 0 (no match) to 1 (perfect match). Recall quantifies the proportion of golden answers (R_{gold}) captured by the model's predictions (R_{model}), defined as:

$$R = \frac{\sum_{r \in R_{\mathrm{gold}}} \mathrm{Judge}(r, R_{\mathrm{model}})}{|R_{\mathrm{gold}}|}$$

The F1-score balances precision and recall and is defined as:

$$F1 = 2 \cdot \frac{p \cdot r}{p + r}$$

The *recall (r), precision (p)*, and *F1-score* were measured both pre & post utilization of SACoD approach on baseline. Results are summarized in Table 3.

The results display substantial improvements across all three metrics after implementing SACoD. The F1-score received a bump from 40.7% to 67.2%, demonstrating the models ability to deliver precise responses with minimal computational resources using SACoD.

---

[1] Using LLM-as-a-judge cookbook: https://huggingface.co/learn/cookbook/en/llm_judge.

Table 3. Model performance before and after applying SACoD

Metric	Before	After
Recall	46.3%	66.5% (+20.2%)
Precision	41.1%	69.9% (+28.8%)
F1-Score	40.7%	67.2% (+26.5%)

8 Evaluating Language Model (LM) Inference Efficiency

Evaluating language model inference efficiency for SACoD involves analyzing various metrics that capture different performance aspects, including accuracy, zero-shot reasoning [6] capabilities, compression ratio, and inference time.

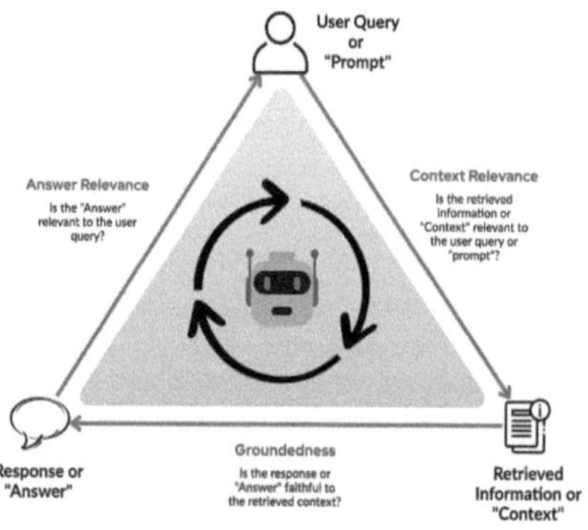

Fig. 3. RAG-Triad

Within the context of incorporating SACoD in RAG-based solutions, the "Triad of Metrics" as visualized in Fig. 3 – *Faithfulness*, *Context Relevance*, and *Answer Relevance* – are among the key metrics (though not exhaustive) used for assessment. Achieving satisfactory performance across these metrics helps ensure that the language model application is reliable and has minimal (or rather free from) hallucinations. Following the same, we thus reviewed several key performance metrics, including the **faithfullness** (or groundedness) of SACoD method, **inference time, self-consistency, contextual** & **answer relevance**.

- **Faithfulness**: This metric evaluates the *"groundedness"*, i.e., how accurately a generated response (produced by an LLM) corresponds to and is backed by the given context.

$$\text{Faithfulness} = \frac{\text{Number of verified statements}}{\text{Total statements made}}$$

- **Inference Time**: Referred to as latency (seconds or milliseconds), represents the duration of how a LLM requires to process input and generate responses.

- **Self-Consistency (SC)**: Wang et al. [16] proposed the concept of self-consistency. This was based on using CoT [17] prompting & later revised to CoD [18] approach to generate multiple reasoning paths and picking the most consistent one. Given a CoD prompt, the model generates multiple answers $a_1, a_2, \ldots$ with corresponding reasoning paths $r_1, r_2, \ldots$, forming pairs (r_i, a_i). It then selects the most consistent answer as:

$$SC = argmax_a \left(\sum_{i=1}^{m} 1(a = a_i) \right)$$

This builds on the intuition that correct answers tend to appear more consistent across different iterations, while hallucinations or errors are likely to be more varied.

- **Answer Relevance (AR)**: AR is assessed by using an LLM to generate potential questions based on the answers and then computing the cosine similarity between these generated questions and the original question. The relevance score is the mean of these similarities, reflecting the degree to which the answers are direct and appropriate.

$$AR = \frac{1}{n} \sum_{i=1}^{n} \text{sim}(q, q_i)$$

where q_i represents questions generated from the answer, and "sim" denotes the cosine similarity between the embeddings of the original question q & q_i.

- **Context Relevance (CR)**: This metric evaluates whether the retrieved context predominantly contains information that is pertinent to answering the question.

$$CR = \frac{\text{Number of contextually relevant sentences}}{\text{Total sentences in the retrieved context}}$$

A higher CR leads to greater context relevance and accuracy gain, while a lower CR reduces accuracy gain due to irrelevant or redundant information.

9   State-of-the-Art (SOTA) and Datasets

We present the average performance on the GSM8K reasoning SOTA benchmarks, derived from 15 randomly chosen samples (Fig. 4). We reproduced the results on SOTA (Table 4) by performing experiments in our own set-up instead of directly inheriting the values from [18]. Accordingly, we observed a tangible improvement in accuracy for our proposed method (SACoD) as compared to the SOTA models applied on relevant datasets[2].

---

[2] Datasets: Arithmetic—GSM8K,   Commonsense—HellaSwag,   Semantic—Wino Grande.

10   Challenges and Future Directions

More Advanced Methods: SACoD is based on the research surrounding Chain-of-Draft (CoD) [18] approach for large language models (LLMs), which is still in its early stages. While earlier studies have demonstrated promising outcomes with methods like self-consistency CoT and ReAct [19], these approaches still fall short of CoD in terms of overall performance. SACoD leverages the internal attention mechanism of LLMs during the second round of reasoning, where the model reviews and refines its outputs through self-assessment (i.e., self-reflection) [8].

Table 4. Performance Across Three Reasoning Datasets

Arithmetic Dataset (GSM8K)				
Model Name	**Baseline**	**CoT**	**CoD**	**SACoD**
Claude-3.7 Sonnet	61.7%	93.2%	91.4%	94.6%
OpenAI GPT-4o	53.3%	92.9%	89.7%	93.5%
DeepSeek-R1-Distill-Llama-70B	52.5%	90.4%	91.2%	92.1%
Gemini 2.0 Flash	54.2%	90.1%	90.4%	91.4%
LLaMA 3.1 70B	50.9%	84.8%	88.7%	88.6%

Commonsense Dataset (HellaSwag)				
Model Name	**Baseline**	**CoT**	**CoD**	**SACoD**
Claude-3.7 Sonnet	67.3%	88.2%	86.1%	89.4%
OpenAI GPT-4o	64.7%	89.1%	87.2%	90.8%
DeepSeek-R1-Distill-Llama-70B	65.7%	87.5%	85.1%	87.1%
Gemini 2.0 Flash	67.8%	87.5%	86.7%	89.2%
LLaMA 3.1 70B	59.1%	85.4%	82.3%	86.5%

Semantic Dataset (WinoGrande)				
Model Name	**Baseline**	**CoT**	**CoD**	**SACoD**
Claude-3.7 Sonnet	68.9%	78.7%	79.3%	80.2%
OpenAI GPT-4o	61.2%	74.1%	73.2%	74.0%
DeepSeek-R1-Distill-Llama-70B	59.3%	72.8%	73.3%	77.8%
Gemini 2.0 Flash	55.2%	76.4%	76.6%	80.8%
LLaMA 3.1 70B	51.4%	71.7%	72.1%	73.9%

Performance-Size Trade-offs: Previous studies shed light on the importance of balancing LLM performance with context size, especially when considering hardware limits and real-world constraints. Despite its significance, the theoretical and empirical foundations of this trade-off remain poorly understood. Future studies should aim to conduct thorough investigations to spur the development of sophisticated techniques capable of addressing the challenges posed by increasingly complex datasets, permitting researchers to create suited methods that effectively explore the design space and achieve optimal performance.

Explainability: For large and complex datasets, where information overlap exists, relying solely on the *self-attention* mechanisms of pre-trained language models can make their decisions difficult to justify, leading to a lack of explainability. We can address this using custom-tailored instructions that can further

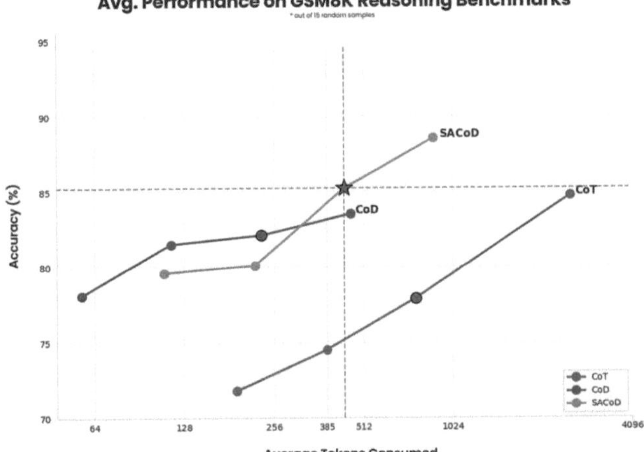

Fig. 4. Average performance on GSM8K Reasoning Benchmarks (over 15 randomly chosen samples)

enhance model interpretability, simplify evaluation, and improve reliability in real-world scenarios.

Inconsistency without Few-shot Examples: We gauged the performance of SACoD in a zero-shot setting, using OpenRouter[3]. The results in Table 5 indicate a slight drop in SACoD's accuracy and, consequently, its overall effectiveness. Moreover, SA-CoD offers more modest token savings compared to the few-shot CoT [17] approach. We speculate that this limitation stems from the scarcity or absence of CoD-style reasoning patterns in the training data of LLMs, making it a significantly challenging task to produce concise and insightful "drafts" without guidance from few-shot examples.

Reduced Performance on Small Models: We benchmarked SACoD on several Small Language Models (SLMs) with fewer than 10B parameters, including Microsoft Phi-2 (2.7B) [10], Gemini 1.5 Flash-8B [15], Mistral 7B (v0.1) [4], Meta Llama-3 8B [2], and Salesforce XGen-7B [11]. The results in Table 5 demonstrate that although SACoD reduces the count of tokens per response & yields higher accuracy than direct answering, its relative underperformance compared to CoT [17] is pronounced in these smaller models.

While our metrics quantitatively evaluate SACoD's performance, a key mathematical insight is that if logical consistency increases monotonically with each self-reflection step $(H_n \geq H_{n-1})$, the process converges. That is, there exists an N beyond which H_n remains stable. This follows from the bounded nature of logical consistency scores, ensuring eventual termination.

Ethical Concerns: As we explore newer prompting methods for LLMs, it's important to address the ethical concerns associated with their usages. A prime

---

[3] OpenRouter: https://openrouter.ai.

Table 5. Zero-shot GSM8K evaluation results across models

Model	Prompt	Accuracy	Avg. Token #	Latency
Microsoft Phi-2 (2.7B)	Standard	42.3%	48	1.0 s
	CoT	77.8%	262	1.3 s
	CoD	67.5%	67	1.8 s
	SACoD	74.1%	156	1.7 s
Gemini 1.5 Flash 8B	Standard	61.9%	46	0.8 s
	CoT	81.4%	318	1.5 s
	CoD	75.5%	103	1.9 s
	SACoD	79.8%	212	1.7 s
Mistral 7B	Standard	59.3%	55	0.7 s
	CoT	79.1%	323	1.5 s
	CoD	75.3%	80	1.8 s
	SACoD	76.2%	191	1.7 s
Meta Llama-3 8B	Standard	54.7%	47	0.8 s
	CoT	88.4%	351	1.7 s
	CoD	83.2%	68	1.9 s
	SACoD	85.1%	198	1.9 s
Salesforce X-Gen 7B	Standard	44.9%	39	1.0 s
	CoT	77.6%	378	2.1 s
	CoD	71.4%	96	2.4 s
	SACoD	76.9%	174	2.3 s

concern is the potential for biases to be embedded in the reasoning processes, which could reinforce existing societal inequalities. Moreover, if the data used to train LLMs is not diverse and representative, or if our approach emphasizes certain types of reasoning over others, it could lead to unfair outcomes for marginalized peers.

Besides, our approach relies on the iterative refinement of reasoning, which does possess a risk where the model may inadvertently amplify errors or biases from initial drafts, especially if the process isn't designed to critically evaluate and adjust for them. This could further perpetuate the biases present in the original training data or introduce new forms of error in reasoning.

Another big ethical concern here is the need for transparency and accountability. As our method enhances reasoning through iterative drafts, it's crucial that the reasoning process & the decisions made at each step remain interpretable and explainable to users. Ensuring that the model's outputs are traceable, and that any errors or biases can be logged and addressed, shall provide clarity for upholding trust and fairness.

Future Perspectives: In future, we will focus on formalizing the conditions required for maximal error correction and on establishing theoretical guarantees for the convergence and optimality of the refinement process. The current analysis provides a solid empirical and structural basis for this direction.

While our experiments show clear improvements in reasoning quality when few-shot exemplars are provided, zero-shot performance remains limited in the absence of explicit reasoning cues. This restricts adaptability in unseen or low-data settings, highlighting a common challenge in zero-shot generalization for large language models. We randomly selected 15 items to reduce bias toward any specific question type. Although this represents a small sample and limits the strength of statistical conclusions, SACoD demonstrated consistent improvements across all major metrics. Statistical significance results should therefore be interpreted with caution. We plan to extend the evaluation to larger datasets to validate these trends and improve generalizability.

This study assesses SACoD's performance across models of varying sizes and few-shot settings, though these factors were not independently controlled. Isolating the effects of model size and shot count is key to understanding their roles in reasoning improvement. Future work will involve controlled experiments and ablation studies to clarify these effects and guide more precise prompt design and model selection (Table 6).

Table 6. GSM8K evaluation results on SLMs

Model	Prompt	Accuracy	Avg. Token #
Mistral 7B (v0.1)	Standard	27.4%	23
	CoT	78.2%	161
	CoD	75.7%	75
	SACoD	77.1%	93
Gemini 1.5 Flash-8B	Standard	36.9%	30
	CoT	81.4%	247
	CoD	78.8%	53
	SACoD	79.2%	77
OpenAI GPT-4.1-nano	Standard	39.4%	24
	CoT	82.8%	205
	CoD	79.7%	104
	SACoD	80.8%	123
LLaMA 3 8B	Standard	35.1%	22
	CoT	78.1%	146
	CoD	75.6%	52
	SACoD	77.3%	75
Salesforce XGen-7B	Standard	28.5%	27
	CoT	78.5%	175
	CoD	72.6%	85
	SACoD	75.4%	102

11   Conclusion

Through this paper, we presented an in-depth analysis of several reasoning methods with SACoD, quantifying its impact on logical consistency, coherence, and error correction rates. This was followed by an evaluation of key performance metrics, including faithfulness, inference time, self-consistency, and contextual and answer relevance, which were critical for benchmarking. These benchmarks assessed the model's accuracy & efficiency across a wide scope of NLP use cases and domains. The findings demonstrate significant improvement in the reasoning process of LLMs by improving both the quality of reasoning and the model's ability for self-revision. It outperforms most traditional reasoning via prompting strategies, offering a more reliable approach for applications requiring accurate, coherent, and consistent reasoning.

References

1. Amatriain, X.: Prompt design and engineering: introduction and advanced methods (2024). https://arxiv.org/abs/2401.14423
2. Grattafiori, A., et al.: The llama 3 herd of models (2024). https://arxiv.org/abs/2407.21783
3. Ji, S., et al.: Mygo multiplex cot: a method for self-reflection in large language models via double chain of thought thinking (2025). https://arxiv.org/abs/2501.13117
4. Jiang, A.Q., et al.: Mistral 7b (2023). https://arxiv.org/abs/2310.06825
5. Khattab, O., et al.: DSPY: compiling declarative language model calls into self-improving pipelines (2023). https://arxiv.org/abs/2310.03714
6. Kojima, T., Gu, S.S., Reid, M., Matsuo, Y., Iwasawa, Y.: Large language models are zero-shot reasoners (2023). https://arxiv.org/abs/2205.11916
7. Lin, Z., Tao, J., Yuan, Y., Yao, A.C.C.: Existing LLMs are not self-consistent for simple tasks (2025). https://arxiv.org/abs/2506.18781
8. Liu, F., AlDahoul, N., Eady, G., Zaki, Y., Rahwan, T.: Self-reflection makes large language models safer, less biased, and ideologically neutral (2025). https://arxiv.org/abs/2406.10400
9. Machlab, D., Battle, R.: LLM in-context recall is prompt dependent (2024). https://arxiv.org/abs/2404.08865
10. Marah Abdin, J.A., et al.: Phi-2: the surprising power of small language models (2023). https://www.microsoft.com/en-us/research/blog/phi-2-the-surprising-power-of-small-language-models
11. Nijkamp, E., et al.: Xgen-7b technical report (2023). https://arxiv.org/abs/2309.03450
12. Ning, X., Lin, Z., Zhou, Z., Wang, Z., Yang, H., Wang, Y.: Skeleton-of-thought: Prompting LLMs for efficient parallel generation (2024). https://arxiv.org/abs/2307.15337
13. Ren, J., Zhao, Y., Vu, T., Liu, P.J., Lakshminarayanan, B.: Self-evaluation improves selective generation in large language models (2023). https://arxiv.org/abs/2312.09300
14. Sahoo, P., Singh, A.K., Saha, S., Jain, V., Mondal, S., Chadha, A.: A systematic survey of prompt engineering in large language models: techniques and applications (2025). https://arxiv.org/abs/2402.07927
15. Team, G., et al.: Gemini 1.5: unlocking multimodal understanding across millions of tokens of context (2024). https://arxiv.org/abs/2403.05530
16. Wang, X., et al.: Self-consistency improves chain of thought reasoning in language models (2023). https://arxiv.org/abs/2203.11171

17. Wei, J., et al.: Chain-of-thought prompting elicits reasoning in large language models (2023). https://arxiv.org/abs/2201.11903
18. Xu, S., Xie, W., Zhao, L., He, P.: Chain of draft: thinking faster by writing less (2025). https://arxiv.org/abs/2502.18600
19. Yao, S., et al.: React: synergizing reasoning and acting in language models (2023). https://arxiv.org/abs/2210.03629
20. Zhang, J., et al.: Draft&verify: lossless large language model acceleration via self-speculative decoding, pp. 11263–11282. (ACL 2024) (2024). http://dx.doi.org/10.18653/v1/2024.acl-long.607. presented at the 62nd Annual Meeting of the Association for Computational Linguistics
21. Zhou, Y., Ye, J., Ling, Z., Han, Y., Huang, Y., et al.: Dissecting logical reasoning in LLMs: a fine-grained evaluation and supervision study (2025). https://arxiv.org/abs/2506.04810

A Novel Explainable Multimodal Edge Framework for Stress Detection

Ojasvi, Kashish, Ravneet Kaur[(✉)], Rajendra Kumar Roul, and Shalini Batra

Thapar Institute of Engineering & Technology, Patiala, Punjab, India
`ravneet.kaur@thapar.edu`

Abstract. This work presents a real-time, edge-deployable system for multimodal stress detection with natural language feedback, prioritizing explainability, privacy, and emotional intelligence. Lightweight machine learning models, including logistic regression and gradient boosting, independently process physiological signals (heart rate variability, skin conductance, skin temperature), behavioral patterns (keystroke dynamics, mouse movements), and facial expressions. Each modality produces an interpretable stress score normalized to the range $[-1, +1]$, allowing users to identify the most influential signals rather than receiving a single opaque output. A local large-language model (Mistral-7B-Instruct) translates these scores into concise two-sentence feedback: the first summarizes stress on a four-level scale from *calm* to *high* stress, while the second suggests a coping strategy such as grounding or breathing exercises. The integration of a local LLM enables context-aware, natural feedback generation while safeguarding user privacy. As all inference runs locally, the system avoids cloud dependency and ensures privacy, making it suitable for resource-constrained or sensitive environments. The preliminary evaluations with synthetic and real sensor inputs demonstrate that the system is modular, interpretable, and effective in providing actionable feedback, paving the way for human-centered and explainable stress-aware technologies.

Keywords: Behavioral Biometrics · Edge Computing · Human-Centered AI · Lightweight Machine Learning · Multimodal Stress Detection

1 Introduction

Stress is a common challenge in modern life, with long-term effects on both mental and physical health if left unmanaged [10]. Various advances in wearable sensors, webcams, and digital traces have led to systems that attempt to detect stress in real time. However, most existing approaches provide only binary outputs, rely on cloud-based processing, or use opaque black-box models with limited interpretability [5]. This lack of transparency reduces user trust, particularly in non-clinical contexts, and raises privacy concerns when sensitive data must be sent to external servers. This work presents a modular, explainable, and

B. Chatterjee et al. (Eds.): ICDCIT 2026, LNCS 16420, pp. 282–298, 2026.
https://doi.org/10.1007/978-3-032-16632-6_18

privacy-preserving system for stress detection. The system integrates multimodal signals such as heart rate variability, skin conductance, temperature, facial cues, and behavioral patterns. Each signal is processed with lightweight models such as logistic regression, gradient boosting *etc.* to generate normalized stress scores, allowing users to see which signals contribute the most to their stress level. A local large-language model (Mistral-7B-Instruct) then summarizes these scores into concise feedback: one sentence describing stress level (calm, neutral, mild stress, or high stress) and another suggesting a simple coping strategy. Importantly, all processing runs fully on-device, ensuring privacy and suitability for edge environments.

The hardware design includes an ESP32 microcontroller that interfaces with physiological sensors such as MAX30100 (heart rate/SpO$_2$), AD8232 (ECG), Galvanic skin response (GSR), and DS18B20 (temperature). These capture physiological responses related to stress that are analyzed in real time to provide interpretable feedback. The modular per-modality design improves transparency without sacrificing performance, while the generated feedback is user-relevant and actionable. This approach demonstrates a path toward human-centered, trustworthy, and deployable stress-aware technologies.

1.1 Motivation

Chronic stress is now an everyday aspect of modern workplace life. Surveys in recent years report that many working adults feel stressed every day and often lack effective coping techniques. Most available solutions rely on cloud-based infrastructure, sophisticated models, or unidimensional methods that either do not respect the privacy of the user or do not address the needs of an individual. The main motivation is to build a system that applies multimodal real-time stress detection, enabling people to be in charge of their mental well-being. The strategy tries not only to precisely measure stress levels, but also to offer explicit, understandable descriptions and customized coping strategies by combining physiological signals, behavioral signs, and emotions. In addition, stress management is made more discreet, efficient, and available even in sensitive or resource-constrained environments such as healthcare, education, or remote work by making sure that the system is capable of operating on-device without requiring constant access to the Internet.

1.2 Contributions

The key contributions of this work are as follows:

- Proposed an explainable multimodal stress detection framework integrating physiological, behavioral, and affective signals for real-time, edge-based operation.
- Designed lightweight, modality-specific models ensuring low latency, high accuracy, and interpretability on resource-constrained devices.

- Introduced a scaled logit-based stress scoring function for continuous, human-understandable stress quantification.
- Integrated an on-device large language model (Mistral-7B-Instruct) for generating natural-language, privacy-preserving feedback and coping suggestions.
- Performed comprehensive evaluation and ablation studies on benchmark datasets, validating robustness, explainability, and feasibility for human-centered stress monitoring.

2   Related Work

Stress detection has gained significant attention in recent years due to its implications in health monitoring, workplace productivity, and human-computer interaction. Several approaches have been proposed using physiological, behavioral, and multimodal data to improve accuracy and reliability. Table 1 shows a summary of the recent works on stress detection.

Table 1. Summary of existing works on stress detection

Author(s)	Approach	Pros	Cons
Kim & Park (2022) [9]	Introduced Local Head Channel Attention for FER.	Detects subtle micro-expressions.	Requires architecture tuning.
Arushi et al. (2022) [4]	Conducted voice stress detection in VR interviews.	Enables real-time and bio-aware sensing.	Sensitive to noise and VR conditions.
Zhou et al. (2023) [21]	Applied Swin Transformer on FER2013 dataset.	Uses hierarchical attention for robustness.	High memory consumption.
Wang et al. (2023) [17]	Used multimodal Weibo data for stress detection.	Reached 88.7% accuracy using text and behavior.	May be biased by posting behavior.
Nguyen et al. (2024) [14]	Used PySpark NLP on Reddit posts for real-time stress detection.	Supports real-time processing.	Moderate performance
Moser et al. (2024) [13]	Used explainable ML on Heart Rate Variability (HRV) data.	Improves model interpretability.	Depends on sensor quality.
Abdelfattah et al. (2025) [1]	Combined LSTM and GAN on EDA signals.	Uses integrated gradients for explanation.	Complex GAN design.
Lee et al. (2025) [11]	Compared DL models on WESAD dataset.	Reached 99% F1-score.	Results are dataset-specific.

3   Preliminaries

3.1   Large Language Models

Large Language Models (LLMs) are advanced AI systems built on the Transformer architecture, enabling tasks such as translation, summarization, and question answering with near-human fluency. Input text is tokenized (e.g., BPE, WordPiece) and mapped into embeddings before being processed by the self-attention mechanism. The attention function that computes contextual dependencies between tokens is given by Eq. 1.

$$\text{Attention}(Q, K, V) = \text{softmax}\left(\frac{QK^T}{\sqrt{d_k}}\right) V \tag{1}$$

Since Transformers lack recurrence, positional encodings are added to embeddings to preserve word order. A commonly used formulation is given in Eq. 2.

$$\text{PE}_{(pos,2i)} = \sin\left(\frac{pos}{10000^{2i/d_{model}}}\right), \quad \text{PE}_{(pos,2i+1)} = \cos\left(\frac{pos}{10000^{2i/d_{model}}}\right) \tag{2}$$

LLMs are typically implemented in encoder-only (BERT), decoder-only (GPT), or encoder-decoder (T5) configurations, incorporating multi-head attention, normalization layers, and activation functions. Their scale ranges from 70B parameters in LLaMA-2 to 175B in GPT-3 and 540B in PaLM, reflecting rapid growth in capability.

4 Proposed Approach

4.1 Hardware Overview

The proposed system enables real-time stress detection entirely at the edge through a multisensor wearable device managed by an ESP32 microcontroller. Physiological signals are non-invasively recorded, locally preprocessed, and analyzed using a lightweight software stack to provide instant feedback. Prioritizing privacy, modularity, and responsiveness, a compact real-time hardware configuration is implemented, and the device integrates four biosensors, MAX30100, GSR, AD8232, and DS18B20, with the ESP32 for efficient on-device stress monitoring.

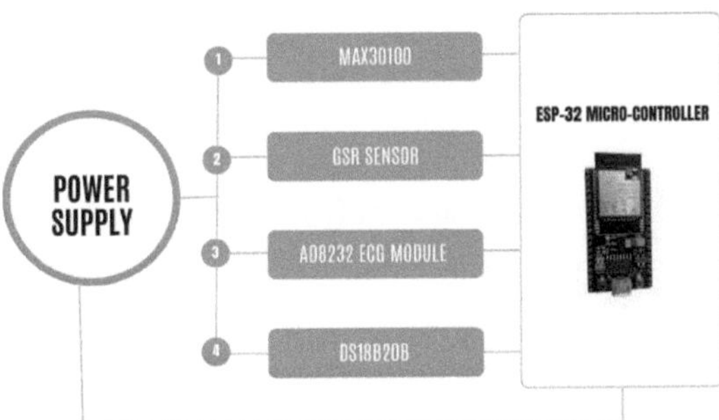

Fig. 1. Modular hardware architecture for multimodal stress sensing and edge processing

The proposed multimodal stress sensing and edge processing architecture is illustrated in Fig. 1, with biosensor-to-marker mappings summarized in Table 2. The ESP32 serves as the core processor, handling signal acquisition, preprocessing,

Table 2. Mapping of biosensors to physiological markers, signal types, and ESP32 interface protocols

Sensor	Parameter Measured	Signal Type	Interface with ESP32
MAX30100	Heart Rate and SpO$_2$	Digital	I^{2}C
AD8232 ECG Module	ECG Signal and HRV	Analog	ADC (Analog Input)
GSR Sensor	Skin Conductance (Electrodermal Activity)	Analog	ADC (Analog Input)
DS18B20	Skin Surface Temperature	Digital	One-Wire Protocol

and wireless transmission. Analog inputs (AD8232, GSR) connect via ADC pins, while DS18B20 (One-Wire) and MAX30100 (I^{2}C) use digital interfaces. Power is managed through 3.3V logic with level shifters for 5V sensors. Real-time features extracted include skin temperature variation, conductance change rate, and RR-intervals. Figure 2 shows the proposed system setup for stress detection.

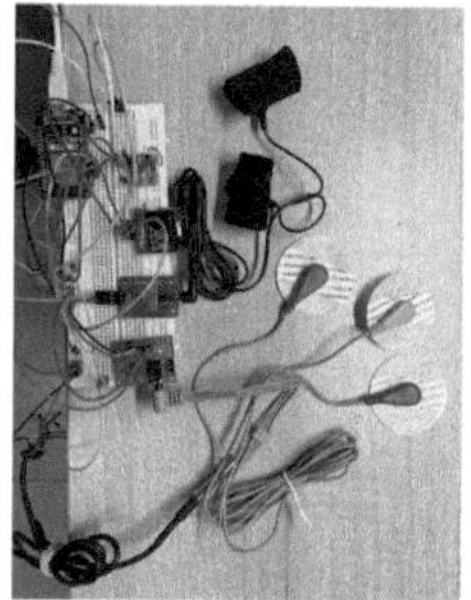

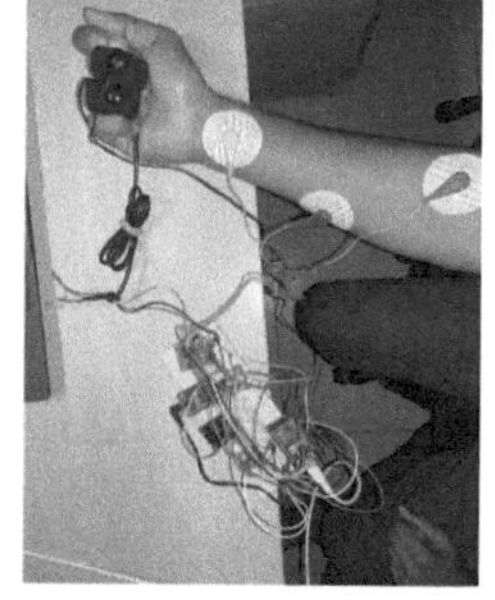

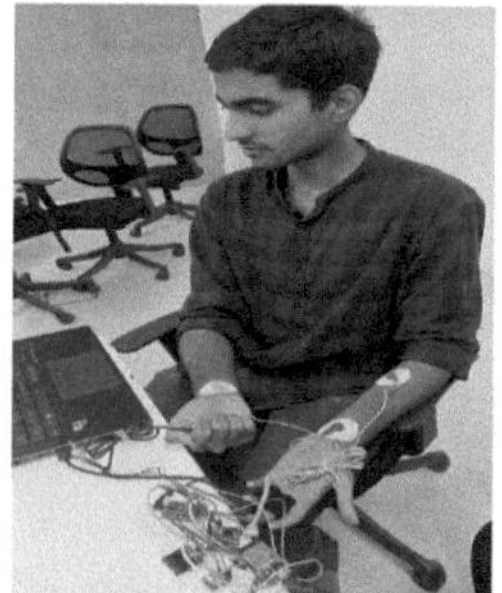

(a)   Sensor   wiring showing connection of GSR, ECG, and temp sensors to ESP32.

(b)   Integration of MAX30100, DS18B20, AD8232, and GSR sensor with ESP32.

(c)   Final   assembled hardware   including ESP32-based setup for stress monitoring.

Fig. 2. System setup: (a) wiring schematic, (b) sensor integration, and (c) final assembled hardware.

4.2   Software Stack and Processing Pipeline

The proposed system is a modular, interpretable, and real-time stress detection framework that fuses multimodal data, physiological (HRV, GSR, Temp, PPG, SpO$_2$), behavioral (keystrokes, mouse movement), and affective (facial and speech emotion). Each signal undergoes tailored preprocessing for noise removal and normalization before parallel processing through optimized ML/DL models. The framework supports efficient, on-device inference with sub-second latency, ensuring edge deployment without cloud dependence. Its key novelty lies in explainability: outputs are integrated into personalized, natural-language summaries via a locally hosted instruction-tuned LLM (Mistral-7B-Instruct). Transparency is further enhanced through feature importance and emoji-tagged feedback, fostering usability, trust, and privacy in continuous mental health monitoring.

4.3   Multi-modal Architecture

The stress detection architecture adopts a multibranch model, where each branch corresponds to a specific physiological or behavioral signal (Fig. 3). This design treats each modality as an independent predictor, enhancing interpretability and robustness to noisy or missing data. Signal pipelines begin with feature extraction time-domain metrics (e.g., RMSSD, SDNN), slope estimates, and derivatives for HRV and GSR; dynamic features (e.g., mouse acceleration, typing speed) for behavioral data; and pre-trained CNNs/Multi-Layer Perceptron (MLPs) for emotion modalities like speech and facial expressions. Each modality is then processed by a tailored model: logistic regression for smooth signals (e.g., conductance, temperature), XGBoost for high-variance behavioral and HRV features, and CNNs/MLPs for emotion classification. The output of each branch is a scalar stress probability.

After z-score normalization and scaling, logits are transformed using a hyperbolic cotangent (coth)-based function, yielding bounded stress scores that preserve semantic granularity. Each score reflects the stress level attributed to its signal source. A locally hosted instruction-tuned LLM (e.g., Mistral-7B-Instruct) then interprets the multidimensional stress vector, computing cumulative intensity and generating natural-language feedback. Outputs typically include descriptive summaries (e.g., "You seem to be moderately stressed") and prescriptive coping advice (e.g., "Try progressive muscle relaxation"). The modular design supports scalability, parallel processing, and graceful degradation, ensuring robustness in dynamic, low-resource, or noisy environments.

4.4   LLM Integration

In the final pipeline stage, a local LLM (Mistral-7B-Instruct) converts quantified stress indicators into natural-language feedback. It (i) integrates per-modality scores (HRV, GSR, temperature) to classify stress on a four-level scale, (ii) enhances explainability by highlighting modality-specific contributions (e.g., "Elevated skin conductance and HRV suggest emotional arousal"), and (iii) provides concise coping strategies such as breathing or grounding exercises. Running the LLM locally ensures privacy, low latency, and edge compatibility, bridging quantitative stress detection with interpretable, human-centered feedback. Figure 4 shows the pipeline of the proposed system for stress classification.

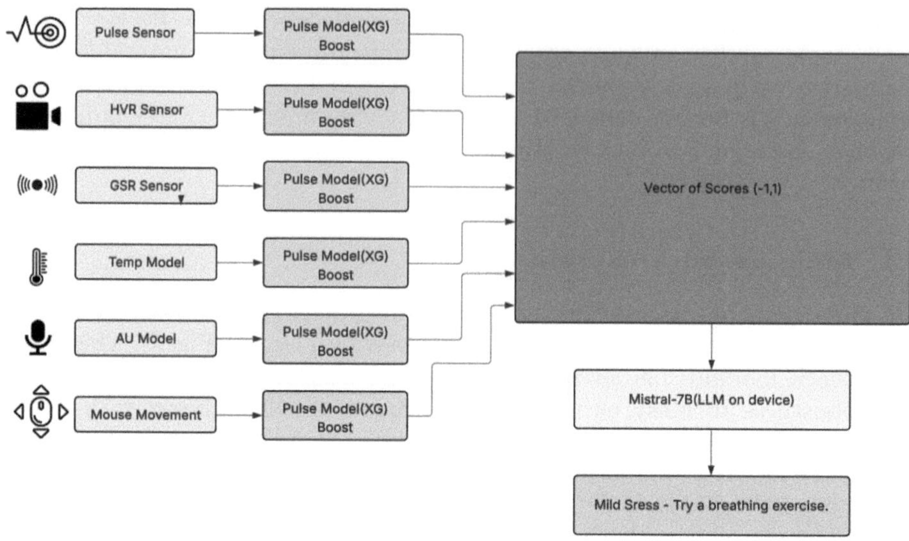

Fig. 3. Sensor-to-LLM Pipeline for Stress Detection and Recommendation

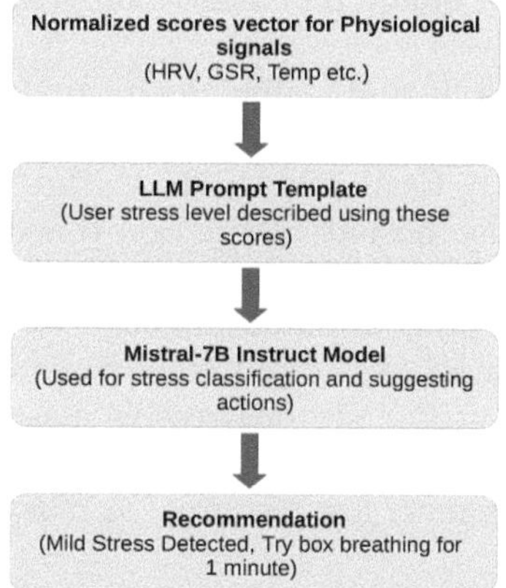

Fig. 4. Stress classification and Calming recommendation pipeline

4.5 Stress Score Transformation via Scaled Logit-Based Nonlinearity

A unique non-linear transformation function motivated by information-theoretic scaling mechanisms is used to transform raw model outputs into a normalized, continuous stress score that can be understood by human stakeholders as well as the downstream LLM. This function is represented in Eq. 3.

$$F\big(\text{scaled}(\text{logit} - \text{center})\big) \tag{3}$$

It is designed to compress the output range while preserving the gradient flow and amplifying semantically relevant deviations. The transformation is defined in Eq. 4.

$$F(x) = \frac{e^x - e^{-x}}{e^x + e^{-x}} = \tanh(x) \tag{4}$$

This is the hyperbolic cotangent (coth) function, which functions as a continuous, sharp, and differentiable mapping. Due to its characteristics, it can be used for stress detection, where slight variations around the center need to be discernible without being unduly pronounced. Crucially, the function gets closer to infinity as $x \to 0$, but in reality, the inputs are scaled to prevent singularities. The function asymptotically approaches ± 1 as $|x|$ grows, compressing extreme values and avoiding over-saturation of stress scores. A centered and scaled logit function is defined in Eq. 5.

$$\text{logit} = \alpha z + \beta \tag{5}$$

In this case, the learnable slope and bias terms are represented by the trainable parameters α and β, respectively. During training or calibration stages, they allow the system to adaptively stretch or shift the stress score's decision boundary based on empirical data. Validation feedback is used to optimize these parameters and adjust the sensitivity of the scoring mechanism. A standardized input feature, the variable z, is obtained in Eq. 6.

$$z = \frac{x - \bar{x}}{\sigma} \tag{6}$$

This formula guarantees that the logit functions on an input space that is unit-variance and zero-centered. The division by the standard deviation σ homogenizes the scale between modalities and subjects, while the normalization step $(x - \bar{x})$ eliminates inter-subject variability and dataset bias. In multimodal systems like ours, where diverse signal types from mouse movement acceleration to heart rate variability must be projected onto a single latent axis for interpretability and model fusion, this standardization is especially crucial. Upon computation, the final scalar stress indicator, represented by the transformed value F, is supplied to the narrative feedback generator (LLM). Smooth interpretation and interpolation are made possible by the function's monotonic and differentiable nature, which is crucial for producing emotionally complex and ongoing feedback phrases (e.g., "Your tension is slightly elevated" vs. "You appear highly stressed").

4.6   System Flow

The proposed system enables real-time, interpretable stress detection using multimodal inputs, physiological (HRV, GSR, temperature), behavioral (keystrokes, mouse movement), and emotional (facial/speech cues). Each modality is processed by a lightweight model to yield a normalized stress score in the range

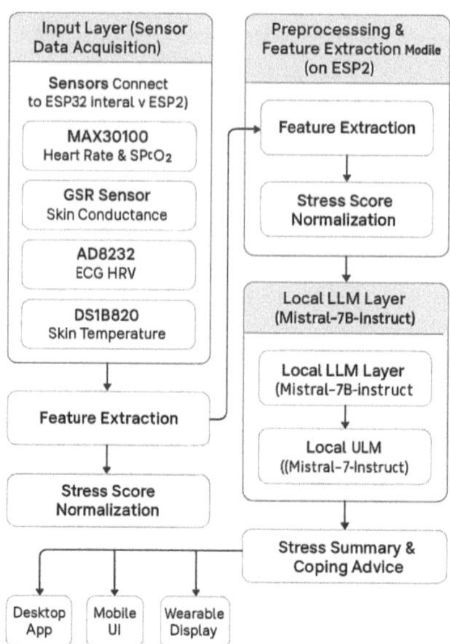

Fig. 5. System flow diagram for stress detection using physiological sensors and machine learning

$[-1, +1]$. These scores are aggregated and interpreted by a local LLM, which generates two-sentence feedback: one summarizing stress severity and another suggesting a coping strategy. With end-to-end latency under one second, the system is suitable for wearables and mental wellness applications. The overall flow is illustrated in Fig. 5.

5 Experimental Evaluation and Performance Analysis

A rigorous experimental setup was established to assess the proposed system's reliability, validity, explainability, and feasibility. HRV, GSR, Skin Temperature, Facial Emotion Recognition, Speech Emotion Recognition, and behavioral inputs such as mouse and keystroke dynamics were some of the different modalities from which the system was designed to read and fuse data. Each of these modalities was subject to personalized training and validation processes with preprocessing methods depending on the type of data. This ensured inter-modal consistency, relevance to the domain, and integrity of signal throughout the pipeline.

5.1 Dataset Description

In order to ensure cross-domain robustness and ecological validity, the evaluation method employs a mixed strategy that integrates user-specific real-time data with existing benchmark datasets. The WESAD dataset [15] contributed the physiological signal data, such as skin temperature, GSR, and HRV. This dataset is commonly used due to its extensive physiological recordings in baseline and stress-induced tasks, providing a good foundation for time-series modeling. The FER-2013 dataset [8] was used for facial emotion recognition. It has thousands of labeled grayscale facial expressions that cover a wide range of affective states, allowing stress-related facial cues such as fear, anger, and disgust to be modeled. Two concurrent speech databases, RAVDESS [12] and TESS [6], are used for vocal emotion recognition. Both provide high-fidelity, labeled speech samples with a variety of emotional expressions, allowing modeling of the prosodic features indicative of vocal stress. Behavioral information is collected from the Keystroke and Mouse Stress Detection dataset [18], which contains session-level input logs recorded in a variety of emotional and cognitive states. Special logging scripts are introduced to log user actions in real time while working on high-cognitive-load tasks for better contextual flexibility. All modalities are annotated with a tripartite labeling scheme of low, moderate, and high stress, derived from physiological thresholds, emotion classification outputs, and subjective user feedback. These categorical labels are additionally normalized into a continuous stress score in the range $[-1, +1]$, facilitating smoother cross-modal integration and continuous stress representation throughout the evaluation pipeline.

5.2   Data Preprocessing Pipeline

Data pre-processing ensures signal quality, robustness, and consistency across modalities. For HRV, interbeat intervals are extracted from ECG using R-peak detection, and Root Mean Square of Successive Differences (RMSSD) is computed, segmented into 60-second windows with 30-second overlap, and standardized by z-score normalization. GSR signals are median-filtered to suppress noise, and Skin Conductance Level (SCL) is derived and normalized per user. Temperature data are baseline corrected to address ambient shifts and sensor drift. Facial data undergo detection, alignment, and resizing before feature extraction using a CNN pre-trained on FER-2013, with stress-related emotions (anger, fear, disgust) logged as features. Speech features include MFCCs, chroma vectors, and spectral contrast descriptors, aggregated into fixed-size embeddings. Finally, behavioral features from keystrokes (inter-key intervals, hold times) and mouse dynamics (velocity, acceleration, jerk) are extracted and normalized using MinMax scaling for cross-user comparability.

5.3   Experimental Setup

An NVIDIA RTX 3070 Ti GPU, 32 GB of RAM, and Python 3.10 were installed on the workstation used for the experimental analysis. TensorFlow/Keras for deep learning-based facial emotion classifiers, XGBoost for gradient-boosted tree models, and scikit-learn for classical machine learning were among the essential libraries utilized. Low-latency text generation without the need for external APIs was made possible by the narrative feedback component's use of Hugging Face's transformer pipeline to run Mistral-7B-Instruct locally. To ensure label balance across stress categories, models were trained independently for each modality using 5-fold stratified cross-validation. Hyperparameters were chosen based on domain heuristics or adjusted using grid search methods. XGBoost classifiers with a conservative learning rate and moderate tree depth were used in HRV and behavioral models. For stability and computational efficiency, logistic regression was used to model the temperature and GSR data because they were smoother and had less variance. A CNN tuned for 30 epochs with dropout regularization to reduce overfitting was used to model facial emotion, while an MLP with two dense hidden layers was used to model speech emotion. Table 3 presents the model configuration and hyperparameters used for each modality.

Table 3. Model configuration and hyperparameters used per modality

Modality	Model Type	Key Hyperparameters
HRV	XGBoost	max_depth=3, learning_rate=0.1, n_estimators=100
GSR	Logistic Regression	penalty='l2', solver='liblinear'
Temperature	Logistic Regression	penalty='l2', solver='liblinear'
Behavior	XGBoost	max_depth=5, learning_rate=0.1, n_estimators=150
Facial Emotion	CNN	30 epochs, dropout=0.3
Speech Emotion	MLP	2 hidden layers, relu activations

5.4   Performance Evaluation

Multiple evaluation metrics, including accuracy, precision, recall, F1 score, ROC-AUC (Receiver Operating Characteristic - Area Under Curve), and inference latency, are used to evaluate performance in a comprehensive manner. These metrics capture both operational viability and statistical robustness. With an ROC-AUC of 0.93%, an F1 score of 0.89%, and an accuracy of 91%, the HRV model demonstrated high temporal sensitivity. The accuracy of the temperature and GSR models was 85% and 82%, respectively, with F1-scores of 0.80% and 0.84%. Although facial and speech emotion classifiers showed respectable accuracy of 86% and 83%, respectively, the behavioral model achieved 88% accuracy. Crucially, all models were able to maintain inference latencies below 15 milliseconds, which made them suitable for real-time implementation in ambient or wearable systems. Table 4 presents the performance metrics obtained for each modality. The confusion matrices were generated for each modality's binary stress classification (low vs. high) as shown in Figs. 6(a), 6(b), and 6(c), respectively.

Tree-based techniques, like XGBoost, outperformed other models when applied to high-variance, interaction-heavy data streams, like behavioral logs and HRV. However, because of its ease of use and interpretability, logistic regression worked well for physiological signals with low noise levels, such as temperature and GSR. When modeled using deep learning architectures like CNNs or dense MLPs, which could successfully capture intricate patterns in affective signals, emotion-based data streams that benefit from spatial (facial) or spectral (audio) repre-

Table 4. Performance Metrics per Modality

Modality	Model	Accuracy	F1-Score	ROC-AUC	Specificity
HRV	XGBoost	0.91	0.89	0.93	0.92
GSR	Logistic Regression	0.85	0.84	0.88	0.87
Temperature	Logistic Regression	0.82	0.80	0.86	0.84
Behavior	XGBoost	0.88	0.86	0.90	0.89
PPG	Logistic Regression	0.86	0.83	0.88	0.86
SpO$_2$	Logistic Regression	0.83	0.81	0.85	0.84

sentations performed better. XGBoost consistently outperformed classical models for temporal and behavioral modalities. Figure 7 shows the clear separation between stress and non-stress states in GSR stress scores, demonstrating the model's ability to capture discriminative patterns.

Table 5. Robustness of Models under Noisy Conditions

Modality	Perturbation	Accuracy Retained
HRV	Gaussian noise in ECG	0.81
Behavioral	Random keypress/mouse jitter	0.83
Facial Emotion	Blurred image input	0.80
Speech Emotion	Pitch-shifted audio	0.78

System profiling showed an average end-to-end latency of 0.9 s, with 0.7 s spent on LLM-based feedback generation and 0.2 s on machine learning inference and feature extraction. This confirms that the system can operate in near real time on CPU-only devices, meeting the latency requirements for wearable and edge-based stress detection. Robustness was evaluated using perturbed datasets that simulate real-world noise. Table 5 presents the robustness analysis of the proposed models under noisy conditions, indicating a consistent accuracy retention across different perturbations. The HRV model maintained an accuracy greater than 80% with Gaussian noise added to the ECG signals, while the behavioral model remained reliable in diverse mouse trajectories and randomized keypress patterns. Speech and facial models also generalized well to pitch-shifted audio and blurred images, showing stability in uncontrolled environments. Table 6 reports the inference time for each modality, highlighting the efficiency of the models for real-time edge-based stress detection. The interpretability was addressed through confusion matrices and feature importance analysis, which identified RMSSD from HRV and cursor jerk from behavioral data as the most informative predictors. Table 7 highlights the most influential features identified by XGBoost across modalities, with RMSSD, jerk, EDA slope, and skin delta emerging as key predictors of stress. Finally, the local LLM generated concise two-line feedback with coping suggestions and emotion tags based on emoji, improving user trust and engagement.

Although many previous stress detection methods have used deep learning or traditional ML models, they tend to utilize monolithic designs, cloud-based

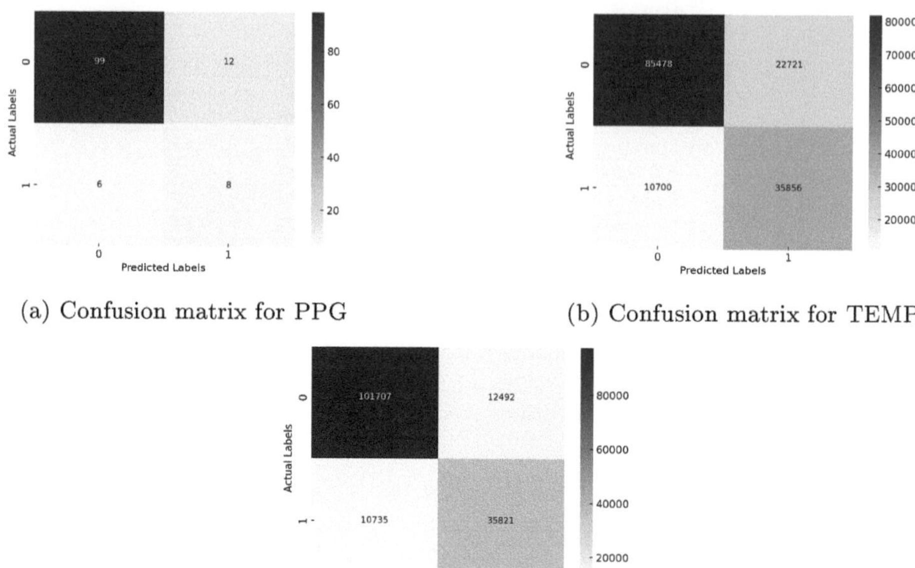

(a) Confusion matrix for PPG

(b) Confusion matrix for TEMP

(c) Confusion matrix for GSR

Fig. 6. Confusion matrices for (a) PPG, (b) TEMP, and (c) GSR under binary stress classification.

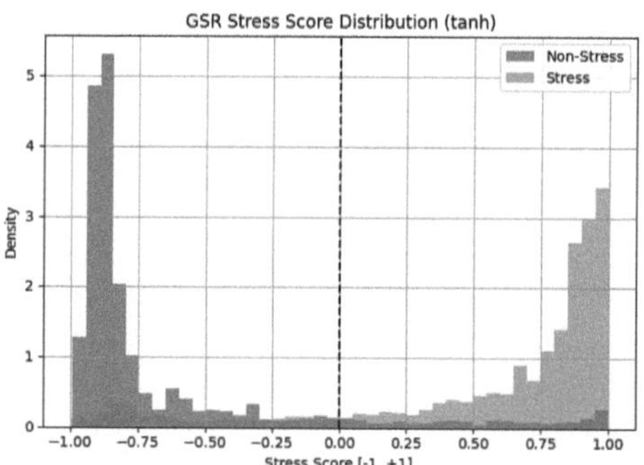

Fig. 7. Distribution of GSR stress scores

Table 6. Inference Time per modality

Modality	Model	Inference Time
HRV	XGBoost	0.007 s
GSR	Logistic Reg	0.003 s
Temp	Logistic Reg	0.003 s
Behavior	XGBoost	0.009 s

Table 7. Top Features by XGBoost Feature Importance

Modality	Top Feature (Importance Score)
HRV	RMSSD (0.31)
Behavioral	Jerk (0.27)
GSR	EDA Slope (0.24)
Temperature	Skin Delta (0.21)

pipelines, or shallow modality coverage. As evident in Table 8, most systems consider only facial, vocal, or physiological inputs, thus constraining their generalizability in real-life applications. The proposed approach, as opposed to others, embraces per-modality modeling with the ability to perform fine-grained feature importance analysis, debug modularity, and real-time deployment on local devices in an efficient manner. It also couples conventional ML for bodily signals and large language models for narrative abstraction, closing the gap between technical prediction and human-understandable feedback in terms of improving interpretability and usability.

Table 8. Comparison of proposed method with existing stress detection approaches

Study/Modality	Model Type	Modalities Used	Accuracy
Zhai and Barreto, 2006 [19]	SVM	ECG, GSR	85%
Aigrain *et al.*, 2016 [2]	CNN (Deep Learning)	Facial Expressions	83%
Gjoreski *et al.*, 2017 [7]	Random Forest	Accelerometer, GSR, HRV	87%
Zhang *et al.*, 2020 [20]	LSTM (Deep RNN)	EEG, HRV	88%
Sethi *et al.*, 2023 [16]	AdaBoost	ECG, PPG (fingertip) and PPG (wrist)	75.7%
AI *et al.*, 2025 [3]	Random Forest	ECG, PPG(fingertip), GSR	89%
Proposed method	Modular ML + LLM	HRV, GSR, Temp, PPG, SpO$_2$, Behavior	91% (HRV)

5.5   Ablation Study

Targeted ablation studies were conducted to assess model dependencies and separate the contribution of individual features. The significance of modeling complex temporal interactions was confirmed by the 7% decrease in classification accuracy that occurred when the maximum depth of the XGBoost classifier in the HRV model was reduced. The behavioral model's F1-score decreased by 5% when jerk, a third-order derivative of position, was excluded. This suggests that higher-order motion dynamics plays a significant role in stress differentiation. Similarly, the ROC-AUC of the facial emotion model decreased by 6% when fear and anger classes were removed, highlighting the importance of affective granularity in enhancing generalizability. Table 9 presents the results of the ablation study.

Table 9. Ablation Study: Feature Impact on Performance

Model	Feature Removed	Δ Accuracy	Δ F1-Score
HRV (XGBoost)	Reduced max depth (3 → 2)	−7%	−6%
Behavioral	Jerk	−6%	−5%
Facial Emotion (CNN)	Fear & Anger classes	−5%	−6%

5.6 Discussion

This work is a significant milestone towards the creation of next-generation interpretable stress monitoring systems that integrate multimodal physiological, behavioral, and affective signals with a modular AI framework. Among the models that were tested, the HRV-based classifier showed the best overall performance with an accuracy of 91% and class-wise balanced metrics. It also achieved consistent F1 scores for the two classes and was therefore most effective in differentiating between stress types in real-time applications. In contrast, the temperature model (TEMP) performed worse, at 82% accuracy and with lower precision and F1 scores for class 1. The PPG model performed at 86% accuracy, but had difficulty with class imbalance, especially for the more difficult to detect class 1. Despite these variations across individual modalities, the combined pipeline worked well overall, with 86% accuracy on the test set and with balanced metrics, affirming its viability as a strong multimodal stress detection solution. In addition to classification performance, the system emphasizes interpretability and usability. Translating raw model predictions into linguistically sensible and emotionally meaningful recommendations, localized LLM-based feedback generation greatly increases its value.

There are certain limitations in deploying the system in the real world. Real-time inference with large models, even locally with models such as Mistral-7B-Instruct, can be demanding in terms of computation and is thus challenging for low-power or mobile deployment. Physical form factor constraints of wearable hardware in terms of size, battery life, and comfort must be resolved for full-day usage. Although current ESP32-based integration is already minimized, miniaturization and power efficiency need to be done even better for complete market readiness. Ultimately, ethical deployment requires careful consideration of privacy, transparency, and user consent.

6 Conclusion and Future Work

This work presents a real-time, explainable stress detection framework that integrates multimodal signals with a modular machine learning pipeline. By combining lightweight classifiers with LLM-based feedback, the system achieves accurate classification while providing transparent, user-friendly explanations. The key innovations include modular explainability, edge-first deployment with privacy preservation, and natural language feedback, addressing a major gap in bio-AI systems. The experiments on benchmark datasets confirm both performance and interpretability, while the design avoids cloud dependency, making it suitable for sensitive contexts such as remote work, learning, and mental health care. Future work will focus on real-world validation, personalization, hardware optimization, multilingual feedback, and longitudinal tracking. With these developments, the system can evolve into a clinically viable and accessible tool for stress awareness and management.

Disclosure of Interests. The authors have no competing interests to declare that are relevant to the content of this article.

References

1. Abdelfattah, S., Liu, C., Ortega, J.: Machine learning for acute stress detection from wearable devices using hybrid LSTM-GAN models. J. Biomed. Inform. **135**, 104392 (2025)
2. Aigrain, J., Spodenkiewicz, M., Dubuisson, S., Detyniecki, M., Cohen, D., Chetouani, M.: Multimodal stress detection from multiple assessments. IEEE Trans. Affect. Comput. **9**(4), 491–506 (2016)
3. Al Hasan, M.N., Noman, N.S., Chowdhury, M.H., Chowdhury, A.: Improving multimodal stress detection using MAUS dataset with PPG, ECG and GSR signal. In: 2025 International Conference on Electrical, Computer and Communication Engineering (ECCE), pp. 1–5. IEEE (2025)
4. Arushi, A., Sharma, K., Patel, M.: Voice-based stress detection in virtual reality public speaking scenarios. In: 2022 International Conference on Affective Computing and Intelligent Interaction (ACII). IEEE (2022)
5. Bhattacharyya, S., Natarajan, S., et al.: Explainable machine learning in health informatics. ACM Comput. Surv. **54**(8), 1–38 (2021)
6. Dupuis, K., Pichora-Fuller, M.K.: Toronto emotional speech set (TESS) (2010)
7. Gjoreski, M., Luštrek, M., Gams, M., Gjoreski, H.: Monitoring stress with a wrist device using context. J. Biomed. Inform. **73**, 159–170 (2017)
8. Goodfellow, I., Erhan, D., Carrier, L., Courville, A., Bengio, Y.: Challenges in representation learning: A report on three machine learning contests. arXiv preprint arXiv:1307.0414 (2013)
9. Kim, J., Park, S.: Local multi-head channel self-attention for facial expression recognition. arXiv preprint arXiv:2111.07224 (2022)
10. Lazarus, R.S., Folkman, S.: Stress, appraisal, and Coping. Springer, Cham (1984)
11. Lee, H., Kim, J., Han, B., Park, S.M., Chang, J.: Developing an explainable deep neural network for stress detection using biosignals and human-engineered features. Biomed. Signal Process. Control **109**, 107960 (2025)
12. Livingstone, S.R., Russo, F.A.: The ryerson audio-visual database of emotional speech and song (RAVDESS). PLoS ONE **13**(5), e0196391 (2018)
13. Moser, M.K., Ehrhart, M., Resch, B.: An explainable deep learning approach for stress detection in wearable sensor measurements. Sensors **24**(16), 5085 (2024)
14. Nguyen, B.M., Pham, B.Q., Nguyen, H.T.T., Do, T.L.: Real-time stress detection on social network posts using big data technology. arXiv preprint arXiv:2411.04532 (2024)

15. Schmidt, P., Reiss, A., Duerichen, R., Marberger, C., Van Laerhoven, K.: Introducing wesad, a multimodal dataset for wearable stress and affect detection. In: Proceedings of the 20th ACM International Conference on Multimodal Interaction, pp. 400–408 (2018)
16. Sethi, A., Walambe, R., Jain, P., Kotecha, K.: Multimodal mental workload classification using maus dataset. In: 2023 International Conference on Advanced Computing Technologies and Applications (ICACTA), pp. 1–6. IEEE (2023)
17. Wang, L., Zhao, T., Sun, F.: Mental health monitoring on weibo: a multimodal fusion approach using text and behavioral signals. IEEE Trans. Affect. Comput. **14**(3), 510–520 (2023)
18. Weerasinghe, C.: Stress detection by keystroke/mouse changes dataset (2023)
19. Zhai, J., Barreto, A.: Stress detection in computer users based on digital signal processing of noninvasive physiological variables. In: 2006 International Conference of the IEEE Engineering in Medicine and Biology Society, pp. 1355–1358. IEEE (2006)
20. Zhang, H., Feng, L., Li, N., Jin, Z., Cao, L.: Video-based stress detection through deep learning. Sensors **20**(19), 5552 (2020)
21. Zhou, L., Wang, Y.: Swin-fer: Swin transformer for facial expression recognition. In: 2023 International Conference on Computer Vision and Pattern Recognition (ICCVPR). IEEE (2023)

AI for Security

A Reverse Reachable Set Based Approach for Motif Oriented Profit Maximization in Social Networks

Poonam Sharma$^{(\boxtimes)}$ and Suman Banerjee

Indian Institute of Technology Jammu, Jammu 181221, J&K, India
{poonam.sharma,suman.banerjee}@iitjammu.ac.in

Abstract. Profit Maximization is one of the key objectives for social media marketing, where the task is to choose a limited number of highly influential nodes such that their initial activation leads to maximum profit. In this paper, we introduce a variant of the Profit Maximization Problem where we consider that instead of nodes, benefits are assigned to some of the motifs of the graph, and these benefit values can be earned once a given threshold count of nodes from the motifs is influenced. The goal here is to choose a limited number of nodes for initial activation (called 'seed nodes') such that the motif-oriented profit gets maximized. Formally, we call our problem the MOTIF ORIENTED PROFIT MAXIMIZATION Problem. We show that the problem is NP-hard to solve optimally. We propose a Reverse Reachable Set-based framework to solve our problem. The proposed methodology broadly divides into three steps: KPT Estimation and $\mathcal{RR}$ Set generation, Seed Set Selection, and Motif Oriented Profit Estimation. The proposed methodology has been analyzed to understand its time and space requirements. It has been implemented with real-world social network datasets, and the results are reported. We observe that the seed set selected by the proposed solution approaches leads to more profit compared to the seed sets selected by the existing methods. The whole implementation and data are available at: https://github.com/PoonamSharma-PY/MotifProfit.

Keywords: Social Networks · Motif · Profit Maximization Problem · Seed Set · Information Diffusion

1 Introduction

In recent times, *Online Social Networks* play a pivotal role in spreading news, ideas, rumors, etc., and this happens due to the diffusion of information [1,2]. People tend to share the information through social media posts, and people who are in the friend (or follower) list may wish to like, share, comment, etc. on the post. If the person is influential, then there is a very high chance that many of the users of the network will come to know about the fact. This phenomenon has been exploited by commercial houses for promoting their brands. For this

B. Chatterjee et al. (Eds.): ICDCIT 2026, LNCS 16420, pp. 301–316, 2026.
https://doi.org/10.1007/978-3-032-16632-6_19

purpose, they choose a limited number of influential people from the network and distribute free (or discounted) products with the hope that they will spread positive words about the product due to word-of-mouth. This notion is called Viral Marketing through Social Media. In recent times, commercial houses spend a significant portion of their revenue on Social Media advertisements.

To study the diffusion process in a social network, several models have been introduced and studied in the literature. Among them, the Independent Cascade Model is the most popular one. In the context of viral marketing, the key computational problem that arises is that given a social network, how can we effectively select a limited number of nodes for initial activation such that the influence gets maximized? Initially, this problem was posed by Domingos and Richardson [4,14]. Later, Kempe et al. [7,8] showed that this problem is NP-hard to solve optimally under the IC Model of diffusion. They proposed an iterative greedy approach based on marginal influence gain computation, which provides a $(1 - \frac{1}{e})$-factor approximate solution. This study triggers a significant amount of research in this direction, and a huge amount of literature is available. The proposed solution approaches for this problem can be classified into the following categories: Approximation Algorithms [12], Heuristic Solutions [3], Soft Computing-based Approaches, Reverse Reachable Set-based Approaches, and many more.

In practice, social networks are formed by rational human beings, which means if a user is acting as a seed user, then (s)he must be incentivized. Also, in commercial advertising, the key objective is to maximize profit. Hence, the following problem is of immense importance: Given a social network, the cost and benefit of each user, and a fixed budget, how can we select a seed set within the budget to maximize the profit? This problem has been referred to as the Profit Maximization Problem. In the past decade, this problem has been studied extensively in the literature. In most of the studies, it has been considered that every user of the network has some benefit value that can be earned if the user is influenced. Now, consider the following scenario. A group of friends wants to dine in a restaurant. Now, any restaurant brand will be able to attract this group and earn some profit if that brand can influence the whole group. A small group of nodes in a network is called a motif. Sometimes it is important to consider influencing a whole motif rather than an individual user. To influence a motif, it may be sufficient to influence the majority of the users present in the motif. In this paper, we consider the problem of maximizing the profit of a commercial campaign by influencing the motifs. We call this problem the MOTIF ORIENTED PROFIT MAXIMIZATION Problem. In this problem, we are given a social network where each user is assigned a selection cost, a set of motifs along with their corresponding benefit value, and a budget. This problem asks to choose a subset of nodes within the allocated budget such that the earned profit by maximizing the influence among the motifs is maximized. To the best of our knowledge, we are the first to study the Profit Maximization Problem under the motif-oriented setup. In particular, we make the following contributions in this paper:

– We introduce and study the MOTIF ORIENTED PROFIT MAXIMIZATION Problem for which there does not exist any literature.
– We propose a reverse reachable set-based solution approach to solve our problem with a detailed analysis and illustration.
– A number of experiments have been conducted on real-world social network datasets, and the results are compared with the existing methods to show the effectiveness and efficiency of the proposed solution approach.

The rest of the paper has been organized as follows. Section 2 describes background information and defines the problem formally. Section 3 describes the proposed solution approaches with a detailed analysis. The experimental evaluation of the proposed solution approaches has been described in Sect. 4. Finally, Sect. 5 concludes our study and gives future research directions.

2 Background and Problem Definition

In this section, we describe the required preliminary concepts and subsequently define our problem formally. Initially, we start by describing the notion of social networks.

2.1 Social Networks

A social network is defined as an interconnected structure among a group of people, which has been formally stated in Definition 1.

Definition 1 (Social Networks). *A social network is often represented as a simple, (un)directed, weighted graph $\mathcal{G}(\mathcal{V}, \mathcal{E}, \mathcal{P})$ where the vertex set $\mathcal{V}$ represents the set of users connected through the network, the edge set represents the social relationships, and the edge weight function $\mathcal{P}$ maps each edge to its corresponding influence probability, i.e., $\mathcal{P} : \mathcal{E} \longrightarrow (0, 1]$.*

For any edge $(u_i u_j) \in \mathcal{E}$, it means that u_i and u_j are in the social relationship. We reserve n and m to denote the number of nodes and edges, respectively. For any edge $(u_i u_j) \in \mathcal{E}$, its influence probability is denoted by $\mathcal{P}(u_i u_j)$. In our study, we assume that every edge has a non-zero influence probability, i.e., for any edge $(u_i u_j) \in \mathcal{E}$, $0 < \mathcal{P}(u_i u_j) \leq 1$.

In graph data analytics, there has always been an interest in understanding how large networks (e.g., Social Networks, Biological Networks, etc.) have been formed. It has been found that a large network is formed using small networks as a building block, which is also called a Motif, as stated in Definition 2.

Definition 2 (Motif). *A motif is a subgraph that appears significantly more often in a real network than would be expected in a randomized network with the same number of nodes and edges.*

2.2   Information Diffusion and Social Influence Maximization

Among many, one of the properties of social networks is the diffusion of information, which says that an individual connected through online social networks tends to share the information. Now, it is expected that if the person is influential, then he will have many social neighbors, and a large number of them will be influenced by the information and share it further. This process will be continued, and the hope is that at the end of the diffusion process, a large number of people will be influenced. The entire process is referred to as the *Information Diffusion*. This process starts from a set of initially active nodes referred to as Seed Nodes. How the information diffusion happens in the network depends on the diffusion model that has been chosen. In this study, we assume that the diffusion of information is happening by the rule of the IC Model, which has been stated in Definition 3.

Definition 3 (Independent Cascade Model). *As per the IC Model, the diffusion process starts from a set of initially active nodes called seed nodes and proceeds in discrete time steps. In the diffusion process, an active node at time step t will get a single chance to activate its inactive neighbors. A node's state can be either 'activated' (also known as influenced) or 'non-activated' (also called non-influenced). A node can change its state from 'non-activated' to 'activated'; however, it cannot do so vice versa. The diffusion process stops when no more node activation is possible.*

At the end of the diffusion process, the number of influenced nodes is called the influence of the seed set. For any given seed set $\mathcal{S} \subseteq \mathcal{V}$, $I(\mathcal{S})$ denotes the set of influenced nodes and $\sigma(\mathcal{S})$ denotes the influence of $\mathcal{S}$, where $\sigma()$ is the social influence function (a set function defined on the ground set $\mathcal{V}$) which maps each subset of the users of the network to their expected influence, i.e., $\sigma : 2^{\mathcal{V}} \longrightarrow \mathbb{R}_0^+$. In the IC Model, for a given seed set, its influence can be computed by constructing 2^m many live graphs and taking the expected value as described in [7]. As mentioned in the literature, the influence under the IC Model of diffusion is non-negative, monotone, and sub-modular. In the context of information diffusion, one well-studied problem is the Social Influence Maximization Problem which has been stated in Definition 4.

Definition 4 (Social Influence Maximization Problem). *Given a social network $\mathcal{G}(\mathcal{V}, \mathcal{E}, \mathcal{P})$, and a positive integer k, the problem of social influence maximization asks to choose k many users to activate initially, such that the maximum number of nodes gets influenced at the end of the diffusion process. Mathematically, this problem can be posed as an optimization problem as mentioned in Eq. 1.*

$$\mathcal{S}^{OPT} \longleftarrow \underset{\mathcal{S} \subseteq \mathcal{V} \ and \ |\mathcal{S}|=k}{argmax} \ \sigma(\mathcal{S}) \tag{1}$$

2.3   Profit Maximization in Social Networks

In commercial campaigns, the users of the network need to be incentivized, and every user of the network is assigned some benefit value, which can be earned if the user is influenced. These notions have been formalized by the Cost and Benefit functions which are denoted by $\mathcal{C}$ and b, respectively, i.e., $\mathcal{C} : \mathcal{V} \longrightarrow \mathbb{R}^+$ and $b : \mathcal{V} \longrightarrow \mathbb{R}_0^+$. For any user $u \in \mathcal{V}$, its cost and benefit are denoted by $\mathcal{C}(u)$ and $b(u)$, respectively. Now, we define the notion of the earned profit by a seed set $\mathcal{S}$ in Definition 5.

Definition 5 (Earned Profit). *Given a seed set $\mathcal{S}$, the earned profit by $\mathcal{S}$ is defined as the difference between the earned benefit by the seed set and the cost of the seed set. This is denoted by $\Phi(\mathcal{S})$ and can be mathematically posed in Eq. 2.*

$$\Phi(\mathcal{S}) = \sum_{u \in I(\mathcal{S})} b(u) - \sum_{u \in \mathcal{S}} \mathcal{C}(u) \tag{2}$$

Naturally, in a commercial campaign, it is important to select a limited number of influential nodes within the budget to maximize the profit. This problem has been referred to as the Profit Maximization Problem in the literature and stated in the Definition 6.

Definition 6 (Profit Maximization Problem). *Given a social network, $\mathcal{G}(\mathcal{V}, \mathcal{E}, \mathcal{P})$ with the Cost and Benefit functions $\mathcal{C} : \mathcal{V} \longrightarrow \mathbb{R}^+$ and $b : \mathcal{V} \longrightarrow \mathbb{R}_0^+$, respectively, and a fixed budget $\mathcal{B}$, the profit maximization problem asks to choose a set of nodes for initial activation such that the earned profit by the seed set is maximized. Mathematically, this problem can be posed as shown in Eq. 3.*

$$\mathcal{S}^{OPT} \longleftarrow \underset{\mathcal{S} \subseteq \mathcal{V} \text{ and } \sum\limits_{u \in \mathcal{S}} \mathcal{C}(u) \leq \mathcal{B}}{argmax} \Phi(\mathcal{S}) \tag{3}$$

$\mathcal{S}^{OPT}$ denotes the optimal seed set for the budget $\mathcal{B}$ in $\mathcal{G}$. As mentioned previously, this problem has been studied in the literature and a number of solution methodologies have been proposed. However, as mentioned in Sect. 1, we study the Motif Oriented Profit Maximization Problem. In this problem, we assume that along with the input social network $\mathcal{G}(\mathcal{V}, \mathcal{E}, \mathcal{P})$, we are also given a set of ℓ motifs $\mathcal{M} = \{m_1, m_2, \ldots, m_\ell\}$ and a benefit function b that maps each of the motifs to its corresponding benefit value, i.e., $b : \mathcal{M} \longrightarrow \mathbb{R}_0^+$. For any arbitrary motif $m_j \in \mathcal{M}$, $|m_j|$ denotes the number of vertices that the motif contains. The associated benefit with the motif is denoted by $b(m_j)$. This benefit can be earned if the motif is influenced. Now, how do we decide whether a motif has been influenced or not? This depends on the influence model. In this study, we assume that a threshold has been given, and if at least the threshold number of nodes of the motif are influenced, for the motif $m_j \in \mathcal{M}$, its threshold is denoted by τ_j, $1 \leq \tau_j \leq |m_j|$. Given a seed set $\mathcal{S} \subseteq \mathcal{V}$, for every motif $m_j \in \mathcal{M}$, we define an indicator boolean variable $I_{m_j}(\mathcal{S})$ which takes the value 1 if the motif is influenced and 0, otherwise. This has been mentioned in the Conditional Eq. 4.

$$I_{m_j}(\mathcal{S}) = \begin{cases} 1, & \text{if } |I(\mathcal{S}) \cap V(m_j)| \geq \tau_j \\ 0, & \text{otherwise} \end{cases} \tag{4}$$

Now, we define the notion of Motif Oriented Earned Profit by a given seed set, which is stated in Definition 7.

Definition 7 (Motif Oriented Earned Profit). *Given a Social Network $\mathcal{G}(\mathcal{V}, \mathcal{E}, \mathcal{P})$, a seed set $\mathcal{S}$, and a set of motifs $\mathcal{M} = \{m_1, m_2, \ldots, m_\ell\}$ with the corresponding benefit function $b : \mathcal{M} \longrightarrow \mathbb{R}_0^+$, and the cost function $\mathcal{C} : \mathcal{V} \longrightarrow \mathbb{R}^+$, the motif oriented earned profit by the seed set $\mathcal{S}$ is defined as the difference between the expected motif oriented earned benefit by the seed set and the cost of the seed set. This has been mathematically represented in Eq. 5.*

$$\Phi_{\mathcal{M}}(\mathcal{S}) = \sum_{g \in L(\mathcal{G})} Pr(g) \sum_{m_j \in \mathcal{M}} I_{m_j}(\mathcal{S}) \cdot b(m_j) - \sum_{u \in \mathcal{S}} \mathcal{C}(u) \tag{5}$$

The following question arises: Given a seed set, how efficiently can we compute its motif-oriented earned profit? Theorem 1 states the fact.

Theorem 1. *Given a Social Network $\mathcal{G}(\mathcal{V}, \mathcal{E}, \mathcal{P})$, a seed set $\mathcal{S}$, and a set of motifs $\mathcal{M} = \{m_1, m_2, \ldots, m_\ell\}$, accurately computing the motif oriented earned profit is a #P-Complete Problem.*

Now, in a commercial campaign, of course, it is important to choose the seed set effectively. Within the allocated budget, we formally state the Motif Oriented Profit Maximization Problem in Definition 8.

Definition 8 (Motif Oriented Profit Maximization Problem). *Given a Social Network $\mathcal{G}(\mathcal{V}, \mathcal{E}, \mathcal{P})$, a set of motifs $\mathcal{M} = \{m_1, m_2, \ldots, m_\ell\}$ with the corresponding benefit function $b : \mathcal{M} \longrightarrow \mathbb{R}_0^+$, cost function $\mathcal{C} : \mathcal{V} \longrightarrow \mathbb{R}^+$, and a fixed budget $\mathcal{B}$, this problem asks to choose a seed set to maximize the Motif Oriented Earned Profit as stated in Definition 7 such that the total cost of the seed set is less than the budget. Mathematically, this problem has been stated in Eq. 6.*

$$\mathcal{S}^{OPT} \longleftarrow \underset{\mathcal{S} \subseteq \mathcal{V} \text{ and } \sum_{u \in \mathcal{S}} \mathcal{C}(u) \leq \mathcal{B}}{argmax} \Phi_{\mathcal{M}}(\mathcal{S}) \tag{6}$$

As mentioned in [13], the Profit Maximization Problem is NP-hard. Motif Oriented Profit Maximization Problem is a generalization of the Profit Maximization Problem; hence, Motif Oriented Profit Maximization Problem will also remain NP-hard. This has been formally stated in Theorem 2.

Theorem 2. *Given a Social Network $\mathcal{G}(\mathcal{V}, \mathcal{E}, \mathcal{P})$, a set of motifs $\mathcal{M} = \{m_1, m_2, \ldots, m_\ell\}$ with the corresponding benefit function $b : \mathcal{M} \longrightarrow \mathbb{R}_0^+$, cost function $\mathcal{C} : \mathcal{V} \longrightarrow \mathbb{R}^+$, and a fixed budget $\mathcal{B}$, finding an optimal seed set to maximize the Motif Oriented earned profit is NP-hard.*

Next, we proceed to describe the solution methodologies subsequently.

3 Proposed Approach

Our proposed solution approach is based on the notion of Reverse Reachable Set, which has been stated in Definition 9.

Definition 9 (Reverse Reachable Set). *[15] Given a Social Network* $\mathcal{G}(\mathcal{V}, \mathcal{E}, \mathcal{P})$*, and a node* v*, the reverse reachable set of* v *is denoted by* $\mathcal{RR}(v)$ *and defined as the set of nodes from which there exists a directed path to the node* v *which has been stated in Eq. 7*

$$\mathcal{RR}(v) = \{u : \text{ There exists a path from } u \text{ to } v\} \tag{7}$$

Algorithm 1 Motif Oriented RIS Framework

Input: Graph $\mathcal{G}(\mathcal{V}, \mathcal{E}, \mathcal{P})$, Cost function $\mathcal{C}(\cdot)$, Benefit function $b(\cdot)$, Motif set $\mathcal{M}$, Budgets $\mathbb{B}$, Thresholds τ, Simulation count T

Output: Seed set $\mathcal{S} \subseteq \mathcal{V}$

1: **for** each budget $\mathcal{B} \in \mathbb{B}$ **do**
2:      $k \leftarrow \lfloor \mathcal{B} / \min_v \mathcal{C}(v) \rfloor$
3:      $\kappa \leftarrow \text{EstimateKPT}(\mathcal{G}, k, \mathcal{C}, b)$
4:      $\theta \leftarrow \text{ComputeTheta}(\kappa, |V|, k)$
5:      $\mathcal{R} \leftarrow \text{GenerateRRsets}(\theta, \mathcal{G})$
6:      $\mathcal{S} \leftarrow \text{GreedySeedSelection}(\mathcal{R}, \mathcal{C}, b, \mathcal{B})$
7:      Perform T Monte Carlo simulations of diffusion from $\mathcal{S}$ to obtain $\{A_1, A_2, \ldots, A_T\}$
8:      Compute average influence benefit: $\Pi \leftarrow \frac{1}{T} \sum_{i=1}^{T} \sum_{v \in A_i} b(v)$
9:      **for** each threshold $\tau \in$ Thresholds **do**
10:        $\text{MotifProfit} \leftarrow \text{ComputeMotifProfit}(\{A_i\}, \mathcal{M}, b, \tau, \mathcal{C}(\mathcal{S}))$
11:        Log result: Budget $\mathcal{B}$, Seed set $\mathcal{S}$, Π, MotifProfit, θ, κ
12:      **end for**
13: **end for**

The Reverse Influence Sampling (RIS) framework enhances classical influence maximization by incorporating motif-aware evaluation. It consists of three main parts: (i) estimation of KPT and generation of $\mathcal{RR}$ sets, (ii) greedy node selection for the seed set, and (iii) computation of motif-based profit. Algorithm 1 illustrates this process. Given a graph $\mathcal{G} = (\mathcal{V}, \mathcal{E}, \mathcal{P})$, node cost $\mathcal{C}(\cdot)$, benefit $b(\cdot)$, motif set $\mathcal{M}$, budgets $\mathbb{B}$, thresholds τ, and simulation count T, the algorithm iteratively processes each budget $\mathcal{B}$. For each budget, it estimates the maximum number of seeds k and computes the influence lower bound κ using the EstimateKPT procedure (Line 4). This value determines the required number of reverse reachable sets θ (Line 5). $\mathcal{RR}$ sets are generated (GenerateRRSets, Line 6), and a greedy strategy then selects the seed set $\mathcal{S}$ under the budget constraint (Line 7). The diffusion process is simulated T times to obtain the average profit (Lines 8–9). Finally, for each threshold τ, motifs activated in the simulations are identified, their motif-based profit is computed (ComputeMotifProfit, Line 11), and results such as seed sets, influence profit, motif profit, and sampling parameters are recorded (Line 12).

Algorithm 2 EstimateKPT

Input: Graph $\mathcal{G}(\mathcal{V}, \mathcal{E}, \mathcal{P})$, Seed count k, Cost function $\mathcal{C}(\cdot)$, Benefit function $b(\cdot)$
Output: Estimated KPT value κ

1: $\eta \leftarrow |\mathcal{V}|$, $m \leftarrow |\mathcal{E}|$
2: Define $p_v \propto \frac{b(v)}{\mathcal{C}(v)}$ for all v
3: **for** $i = 1$ to $\log_2(n) - 1$ **do**
4:      $c_i \leftarrow$ Required samples at round i
5:      Initialize $sum \leftarrow 0$
6:      **for** $j = 1$ to c_i **do**
7:          Sample node v using p_v
8:          Generate $\mathcal{RR}(v)$ set
9:          Estimate $\kappa_v = 1 - (1 - (|\mathcal{RR}(v)|/m))^k$
10:          $sum \leftarrow sum + \kappa_v$
11:      **end for**
12:      **if** $\frac{sum}{c_i} > \frac{1}{2^i}$ **then**
13:          **return** $\kappa = \frac{n \cdot sum}{2c_i}$
14:      **end if**
15: **end for**
16: **return** $\kappa = 1$

3.1   Part (i): Estimation of KPT and Generation of $\mathcal{RR}$ Sets

The ESTIMATEKPT procedure (Algorithm 2) estimates the KPT value, a key parameter for determining the number of reverse reachable ($\mathcal{RR}$) sets needed in RIS-based algorithms. It first identifies the number of nodes $n = |V|$ and edges $m = |E|$ (Line 3). To emphasize nodes with higher influence, an importance sampling distribution is defined with probabilities proportional to $b(v)/\mathcal{C}(v)$ (Line 4). The estimation runs iteratively over logarithmic rounds $i = 1$ to $\log_2(n) - 1$ (Line 5). In each round, c_i samples are drawn (Line 6), and for each sample a node v is selected (Line 9), its $\mathcal{RR}$ set $\mathcal{RR}(v)$ is generated (Line 10), and the contribution $\kappa_v = 1 - (1 - |\mathcal{RR}(v)|/m)^k$ is computed (Line 11). The results are aggregated (Line 12), and the average $\frac{sum}{c_i}$ is compared with $1/2^i$ (Line 14). If satisfied, the algorithm returns $\kappa = \frac{n \cdot sum}{2c_i}$ (Line 15); otherwise, if no threshold is met in any round, it returns $\kappa = 1$ (Line 18).

Complexity Analysis. In Algorithm 2, the main cost lies in the inner loop (Lines 6–10), where each of the c_i samples requires generating an $\mathcal{RR}$ set. A single $\mathcal{RR}$ set generation may, in the worst case, traverse all $n = |\mathcal{V}|$ nodes and $m = |\mathcal{E}|$ edges. The outer loop (Line 3) executes for $\mathcal{O}(\log n)$ rounds, so the overall time complexity is $\mathcal{O}((n + m) \log n)$, as proved in [17]. The space complexity is $\mathcal{O}(n + m)$, dominated by storing the graph and temporary $\mathcal{RR}$ sets.

The GENERATERRSETS procedure (Algorithm 3) generates a collection of Reverse Reachable ($\mathcal{RR}$) sets, the core data structure in RIS-based influence maximization. The number of sets is given by $\theta = \frac{(8+2\epsilon)\, n\, (l \log n + \log \binom{n}{k} + \log 2)}{\mathrm{KPT}\, \epsilon^2}$, with $\epsilon = 0.3$ and $l = 1$ as in [17]. Given θ, the algorithm samples nodes using an

---

Algorithm 3 GenerateRRsets

Input: θ, $\mathcal{G}(\mathcal{V}, \mathcal{E}, \mathcal{P})$
Output: Set of $\mathcal{RR}$ sets $\mathcal{R}$
1: Sample θ start nodes using importance probabilities
2: For each node, perform reverse BFS
3: **return** $\mathcal{R}$

---

importance distribution proportional to their influence potential (Line 3). For each sampled node, a reverse BFS is performed (Line 4) to identify nodes that could reach it under the IC diffusion model. After all samples are processed, the complete set of θ many $\mathcal{RR}$ sets in $\mathcal{R}$ is returned (Line 5) for evaluating seed coverage in later steps.

Complexity Analysis. In Algorithm 3, each $\mathcal{RR}$ set is constructed by performing a reverse breadth-first search (BFS) on a randomly sampled live-edge graph under the IC model (Line 2). A single reverse BFS may, in the worst case, traverse all $n = |\mathcal{V}|$ nodes and $m = |\mathcal{E}|$ edges of the graph, leading to a cost of $O(n + m)$ per $\mathcal{RR}$ set. Since the algorithm generates θ many $\mathcal{RR}$ sets, the total worst-case time complexity is $O(\theta(n + m))$. The space complexity is $\mathcal{O}(\theta \cdot |\mathcal{RR}|)$ $= \mathcal{O}(\theta \cdot n)$ (when in the worst case, the size of an $\mathcal{RR}$ set is n), for storing all generated $\mathcal{RR}$ sets.

Algorithm 4 GreedySeedSelection

Input: $\mathcal{RR}$ sets $\mathcal{R}$, Cost function $\mathcal{C}(\cdot)$, Benefit function $b(\cdot)$, Budget $\mathcal{B}$
Output: Seed set $\mathcal{S}$
1: Initialize $\mathcal{S} \leftarrow \emptyset$, RemainingBudget $\leftarrow \mathcal{B}$
2: **while** RemainingBudget > 0 **do**
3:     **for all** nodes $v \notin \mathcal{S}$ **do**
4:         Compute coverage score: number of $\mathcal{RR}$ sets containing v
5:         Compute normalized score: score$/\mathcal{C}(v)$
6:     **end for**
7:     Select node v^* with highest normalized score within budget
8:     **if** no such node exists **then**
9:         **break**
10:     **end if**
11:     $\mathcal{S} \leftarrow \mathcal{S} \cup \{v^*\}$, RemainingBudget $\leftarrow$ RemainingBudget - $\mathcal{C}(v^*)$
12:     Mark RR sets covered by v^*
13: **end while**
14: **return** $\mathcal{S}$

3.2 Part (ii): Greedy-Based Approach for Node Selection of the Seed Set

The GREEDYSEEDSELECTION procedure (Algorithm 4) selects an optimal seed set under a budget constraint using precomputed $\mathcal{RR}$ sets. It starts with an empty seed set $\mathcal{S}$ and budget $\mathcal{B}$ (Line 1), then iteratively adds nodes while the budget remains (Line 2). In each round, all candidate nodes $v \notin \mathcal{S}$ are evaluated: their coverage score is the number of $\mathcal{RR}$ sets containing v (Line 4), normalized by cost $\mathcal{C}(v)$ (Line 5). The node v^* with the highest affordable normalized score is chosen (Line 7). If no node fits the budget, the loop terminates (Lines 8–10). Otherwise, v^* is added to $\mathcal{S}$, its cost subtracted, and its covered $\mathcal{RR}$ sets marked (Lines 11–12) to avoid double counting. This process repeats until the budget is exhausted or no nodes remain, and the final seed set $\mathcal{S}$ is returned (Line 14).

Complexity Analysis. In Algorithm 4, initialization (Line 1) takes $\mathcal{O}(1)$ time. The main cost is the `while` loop (Lines 2–13), which may run up to $\mathcal{B}/C_{\min}$ times, where $C_{\min} = \min_{v \in \mathcal{V}} \mathcal{C}(v)$. In each iteration, computing coverage scores for all $n = |\mathcal{V}|$ nodes requires processing θ $\mathcal{RR}$ sets, giving $\mathcal{O}(n \cdot \theta \cdot |\mathcal{RR}(v)|)$. In the worst case $|\mathcal{RR}(v)| = n$, i.e., $\mathcal{O}(\theta \cdot n^2)$. Normalized score computation (Line 5) and node selection (Line 7) add $\mathcal{O}(n)$ each, but are dominated as well. Marking covered $\mathcal{RR}$ sets (Line 12) takes $\mathcal{O}(\theta \cdot n)$. Hence, each iteration costs $\mathcal{O}(\theta \cdot n^2)$, and the overall time complexity is $\mathcal{O}\left(\frac{\mathcal{B}}{C_{\min}} \cdot \theta \cdot n^2\right)$. The space complexity is $\mathcal{O}(n + \theta \cdot n) = \mathcal{O}(\theta \cdot n)$ (as $\mathcal{RR}$ sets dominate the overall cost), for maintaining node scores and marked $\mathcal{RR}$ sets.

Algorithm 5 ProcessMotifProfit

    Input: Simulation results $\{A_i\}$, Motifs $\mathcal{M}$, Benefit $b(\cdot)$, Threshold τ, Seed cost $\mathcal{C}(\mathcal{S})$

    Output: Average motif-based profit

1: **for** each simulation A_i **do**
2:     Identify $\mathcal{M}_i \leftarrow \{m \in \mathcal{M} \mid |m \cap A_i| \geq \tau\}$
3:     $B_i \leftarrow \sum_{v \in \cup \mathcal{M}_i} b(v)$
4:     $\Pi_i \leftarrow B_i - \mathcal{C}(\mathcal{S})$
5: **end for**
6: **return** $\frac{1}{T} \sum_i \Pi_i$

3.3   Part (iii): Computation of Motif-Based Profit

The PROCESSMOTIFPROFIT procedure (Algorithm 5) concludes the RIS framework by computing the average motif-based profit from a given seed set using multiple diffusion simulations under the IC model. It takes as input the simulation results $\{A_i\}$, a motif set $\mathcal{M}$, benefit function $b(\cdot)$, threshold τ, and seed cost C. For each simulation A_i, motifs $\mathcal{M}_i$ are considered active if $|m \cap A_i| \geq \tau$ (Line 1–2). The benefit B_i is then the sum of $b(v)$ over all nodes in the union of active motifs (Line 3), and the net profit Π_i is $B_i - \mathcal{C}(\mathcal{S})$ (Line 4). After T simulations, the average profit $\frac{1}{T} \sum_i \Pi_i$ is returned (Line 6).

Complexity Analysis. The time complexity of Algorithm 5 depends on the number of simulations T, motifs $|\mathcal{M}|$, motif size s, and nodes n. In each simulation, checking threshold activation costs $\mathcal{O}(s)$ per motif, or $\mathcal{O}(|\mathcal{M}|\,s)$ in total. Computing the benefit B_i then requires at most $\mathcal{O}(n)$ time. Hence, the per-simulation cost is $\mathcal{O}(|\mathcal{M}|\,s + n)$, and over T simulations the total runtime is $\mathcal{O}(T(|\mathcal{M}|\,s + n))$. The space complexity is $\mathcal{O}(|\mathcal{M}|s + n)$, for storing motif definitions and activated nodes.

Therefore, the overall time complexity of our proposed approach (Algorithm 1) is $\mathcal{O}\left((n+m)\log n + \theta(n+m) + \frac{\mathcal{B}}{C_{\min}} \cdot \theta \cdot n^2 + T(|\mathcal{M}|\,s+n)\right)$. The overall space complexity is $\mathcal{O}(n + m + \theta \cdot n + |\mathcal{M}|\,s + T \cdot n)$.

4   Experimental Evaluation

We next present the experimental evaluation of the proposed approach, beginning with the datasets.

4.1   Dataset Description

Our experiments use the following networks:

- **US Congress** (Congress) [5,6]: Twitter interaction network for the 117th United States Congress (House and Senate).
- **Email-Eu-Core** (Euemail) [11,16]: Built from email exchanges in a large European research institution; an edge (u,v) exists if u sent v at least one email.
- **Wikipedia Vote** (Wikivote) [9,10]: Voting data from Wikipedia's inception to Jan 2008; nodes are users and a directed edge (u,v) means u voted on v.

Table 1. Basic statistics of the datasets used in our experiments.

Dataset Name	Type of Graph	Number of Nodes $|\mathcal{V}|$	Number of Edges $|\mathcal{E}|$	Maximum Degree $d_{\max}$	Average Degree d_{avg}
US Congress	Directed	475	13289	284	55.95
Email-Eu-Core	Directed	1005	25571	546	50.89
Wiki-Vote	Directed	7115	103689	1167	29.15

All the datasets have been downloaded from Stanford Large Network Dataset Collection[1]. Table 1 describes the basic statistics of the datasets.

---

[1] https://snap.stanford.edu/data/index.html.

4.2   Experimental Setup

In our study, several parameters need to be defined, beginning with the influence probability setting. *Influence Probability*: We consider two settings:

- **Trivalency**: Each edge is assigned a probability uniformly at random from $\{0.1, 0.01, 0.001\}$.
- **Weighted Cascade**: Each edge (u, v) has probability inversely proportional to the in-degree of v, i.e., $\frac{1}{deg^{in}(v)}$.

Cost and Benefit Values: We use a degree-proportional cost setting, where a higher out-degree implies a higher cost, as in practice (e.g., celebrities with more followers demand higher fees). The benefit of each node is then assigned by scaling its cost.

4.3   Baseline Methods

We compare our proposed methodology against the following baselines:

- **Random**: Nodes are selected randomly until the budget is exhausted.
- **High Degree**: Nodes are ranked by degree and selected in order until the budget is exhausted.
- **CELF**: A popular influence maximization algorithm by Leskovec et al. [12], adapted here for profit maximization.
- **Simple Greedy**: Starting with an empty set, nodes are added iteratively based on marginal profit gain [7].

All baselines were implemented in Python 3.0.1+ with NetworkX 2.2.1, and experiments were run on a Linux desktop with 64 GB RAM and a 32-core Intel i9 processor.

4.4   Experimental Results and Discussions

We have analyzed three datasets for our experiments, which are listed in Table 1. Our research objective is to evaluate how well the algorithms work with the structural pattern of the graph, i.e., motifs. The metric used for comparison is the motif-based profit earned under a given budget. We also aim to understand which threshold values are effective in maximizing motif-based profit. For the Congress dataset (Figs. 1 and 2), experiments were conducted for motif sizes 2, 3, and 4. We compared Random, High Degree, CELF, and Simple Greedy with the Motif Oriented RIS approach. Across all probability settings, motif profit increases monotonically with budget, and RIS consistently outperforms all other algorithms. Simple Greedy and CELF are often competitive, while Random and High Degree perform similarly. For instance, at budget 10 under Trivalency probability settings, RIS achieves 1323.8 units of profit, compared to 794.9 for Simple Greedy (66% less) and 770.5 for CELF (71% less). High Degree and Random perform much worse, with RIS producing 110% and 153% higher profits, respectively. Similar trends are observed across other budgets and motif sizes. In the Weighted Cascade probability setting, RIS again outperforms all approaches by large margins (Figs. 2(a)–(f)). On average, RIS generates about 10990% more profit than Random, 4644% more than High Degree, 2222% more than CELF, and 5873% more than Simple Greedy. The Euemail dataset shows even more striking results (Figs. 3, 4). Under Trivalency, RIS outperforms by 260% over Random, 229% over High Degree, 188% over CELF, and 193% over Simple Greedy. Under Weighted Cascade, RIS gains are enormous, reaching up to 85586% compared to Random, 22509% over High Degree, 16105% over CELF, and 81017% over Simple Greedy. The Wikivote dataset (Fig. 5) further confirms this trend. Random, High Degree, and Simple Greedy perform about 105% worse than RIS, while CELF is 102% worse.

We next analyze the impact of threshold values of different motif sizes. In the Congress dataset, at threshold 2, motif profits are higher as motifs are activated more easily. RIS remains the best performer, e.g., achieving 1755 units at budget 50 under Weighted Cascade probability setting for motif size 2 (Fig. 2(a)). CELF and Simple Greedy reach about 60–100% of RIS's performance, while Random and High Degree remain significantly lower. At threshold 3, profits decline for all algorithms, though RIS still leads. Stricter thresholds reduce overall profits since fewer motifs activate, but RIS continues to dominate. For example, at budget 40 under Weighted Cascade, RIS profits are reduced but still higher than all baselines, with Random and High Degree nearly negligible. In Fig. 1, CELF achieves up to 79% of RIS at threshold 2 for motif size 2 and remains closer to RIS in motif sizes 3 and 4 for thresholds 2 and 3. The Euemail dataset shows similar threshold effects. Lower thresholds yield higher profits, while values closer to motif size reduce profits. For example, in Trivalency with motif size 4 at budget 10 (Fig. 3(d)–(f)), Random achieves 8410.31 at threshold 2, 5403.61 at threshold 3, and only 1997.59 at threshold 4. RIS consistently leads: in Weighted Cascade with motif size 4 at budget 10 (Fig. 4(d)–(f)), it performs 326% better than Simple Greedy at threshold 2, 1506% better at threshold 3, and 20483% better at threshold 4. The Wikivote dataset also reflects these effects (Fig. 5(b)–(c)): at budget 30 for motif size 3, Simple Greedy performs 97% worse (threshold 2) and 103% worse (threshold 3) than RIS.

Across all datasets, RIS consistently outperforms Random, High Degree, CELF, and Simple Greedy, confirming its superiority in exploiting motifs. While CELF and Simple Greedy are occasionally competitive, Random and High Degree perform poorly, especially under the Weighted Cascade probability setting. Threshold analysis shows that smaller thresholds give higher profits, while stricter ones reduce them across all algorithms. Nonetheless, RIS remains the clear leader, showing robustness under varying activation criteria.

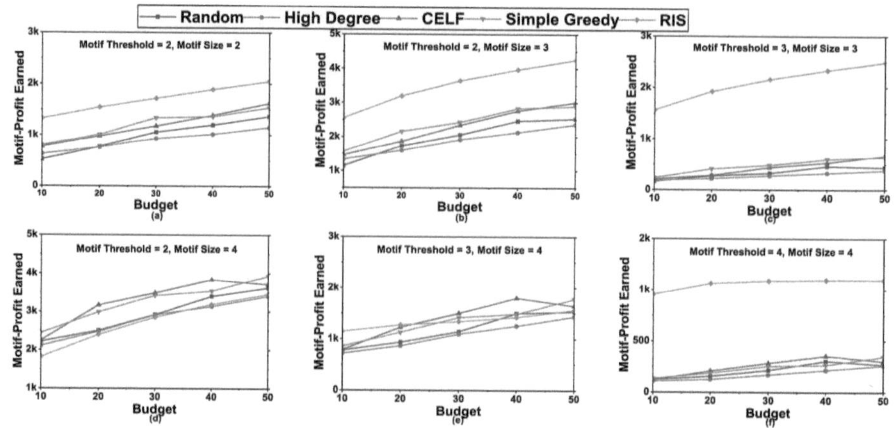

Fig. 1. Budget vs. Motif-Profit for Congress (Trivalency).

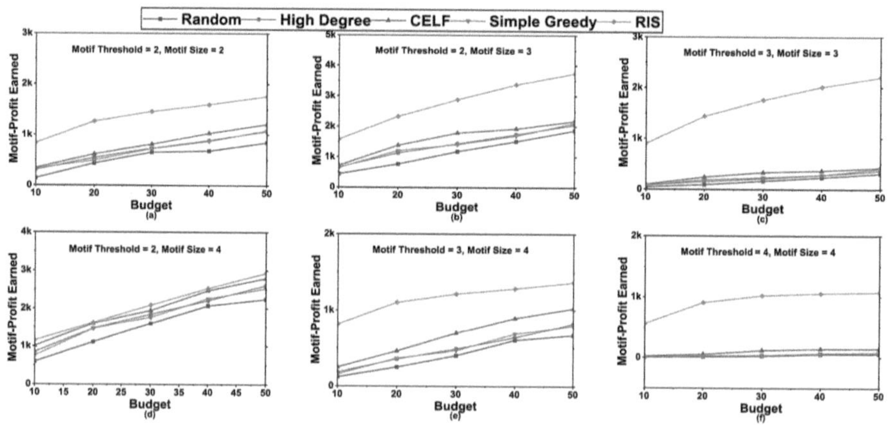

Fig. 2. Budget vs. Motif-Profit for Congress (Weighted Cascade).

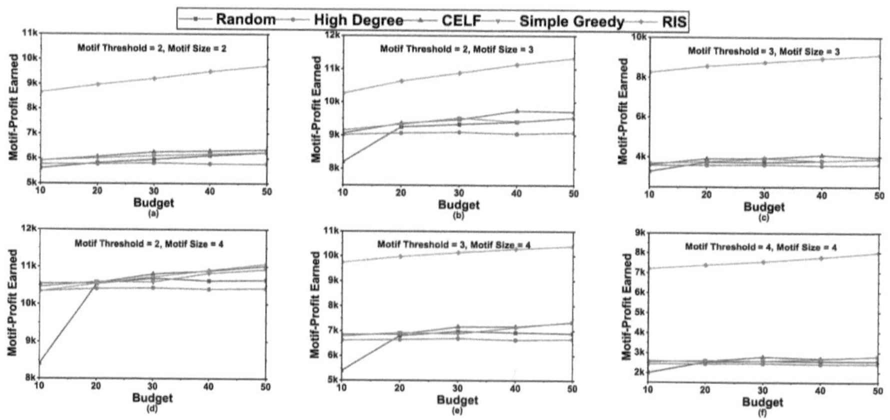

Fig. 3. Budget vs. Motif-Profit for Euemail (Trivalency).

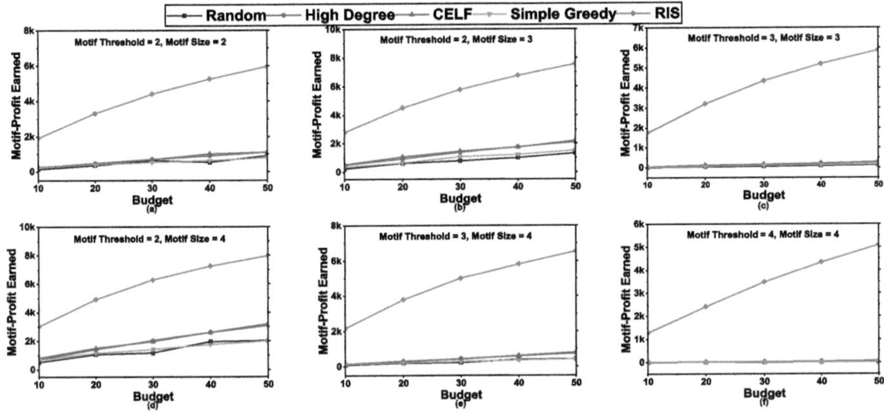

Fig. 4. Budget vs. Motif-Profit for Euemail (Weighted Cascade).

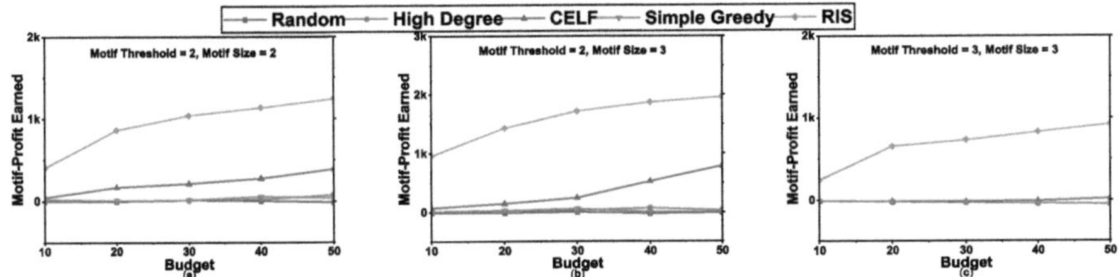

Fig. 5. Budget vs. Motif-Profit for Wikivote (Weighted Cascade).

5   Concluding Remarks

In this paper, we have studied the Motif-Oriented Profit Maximization Problem, where, given a social network with the selection cost of the nodes and a set of motifs with their corresponding benefit value, this problem asks to choose a limited number of highly influential nodes within a budget such that the motif oriented earned profit gets maximized. This problem is NP-hard to solve optimally. We have proposed a reverse reachable set-based solution approach. The experimental results with real-world social network datasets show the effectiveness of the proposed solution approach, motif oriented RIS. Our approach proves to be robust across datasets, probability settings, and threshold values, establishing its effectiveness in exploiting motif structures for profit maximization. Now, our future study on this problem will remain concentrated on developing more efficient solution methodologies.

References

1. Arnaboldi, V., Conti, M., Passarella, A., Dunbar, R.I.: Online social networks and information diffusion: the role of ego networks. Online Soc. Netw. Media **1**, 44–55 (2017)

2. Bakshy, E., Rosenn, I., Marlow, C., Adamic, L.: The role of social networks in information diffusion. In: Proceedings of the 21st International Conference on World Wide Web, pp. 519–528 (2012)
3. Chen, W., Wang, C., Wang, Y.: Scalable influence maximization for prevalent viral marketing in large-scale social networks. In: Proceedings of the 16th ACM SIGKDD International Conference on Knowledge Discovery and Data Mining, pp. 1029–1038. ACM (2010)
4. Domingos, P., Richardson, M.: Mining the network value of customers. In: Proceedings of the Seventh ACM SIGKDD International Conference on Knowledge Discovery and Data Mining, pp. 57–66. ACM (2001)
5. Fink, C.G., et al.: A centrality measure for quantifying spread on weighted, directed networks. Physica A (2023)
6. Fink, C.G., Omodt, N., Zinnecker, S., Sprint, G.: A congressional twitter network dataset quantifying pairwise probability of influence. Data Brief (2023)
7. Kempe, D., Kleinberg, J., Tardos, É.: Maximizing the spread of influence through a social network. In: Proceedings of the Ninth ACM SIGKDD International Conference on Knowledge Discovery and Data Mining, pp. 137–146. ACM (2003)
8. Kempe, D., Kleinberg, J., Tardos, É.: Influential nodes in a diffusion model for social networks. In: International Colloquium on Automata, Languages, and Programming, pp. 1127–1138. Springer (2005)
9. Leskovec, J., Huttenlocher, D., Kleinberg, J.: Predicting positive and negative links in online social networks. In: Proceedings of the 19th International Conference on World Wide Web, pp. 641–650 (2010)
10. Leskovec, J., Huttenlocher, D., Kleinberg, J.: Signed networks in social media. In: Proceedings of the SIGCHI Conference on Human Factors in Computing Systems, pp. 1361–1370 (2010)
11. Leskovec, J., Kleinberg, J., Faloutsos, C.: Graph evolution: densification and shrinking diameters. ACM Trans. Knowl. Discov. Data (TKDD) $1(1)$, 2 (2007)
12. Leskovec, J., et al.: Cost-effective outbreak detection in networks. In: Proceedings of the 13th ACM SIGKDD International Conference on Knowledge Discovery and Data Mining, pp. 420–429. ACM (2007)
13. Lu, W., Lakshmanan, L.V.: Profit maximization over social networks. In: 2012 IEEE 12th International Conference on Data Mining, pp. 479–488. IEEE (2012)
14. Richardson, M., Domingos, P.: Mining knowledge-sharing sites for viral marketing. In: Proceedings of the Eighth ACM SIGKDD International Conference on Knowledge Discovery and Data Mining, pp. 61–70. ACM (2002)
15. Tang, Y., Xiao, X., Shi, Y.: Influence maximization: near-optimal time complexity meets practical efficiency. In: Proceedings of the 2014 ACM SIGMOD International Conference on Management of Data, pp. 75–86. ACM (2014)
16. Yin, H., Benson, A.R., Leskovec, J., Gleich, D.F.: Local higher-order graph clustering. In: Proceedings of the 23rd ACM SIGKDD International Conference on Knowledge Discovery and Data Mining, pp. 555–564 (2017)
17. Zhou, M., Cao, W., Liao, H., Mao, R.: Motif-oriented influence maximization for viral marketing in large-scale social networks. In: Globerson, A., et al. (eds.) Advances in Neural Information Processing Systems, vol. 37, pp. 135861–135882. Curran Associates, Inc. (2024)

AI-INT: An AI-Driven Telemetry Framework for Programmable Networks

Amit Kumar Singh$^{(\boxtimes)}$ [iD] and Mayank Pandey [iD]

Department of Computer Science and Engineering, MNNIT Allahabad,
Prayagraj, India
`{amit.2021rcs02,mayankpandey}@mnnit.ac.in`

Abstract. The growing demand for real-time and application-specific insights in modern networks has elevated the significance of In-band Network Telemetry (INT). INT, enabled by programmable data planes and a domain-specific programming language, P4 provides fine-grained, hop-by-hop insights into network traffic. While INT enables fine-grained packet monitoring across programmable switches, its uniform deployment across all traffic flows can lead to substantial overhead and inefficient resource consumption. To address this challenge, we propose a novel AI-driven telemetry framework that combines flow intelligence with INT activation. This paper proposes an AI-assisted INT (AI-INT) framework that leverages the programmable data plane using P4 and ONOS, in combination with a Multi-Layer Perceptron (MLP) model for real-time traffic classification. Upon flow detection, the classifier predicts the traffic class, and ONOS installs appropriate telemetry and forwarding rules on the BMv2 switch, accounting for the current network state. This integrated system enables efficient, dynamic, and application-aware telemetry that minimizes overhead while maintaining observability. We present the architecture, implementation details, and evaluation results that demonstrate significant gains in overhead reduction and resource utilization.

Keywords: In-band Network Telemetry (INT) · Programmable Data Plane · P4 · ONOS · Traffic Classification · Multi-Layer Perceptron (MLP) · Resource Optimization

1 Introduction

Modern communication networks are the backbone of a digitally interconnected world, facilitating an ever-increasing volume and diversity of applications. From latency-sensitive financial transactions to bandwidth-intensive video streaming, each application presents unique demands on network resources. To ensure optimal performance, security, and service quality, network operators require **real-time, fine-grained, granular insights** about the network behavior. Traditional network monitoring approaches, often relying on passive methods like SNMP [10] or NetFlow [11], provide aggregated views that lack the per-packet,

B. Chatterjee et al. (Eds.): ICDCIT 2026, LNCS 16420, pp. 317–330, 2026.
https://doi.org/10.1007/978-3-032-16632-6_20

hop-by-hop detail crucial for diagnosing microbursts, identifying bottlenecks, or detecting anomalies with precision. **INT** [14] has emerged as a transformative technology to address this gap. INT is enabled by the advent of programmable data planes and domain-specific languages like P4 [8]. INT allows network devices to collect and insert telemetry metadata directly into data packets as they traverse the network, as shown in Fig. 1.

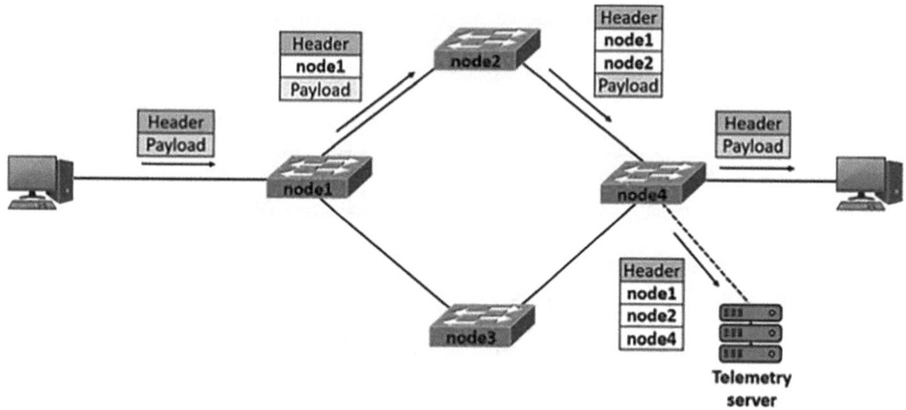

Fig. 1. INT Process.

However, the power of INT comes with a significant challenge **overhead**. Applying INT to all network traffic can lead to substantial increases in packet size, reduced throughput, increased latency, and heightened processing loads on network devices. This overhead problem is due to the uniform development of the model without considering the application requirements and the current network conditions. Not all traffic flows require the same level of detailed monitoring; we need a solution to reduce this overhead issue. To mitigate this challenge, we propose **AI-INT**. This AI-assisted INT framework intelligently and dynamically activates INT based on the specific characteristics and importance of network traffic flows. By integrating flow intelligence with programmable data planes, AI-INT aims to provide **application-aware telemetry** that optimizes resource utilization without compromising essential observability. Our framework leverages a Multi-Layer Perceptron (MLP) model for real-time traffic classification, deployed in conjunction with an ONOS controller [7] and P4-programmable switches (BMv2). This synergy enables the network to learn, adapt, and make intelligent decisions about which flows warrant deep, in-band inspection and which do not, reducing telemetry overhead significantly while maintaining high diagnostic fidelity for critical traffic. The primary contributions of this paper are:

- The design and architecture of AI-INT, a novel framework for intelligent, dynamic INT activation in programmable networks.

- The integration of a real-time MLP-based traffic classifier with an SDN controller (ONOS) and P4 data plane.
- Demonstrating the framework's effectiveness in reducing telemetry overhead and resource utilization.

The remainder of this paper is structured as follows: Sect. 2 discusses background concepts and related work. Section 3 presents the detailed architecture of the AI-INT framework. Section 4 elaborates on the algorithms underpinning AI-INT. Section 5 describes our implementation details. Section 6 provides an evaluation of the framework. Finally, Sect. 7 concludes the paper and outlines future research directions.

2   Background and Related Work

This section provides an overview of the foundational technologies underpinning AI-INT and surveys some existing efforts in network telemetry and intelligent network management.

2.1   Software-Defined Networking (SDN) and ONOS

SDN [9] decouples the network's control plane from its data plane, centralizing network intelligence and management. An SDN controller provides a holistic view of the network and an API for applications to program network behavior. This centralized control enables dynamic policy enforcement, traffic engineering, and agile service deployment. **ONOS** [7] is an open-source SDN controller specifically designed for service providers and enterprises, offering high performance, scalability, and robust APIs. ONOS can interact with programmable switches via protocols like P4 Runtime [12], which allows the controller to install and modify P4 programs and flow rules on the data plane. In our proposed approach, ONOS is the orchestrator, translating AI-driven insights into actionable P4 flow rules for dynamic INT activation.

2.2   Programmable Data Planes and P4

The concept of a **programmable data plane** [16]has revolutionized network device functionality. P4 [8] emerged as a high-level, domain-specific programming language that allows developers to precisely define how packets are parsed, processed, and forwarded by network devices. P4 programs are compiled into device-specific configurations such as Intel's Tofino [2] and BMv2 (Behavioral Model version 2) [1] software switch. This programmability empowers network operators to deploy custom protocols, implement novel forwarding behaviors, and embed advanced telemetry mechanisms directly within the data packets. P4's match-action table abstraction provides a flexible and efficient way to define packet processing logic, making it ideal for implementing INT operations.

2.3   In-band Network Telemetry (INT)

INT [3]leverages programmable data planes to insert telemetry metadata into packet headers as they traverse a network. Each hop capable of INT processing can add its local state to a designated metadata field within the packet. Upon reaching an egress point or a designated telemetry sink, this enriched packet is either forwarded normally or sent to a collector for analysis. The working in INT is shown in Fig. 1.

2.4   AI/ML in Network Management

The application of Artificial Intelligence (AI) and Machine Learning (ML) in network management has gained significant traction [5]. ML models can identify complex patterns in network data that are difficult for human operators or rule-based systems to detect. Typical applications of AI/ML in networking are **Traffic Classification** [20],**Anomaly Detection** [18], **Resource Management** [15], and **Predictive Maintenance** [13] and forecasting network failures to enable proactive intervention. Various ML models have been employed, but for real-time, low-latency classification, simpler neural networks like **Multi-Layer Perceptrons (MLPs)** [19] offer a good balance of accuracy and computational efficiency.

2.5   Related Work

Several research efforts have attempted to address the INT overhead problem based on sampling such as PINT [6] DINT [17] suggest sampling traffic flows and applying INT only to sampled packets or flows. While reducing overhead, sampling inherently sacrifices granularity and may miss short-lived anomalies some approaches based on **Policy-driven INT** [4] which involves predefined policies based on application types or critical network segments to activate INT. While effective for known critical flows, it lacks adaptability to dynamic network conditions or emerging threats. However, many focus on static optimization or require significant offline analysis. Our AI-INT framework offers a **closed-loop, real-time, and application-aware dynamic INT activation system**. It uniquely combines the strengths of P4's data plane programmability, ONOS's centralized control, and an MLP's real-time classification capabilities to make informed, adaptive decisions about INT deployment, explicitly considering the current network state to avoid global performance degradation.

3   AI-INT Framework Architecture

The AI-INT framework integrates a programmable data plane, an SDN controller, and an AI-driven classification engine to provide dynamic and intelligent INT. The architecture consists of three primary logical components: the **Programmable Data Plane**, the **SDN Control Plane**, and the **AI/ML Decision Plane** connected as shown in Fig. 2.

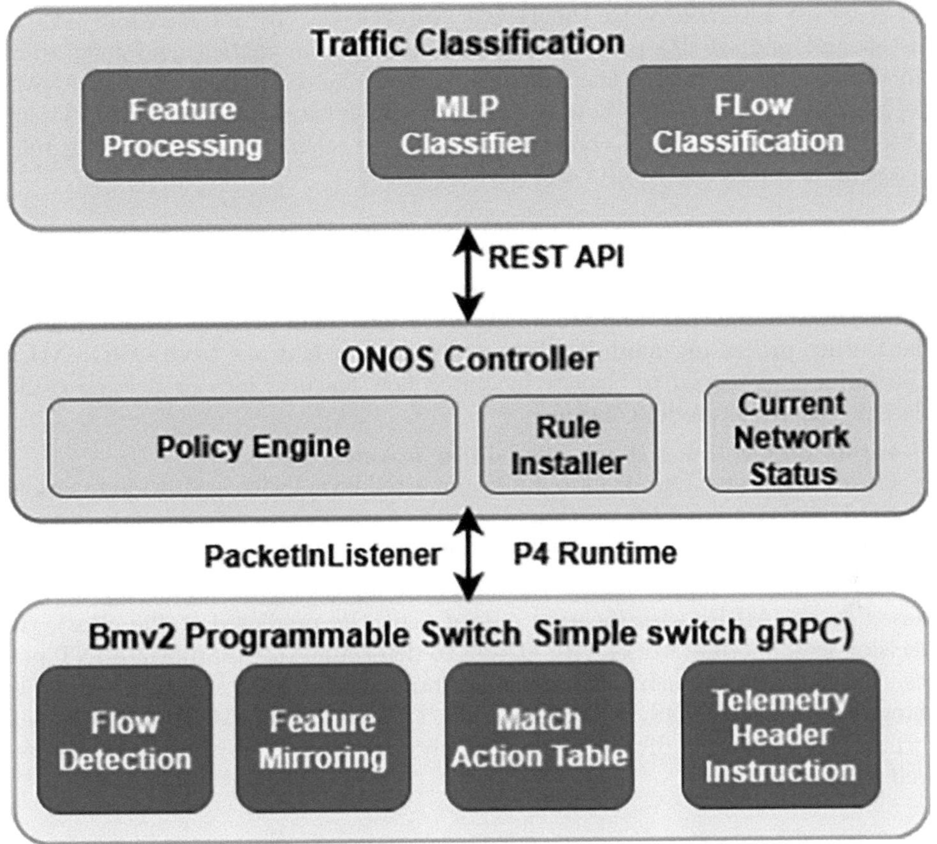

Fig. 2. AI-INT Framework Architecture.

3.1 Working at Programmable Data Plane

Each switch contains a basic P4 program which is responsible for **Flow Identification** by extracting key header fields (e.g., source/destination IP, port numbers, protocol) to identify unique traffic flows and **Feature Extraction** for new or unknown flows. Specific fields are extracted, calculated, and mirrored to the SDN controller for classification and **INT Metadata Insertion/Extraction** for a flow. The P4 program inserts relevant INT metadata into the packet header if it is marked for telemetry. It forwards the packet based on installed rules.

3.2 Working at SDN Control Plane

The **ONOS controller** is the central orchestrator of our proposed AI-INT framework. Its responsibilities include network topology management to maintain a comprehensive, real-time view of the network topology, including switch capabilities and link states. This plane is also responsible for configuring the

P4 Runtime Interface with the BMv2 switches via the P4 Runtime API to install and manage P4 programs, match-action table entries, and forwarding rules. This plane serves as the interface between the data plane and the AI/ML decision plane, forwarding flow features for classification and receiving classification results. The ONOS controller installs the telemetry or forwarding rules based on classification results and network state.

3.3   Working at AI Driven Traffic Classifier Plane

The **AI/ML Decision Plane** is the core of the AI-INT framework, primarily responsible for real-time traffic classification. This plane is responsible for the feature processing module when receiving flow features from ONOS.**MLP Classifier** is deployed to classify incoming flow features into predefined traffic classes. The MLP model contains:

- **Input Layer:** Takes the processed flow features.
- **Hidden Layers:** One or more fully connected layers with activation functions ReLU to learn complex patterns.
- **Output Layer:** Typically a softmax activation function, providing probabilities for each traffic class.

Based on the MLP's classification output (i.e., the predicted traffic class), the decision logic module works with ONOS to determine the appropriate INT policy. The AI/ML Decision Plane can be implemented as a separate service or integrated as an ONOS application. The training of the MLP model is performed offline using a diverse dataset of network traffic, ensuring it generalizes well to unseen flows.

3.4   Workflow Model

This section discusses the workflow model of our proposed method (AI-INT). The interaction between the components of our proposed framework follows a structured workflow explained in the following steps.

- **Flow Detection:** A new packet arrives at P4 switch. The switch identifies it as a new flow based on flow rules.
- **Feature Mirroring:** The P4 switch extracts initial features of the new flow's first few packets and mirrors them to the ONOS controller.
- **Classification Request:** ONOS receives the features and forwards them to the AI/ML Decision Plane.
- **Real-time Classification:** The Feature Processing Module preprocesses the features, and the MLP Classifier predicts the traffic class.
- **Policy Decision:** The Decision Logic Module, in conjunction with ONOS, determines the appropriate INT activation policy and forwarding strategy based on the predicted traffic class and current network state.
- **Rule Installation:** ONOS uses P4 runtime to install or modify flow rules on the P4 switch.
- **Telemetry Reporting:** If INT is enabled, the collected telemetry data is sent to a central collector for analysis.

4   Methodology

The AI-INT framework operates through a series of interconnected algorithmic steps, orchestrating the programmable data plane, SDN controller, and AI/ML engine. When a new flow is detected at the data plane, the initial set of packets is analyzed to extract relevant features. These features form an input vector for a trained machine learning classifier that predicts the flow type. Based on the predicted category, the algorithm selects an appropriate telemetry policy that specifies which metadata fields should be inserted into the packets. The complete process is explained in Algorithm 1.

4.1   Algorithm 1: AI-INT Framework Orchestration

This algorithm describes the high-level workflow of the AI-INT framework, managed primarily by the ONOS controller.
Input: Network traffic, Pre-trained MLP Model, P4 Switch Capabilities
Output: Dynamically updated P4 flow rules for intelligent INT activation

Initialization Phase (Controller Startup):

1. **Load P4 Program:** ONOS compiles and loads the base P4 program (defining INT header formats, basic forwarding, and feature extraction mechanisms) onto all participating BMv2 switches via P4 Runtime.
2. **Initialize MLP:** Load the pre-trained MLP model into the AI/ML Decision Plane.
3. **Establish Data Plane Communication:** ONOS establishes control channels with all P4 switches.
4. **Network State Monitoring:** ONOS starts monitoring network-wide metrics periodically.

Main Loop (Event-Driven Phase):

Algorithm 1 AI-INT Framework Orchestration

1: **while** network operating **do**
2:     $EVENT$ = LISTEN_FOR_NETWORK_EVENTS()
3:     **if** $EVENT$ == "NEW_FLOW" at Switch S, with $Flow\_Features$ F **then**
4:         $Flow\_ID$ = EXTRACT_FLOW_ID(F)
5:         $Network\_State$ = GET_CURRENT_NETWORK_STATE()
6:         $Predicted\_Class$ = CLASSIFY_FLOW(F, MLP_Model)
7:         INT_Policy = DETERMINE_INT_POLICY($Predicted\_Class$, $Network\_State$)
8:         INSTALL_TELEMETRY_RULES($Switch$ S, $Flow\_ID$, INT_Policy)
9:     **else if** $EVENT$ == "FLOW_UPDATE"or"NETWORK_STATE_CHANGE"
        then
10:         **for** each $Active\_Flow$ in Network **do**
11:             **if**   CONDITION_REQUIRES_RE_EVALUATION($Active\_Flow$, Net-
                $work\_State$) **then**
12:                 $Re\_Predicted\_Class$ =   CLASSIFY_FLOW($Active\_Features\_of\_Flow$,
                    MLP_Model)
13:                 New_INT_Policy =   DETERMINE_INT_POLICY($Re\_Predicted\_Class$,
                    $Network\_State$)
14:                 UPDATE_TELEMETRY_RULES($Actie\_Flow$.Switch,$Active\_Flow$.ID,
                    New_INT_Policy)
15:             **end if**
16:         **end for**
17:     **else if** $EVENT$ == "TELEMETRY_REPORT_RECEIVED" **then**
18:         PROCESS_TELEMETRY_REPORT($EVENT$.Dat)
19:     **end if**
20: **end while**

The orchestration Algorithm 1 governs the operation of the AI-INT framework through two phases. When a new flow is detected, its features are classified by the MLP, and the appropriate telemetry policy is derived based on both flow characteristics and current network state. The policy is then enforced through updated P4 rules. If flows or network conditions change, policies are re-evaluated and adjusted dynamically.

5   Implementation Details

Implementing the AIINT framework involves careful integration of several open-source and custom components. This section outlines the practical aspects of our prototype implementation. We developed a custom P4 program (`ai_int.p4`) for the BMv2 software switch. This program includes: **Custom INT Header** to carry various telemetry metadata fields (e.g., timestamp, ingress_port, egress_port, queue_depth, switch_id, CPU_utilization) and a **Flow Match-Action Tables** `flow_lookup` table to match on 5-tuple (sourcedestination IP, sourcedestination port, protocol) and a `int_control` table to enabledisable INT based on a policy ID. P4 `clone` actions are used to send the first few packets of a new flow to a designated controller port. The P4 program extracts initial packet length, IP protocol, TCP flags, and TCP window size before mirroring. The P4 program is utilized to push the custom INT header and populate its fields with runtime data plane values. An additional action of the P4 program is to encapsulate INT-enabled packets into a report format and forward them to a separate telemetry collector. We used `simple_switch_grpc` instances from the behavioral model, running on Ubuntu Linux virtual machines. Each switch instance is launched with the compiled `ai_int.json` generated using the p4c compiler to simulate a network topology. **ONOS** is utilized in our implementation, which is used to manage the network. It provides native support for P4 Runtime. We developed an ONOS application that uses the `P4RuntimeController` and `FlowRuleService` APIs. The ONOS application includes an `PacketInListener`, a custom P4Runtime stream channel listener, to receive mirrored packets and flow feature notifications from the P4 switches. A REST API is used by the ONOS application to communicate with the external AI/ML decision plane. This API allows ONOS to send flow features and receive classification results. Upon receiving a classification result, the ONOS application dynamically constructs P4 Runtime `TableEntry` messages (using the `p4info.txt` generated by p4c) and installs them on the relevant BMv2 switch's `flow_lookup` and `int_control` tables. Rules include `idle_timeout` values to enable re-evaluation if a flow remains active for an extended period. A separate ONOS module periodically queries switch statistics to gather real-time link utilization, queue occupancy, and CPU load, making this information available to the decision logic module.

A Multi-Layer Perceptron (MLP) is implemented using **TensorFlow**. We experimented with different configurations, ultimately settling on an MLP with two hidden layers with 64 and 32 neurons, respectively, using ReLU activation functions, and a softmax output layer for multi-class classification. The model was trained offline using a custom dataset generated from a mix of publicly available traffic traces, MAWI, and synthetically generated traffic representing various application types (HTTP, FTP, VoIP, Video, and Gaming). Data was carefully labeled into target classes. The model was trained using a standard categorical cross-entropy loss function and the Adam optimizer. A separate module running on the control plane determines the INT policy based on the MLP's output and the current network state. This logic is configurable via a simple JSON file, allowing operators to easily define thresholds and priorities for INT activation based on predicted class and network conditions. The AI/ML decision plane runs as a standalone Python Flask application, making it accessible to the ONOS controller via REST API calls.

5.1 Testbed Setup

Our experimental testbed comprised an Ubuntu Linux VM where several software programs, like ONOS controller, BMv2 switches, and others, as traffic generators/receivers utilities are installed. Mininet was used to construct custom network topologies, allowing us to connect BMv2 instances and client/server applications within a controlled environment. `iPerf3`, `hping3`, and custom

Python scripts are used to generate diverse traffic patterns mimicking different applications. A simple Python script acted as an INT collector, receiving and parsing telemetry reports from the P4 switches. This setup allowed us to rigorously test the AI-INT framework under various network conditions and evaluate its performance against predefined metrics.

6   Evaluation

The evaluation of the AI-INT framework focused on validating its core objectives, reducing telemetry overhead, optimizing resource utilization, and demonstrating adaptability to application-specific monitoring needs. We conducted experiments in a Mininet-emulated environment with BMv2 switches controlled by ONOS and the AI/ML Decision Plane. A topology shown in Fig. 3 was used to simulate our proposed method in a controlled environment.

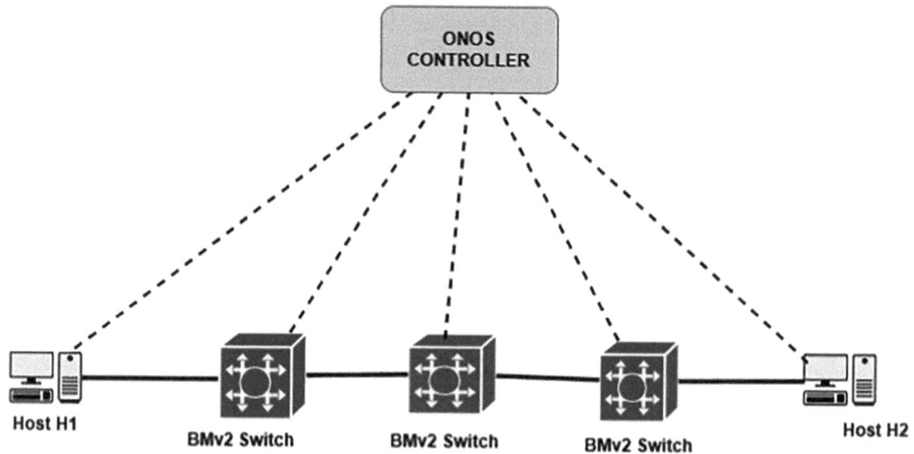

Fig. 3. Topology Used for Experiment.

We generated a diverse set of network traffic flows, encompassing **high-priority and latency-sensitive traffic** (e.g., VoIP and online gaming), **bandwidth-intensive traffic** (e.g., video streaming and bulk data transfer), and **interactive or best-effort traffic** (e.g., web browsing). The proposed AI-INT framework was evaluated by comparing its performance in terms of **telemetry overhead** and **resource utilization** to demonstrate and compare the effectiveness of the proposed methodology.

6.1   Result and Discussion

Based on the experiments performed on our testbed, we compare the outcomes of the experiment of the various parameters and come to the decision that our proposed approach (AI-INT) performed well in my small topology, and it should also work for bigger networks. The Comparisons are shown below.

Telemetry Overhead Comparison. AI-INT achieved a **significant reduction in telemetry overhead**, ranging from **60% to 85%** compared to the Full INT baseline, depending on the traffic mix. This reduction directly correlated with the proportion of non-critical traffic flows for which INT was intelligently disabled or limited (Fig. 4).

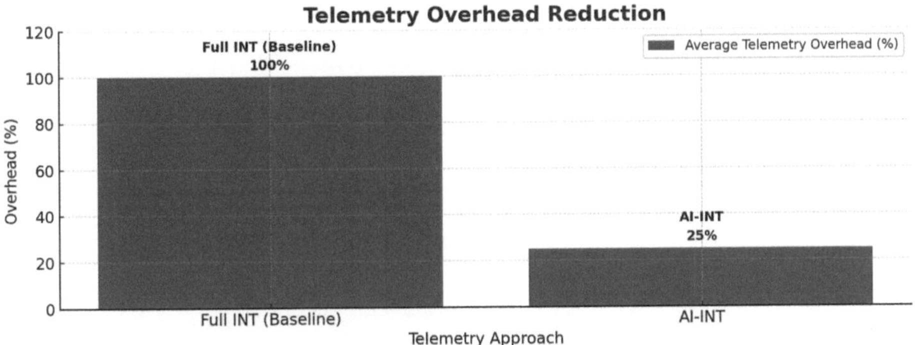

Fig. 4. Telemetry Overhead Reduction Chart.

Resource Utilization of the Programmable Switch: The CPU and memory utilization measurements on BMv2 switches showed that AI-INT significantly **lowered the processing burden** associated with INT metadata insertion and extraction. Switches running AI-INT exhibited CPU utilization profiles closer to the "No INT" scenario for average traffic, while still providing detailed telemetry for prioritized flows. This suggests more efficient utilization of programmable data plane resources. The ONOS controller and AI/ML Decision Plane showed acceptable resource usage, demonstrating that the real-time classification capability does not overwhelm the control plane and data plane. The resource utilization details with different telemetry approaches are shown in Fig. 5, 6, and we can see our proposed approach utilizing the resources in an efficient manner.

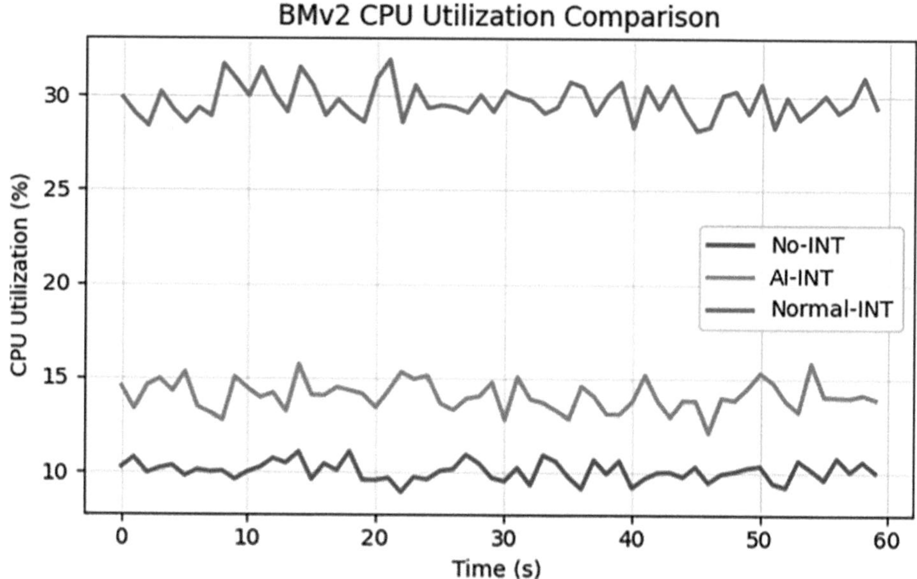

Fig. 5. CPU Utilization Comparison.

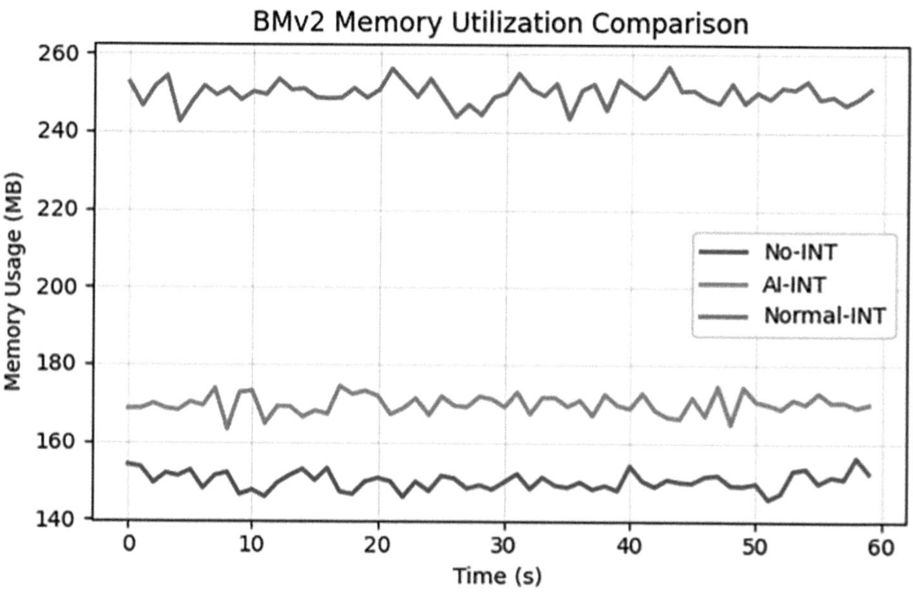

Fig. 6. Memory Utilization Comparison.

6.2   Limitations and Future Work

While AI-INT demonstrates significant advantages, certain limitations are also present. The accuracy of the MLP classifier depends on the training dataset's quality and diversity; new or encrypted applications might pose challenges. The latency of the AI/ML Decision Plane can still be a factor in extremely high-speed, ultra-low-latency networks. Future work will explore more sophisticated deep learning models to handle encrypted traffic or achieve even higher classification accuracy than existing classifiers. Investigating the feasibility of deploying lightweight ML models directly on programmable switches for ultra-low-latency classification, reducing reliance on the external AI/ML Decision Plane for certain decisions.

7   Conclusion

INT offers unparalleled visibility into network behavior, but its indiscriminate application can introduce significant overhead. This paper introduced **AI-INT**, an innovative AI-driven framework that intelligently and dynamically activates INT in programmable networks. By combining the power of P4-programmable data planes, the centralized control of ONOS, and the real-time classification capabilities of an MLP model, AI-INT enables application-aware telemetry that significantly minimizes overhead while maintaining critical observability. Our architecture and detailed algorithmic description highlight a closed-loop system where network flows are detected and classified in real-time, and their telemetry policies are dynamically installed based on their predicted class and the current network state. Evaluation results demonstrate substantial reductions in telemetry overhead, improved throughput, and resource utilization with rapid responsiveness. AI-INT's adaptability to changing network conditions underscores its potential to revolutionize network monitoring by making it more efficient, intelligent, and aligned with application-specific requirements. This work paves the way for truly self-optimizing and observable next-generation networks.

References

1. GitHub - p4lang/behavioral-model: The reference P4 software switch — github.com. https://github.com/p4lang/behavioral-model. Accessed 28 Aug 2025
2. Intel&x2019;s Tofino P4 Software is Now Open Source &x2013; P4 &x2013; Language Consortium — p4.org. https://p4.org/intels-tofino-p4-software-is-now-open-source/. Accessed 28 Aug 2025
3. p4.org. https://p4.org/p4-spec/docs/INT_v2_1.pdf. Accessed 28 Aug 2025
4. Abhashkumar, A., et al.: P5: policy-driven optimization of P4 pipeline. In: Proceedings of the Symposium on SDN Research, pp. 136–142 (2017)
5. Alam, Q.M., Kolar, V., Thottan, M.: Towards AI/ML-driven network traffic engineering. In: Proceedings of the 4th International Conference on AI-ML Systems, pp. 1–8 (2024)

6. Ben Basat, R., Ramanathan, S., Li, Y., Antichi, G., Yu, M., Mitzenmacher, M.: Pint: probabilistic in-band network telemetry. In: Proceedings of the Annual Conference of the ACM Special Interest Group on Data Communication on the Applications, Technologies, Architectures, and Protocols for Computer Communication, pp. 662–680 (2020)

7. Berde, P., et al.: ONOS: towards an open, distributed SDN OS. In: Proceedings of the Third Workshop on Hot Topics in Software Defined Networking, pp. 1–6 (2014)

8. Bosshart, P., Daly, D., Gibb, G., et al.: P4: programming protocol-independent packet processors. ACM SIGCOMM Comput. Commun. Rev. **44**(3), 87–95 (2014)

9. Casado, M., Freedman, M.J., Pettit, J., Luo, J., McKeown, N., Shenker, S.: Ethane: taking control of the enterprise. ACM SIGCOMM Comput. Commun. Rev. **37**(4), 1–12 (2007)

10. Case, J.D., Fedor, M., Schoffstall, M.L., Davin, J.: Simple network management protocol (SNMP). Technical report (1989)

11. Cisco: Introduction to cisco netflow (2014). https://www.cisco.com/c/en/us/products/ios-nx-os-software/ios-netflow/index.html

12. P4Runtime Specification — p4.org. https://p4.org/p4-spec/p4runtime/main/P4Runtime-Spec.html. Accessed 25 Aug 2025

13. Khawar, M.W., Salman, W., Shaheen, S., Shakil, A., Iftikhar, F., Faisal, K.M.I.: Investigating the most effective AI/ML-based strategies for predictive network maintenance to minimize downtime and enhance service reliability. Spectrum Eng. Sci. **2**(4), 115–132 (2024)

14. Kim, C., et al.: In-band network telemetry via programmable dataplanes. In: ACM SIGCOMM, vol. 15, pp. 1–2 (2015)

15. Lin, M., Zhao, Y.: Artificial intelligence-empowered resource management for future wireless communications: a survey. China Commun. **17**(3), 58–77 (2020)

16. Michel, O., Bifulco, R., Rétvári, G., Schmid, S.: The programmable data plane: abstractions, architectures, algorithms, and applications. ACM Comput. Surv. (CSUR) **54**(4), 1–36 (2021)

17. Papadopoulos, K., Papadimitriou, P., Papagianni, C.: Deterministic and probabilistic P4-enabled lightweight in-band network telemetry. IEEE Trans. Netw. Serv. Manage. **20**(4), 4909–4922 (2023)

18. PM, V.P., Soumya, S.: Advancements in anomaly detection techniques in network traffic: the role of artificial intelligence and machine learning. J. Sci. Res. Technol. 38–48 (2024)

19. Riedmiller, M., Lernen, A.: Multi layer perceptron. Machine learning lab special lecture, University of Freiburg, vol. 24, pp. 11–60 (2014)

20. Vulpe, A., Dobrin, C., Stefan, A., Caranica, A.: AI/ML-based real-time classification of software defined networking traffic. In: Proceedings of the 18th International Conference on Availability, Reliability and Security, pp. 1–7 (2023)

Temporal Analysis Based Exploratory Data Analysis for Phishing Email Detection via Machine Learning

Tanmoy Chanda, Biva Mondal, Subhashis Das, Soumendu Banerjee, and Bappaditya Mondal[✉]

Academy of Technology, Adisaptagram 712121, West Bengal, India
{tanmoy.chanda.23,biva.mondal.23,subhashis.das,
soumendu.banerjee,bappaditya.mondal}@aot.edu.in

Abstract. Phishing attacks are on the rise in current society where attackers try to steal sensitive information from the user using any means necessary. Majority of the attacks leverage electronic mails to trick unsuspecting users to click a link or urge a sense of urgency. Thus this research work aims to explore key features of phishing emails for the detection of the phishing attacks. The main focus was to apply Exploratory Data Analysis (EDA) on key features like URL Patterns, timestamps, sentiment of sender, grammar and TF-IDF (Term Frequency-Inverse Document Frequency) which can be leveraged in detection of phishing attacks. Using these features, machine learning models like Random Forest (RF), XG Boost (eXtreme Gradient Boosting) were evaluated on the dataset mentioned in Sect. 3.1 and it was found that XG Boost provided the False Positive Rate of just 1.76% with the lowest execution time of just **27.85 s**. In comparison, the best performing Bidirectional Long Short-Term Memory (Bi-LSTM) model had a False Positive Rate of **1.20%** and had a very high execution time. The results highlight XGBoost as the optimal choice for balancing performance and computational efficiency for the detection of phishing emails.

Keywords: Phishing Detection · EDA · Temporal Trends · Phishing Patterns · comparative analysis · TF-IDF vectorization · CNN · Bi-LSTM

1 Introduction

Emails have now become an integral part of modern society and the modern society is highly dependent on technology. Unlike other modes of non-verbal communication like Whatsapp, Facebook and other platforms that are used for casual communication, emails are used mainly as formal mode of communication. Thus, it is used in various private and public industries, schools and government agencies to convey some message to the sender. However, relying too much in emails as a primary source of non-verbal communication have led to the rise of cybersecurity risks in the form of spam and phishing emails. Phishing emails tend to attack users by trying to steal sensitive information by acting as a trusted entity.

B. Chatterjee et al. (Eds.): ICDCIT 2026, LNCS 16420, pp. 331–340, 2026.
https://doi.org/10.1007/978-3-032-16632-6_21

As per the report shared by the *Anti-Phishing Working Group (APWG)* [5], the first quarter of 2025 has recorded 1,003,924 phishing attacks, making it the highest in volume since 2023. Cybercriminals have increasingly incorporated QR codes into phishing emails, leveraging their widespread use to redirect victims to malicious websites or malware. Attacks targeting the online payment and banking sectors rose sharply, consisting of 30.9% of all the incidents.

Recent findings from the 2025 IBM *Cost of a Data Breach Report* reveal a complex cybersecurity landscape, where artificial intelligence (AI) delivers both defensive and offensive power. Globally, the average cost of a data breach decreased to USD 4.44 million, a 9% reduction from the previous year, largely due to faster detection and containment enabled by AI and automation [1].

Attackers targeted customer PII over other types of data by a wide margin. At 53%, it was the most stolen or compromised data type. Customer PII can include tax identity (ID) numbers, emails and home addresses, and can be used in identity theft and credit card fraud whereas company intellectual property (IP), while less commonly stolen or compromised, was the most costly (USD 178 per record) [1] (Figs. 1 and 2).

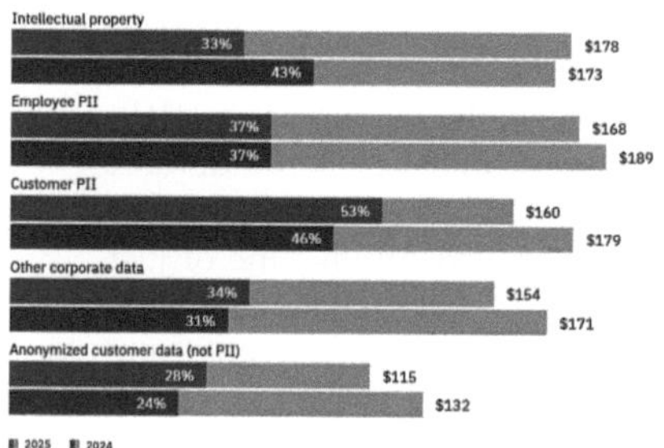

Fig. 1. Breach-cost comparison by data category and year [1].

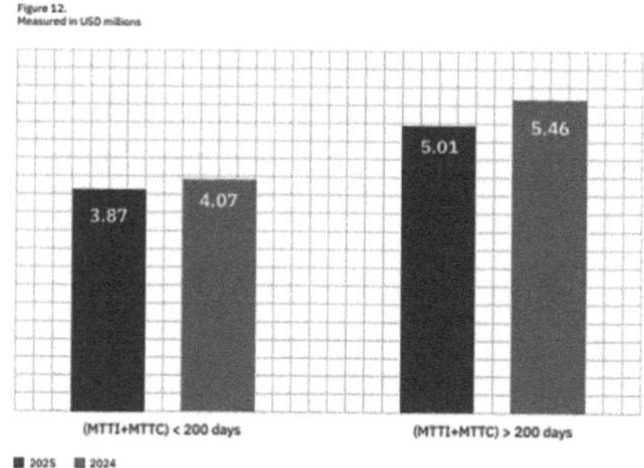

Fig. 2. Regulatory Fines on Industry [1].

However, this progress is shadowed by glaring security gaps. Among organizations that suffered AI-related security incidents, 97% lacked proper AI access controls, and 63% had no established AI governance policies [1]. Moreover, breaches involving unapproved AI tools ("shadow AI") added an average of USD 670,000 to breach costs, and compelled broader data compromises and operational [1]. Alarmingly, attackers are increasingly using AI to increase effectiveness of phishing campaigns - 16%breaches involved AI-driven attacks, most commonly AI-generated phishing (37%) and deepfake impersonations (35%) [1]. This dual-use nature of AI, both as a security enabler and a rising attack vector, underscores the urgency of integrating robust AI governance into cybersecurity strategies. The interplay of advanced phishing methods and weak oversight presents a growing threat landscape that this paper aims to explore.

2   Related Work

There has been a lot of research work which has already been done related to phishing or spam detection due to the importance of this work in modern society. The most recent work was done in 2025 by Sabitha Banu et al. where the researchers proposed a framework involving phishing simulation, email header and URL analysis and achieved a 91% correlation accuracy between forged headers and malicious URLs [6]. Another work by Al-Subaiey et al. proposed a phishing email detection model where they merged six different spam datasets and applied different machine learning models and obtained an accuracy of 99.1% with the Support Vector Machine(SVM) [2]. Heiding et al. experimented with the generation and detection of phishing emails with different LLMs and concluded that the hybrid GPT + V-Triad achieved a success rate up to 81% compared to other models [14].

Guo et al. in 2023 [12] used the Enron-Spam (33,716 emails) and Spam or Not Spam (2,999 emails) datasets with a BERT-based model and classifiers (Logistic Regression, SVM, RF, KNN). Logistic Regression performed best, achieving up to 97.8% F1-score, showing that BERT embeddings enhance spam detection.

Sarno et al. tried a different approach using signal detection theory, regression models, and frameworks such as Truth-Default Theory, System 1 & 2 processing, and the SCAM model to detect phishing attacks and they concluded that the detection was highest for headlines (d≐ 2.67), moderate for texts (d≐ 1.91), and lowest for phishing emails (d≐ 1.33). Digital literacy and cognitive reflectiveness predicted stronger performance, while age was not significant [17]. Alsuwit et al. in 2024 studied email spam classification using a merged dataset of 83,448 emails from the TREC Public Spam Corpus (2007) and Enron-Spam where they leveraged Logistic Regression, Naïve Bayes, Random Forest, and a Keras-based Artificial Neural Network (ANN) and found the highest accuracy with ANN(98%, F1 = 97.5%) [3]. Reinforcement Learning based approach was proposed by Ajay Kumar et al. to detect phishing attacks using reinforcement learning where the researchers used a synthetic dataset of 2,000 URLs (balanced between phishing and legitimate) generated by a URL Dataset Generator. The best performance was achieved with the RL-based system, reporting Accuracy (96%) [15]. Exploratory Data Analysis of Phishing Emails was done by Daniel in 2019 where they performed text analysis on phishing emails which reveal different text patterns when compared with non-phishing emails [16]. Bliss [7] analyzed temporal patterns in phishing email detection and tried to forecast the occurrence of phishing emails when coupled with external events but could not find a meaningful results were obtained from intervention analysis.

Mahmood et al. [4] used temporal information to forecast phishing attack volumes weeks or months in advance rather than relying on reactive detection mechanisms. Their mean classification accuracy is 64% which is better than existing forecasting techniques.

Medhasree Ghosh et al. [11] in 2023 analyzed phishing detection using 14 machine learning classifiers on datasets from UCI Spambase, Enron, SpamAssassin, Nazario, and PhishTank. The models included Naïve Bayes, J48, Random

Forest, SVM, AdaBoost, and Rotation Forest, implemented in WEKA 3.9. During transactional feature extraction, they used email header metadata such as sender, receiver, IP path, and timestamp. The timestamp was treated as a static header attribute, not for temporal or trend analysis.

In most of these approaches, the researchers focused on extracting URL information to detect phishing attacks or they performed TF-IDF vectorization to extract the information. Few approaches used powerful Deep Learning Based Models or Reinforcement Learning for the detection of phishing attacks. Few of these research papers leveraged timestamp information to forecast the phishing attack volumes but did not use it for phishing email detection. Our work focuses on obtaining monthly, weekly and hourly information, along with URL embeddings, email sentiment, grammatical issues, suspicious domains and TF-IDF vectorizations to detect the presence of phishing attacks.

3   Proposed Methodology

3.1   Dataset Collection

Initially, the data set was collected from *Seven Phishing Email Datasets* [9] [8] where they have curated to prevent data leakage and ensure readability. The dataset include data from seven different phishing campaigns covering a broad range of email content, including seven fields for each mail which are sender, receiver, date, subject, body, label & urls including spam, scam & other phishing techniques.

3.2   Exploratory Data Analysis on Temporal Trends

Exploratory data analysis(EDA) was performed on the given dataset based on timestamp information focusing on monthly patterns, which revealed that the rate of phishing emails was high in the month of August as compared to the other months which might be the effect of higher volumes of emails sent during that period. Overall, the highest rate of phishing emails sent per email is in the month of April which remains at an elevated state till the month of August and gradually decreases to its minimum in the month of October and finally increases in the month of December, due to the holiday season where people tend to spend money. This is depicted in Fig. 3.

Furthermore, EDA was performed on the email dataset, where the trend of phishing emails was analyzed based on two key aspects:

1. **Temporal Behavioral Analysis of Phishing Emails by Hour-of-Day**: The first analysis focused on the occurrence of phishing emails at each hour of the day. As shown in Fig. 4(a), the analysis revealed a significant increase in phishing emails around the *early hours (before office hours)* and the *late hours (after office hours)*. This suggests that phishing attacks tend targets individuals during these times, potentially exploiting lower levels of vigilance. The data indicates that phishing emails are less frequent during peak working hours (9 AM to 5 PM), which can be attributed to individuals being more attentive to suspicious emails during the workday.

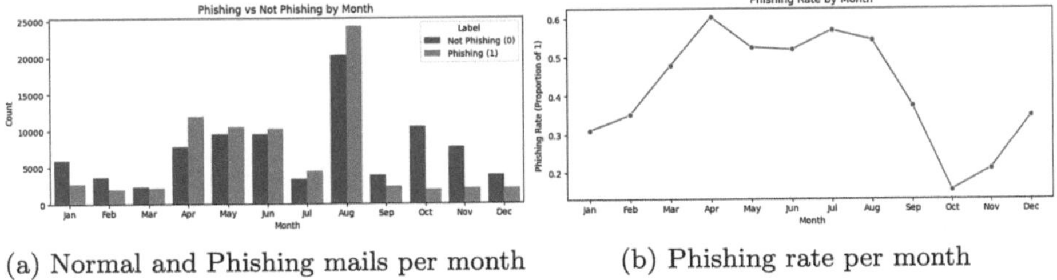

(a) Normal and Phishing mails per month   (b) Phishing rate per month

Fig. 3. Comparison of Phishing Email Patterns Month-wise.

2. **Temporal Behavioral Analysis of Phishing Emails by Day-of-Month**:
   The second analysis explored phishing trends by day of the month. Figure 4(b)
   shows that phishing emails are most frequent during the *first two weeks* of
   each month. This could be indicative of phishing campaigns aligned with
   payroll cycles, tax season, or other monthly activities when individuals may
   be more likely to click on suspicious links or open fraudulent attachments.

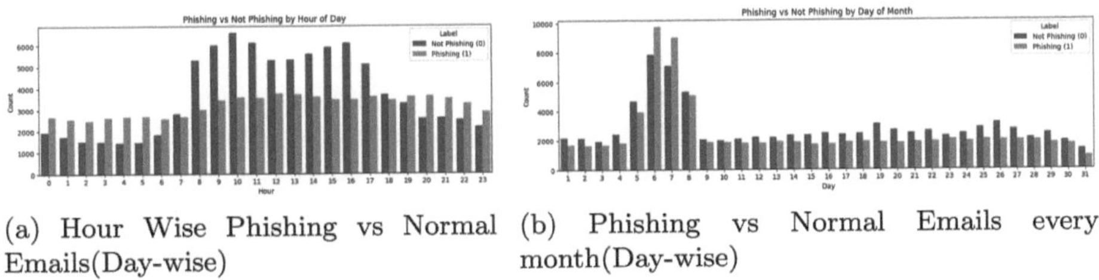

(a) Hour Wise Phishing vs Normal   (b) Phishing vs Normal Emails every
Emails(Day-wise)   month(Day-wise)

Fig. 4. Comparison of Phishing Email Patterns day-wise.

3. **EDA on Weekday Trends in Phishing Emails:**The analysis on phishing
   emails by *weekday* shown in Fig. 5 revealed that:

(a) The average phishing email ratio is higher on *weekends*, indicating less vigi-
    lance during these times.
(b) The *middle of the week* (Wednesday and Thursday) shows a higher overall
    phishing rate, likely due to reduced alertness during busy workdays.

These findings suggest that phishing emails are more likely to target individuals
during times of reduced alertness. Thus, these features can be used to predict
the presence of phishing emails and feature weights are computed based on this
information.

3.3   Exploratory Data Analysis on URLs and Phishing Trends

Phishing emails have some source of links which are used by the malicious actors
to perform some financial/identity theft. Thus, the analysis was performed and

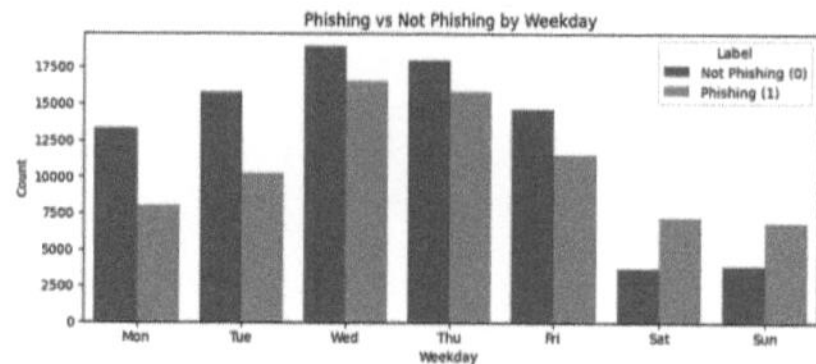
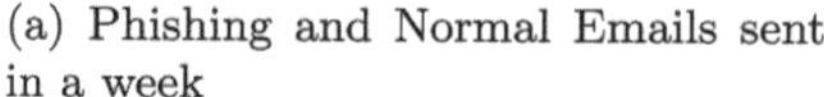

(a) Phishing and Normal Emails sent in a week

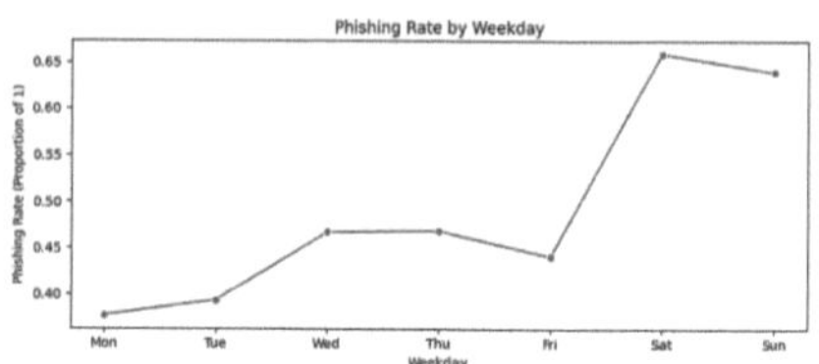

(b) Normalized rate of Phishing Emails sent in a week

Fig. 5. Phishing Trends every Week.

the results are shown in Fig. 6a & Fig. 6b, suggesting that most phishing emails have a URL and therefore can be a valid indicator to detect phishing attempts.

3.4   Exploratory Data Analysis Based on Email Sentiment

Sentiment Analysis was performed individually on subject and body of the email. The sentiment obtained was tested against the phishing emails to determine whether sentiment of the sender could determine the phishing emails. For sentiment analysis, Bidirectional Encoder Representations from Transformers(BERT) [10] model was used to extract the sentiment. The sentiment analysis module uses the pretrained BERT model [18] which has 12 transformer layers, 12 attention heads, a hidden size of 768, intermediate size of 3072, GELU activation, dropout of 0.1, maximum sequence length of 512, and a multilingual uncased WordPiece vocabulary of 105,879 tokens. The model was chosen since emails can be written in complex tone and may also contain both formal and informal languages which are well handled by the chosen model. The result, shown in Fig. 6c indicates that malicious actors often use positive tone like flattery, urgency or use rewards as a way to gather sensitive user information. This information is utilized in the model detection.

3.5   Exploratory Data Analysis on Grammatical Issues

Phishing Emails generally do not follow a formal tone and have a ton of grammatical, punctuation and readability issues. Thus, different grammatical issues are correlated with occurrence of phishing which are shown in Fig. 7(a).

Body punctuation ratio, subject punctuation count and subject punctuation ratio showed a negative weak correlation in detection of phishing emails. These features are retained since they still meaningfully contribute to the model's overall performance in detection of phishing emails.

3.6   Exploratory Data Analysis on Suspicious Domains

The phishing emails tend to use suspicious domains and tries to mimick the legitimate organizations. Thus, the focus was to find out the relationship between

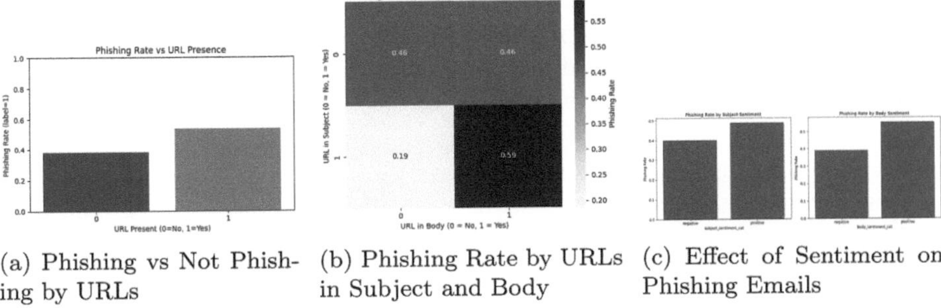

(a) Phishing vs Not Phishing by URLs

(b) Phishing Rate by URLs in Subject and Body

(c) Effect of Sentiment on Phishing Emails

Fig. 6. Phishing trends based on URLs and sentiment features.

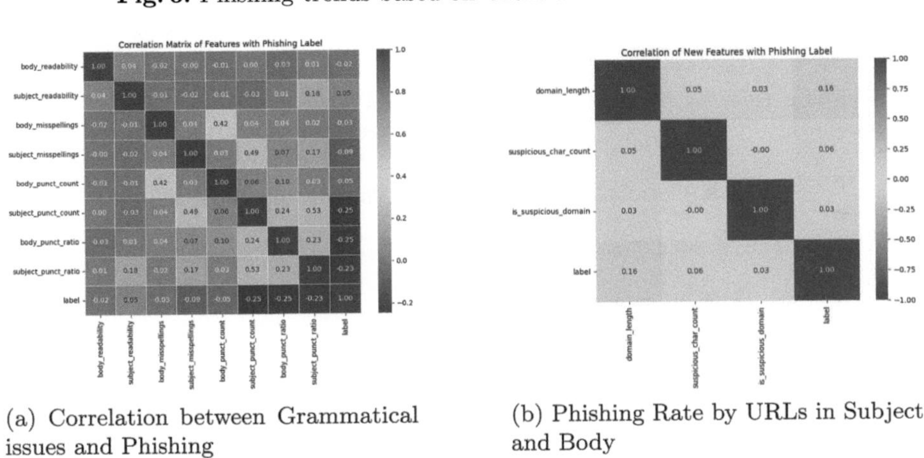

(a) Correlation between Grammatical issues and Phishing

(b) Phishing Rate by URLs in Subject and Body

Fig. 7. Correlation of sender domains and phishing.

domain addresses and phishing attempts. The analysis shown in Fig. 7(b) indicates that only the domain length has some meaningful correlation with the phishing label. The weights of these features are computed to be fed in the models for further detection.

3.7   TF-IDF Vectorization

TF-IDF (Term Frequency-Inverse Document Frequency) [13] vectorization is used to measure the importance of keywords in the collection of documents. Here, the same technique is applied in email body and subject to determine the important keywords that can be used to identify phishing attempts. To ensure that only the most informative and discriminative features were retained, a feature selection process was applied using the Chi-square statistical test, which ranks terms based on their correlation with the phishing label & Truncated Singular Value Decomposition (SVD) was employed as a dimensionality reduction technique to handle the high-dimensional TF-IDF space efficiently, compressing the feature vectors into a lower-dimensional latent space while preserving key semantic relationships. The top-ranked features were then retained for model training, thereby reducing noise and improving generalization. The *top 10* correlations *(positive/negative)* is shown in Fig. 8(a) and 8(b).

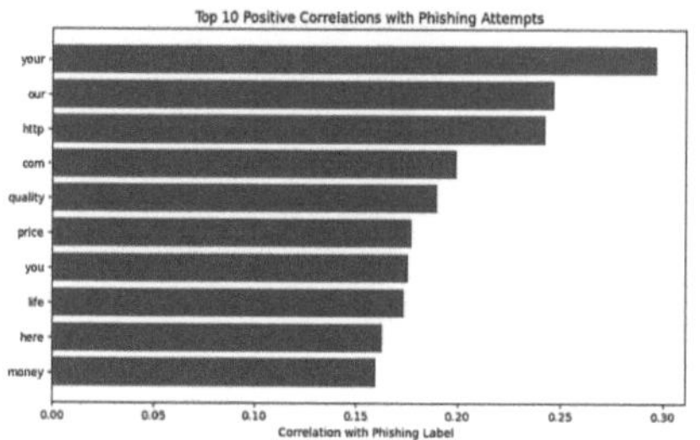

(a) Phishing Rate by Words(Positive Correlation)

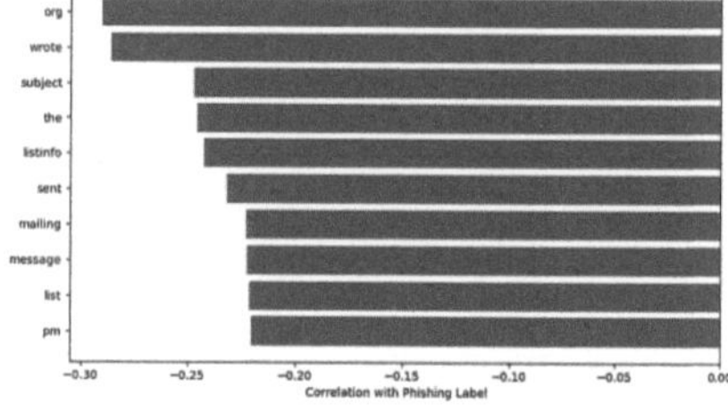

(b) Phishing Rate by Words(Negative Correlation)

Fig. 8. Correlation of phishing emails with top 10 labels.

4   Model Training and Results

For this study, the ML models include the Random Forest Classifier (RF) & eXtreme Gradient Boosting Classifier (XGBoost) & DL models comprises Convolutional Neural Network (CNN) & Bidirectional Long Short-term Memory (Bi-LSTM). The dataset mentioned in Sect. 3.1 was split into training (80%) and testing (20%) sets using stratified sampling to preserve the label distribution and ensure class balance between phishing and legitimate emails. For feature scaling, StandardScaler was applied to numeric features, and LabelEncoder was used for categorical attributes. The text features from email subjects and bodies were transformed into TF-IDF vectors (with 500 features) to capture keyword relevance. Hyperparameter tuning was performed empirically through grid-based exploration, optimizing parameters such as the number of estimators, learning rate, and maximum tree depth for Random Forest and XGBoost models. The moddels were then trained & evaluated on standard metrics of precision, recall, F1-Score & shown in Table 1.

The results in Table 1 shows that all the models performed well in detecting the phishing emails with very minimal False Positive Rates. Among these, Bi-LSTM has the least False Positive Rate among all the models used in the work. Additionally, the total training and evaluation times were also recorded for each models as shown in Table 2. The tests were carried out on Ryzen 7 6800H with 16GB of RAM. The results show that the XG Boost provided the fastest execution time of just 27.85 s across all the different models compared in this study. Bi-LSTM model had the longest execution time with **1274.48** seconds which

Table 1. Classification Metrics for Different Models

Model	Precision	Recall	F1-Score	Accuracy	False Positive Rate
Random Forest	0.9810	0.9821	0.9815	**0.9829**	0.0164
XGBoost	0.9798	0.9860	0.9829	0.9826	0.0176
CNN	0.9794	**0.9888**	**0.9841**	0.9821	0.0180
Bi-LSTM	**0.9860**	0.9770	0.9814	0.9819	**0.0120**

is **45** times slower than XG Boost. Thus, it can be said that XG Boost can be reliably used in phishing detection in practical scenarios where training time and inference speeds are critical.

Table 2. Model Training and Evaluation Time

Model	Time Taken (s)
Random Forest	265.12
XGBoost	**27.85**
CNN	319.24
Bi-LSTM	1274.48

5 Conclusion

This work reveals that using powerful models are not the only solution to detect phishing attacks. It has been shown that the extracted features obtained from the phishing emails can help even the weaker models to perform well. However, the benefit of using weaker models for the detection purpose is that it can be deployed in portable devices with resource constraints for easier detection. Our analysis has shown that XGBoost performed very well and its results are close to the best performing model in our research. However, the training and inference times are 46 times lesser when compared to the top performing model. The future scope of this work to look for model explainability and identify hidden patterns from the emails which can further strengthen the model prediction.

References

1. 2025 Cost of a Data Breach Report: Navigating the AI rush without sidelining security | IBM (2025). https://www.ibm.com/think/x-force/2025-cost-of-a-data-breach-navigating-ai
2. Al-Subaiey, A., Al-Thani, M., Alam, N.A., Antora, K.F., Khandakar, A., Zaman, S.A.U.: Novel interpretable and robust web-based AI platform for phishing email detection. Comput. Electr. Eng. **120**, 109625 (2024)

3. Alsuwit, M.H., Haq, M.A., Aleisa, M.A.: Advancing email spam classification using machine learning and deep learning techniques. Eng. Technol. Appl. Sci. Res. **14**(4), 14994–15001 (2024)

4. Amin Mahmood, S.H., Mustafa Ali Abbasi, S., Abbasi, A., Zaffar, F.: Phishcasting: deep learning for time series forecasting of phishing attacks. In: 2020 IEEE International Conference on Intelligence and Security Informatics (ISI), pp. 1–6 (2020). https://doi.org/10.1109/ISI49825.2020.9280509

5. Anti-Phishing Working Group: Phishing Activity Trends Report, Q1 2025 (2025). https://apwg.org/trendsreports/

6. Banu, S., et al.: Phishing attack simulation, email header analysis, and URL scrutiny: a comprehensive approach to cyber threat mitigation. Comput. Netw. Commun. 1–20 (2025)

7. Bliss, E.: Analyzing temporal patterns in phishing email topics. Rochester Institute of Technology (2021)

8. Champa, A.I., Rabbi, F., Zibran, M.F.: Why phishing emails escape detection: a closer look at the failure points. In: 2024 12th International Symposium on Digital Forensics and Security (ISDFS), pp. 1–6. IEEE (2024)

9. Champa, A.I., Rabbi, M.F., Zibran, M.F.: Curated datasets and feature analysis for phishing email detection with machine learning. In: 3rd IEEE International Conference on Computing and Machine Intelligence (ICMI), pp. 1–7 (2024)

10. Devlin, J., Chang, M.W., Lee, K., Toutanova, K.: Bert: pre-training of deep bidirectional transformers for language understanding (2019). https://arxiv.org/abs/1810.04805

11. Ghosh, M., Ghosh, D., Halder, R., Chandra, J.: Investigating the impact of structural and temporal behaviors in ethereum phishing users detection. Blockchain Res. Appl. **4**(4), 100153 (2023)

12. Guo, Y., Mustafaoglu, Z., Koundal, D.: Spam detection using bidirectional transformers and machine learning classifier algorithms. J. Comput. Cogn. Eng. **2**(1), 5–9 (2023)

13. Havrlant, L., Kreinovich, V.: A simple probabilistic explanation of term frequency-inverse document frequency (TF-IDF) heuristic (and variations motivated by this explanation). Int. J. General Syst. **46**(1), 27–36 (2017). https://doi.org/10.1080/03081079.2017.1291635. https://www.tandfonline.com/doi/full/10.1080/03081079.2017.1291635

14. Heiding, F., Schneier, B., Vishwanath, A., Bernstein, J., Park, P.S.: Devising and detecting phishing emails using large language models. IEEE Access **12**, 42131–42146 (2024)

15. Kumar, C.V.R.A., Yakkaladevi, S.L., Pandiri, S., Godugu, Y.: Reinforcement learning-based phishing detection model. World J. Adv. Res. Rev. **25**(1), 2291–2295 (2025)

16. O'Leary, D.E.: What phishing e-mails reveal: an exploratory analysis of phishing attempts using text analysis. J. Inf. Syst. **33**(3), 285–307 (2019). https://doi.org/10.2308/isys-52481

17. Sarno, D.M., Black, J.: Who gets caught in the web of lies?: understanding susceptibility to phishingemails, fake news headlines, and scam text messages. Hum. Factors **66**(6), 1742–1753 (2024)

18. Town, N.: BERT-base-multilingual-uncased-sentiment (revision edd66ab) (2023). https://doi.org/10.57967/hf/1515. https://huggingface.co/nlptown/bert-base-multilingual-uncased-sentiment

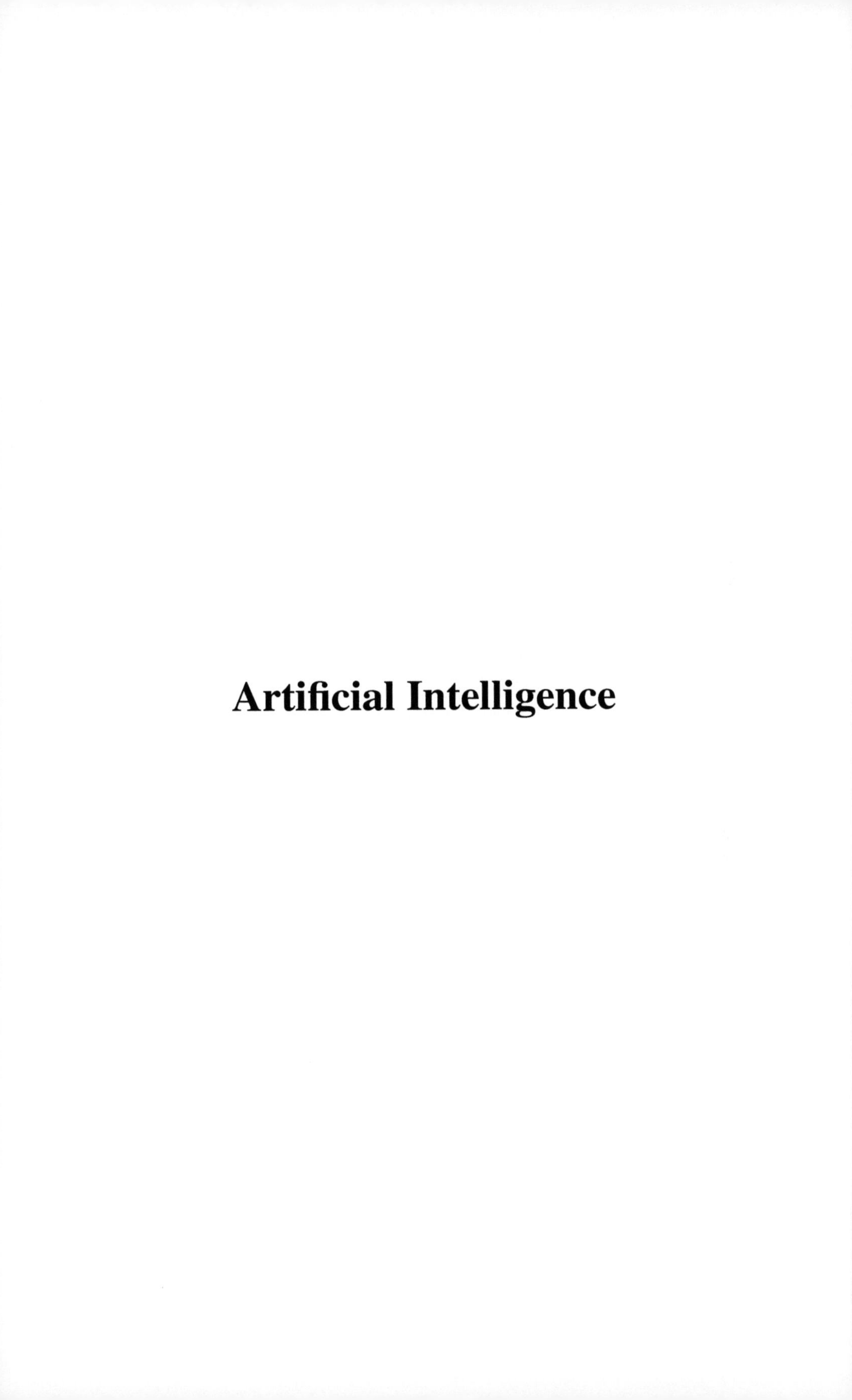

Artificial Intelligence

Bhāluk: Learning the Unknown Basis of Human Olfactory System Using Deep Learning

Avinash Kushwaha[✉][iD], Prashant D. Kulkarni[iD], Richa Thakur[iD],
Shubhajit Roy Chowdhury[iD], Aditya Nigam[iD], and Dinesh Singh[iD]

Visual Intelligence and Machine Learning (VIML) Group, School of Computing and
Electrical Engineering, Indian Institute of Technology Mandi, Mandi, India
{s23108,t22058,d23151}@students.iitmandi.ac.in,
{src,aditya,dineshsingh}@iitmandi.ac.in

Abstract. The artificial human olfactory system mimics the human
olfactory system using a sensor array and AI algorithms to identify and
quantify volatile compounds. This technology has shown promise in various
fields, including agriculture, food and beverage, cosmetics, healthcare, and environmental monitoring. However, it remains underdeveloped
due to the complexity of odors and the limitations of current sensors in
distinguishing specific odors. Odor is a mixture of gases and volatile
organic compounds, presenting significant classification challenges due
to their low concentrations and complex chemical structures. Our study
utilizes multiple sensors to convert gas molecular signals into electrical
signals, identifying specific gases and their physicochemical characteristics. This paper introduces a novel study leveraging a unique dataset,
comprising 20 distinct olfactory signatures captured with 11 sensors.
Additionally, we have developed an artificial olfactory system capable
of sensing the concentration of various gases and volatile organic compounds, learning the unknown basis of the olfactory signature based on
the received time-series data, and finally classifying it as a smell. Developing such a system involves overcoming challenges related to complex
gas interactions, sensor accuracy, and the analysis of the sensor-generated
data. We evaluate a range of deep learning models, including 1DCNNs,
ResidualCNNs, RNNs with attention, GRU, and LSTM, to classify these
signatures across a carefully prepared dataset.

Keywords: Odor detection · Olfactory system · Sensors

1 Introduction

Odors consist of volatile organic compounds (VOCs) with highly diverse chemical
structures making their classification challenging and complex [5]. Also, identifying and quantifying the gases in a compound is difficult due to their low
concentrations. An artificial olfactory system is a sophisticated device designed

B. Chatterjee et al. (Eds.): ICDCIT 2026, LNCS 16420, pp. 343–357, 2026.
https://doi.org/10.1007/978-3-032-16632-6_22

to mimic the human olfactory system. It utilizes an array of sensors combined with pattern recognition algorithms to identify and quantify volatile compounds. The advancement of this technology has demonstrated promising results in the fields such as agriculture, food and beverage, cosmetics, healthcare, and environmental monitoring [4,11,20,27,32,37], and beyond. However, the technology for olfactory detection is still significantly underdeveloped due to the complexity of odors, and the current ability of sensors to correctly and effectively distinguish a specific odor. An artificial olfactory system contains a sensor array to transform the gas molecular signals into electric signals. It is different from other instruments used in chemical analysis in that they are mainly designed to recognize gas mixtures as a whole, while our artificial olfactory system is most useful for determining the sources from which the gas mixtures were derived of the gases [36].

However, developing an artificial olfactory system poses significant challenges due to the complex interactions of gases involved, the sensor technology used to accurately detect the gases, and the use of deep learning models to capture the relation between the time-series data generated by the sensors. Although the use of deep learning models for olfactory detection has increased over time. The primary models used in olfaction detection and classification are support vector machines (SVM) [14], fully connected neural networks (FCNNs) [8], and convolutional neural networks (CNNs) [19]. Our study explores the advanced deep learning models such as RNNs with attention [25], 1D convolutional neural networks [19], ResidualCNNs [13], long short-term memory (LSTM) [16], and gated recurrent unit (GRU) [7] to analyze the time-series data in the proposed olfactory system.

Olfactory adaptation [9], where sensitivity to an odor decreases with prolonged exposure, adds complexity to olfactory systems. Additionally, environmental factors like pressure, temperature, and humidity can alter chemical properties, complicating accurate detection. Odor profiles [5], which are the smells and their characteristics, can also change over time due to these changing environmental conditions like airflow, temperature, and humidity. To address the issues stemming from environmental conditions, we devise a suitable protocol for the data collection. Also, an additional background class is incorporated to cope with the influence of ambient conditions on the olfactory detection system. Developing olfactory systems is particularly challenging due to the limited number of sensors available relative to the vast range of odors. The lack of standard datasets is another problem for a comparative analysis. It is also known that there are no primary odors that can represent any other odors with their combination [38]. Due to these challenges, and the advancement of artificial intelligence, our study on olfactory detection systems elucidates valuable insights related to the development and optimization of olfactory technologies. Following are the main contributions of our work

- Developed an artificial olfactory system by incorporating a large number of sensors to enable more accurate and diverse odor detection capabilities.

– Collected a dataset of 20 distinct odors related to food, cosmetics, aroma, and healthcare items by following a standardized data collection protocol.
– Investigated several state-of-the-art deep learning methods for the identification of odors, unlike traditional machine learning models by existing works.

2 Related Work

The existing work on odor classification with artificial nose used application-specific sensors and often relies on traditional machine learning models like k-nearest neighbors, linear discriminant analysis, fully connected neural networks [8], support vector machines [12,15,40]. However, work on the general understanding of the olfactory system is limited. Ma *et al.* [22] used algorithms such as k-NN, SVM, and pre-trained VGG19 model to classify odor. Peng *et al.* [26] used deep convolutional neural networks along with SVM and multi-layered perceptron models for classification purposes. Shi *et al.* [30] proposed a CNN-SVM model to classify olfactory information using only five different types of beer samples using the PEN3 E-nose, developed by the Airsense Analytics Inc.(Schwerin, Germany). Wijaya *et al.* [33] Explored ensemble machine learning approaches for electronic nose signal processing, employing models such as SVM, decision trees, random forests, and AdaBoost to assess beef quality, from fresh to spoiled, using 11 sensors. While these traditional models achieved good accuracy, they could limit scalability for larger or more complex datasets.

Table 1. Available Datasets in Artificial Nose study

No.	Impact area	Number of Classes	#Samples
1.	Beef Quality Monitoring [34]	4 (excellent, good, acceptable, spoiled)	5 (36 hrs. each)
2.	Wine Spoilage Detection [28]	4 (LQ, HQ, AQ, Ethanol)	235
3.	COPD [3]	4 (COPD, smokers, air, healthy)	78
4.	Pork Adulteration [29]	7 (Class1-Class7)	420
5.	**Our:** General day-to-day	20	320 (10 min each)

The studies in the olfactory domain are mostly carried around some specific area of aromatic substances. Although there have been a few public E-Nose datasets available as shown in Table 1, they have a limited number of samples and focus on specific target gases. As an instance, the paper [34] has used 500g of fresh extra-lean beef for testing using an e-nose in uncontrolled ambient conditions. Another study [28] is conducted on *wine spoilage* taking 25 different types of wines and classifying them in average-quality (AQ), low-quality (LQ), high-quality (HQ), or simply alcohol. *Tea Quality evaluation* is done in [39] which takes the tea samples and divides them into 6 grades from high-quality to poor quality. A different area of impact in healthcare is done by the dataset [3] which takes the sample of 78 people detecting *Chronic Obstructive Pulmonary Disease*. While all these studies report good performance, their application usually has limited scope. Also, the studies suggest a need for building a benchmark dataset for the olfactory system with a standard system setup and data collection scheme.

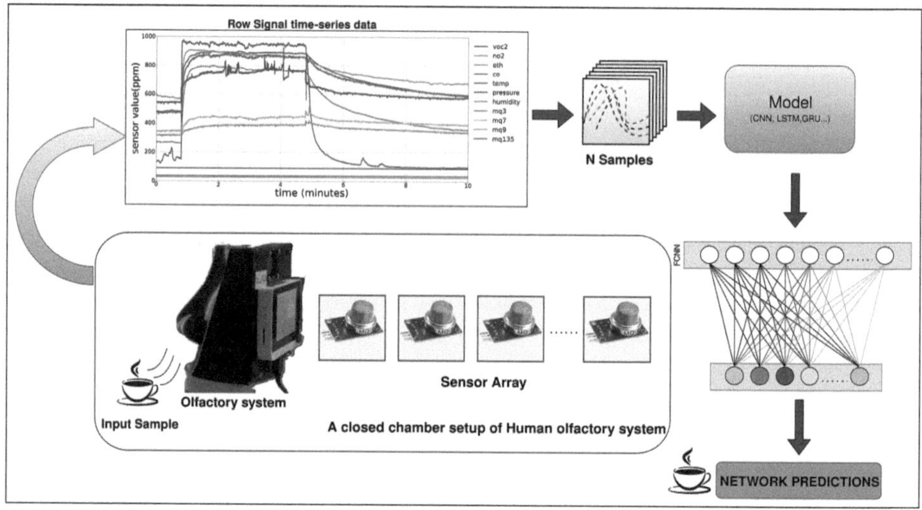

Fig. 1. Block diagram showing the composition and the working process of the proposed artificial olfactory system. The black enclosure contains sensor arrays used in olfactory detection. The received time-series data is further analyzed for representation of the olfactory system and classification of smell using the GRU model.

3   Proposed Methodology

The olfactory system described captures time-series data from environmental odors through an array of sensors as shown in Fig. 1. This raw data undergoes preprocessing to remove noise, normalize values, and extract meaningful features. The processed data is then passed through a machine learning model, which could include LSTM [16], GRU [7], RNNs with attention [25], ResidualCNNs [13], and 1D CNNs [19], all designed to identify patterns in the time-series data and classify it into predefined categories. The final layer of the model outputs a classification result, predicting the type of odor or chemical sample detected. This system facilitates real-time odor detection and classification, with applications [35] in environmental monitoring, quality control, and other fields.

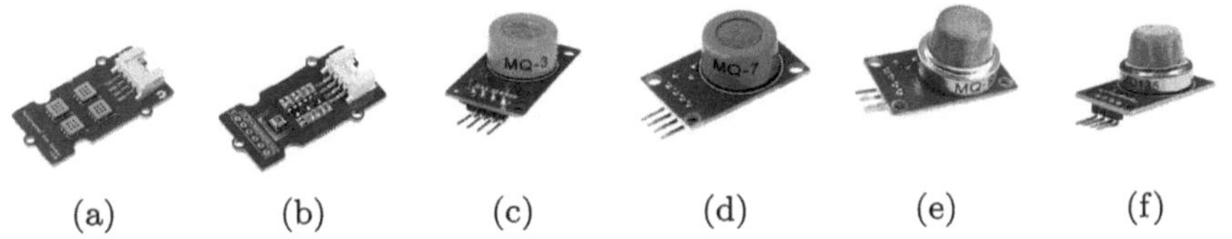

Fig. 2. Sensors array used in the olfactory system- (a). Multichannel Gas Sensor, (b). BME-680, (c). MQ-3, (d). MQ-7, (e). MQ-9, and (f). MQ-135.

3.1 Sensor Selection

After qualitatively evaluating the gas sensors and the ingredients present in the samples selected for the study, 9 sensors, which sense 11 characteristics of a sample, are selected. Table 2 shows the list of gas sensors used in constructing our olfactory system. The first one is Grove - Multichannel Gas Sensor [1]. It has the 4 sensors on a single chip Fig. 2(a): GM-102B (for NO_2 gas), GM-302B (for C_2H_5OH gas), GM-502B (VOC gas sensor), and GM-702B (for CO gas). Additionally, four MQ gas sensors were utilized: MQ3 Fig. 2(c) detects H_2, LPG, CH_4, CO, alcohol, smoke, or propane. MQ7 Fig. 2(d) is primarily used for CO, MQ9 Fig. 2(e) for detecting CO and Methane, and MQ135 Fig. 2(f) for Ammonia (NH_3), Sulfur (S), Benzene (C_6H_6), CO_2, and other harmful gases and smoke. For pressure, humidity, and temperature, we used a BME680 sensor as shown in Fig. 2(b).

Table 2. List of gas sensors used in our Electronic Nose

Sensor	Detects gases
GM-102B	NO_2
GM-302B	C_2H_5OH
GM-502B	VOC
GM-702B	CO
MQ3	Methane (CH_4), Hexane, LPG, CO, Alcohol, Benzene
MQ7	CO
MQ9	Propane, methane, CO
MQ135	Ammonia (NH_3), Sulfur (S), Benzene (C_6H_6), CO_2
BME680	Pressure, Humidity, Temperature

3.2 Data Acquisition Protocol

The data acquisition phase is the most important step in constructing an olfactory system. In our protocol, the sample is positioned near the nostrils of the

Table 3. Samples list with their ingredients (as mentioned on the product)

SN	Sample	Ingredients
1.	Nescafe Classic Coffee	100% pure coffee beans.
2.	Garlic	Natural
3.	Incense Stick (Zed black Charlie)	Lavender
4.	POLO Mint with the hole	Sugar, Edible Starch, Liquid glucose, Anticaking agent (470(i)), Natural flavour and Natural flavouring substance
5.	Sanitizer (Dettol)	Alcohol Denat., Water, PEG/PPG-17/6 Copolymer, Propylene Glycol, Acrylates/C10-30 Alkyl Acrylate Crosspolymer, Tetrahydroxypropyl Ethylenediamine, Fragrance, Limonene
6.	Shampoo (Clinic Plus Milk Protein & Multivitamin)	Water, Sodium Laureth Sulphate, Dimethiconol (And) Tea-Dodecylbenzene Sulfonate, Cocoamidopropyl Betaine, Sodium Chloride, Perfume, CarbomeUnisex.
7.	Soap (Medimix)	Chitraka, Vanardraka, Sariba, Chopchini, Nimba Twak, Daru Haridra, Vacha, Usheeram, Dhanyaka, Jeeraka, Vidangam, Yashtimadhu, Kutaja, Jyothishmathi, Devadaru, Krishna Jeeraka, Bakuchi, Guggulu
8.	Vicks (Menthol Lozenges)	Ascorbic Acid, Caramel, Corn Syrup, Eucalyptus Oil, Sucrose.
9.	Volini (spray)	Diclofenac Diethylamine Methyl Salicylate Menthol And Linseed Oil
10.	Turmeric	Natural
11.	Cumin seeds	Natural
12.	Coriander (seeds)	Natural
13.	Onion	Natural
14.	Cardamom	Natural
15.	Ginger	Natural
16.	Honey	Natural
17.	Chocolate (Dairy Milk)	Sugar, Milk Solids (23%*), Cocoa Butter, Cocoa Solids, Emulsifiers (442,476), Flavour (Natural, Nature Identical And Artificial (Vanilla) Flavouring Substances).
18.	Camphor (Saraswati)	Pinene
19.	Red chilli	Natural
20.	Background	Natural

artificial olfactory system in a controlled room-temperature environment. For each class, we selected 10Hz (one sample every 0.1 seconds) sampling rate to ensure high temporal resolution, capturing subtle sensor signal changes, which allowing the model to detect subtle dynamic patterns in volatile organic compounds across all 20 distinct classes. This rate aligns with domain standards for environmental monitoring, and also it compromise between capturing and dynamics and minimizing high-frequency noise. A higher rate may introduce noise, while lower rate might miss the critical variations.

After a 1-min warm-up period, the sample is exposed to the sensors for 4 min, in which the sensor reaches its saturation phase for a specific gas. The duration of 4 min was determined through empirical testing. After this exposure, the sample is removed, and the sensor is allowed for 5 min to purge out the gases and return to its initial state. This makes it a 10-min process. The next sample is introduced after (at least) 1 min of this entire process to purge out the gas presented, as illustrated in Fig. 3. Another important thing to strictly follow in the data collection process is to make the impact of the outside environment as minimal as possible. As metal-oxide sensors are highly sensitive to changes, particularly airflow [21], to address this, we enclosed the entire setup in a glass chamber to collect the data. The final collected odor data is a time-series array data, with the 11 dimensions representing various gases listed in Table 2.

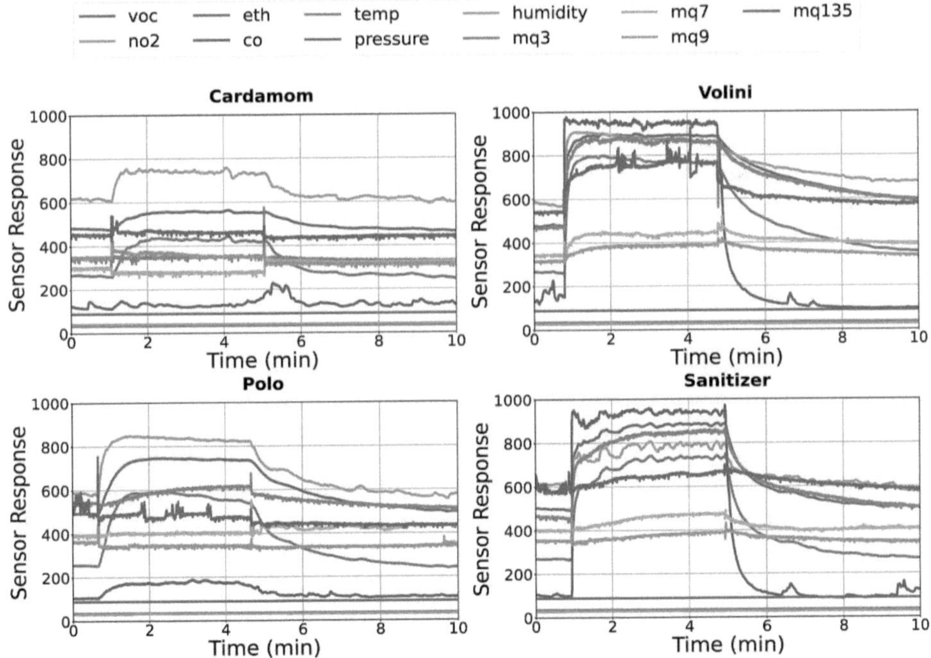

Fig. 3. Response curves from different raw samples.

We collected a large dataset using various sensors, which included samples of 20 different classes as mentioned in Table 3, Each class represents a unique product, with its corresponding composition detailing the specific ingredients present in that particular sample. These classes are background *(air/no odor)*, cardamom, camphor, chocolate *(dairy milk)*, nescafe classic coffee, coriander, cumin seeds, garlic, ginger, honey, incense stick *(zed black charlie)*, polo mint with hole, onion, red chilli, sanitizer *(dettol)*, shampoo *(clinic plus)*, soap *(medimix)*, turmeric, vicks *(menthol lozenges)*, and volini *(spray)* as shown in Table 3 with their ingradients. The choice of samples aimed to encompass a range of olfactory profiles representative of everyday substances. For each class, a sample reading is collected 16 times at different times over several days (usually 3 to 4 days). Each sample of a class consists of 6000 rows of 10-bit Analog-to-Digital Converter (ADC) readings were converted in to meaningful voltage scale using a reference voltage V_{ref} of 3.3V. The conversion is given by:

$$V_{\text{out}} = \frac{\text{ADC}_{reading}}{1024} \times V_{\text{ref}} \tag{1}$$

Sensors data often contains noise and sudden spikes. To reduce this, we use a rolling Z-score to detect the outliers, Z-score [6] calculated as:

$$Z = \frac{x - \mu_{window}}{\sigma_{window}} \tag{2}$$

Any data point x where the Z-score exceeded a threshold of 2 then it replaced by the window's local mean (μ_{window}). Then we formally define the dataset $\mathcal{D} = \{(\mathbf{X}_i, y_i), i \in [1, 320]\}$, where $\mathbf{X}_i \in \mathbb{R}^{6000 \times 11}$ is the time-series data from sensors and $y_i \in \{1, 2, \cdots, 20\}$ is the corresponding odor label. In our quest to develop a robust model, we initially worked with 11 features. However, we identified that certain features *(MQ135, MQ3, and Pressure)*, which have a high correlation with others, lead to redundant information. To enhance our model, we conducted feature selection and eliminated these redundant attributes, allowing the model to concentrate on the most relevant and independent features. This optimization significantly improved the model's accuracy, interpretability, and overall efficiency. To determine the best data segmentation approach, we conducted multiple experiments using different time intervals, including 2 min, 4 min, and 6 min. Each experiment yielded different outcomes, making it challenging to pinpoint a consistent pattern. After extensive analysis, the 4-min segment emerged as the most reliable and accurate among all. With this insight, we refined our dataset even further. The reading from the range $600 - 3001$, *i.e.*, total 2400 readings for the 4 min duration starting after 1st min till the 5th min are considered, yielding a matrix of $\mathbf{X}_i \in \mathbb{R}^{2400 \times 8}$. We applied a sliding window technique with window size w and stride s to further refine the data for better accuracy. The number of samples n generated from this technique is calculated as $n = \lfloor \frac{2400 - w}{s} \rfloor + 1$. We normalize the data based on the training set to ensure consistency, applying zero mean and unit variance normalization. Thus, transforming each $\mathbf{X}_i$ into several windows $\mathbf{Z}_{i,1}, \mathbf{Z}_{i,2}, \mathbf{Z}_{i,3}, \ldots, \mathbf{Z}_{i,n}$, where $\mathbf{Z}_{i,j} \in \mathbb{R}^{w \times 8}$, while having the same odor label y_i for each of these windows.

3.3 Hardware Assembly

We used 3D printing technology to construct the physical framework of our olfactory system, as shown in Fig. 1. This ensured a precise and tailored design optimizing the integration of subsequent components. Our system consists of:

- A SAMD51-based microcontroller with wireless connectivity (also known as the Wio Terminal) [2]. It is compatible with Arduino and MicroPython and comes with an LCD.
- Sensor array consisting of 9 sensors (on 6 chips): GM-102B, GM-302B, GM-502B, GM-702B, MQ3, MQ7, MQ9, MQ135, and BME680 as shown in Fig. 2.
- A breadboard for directly connecting the sensor array to the Wio Terminal Controller.
- The enclosure has exactly the shape of a human nose, and a small fan at the back helps with the inhalation and exhalation of gas from the nose enclosure.

4 Experiments and Results

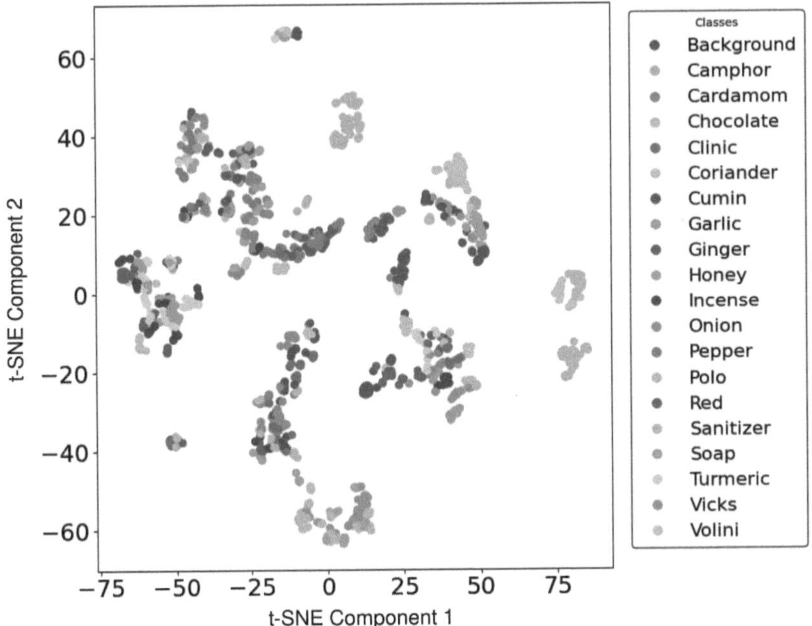

Fig. 4. t-SNE visualization of Test Features.

4.1 Implementation Detail

All models were implemented in Pytorch 2.5.1+$cuda$12.4 and trained on a server equipped with Nvidia RTX A6000 with 48GB of memory. The model was trained on 500 epochs with Adam optimizer, learning rate of 0.00002, weight decay $1e-3$, and batch size of 64. To mitigate overfitting, we employed a dropout of 0.2 and utilized cross-entropy loss with computed class weight. We also leveraged the early stopping mechanism with a patience of 10 epochs based on validation accuracy.

4.2 Experiment

We have curated a diverse dataset comprising 20 distinct classes for odor classification. Experiments were conducted with varying window size and stride, as can be seen in Table 4, it's shows that a smaller window size and stride may include redundant information, hindering the model's ability to classify effectively, as this can lead to oversampling of similar data points, reducing the diversity of temporal patterns available for learning. So we opted for 250/250 windows with a non-overlapped stride, which ensures comprehensive temporal context for the timeseries data. Moreover, this approach offers two key benefits: A larger window, more likely to capture a better signature of the gas. Using an equal stride to a window ensures that the windows are statistically independent, avoiding the redundancy from overlapping data. Thus, the 250/250 setup produces clean, non-correlated samples, captures a sufficient portion of the gas response dynamics, and offers a fair and interpretable baseline. Additionally, we applied advanced time-series augmentation techniques to enhance the robustness and generalization of our model. The augmentation pipeline includes adding Gaussian noise [31] to simulate sensor variability, time warping [18] to introduce temporal distortions, magnitude warping [17] to vary signal intensity, and random window slicing [10] to mimic missing or partial data. By applying these transformations in random combinations, we increase data diversity and reduce overfitting, ensuring the model performs reliably under real-world variations.

Our comprehensive results revealed that the task is quite challenging, as we can see in the confusion matrix, as referred in Fig. 6, we noticed that classes like *onion, clinic, vicks, polo, turmeric, cardamom* got mixed up with other classes, and some were not classifiable. This shows these classes are too similar and have unclear differences. These challenges were attributed to potential factors such as class overlap, ambiguous class definitions, or insufficient discriminative features in the input representation.

These architectures captured valuable spatiotemporal dependencies from sequential sensor data, making them effective for this challenging odor classification task. We have selected models like CNNs, ResidualCNNs, GRU, LSTM, and RNNs with Attention. These architectures form sequential sensor data, making them effective for this challenging odor classification task, and all models were

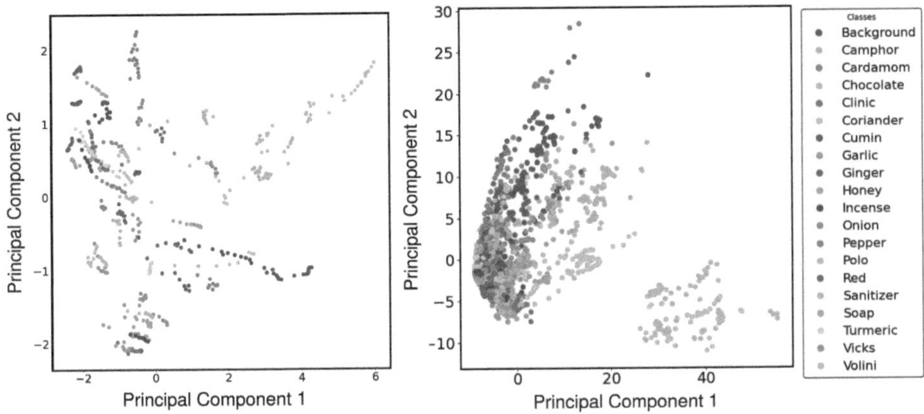

Fig. 5. PCA visualization of test data (left) and test features (right).

trained for up to 500 epochs with lr 0.00002 with dropout of 0.2 and weight decay $1e - 3$. Training was conducted with the same hyperparameters across all models, with applying an early stop with patience of 10 based on validation accuracy to prevent overfitting. However, the CNN model delivered the best performance among all evaluated models on 250/250 window size and stride. The architecture features an initial convolutional layer with 64 filters, followed by a second layer with 128 filters, both leveraging $3 * 3$ kernel size and 1 padding to preserve the spatial dimensions. A max pooling layer with a stride of 2 reduces the temporal resolution.

As shown in Table 4, the CNNs model demonstrates strong performance for our dataset comprising 20 classes. Where, The confusion matrix in Fig. 6 revealed that the model struggles with certain classes like *onion, clinic plus, vicks, polo, turmeric, and cardamom,* where missclassification occurs. This is likely due to similarities between some odors, which makes it harder to distinguish. Apart from this, the results in a notable for other classes with this CNNs achieving a high F1 score on 250/250 window size and stride. To gain deeper insights into the learned representations of the CNNs model, we visualize the extracted test set embeddings using t-Distributed Stochastic Neighbor Embedding (t-SNE) [23] as illustrated in Fig. 4, where each point represents a sample from the test dataset. The color-coded labels indicate different classes, offering a visual assessment of how well the model distinguishes them in the feature space. Also, we also examine the structure of learned feature space by projecting the embeddings onto the first two principal components [24], as illustrated in Fig. 5. This linear dimensionality reduction technique highlights the global structure and variance within the data, providing a clear representation of how the CNNs model transforms the original 8-sensor time-series into a more separable feature space.

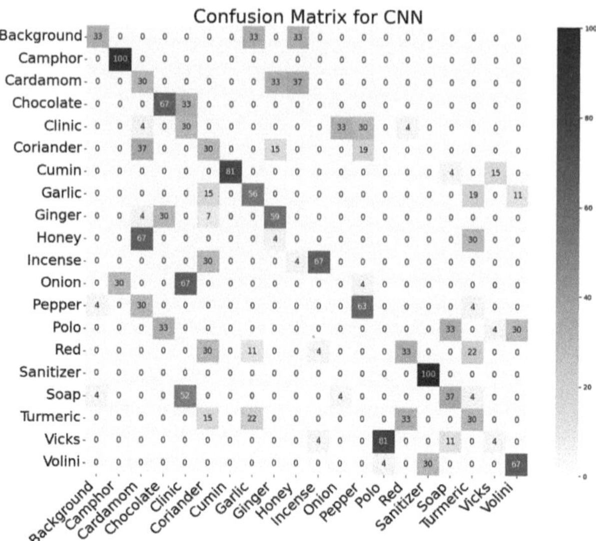

Fig. 6. Confusion matrix of CNNs model.

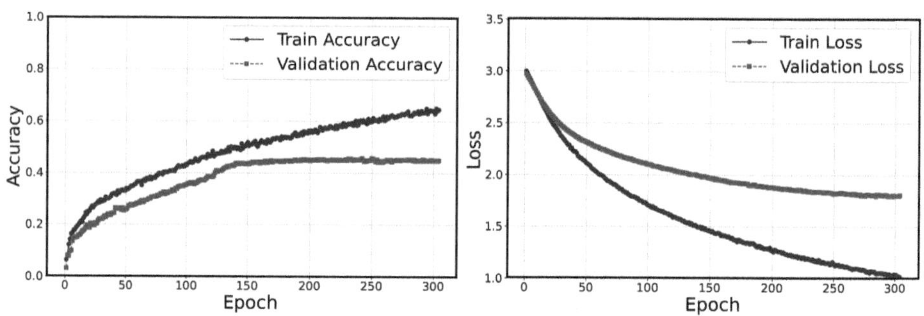

Fig. 7. Accuracy and Loss plot for the CNN model.

Results in Table 4 show the accuracy comparison among 1D-CNNs, Residual CNNs, LSTM, GRU, and RNNs with attention. Notably, the CNNs model achieved good accuracy and F1 scores. We fine-tuned the window sizes and strides alongside carefully optimized hyperparameters to achieve the best accuracy across different models. To better understand the optimization process and generalization capability of the model, we plot the training and validation accuracy and loss curve in Fig. 7, which illustrates its convergence behaviour and effectiveness of the chosen hyperparameters.

Table 4. Performance comparison of models in terms of accuracy and F1 score.

	CNNs		ResidualCNNs		GRU		LSTM		RNNs+Attention	
	Acc (%)	F1	Acc (%)	F1	Acc (%)	F1	Acc (%)	F1	Acc (%)	F1
w 300, s 300	44.58	42.72	43.95	41.74	43.75	42.84	32.70	27.08	40.62	37.29
w 300, s 250	43.33	41.97	45.92	45.15	47.03	46.02	28.14	23.66	40.55	36.32
w 300, s 200	44.84	38.06	47.72	46.40	42.42	40.85	28.84	21.90	41.21	38.87
w 250, s 250	44.25	**42.90**	43.51	42.06	37.40	35.12	36.85	36.60	41.29	38.32
w 200, s 200	43.75	42.51	41.25	41.30	37.08	36.26	32.50	29.65	42.36	39.82

5   Conclusion

In this work, we developed a sensor array to capture the olfactory signature of different odors capable of sensing the smell from various generic application domains instead of specific odor application sensors used by the existing works. Also, we used several advanced deep learning models to learn the unknown basis of the olfactory space. We achieved the best results 42.90% F1 score, with accuracy 44.25% with the CNNs model. Also, we collected a large dataset for 20 different odors with a standard protocol that will be very helpful for the further advancement of olfactory research. The proposed dataset can serve as a valuable resource for advancing research in odor classification. It provides a foundation for developing robust models. This proposed dataset can help reduce confusion among the olfactory signatures of the various smells.

Acknowledgment. This work is supported by the iHub an HCI foundation, IIT Mandi through grant number project no. IITM/iHub & HCIF-IIT Mandi/SRC/418. Also, we would like to thank and acknowledge the use of the CHEETAH: A GPU-based computational facility developed under research grant No. IITM/SG/DIS-ROS-SPA/111 of the Indian Institute of Technology Mandi, Department of Higher Education, Ministry of Education, Government of India for the computational requirements of this research work.

References

1. Grove-multichannel-gas-sensor-v2. https://wiki.seeedstudio.com/Grove-Multichannel-Gas-Sensor-V2. Accessed 28 Aug 2025
2. Wio-terminal-getting-started. https://wiki.seeedstudio.com/Wio-Terminal-Getting-Started/. Accessed 28 Aug 2025
3. Acevedo, C.M.D., Vasquez, C.A.C., Gómez, J.K.C.: Electronic nose dataset for COPD detection from smokers and healthy people through exhaled breath analysis. Data Brief **35**, 106767 (2021)
4. Aghoutane, Y., Brebu, M., Moufid, M., Ionescu, R., Bouchikhi, B., El Bari, N.: Detection of counterfeit perfumes by using GC-MS technique and electronic nose system combined with chemometric tools. Micromachines **14**, 524 (2023)

5. Buettner, A.: Springer Handbook of Odor. Springer (2017)
6. Chikodili, N.B., Abdulmalik, M.D., Abisoye, O.A., Bashir, S.A.: Outlier detection in multivariate time series data using a fusion of k-medoid, standardized euclidean distance and z-score. In: ICTA 2020. CCIS, vol. 1350, pp. 259–271. Springer, Cham (2021). https://doi.org/10.1007/978-3-030-69143-1_21
7. Dey, R., Salem, F.M.: Gate-variants of gated recurrent unit (GRU) neural networks. In: 2017 IEEE 60th International Midwest Symposium on Circuits and Systems (MWSCAS), pp. 1597–1600. IEEE (2017)
8. Dong, W., Zhao, J., Rongsuo, H., Dong, Y., Tan, L.: Differentiation of Chinese robusta coffees according to species, using a combined electronic nose and tongue, with the aid of chemometrics. Food Chem. **229**, 743–751 (2017)
9. Doty, R.L.: Handbook of Olfaction and Gustation. Wiley (2015)
10. Forestier, G., Petitjean, F., Dau, H.A., Webb, G.I., Keogh, E.J.: Generating synthetic time series to augment sparse datasets. In: Raghavan, V., Aluru, S., Karypis, G., Miele, L., Wu, X. (eds.) 2017 IEEE International Conference on Data Mining, ICDM 2017, New Orleans, LA, USA, 18–21 November 2017, pp. 865–870. IEEE Computer Society (2017)
11. Fundurulic, A., Faria, J.M.S., Inácio, M.L.: Advances in electronic nose sensors for plant disease and pest detection. Eng. Proc. **48**, 14 (2023)
12. Gharibzahedi, S.M.T., Barba, F.J., Zhou, J., Wang, M., Altintas, Z.: Electronic sensor technologies in monitoring quality of tea: a review. Biosensors **12**, 356 (2022)
13. He, K., Zhang, X., Ren, S., Sun, J.: Deep residual learning for image recognition. CoRR, abs/1512.03385 (2015)
14. Hearst, M.A., Dumais, S.T., Osuna, E., Platt, J., Scholkopf, B.: Support vector machines. IEEE Intell. Syst. Appl. **13**, 18–28 (1998)
15. Hearst, M.A., Dumais, S.T., Osuna, E., Platt, J., Scholkopf, B.: Support vector machines. IEEE Intell. Syst. Appl. **13**, 18–28 (1998)
16. Hochreiter, S., Schmidhuber, J.: Long short-term memory. Neural Comput. **9**, 1735–80 (1997)
17. Iwana, B.K., Uchida, S.: An empirical survey of data augmentation for time series classification with neural networks. PLoS ONE **16**, e0254841 (2021)
18. Le Guennec, A., Malinowski, S., Tavenard, R.: Data augmentation for time series classification using convolutional neural networks. In: ECML/PKDD Workshop on Advanced Analytics and Learning on Temporal Data (2016)
19. LeCun, Y., et al.: Handwritten digit recognition with a back-propagation network. In: Touretzky, D.S. (ed.) Advances in Neural Information Processing Systems 2, [NIPS Conference, Denver, Colorado, USA, 27–30 November 1989], pp. 396–404. Morgan Kaufmann (1989)
20. Li, Y., Wei, X., Zhou, Y., et al.: Research progress of electronic nose technology in exhaled breath disease analysis. Microsyst. Nanoeng. **9**, 129 (2023)
21. Liu, X., Cheng, S., Liu, H., Sha, H., Zhang, D., Ning, H.: A survey on gas sensing technology. Sensors **12**, 9635–9665 (2012)
22. Ma, D., Gao, J., Zhang, Z., Zhao, H.: Gas recognition method based on the deep learning model of sensor array response map. Sens. Actuators B Chem. **330**, 129349 (2021)
23. van der Maaten, L., Hinton, G.: Visualizing data using t-SNE. J. Mach. Learn. Res. **9**, 2579–2605 (2008)
24. Maćkiewicz, A., Ratajczak, W.: Principal components analysis (PCA). Comput. Geosci. **19**, 303–342 (1993)
25. Olah, C., Carter, S.: Attention and augmented recurrent neural networks. Distill **1**, e1 (2016)

26. Peng, P., Zhao, X., Pan, X., Ye, W.: Gas classification using deep convolutional neural networks. Sensors **18**, 157 (2018)
27. Prasad, P., Raut, P., Goel, S., et al.: Electronic nose and wireless sensor network for environmental monitoring application in pulp and paper industry: a review. Environ. Monit. Assess. **194**, 855 (2022)
28. Gamboa, J.C.R., et al.: Wine quality rapid detection using a compact electronic nose system: application focused on spoilage thresholds by acetic acid. LWT Food Sci. Technol. **108**, 377–384 (2019)
29. Sarno, R., Sabilla, S.I., Wijaya, D.R., Sunaryono, D., Fatichah, C.: Electronic nose dataset for pork adulteration in beef. Data Brief **32**, 106139 (2020)
30. Shi, Y., Gong, F., Wang, M., Liu, J., Yinong, W., Men, H.: A deep feature mining method of electronic nose sensor data for identifying beer olfactory information. J. Food Eng. **263**, 437–445 (2019)
31. Um, T.T., et al.: Data augmentation of wearable sensor data for Parkinson's disease monitoring using convolutional neural networks. In: Proceedings of the 19th ACM International Conference on Multimodal Interaction, pp. 216–220 (2017)
32. Wang, M., Chen, Y.: Electronic nose and its application in the food industry: a review. Eur. Food Res. Technol. **250**, 21–67 (2024)
33. Wijaya, D.R., Afianti, F., Arifianto, A., Rahmawati, D., Kodogiannis, V.S.: Ensemble machine learning approach for electronic nose signal processing. Sens. Bio-Sens. Res. **36**, 100495 (2022)
34. Wijaya, D.R., Sarno, R., Zulaika, E.: Electronic nose dataset for beef quality monitoring in uncontrolled ambient conditions. Data Brief **21**, 2414–2420 (2018)
35. Wilson, A.D., Baietto, M.: Applications and advances in electronic-nose technologies. Sensors **9**, 5099–5148 (2009)
36. Wilson, A.D.: Review of electronic-nose technologies and algorithms to detect hazardous chemicals in the environment. Procedia Technol. **1**, 453–463 (2012)
37. Wojnowski, W., Kalinowska, K.: Machine learning and electronic noses for medical diagnostics, pp. 1203–1218. Springer, Cham (2022)
38. Xu, H., Kitai, K., Minami, K., et al.: Determination of quasi-primary odors by endpoint detection. Sci. Rep. **11**, 12070 (2021)
39. Min, X., Wang, J., Zhu, L.: Tea quality evaluation by applying e-nose combined with chemometrics methods. J. Food Sci. Technol. **58**, 1549–1561 (2021)
40. Zhi, R., Zhao, L., Zhang, D.: A framework for the multi-level fusion of electronic nose and electronic tongue for tea quality assessment. Sensors **17**, 1007 (2017)

Sanjeev Chauhan[1]([✉]) [iD], Alok Singh[1] [iD], and Rammohan Mallipeddi[2] [iD]

[1] School of Computer and Information Sciences, University of Hyderabad,
Hyderabad 500046, India
`isitsanjeev@gmail.com, alok@uohyd.ac.in`
[2] Department of Artificial Intelligence, School of Electronics Engineering,
Kyungpook National University, Daegu 41566, Republic of Korea

Abstract. Single depot multiple traveling salesman problem (MTSP) is widely studied in the literature. However, multi-depot multiple traveling salesman problem (MD-MTSP) has not gained much attention. Only a few approaches exist in the literature for MD-MTSP. In this paper, we have proposed two hybrid evolutionary approaches for MD-MTSP. Our first approach is based on grouping genetic algorithm (GGA), whereas the other approach utilizes discrete differential evolution (DDE). Chromosome encoding and variation operators in these two approaches are designed considering the characteristics of MD-MTSP. The solutions obtained through variation operators in these approaches are improved further through a local search. We have compared the performance of our approaches with the best approach available in the literature on standard benchmark instances. In addition, we have reported the performance of our approaches on some large instances also. Computational results show the effectiveness of our two approaches in solving MD-MTSP as these two consistently outperform the existing best approach.

Keywords: Multi-depot multiple travelling salesman problem ·
Grouping genetic algorithm · Discrete differential evolution · Intelligent optimization

1 Introduction

The multiple traveling salesman problem (MTSP) is a generalization of the well-known traveling salesman problem (TSP). In the TSP, the objective is to determine a tour for a single salesman that visits each of the n cities exactly once and return to the starting city while minimizing the total travel distance. In contrast, the MTSP involves m salespersons tasked with visiting $n > m$ cities. The problem requires partitioning the n cities into m subsets and determining the visiting order within each subset, such that every city is visited exactly once

B. Chatterjee et al. (Eds.): ICDCIT 2026, LNCS 16420, pp. 358–376, 2026.
https://doi.org/10.1007/978-3-032-16632-6_23

by only one salesman, and the overall travel distance of all salesmen combined is minimized. In contrast to TSP where a single tour needs to be determined, MTSP involves determining m tours. MTSP has numerous real-world applications in logistic, routing, scheduling, manufacturing, disaster management, satellite surveying system and so on [1,2]. Being a generalization of TSP, which is an $\mathcal{NP}$-hard problem, MTSP is also $\mathcal{NP}$-hard.

In the MTSP framework, the cities where tours begin and end are termed depots, while all other cities are classified as intermediate cities. Variants of MTSP are distinguished by the number of depots involved. In the single-depot variant, all m salesmen must start and finish their tours at the same common depot. In the multi-depot variant, each salesman begins and ends their journey at their own designated depot. Both variants put the restriction that each salesman must visit at least one city in addition to its depot in order to utilize all the salesmen and to prevent the problem from reducing to TSP. Former variant is widely studied and there exists a copious literature describing metaheuristic approaches for this variant (e.g., [2,6,8,13,16,18]). On the other, latter variant referred to as multi-depot multiple traveling salesman problem (MD-MTSP) has not gained much attention specially from metaheuristic perspective despite real-world applications (e.g., [7,17]).

Only a few approaches based on ant colony optimization exist (ACO) in the literature for MD-MTSP [9,11,12]. Among these ACO approaches, the ACO approach proposed by Pérez-Carabaza et al. [11] is the most recent and best approach. This ACO approach is based on ant colony system (ACS) [4] and utilizes dynamically updated Voronoi regions to efficiently organize the assignment and routing of salesmen. Three variants of the ACO approach have been evaluated in [11]. Among the three variants, dynamic-yield variant achieves the best results. This variant leverages the dynamic nature of Voronoi regions to adaptively update or skip city assignments using a yield-turn strategy. This mechanism allows a salesman to skip their turn if no unvisited city remains within its Voronoi region, thereby enabling more efficient assignments in subsequent iterations. This variant will be referred to as ACS-V-DY. In comparison to previous best performing ACO approach [12], ACS-V-DY obtained better results on a set of 20 benchmark instances introduced by Pérez-Carabaza et al. [11].

In this paper, we have proposed two hybrid evolutionary approaches for MD-MTSP. Our first approach is based on grouping genetic algorithm (GGA), whereas second approach is based on discrete differential evolution approach (DDE). We have designed the chromosome encoding and variation operators in these two approaches keeping in mind the structure of MD-MTSP. The solutions obtained after applying variation operators are enhanced further by making use of a 2-opt based local search. We have compared the performance of the proposed approaches with the best approach available in the literature, namely ACS-V-DY on the same set of 20 benchmark instances as used in [11]. Computational results clearly demonstrate the superiority of our two approaches over ACS-V-DY in terms of best as well as average solution quality. To facilitate future research, we have also introduced 140 large benchmark instances for MD-

MTSP and reported the performance of our GGA and DDE approach on these instances.

The remainder of this paper is organized in the following manner: Sect. 2 presents our grouping genetic algorithm approach for MD-MTSP. Section 3 is devoted to our discrete differential evolution approach for MD-MTSP. Experimental results and analysis thereof are presented in Sect. 4. Finally, Sect. 5 concludes the paper by listing the contributions made and a few directions for future research.

2   Grouping Genetic Algorithm for MD-MTSP

A grouping problem is a problem which calls for partitioning a given set of items into groups subject to some constraints so that a given cost function is optimized. Clearly, MD-MTSP is a grouping problem as we need to partition the set of cities into groups where each group of cities is assigned to a salesman. To effectively solve grouping problems, Falkenauer [5] developed grouping genetic algorithm, which was later extended in [13, 14]. Considering the grouping nature of MD-MTSP, we have developed a grouping genetic algorithm (GGA) for MD-MTSP which employs crossover and mutation operators that are tailor-made for MD-MTSP keeping in mind the structure of MD-MTSP. Subsections that follow provide the details of various components of our GGA.

2.1   Chromosomes Representation and Fitness

This work adopts a chromosome structure, where depots are not part of the chromosome, but stored separately in an ordered list. Each chromosome is an ordered sequence of m tours, where i^{th} tour in the chromosome corresponds to i^{th} depot in the ordered list of depots. A tour in the chromosome contains only intermediate cities and its position in the chromosome serves as an index into the ordered list of depots to get the complete tour. For example, consider an example with a total of 15 cities, where 3 cities, namely 4, 9 and 12 are depots. The remaining 12 cities are intermediate cities and are allocated among the 3 salesmen. If the depots are stored in the ordered list in the order 4, 9 and 12, a sample chromosome is illustrated in Fig. 1. In this chromosome, tour 6, 15, 5, 1 corresponds to first depot in the ordered list of depots, i.e., depot 4 and salesman 1 (complete tour is $4 \rightarrow 6 \rightarrow 15 \rightarrow 5 \rightarrow 1 \rightarrow 4$), tour 8, 10, 3, 2, 7 corresponds to depot 9 and salesman 2 (complete tour is $9 \rightarrow 8 \rightarrow 10 \rightarrow 3 \rightarrow 2 \rightarrow 7 \rightarrow 9$) and tour 14, 11, 13 corresponds to depot 12 and salesman 3 (complete tour is $12 \rightarrow 14 \rightarrow 11 \rightarrow 13 \rightarrow 12$). Each solution is uniquely represented in this representation. A chromosome representation where it is possible to represent a solution in more than one way is said to suffer from problem of redundancy, which may have a negative impact on the performance of a GA. Actually, GA works in the representation space (set of all possible solution representations) rather than solution space (set of all possible solution to the problem). If size of the former is larger than the latter then GA is forced to search a larger space than actually needed, which can negatively impact its performance. Our chromosome representation do not suffer from the problem of redundancy. This is possible because of two factors. First the position of each salesman's tour in the chromosome is fixed. Second, the depot for each tour is not explicitly stored along with the tour allowing an unique representation for each tour. The objective of MD-MTSP is to minimize the total distance travelled by all the salesman. Accordingly, the fitness of a solution is defined as the total distance travelled by all the salesman in that solution. A lower value implies a better fitness.

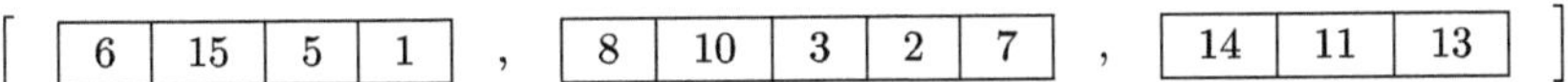

Fig. 1. Our Chromosomes Representation

2.2   Initial Population Generation

Each solution of the initial population is generated via an iterative process that is a proper mix of greediness and randomness. Before this iterative process begins, it is assumed that salesman are at their respective depots and their tours are empty. During each iteration, first a salesman is randomly selected and then an unassigned city is chosen at random. The chosen city is inserted into the most suitable position in the tour of the selected salesman. The most suitable position is the position where inserting the city yields the smallest increase in cost. These iterations continue till all cities are assigned. The resulting solution is verified for uniqueness in relation to the population members that are already generated. Solution that meet this condition is added to the initial population. If this condition is not met, then resulting solution is discarded and process starts afresh. This procedure ensures a diverse and high-quality initial population, increasing the likelihood of obtaining an optimal or near-optimal solution with fewer iterations.

2.3   Selection

The selection procedure plays a critical role in maintaining solution diversity and guiding the search toward optimal solutions. We have used two different variants of tournament selection for parent selection in mutation and crossover. For selecting a parent for mutation, we have used ternary tournament selection where best solution among the three randomly chosen solutions is always selected as parent for mutation. On the other hand, for selecting a parent for crossover, we have used probabilistic binary tournament selection where the best solution between two randomly chosen solutions is selected with probability π_b. So the worst solution between the two solutions also has a chance of selection with probability $1 - \pi_b$. The reason for using two different variants of tournament selection for mutation and crossover is that we got better results in this manner in comparison to using a single variant for both crossover and mutation.

2.4 Crossover

Crossover generates offspring by combining the best characteristics of two parent solutions. The crossover operator used in this work is an adapted version of the crossover operator used in [13]. This crossover consists of two distinct phases. The first phase follows an iterative process. During each iteration, the best tour (as per the below mentioned criteria) from among the two parents is determined and copied to the corresponding position in the child. The cities belonging to this best tour are deleted from their respective positions in both the parents. This deletes the selected tour in the parent from which it is selected. The corresponding salesman's tour in other parents is also deleted. This process is repeated till either all m tours have been copied or all tours in both the parents are empty. The criteria for selecting the best tour is the length of the tour divided by number of cities (excluding the depot) in that tour.

After the first phase, if there are unassigned cities or some tours are empty then second phase is executed. This phase first deals with the unassigned cities and then with the empty tours. It also follows an iterative process where during each iteration, an unassigned city is chosen randomly and inserted into its most suitable possible position over all the tours. The most suitable position is the position among all positions in all the tours where inserting the city yields the smallest increase in cost. This process continues till every city is assigned. If after this process, some tours still remain empty, then these empty tours are converted into non-empty tours by following an iterative process where during each iteration a city whose removal decreases the corresponding tour's cost by maximum amount and does not make this tour empty is removed, and inserted into an empty tour where cost increases by the least amount. This process continues till no empty tour remains.

2.5 Mutation

In mutation, each city is removed from its respective tour with probability π_{copy}, thereby creating a set of unassigned cities and possibly some empty tours. These unassigned cities are reinserted into the solution using the same strategy as in the second phase of the crossover operation. Notably in GGA, crossover and mutation are utilized in a mutually exclusive way, with the choice of operator determined by the crossover probability π_c. So with probability $1 - \pi_c$ mutation is used.

2.6 2-Opt

The 2-Opt local search is widely used technique in solving the TSP and its variants. It improves a solution by deleting two non-adjacent edges from a tour and reconnecting the two resulting segments via two new edges, thereby forming a valid tour. 2-Opt local search is applied one-by-one to all the tours to improve their cost.

Algorithm 1: GGA for MD-MTSP

Input: Parameters of GGA and a MD-MTSP instance
Output: Best solution found
Initialize population P;
$s_{best} \leftarrow$ best solution in P;
$i_{worst} \leftarrow find\_worst\_index(P)$;
$t \leftarrow 0$;
while $(t < T)$ **do**
    if $u01 \leq \pi_c$ **then**
        $s_1 \leftarrow binary\_selection()$;
        repeat
            $s_2 \leftarrow binary\_selection()$;
        until $(s_1 \neq s_2)$;
        $offspring \leftarrow crossover(s_1, s_2)$;
    else
        $s_1 \leftarrow ternary\_selection()$;
        $offspring \leftarrow mutation(s_1)$;
    $offspring \leftarrow 2 - opt(offspring)$;
    if $((f(offspring) < f(P[i_{worst}])$ **and** $isunique(offspring, P))$ **then**
        $P[i_{worst}] \leftarrow offspring$;
        if $(f(offspring) < f(s_{best}))$ **then**
            $s_{best} \leftarrow offspring$;
        $i_{worst} \leftarrow find\_worst\_index(P)$;
    $t \leftarrow t + 1$;
return s_{best};

2.7   Replacement Policy

The replacement phase is the final yet critical step in the GGA process, and it is responsible for ensuring the best solutions generated during evolution. Each newly produced offspring is first evaluated for uniqueness with respect to the existing population. If found unique as well as having fitness better than the worst solution of the population, it replaces the worst solution in the population. If offspring is either not unique or have fitness worse than the worst member of the population then, it is discarded. This mechanism ensures that population diversity is maintained while steadily improving the overall fitness across generations.

Algorithm 1 provides the pseudo-code of GGA, where $u01$ is a uniform variate in $[0, 1]$. In this algorithm, functions *binary_ selection()* and *ternary_ selection()* perform parent selection for crossover and mutation respectively as per their description in Sect. 2.3. The functions *crossover()* and *mutation()* perform crossover and mutation respectively as per the description provided in Sect. 2.4 and Sect. 2.5. The function *2-opt()* performs the 2-opt local search as per the description provided in Sect. 2.6. The *isunique()* function checks whether generated offspring is unique with regard to present population. The function *find_ worst_ index()* returns the index of the worst solution in the population.

3   Discrete Differential Evolution for MD-MTSP

This section is devoted to our discrete differential evolution (DDE) approach for solving the MD-MTSP. Readers unfamiliar with differential evolution may refer to [3], while those unfamiliar with discrete differential evolution can refer to [10, 15].

Algorithm 2: DDE for MD-MTSP

Input: Parameters of DDE and a MD-MTSP instance
Output: Best solution found
Initialize population P;
$s_{best} \leftarrow$ best solution in P;
$t \leftarrow 0$;
while $(t < T)$ **do**
    foreach $(s \in population)$ **do**
        $s_1 \leftarrow ternary\_selection()$;
        $mutant \leftarrow mutation(s_1)$;
        $trial \leftarrow crossover(s, mutant)$;
        $trial \leftarrow$ 2-opt$(trial)$;
        if $(f(trial) < f(s))$ **then**
            $s \leftarrow trial$;
            if $(f(s) < f(s_{best}))$ **then**
                $s_{best} \leftarrow s$;
    $t \leftarrow t + 1$;
return s_{best};

Our approach starts with the generation of an initial population. Then, an iterative process is carried out in which each solution in the population is examined sequentially. The solution under consideration is termed the target solution and serves as one parent in the crossover operation. The second parent for crossover, known as the mutant solution, is generated through mutation. In DDE, the mutant solution can be created in the following manner [10]:

- By applying mutation on the target solution itself,
- By applying mutation on the best solution discovered so far
- By applying mutation on a randomly chosen population member

In our approach, we have followed the last option albeit in a slightly modified way. To create the mutant, we first select a parent solution through ternary tournament selection (Sect. 2.3), and then performed the mutation on the selected solution to get the mutant. Next, the target and mutant solutions undergo crossover to produce a trial solution. This trial solution is further refined using 2-opt local search. If the trial solution outperforms the target solution in terms of fitness, it replaces the target solution. Once all population members are processed, the algorithm moves to the next iteration. The process continues until a stopping condition is reached, after which the best solution found across all iterations is returned.

The pseudo-code for the proposed DDE approach is presented in Algorithm 2. Our DDE framework incorporates elements from GGA, utilizing the same chromosome representation and fitness function, as well as identical procedures for population initialization, selecting a single parent for mutation, crossover, mutation, and local search (see Sects. 2.2, 2.3, 2.4, 2.5, and 2.6).

Table 1. Performance comparison of GGA, DDE and ACS-V-DY on 20 benchmark instances from the literature

Name	Depots	ACS-V-DY		GGA		DDE	
		Avg	Best	Avg	Best	Avg	Best
berlin52	22-38-1	8262	8188	7890.1	7775	**7735.5**	**7637**
	16-8-5	8080	7798	7914.8	**7758**	**7910.2**	7794
	10-18-21-29	8333	8465	7727.4	**7698**	**7711.5**	7699
	22-36-11-46	7903	7788	**7703.6**	**7639**	7785.6	7673
kroA100	42-73-1	21964	21502	**21505.8**	21409	21573.6	21427
	31-15-10	24481	23342	21618.0	**21415**	**21559.3**	21429
	54-42-69-21	22871	22140	22003	21517	**21926.8**	**21240**
	88-3-68-42	23016	22713	22213	**21332**	**22042.4**	**21314**
ch130	55-94-1	6362	6207	6299.4	**6191**	**6258.9**	6210
	40-20-13	6818	6553	6301.1	6159	**6283.8**	**6148**
	71-55-90-27	6726	6372	6326.1	**6135**	**6218.0**	6139
	115-4-88-55	6661	6364	6386.8	6247	**6324.3**	**6198**
ch150	63-109-1	6948	6719	6718.2	6592	**6633.6**	**6565**
	28-52-60	6811	6632	6742.3	**6544**	**6699.6**	6562
	81-63-103-31	6922	6685	6779.2	6642	**6633.0**	**6544**
	132-5-101-63	6936	6680	6750.4	**6554**	**6706.5**	6559
kroB200	84-145-1	31799	30540	30356.6	29813	**30256.7**	**29737**
	61-30-19	30948	30179	30959.6	30231	**30800.8**	**30046**
	108-84-138-41	31596	30762	30983.8	30615	**30601.4**	**29808**
	176-6-135-84	33258	31358	30808.6	30034	**30215.1**	**29330**

4 Experimental Results

Our GGA and DDE approaches have been coded in C and tested on a desktop machine equipped with a 3.10GHz Intel Core i5-8600 processor & 8 GB of RAM, and running the Ubuntu 24.04.2 operating system. The implementations were compiled using gcc version 13.3.0 with the -O3 optimization flag enabled.

The GGA and DDE parameters were configured as follows: In GGA, population size is 100, crossover probability $\pi_c = 0.8$ (so mutation probability is 0.2), probability of selecting the best solution in probabilistic binary tournament selection $\pi_b = 0.7$, and probability of removing a city in mutation $\pi_{copy} = 0.66$. The GGA was executed for 20,000 iterations. DDE also uses a population of 100, and the probability of removing a city in mutation is also same as GGA, i.e., $\pi_{copy} = 0.66$. We have executed DDE for 200 iterations. This ensures that both GGA and DDE generate the same number of solutions. It is to be noted that DDE generates 100 solutions in an iteration, whereas GGA generates a single solution in an iteration. Both GGA and DDE have been executed 20 times independently on each test instance.

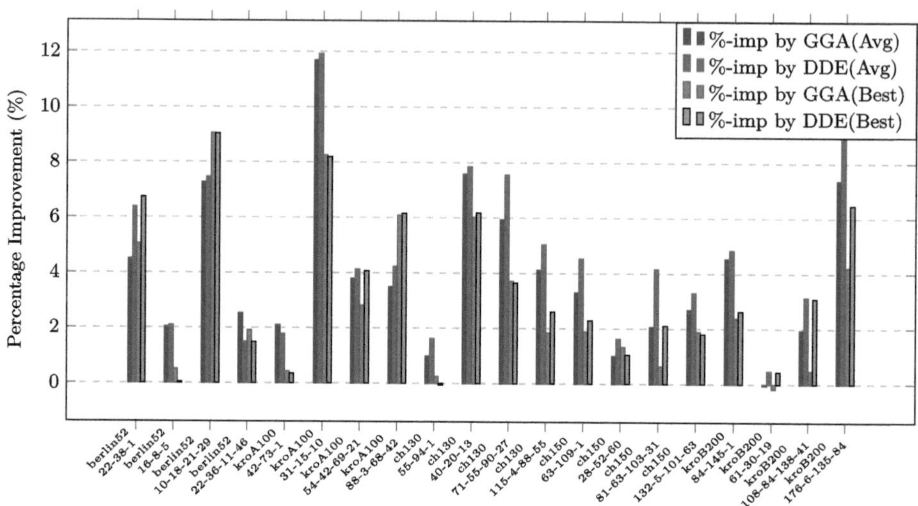

Fig. 2. %-improvement in best and average solution quality of ACS-V-DY by GGA and DDE

We have evaluated the performance of GGA and DDE approaches on two sets of instances. First set of instances are same as used in [11] and consists of 20 instances derived from 5 TSPLIB instances, namely *berlin52*, *kroA100*, *ch130*, *ch150*, and *kroB200*. For each of these 5 instances, the number of depots is taken to be 3 or 4 and there are two different instances with different set of cities as depot for same number of depot thereby leading to 20 (5 × 2 × 2) instances. As the number of cities in first set of instances is limited to 200 and number of depots to either 3 or 4, we have created an additional set of 140 large instances with upto 1889 cities and number of depots 5, 8, 10 and 15. For creating this set, we have taken 35 additional instances from TSPLIB with number of cities ranging from 200 to 1889. For each of these 35 TSPLIB instances, 4 MD-MTSP instances are derived by choosing 5 or 8 or 10 or 15 cities randomly as depot, thereby leading to a set of 140 instances. We have compared the performance of our two approaches on these instances.

On the first set of 20 instances, we have compared the performance of our GGA and DDE approaches with the best method available in the literature, namely ACS-Vornoi based method with dynamic-yield (ACS-V-DY) [11]. Table 1 and Fig. 2 present the results of ACS-V-DY, GGA and DDE. Results of ACS-V-DY are taken from [11]. On each instance, best solution and average solution obtained over 20 runs by ACS-V-DY, GGA and DDE are reported in Table 1. Best values are shown in bold-face for easy identification in this table. Figure 2 shows the percentage improvement in best and average solution quality obtained through ACS-V-DY by GGA and DDE approaches. These table and figure clearly demonstrate the superiority of GGA and DDE over ACS-V-DY as except for one instance (kroB200 with 61, 30 and 19 as depots) where ACS-V-DY performs better than both GGA and DDE in terms of average solution quality and better than GGA in terms of best solution quality, and another instance (ch130 with 55, 94 and 1 as depots) where ACS-V-DY performs better than DDE in terms of best solution quality, in all other cases, results of GGA and DDE are individually better than ACS-V-DY. Our approaches achieve superior solutions, producing solutions up to 9.06% shorter in terms of best solution and 11.83 shorter in terms of average solution than those obtained by the ACS-V-LS.

We can not perform the comparison of execution times of GGA and DDE with ACS-V-DY as no execution times were reported in [11]. However, as ACS-V-DY uses 10 ants and executed for 20000 iteration, it generates 200000 solutions which is 10 times more than the number of solutions generated by GGA and DDE. Further, ant-colony optimization based approaches are inherently computationally expensive as each and every solution is constructed from scratch based on pheromone values. Due to these two factors, ACS-V-DY is expected to be much slower. As far as comparison between our two approaches on these 20 instances is concerned, both perform similar though DDE performed slightly better in terms of average solution quality, whereas GGA performed slightly better in terms of best solution quality.

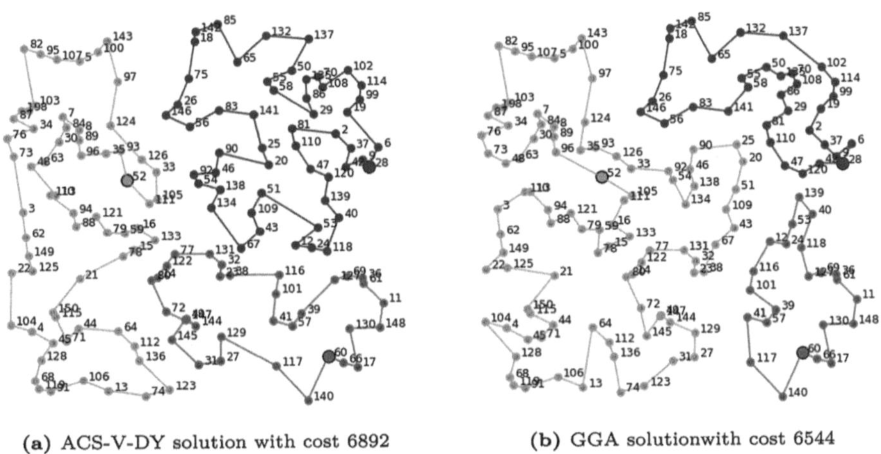

(a) ACS-V-DY solution with cost 6892   (b) GGA solutionwith cost 6544

Fig. 3. Composition of solutions obtained by ACS-V-DY and GGA on *ch150* instance with 28, 52, & 60 as depots

Figure 3 shows the composition of solution obtained by the ACS-V-DY (Fig. 3a) and GGA (Fig. 3b) for the *ch150* instance with cities 28, 52, & 60 serving as depots. As illustrated, the GGA achieves compact tours across all the salesmen in comparison to ACS-V-DY, thereby leading to a better solution.

Table 2. Performance comparison of GGA and DDE on 140 large instances

Name	Depots	GGA			DDE		
		Best	Avg	Time	Best	Avg	Time
kroA200	128-79-129-170-171	30608	31139.8	0.55	**30444**	**30724.2**	1.06
kroA200	28-199-121-164-22-61-84-17	**30325**	31252.4	0.46	30482	**30989.7**	0.91
kroA200	68-24-183-93-112-36-154-164-9-63	**30945**	31831.2	0.44	31144	**31551.7**	0.89
kroA200	169-96-199-61-177-10-174-104-88-55-74-58-82-24-130	30446	31060.3	0.49	**30118**	**30486.6**	1.03
kroB200	126-153-197-176-189	30477	30979.7	0.47	**29821**	**30460.8**	0.92
kroB200	158-130-37-61-15-122-105-29	30384	31076.9	0.45	**29803**	**30698.1**	0.89
kroB200	28-51-149-157-103-195-98-100-44-40	**30640**	31377.3	0.47	30932	**31172.7**	0.93
kroB200	3-29-4-101-82-48-139-160-152-136-135-140-93-16-128	**31102**	**31846.9**	0.50	31430	31922.7	1.11
gr202	179-202-14-180-25	**40252**	**41360.9**	0.78	40881	41741.1	1.17
gr202	82-126-84-128-193-19-104-3	41631	**42454.3**	0.48	**41604**	42589.2	0.91
gr202	15-127-48-8-73-11-84-112-120-198	41720	42617.8	0.43	**41543**	**42237.4**	0.93
gr202	26-66-43-79-94-118-134-71-117-113-48-107-160-173-191	42665	43548.1	0.45	**42553**	**43372.6**	0.99
ts225	119-176-135-140-25	130924	137175.0	0.68	**129766**	**134739.8**	1.23
ts225	215-213-207-169-217-153-41-10	133950	141413.6	0.56	**130902**	**137275.3**	1.16
ts225	62-158-102-63-29-51-183-175-197-9	138819	144783.7	0.63	**137018**	**141081.6**	1.41
ts225	71-180-38-211-44-69-129-94-187-79-55-102-155-89-189	144342	147746.5	0.62	**143162**	**145996.3**	1.30
tsp225	148-214-27-26-13	4103	4221.4	0.60	**4013**	**4086.6**	1.36
tsp225	212-55-214-176-209-148-42-51	**4067**	4142.6	0.69	4067	**4132.3**	1.28
tsp225	108-20-191-96-2-19-116-120-225-135	4101	4215.1	0.54	**4096**	**4143.0**	1.19
tsp225	222-134-54-188-179-162-118-133-85-158-211-110-170-197-216	**4052**	**4144.0**	0.65	4123	4173.6	1.34
pr226	77-52-106-134-137	**79363**	81891.8	0.53	79547	**80959.7**	1.00

(continued)

Table 2. (*continued*)

Name	Depots	GGA			DDE		
		Best	Avg	Time	Best	Avg	Time
pr226	116-195-135-213-70-187-139-223	76353	78711.4	0.54	**75980**	**77625.9**	1.08
pr226	168-108-2-31-196-11-210-29-170-28	**80595**	85796.8	0.48	81168	**84065.3**	1.05
pr226	14-210-77-123-172-102-55-176-170-107-78-17-163-38-151	**73095**	**74029.8**	0.51	74373	75465.5	1.12
gr229	15-184-128-53-56	138706	141007.5	0.67	**136973**	**139370.7**	1.36
gr229	41-3-76-64-167-187-181-129	**137291**	**139904.5**	0.63	137734	141259.8	1.39
gr229	223-122-104-212-57-182-38-91-68-90	**139033**	**141733.8**	0.56	140850	142719.8	1.12
gr229	132-93-214-152-11-60-65-87-75-19-215-127-109-129-184	**141857**	**145133.2**	0.59	142238	146440.7	1.29
gil262	188-240-221-260-56	2464	2526.8	0.88	**2441**	**2483.4**	1.79
gil262	77-142-69-227-171-249-95-187	2532	2588.4	0.65	**2481**	**2515.3**	1.55
gil262	238-89-220-183-147-189-179-103-110-180	2575	2637.8	0.77	**2509**	**2577.6**	1.79
gil262	133-78-159-89-261-134-247-63-111-81-198-42-158-77-260	2621	2684.2	0.75	**2617**	**2683.4**	1.74
pr264	58-190-189-180-140	**45619**	**46635.4**	0.88	45987	47029.5	1.67
pr264	216-44-155-186-203-6-11-127	**44206**	**45050.2**	0.69	44748	45142.8	1.42
pr264	244-94-9-37-214-44-162-140-185-46	44119	44957.7	0.67	**44098**	**44876.6**	1.41
pr264	175-66-226-237-185-30-42-56-19-221-195-234-64-150-219	**43621**	**44385.1**	0.73	45000	45530.1	1.61
a280	62-123-166-244-100	2701	2763.6	0.85	**2672**	**2726.4**	1.84
a280	122-249-179-128-21-46-203-188	2769	2859.4	0.80	**2728**	**2797.8**	1.80
a280	100-72-70-107-114-147-149-195-197-67	2811	2940.8	0.71	**2810**	**2857.5**	2.28
a280	68-253-258-225-122-21-81-247-235-75-4-198-174-125-38	2829	2884.2	0.79	**2809**	**2844.7**	1.77
pr299	274-194-285-60-22	50467	51829.2	0.93	**50127**	**50698.8**	1.85
pr299	122-170-286-243-247-205-79-47	52208	53547.8	0.83	**50925**	**52234.9**	1.74

(*continued*)

Table 2. (*continued*)

Name	Depots	GGA			DDE		
		Best	Avg	Time	Best	Avg	Time
pr299	47-201-209-206-113-298-41-142-256-20	**50269**	53351.2	0.82	51473	**52797.4**	1.82
pr299	156-233-100-216-4-118-105-277-12-90-170-165-45-40-151	**52225**	53776.4	0.89	52526	**53317.8**	1.84
lin318	5-32-240-11-54	43036	43719.1	1.64	**42698**	**43494.6**	2.84
lin318	276-22-173-21-144-35-222-152	**43935**	44825.8	1.02	44081	**44630.5**	2.17
lin318	151-282-245-264-249-294-197-154-270-309	**44526**	**45912.1**	1.05	45569	46101.6	2.26
lin318	278-169-101-303-61-188-317-225-118-31-73-54-84-30-76	**43426**	**44483.9**	1.01	44487	45106.9	2.33
rd400	274-12-66-369-282	15806	16251.8	2.11	**15508**	**15840.5**	4.37
rd400	14-84-100-178-136-215-265-370	16093	16307.8	1.66	**15838**	**15946.3**	3.30
rd400	347-108-273-192-141-12-224-388-258-237	16230	16541.0	1.87	**15968**	**16131.2**	3.77
rd400	394-240-82-221-115-372-172-219-197-135-284-165-368-298-201	16118	16304.3	1.79	**15971**	**16164.5**	3.92
fl417	237-341-103-22-263	11231	11560.0	1.71	**10970**	**11265.8**	3.02
fl417	56-147-93-328-136-159-348-63	**12057**	13320.0	1.84	12262	**12815.7**	3.39
fl417	8-134-140-90-205-274-304-306-253-353	11447	11901.3	1.42	**11266**	**11569.2**	3.44
fl417	245-374-170-346-313-301-342-360-315-45-240-160-150-386-302	11608	11960.8	1.52	**11494**	**11805.2**	3.53
gr431	57-415-217-50-214	**175652**	180535.5	2.76	177982	**180196.1**	5.10
gr431	192-81-30-258-202-32-260-185	177336	181117.1	2.61	**176888**	**179659.6**	5.56
gr431	43-6-355-161-339-169-346-21-93-98	179419	181062.0	2.21	**177354**	**179567.2**	4.97
gr431	406-99-150-217-179-389-18-236-84-234-428-298-426-77-327	177066	178526.9	2.08	**175501**	**178038.4**	4.16
pr439	112-239-368-267-164	114134	116567.2	2.06	**113213**	**114793.0**	4.26
pr439	430-337-82-426-328-101-78-213	**113232**	115843.9	2.06	113846	**115359.9**	4.18
pr439	59-228-123-127-302-352-362-75-131-74	**112194**	116407.0	1.88	113718	**114886.8**	4.18

(*continued*)

Table 2. (*continued*)

Name	Depots	GGA			DDE		
		Best	Avg	Time	Best	Avg	Time
pr439	364-16-180-230-302-410-83-413-79-11-241-243-2-138-194	115066	116642.1	1.76	**113711**	**115515.7**	3.83
pcb442	430-144-93-344-75	**51947**	54180.1	2.51	52236	**53459.6**	5.07
pcb442	38-202-205-296-144-222-230-184	53672	54987.8	1.91	**52938**	**53575.0**	4.03
pcb442	153-296-107-11-108-13-317-119-359-177	54825	56058.9	2.14	**53086**	**54296.2**	4.96
pcb442	364-60-285-360-424-85-126-283-229-218-184-303-128-258-380	54883	56653.3	1.73	**54086**	**54733.0**	3.77
d493	256-445-379-452-176	36971	37790.0	3.45	**36340**	**37314.3**	6.22
d493	304-233-181-455-354-66-359-222	37252	38053.9	2.12	**36324**	**36995.1**	4.63
d493	16-191-417-307-207-356-288-210-238-42	36867	37675.8	2.85	**36510**	**36896.8**	5.69
d493	490-318-280-364-177-119-118-351-374-264-237-333-142-47-267	37312	38368.9	2.17	**36940**	**37793.7**	4.56
att532	286-191-222-103-389	29348	29953.9	3.25	**28780**	**29312.5**	6.58
att532	528-208-482-496-69-172-518-526	**29447**	30528.5	4.46	29493	**30078.0**	7.33
att532	269-447-360-439-263-409-193-279-313-25	28987	29963.7	2.77	**28799**	**29142.1**	6.41
att532	507-229-308-362-125-352-323-260-425-513-269-316-370-265-311	**29980**	30442.8	2.61	30039	**30360.8**	5.87
ali535	355-230-528-89-428	207123	213815.5	4.25	**206681**	**210064.0**	9.50
ali535	236-514-425-470-153-376-282-330	212695	216456.3	3.22	**210665**	**213237.7**	6.14
ali535	437-223-422-198-416-453-419-257-332-235	211762	215513.8	3.63	**209717**	**212595.2**	8.97
ali535	101-56-237-128-203-475-186-22-170-178-110-529-346-89-418	**215188**	**219358.0**	2.67	216317	219905.8	6.83
si535	522-445-533-166-193	48616	48757.4	3.88	**48581**	**48696.4**	7.36
si535	65-111-128-210-532-140-50-62	48696	48890.9	2.90	**48557**	**48707.7**	5.75
si535	433-194-47-339-322-164-14-295-148-340	48943	49138.2	2.44	**48735**	**49005.1**	5.66
si535	301-327-326-216-322-209-14-341-196-391-338-293-48-335-403	48877	49059.8	2.51	**48867**	**49016.8**	5.56

(*continued*)

Table 2. (*continued*)

Name	Depots	GGA			DDE		
		Best	Avg	Time	Best	Avg	Time
pa561	443-68-116-438-493	2924	3002.8	3.44	**2878**	**2933.1**	8.43
pa561	205-551-452-471-16-395-393-559	2999	3055.6	3.75	**2951**	**2987.6**	9.08
pa561	114-166-251-333-318-180-295-557-419-250	2969	3025.9	3.05	**2894**	**2952.6**	7.71
pa561	376-20-304-544-178-215-549-86-96-55-430-201-74-190-334	2999	3065.3	2.81	**2977**	**3020.5**	7.37
u574	198-358-266-54-99	38712	39219.2	4.60	**38086**	**38644.9**	8.27
u574	465-199-405-344-561-418-45-379	38606	39281.4	4.16	**37847**	**38725.6**	7.58
u574	253-176-298-234-179-109-122-515-251-529	40061	40939.1	2.97	**39692**	**40659.0**	7.03
u574	129-365-536-263-392-283-155-73-72-104-338-126-203-394-490	39779	40870.6	2.61	**39604**	**40228.6**	6.12
rat575	237-351-222-452-545	7267	7378.5	3.78	**7146**	**7244.0**	8.53
rat575	317-3-454-80-372-241-73-396	7059	7255.4	3.82	**6954**	**7072.5**	8.74
rat575	52-281-57-319-33-478-113-387-565-106	7162	7327.2	4.06	**7082**	**7187.0**	10.09
rat575	488-216-163-405-211-545-90-225-206-342-446-559-213-89-464	7372	7493.9	3.07	**7292**	**7386.4**	7.88
p654	561-264-244-18-78	37001	38155.1	5.59	**36712**	**37518.9**	9.72
p654	51-231-500-82-228-363-258-378	36080	37194.5	4.27	**35907**	**36666.4**	8.17
p654	548-618-138-327-465-600-479-254-510-303	**33590**	35132.9	3.66	33788	**34855.7**	8.22
p654	188-10-412-125-133-25-637-431-585-154-20-511-232-71-87	**33196**	34115.5	3.23	33586	**34062.9**	7.42
d657	389-441-37-376-225	51306	52632.4	5.39	**50709**	**51558.3**	9.56
d657	7-430-621-588-322-478-495-525	**51367**	52594.2	4.44	51416	**52061.6**	8.78
d657	195-386-54-130-595-606-594-63-482-19	52278	52968.9	4.42	**51643**	**52118.3**	9.12
d657	278-303-112-528-518-215-608-12-603-84-397-13-657-95-135	53196	54507.1	4.12	**52456**	**53390.0**	9.42
gr666	618-220-473-663-365	309354	317609.9	6.73	**308991**	**315399.8**	13.75

(*continued*)

Table 2. (*continued*)

Name	Depots	GGA			DDE		
		Best	Avg	Time	Best	Avg	Time
gr666	599-558-587-322-494-500-601-233	311362	318685.9	7.49	**304878**	**312228.7**	16.63
gr666	132-121-621-449-643-151-108-33-443-169	314830	318821.1	5.69	**311881**	**316456.3**	13.37
gr666	327-231-358-313-465-469-13-459-420-232-317-417-648-250-360	**315795**	320857.8	4.29	316276	**320451.3**	11.15
u724	486-210-17-555-434	45160	45495.2	6.01	**43933**	**44590.8**	11.70
u724	374-463-219-245-166-54-197-50	44969	45563.6	5.09	**43624**	**44724.4**	11.66
u724	355-518-240-379-601-563-405-592-265-406	45187	46629.2	7.08	**45014**	**45985.1**	15.98
u724	283-643-225-87-536-114-573-689-600-59-246-694-32-619-433	45304	45965.1	4.51	**44448**	**44956.7**	11.35
rat783	375-520-393-89-511	9249	9441.8	8.51	**9161**	**9272.8**	16.93
rat783	259-504-321-283-196-750-225-245	9429	9590.5	7.55	**9208**	**9336.2**	17.77
rat783	664-286-342-181-524-317-449-523-49-228	9323	9542.3	6.00	**9203**	**9291.5**	15.74
rat783	28-164-750-371-477-346-348-633-277-424-242-705-152-57-765	9414	9633.2	6.10	**9315**	**9472.2**	16.09
nrw1379	1103-582-347-812-69	59280	60250.8	53.96	59018	59663.3	114.75
nrw1379	317-914-191-48-1011-261-172-142	59737	60656.4	49.33	59680	**60293.8**	137.14
nrw1379	1358-1001-753-304-1336-1230-335-225-549-1089	60173	61178.1	40.72	59184	**59888.4**	115.27
nrw1379	413-561-1079-1232-1333-681-603-472-404-1140-819-1215-1208-1091-706	60872	62228.4	40.47	**60038**	**61060.9**	113.58
fl1577	112-999-913-633-742	23614	24696.0	62.42	**22890**	**24182.2**	155.78
fl1577	1051-97-211-226-728-1239-466-1250	23374	24099.3	56.28	**22958**	**23547.2**	132.47
fl1577	770-791-225-649-819-1399-1388-254-263-1465	24168	24800.8	52.98	**23272**	**23801.2**	148.02
fl1577	861-904-1364-1198-100-525-452-790-637-706-958-1447-432-621-914	23887	24522.8	44.52	**23455**	**23916.3**	123.22
d1655	356-595-500-1594-975	65714	67183.5	68.45	**65636**	**66783.9**	148.45
d1655	607-405-1008-250-726-899-821-1174	66974	68113.6	58.03	**65487**	**66722.0**	145.13

(*continued*)

Table 2. (*continued*)

Name	Depots	GGA			DDE		
		Best	Avg	Time	Best	Avg	Time
d1655	1534-1533-825-505-300-810-1632-520-260-1653	66890	68624.1	58.68	**66495**	**67743.0**	146.77
d1655	551-42-931-520-626-847-667-417-870-929-583-808-248-1189-879	67273	68307.0	54.54	**66148**	**67024.1**	150.70
vm1748	714-1024-444-661-582	359511	365375.0	114.06	**348968**	**356277.8**	218.15
vm1748	1251-946-1256-1310-1082-596-644-1417	365694	374995.1	92.61	**359683**	**363751.8**	203.72
vm1748	655-1294-1021-289-669-259-1215-1252-745-383	364482	370374.3	75.58	**355798**	**358882.2**	178.23
vm1748	620-425-528-66-1568-1207-1327-805-949-1378-276-1609-211-554-1582	370460	377826.8	66.41	**362718**	**365979.1**	187.42
u1817	1219-1653-790-23-1738	61280	62073.1	86.57	**60277**	**61402.2**	238.85
u1817	18-330-1544-513-195-594-1701-260	61561	62703.2	79.09	**61107**	**62143.6**	208.64
u1817	314-1630-1221-1175-1315-1595-139-1123-1209-998	62241	63813.4	78.57	**61824**	**62753.8**	222.40
u1817	1139-565-739-1787-24-352-1168-1565-1151-584-117-753-84-1531-1082	63375	64237.6	67.90	**61642**	**62961.2**	214.28
rl1889	1395-1637-1499-1575-50	342139	350837.6	128.35	**334985**	**342590.9**	310.42
rl1889	56-1824-81-1750-1208-442-248-294	340493	347321.2	123.07	**333081**	**337596.4**	307.24
rl1889	116-1517-245-954-986-1176-1484-1620-1825-1244	351385	357011.4	86.11	**339646**	**344800.9**	240.84
rl1889	909-72-271-566-311-838-22-1699-1789-1215-1309-1030-820-920-964	354404	362294.3	79.23	**344715**	**349172.4**	235.68

Table 2 presents the results of GGA and DDE approaches on 140 large instances created by us. On each instance, we have reported the best and average solution quality as well as average execution time over 20 runs for GGA and DDE. This table clearly show DDE to be slower. This is due to the fact that DDE applies crossover and mutation both to produce a solution, whereas GGA either applies crossover or mutation, but never both to produce a solution. Further, DDE performed better than GGA in terms of both best and average solution quality on large majority of instances (out of 140 instances, DDE performed better than GGA on 107 and 126 instances in terms of best and average solution quality respectively) though there are many instances where reverse is true.

5   Conclusions and Future Work

Single-depot multiple traveling saleman problem (MTSP) is a widely studied problem in the literature. On the other hand, only a few approaches exist in the literature for multi-depot multiple traveling salesman problem (MD-MTSP) despite several real-world applications. In this paper, we have presented two hybrid evolutionary approaches, namely a grouping genetic algorithm (GGA) and a discrete differential evolution approach (DDE) for MD-MTSP. Chromosome encoding and variation operators in these two approaches are tailor made for MD-MTSP considering the structure of MD-MTSP. The solutions obtained through variation operators are improved further via 2-opt based local search. We have compared the performance of the proposed approach with the best approach available in the literature on 20 benchmark instances available in the literature. Computational results clearly demonstrate the superiority of our two approaches in terms of best as well as average solution quality.

We have also reported the performance of GGA and DDE on an additional set of instances containing 140 large instances. Computational results clearly show DDE to be better than GGA in terms of both best and average solution quality. However, it is slower than GGA. These newly introduced 140 benchmark instances are derived from 35 TSPLIB instances. We have provided all the additional details for these instances so that they can be used by future researchers working on MD-MTSP without any difficulty to evaluate the performance of their approaches.

As a future work, we would like to explore other variants of MD-MTSP and develop similar approaches. Another possible future work is to explore other local searches for MD-MTSP. For example, we have only utilized 2-opt local search which improves each tour separately and relying on variation operators to do inter-tour improvements. Some explicit inter-tour local searches like swapping the two cities between two different tours in case doing so improves the objective function can be tried in a bid to further improve the solution quality.

References

1. Bektas, T.: The multiple traveling salesman problem: an overview of formulations and solution procedures. Omega **34**(3), 209–219 (2006)
2. Cheikhrouhou, O., Khoufi, I.: A comprehensive survey on the multiple traveling salesman problem: applications, approaches and taxonomy. Comput. Sci. Rev. **40**, 100369 (2021)
3. Das, S., Suganthan, P.N.: Differential evolution: a survey of the state-of-the-art. IEEE Trans. Evol. Comput. **15**(1), 4–31 (2011)
4. Dorigo, M., Gambardella, L.: Ant colony system: a cooperative learning approach to the traveling salesman problem. IEEE Trans. Evol. Comput. **1**(1), 53–66 (1997)
5. Falkenauer, E.: Genetic Algorithms and Grouping Problems. John Wiley & Sons, Inc., Hoboken (1998)
6. He, P., Hao, J.K.: Hybrid search with neighborhood reduction for the multiple traveling salesman problem. Comput. Oper. Res. **142**, 105726 (2022)
7. Ho, W., Ji, P., Dey, P.K.: A multi-depot travelling salesman problem and its iterative and integrated approaches. Int. J. Oper. Res. **1**(4), 382–395 (2006)
8. Liu, W., Li, S., Zhao, F., Zheng, A.: An ant colony optimization algorithm for the multiple traveling salesmen problem. In: 2009 4th IEEE Conference on Industrial Electronics and Applications, pp. 1533–1537 (2009)
9. Necula, R., Breaban, M., Raschip, M.: Tackling the bi-criteria facet of multiple traveling salesman problem with ant colony systems. In: 2015 IEEE 27th International Conference on Tools with Artificial Intelligence (ICTAI 2015), pp. 873–880 (2015)
10. Pan, Q.K., Tasgetiren, M.F., Liang, Y.C.: A discrete differential evolution algorithm for the permutation flowshop scheduling problem. Comput. Ind. Eng. **55**(4), 795–816 (2008)
11. Pérez-Carabaza, S., Gálvez, A., Iglesias, A.: Ant colony based dynamic voronoi method for the multi-depot multiple tsp. In: 2024 IEEE Congress on Evolutionary Computation (CEC 2024), pp. 1–8. IEEE (2024)
12. Ramadhani, T., Hertono, G.F., Handari, B.D.: An ant colony optimization algorithm for solving the fixed destination multi-depot multiple traveling salesman problem with non-random parameters. In: AIP Conference Proceedings, vol. 1862, no. 1, p. 030123 (2017)
13. Singh, A., Baghel, A.S.: A new grouping genetic algorithm approach to the multiple traveling salesperson problem. Soft Comput. **13**, 95–101 (2009)
14. Singh, A., Gupta, A.K.: Two heuristics for the one-dimensional bin-packing problem. OR Spectrum **29**, 765–781 (2007)
15. Tasgetiren, M.F., Pan, Q.K., Liang, Y.C.: A discrete differential evolution algorithm for the single machine total weighted tardiness problem with sequence dependent setup times. Comput. Oper. Res. **36**(6), 1900–1915 (2009)
16. Venkatesh, P., Singh, A.: Two metaheuristic approaches for the multiple traveling salesperson problem. Appl. Soft Comput. **26**, 74–89 (2015)
17. Yang, R., Fan, C.: A hierarchical framework for solving the constrained multiple depot traveling salesman problem. IEEE Robot. Autom. Lett. **9**(6), 5536–5543 (2024)
18. Yuan, S., Skinner, B., Huang, S., Liu, D.: A new crossover approach for solving the multiple travelling salesmen problem using genetic algorithms. Eur. J. Oper. Res. **228**(1), 72–82 (2013)

Optimization of Latent-Space Compression Using Game-Theoretic Techniques for Transformer-Based Vector Search

Kushagra Agrawal$^{(\boxtimes)}$, Nisharg Nargund , and Oishani Banerjee

School of Computer Engineering, KIIT Deemed to be University, Bhubaneswar, Odisha, India
`2205044@kiit.ac.in`

Abstract. Vector similarity search is a crucial component of modern information retrieval systems, in particular using transformer-based embeddings. Nevertheless, scalability and efficiency of these systems is limited owing to the high dimensional latent representations. In this paper, we introduce **NashVec**, a new game-theoretic approach for learning how to compress the latent space in order to improve the efficiency and semantic relevance of vector search. By casting the compression strategy as a zero-sum game in retrieval accuracy and storage efficiency, we obtain a hidden transformation preserving the semantic similarity but decrease redundancy. We compare **NashVec** against FAISS, a state-of-the-art vector search library, and show that we achieve much higher average similarity (0.9981 vs. 0.5517) and utility (0.8873 vs 0.5194) at the expense of a slightly slower query time. This trade-off demonstrates the utility of game-theoretic latent compression for high-utility, transformer-based search applications. The approach can be easily integrated with the traditional LLM pipelines while achieving more semantically correct and efficient retrieval. (The code for NashVec can be accessed publicly at: https://github.com/KushagraIsTaken/NashVec).

Keywords: Vector Database · Game Theory · Semantic Similarity · Latent Space Compression

1 Introduction

The development of transformer-based language models has radically changed natural language processing (NLP) and brought significant advancements in tasks such as question answering, semantic search, and information extraction. Crucial to these developments is the capability of extracting semantically relevant information from large text corpora in an effective and efficient manner via its underlying latent-space representations. These embeddings coming from pretrained transformers hidden layers carry complex semantics in a 768-dimensional vector space. But when the number of vector databases increases to billions, space efficiency and a fast lookup operation are very difficult to maintain [1].

B. Chatterjee et al. (Eds.): ICDCIT 2026, LNCS 16420, pp. 377–389, 2026.
https://doi.org/10.1007/978-3-032-16632-6_24

Large Lucene indexes are in widespread use, and similarity search libraries such as FAISS (Facebook AI Similarity Search) are popular due to their speed and scalability. However, they often fail to retain fine-grained semantic subtleties, especially under embedding compression and efficient low-latency retrieval. Compression techniques, while successful in reducing the memory requirement, usually cause distortions to vector quality that impair precise retrieval. This compromise between efficiency and semantic fidelity has driven the investigation of novel compression techniques that could reduce information loss with acceptable performance.

In this work, we propose a game-theoretic approach for analytically and optimally model the interaction between compression schemes and retrieval techniques. We formulate the problem as a traditional zero-sum game, in which the two players (encoder and retriever) are designed to play this adversarial game: The objective of the encoder is to maximize compressibility of data and that of retriever is opposite for maximum semantic matching. This adversarial setup leads to adaptive equilibrium solutions, and result in the construction of small but semantically relevant spaces of vectors.

We also propose a new Custom DB that optimizes compression methods customized to transformer-generated embeddings. In contrast to traditional approaches where uniform quantization or reduction is directly employed, our method can effectively preserve some semantic structures which are crucial for the subsequent retrieval. This is accomplished by iteratively training the compression scheme based on retrieval system feedback. The performance of the retriever is also an important utility signal, which provides guidance for compression parameter adapting. So we focus on recovering the successfule retrive as our first goal of compression.

To assess the performance and effectiveness of our method, we benchmark compared our custom database with FAISS over query time, avg cosine similarity, and a custom defined semantic utility score. In our experiments, we consistently observe a clear and robust improvement on retrieval accuracy and contextual alignment even with very small hidden dimensions. The custom database achieved an increase in average similarity of 0.9981 with a utility of 0.8873 (as well as a reduced similarity and retrieval time on FAISS. The observations suggest that a game-theoretic optimization framework is necessary to balance the tension between retrieval speed at scale and semantic quality in a large-scale vector search system.

To sum up, we propose here a principled and practical method for compressing the latent space based on game-theoretic reasoning. Defining compression and retrieval objectives in a joint adversarial setting, we show that lossy semantic retrieval is tractable in compressed space. The purpose of the method is not only to serve as an alternative to testing directly on the traditional benchmarks, but also sets stage for future work in cooperative-competitive optimization in generative AI systems.

2   Related Works

With the rise of deep learning, vector search has become an integral element of contemporary information retrieval, particularly for tasks that require semantic similarity. We now see growing traction of dense retrieval methods leveraging transformer -based embeddings, replacing traditional sparse vector space models such as TF-IDF and BM25.

Vector-based search permits word retrieval not only by means of lexical overlap at the surface lexis level but also semantic similarity. Karpukhin et al. (2020) proposed a dual-encoder model with dense representations for passage retrieval in open-domain Question Answering, achieving notable gains compared to traditional sparse retrievers [2] Their work constituted a significant shift towards embedding-centric methods which emphasis on semantic understanding.

Furthermore, since text is modelled as vectors or embeddings, retrieval systems can more effectively capture semantic relatedness by incorporating features based on word embeddings. Kenter and de Rijke demonstrated that capturing these semantic relationship results in a retrieval is being much more accurate [3]. Therefore, vector search has become a hot trend in the new generation of information retrieval systems. It's a way for systems to look past the superficial level of keyword matching in order to discover and exploit deeper semantic relationships between documents and queries.

While we have already come quite far with dense retrieval methods, classic vector search frameworks such as FAISS still struggle in a number of cases, particularly if they are faced with high-dimensional embeddings and tight efficiency constraints. Karpukhin et al. (2020) argue that dense retrieval could increase the accuracy, however high computing cost limits system's scalability for real data on this task [2]. Traversing the computational retrieval quality trade-off in high dimensional spaces remains to be an open problem.

Moreover, other works have considered alternatives such as supervised hashing techniques for image retrieval [25]. But these techniques aren't really addressing the problems that arise when plugging high-dimensional vector spaces into typical search systems. This gap indicates that we require novel ways to integrate the speed of existing vector search engines with the density and strength of transformer-based embeddings for data representation.

2.1   Dimensionality Reduction Techniques

PCA Vs Autoencoders. Principal Component Analysis (PCA) has been commonly used for a long time to reduce dimensionality, in particular in classification and clustering. In addition to the computational inefficiency of computation, PCA is a linear method and so can only approximate more complicated data manifolds. In recent studies, the autoencoder, which is a type of neural network trained to learn compressed representation has significant advantages over linear techniques such as PCA. As a result of being able to learn nonlinear relationships between data, autoencoders are very capable of catching nuanced anomalies that PCA often misses [4]. This kind of flexibility means that autoencoders are likely to be capturing more complex semantic patterns in high-dimensional feature spaces.

On the other hand, nonlinear dependencies found in many real-world datasets may be missed by classical PCA, which would reduce semantic fidelity [5]. This reveals a basic trade-off: autoencoders produce more accurate and semantically meaningful representations, but at the expense of increased computational complexity, whereas PCA offers efficiency and simplicity.

Nonlinear Methods and Advanced Architectures. The significance of architectural design to the performance results (speed and compression effectiveness) has been shown by recent advances in learned image compression [6]. The introduction of unbalanced channel-conditional adaptive coding can be taken as another interesting alternative to improve the performance without loosing speed, which is important for practical applications. The trade-off between efficiency and semantics continues to be an issue since the preservation of the original images properties during compression is a problem.

Techniques such as UMAP have received much attention for better preserving local data structures than linear techniques [7]. Although they have benefits, the difficulty of preserving fine-grained and semantic relationships when compressing representations still shows that even these sophisticated methods also have limitations.

2.2   Challenges in Preserving Semantic Relationships

True to form, the difficulty of de-noising complex semantic connections as latent representations is an enduring challenge and accounts for many struggles in countless applications across domains. In analyzing genomic data, for instance, Griffiths and Steyvers [8] show that different ways to reduce the data can yield different interpretations of population structures, highlighting how sensitive results are to methodological decisions. One major shortcoming of the current methods becomes evident in this tradeoff between representational precision and compact data representation.

Autoencoders have become indispensable in learning salient latent representations in clinical data. Balancing between density-based and distance-based measures in order to capture semantic fidelity is difficult. Autoencoders can improve interpretability and clustering, however they often have difficulty combining retrieval accuracy and storge efficiency.

2.3   Gaps in Conventional Techniques

Despite the considerable progress in the area, conventional dimensionality reduction methods often can not solve both accurate retrieval and efficient storage simultaneously. That limitation is especially pronounced in high-dimensions, where even the subtlest perturbation can change results drastically. Like in the case of predicting concrete compressive strength using machine learning models, they struggle in capturing fine-grain features [9]. As a second important example, the insistence on a limited type of self-reported performance metrics in the analysis of scRNA-seq data has raised questions on the generalizability and robustness of existing methods [10].

Batch Normalization outperforms the state of the art in video compression; however, efforts to learn compact, lower-dimensional embeddings have achieved state-of-the-art results in video compression as well. Even so, the gap still is persistent since existing approaches seldom achieve an optimal trade-off between storage reduction and retrieval precision. This semantic gap is also illustrated by the limitations of prototype learning in deep neural networks due to compound difficulty of creating shared representations [11].

2.4   Game-Theoretic Optimization Methods

Game theory has arisen as a powerful framework for addressing optimization problems in a variety of domains, including energy systems, supply chains, and information retrieval [12]. This field is based on the notions of cooperative and non-cooperative games, the latter being an imitation of interactions by agents/players who either cooperate or compete to maximize system outcomes.

2.5   Game Theory Applications in Optimization

The game-theoretic frameworks are widely applied to solve optimality problems, such as the power control and routing in wireless sensor networks (WSNs). Game-theoretic frameworks enable coordination among sensors by allowing them to form coalitions that improve coverage and reduce energy spending. However, in non-cooperative environments, sensors behave independently, thus can perform conflicting behaviours [13]. This difference indicates when strategic interaction is important in optimization in as much as it represents the notions of zero-sum game, where the success of one player is equivalent to failure of another.

Game theory has become one of the important frameworks for optimization problems in different fields, such as information retrieval and distributed systems. The most fundamental elements consist in modeling agent (or process) interaction, where the agents compete (or cooperate) for the purpose of maximizing their utility [14].

Such as, in resource-constrained environment like wireless sensor networks (WSNs), mobile-edge computing (MEC), game-theoretic frameworks are broadly employed for power control, routing, and task offloading problems. These applications have individual agents that seek to maximize their own benefit (e.g., computational throughput) but minimize cost (e.g., latency or energy use), causing competition among them, one agent's optimization can not be isolated from the others [15].

This paradigm of conflicting objectives is directly analogous to the challenge in vector search. We frame our problem as a zero-sum game between retrieval accuracy and storage efficiency, where gains in one area often lead to compromises in the other. Furthermore, developments in constrained optimization have explored non-zero-sum formulations of Lagrangian methods, showing how game-theoretic insights can effectively solve problems with conflicting objectives in multi-objective environments [16].

2.6   Hybrid Search Architectures

Hybrid search architectures are designed to integrate the strengths of dense retrieval methods with approximate nearest neighbor (ANN) algorithms, such as Hierarchical Navigable Small World (HNSW). The Hybrid Search Architecture system have become well-known due to their capacity to successfully balance the trade-off between accuracy in locating pertinent documents and retrieval efficiency.

Dense Retrieval and Approximate Nearest Neighbor Algorithms : A novel and major development in hybrid search systems is the ability of the system to combine sparse and dense retrieval methods. It becomes feasible to strategically maximize their complementary strengths for better retrieval results when the interaction between these two approaches is viewed as a competitive process [17]. By considering them as rivals, systems that can capitalize on this dynamic can be created, which will ultimately increase retrieval accuracy due to their structured interaction.

Re-Ranking Methods : Re-Ranking is a key part of a hybrid retrieval system. Its purpose is to re-rank search-result documents based on the semantic similarity of the query and documents. One significant instance of this is the Unified Ensemble Diffusion (UED) framework that aggregates a large number of similarity measures in a single ensemble to yield better performance [18]. From a game-theoretic viewpoint, these individual metrics can be seen as contributors in a cooperative-competitive framework, where their collective interaction benefits the entire system by achieving a higher degree of accuracy.

3   Methodology

This section outlines the pipeline and formal definitions used in comparing the performance of a standard FAISS-based vector retrieval system with a proposed hybrid architecture combining deep autoencoders and Hierarchical Navigable Small World (HNSW) indexing. The methodology can be summarized as a sequence of transformations and retrievals over vectorized natural language instructions (as shown is Fig. 1).

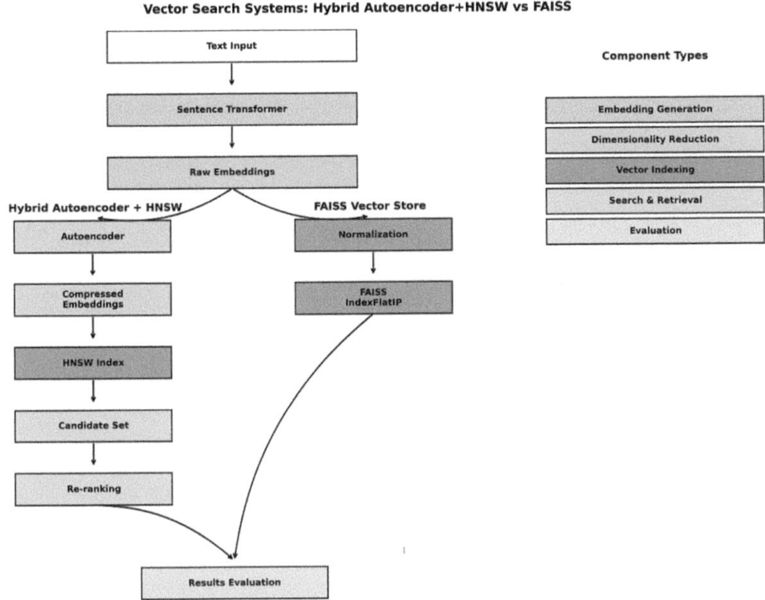

Fig. 1. Vector Search Systems: A comparison between Hybrid Autoencoder + HNSW and FAISS-based retrieval pipelines. The hybrid method utilizes deep autoencoders for dimensionality reduction followed by HNSW indexing and re-ranking. In contrast, the FAISS method applies normalization with flat inner product indexing.

3.1 Dataset Selection and Preprocessing

Let $\mathcal{D} = \{x_i\}_{i=1}^{N}$ denote the dataset of $N = 500$ instruction-style prompts selected from the open-source Alpaca dataset $\mathcal{D}_{\text{Alpaca}}$. The subset $\mathcal{D}$ is chosen to preserve semantic diversity while maintaining computational feasibility. Each instruction x_i is a sequence of natural language tokens and does not require preprocessing beyond initial tokenization.

3.2 Sentence Embedding Generation

Each instruction $x_i \in \mathcal{D}$ is passed through a transformer-based encoder function:

$$\mathbf{e}_i = f_{\text{SBERT}}(x_i) \in \mathbb{R}^{384}$$

where $f_{\text{SBERT}} : \mathcal{X} \to \mathbb{R}^{384}$ is the pre-trained `all-MiniLM-L6-v2` model from the SentenceTransformers suite, mapping natural language text to dense semantic vectors. The complete embedding matrix is:

$$\mathbf{E} = [\mathbf{e}_1, \mathbf{e}_2, \ldots, \mathbf{e}_N]^{\top} \in \mathbb{R}^{N \times 384}$$

3.3 Autoencoder-Based Latent Compression

To reduce dimensionality and enhance indexing efficiency, we train an autoencoder $\mathcal{A} : \mathbb{R}^{384} \to \mathbb{R}^{128}$, parameterized by encoder f_θ and decoder g_ϕ:

$$\mathbf{z}_i = f_\theta(\mathbf{e}_i) \in \mathbb{R}^{128}, \quad \hat{\mathbf{e}}_i = g_\phi(\mathbf{z}_i) \in \mathbb{R}^{384}$$

The objective is to minimize the reconstruction loss over all samples:

$$\mathcal{L}_{\mathrm{AE}}(\theta, \phi) = \frac{1}{N} \sum_{i=1}^{N} \|\mathbf{e}_i - \hat{\mathbf{e}}_i\|_2^2$$

Optimization is performed using the Adam optimizer with learning rate $\eta = 10^{-3}$, for $E = 10$ epochs and batch size $B = 32$.

3.4 Index Construction

Two distinct indices are constructed for comparative evaluation:

FAISS Flat Index. Let $\tilde{\mathbf{e}}_i = \frac{\mathbf{e}_i}{\|\mathbf{e}_i\|_2}$ denote the L2-normalized embedding. The FAISS index $\mathcal{I}_{\mathrm{FAISS}}$ is built using inner-product similarity:

$$\mathrm{sim}_{\cos}(\mathbf{q}, \mathbf{e}_i) = \langle \tilde{\mathbf{q}}, \tilde{\mathbf{e}}_i \rangle$$

Hybrid HNSW Index. Let $\mathbf{z}_i = f_\theta(\mathbf{e}_i)$ denote the compressed latent vector. These are indexed using HNSW via the `hnswlib` library. Formally, the index $\mathcal{I}_{\mathrm{HNSW}}$ supports approximate nearest neighbor queries:

$$\mathrm{HNSWQuery}(\mathbf{z}_q) = \{\mathbf{z}_{j_1}, \ldots, \mathbf{z}_{j_K}\},$$
$$K = \mathrm{candidate\_multiplier} \times k$$

3.5 Hybrid Search and Re-Ranking

Given a query q, its embedding $\mathbf{e}_q = f_{\mathrm{SBERT}}(q)$ is compressed to $\mathbf{z}_q = f_\theta(\mathbf{e}_q)$. The hybrid search pipeline performs:

1. Candidate Retrieval:

$$\mathcal{C} = \mathrm{HNSWQuery}(\mathbf{z}_q) = \{\mathbf{z}_{j_1}, \ldots, \mathbf{z}_{j_K}\}$$

2. Re-ranking via cosine similarity in the latent space:

$$\mathrm{sim}_{\cos}(\mathbf{z}_q, \mathbf{z}_j) = \frac{\langle \mathbf{z}_q, \mathbf{z}_j \rangle}{\|\mathbf{z}_q\|_2 \|\mathbf{z}_j\|_2}$$

3. Final top-k retrieval:

$$\mathcal{R}_k = \arg\max_{\mathbf{z}_j \in \mathcal{C}} \mathrm{sim}_{\cos}(\mathbf{z}_q, \mathbf{z}_j)$$

3.6   Performance Metrics and Utility Modeling

Two primary evaluation metrics are defined:

- **Average Similarity:**

$$\bar{s} = \frac{1}{k} \sum_{i=1}^{k} \mathrm{sim}_{\cos}(\mathbf{q}, \mathbf{e}_i)$$

- **Query Time:** Let t_q denote the elapsed time (in seconds) for the retrieval process.

A utility function $\mathcal{U}$ is formulated to capture the trade-off between speed and semantic accuracy:

$$\mathcal{U} = \alpha \cdot \bar{s} - \beta \cdot t_q, \quad \alpha, \beta \in \mathbb{R}_{\geq 0}$$

where α and β are tunable hyperparameters. For equal importance, we set $\alpha = \beta = 1.0$.

To evaluate, we issue a query such as:

$$q := \texttt{``Explain the process of photosynthesis.''}$$

and compute $\mathcal{U}_{\mathrm{FAISS}}$ and $\mathcal{U}_{\mathrm{Hybrid}}$ for comparison.

4   Results

To evaluate the effectiveness of the proposed hybrid search architecture (Autoencoder + HNSW + Re-ranking), a comparative analysis was conducted against the traditional FAISS-based vector store. The evaluation used a representative query: *"Explain the process of photosynthesis."* Both systems were assessed based on query performance, retrieval quality, and overall utility using a balanced game-theoretic framework. The results are summarized and discussed below.

4.1   Game-Theoretic Training and Convergence

To cast the optimization explicitly as a multi-objective game, we created a custom autoencoder trained with a composite loss function. This model has two directly competing objectives, which we define as the **players** within our game-theoretic framework:

- **Player 1 (Storage Efficiency):** Minimizes the **Reconstruction Loss** (MSE) to achieve a compact, high-fidelity representation of the original 384-dimensional vector.
- **Player 2 (Retrieval Accuracy):** Minimizes the **Retrieval Loss** (Triplet loss), ensuring that the new 128-dimensional latent space is semantically aligned, with nearby vectors being similar.

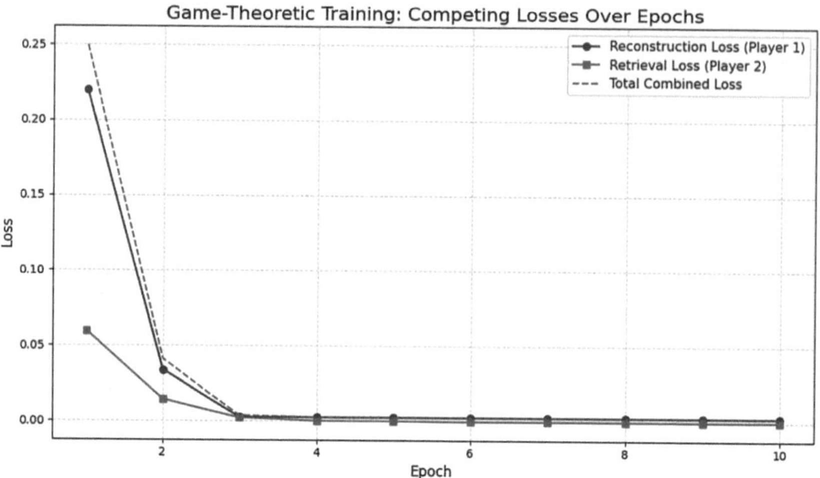

Fig. 2. The convergence of the game-theoretic autoencoder over 10 epochs. The "game" is the simultaneous optimization of the two competing losses: **Player 1 (Reconstruction Loss)** and **Player 2 (Retrieval Loss)**. Both losses, along with the **Total Combined Loss**, find a stable equilibrium after Epoch 3, indicating the model successfully learned a latent space that is both compact and semantically accurate.

Figure 2 illustrates the training process, which aims to find a stable equilibrium between these two adversarial players. The input to the autoencoder consisted of 500 sentence embeddings obtained from the Alpaca instruction dataset [19].

As shown in the figure, the model demonstrates rapid convergence. Both competing losses, and consequently the Total Combined Loss, plummet in the first three epochs and stabilize at a minimal value. This validates our game-theoretic approach, demonstrating that the model successfully found an optimal balance between the two objectives. The final reconstruction loss component settled at a minimal 0.0026, confirming the original embedding's structure was preserved with high fidelity.

The encoder from this trained model was subsequently used to project all sentence vectors into the 128-dimensional latent space. This reduced, yet now semantically-optimized, embedding was then utilized for high-performance approximate nearest neighbor (ANN) search via the HNSW algorithm.

4.2   Quantitative Evaluation

The two systems were evaluated on three key metrics: **Query Time, Average Similarity**, and a combined **Utility Score**. These are defined as follows:

- **Query Time (in seconds):** The latency between query initiation and retrieval of the top-k results.

- **Average Similarity:** The mean cosine similarity between the top-5 results and the query embedding.
- **Utility Score:** A combined score calculated using the linear game-theoretic model:

$$\text{Utility} = \alpha \cdot \text{Accuracy} - \beta \cdot \text{Query Time}$$

where both α and β are set to 1.0 to maintain a balanced trade-off between accuracy and speed.

Hybrid Autoencoder-HNSW System. The hybrid system demonstrated superior performance across all evaluation metrics:

- **Query Time:** 0.1108 s
- **Average Similarity:** 0.9981
- **Utility Score:** 0.8873

The top-5 retrievals were semantically coherent and highly relevant to the query. For instance:

- *"What is the process of photosynthesis and why is it important?"* - Similarity Score: 0.9994
- *"Explain the process of cellular respiration in plants."* - Similarity Score: 0.9981

Two important actions enable this high performance: (1) the autoencoder (as shown in Fig. 2) retains semantic meaning when compressing vectors, and (2) the re-ranking step that makes use of cosine the similarity in the embedding space of the HNSW outputs.

FAISS-Based System. In contrast, though faster, the semantically poorer embeddings used with the traditional FAISS based vector store:

- **Query Time:** 0.0323 s
- **Average Similarity:** 0.5517
- **Utility Score:** 0.5194

While the query latency was lower with the FAISS system, the reduced similarity scores suggest the system's limitations in capturing more nuanced semantic relationships without a latent re-ranking component. For example:

- *What are the steps to photosynthesis and why it matters.* - Similarity Score: 0.8708
  Otherwise the rest - Similarity Scores: less than 0.70, some even 0.38

Such lower similarity values from the similarity retrieval suggest FAISS is efficient but the trade-off is the low retrieval quality, in particular, when queries need more semantic insight about the phrases

4.3 Game-Theoretic Outcome

The hybrid system also surpassed the FAISS-based system under the balanced assumption ($\alpha = \beta = 1.0$) with a widening margin of 0.3679 in aggregate utility scores. Even though query latencies were marginally longer, the trade-off was well worth it as similarity scores detracted more from total utility than raw speed of retrieval—at least for use cases where the quality of results made all the difference.

Under the above landscape of assumptions and evaluation, the **Custom DB (Autoencoder + HNSW)** emerges as the **game-theoretically absolute dominant strategy** for vector-based semantic search.

5 Conclusion

We show in this paper that a game-theoretic variational framework to latent-space compression, based on deep autoencoders and hybrid HNSW indexing, gives a remarkable improvement to the semantic correctness and usefulness of transformer-based vector search systems over classical methods such as FAISS. We then propose a zero-sum game between retrieval accuracy and storage efficiency, which results in the Semantic retrieval in compressed space with the retrieval-trade off framework achieving near-lossless semantic retrieval with increasing average similarity and utility in exchange for little accuracy at the cost of increased query time. Such results underscore the practical value of game-theoretic optimization in large-scale, high-utility search, and should enable a deeper integration of smarter and more capable compression-pipeline and search algorithms in upcoming LLM pipelines.

References

1. Agrawal, K., Nargund, N.: Deep Learning in Industry 4.0: Transforming Manufacturing Through Data-Driven Innovation, pp. 222–236. Springer, Switzerland (2024). https://doi.org/10.1007/978-3-031-50583-615
2. Karpukhin, V., et al.: Dense passage retrieval for open-domain question answering. In: Proceedings of the 2020 Conference on Empirical Methods in Natural Language Processing (EMNLP). Association for Computational Linguistics (2020). http://dx.doi.org/10.18653/v1/2020.emnlp-main.550
3. Kenter, T., de Rijke, M.: Short text similarity with word embeddings. In: Proceedings of the 24th ACM International on Conference on Information and Knowledge Management, pp. 1411–1420. CIKM'15, ACM (2015). http://dx.doi.org/10.1145/2806416.2806475
4. Sakurada, M., Yairi, T.: Anomaly detection using autoencoders with nonlinear dimensionality reduction. In: Proceedings of the MLSDA 2014 2nd Workshop on Machine Learning for Sensory Data Analysis, pp. 4–11. MLSDA'14, ACM (2014). http://dx.doi.org/10.1145/2689746.2689747
5. Alkhayrat, M., Aljnidi, M., Aljoumaa, K.: A comparative dimensionality reduction study in telecom customer segmentation using deep learning and pca. J. Big Data **7**(1) (2020). http://dx.doi.org/10.1186/s40537-020-0286-0

6. He, D., Yang, Z., Peng, W., Ma, R., Qin, H., Wang, Y.: Elic: efficient learned image compression with unevenly grouped space-channel contextual adaptive coding. In: 2022 IEEE/CVF Conference on Computer Vision and Pattern Recognition (CVPR), pp. 5708–5717 (2022)

7. Yang, Y., et al.: Dimensionality reduction by umap reinforces sample heterogeneity analysis in bulk transcriptomic data. Cell Reports **36**(4), 109442 (2021). https://www.sciencedirect.com/science/article/pii/S2211124721008597

8. Griffiths, T.L., Steyvers, M.: A probabilistic approach to semantic representation, pp. 381–386. Routledge (2019). http://dx.doi.org/10.4324/9781315782379-102

9. In, M.H., Speck, O.: Highly accelerated psf-mapping for epi distortion correction with improved fidelity. Magn. Reson. Mater. Phys. Biol. Med. **25**(3), 183–192 (2011). http://dx.doi.org/10.1007/s10334-011-0275-6

10. Trozzi, F., Wang, X., Tao, P.: Umap as a dimensionality reduction tool for molecular dynamics simulations of biomacromolecules: a comparison study. J. Phys. Chem. B **125**(19), 5022–5034 (2021). http://dx.doi.org/10.1021/acs.jpcb.1c02081

11. Hernandez, B., et al.: Learning meaningful latent space representations for patient risk stratification: model development and validation for dengue and other acute febrile illness. Front. Digit. Health 5 (2023). http://dx.doi.org/10.3389/fdgth.2023.1057467

12. Agrawal, K., Goktas, P., Sahoo, B., Swain, S., Bandyopadhyay, A.: IoT-Based Service Allocation in Edge Computing Using Game Theory, pp. 45–60. Springer, Switzerland (2024). http://dx.doi.org/10.1007/978-3-031-81404-44

13. Shi, H.Y., Wang, W.L., Kwok, N.M., Chen, S.Y.: Game theory for wireless sensor networks: a survey. Sensors **12**(7), 9055–9097 (2012). http://dx.doi.org/10.3390/s120709055

14. Han, L., Morstyn, T., McCulloch, M.: Incentivizing prosumer coalitions with energy management using cooperative game theory. IEEE Trans. Power Syst. **34**(1), 303–313 (2019)

15. Bai, S., Tang, P., Torr, P.H., Latecki, L.J.: Re-ranking via metric fusion for object retrieval and person re-identification. In: 2019 IEEE/CVF Conference on Computer Vision and Pattern Recognition (CVPR), pp. 740–749 (2019)

16. Daskalakis, C., Panageas, I.: Last-iterate convergence: Zero-sum games and constrained min-max optimization. Schloss Dagstuhl – Leibniz-Zentrum für Informatik (2019). https://drops.dagstuhl.de/entities/document/10.4230/LIPIcs.ITCS.2019.27

17. Lin, J., Ma, X., Lin, S.C., Yang, J.H., Pradeep, R., Nogueira, R.: Pyserini: a python toolkit for reproducible information retrieval research with sparse and dense representations. In: Proceedings of the 44th International ACM SIGIR Conference on Research and Development in Information Retrieval, pp. 2356–2362. SIGIR '21, ACM (2021). http://dx.doi.org/10.1145/3404835.3463238

18. Bacci, G., Lasaulce, S., Saad, W., Sanguinetti, L.: Game theory for networks: a tutorial on game-theoretic tools for emerging signal processing applications. IEEE Signal Process. Mag. **33**(1), 94–119 (2016)

19. Taori, R., et al.: stanford alpaca: an instruction-following llama model (2023). https://github.com/tatsu-lab/stanford_alpaca

Symbolic-Regression Driven User Profiling for Hierarchical Intersection Collaborative Filtering

Pushya Chaparala[1]([email]) and P. Nagabhushan[1,2]

[1] Vignan's Foundation for Science, Technology and Research, Vadlamudi, Guntur 522213, Andhra Pradesh, India
pushyachaparala@gmail.com, pnbhushan@vignan.ac.in

[2] Indian Institute of Information Technology Allahabad, Jhalwa, Prayagraj 211012, Uttar Pradesh, India

Abstract. Personalization, the de facto standard for modern recommendation systems, requires user profiling based on item interactions. However, existing models struggle to condense extensive user preferences into a single representation, leading to computational inefficiencies. To address these, this paper proposes the *Symbolic*-Regression Based User Profiling (SRBUP) framework, which represents user profiles using just two parameters: slope and intercept, forming *symbolic* objects that reduce storage and computational complexity. Similarity between users is then measured using the area (A) between those *symbolic* regression lines and behavioral (B) differences they convey. These similarity scores are leveraged to generate recommendations. Beyond profiling, generating relevant recommendations is another key focus of this paper. Towards this, four recommendation strategies with hierarchical intersections are devised, each examining the impact of different thresholds on predicted ratings. Experimental results show that selecting an optimal threshold depends on balancing quality, diversity, and consensus filtering. A comparative analysis using Normalized Discounted Cumulative Gain (NDCG) and Mean Reciprocal Rank (MRR) confirms that SRBUP outperforms existing models in ranking quality and relevance.

Keywords: Personalization · Recommendation Systems · Regression-Based User Profiling · Symbolic Objects

1 Introduction

Users increasingly seek personalized experiences on streaming platforms like Netflix, YouTube, and Spotify, as well as on e-commerce sites such as Amazon, Flipkart, and Myntra. To meet these expectations, companies employ Content-Based Recommendation Systems (CBRS) [6] and Collaborative Filtering Recommendation Systems (CFRS) [6]. CBRS recommends items by matching item properties (e.g., genre, director, brand) with user preferences, while CFRS analyzes user's

© The Author(s), under exclusive license to Springer Nature Switzerland AG 2026
B. Chatterjee et al. (Eds.): ICDCIT 2026, LNCS 16420, pp. 390–405, 2026.
https://doi.org/10.1007/978-3-032-16632-6_25

behavioral patterns by leveraging explicit (ratings, reviews) and implicit (click behavior, watch time) data.

CFRS can be classified into model-based and memory-based approaches. Model-based includes techniques such as Matrix Factorization [18], Bayesian Networks [30], and deep learning models [18,27], which uncover latent factors that drive user preferences. In contrast, memory-based CFRS, including User-Based and Item-Based Collaborative Filtering (UBCF, IBCF) [18], computes similarities between users or items based on the interaction history. Similarity measures [1,10,19] such as Cosine Similarity, Pearson Correlation, and Adjusted Cosine Similarity are commonly used in this category.

While CFRS is effective, it struggles to capture evolving user preferences. As user interactions increase [18], moving from no interactions with items (Cold Start) to engaging more frequently (Warm State), profiles grow, making it challenging to optimize profile size and extract meaningful patterns. Traditional approaches simplify preferences by averaging interactions, but this often fails to retain user interest variability [11]. Symbolic Data Analysis (SDA) [7,8,11] offers a more structured profiling approach that better preserves variability, while histogram-based profiling [5] enhances adaptability but remains storage-intensive.

To address these limitations, this paper proposes the *Symbolic*-Regression Based User Profiling (*S*RBUP) framework, which represents user profiles as *Symbolic*-Regression objects [17]. Unlike histograms, *S*RBUP reduces storage needs by encoding interactions into just two parameters: slope and intercept, while retaining essential behavioral patterns. The AB distance measure [17] is then applied to compute similarities, producing a similarity matrix to identify the Top_N similar users for generating personalized recommendations.

*S*RBUP employs four recommendation strategies. *Quality-driven filtering* prioritizes highly rated items from hierarchical intersections of similar users, including full (all Top_N users) and pairwise (at least two users), before selecting top-rated non-intersecting items. *Relaxed rating thresholds* lower constraints to balance quality and quantity while maintaining intersection-based ranking. *Diverse inclusion* further relaxes thresholds to increase coverage, expanding recommendations beyond strict intersections. Finally, *Consensus-based filtering* emphasizes user agreement, ranking items from full intersections, pairwise intersections, and non-intersecting sets according to predicted ratings.

To evaluate the framework, experiments are conducted using *The Movies* [2] *MovieLens-100K* [12], and *TripAdvisor Restaurant Reviews for New York (NYC) City* [21] Datasets. The relevance of generated recommendations is assessed using Normalized Discounted Cumulative Gain (NDCG) and Mean Reciprocal Rank (MRR) [26] to ensure both ranking quality and retrieval effectiveness.

The rest of the paper is organized as follows: Sect. 2 reviews related work, Sect. 3 introduces the *S*RBUP framework with a running example, Sect. 4 describes the experimental setup, Sect. 5 presents results and discussions, and Sect. 6 concludes with future directions.

2 Related Work

With the proliferation of data, recommendation systems have become essential for personalizing user experiences across various domains. Central to these systems is user profiling [4,9,13,15,23–25,29], which captures preferences and behaviors to enhance recommendations. User profiling methods vary in complexity, ranging from explicit attribute mapping to implicit feature extraction and hybrid techniques that integrate multiple data sources.

A key challenge in profiling is uncovering latent preferences from implicit interactions. Wilson et al. [29] modeled users with Latent Dirichlet Allocation (LDA) and generated Top_K recommendations from topic weights. The approach is effective, but storage and compute costs limit large-scale use. For contextual adaptation, CAPS [13] combines user preferences with contextual personalized ontological profiles (CPOPs) and refines results using enhanced spreading activation (ESAT) and graph-based semantic relatedness (GBS-ROC). However, its reliance on high-quality ontologies and substantial computation and storage limits its scalability.

Beyond context, balancing novelty and popularity is critical [26]. The UPOD model [4] employs K-Modes clustering and Mass Diffusion Heat Spreading to optimize the novelty–popularity trade-off, using SVMs to predict optimal λ values for new users. However, treating all interactions equally may overlook rating relevance. CISER [15] enhances recommendations by integrating sentiment analysis and reviewer credibility, leveraging fastText and PageRank. Despite improved personalization, processing sentiment and credibility scores still poses scalability challenges.

Sentiment-aware profiling is further refined in Chen's dual-profile framework [9], which differentiates highly rated (Positive Profile) and poorly rated (Negative Profile) items using LDA and Jensen-Shannon Divergence (JSD). Prioritizing alignment with the Positive Profile improves precision but introduces high computational and storage overhead. To tackle sparsity, Singh et al. [24] applied the Apriori algorithm to construct positive and negative profiles, enhancing collaborative filtering with attribute-based similarities. While effective, reliance on frequent attributes may limit serendipitous discoveries.

Beyond sparsity, user rating dispositions significantly impact recommendation quality. Sun et al. [25] partitioned users based on rating tendencies, revealing that KNNWithMeans is highly sensitive to rating dispositions, whereas SVD remains robust across groups. Their findings highlight the impact of user behavior on collaborative filtering performance.

Despite advancements, challenges remain in balancing personalization, scalability, storage optimization and computational efficiency. To address these, this paper proposes $Symbolic$-Regression Based User Profiling (SRBUP) within the framework of Symbolic Data Analysis (SDA) [3,5]. By structuring profiles using linear regression lines, SRBUP preserves user individuality while offering a lightweight, scalable approach. Experimental results validate its effectiveness, demonstrating its potential for real-world recommendation systems.

3   Proposed Framework

3.1   *Symbolic*-Regression Based User Profiling (*SRBUP*)

Users exhibit distinct rating behaviors on the Likert scale (i.e., 1 to 5); some give consistently high scores, while others are more critical. Traditional models normalize ratings to adjust for these variations, but research [25] suggests that rating behavior reflects user personality and should be preserved to enhance personalization.

The *Symbolic*-Regression Based User Profiling (*SRBUP*) framework addresses this by mapping rating patterns to item descriptors instead of averaging ratings. Histograms capture frequency distributions, with ratings as bins and counts as frequencies. For computational efficiency, these histograms are transformed into regression lines, retaining distributional properties in two key parameters: slope and intercept. By maintaining individual variability [5], these *Symbolic Objects* [3,5] offer a deeper understanding of user preferences, improving recommendation quality.

To demonstrate *SRBUP*, a running example from the movie domain is used. Table 1 shows a user–item interaction matrix in long format, where each record contains a `UserID`, an `ItemID`, the corresponding `Rating`, and binary indicators for the genres associated with that movie. For instance, if a movie belongs to the "Thriller" genre, the respective column is marked as 1, otherwise 0.

Formally, let $D \in d^{n \times m}$ denote the user–item matrix, with users $U = \{u_1, \dots, u_n\}$ and items $I = \{i_1, \dots, i_m\}$. Genres (G) serve as the item descriptors: $G = \{g_1, \dots, g_k\}$, k being the total number of genres.

These categorical attributes effectively capture user interests. Ratings r are defined as: $r = \{1, 2, 3, 4, 5\}$, where 1 represents the lowest preference, 5 the highest, and $r = 0$ denotes unrated movies. The dataset used here covers the following genres:

$$G = \left\{ \begin{array}{l} \text{Unknown, Action, Adventure, Animation, Children, Comedy, Crime,} \\ \text{Documentary, Drama, Fantasy, Film-Noir, Horror, Musical, Mystery,} \\ \text{Romance, Sci-Fi, Thriller, War, Western} \end{array} \right\}$$

Note: The "Unknown" category accounts for items lacking a specific genre classification.

Figure 1 illustrates the *SRBUP* process. The first two steps, constructing histogram profiles and converting them into regression profiles, form the core of user profiling. The remaining steps extend these profiles to compute similarities and generate personalized recommendations. The process can be summarized as follows:

1. **Histogram Profiles:** Captures the frequency distribution of ratings for each item descriptor.
2. **Linear Regression Profiles:** Converts histogram profiles into regression lines by fitting a first-order polynomial.
3. **User Similarities:** Computes similarity scores based on regression profiles.

4. **Generating Recommendations:** Uses similarity scores to generate personalized recommendations.

The following subsections describe each step in detail, beginning with histogram profiles.

Table 1. Sample user $\times$ item dataset with genre descriptors

UserID	ItemID	Rating	Unknown	Action	Adventure	Thriller	War	Western
13	242	2	0	0	0	0	0	0
13	302	5	0	0	0	1	0	0
13	377	1	0	0	0	0	0	0
13	51	3	0	0	0	0	1	1
13	346	4	0	0	0	0	0	0
13	474	4	0	0	0	0	1	0
13	265	4	0	1	0	1	0	0

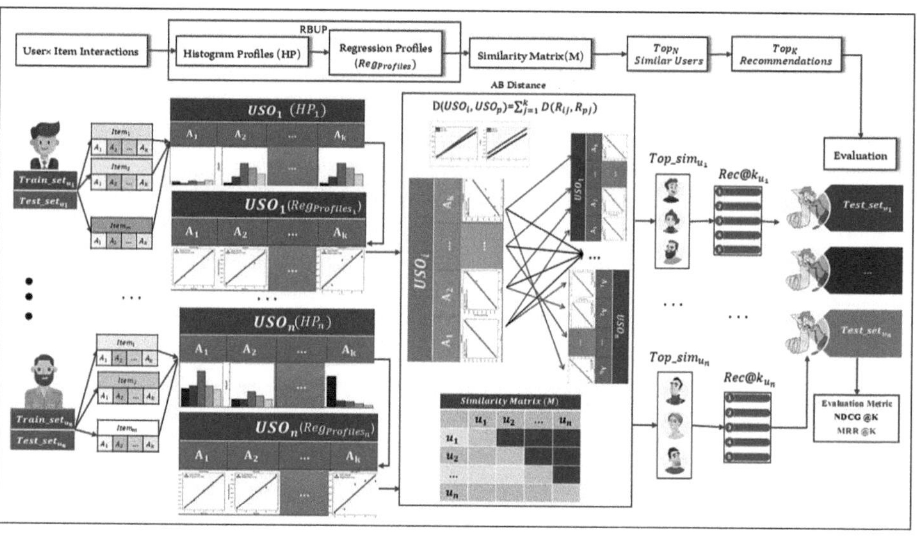

Fig. 1. Overview of the $SRBUP$ Framework.

1. **Histogram Profiles:** In this step, user interactions are represented as the distribution of ratings across item descriptors, here genres (G). These distributions, expressed as histograms, provide a structured view of user preferences. For each user u, the frequency of each rating r per genre $g \in G$ is denoted as $H_{u,g}(r)$, where $H_{u,g}(r)$ captures how often user u assigns rating r to items belonging to genre g.

$$\mathrm{HP}_{u,g}(r) = \mathrm{count}\left(\{(g,r) \mid g \in G, \text{ rating} = r \text{ for } u\}\right) \tag{1}$$

The profile is structured by sorting r in ascending order for each genre g and stored as a nested mapping $\{u : \{g : \{r : c\}\}\}$, where c is the count of rating r. Table 2 presents this structure for UserID-13 from Table 1, showing raw histograms $(HP_{u,g}(r))$, cumulative counts $(C_{u,g}(r))$, and normalized distributions $(N_{u,g}(r))$.

Table 2. User u's histogram (HP), cumulative (C), and normalized (N) distributions across genres. Vectors are ordered by rating bins $r = 1, \ldots, 5$.

Genres	$HP_{u,g}(r)$	$C_{u,g}(r)$	$N_{u,g}(r)$
Unknown	[0,0,0,0,0]	[0,0,0,0,0]	[0.00,0.00,0.00,0.00,0.00]
Action	[21,24,41,24,20]	[21,45,86,110,130]	[0.16,0.35,0.66,0.85,1.00]
Adventure	[9,9,18,13,9]	[9,18,36,49,58]	[0.16,0.31,0.62,0.84,1.00]
...	...	...	...
War	[3,4,8,9,10]	[3,7,15,24,34]	[0.09,0.21,0.44,0.71,1.00]
Western	[0,0,3,3,5]	[0,0,3,6,11]	[0.00,0.00,0.27,0.55,1.00]

These histogram profiles capture detailed user preferences but pose challenges such as high storage and computational complexity [17], requiring $O(k\,|R|)$ space and processing per user, where k is the number of item descriptors and $|R|$ is the number of distinct rating bins. To improve efficiency, these profiles are transformed into regression lines that reduce high-dimensional histograms to just two parameters, slope and intercept [17]. This transformation minimizes storage needs, simplifies computations, and enables efficient manipulation of large datasets. Additionally, they serve as versatile symbolic representations, making them suitable for mixed and symbolic datasets [17]. The conversion process is detailed in next step.

2. *Symbolic*-Regression Profiles: To optimize storage and support advanced computations, histogram-based profiles (HP) are transformed into regression profiles [17], reducing dimensionality while preserving preference patterns. The transformation begins with cumulative frequency (C) distributions, derived from histogram counts using Eq. (2):

$$C_{u,g}(r_k) = \sum_{i=1}^{k} \mathrm{HP}_{u,g}(r_i) \tag{2}$$

where $r_1, r_2, \ldots, r_k$ are sorted ratings for genre g. To ensure consistency across genres, cumulative distributions are normalized (Eq. 3):

$$N_{u,g}(r) = \frac{C_{u,g}(r_k)}{C_{u,g}(r_n)} \tag{3}$$

where $C_{u,g}(r_n)$ is the total cumulative frequency for the highest rating r_n. These normalized distributions, summarized in Table 2 are then used for regression fitting.

Table 3. User-13 Regression Profiles

User-13 Regression Profiles
Unknown: {slope: 0.0, intercept: 0.0, $X_{\min}$ (Y = 0): None, $X_{\max}$ (Y = 1): None}
Action: {slope: 0.22, intercept: -0.05, $X_{\min}$ (Y = 0): 0.23, $X_{\max}$ (Y = 1): 4.82}
Adventure: {slope: 0.22, intercept: -0.08, $X_{\min}$ (Y = 0): 0.35, $X_{\max}$ (Y = 1): 4.87}
... (Other genres omitted for brevity) ...
Western: {slope: 0.26, intercept: -0.40, $X_{\min}$ (Y = 0): 1.57, $X_{\max}$ (Y = 1): 5.49}

Regression profiles (Table 3) are obtained by fitting normalized cumulative frequencies $N_{u,g}(r)$ (Table 2) against rating bin centers using standard linear regression [20]. Each genre is thus represented by a slope (m) and intercept (c) and valid rating range ($X_{\min}, X_{\max}$). Genres without user ratings (e.g., *Unknown*) remain zero, resulting in $m = 0$, $c = 0$, and $X_{\min}, X_{\max} =$ None, indicating no inferred preferences.

$$\text{Reg}_{\text{profiles}} = \left\{ u : \left\{ g : \{\text{slope}, \text{intercept}, X_{\min}, X_{\max}\} \right\} \right\} \tag{4}$$

The regression profiles presented in Table 3 constitute the *Symbolic* Regression-Based User Profiles (*SRBUP*), serving as their core representation. These profiles offer a compact and expressive summary of user preferences across genres, requiring only $O(k)$ storage and computation per user, as each descriptor is represented by two symbolic parameters, slope and intercept.

This compact representation minimizes memory usage and allows constant-time comparisons per descriptor. Importantly, the regression here is not a predictive model in the conventional sense but a symbolic linear fit applied over the normalized cumulative histogram, serving as a behavioral signature of each user's rating distribution. In the subsequent stage, they are employed to compute similarity scores, allowing for direct comparison of user preference trends.

3. User Similarities: After constructing regression profiles for each user, the next step is to compute the inter-user similarity matrix. This is central to user-based collaborative filtering, where recommendations are derived from the preferences of similar users. Regression profiles serve as compact representations of user behavior, capturing both geometric proximity (slope–intercept characteristics) and behavioral trends (line segment length), which enable more robust similarity estimation [17].

A symmetric distance matrix M is defined for the user set U, where each entry d_{ij} denotes the distance between users u_i and u_j:

$$M = \begin{bmatrix} 0 & d_{12} & \dots & d_{1n} \\ d_{21} & 0 & \dots & d_{2n} \\ \vdots & \vdots & \ddots & \vdots \\ d_{n1} & d_{n2} & \dots & 0 \end{bmatrix} \tag{5}$$

Each d_{ij} is obtained by summing the genre-specific distances across all genres:

$$d_{ij} = \sum_{g \in G} d_{ij}^g \qquad (6)$$

where d_{ij}^g is computed using the AB Distance Measure [17], which distinguishes between intersecting and non-intersecting regression lines. This measure has α as a tunable parameter to balance proximity and behavioral similarity; experiments on *The Movies* [2] dataset with 100 users (varying α from 0.1 to 1.0) indicated $\alpha = 0.5$ as yielding balanced and relevant recommendations (results omitted due to space constraints).

Table 4. Symmetric Distance Matrix M

User ID	13	276	405	450	655
13	0.00	15.1	79.3	18.6	15.7
276	15.1	0.00	93.3	6.38	7.12
405	79.3	93.3	0.00	93.2	88.7
450	18.6	6.38	93.2	0.00	10.6
655	15.7	7.12	88.7	10.6	0.00

Table 5. Top Recommendations for User 13

Movie ID	Predicted Rating
127	5.00
427	4.67
237	4.33
196	4.00
204	4.00

Illustrative Example: While Table 2 and Table 3 highlighted regression profiles for a single user (User 13), Table 4 extends the analysis by reporting distances between User 13 and four other users. The diagonal entries are zero, while off-diagonal entries reflect computed dissimilarities. Finally, by sorting the distances in each row of M, the Top_N most similar users (S_i) are identified for every individual. For instance, with $N = 3$, User 13 is closest to Users 276, 655, and 450. These nearest neighbors provide the basis for generating personalized recommendations grounded in shared behavioral patterns across genres.

4. Recommendation Strategies (Rec.Strat.): Building upon the similarity insights from Step 3, Step 4 generates Top_K personalized recommendations, where K is the number of items suggested. This step introduces a hierarchical intersection framework, which progressively analyzes the overlap in similar users' viewing histories, beginning with full intersections, then pairwise intersections, and finally the non-intersection pool, to balance recommendation quality and coverage.

In connection with the running example from the movie domain, Table 6 defines the notations used throughout this step. Using these notations, four recommendation strategies are formulated, each grounded in the hierarchical intersection principle but differing in their filtering thresholds. Table 7 provides a comparative summary of these strategies.

Table 6. Notation and Definitions

Notation	Definition
$S(u_i)$	Top_N similar users for u_i, derived from the distance matrix.
$M(u_i)$	Movies watched by target user u_i.
$M(S(u_i))$	Movies watched by similar users: $\bigcup_{s \in S(u_i)} M(s)$.
$M_{\text{filtered}}(S(u_i))$	Filtered movies: $M(S(u_i)) \setminus M(u_i)$.
$M_\cap(S(u_i))$	Movies watched by all similar users: $\bigcap_{s \in S(u_i)} M(s)$.
$M_\cap(s_1, s_2)$	Pairwise intersection between two users: $M(s_1) \cap M(s_2)$, $\forall s_1, s_2 \in S(u_i)$.
$M_{\text{non-intersection}}$	Movies in the union but not in the full intersection: $M(S(u_i)) \setminus M_\cap(S(u_i))$.
$R(m)$	Average rating for a movie m: $R(m) = \frac{\sum_{r \in R(m)} r}{|R(m)|}$

Table 7. Comparison of Recommendation Strategies Based on Selection Criteria

Strategy	$M_\cap(S(u_i))$	$M_\cap(s_1, s_2)$	$M_{\text{non-intersection}}$
1	$R(m) > 3.5$	$R(m) > 4.0$	Movies are sorted by $R(m)$, and the highest-rated ones are selected.
2	$R(m) \geq 3.5$	$R(m) \geq 4.0$	
3	$R(m) \geq 3.0$	$R(m) \geq 4.0$	
4	$R(m)$ from all movies	Sorted by $R(m)$	

Note: Strategies progress from full intersection $M_\cap(S(u_i))$ to pairwise intersection $M_\cap(s_1, s_2)$, and finally to the non-intersection set $M_{\text{non-intersection}}$, only if earlier criteria do not provide enough recommendations to reach K.

Table 7 highlights how the four strategies apply rating thresholds across hierarchical intersections. Strategy 1 prioritizes highly rated movies from the full intersection, ideal for users with consistent preferences but yielding fewer options when overlap is limited. Strategy 2 slightly relaxes thresholds to balance quality and coverage, making it suitable for moderate alignment. Strategy 3 lowers thresholds further, broadening diversity and offering more varied recommendations. Strategy 4 maximizes collaborative consensus by including all movies from intersections and extending to non-intersection sets, effective when user overlap is high but less so for sparse alignments.

An illustrative example for Strategy 1 is shown in Table 5, listing the Top_K ($K = 5$) recommendations for User 13. The hierarchical intersection principle prioritizes full intersections $M_\cap(S(u_{13}))$ with ratings above 3.5; if insufficient, pairwise intersections $M_\cap(s_1, s_2)$ under stricter thresholds (e.g., $R(m) > 4.0$) are added, and the highest-rated movies from the non-intersection pool complete the list. For instance, Movie 127 (5.00) reflects unanimous agreement among similar users, while Movie 427 (4.67) indicates strong consensus, illustrating how the strategy preserves both personalization and quality even with varying user overlaps.

Table 8. User Group Classifications Across Selected Datasets

Dataset	UG	Criteria	Level	# Users	# Items
MovieLens-100K					
	ML_UG$_1$	$u \le 50$	ML_PU_L0	380	980
	ML_UG$_2$	$50 < u \le 100$	ML_PU_L1	199	1,189
	ML_UG$_3$	$100 < u \le 250$	ML_PU_L2	579	1,273
	ML_UG$_4$	$u \ge 100$	ML_WU_L0	364	1,668
	ML_UG$_5$	$u \ge 250$	ML_WU_L1	91	1,609
	ML_UG$_6$	$u \ge 500$	ML_WU_L2	5	1,344
	ML_100K	Complete dataset	–	943	1,682
TripAdvisor NYC					
	TA_UG$_1$	$u \le 10$	TA_PU_L0	418,711	7,047
	TA_UG$_2$	$10 \le u \le 25$	TA_PU_L1	6,656	5,886
	TA_UG$_3$	$26 \le u \le 50$	TA_PU_L2	1,030	5,043
	TA_UG$_4$	$50 \le u \le 100$	TA_PU_L3	235	4,125
	TA_UG$_5$	$u > 101$	TA_WU	64	3,774

4   Experiment Setup

4.1   Datasets and User Groups (UG)

To demonstrate SRBUP's versatility, datasets from both movies and restaurants were used. For movies, *MovieLens-100K* [12] (100K ratings from 943 users on 1,682 movies) served as the benchmark, while for restaurants, the *TripAdvisor NYC Reviews* dataset [21] (166,920 reviews from 43,083 users on 10,488 restaurants) captured localized real-world preferences.

To test performance under partial cold-start conditions, users were segmented by interaction counts: those with ≤ 10 rated items as partial cold-start users (PU) and those with ≥ 100 as warm users (WU), with finer levels based on thresholds (Table 8). This segmentation enables evaluation across sparse (PU) and dense (WU) environments, highlighting SRBUP's robustness in handling cold-start challenges and modeling active user behavior.

4.2   Evaluation Metrics

This paper evaluates recommendation relevance using Normalized Discounted Cumulative Gain (NDCG) and ranking effectiveness using Mean Reciprocal Rank (MRR). NDCG quantifies ranking quality by comparing Discounted Cumulative Gain (DCG) to Ideal DCG (IDCG), representing a perfect ranking [26]. This paper introduces Success NDCG (SNDCG), a variation designed for static datasets, emphasizing successfully matched recommendations. MRR measures ranking effectiveness based on the position of the first relevant item, averaging reciprocal ranks across users [26].

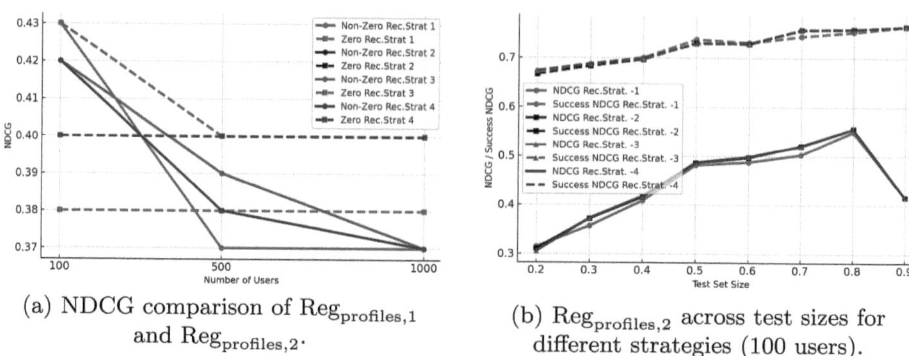

(a) NDCG comparison of $Reg_{profiles,1}$ and $Reg_{profiles,2}$.

(b) $Reg_{profiles,2}$ across test sizes for different strategies (100 users).

Fig. 2. Performance of $Reg_{profiles}$ variants.

5   Results and Discussions

5.1   Impact of Non-Zero and Zero Ratings on User Profile Construction

A central challenge in regression-based profiling is data sparsity, especially when users engage with only a few genres or items. For example, User 7187, who rated only one movie in the Animation genre, produces the following histogram using Eq. 1:

$$HP_{7187,\text{Animation}} = \{0.5:0, 1.0:0, 1.5:0, 2.0:0, 2.5:0, 3.0:0, 3.5:0, 4.0:0, \mathbf{4.5:1}, 5.0:0\}$$

This raises a key design choice: should profiles rely only on non-zero ratings (active engagement) or also include zeros to represent absence of interest? The answer directly influences recommendation quality.

Experiments on *The Movies* [2] dataset (100, 500, 1,000 random users, test size = 0.3) compare two profiles: (i) $Reg_{profiles_1}$ using only rated items, and (ii) $Reg_{profiles_2}$ including zeros for unrated items.

As shown in Fig. 2a, $Reg_{profiles_2}$ is more stable and scalable, while $Reg_{profiles_1}$ fluctuates with user size. Further, Fig. 2b confirms robustness under varying train/test splits: NDCG and SNDCG peak at 70–80% test size, with only a slight drop at 90% due to reduced training data. These results highlight that incorporating zeros yields balanced profiles and improves reliability under sparse and cold-start conditions.

5.2   Evaluation Across Different Datasets:

"MovieLens-100K" Dataset: For all experiments, the test_set was constructed at the user level by splitting each user's interactions into 70% training and 30% testing, with random seed fixed at 42. User groups (PU and WU) follow the classification shown in Table 8. Experiments used standardized settings: $\alpha = 0.5$, $Top_N = 3$ (similar users), and $Top_K = 5$ (recommendations).

Table 9 reports NDCG, SNDCG, and MRR values across (ML_UG)user groups and recommendation strategies. Results show that performance improves

Table 9. NDCG, SNDCG, and MRR values for different User Groups and Recommendation Strategies

UG/Rec. Strat.	NDCG				SNDCG				MRR			
	1	2	3	4	1	2	3	4	1	2	3	4
ML_UG_1	0.10	0.12	0.12	0.15	0.53	0.54	0.54	0.56	0.07	0.09	0.09	0.11
ML_UG_2	0.21	0.26	0.26	0.29	0.60	0.65	0.66	0.70	0.17	0.22	0.22	0.25
ML_UG_3	0.12	0.14	0.15	0.17	0.57	0.56	0.56	0.58	0.09	0.11	0.11	0.13
ML_UG_4	0.57	0.57	0.56	0.58	0.73	0.74	0.75	0.76	0.50	0.51	0.51	0.52
ML_UG_5	0.78	0.78	0.78	0.77	0.82	0.82	0.82	0.82	0.74	0.74	0.75	0.74
ML_UG_6	0.97	0.97	0.97	0.97	0.97	0.97	0.97	0.97	1.00	1.00	1.00	1.00
ML_100K	0.18	0.19	0.19	0.22	0.58	0.58	0.58	0.59	0.14	0.15	0.15	0.17

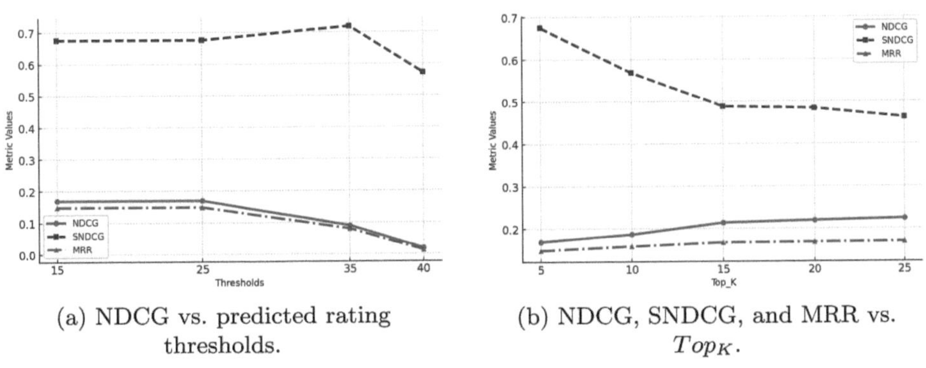

(a) NDCG vs. predicted rating thresholds.

(b) NDCG, SNDCG, and MRR vs. Top_K.

Fig. 3. TA_WU performance analysis.

with increased user interactions: PU users consistently achieve lower values, while WU users obtain substantially higher scores. This highlights the strong correlation between user engagement and recommendation accuracy, with SNDCG particularly reflecting the higher success rate of relevant matches among WU users. The overall dataset performance (NDCG: 0.18–0.22) is suppressed by the prevalence of PU users, underscoring the influence of engagement on accuracy.

The performance of the proposed recommendation strategies (Table 7) can also be interpreted in this context from Table 9. Strategies with relaxed thresholds on predicted ratings $R(m)$ (3 and 4) achieve better relevance and ranking than stricter thresholds (1 and 2). This indicates that incorporating flexibility in rating thresholds expands the search space without sacrificing recommendation quality, thereby improving ranking performance.

Here, user profiles are constructed using the *Cuisine Type* of restaurants as the item descriptor, and users are grouped into five categories as summarized in Table 8. An initial experiment on warm users (TA_WU, $u > 100$) was conducted with test split 30 at user level (random seed = 42), $Top_N = 3$, and $Top_K = 5$, to

Table 10. (a) Optimal Top_N values and (b) CBRP results

(a) Optimal Top_N

Top_N	NDCG	SNDCG	MRR
10	0.1005	0.6431	0.0826
7	0.1479	0.6311	0.1164
3	0.1688	0.6752	0.1482
5	0.1704	0.6415	0.1482

b) CBRP Results

Classification	NDCG	SNDCG	MRR
TA_PU_L0 (1000)	0.0011	0.5308	0.0008
TA_PU_L1 (1000)	0.0110	0.4574	0.0071
TA_PU_L2	0.0369	0.5208	0.0272
TA_PU_L3	0.0508	0.5195	0.0395
TA_WU	0.1965	0.5467	0.1520

Table 11. Performance Comparison of Models on NDCG@10

S.No	Models	NDCG@10 (Epochs)				
		1	5	10	15	50
1	Proposed	**0.2725**	**0.2725**	**0.2725**	**0.2725**	**0.2725**
2	BPR	0.137	0.199	0.204	0.204	0.204
3	SASRec	0.019	0.054	0.063	0.065	0.069
4	LightGCN	0.122	0.122	0.122	0.137	0.177
5	NGCF	0.059	0.105	0.120	0.141	0.219

determine the optimal threshold for recommendations. Thresholds were drawn from the dataset's rating range (10–50).

Results (Fig. 3a) show that as the threshold increases, recommendation relevance declines, making Strategy–4, which emphasizes consensus filtering, the most effective. A further analysis (Fig. 3b) reveals that while NDCG improves with higher Top_K, SNDCG decreases, indicating that not all additional recommendations remain highly relevant. This highlights the trade-off between ranking performance and recommendation quality.

Based on these findings (optimal threshold = 25, $Top_K = 5$), an additional study (Table 10a) identified $Top_N = 5$ as optimal. Using this configuration ($Top_N = 5$, $Top_K = 10$, threshold = 25), experiments were extended to all (TA_UG) user groups in Table 8. For the first two groups with very large user populations (TA_PU_L0 and TA_PU_L1), a random subset of 1,000 users (seed = 42) was selected to ensure computational feasibility, while all users from the remaining groups were included. The results (Table 10b) confirm that as user interactions increase, both relevance and ranking improve, consistent with the trends observed in the *MovieLens-100K* dataset.

5.3   Comparative Analysis of Existing Models

This paper employs the RecBole framework [31] for standardized evaluation, using *MovieLens-100K* with a global 0.2 split (20% testing, 80% training). To establish a fair comparison with other models, the optimal configuration for the dataset is first identified, yielding an NDCG of 0.2725 with $Top_N = 5$, $R(m) = 3$, and $Top_K = 10$.

For comparison, four benchmark models are considered: BPR [22] (pairwise ranking), SASRec [16] (self-attention for sequential behavior), NGCF [28] (graph neural networks for high-order interactions), and LightGCN [14] (efficient GNN aggregation).

Table 11 shows that proposed framework attains optimal performance in a single epoch, unlike matrix factorization and neural models that require multiple epochs to converge. Even after 50 epochs, BPR, SASRec, NGCF, and LightGCN fail to surpass proposed NDCG, highlighting its fast convergence and lightweight *symbolic* design. These results confirm proposed as an efficient and scalable solution, combining relevance with computational efficiency.

6   Conclusion

The results highlight the potential of the *Symbolic*-Regression Based User Profiling (*S*RBUP) framework as an effective alternative to conventional recommendation approaches. Experiments on benchmark (MovieLens-100K) and real-world (TripAdvisor) datasets confirm its ability to achieve higher NDCG, SNDCG, and MRR scores, particularly for warm users (WU), while reducing computational costs through compact symbolic profiles that eliminate iterative training.

Findings also show that recommendation strategies with relaxed thresholds on predicted ratings, especially those leveraging full and pairwise intersections of similar users, improve ranking quality by broadening the search space without sacrificing relevance. This is particularly valuable in real-time settings where sparsity and recommendation reliability are key challenges.

Future work will extend the framework to diverse datasets and explore hybrid designs by integrating content-based signals to further enhance ranking and relevance.

References

1. Amer, A., Abdalla, H., Nguyen, L.: Enhancing recommendation systems performance using highly-effective similarity measures. Knowl.-Based Syst. **217**, 106842 (2021). https://doi.org/10.1016/j.knosys.2021.106842
2. Banik, R.: The movies dataset (2024). https://www.kaggle.com/datasets/rounakbanik/the-movies-dataset. Accessed Aug 2024
3. Beranger, B., Lin, H., Sisson, S.: New models for symbolic data analysis. Adv. Data Anal. Classif. **17**, 659–699 (2023). https://doi.org/10.1007/s11634-022-00520-8
4. Bertani, R., Bianchi, R., Costa, A.: Combining novelty and popularity on personalised recommendations via user profile learning. Expert Syst. Appl. **146**, 113149 (2020). https://doi.org/10.1016/j.eswa.2019.113149
5. Billard, L., Diday, E.: Symbolic data analysis: definitions and examples. Technical report (2003)

6. Bobadilla, J., Ortega, F., Hernando, A., Gutiérrez, A.: Recommender systems survey. Knowl.-Based Syst. **46**, 109–132 (2013). https://doi.org/10.1016/j.knosys.2013.03.012

7. Chaparala, P., Nagabhushan, P.: Symbolic data analysis framework for recommendation systems: Sda-recsys. In: Trejos, J., Chadjipadelis, T., Grané, A., Villalobos, M. (eds.) Data Science, Classification, and Artificial Intelligence for Modeling Decision Making, pp. 71–79. Springer, Cham (2025). https://doi.org/10.1007/978-3-031-85870-3_8

8. Chaparala, P., Nagabhushan, P., Ponduri, L., Kummari, P.: Mapping item-wise rating into attribute-wise ratings for enhanced personalized recommendations. In: Proceedings of 15th International Conference on Computing Communication and Networking Technologies (ICCCNT 2024), pp. 1–6. IEEE (2024). https://doi.org/10.1109/ICCCNT61001.2024.10724325

9. Chen, Y., Yeh, Y., Ma, M.: A movie recommendation method based on users' positive and negative profiles. Inf. Process. Manage. **58**, 102531 (2021). https://doi.org/10.1016/j.ipm.2021.102531

10. Choi, K., Suh, Y.: A new similarity function for selecting neighbors for each target item in collaborative filtering. Knowl.-Based Syst. **37**, 146–153 (2013). https://doi.org/10.1016/j.knosys.2012.07.019

11. Dantas Bezerra, B., Tenorio de Carvalho, F.A.: Symbolic data analysis tools for recommendation systems. Knowl. Inf. Syst. **26**, 385–418 (2011). https://doi.org/10.1007/s10115-009-0282-3

12. Harper, F., Konstan, J.: The movielens datasets: history and context. ACM Trans. Interact. Intell. Syst. **5**(4) (2015). https://doi.org/10.1145/2827872

13. Hawalah, A., Fasli, M.: Utilizing contextual ontological user profiles for personalized recommendations. Expert Syst. Appl. **41**, 4777–4797 (2014). https://doi.org/10.1016/j.eswa.2014.01.039

14. He, X., Deng, K., Wang, X., Li, Y., Zhang, Y., Wang, M.: Lightgcn: simplifying and powering graph convolution network for recommendation. In: Proceedings of 43rd International ACM SIGIR Conference on Research and Development in Information Retrieval (SIGIR 2020), pp. 639–648. ACM (2020). https://doi.org/10.1145/3397271.3401063

15. Hu, S., Kumar, A., Al-Turjman, F., Gupta, S., Seth, S.: Shubham: reviewer credibility and sentiment analysis based user profile modelling for online product recommendation. IEEE Access **8**, 26172–26189 (2020). https://doi.org/10.1109/ACCESS.2020.2971087

16. Kang, W.C., McAuley, J.: Self-attentive sequential recommendation. In: Proceedings of IEEE International Conference on Data Mining (ICDM 2018), pp. 197–206 (2018). https://doi.org/10.1109/ICDM.2018.00035

17. Kumar, R.: Wavelets for knowledge mining in multi-dimensional generic databases. Ph.D. thesis, University of Mysore (2006)

18. Papadakis, H., Papagrigoriou, A., Panagiotakis, C., Kosmas, E., Fragopoulou, P.: Collaborative filtering recommender systems taxonomy. Knowl. Inf. Syst. **64**(1), 35–74 (2022). https://doi.org/10.1007/s10115-021-01628-7

19. Patra, B., Launonen, R., Ollikainen, V., Nandi, S.: A new similarity measure using bhattacharyya coefficient for collaborative filtering in sparse data. Knowl.-Based Syst. **82**, 163–177 (2015). https://doi.org/10.1016/j.knosys.2015.03.001

20. Pedregosa, F., et al.: Scikit-learn: machine learning in python. J. Mach. Learn. Res. **12**, 2825–2830 (2011). https://doi.org/10.5555/1953048.2078195

21. Pérez-Núñez, P., Luaces, O., Díez, J., Remeseiro, B., Bahamonde, A.: Tripadvisor restaurant reviews. Zenodo (2021). https://doi.org/10.5281/zenodo.5644892

22. Rendle, S., Freudenthaler, C., Gantner, Z., Schmidt-Thieme, L.: BPR: Bayesian personalized ranking from implicit feedback. arXiv preprint arXiv:1205.2618 (2012). https://doi.org/10.48550/arXiv.1205.2618
23. Roy, A., Ludwig, S.A.: Genre based hybrid filtering for movie recommendation engine. J. Intell. Inf. Syst. **56**(3), 485–507 (2021). https://doi.org/10.1007/s10844-021-00637-w
24. Singh, P., Othman, E., Ahmed, R., Mahmood, A., Dhahri, H., Choudhury, P.: Optimized recommendations by user profiling using apriori algorithm. Appl. Soft Comput. **106**, 107272 (2021). https://doi.org/10.1016/j.asoc.2021.107272
25. Sun, R., Kong, R., Jin, Q., Konstan, J.: Less can be more: exploring population rating dispositions with partitioned models in recommender systems. In: Proceedings of 31st ACM Conference on User Modeling, Adaptation and Personalization – Adjunct (UMAP 2023), pp. 291–295. ACM (2023). https://doi.org/10.1145/3563359.3597390
26. Valcarce, D., Bellogín, A., Parapar, J., Castells, P.: Assessing ranking metrics in top-N recommendation. Inf. Retrieval J. **23**(4), 411–448 (2020). https://doi.org/10.1007/s10791-020-09377-x
27. Wang, C., Guo, Z., Li, G., Li, J., Pan, P., Liu, K.: A light heterogeneous graph collaborative filtering model using textual information. Knowl.-Based Syst. **234**, 107602 (2021). https://doi.org/10.1016/j.knosys.2021.107602
28. Wang, X., He, X., Wang, M., Feng, F., Chua, T.: Neural graph collaborative filtering. In: Proceedings of 42nd International ACM SIGIR Conference on Research and Development in Information Retrieval (SIGIR 2019), pp. 165–174. ACM (2019). https://doi.org/10.1145/3331184.3331267
29. Wilson, J., Chaudhury, S., Lall, B.: Improving collaborative filtering based recommenders using topic modelling. In: Proceedings of IEEE/WIC/ACM International Joint Conference on Web Intelligence and Intelligent Agent Technology – Workshops (WI-IAT 2014), pp. 340–346. IEEE (2014). https://doi.org/10.1109/WI-IAT.2014.54
30. Zhang, Q., Ren, F.: Double Bayesian pairwise learning for one-class collaborative filtering. Knowl.-Based Syst. **229**, 107339 (2021). https://doi.org/10.1016/j.knosys.2021.107339
31. Zhao, W., et al.: Recbole: towards a unified, comprehensive and efficient framework for recommendation algorithms. In: Proceedings of ACM International Conference on Information and Knowledge Management (CIKM 2021), pp. 4653–4664. ACM (2021). https://doi.org/10.1145/3459637.3482016

High Utility Itemset Mining Using Roaring Bitmaps and Ant Colony Optimization

Het Dharmendra Dhinoja[1], Kuldeep Singh[1]([✉]), and Rajiv Kumar[2]

[1] University of Delhi, New Delhi, India
`hetdhinoja1@ce.du.ac.in`, `ksingh@cs.du.ac.in`
[2] Bennett University, Greater Noida, India
`rajiv.kumar@bennett.edu.in`

Abstract. High utility itemset mining (HUIM) is a powerful data mining technique that extracts information from transactional datasets. This paper proposes a new approach to mining high utility itemsets (HUIs), based on Ant Colony Optimization (ACO), which uses Roaring Bitmaps as the core data structure for managing transaction sets and Remaining Transaction Weighted Utility (RTWU) for negative utility support. The algorithm works with the help of iterative ants, which construct HUIs by selecting items probabilistically. The ants are guided by pheromones and heuristic information, while leveraging EUCS for effective pruning and Roaring Bitmaps for fast utility calculations. The overall architecture of this algorithm preserves the constructive nature of ACO but significantly enhances the internal mechanics of each phase. In each iteration, multiple ants select items randomly guided by probabilistic information and then construct a high utility itemset by selecting those itemsets that are likely to lead to the highest utility itemset. In addition, the algorithm employs the Estimated Utility Co-occurrence Pruning strategy (EUCS) to prune all paths that couldn't potentially lead to HUIs. The experimental results are compared with five recent state-of-the-art algorithms.

Keywords: High-utility itemset mining · Utility mining ·
Evolutionary computation · Ant colony optimization · Negative utility

1   Introduction

In today's world, the ability to extract information from transactional datasets has become an important task for competitive advantage across numerous fields, from e-commerce to bioinformatics. A primary task within the field of data mining is pattern mining. The technique we will be discussing falls under high utility itemset mining (HUIM), which is an extension of frequent itemset mining (FIM) [1].Diving into the history of FIM, it was introduced to identify a set of items that frequently occurred in a transaction dataset. FIM, however, works on a very simple principle, according to Agrawal et al. [1] "it assumes that all the items hold equal importance (weight, unit profit or value)" and that each item cannot appear more than once in a transaction. This logic is flawed when we consider real life examples, thus it was extended to introduce HUIM. The goal of HUIM is to discover high-utility itemsets (HUIs) [4,5], groups of items which, when purchased together, generate a total utility exceeding a user-defined threshold, which is also called minimum utility. HUIM allows businesses to identify the most profitable product combinations.

Further research was focused on improving efficiency by eliminating the need for explicit candidate generation and reducing the number of dataset scans. This led to the development of single-phase algorithms, which use advanced data structures to store the information of the items. The popular tree-based algorithms, UP-Growth [20] and UP-Growth+ [19]. Both of the tree-based algorithms adapt the FP-Tree [8] concept from FIM (Frequent Itemset Mining) [1] to compress dataset information and mine HUIs with fewer dataset scans. More popular, list-based algorithms, HUI-Miner [11], FHM [7], and HUP-Miner [10] have emerged as the state-of-the-art, utilizing vertical data structures (utility-lists) to store the item's information for utility calculation, thereby avoiding repeated dataset scans and costly tree traversals.

Meanwhile, researchers have also explored the application of evolutionary computation (EC) and metaheuristics as a powerful alternative for dealing with the enormous search-space of potential itemsets, which grows exponentially with the number of items. Techniques such as Genetic Algorithms (GA) [2] and Particle Swarm Optimization (PSO) [9] have been adapted for HUIM to find near-optimal solutions efficiently. Among these, Ant Colony Optimization [18] (ACO) presents a particularly compelling approach. It simulates the foraging behavior of ants to constructively build solutions (candidate itemsets), offering a promising method to avoid the combinatorial explosion as seen in exhaustive search methods.

1.1 The Unresolved Challenges in HUIM-ACO

Although Ant Colony Optimization (ACO) has been applied to HUIM, its effectiveness is constrained by high computational cost, memory inefficiency, and the inability of classical pruning techniques to handle negative utility items, which are common in real-world datasets [4,5]. These limitations, as highlighted in prior work [18], restrict the performance of HUIM-ACO.

1. ACO algorithms, while effective in reducing search space, are computationally and memory intensive. Their performance is sensitive to parameters like iterations and ant count, often leading to premature convergence. The quadratic growth of the pheromone matrix further limits scalability, causing HUIM-ACO [18] to perform poorly on large datasets.
2. The pruning strategy in HUIM-ACO [18] is inefficient due to the lack of anti-monotonicity in HUIM. Although the commonly used Transaction-Weighted Utility (TWU) model [12] provides an upper bound to enable pruning, its loose overestimation generates numerous unpromising candidates, resulting in computational waste and reduced effectiveness.

3. A major limitation of the TWU model is its inability to handle negative-utility items, common in real-world retail scenarios such as loss leaders or promotions. In such cases, TWU may underestimate true utility, causing genuine high-utility itemsets to be missed and leading to incomplete results. Consequently, HUIM algorithms, including HUIM-ACO [18], become unsuitable, and although specialized methods exist [4,5,14], they are yet to be integrated into an efficient ACO framework.

To target the limitations of the current state-of-the-art approaches, we have proposed HUIM-ACO-Neg-EUCS algorithm. The key contributions of the proposed work are as follows:

1. Utilize Roaring Bitmaps [3] a highly efficient compressed bitmap data structure, into the HUIM-ACO framework for representing sets of transactions. By replacing less efficient methods of managing transaction sets, this integration is designed to drastically accelerate core set-based computations, particularly for the sparse datasets.
2. Employ RTWU [4] which ensures accurate mining with respect to negative utility items.
3. Utilize EUCS [7] and modify it according to the negative utility. EUCS is a lookahead pruning mechanism that discards unpromising item pairs early in the construction process, minimizing costly computations.

2   Preliminaries and Problem Statement

Let $\mathcal{I} = \{i_1, i_2, \ldots, i_m\}$ be a finite set of distinct items. A subset of items $X \subseteq \mathcal{I}$ is called an **itemset**. A transaction dataset is a collection of transactions $\mathcal{D} = \{T_1, T_2, \ldots, T_n\}$, where each transaction T_d is a unique identifier associated with an itemset purchased on a visit to the retail store.

In the context of HUIM, two types of utility are defined:

- **Internal utility:** For each transaction $T_d \in \mathcal{D}$ where item i_p appears, a positive real number $q(i_p, T_d)$ represents the quantity of item i_p in the transaction.
- **External utility:** Each item $i_p \in \mathcal{I}$ is associated with a number $p(i_p)$, which can be positive, zero, or negative, representing its unit utility (e.g., profit or price of an item).

Using these, we define the following utility measures:

Definition 1 (Utility of an item in a transaction). *The utility of an item i_p in a transaction T_d is denoted as $u(i_p, T_d)$ and is defined as:*

$$u(i_p, T_d) = p(i_p) \times q(i_p, T_d) \tag{1}$$

This represents the total value contributed by item i_p in transaction T_d.

Definition 2 (Utility of an itemset in a transaction). *The utility of an itemset $X \subseteq \mathcal{I}$ in a transaction T_d is given by:*

$$u(X, T_d) = \begin{cases} \sum\limits_{i_p \in X} u(i_p, T_d), & if \ X \subseteq T_d \\ 0, & otherwise \end{cases} \tag{2}$$

Definition 3 (Utility of an itemset in a dataset). *The utility of an itemset X in the dataset $\mathcal{D}$ is the sum of its utilities in all transactions where it appears:*

$$u(X) = \sum_{\substack{T_d \in \mathcal{D} \\ X \subseteq T_d}} u(X, T_d) \tag{3}$$

This represents the total value generated by itemset X across the entire dataset.

2.1   The High-Utility Itemset Mining Problem

Definition 4 (High utility itemset mining (HUIM)). *Given a transaction dataset $\mathcal{D}$, an external utility table for all items in $\mathcal{I}$, and a user-specified minimum utility threshold min_util, the task of high utility itemset mining is to discover the complete set of high utility itemsets (HUIs).*

An itemset X is considered a high-utility itemset if and only if: $u(X) \geq min\_util$

2.2   Extending the Problem for Negative Utility

Classical HUIM algorithms assume the external utility $p(i)$ are always positive, but real-world scenarios often include loss-leading products (e.g., discounted or gift items) with negative utility for the purpose of customer acquisition. Handling these negative values [4,5,14,15] is a significant algorithmic challenge, particularly for pruning strategies. This problem, as well as our solution, forms a main contribution of this work.

2.3   Roaring Bitmaps

One of the key contributions of this research is the use of Roaring Bitmaps [3] as the data structure of sets of transactions. Roaring Bitmaps is a compact bitmap data structure that is already used as the de facto standard in high-speed data systems like Apache Spark [22], Lucene, and Druid [21], due to their superior efficiency and compression ratio. This efficiency is achieved using a hybrid internal setup consisting of three types of containers, as depicted in Fig. 1.

Array Containers: For sparse segments holding 4096 or fewer integers, a sorted array of 16-bit integers is adequate. It keeps memory usage low in sparse data.

Bitmap Containers: For highly concentrated segments with more than 4096 integers, a regular 216-bit (8KB) bitmap is used. This allows for extremely fast and easy access and uses bit-level parallelism in performing logical operations.

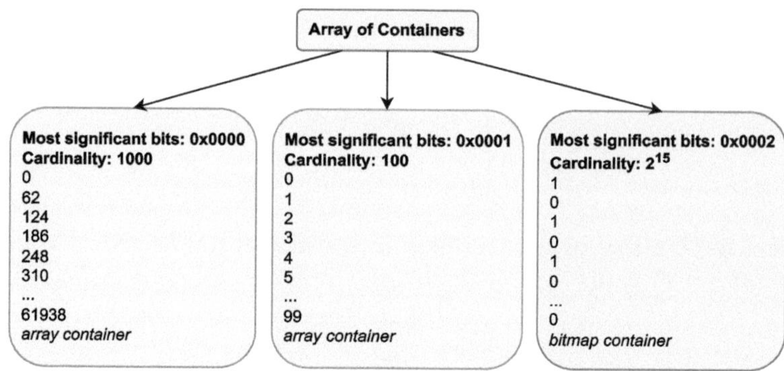

Fig. 1. Structure of a Roaring Bitmap. A Roaring Bitmap stores data in an array of containers, each identified by its most significant bits. The containers may be array or bitmap-based, depending on the cardinality.

Run Containers: Furthermore, Roaring Bitmaps also offer run-length encoding for containers with long consecutive runs of integers, thus providing better compression in these particular situations.

In the initialization phase, for each promising item i, we create and populate a `RoaringBitmap` object, denoted $RB(i)$, which stores the set of transaction IDs (TIDs) for all transactions containing item i.

An ant must maintain the set of transactions, TS, that contain its current path P_a. If the path is: $P_a = \{i_1, i_2, \ldots, i_k\}$, then its corresponding transaction set is the intersection of the transaction sets of its constituent items: $TS(P_a) = RB(i_1) \cap RB(i_2) \cap \cdots \cap RB(i_k)$.

In this paper, this is computed with extreme efficiency. When an ant at path P_a with transaction set $TS(P_a)$ considers adding a new item i_{new}, the transaction set for the new, extended path is calculated simply as:

$$TS(P_a \cup \{i_{\text{new}}\}) = \texttt{RoaringBitmap.and}(TS(P_a), RB(i_{\text{new}})).$$

The *and*() operation in Roaring Bitmaps is highly optimized and often uses SIMD instructions, and is much faster than the intersection of sorted lists or doing *bitwise* operations on big, uncompressed bitmaps. This significantly speeds up the most common and expensive operation within the ant's search process. Additionally, the inherent compression of Roaring Bitmaps substantially reduces the overall memory space necessary for keeping the original transaction record of all products in comparison with other data structures.

2.4   Algorithm Framework

The overall structure of the algorithm also still retains the constructive and iterative processes of Ant Colony. Optimization significantly enhances the internal mechanics of each phase. The algorithm proceeds into three general phases:

Initialization Phase: The algorithm runs once through the transaction dataset. It calculates the redefined transaction-weighted utility (RTWU) [4] of every itemset through scanning. Then, eliminates all items with RTWU less than the minimum utility. For all the remaining potential items, it builds the Estimated Utility Co-occurrence Structure (EUCS) matrix [7] and starts a `RoaringBitmap` [3] for each item and populates it with the TIDs of the transactions it appears in.

Iterative Path Construction: An artificial colony of ants must search the search-space. Each ant builds a candidate HUI (a path) by choosing items successively. The decision is informed by the pheromone matrix and pruned by the EUCS in an aggressive manner. The transaction set for growing paths is accelerated by Roaring Bitmap operations.

Pheromone Update: The pheromone matrix is updated at each step. In addressing the trails that develop high-utility itemsets, a reinforcement occurs, which systematically inclines subsequent ants towards increased potential fields in the search-space. This build creates a chain of upgrades, RTWU [4] places the proper base upper-bound, coarse-grained lookahead pruning is done by EUCS [7], and Roaring Bitmaps provide the high- performance engine for the remaining fine-grained computations.

2.5 Advanced Pruning for a Reduced Search-Space

Negative-Aware Pruning with Redefined Transaction-Weighted Utility (RTWU). To ensure correctness and completeness in the presence of negative-utility items, our algorithm replaces the traditional TWU [12] model with the *Redefined Transaction-Weighted Utility* (RTWU) [4] model.

Definition 5 (Redefined Transaction Utility). *The Redefined Transaction Utility (RTU) of a transaction T_d is the sum of the utilities of only the positive-profit items within it:*

$$\mathrm{RTU}(T_d) = \sum_{\substack{i \in T_d \\ p(i) > 0}} u(i, T_d)$$

Definition 6 (Redefined Transaction-Weighted Utility). *The Redefined Transaction-Weighted Utility (RTWU) of an itemset X is the sum of the RTUs of all transactions containing X:*

$$\mathrm{RTWU}(X) = \sum_{\substack{T_d \in D \\ X \subseteq T_d}} \mathrm{RTU}(T_d)$$

The RTWU [4] restores the crucial upper-bound property, ensuring that: $RTWU(X) \geq u(X)$ for any itemset X, even when $u(X)$ is influenced by negative-profit items. Moreover, RTWU is *anti-monotonic*.

Implementation: The RTWU [4] is employed as the primary pruning mechanism in the initialization phase. After the first dataset scan, any itemset i where:

$RTWU(\{i\}) < min\_util$ is immediately discarded. This enables a powerful first-pass reduction of the search-space before any ants are deployed.

Correctness and Completeness: The guarantee that our Algorithm discovers the complete and correct set of all HUIs rests on the validity of its pruning strategies. We must prove that no valid HUI is ever erroneously discarded.

Furthermore, the RTWU [4] value is used as the heuristic information guiding the ants' probabilistic choices and in the pheromone update rule, replacing TWU [12] in all aspects of the baseline ACO [18] algorithm.

Theorem 1 (Correctness of the RTWU Upper Bound). *For any itemset X, its $RTWU(X)$, is an upper bound on its true utility, $u(X)$, i.e.,*

$$RTWU(X) \geq u(X),$$

even in the presence of items with negative utility.

Proof. The utility of an itemset X is

$$u(X) = \sum_{T_d \in D,\ X \subseteq T_d} u(X, T_d).$$

The utility of X in a single transaction T_d is

$$u(X, T_d) = \sum_{i \in X} u(i, T_d).$$

Partition X into positive-profit items X^{pos} and negative-profit items X^{neg}. Then,

$$u(X, T_d) = \sum_{i \in X^{pos}} u(i, T_d) + \sum_{j \in X^{neg}} u(j, T_d).$$

By definition, the second term is non-positive, so

$$u(X, T_d) \leq \sum_{i \in X^{pos}} u(i, T_d).$$

The Redefined Transaction Utility (RTU) of T_d is

$$RTU(T_d) = \sum_{\substack{k \in T_d \\ p(k) > 0}} u(k, T_d).$$

Since $X^{pos} \subseteq \{k \in T_d \mid p(k) > 0\}$, it follows that

$$\sum_{i \in X^{pos}} u(i, T_d) \leq RTU(T_d).$$

Thus,

$$u(X, T_d) \leq RTU(T_d).$$

Summing over all T_d containing X, we obtain

$$u(X) \leq \sum_{T_d \in D,\ X \subseteq T_d} RTU(T_d) = RTWU(X).$$

Hence, $RTWU(X)$ is a valid upper bound on $u(X)$.

Lookahead Pruning with Estimated Utility Co-occurrence Structure (EUCS). To further reduce unnecessary computations, our algorithm incorporates a lookahead pruning strategy based on the Estimated Utility Co-occurrence Structure (EUCS) [7]

Implementation: During the initialization phase, after the initial pruning of itemsets using RTWU [4], an $H \times H$ symmetric matrix, the EUCS, is constructed, where H is the number of remaining promising items. Each entry $EUCS[j][k]$ stores the pre-computed value of $RTWU(\{i_j, i_k\})$.

EUCS Strategy Integration: This pre-computed matrix enables the Estimated Utility Co-occurrence Strategy(EUCS), which is integrated directly into the ant's state transition logic. Before an ant currently at an item i_c expends computational resources to evaluate a potential next item i_n, it performs a simple and extremely fast lookup in the EUCS matrix. The pruning rule is as follows:

$$\text{If } EUCS[c][n] < \text{min\_util, then prune } i_n \text{ from the set of possible next steps.} \tag{4}$$

This check is valid because if the RTWU of the pair $\{i_c, i_n\}$ is already below the threshold, no superset containing this pair can possibly be an HUI. This strategy effectively acts as a powerful second-layer filter, pruning entire branches of the search-space without performing the more costly Roaring Bitmap intersection and subsequent utility calculations. Consequently, this significantly reduces the branching factor for each ant and focuses its search on more promising paths

Correctness and Completness:

Theorem 2 (Safety of EUCS). *The Estimated Utility Co-occurrence Pruning strategy (EUCS) is safe, meaning it does not prune any path that could potentially lead to an HUI.*

Proof. EUCS prunes the extension of a path with item i_n if $EUCS[c][n] < min\_util$, where i_c is the last item in the current path. The value $EUCS[c][n]$ equals $RTWU(\{i_c, i_n\})$.

From Theorem 1, for any itemset $Y \supseteq \{i_c, i_n\}$, we have $u(Y) \leq RTWU(Y)$. Due to the anti-monotonicity of $RTWU$, $RTWU(Y) \leq RTWU(\{i_c, i_n\})$. Thus,

$$u(Y) \leq RTWU(Y) \leq RTWU(\{i_c, i_n\}).$$

If $RTWU(\{i_c, i_n\}) < min\_util$, it directly implies $u(Y) < min\_util$ for any superset Y. Therefore, no superset of $\{i_c, i_n\}$ can be an HUI, and pruning this path extension is safe.

Conclusion on Completeness: Our Algorithm relies on two primary pruning mechanisms: (1) the initial filtering of itemsets based on their $RTWU$ [4], and (2) EUCS [7] during path construction.

As proven above, both strategies are safe and do not discard any potential HUIs. The underlying ACO [18] search mechanism explores the entire pruned search-space. Therefore, our algorithm is guaranteed to find the complete set of high utility itemsets.

2.6   Algorithm Pseudo-code

The Pseudo-code for the complete algorithm is presented below, illustrating the integration of these components.

Algorithm 1: Main-procedure

Input: Dataset D, min_util, ACO parameters $(\alpha, \beta, \rho, Q, num\_ants, num\_iterations)$
Output: Set of high utility itemsets HUI_set

1   $HUI\_set \leftarrow \emptyset$;
2   $(H_1, EUCS, RB\_maps) \leftarrow Initialize(D, P, min\_util)$;
3   pheromone_matrix $\leftarrow$ Initialize pheromones for items in H_1;
4   **for** $iter \leftarrow 1$ **to** $num\_iterations$ **do**
5   **for** each ant $k \leftarrow 1$ **to** num_ants **do**
6       $path_k \leftarrow$
       $ConstructSolution(k, H_1, EUCS, RB\_maps, pheromone\_matrix, min\_util)$;
7       $HUI\_set \leftarrow HUI\_set \cup \{HUIs\ found\ in\ path_k\}$;
8   Update pheromone_matrix based on HUI_set found in this iteration (evaporation and reinforcement);
9   **return** HUI_set;

Main Procedure: First, itemsets with sufficient transaction weighted utility (H_1), an estimated utility co-occurrence structure (EUCS) [7], and roaring bitmap representations [3] (RB_maps) are taken from the dataset. A pheromone matrix, representing learned selection probabilities for each item, is created. In each iteration, some ants create candidate itemsets by probabilistic selection of items from the pheromones and heuristic knowledge, employing EUCS for effective pruning and Roaring Bitmaps for utility calculation at high speed. High-utility itemsets discovered by the ants are collected, and the pheromone matrix is updated by evaporation and reinforcement, according to the quality of the discovered itemsets.

Initialize Procedure: The initial procedure prepares the data for high-utility itemset mining using Roaring Bitmaps. It scans the dataset to compute item utilities and transaction utilities, calculates the transaction weighted utility (RTWU) [4] for each item, and selects promising items (H_1) whose RTWU meets the minimum utility threshold. For each promising item, it creates a Roaring Bitmap recording the IDs of transactions where the item appears. An empty EUCS [7] matrix is set up, then for every pair of promising items, it computes their shared transactions using bitmap intersection, sums their transaction utilities, and records this in the EUCS matrix. The procedure returns the set of promising items (H_1), the EUCS matrix, and the Roaring Bitmap maps.

Algorithm 2: Initialize-procedure

Input: Dataset D, min_util

Output: Promising itemsets H_1, EUCS matrix, Roaring Bitmap maps RB_maps

1 Scan D once to compute $u(i, T_d)$ and $RTU(T_d)$ for all items i and transactions T_d;

2 Compute $RTWU(\{i\})$ for every item $i \in I$;

3 $H_1 \leftarrow \{i \in I \mid RTWU(\{i\}) \geq min\_util\}$;

4 $RB\_maps \leftarrow$ Create a `RoaringBitmap` for each item $i \in H_1$, storing its $TIDs$;

5 $EUCS \leftarrow$ Initialize an empty $|H_1| \times |H_1|$ matrix;

6 **for** *each pair of items* $\{i_j, i_k\} \subseteq H_1$ **do**

7 $\quad\quad TS_{jk} \leftarrow$ `RoaringBitmap`.$and(RB\_maps[i_j], RB\_maps[i_k])$;

8 $\quad\quad RTWU_{jk} \leftarrow \sum_{t \in TS_{jk}} RTU(T_t)$;

9 $\quad\quad EUCS[j][k] \leftarrow RTWU_{jk}$;

10 **return** $(H_1, EUCS, RB\_maps)$;

Algorithm 3: Construct-solution-procedure (Ant's Logic)

Input: Ant ID k, H_1, EUCS, RB_maps, $pheromone\_matrix$, min_util

Output: Path constructed by ant k

1 Select a starting item $i_{start} \in H_1$ based on probability proportional to its $RTWU$;

2 $current\_path \leftarrow \{i_{start}\}$;

3 $current\_TS \leftarrow RB\_maps[i_{start}]$;

4 **while** *true* **do**

5 $\quad\quad successors \leftarrow$ Get potential next items from H_1 not in $current\_path$;

6 $\quad\quad valid\_successors \leftarrow \emptyset$;

7 $\quad\quad last\_item \leftarrow$ last item in $current\_path$;

8 $\quad\quad$**foreach** $next\_item \in successors$ **do**

9 $\quad\quad\quad\quad$**if** $EUCS[last\_item][next\_item] \geq min\_util$ **then**

10 $\quad\quad\quad\quad\quad\quad$add $next\_item$ to $valid\_successors$;

11 $\quad\quad$**if** $valid\_successors$ *is empty* **then**

12 $\quad\quad\quad\quad$break;

13 $\quad\quad$Select $chosen\_item$ from $valid\_successors$ using ACO state transition rule (pheromones, RTWU heuristic);

14 $\quad\quad current\_path \leftarrow current\_path \cup \{chosen\_item\}$;

15 $\quad\quad current\_TS \leftarrow$ `RoaringBitmap`.$and(current\_TS, RB\_maps[chosen\_item])$;

16 $\quad\quad$Calculate actual utility $u(current\_path)$ using $current\_TS$;

17 $\quad\quad$**if** $u(current\_path) \geq min\_util$ **then**

18 $\quad\quad\quad\quad$Add $current\_path$ to this ant's list of found HUIs;

19 **return** $current\_path$;

Ant Logic: The ant starts by probabilistically selecting an initial item from H_1, weighted by each item's transaction weighted utility (RTWU) [4]. The current path is set to this item, and the set of supporting transactions is initialized using its Roaring Bitmap. While possible, the ant considers potential successor items not already in the path. For each candidate, it checks via the EUCS [7] matrix if the combined RTWU with the last path item meets the minimum utility threshold; only such valid successors are kept. If there are no valid successors, the process ends.

If valid successors exist, the next item is chosen using an ACO [18] rule based on pheromone values and heuristic information (like RTWU [4]). The chosen item is added to the path, and the transaction set is updated via intersection of Roaring Bitmaps [3]. The utility of the current path is then calculated. If it meets or exceeds the minimum utility, this path is recorded as a high-utility itemset for the ant. The process returns the constructed path.

2.7   Complexity Analysis

- **Initialization Phase:** Requires one scan of the dataset: $O(|D| \times L_{max})$, where L_{max} is the maximum transaction length.
- **EUCS Construction:** Takes $O(H^2 \times Cand)$, where $Cand$ is the cost of a Roaring Bitmap AND operation (typically very efficient).
- **Path Construction Phase:**
  - For each of *num_iterations* $\times$ *num_ants*, an ant constructs a path of length at most H.
  - At each step, up to H successors are considered; EUCS drastically reduces this branching factor.
  - For each valid successor, one AND operation between bitmaps and a utility computation is required.
  - The cost of AND between bitmaps of cardinalities $|B_1|$ and $|B_2|$ is $O(|B_1| + |B_2|)$ in the worst case, but usually faster.

The overall time complexity can be approximated as:

$$O\big(InitCost + Iter \times Ants \times PathLength \times BranchFactor \times (Cost_{EUCS} + Cost_{ACO} + Cost_{AND})\big).$$

Our Algorithm achieves performance gains by:

- Reducing the *BranchFactor* via EUCS.
- Lowering cost of AND operations via Roaring Bitmap compression.

This leads to substantial practical improvements compared to baseline HUIM algorithms.

2.8   Experimental Evaluation

This section presents the experimental evaluation of the proposed algorithm, HUIM-ACO-Neg-EUCS. All experiments were performed on a machine equipped with an Intel Core i7-10700 CPU, 64 GB of DDR5 RAM, running Windows 11. The algorithms were implemented in Java. The execution time and peak memory usage were measured using standard Java APIs to ensure consistency and reproducibility.

Parameter Settings. For all experiments, the ant colony size was set to 10,000. This large number promotes a wide breadth of exploration across the search space in each cycle. The total number of iterations was fixed at 20, prioritizing a rapid search over deep convergence. Our algorithm also utilizes two selection thresholds, $\tau_1 = 0.1$ and $\tau_2 = 0.7$. These thresholds are critical for managing the exploration-exploitation trade-off. They partition the probability space to stochastically determine which search method an ant employs, balancing greedy, probabilistic, and random selection strategies.

Datasets. A diverse set of publicly available datasets was used to evaluate the algorithms under different conditions. For all datasets, external utilities for items are generated between $-1,000$ and $1,000$ by using a log-normal distribution and quantities of items are generated randomly between 1 and 5, similarly to the settings of [3, 4, 9, 12]. All the datasets are publicly available at SPMF [6].

- Dense Datasets:
    - mushroom_negative: Prepared based on the UCI mushrooms dataset
    - chess_negative: Prepared based on the UCI chess dataset
    - pumsb_negative: census data for population and housing
- Sparse Dataset:
    - Foodmart dataset of customer transactions from a retail store, obtained and transformed from SQL-Server 2000.

Algorithms

- **HUIM-ACO-Neg-EUCS:** Our proposed algorithm which uses EUCS on top of RTWU for pruning and negative utility support and Roaring Bitmaps.
- **HUIM-ACO-Neg:** This is the modified version of the HUIM-ACO algorithm which uses Roaring Bitmaps and RTWU.
- **HUIM-AF-Neg:** HUIM-AF-Neg [16] is an Artificial Fish Swarm algorithm modified to handle negative utilities, simulating behaviors like preying and swarming to efficiently discover high utility itemsets.
- **HUIM-HC-Neg and HUIM-SA-Neg:** We modified the heuristic algorithms HUIM-SA [13] and HUIM-HC [13] to support negative utilities. These bitmap-based algorithms iteratively generate, prune, and select candidate itemsets using a fitness function over multiple cycles.
- **HUIM-SetPSO-Neg:** HUIM-SPSO [17] uses a Set-Based Particle Swarm Optimization (S-PSO) to discover High Utility Itemsets. It efficiently finds a diverse set of itemsets by focusing modifications on elements with the highest velocities (most potential for improvement.)

Further Analysis. HUIM-HC's apparent speed advantage is misleading, as it results from an incomplete search that fails to discover the full set of high-utility itemsets (HUIs) as shown in the table below (Tables 1 and 2).

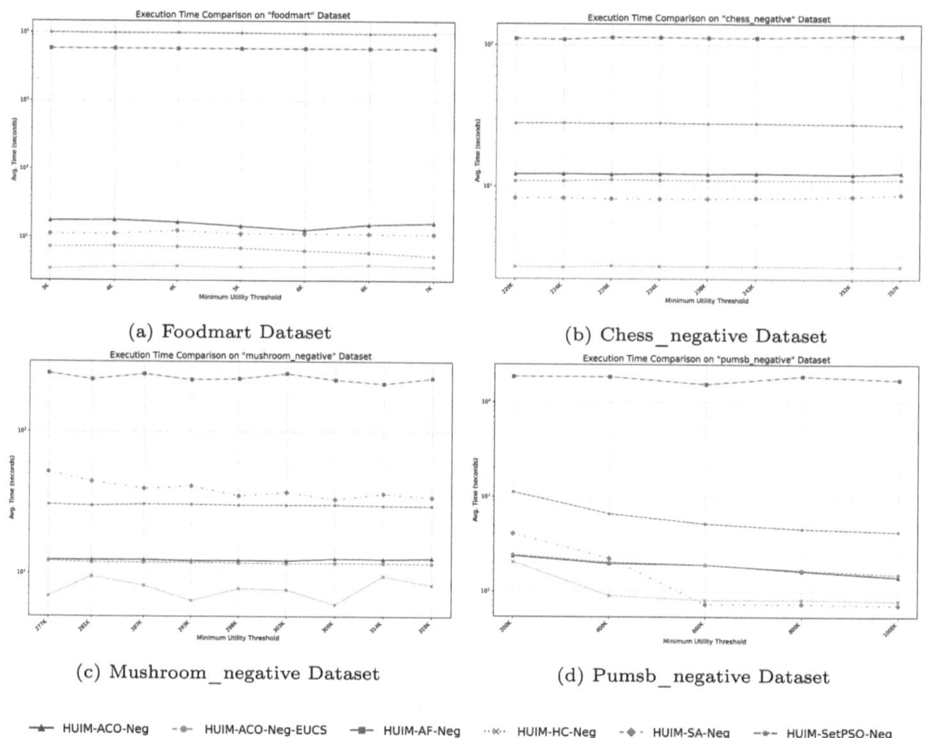

(a) Foodmart Dataset

(b) Chess_negative Dataset

(c) Mushroom_negative Dataset

(d) Pumsb_negative Dataset

Fig. 2. Execution Time Comparison on Various Datasets

– A closer examination of the results validates our claim. While HUIM-HC-Neg (represented as HC-Neg) may complete its execution faster on datasets like Mushroom, Foodmart, Chess and pumsb, this speed comes at the steep price of correctness and completeness. The data shows it consistently discovers only a small fraction of the HUIs found by our proposed algorithm, HUIM-ACO-Neg-EUCS (represented as ACO-Neg-EUCS).
– On the Mushroom (neg) dataset, at a *min_util* of 277,088, HC-Neg finds a mere 17 HUIs, whereas our ACO-Neg-EUCS discovers 237, over 13 times more. This pattern of drastic underperformance by HC-Neg persists across all tested utility thresholds.
– The trend is even more pronounced on the Foodmart dataset. At a *min_util* of 3,603, HC-Neg identifies 240 HUIs. In contrast, our algorithm successfully mines 1,363 HUIs, demonstrating a fundamentally more robust search capability.
This evidence strongly suggests that HUIM-HC achieves its speed by prematurely halting its search, thereby failing in its primary objective to comprehensively identify high-utility patterns.

Our algorithm, HUIM-ACO-Neg-EUCS, operates on a more scientifically sound principle. It invests a comparable amount of runtime to conduct a far

Table 1. Comparison of HUIs mined by our algorithm vs other algorithms on *Mushroom (neg)* dataset.

min_util	ACO-Neg-EUCS	HC-Neg	SetPSO-Neg	AF-Neg	SA-Neg
277088	237	17	80	80	365
281883	213	22	73	73	289
287745	170	13	60	60	161
293073	160	5	64	54	173
298402	120	14	62	49	70
303731	112	9	40	44	95
309059	81	4	40	45	32
314388	80	13	32	35	24
319717	56	10	36	32	23

Table 2. Comparison of HUIs mined by our algorithm vs other algorithms on *Foodmart* dataset.

min_util	ACO-Neg-EUCS	HC-Neg	SetPSO-Neg	AF-Neg	SA-Neg
3603	1363	240	29	1189	677
4203	1235	134	13	600	458
4804	1121	126	13	329	378
5404	1027	92	14	237	350
6005	917	83	8	235	317
6606	825	89	7	177	271
7206	742	90	7	141	247

more thorough exploration of the search-space. This slight increase in computational time is a justified trade-off for the significant gain in completeness, ensuring that the results are not just fast, but also reliable and comprehensive.

Our approach remains highly competitive. While HUIM-SA (SA-Neg) is slightly faster on the Chess dataset, our method demonstrates clear superiority on others, finding nearly double the HUIs on Foodmart and outperforming SA-Neg on most Mushroom thresholds, as depicted in Fig. 2. In conclusion, HUIM-ACO-Neg-EUCS provides a superior balance of efficiency and effectiveness, delivering a significantly more complete HUI set in a comparable timeframe.

2.9   Conclusion

This paper addresses key challenges in high utility itemset mining (HUIM) using ant colony optimization (ACO), including computational inefficiency, memory issues, reliance on weak pruning bounds, and difficulties handling negative utility items. We propose a novel solution integrating three innovations: Roaring

Bitmaps for efficient transaction management; a unified pruning strategy combining Redefined Transaction-Weighted Utility (RTWU) for correctness with negative utilities and the Estimated Utility Co-occurrence Structure (EUCS) for aggressive pruning; and a robust framework delivering accurate results. Our theoretical analysis confirms the correctness and completeness of our pruning strategies. Experimental results show our algorithm outperforms baselines in speed and correctness, and is competitive with leading methods, although we can acknowledge that as meta heuristic algorithm, the algorithm's performance is sensitive to the tuning of ACO-specific parameters (such as colony size and selection thresholds), and the computational overhead, while significantly reduced by our optimizations, can still be considerable on certain dataset distributions. The proposed work can be utilized in dynamic environments, such as streaming and incremental datasets.

Acknowledgments. This work was conducted as part of the project titled "Mining of High Utility Sequential Patterns using Evolutionary Techniques" under the Major Research Project (MRP) scheme - Institute of Eminence, University of Delhi, Sanctioned on 1st August 2022, File Number: IoE-DU/MRP/2022/056.

References

1. Agrawal, R., Srikant, R.: Fast algorithms for mining association rules. In: Proceedings of 20th International Conference on Very Large Data Bases VLDB, vol. 1215 (2000)
2. Beasley, D., Bull, D., Martin, R.: An overview of genetic algorithms: PT1, fundamentals. Univ. Comput. **15**, 58–69 (1993)
3. Chambi, S., Lemire, D., Kaser, O., Godin, R.: Better bitmap performance with roaring bitmaps. Softw. Pract. Exp. **46** (2014). https://doi.org/10.1002/spe.2325
4. Chu, C.J., Tseng, V.S., Liang, T.: An efficient algorithm for mining high utility itemsets with negative item values in large databases. Appl. Math. Comput. **215**(2), 767–778 (2009). https://doi.org/10.1016/j.amc.2009.05.066
5. Fournier-Viger, P.: FHN: efficient mining of high-utility itemsets with negative unit profits. In: Luo, X., Yu, J.X., Li, Z. (eds.) ADMA 2014. LNCS (LNAI), vol. 8933, pp. 16–29. Springer, Cham (2014). https://doi.org/10.1007/978-3-319-14717-8_2
6. Fournier-Viger, P., et al.: The SPMF open-source data mining library version 2. In: Berendt, B., et al. (eds.) ECML PKDD 2016. LNCS (LNAI), vol. 9853, pp. 36–40. Springer, Cham (2016). https://doi.org/10.1007/978-3-319-46131-1_8
7. Fournier-Viger, P., Wu, C.-W., Zida, S., Tseng, V.S.: FHM: faster high-utility itemset mining using estimated utility co-occurrence pruning. In: Andreasen, T., Christiansen, H., Cubero, J.-C., Raś, Z.W. (eds.) ISMIS 2014. LNCS (LNAI), vol. 8502, pp. 83–92. Springer, Cham (2014). https://doi.org/10.1007/978-3-319-08326-1_9
8. Han, J., Pei, J., Yin, Y.: Mining frequent patterns without candidate generation. In: ACM Sigmod Record, vol. 29, pp. 1–12. ACM (2000)
9. Kennedy, J., Eberhart, R.: Particle swarm optimization. In: Proceedings of ICNN'95 - International Conference on Neural Networks, vol. 4, pp. 1942–1948 (1995). https://doi.org/10.1109/ICNN.1995.488968

10. Krishnamoorthy, S.: Pruning strategies for mining high utility itemsets. Expert Syst. Appl. **42**(5), 2371–2381 (2015). https://doi.org/10.1016/j.eswa.2014.11.001

11. Liu, M., Qu, J.: Mining high utility itemsets without candidate generation. In: 21st ACM International Conference on Information and Knowledge Management, pp. 55–64. ACM, NY, USA (2012). https://doi.org/10.1145/2396761.2396773

12. Liu, Y., Liao, W., Choudhary, A.: A two-phase algorithm for fast discovery of high utility itemsets. In: Ho, T.B., Cheung, D., Liu, H. (eds.) PAKDD 2005. LNCS (LNAI), vol. 3518, pp. 689–695. Springer, Heidelberg (2005). https://doi.org/10.1007/11430919_79

13. Nawaz, M.S., Fournier-Viger, P., Yun, U., Wu, Y., Song, W.: Mining high utility itemsets with hill climbing and simulated annealing. ACM Trans. Manage. Inf. Syst. **13**(1) (2021). https://doi.org/10.1145/3462636

14. Singh, K., Shakya, H.K., Abhimanyu, S., Biswas, B.: Mining of high utility itemsets with negative utility. Expert Syst. **35**(6), e12296 (2018). https://doi.org/10.1111/exsy.12296

15. Singh, K., Singh, S.S., Kumar, A., Biswas, B.: High utility itemsets mining with negative utility value: a survey. J. Intell. Fuzzy Syst. **35**(6), 6551–6562 (2018). https://doi.org/10.3233/JIFS-18965

16. Song, W., Li, J.: Discovering high utility itemsets using set-based particle swarm optimization. In: Yang, X., Wang, C.-D., Islam, M.S., Zhang, Z. (eds.) ADMA 2020. LNCS (LNAI), vol. 12447, pp. 38–53. Springer, Cham (2020). https://doi.org/10.1007/978-3-030-65390-3_4

17. Song, W., Li, J.: Discovering high utility itemsets using set-based particle swarm optimization. In: Yang, X., Wang, C.-D., Islam, M.S., Zhang, Z. (eds.) ADMA 2020. LNCS (LNAI), vol. 12447, pp. 38–53. Springer, Cham (2020). https://doi.org/10.1007/978-3-030-65390-3_4

18. Song, W., Nan, J.: Mining high utility itemsets using ant colony optimization. In: Meng, H., Lei, T., Li, M., Li, K., Xiong, N., Wang, L. (eds.) ICNC-FSKD 2020. LNDECT, vol. 88, pp. 98–107. Springer, Cham (2021). https://doi.org/10.1007/978-3-030-70665-4_12

19. Tseng, V.S., Shie, B.E., Wu, C.W., Yu, P.S.: Efficient algorithms for mining high utility itemsets from transactional databases. IEEE Trans. Knowl. Data Eng. **25**(8), 1772–1786 (2013). https://doi.org/10.1109/TKDE.2012.59

20. Tseng, V.S., Wu, C.W., Shie, B.E., Yu, P.S.: Up-growth: an efficient algorithm for high utility itemset mining. In: Proceedings of the 16th ACM SIGKDD International Conference on Knowledge Discovery and Data Mining, KDD 2010, pp. 253–262. ACM, NY, USA (2010). https://doi.org/10.1145/1835804.1835839

21. Yang, F., Tschetter, E., Léauté, X., Ray, N., Merlino, G., Ganguli, D.: Druid: a real-time analytical data store. In: Proceedings of the 2014 ACM SIGMOD International Conference on Management of Data, SIGMOD 2014, pp. 157–168. ACM, NY, USA (2014). https://doi.org/10.1145/2588555.2595631

22. Zaharia, M., Chowdhury, M., Franklin, M.J., Shenker, S., Stoica, I.: Spark: cluster computing with working sets. In: Proceedings of the 2nd USENIX Conference on Hot Topics in Cloud Computing, p. 10. USENIX Association, USA (2010)

AI for Medical Diagnostics

CAMF-SkinNet: Cross-Attention Multimodal Fusion of Visual, Textual, and Dermatology-Specific Embeddings for Skin Disease Classification

Routhu Srinivasa Rao[✉], Aradhana Mishra, and Sanjay Swain

CureBay, Bhubaneswar 751022, Odisha, India
{routhu.srinivasa,aradhana.mishra,sanjay.swain}@curebay.com

Abstract. Accurate diagnosis of dermatological conditions remains a critical challenge in medical imaging, primarily due to visual similarities across diseases and limited annotated data. We introduce CAMF-SkinNet, a Cross-Attention Multimodal Fusion framework that integrates visual, textual, and dermatology-specific expert knowledge for robust and clinically relevant diagnosis. CAMF-SkinNet combines three complementary modalities: (i) visual features extracted from skin lesion images using MedSigLIP, (ii) dermatology-specific embeddings from the Google Derm Foundation model, and (iii) context-rich medical captions automatically generated by MedGemma-4B, a large-scale medical vision-language model. Partial fine-tuning of the vision and language backbones, coupled with hierarchical cross-attention modules, enables effective cross-modal alignment and interaction. A lightweight Transformer encoder refines the fused features, and multi-branch classification heads provide auxiliary supervision to preserve modality-specific discriminability. Focal Loss mitigates class imbalance, while early stopping ensures efficient convergence. On a challenging 20-class skin disease dataset, CAMF-SkinNet achieves superior accuracy, macro-F1, and Top-K performance over unimodal and naive fusion baselines, demonstrating the promise of cross-attention-driven multimodal integration for automated dermatological diagnosis.

Keywords: Skin disease classification · Multimodal learning · Cross-attention · Vision-language models · Dermatology AI

1 Introduction

Skin diseases are among the most common health concerns globally, affecting nearly 900 million people at any given time [4]. Over 3,000 distinct dermatological conditions have been identified, ranging from benign ailments like acne and eczema to malignant disorders such as melanoma and non-melanoma skin cancers [5]. According to the World Health Organization (WHO), one in three cancers diagnosed worldwide is skin cancer, and early detection dramatically improves

© The Author(s), under exclusive license to Springer Nature Switzerland AG 2026
B. Chatterjee et al. (Eds.): ICDCIT 2026, LNCS 16420, pp. 425–435, 2026.
https://doi.org/10.1007/978-3-032-16632-6_27

survival rates [12]. Despite this, access to qualified dermatologists remains limited especially in rural and underserved regions leading to delayed diagnosis, misclassification, and poor treatment outcomes. Accurate dermatological assessment is a complex task requiring the interpretation of nuanced visual patterns alongside clinical metadata such as patient history, symptom progression, lesion distribution, and comorbidities. Traditional AI-based approaches in dermatology, particularly those using convolutional neural networks (CNNs), focus solely on visual inputs. While successful in many image classification tasks, these models often falter in scenarios where visual similarity masks underlying differences, such as differentiating between seborrheic keratosis and melanoma, or psoriasis and eczema [2].

Another challenge lies in the limited explainability of vision-only models, which can hinder clinical trust and adoption. In teledermatology, where remote consultations are increasingly common, the lack of contextual integration (e.g., patient narrative, symptom descriptions) further limits diagnostic reliability. Recent advances in multimodal AI–which combine visual and language understanding–have shown promise in addressing these limitations. Visionlanguage models such as CLIP, MedCLIP, and SigLIP align image features with textual semantics, improving both accuracy and interpretability in medical imaging tasks [8,13]. Furthermore, biomedical language models like BioBERT can capture nuanced medical semantics from textual descriptions, while dermatology-specific embeddings derived from expert models encapsulate domain knowledge often overlooked by general-purpose vision architectures.

Building on these advances, we propose CAMF-SkinNet (Cross-Attention Multimodal Fusion for Skin Disease Classification), a framework that mimics a dermatologist's reasoning process by integrating three complementary modalities:

- High-quality visual features extracted from skin lesion images via MedSigLIP;
- Descriptive medical captions generated using MedGemma-4B, providing narrative lesion context;
- Dermatology-specific expert embeddings from the Google Derm Foundation model, encoding clinical priors.

These modalities are fused using hierarchical cross-attention modules and refined via a lightweight Transformer encoder to produce robust, context-aware predictions. Auxiliary classification heads for individual modalities encourage each representation to remain discriminative, while Focal Loss mitigates class imbalance. CAMF-SkinNet is designed to support not only accurate diagnosis but also explainable pre-assessment workflows, enabling intelligent triage, second-opinion support, and scalable, equitable dermatological care delivery.

2 Related Work

Recent advances in deep learning have enabled the development of AI-based diagnostic tools for dermatology, with most early successes driven by convolutional neural networks (CNNs). Models trained on large publicly available datasets–such as Fitzpatrick17k [3], HAM10000 [10], and Derm7pt [6]–have demonstrated strong performance in skin disease classification tasks. However, despite these achievements, CNN-based systems often face generalization challenges across diverse skin tones, rare disease classes, and varying image acquisition conditions. For example, although Fitzpatrick17k was curated to include a range of skin tones, CNNs still tend to underperform on darker skin types due to underlying data imbalance. Additionally, CNN-only pipelines typically lack the ability to incorporate non-visual clinical context and offer limited explainability, both of which are critical for building trust in clinical applications.

To address these limitations, multimodal AI has emerged as a promising direction. Visionlanguage models such as CLIP [8], MedCLIP [11], and BioViL [1] align image features with natural language representations, enabling zero-shot transfer and improving semantic grounding. While powerful, these models are not dermatology-specific and may misinterpret subtle lesion patterns or fail to capture domain-specific diagnostic cues. Moreover, their alignment mechanisms are often coarse-grained, lacking structured fusion strategies tailored for fine-grained clinical reasoning. In the biomedical text domain, BioBERT [7] has demonstrated strong performance on tasks such as clinical document classification, named entity recognition (NER), and medical question answering. Generative models like MedGemma [9] extend these capabilities by producing context-rich medical captions, which enhance interpretability in radiology and pathology but remain largely unexplored in dermatology applications.

A few recent studies have attempted to integrate image and text for dermatological AI. However, these often rely on early fusion or simple concatenation, limiting the model's ability to learn fine-grained, bidirectional dependencies between modalities. In contrast, CAMF-SkinNet introduces a structured, hierarchical cross-attention fusion pipeline that explicitly integrates: (i) MedSigLIP-based visual embeddings, (ii) MedGemma-generated descriptive captions, and (iii) BioBERT-encoded language features, along with (iv) dermatology-specific expert embeddings from the Google Derm Foundation model. This approach enables clinically grounded, context-aware reasoning by modeling rich inter-modal dependencies, going beyond the capabilities of existing multimodal frameworks in dermatology.

3   Proposed Methodology

We propose **CAMF-SkinNet** (**C**ross-**A**ttention **M**ultimodal **F**usion for Skin Disease Classification), a framework designed to learn synergistic representations from heterogeneous medical modalities–skin images, generated medical captions, and dermatology-specific expert embeddings. The architecture is built to explicitly model fine-grained dependencies between modalities through a hierarchical cross-attention mechanism, enabling context-aware and clinically relevant diagnostic predictions.

3.1   Overview

Let $\mathcal{I}$ be the input lesion image, $\mathcal{T}$ the generated descriptive caption, and $\mathcal{D}$ the dermatology embedding vector. CAMF-SkinNet projects all modalities into a shared embedding space and fuses them via a two-stage cross-attention pipeline followed by a lightweight Transformer encoder. Figure 1 illustrates the overall architecture.

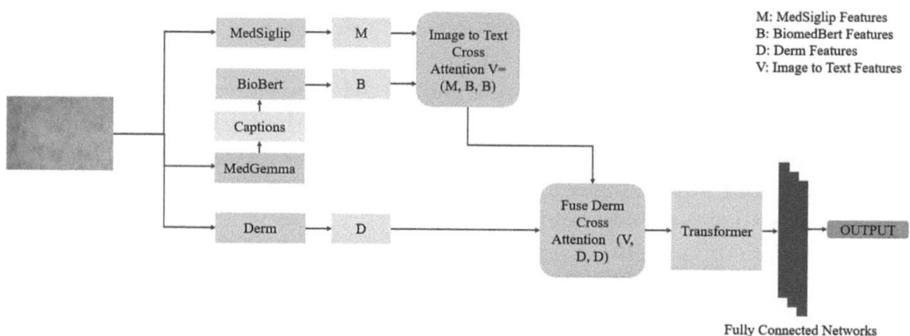

Fig. 1. Overview of CAMF-SkinNet: Visual features from MedSigLIP, textual features from MedGemma-4B/BioBERT, and dermatology embeddings are aligned via hierarchical cross-attention and refined using a Transformer encoder.

3.2   Multimodal Feature Encoding

Image Encoder: We adopt MedSigLIP-448, a visionlanguage pretrained transformer, as the visual backbone. All layers are frozen except the final four transformer blocks to preserve general visuallanguage alignment while allowing dermatology-specific adaptation. The pooled output (1152-D) is projected to a 512-D common space:

$$\mathbf{v} = \mathrm{Proj}_{\mathrm{img}}(\mathrm{MedSigLIP}(\mathcal{I})) \in \mathbb{R}^{512}.$$

Text Encoder (Captions): Captions are generated using MedGemma-4B, a large-scale medical visionlanguage model optimized for structured medical description generation. These captions are encoded by BioBERT, producing contextual token embeddings projected to the shared space:

$$\mathbf{T} = \mathrm{Proj}_{\mathrm{text}}(\mathrm{BioBERT}(\mathcal{T})) \in \mathbb{R}^{L \times 512},$$

where L is the token sequence length.

Dermatology Expert Embeddings: We incorporate expert clinical priors as 6144-D embeddings extracted from the Google Derm Foundation model. These are projected to the shared 512-D space:

$$\mathbf{d} = \mathrm{Proj}_{\mathrm{derm}}(\mathcal{D}) \in \mathbb{R}^{512}.$$

3.3 Hierarchical Cross-Attention Fusion

We design a two-stage cross-attention mechanism to model inter-modal dependencies:

- **Stage 1 (Image $\leftrightarrow$ Text):** Image tokens $\mathbf{v}$ query textual tokens $\mathbf{T}$ via multi-head cross-attention:

$$\mathbf{v}^* = \text{CrossAttn}_{\text{img-text}}(\mathbf{v}, \mathbf{T}).$$

  This stage aligns visual lesion features with their descriptive semantics.
- **Stage 2 (Fused $\leftrightarrow$ Dermatology):** The aligned imagetext representation queries the dermatology expert embedding:

$$\mathbf{z} = \text{CrossAttn}_{\text{fused-derm}}(\mathbf{v}^*, \mathbf{d}),$$

  incorporating domain-specific priors into the fused representation.

3.4 Fusion Transformer Encoder

The fused token $\mathbf{z}$ is passed through a lightweight Transformer encoder to capture higher-order relationships and global context:

$$\tilde{\mathbf{z}} = \text{TransformerEncoder}(\mathbf{z}).$$

3.5 Classification Module

The refined embedding $\tilde{\mathbf{z}}$ is fed to:

- A **primary classification head** producing the final disease prediction:

$$\hat{y} = \text{Softmax}(\text{MLP}(\tilde{\mathbf{z}})).$$

- **Auxiliary heads** applied to the image token and dermatology embedding to preserve modality-specific discriminability and prevent representation collapse.

3.6 Training Objective

We optimize a weighted combination of focal losses:

$$\mathcal{L}_{\text{total}} = \mathcal{L}_{\text{main}} + 0.4 \cdot (\mathcal{L}_{\text{aux-img}} + \mathcal{L}_{\text{aux-derm}}),$$

where each term is computed as:

$$\mathcal{L}_{\text{focal}} = \alpha(1 - p_t)^{\gamma} \cdot \mathcal{L}_{\text{CE}}, \quad \gamma = 2, \ \alpha = 1.$$

Focal loss mitigates severe class imbalance, improving minority-class sensitivity.

3.7   Training Strategy

- **Data Augmentation:** Training images undergo random resized cropping, horizontal flipping, rotation, and color jittering. Validation/test images are resized and center-cropped to 224×224.
- **Data Split:** Stratified 80/20 trainingvalidation split; an independent hold-out set is used for final testing.
- **Optimization:** Adam optimizer, initial LR 1e−4, ReduceLROnPlateau scheduler; mixed-precision (AMP) training for efficiency.
- **Early Stopping:** Monitors validation macro-F1; stops if no improvement for 10 epochs.
- **Evaluation Metrics:** We evaluate the model using traditional metrics such as accuracy, macro F1-score, top-2 and top-3 accuracy, confusion matrix, and per-class classification report.

4   Experimentation and Results

4.1   Evaluation on Pretrained Baseline Models

We evaluated a diverse set of pretrained CNN and Vision Transformer architectures on the Fitzpatrick17k dataset under two settings: the full 114-class setting and the Top-20 most frequent classes setting. These models were fine-tuned end-to-end using the same preprocessing and augmentation strategies. The results are shown in Tables 1 and 2, with our proposed model clearly outperforming all baselines.

Table 1. Test results for pretrained baseline models with 114 classes.

Model	F1 Score	Accuracy	Top-2 Acc	Top-3 Acc
EfficientNetV2-B0	0.3463	0.3716	0.4785	0.5382
MobileNetV2	0.3300	0.3499	0.4576	0.5197
ResNet50	0.2854	0.3242	0.4349	0.5012
InceptionV3	0.2445	0.2657	0.3615	0.4287
ViT-Base (patch16-224)	0.4140	0.4361	0.5627	0.6337
Swin-Base (patch4-window7)	0.4947	0.5140	0.6260	0.6857
ConvNeXt-Base	0.5125	0.5275	0.6385	0.6976
BEiT-Base (patch16-224)	0.2542	0.2916	0.3857	0.4501
DeiT-Base (patch16-224)	0.4257	0.4487	0.5630	0.6331
CoaT-Lite Small	0.2897	0.3337	0.4516	0.5209
Proposed Model	**0.6458**	**0.6693**	**0.7657**	**0.8072**

Table 2. Test results for pretrained baseline models with top-20 most frequent classes.

Model	F1 Score	Accuracy	Top-2 Acc	Top-3 Acc
ConvNeXt-Base	0.6004	0.6155	0.7493	0.8141
Swin-Base ($4\times7/224$)	0.5920	0.6021	0.7465	0.8141
DeiT-Base/16	0.5195	0.5310	0.6761	0.7613
ViT-Base/16	0.4906	0.5042	0.6592	0.7472
EfficientNetV2-B0	0.4446	0.4563	0.5901	0.6690
ResNet-50	0.4230	0.4352	0.5845	0.6810
MobileNetV2	0.4086	0.4310	0.5873	0.6725
CoaT-Lite Small	0.3986	0.4218	0.5754	0.6697
BEiT-Base/16	0.3835	0.3993	0.5521	0.6430
Inception-v3	0.3054	0.3296	0.4669	0.5754
Proposed Model	**0.7260**	**0.7338**	**0.8366**	**0.8908**

4.2   Ablation Study: Fusion Strategies and Component Analysis

To quantify the contribution of each modality and the effectiveness of our cross-attention fusion mechanism, we conducted an ablation study under both the **114-class** and **Top-20** settings. The modalities considered include MedSigLIP (visual), caption embeddings (language), and dermatology-specific embeddings (domain knowledge). Fusion strategies include simple concatenation and our proposed bidirectional cross-attention with auxiliary supervision.

Table 3. Ablation study results (concatenation vs. cross-attention fusion) with 114 classes.

Fusion Strategy/Model	F1 Score	Accuracy	Top-2 Acc	Top-3 Acc
Proposed (MedSigLIP + BioBERT + Derm)	0.6458	0.6693	0.7657	0.8072
MedSigLIP	0.5608	0.5785	0.6886	0.7480
BioBERT	0.2245	0.2564	0.4010	0.5173
Derm	0.5085	0.5370	0.6626	0.7202
MedSigLIP + BioBERT	0.5075	0.5286	0.6668	0.7331
MedSigLIP + Derm	0.5829	0.6017	0.7262	0.7823
BioBERT + Derm	0.5113	0.5265	0.6614	0.7197
BioBERT + MedSigLIP + Derm (Concat)	0.5935	0.6122	0.7247	0.7767

4.3   Performance Analysis

The results in Tables 1, 2, 3 and 4 demonstrate that the proposed cross-attention multimodal fusion model consistently outperforms all evaluated baselines across

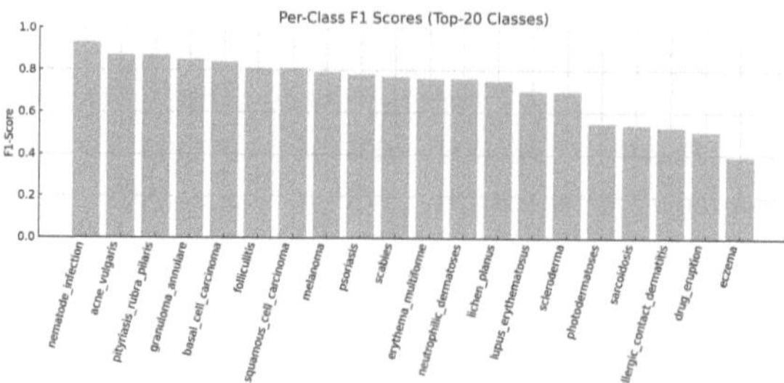

(a) Per-class F1-scores for the Top-20 most frequent classes in Fitzpatrick17k. The model achieves consistently high performance for several rare conditions such as *pityriasis rubra pilaris* (0.87) and *nematode infection* (0.93), demonstrating robustness to limited data availability.

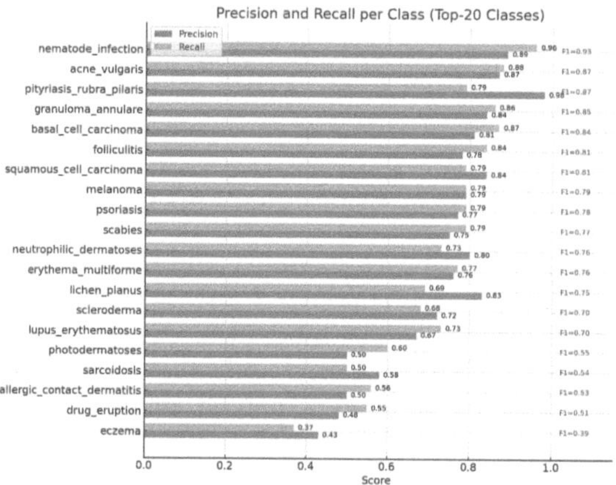

(b) Precision vs Recall trade-off for each class. Bubble size denotes the number of samples (*support*) and color intensity reflects the F1-score. Larger bubbles at high precision and recall indicate strong performance for both frequent and rare classes.

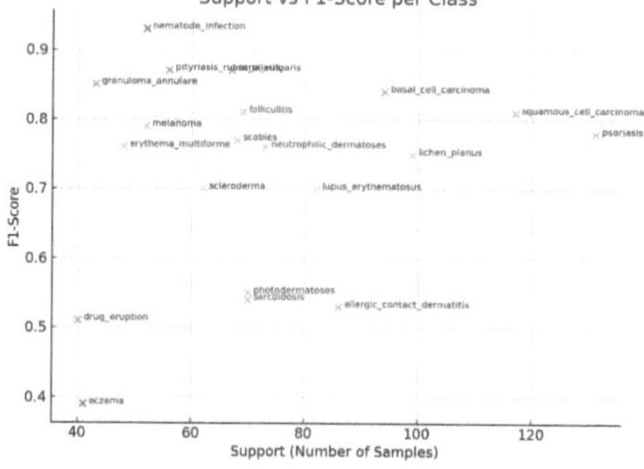

(c) Relationship between class support and F1-score. The model maintains strong predictive performance even for low-support classes, indicating effective handling of severe class imbalance.

Fig. 2. Per-class performance analysis for Top-20 classes. The proposed cross-attention multimodal fusion model achieves balanced performance across both common and rare conditions, highlighting its generalization capability and robustness to imbalanced datasets.

Table 4. Ablation study results (concatenation vs. cross-attention fusion) with top-20 classes.

Fusion Strategy/Model	F1 Score	Accuracy	Top-2 Acc	Top-3 Acc
Proposed (MedSigLIP + BioBERT + Derm)	**0.7260**	**0.7338**	**0.8366**	**0.8908**
MedSigLIP only	0.6536	0.6584	0.7809	0.8323
BioBERT only	0.2483	0.2929	0.4457	0.5535
Derm only	0.6262	0.6408	0.7619	0.8176
MedSigLIP + BioBERT	0.6467	0.6500	0.7919	0.8464
MedSigLIP + Derm	0.6843	0.6936	0.8161	0.8718
BioBERT + Derm	0.6183	0.6408	0.7781	0.8309
MedSigLIP + BioBERT + Derm (Concat)	0.6909	0.6929	0.8260	0.8774

both the 114-class and Top-20 class settings. In the 114-class scenario, our approach achieves an F1 score of 0.6458, representing a relative improvement of approximately 26% over the strongest pretrained baseline (ConvNeXt-Base, F1 = 0.5125). In the Top-20 setting, the proposed model achieves an F1 score of 0.7260, surpassing ConvNeXt-Base by over 12 percentage points. Gains are consistent across accuracy, Top-2, and Top-3 metrics, suggesting superior clinical decision-support capability when multiple ranked predictions are considered.

Figures 2a–2c provide a deeper analysis of per-class performance in the Top-20 setting. Figure 2a shows the per-class F1 scores, revealing that the model maintains high performance across both common and rare conditions. Notably, *nematode infection* achieves an F1 score of 0.93 and *pityriasis rubra pilaris* achieves 0.87, despite limited training samples, highlighting the model's robustness to low-data scenarios.

Figure 2b visualizes the precision-recall trade-off, where bubble size denotes class support and color intensity reflects the F1 score. Larger bubbles positioned at high precision and recall indicate strong and balanced performance for high-support classes such as *psoriasis* and *basal cell carcinoma*. Meanwhile, several smaller bubbles corresponding to rare conditions also occupy the high precision-recall region, confirming generalization to underrepresented classes.

Finally, Fig. 2c illustrates the relationship between class support and F1 score. The relatively flat trend suggests that performance is not overly dependent on class size, and that the fusion mechanism effectively mitigates the typical drop in accuracy for rare classes. This balance in performance across the spectrum of disease prevalence is critical for clinical applicability, where both common and rare dermatological conditions must be identified reliably.

Overall, the combination of high overall F1 scores and consistent per-class performance indicates that the proposed cross-attention fusion strategy effectively integrates visual, textual, and dermatology-specific embeddings, enabling robust and generalizable skin disease classification under severe class imbalance.

5   Conclusion

In this work, we proposed a multimodal skin disease classification framework integrating MedSigLIP visual embeddings, caption-based language features, and dermatology-specific expert embeddings via a bidirectional cross-attention fusion mechanism with auxiliary supervision. The proposed model demonstrates substantial gains over both CNN and Transformer baselines, achieving state-of-the-art performance on the Fitzpatrick17k dataset in both 114-class and Top-20 class evaluations. Our results validate that leveraging complementary modality-specific priors and dynamically aligning them through cross-attention enables more robust and generalizable diagnostic predictions, even under severe class imbalance. Future work will explore integrating structured clinical metadata, extending the approach to temporal skin disease progression modeling, and leveraging generative data augmentation to further enhance generalization in low-data regimes.

References

1. Bannur, S., et al.: Learning to exploit temporal structure for biomedical vision-language processing. In: Proceedings of the IEEE/CVF Conference on Computer Vision and Pattern Recognition, pp. 15016–15027 (2023)
2. Esteva, A., Kuprel, B., Novoa, R.A., et al.: Dermatologist-level classification of skin cancer with deep neural networks. Nature **542**(7639), 115–118 (2017). https://doi.org/10.1038/nature21056
3. Groh, M., et al.: Evaluating deep neural networks trained on clinical images in dermatology with the fitzpatrick 17k dataset. In: Proceedings of the IEEE/CVF Conference on Computer Vision and Pattern Recognition, pp. 1820–1828 (2021)
4. Hay, R., Johns, N., Williams, H., et al.: The burden of skin diseases in India: global burden of disease study 2017. Br. J. Dermatol. **185**(5), 937–938 (2021). https://doi.org/10.1111/bjd.20602, https://pubmed.ncbi.nlm.nih.gov/34877854/
5. Karimkhani, C., et al.: Global skin disease morbidity and mortality: an update from the global burden of disease study 2013. JAMA Dermatol. **153**(5), 406–412 (2017)
6. Kawahara, J., Daneshvar, S., Argenziano, G., Hamarneh, G.: Seven-point checklist and skin lesion classification using multitask multimodal neural nets. IEEE J. Biomed. Health Inform. **23**(2), 538–546 (2018)
7. Lee, J., et al.: Biobert: a pre-trained biomedical language representation model for biomedical text mining. Bioinformatics **36**(4), 1234–1240 (2020)
8. Radford, A., Kim, J.W., Hallacy, C., et al.: Learning transferable visual models from natural language supervision. In: Proceedings of the 38th International Conference on Machine Learning (ICML) (2021). https://arxiv.org/abs/2103.00020
9. Sellergren, A., et al.: Medgemma technical report. arXiv preprint arXiv:2507.05201 (2025)
10. Tschandl, P., Rosendahl, C., Kittler, H.: The ham10000 dataset: a large collection of multi-source dermatoscopic images of common pigmented skin lesions. Scientific Data **5**, 180161 (2018). https://doi.org/10.1038/sdata.2018.161

11. Wang, Z., Wu, Z., Agarwal, D., Sun, J.: Medclip: contrastive learning from unpaired medical images and text. In: Proceedings of the Conference on Empirical Methods in Natural Language Processing. Conference on Empirical Methods in Natural Language Processing, vol. 2022, p. 3876 (2022)
12. World Health Organization: Skin cancers (2022). https://www.iarc.who.int/cancer-type/skin-cancer/. Accessed 01 Aug 2025
13. Zhang, Y., Jiang, H., Miura, Y., Manning, C.D., Langlotz, C.P.: Contrastive learning of medical visual representations from paired images and text. In: Machine Learning for Healthcare Conference, pp. 2–25. PMLR (2022)

FusePolyp: Complementary Dual Encoder Design and Fusion Strategy Analysis for Medical Polyp Segmentation

Panigrahi Srikanth[1]([✉]), Kaushal Sambanna[1], Sanjana Jhansi Ganji[1], and Routhu Srinivasa Rao[2]

[1] Department of Artificial Intelligence and Machine Learning (AI&ML), Chaitanya Bharathi Institute of Technology, Gandipet, Hyderabad 500075, India
srikanth.panigrahi@gmail.com
[2] CureBay, Acharya Vihar, Bhubaneswar, Odisha, India

Abstract. Accurate segmentation of colorectal polyps is critical for the early detection and prevention of colorectal cancer, yet remains challenging due to significant variability in polyp shape, size, texture, and boundary ambiguity. To address these challenges, we propose FusePolyp, a novel Complementary Dual Encoder Framework that integrates the global semantic modeling ability of transformers with the spatial precision of convolutional features. The architecture leverages a pretrained PVTv2-B3 encoder to capture rich hierarchical semantic representations, complemented by a custom ReSEVM encoder that focuses on local detail through Residual connections, Squeeze-and-Excitation recalibration, and lightweight Visual State-Space Mamba blocks. To effectively combine features from both branches, we introduce the Cross-Mamba Channel-Spatial Fusion (CMCSF) module, which dynamically modulates channel and spatial dependencies while modeling long-range interactions. The fused features are further enhanced through a dual-branch bottleneck consisting of a lightweight transformer and an ASPP module, while a gated decoder with skip connections enables precise boundary reconstruction. Extensive experiments conducted on five benchmark datasets–Kvasir-SEG, CVC-ClinicDB, BKAI-IGH, ETIS, and ColonDB– demonstrate that FusePolyp consistently outperforms state-of-the-art methods, achieving the highest mIoU, Dice, and F_2 scores across all datasets. Notably, FusePolyp delivers improvements of up to 2.0–3.5% in Dice, 2.0–3.8% in mIoU, and 1.5–3.8% in F_2 compared to the best competing models, highlighting its superior segmentation accuracy, robustness, and generalization capability across diverse colonoscopic imaging conditions.

Keywords: Polyp Segmentation · Medical Image Segmentation · Deep Learning · Dual-Encoder Network · Cross Fusion · Transformer · Visual State-Space (VSS) with Mamba · Medical Image Analysis

K. Sambanna, S. J. Ganji and R. S. Rao–These authors contributed equally to this work.

1   Introduction

Colorectal cancer (CRC) remains one of the most prevalent and deadly cancers globally, with over 1.9 million new cases and 930,000 deaths reported in 2020 alone [1]. Early detection of colorectal polyps through colonoscopy is critical for reducing CRC-related mortality. However, traditional colonoscopy is often operator-dependent and susceptible to missing small, flat, or poorly contrasted lesions–especially under complex visual conditions [2]. To mitigate these limitations, deep learning-based computer-aided diagnostic (CAD) systems have gained momentum for their ability to provide real-time, automated polyp segmentation, improving diagnostic consistency and efficiency.

The evolution of deep learning methods for polyp segmentation has progressed from early encoder-decoder architectures to sophisticated attention- and transformer-based models. U-Net [3] and U-Net++ [4] laid a strong foundation with efficient spatial representation and skip connections. Enhancements such as ResUNet++ [5] and DeepLabv3+ [6] introduced residual units, ASPP, and decoder refinements to improve multiscale feature aggregation and boundary precision. More recent works like UACANet [7] and CaraNet [8] incorporated uncertainty-aware and reverse attention mechanisms to address challenges in low-saliency or ambiguous polyp regions. Meanwhile, transformer-inspired frameworks such as TransNetR [9] and FANetv2 [10] have emphasized long-range context modeling and adaptability across multi-center datasets. In light of this growing body of work, we introduce FusePolyp–a dual-encoder segmentation framework that offers a unique architectural perspective by integrating complementary global and local features, and effectively combining them through a custom fusion module–striving to remain competitive with state-of-the-art models.

The main contributions of this work are as follows:

1. We propose **FusePolyp**, a complementary dual-encoder architecture that integrates a transformer-based PVTv2-B3 encoder with a custom ReSEVM encoder to jointly capture global semantic context and fine-grained spatial details for precise polyp segmentation.
2. We design and analyze multiple cross-encoder fusion strategies, including transformer and Mamba-based modules, and identify the Cross-Mamba Channel-Spatial Fusion (CMCSF) as the most effective mechanism for harmonizing multiscale features from both encoder branches.
3. We evaluate the proposed architecture on five benchmark datasets–Kvasir-SEG, CVC-ClinicDB, BKAI-IGH, ETIS, and ColonDB–demonstrating its strong generalization ability and robustness across diverse clinical domains.

2   Literature Survey

Polyp segmentation has emerged as a critical component of computer-aided diagnosis for colorectal cancer screening. Foundational architectures such as

Fully Convolutional Networks (FCNs) and U-Net [3] laid the groundwork for biomedical segmentation by utilizing encoder-decoder frameworks with skip connections to retain fine-grained spatial details. U-Net's design effectively leverages data augmentation strategies and small datasets, making it highly suitable for medical imaging. Subsequent variants like ResUNet++ [5] have introduced residual connections, attention blocks, and Atrous Spatial Pyramid Pooling (ASPP) to enhance the model's ability to capture multi-scale contextual features. DeepLabv3+ [6] advanced this further through atrous separable convolutions and an improved decoder that enhances boundary delineation while remaining computationally efficient.

With the goal of achieving high performance in real-time applications, lightweight and hybrid models have gained popularity. HarDNet-MSEG [11] employs a HarDNet68 backbone combined with partial decoders, enabling it to achieve over 0.90 Dice on Kvasir-SEG while maintaining 86 FPS, exemplifying a balance between speed and accuracy. UNeXt [12] introduces a hybrid CNN-MLP architecture that significantly reduces parameter count (by up to 72×) while preserving segmentation fidelity, making it ideal for deployment in resource-constrained environments. Transformer-based models such as TransNetR [9] and FANetv2 [10] extend this trend by incorporating long-range dependency modeling and attention feedback mechanisms. These models have demonstrated strong robustness to domain shifts across multi-center datasets, outperforming conventional CNNs in generalization ability.

To address segmentation challenges in complex cases such as low-contrast, small, or ambiguous polyps, researchers have turned to attention mechanisms and dynamic learning paradigms. UACANet [7] utilizes Uncertainty Augmented Context Attention and axial attention to refine predictions in uncertain zones, achieving notable Dice improvements on difficult cases. CaraNet [8] adopts Context Axial Reverse Attention, specifically targeting small polyp detection and outperforming earlier methods like PraNet [13]. TGANet [14] integrates text-guided auxiliary supervision based on polyp attributes (e.g., count, size), enhancing segmentation performance across varied scenarios. Recent approaches such as G-CASCADE [15] and LDNet [16] leverage graph attention and lesion-aware dynamic kernels, respectively, further advancing the generalization and accuracy of polyp segmentation models.

3 Proposed Methodology

This paper proposes FusePolyp, a novel dual-encoder architecture for polyp segmentation that effectively combines semantic abstraction with spatial precision. The model employs a pretrained PVTv2-B3 as the primary encoder and a custom ReSEVM encoder as a complementary branch, allowing rich hierarchical features to be captured from diverse representational spaces. To integrate features from both encoders, we conduct a systematic fusion study exploring multiple designs, ultimately selecting the Cross-Mamba Channel-Spatial Fusion (CMCSF) module for its superior performance. The fused features are further processed through a dual-branch bottleneck comprising a transformer and ASPP, and decoded via a gated decoder with skip connections to generate accurate segmentation masks (Fig. 1).

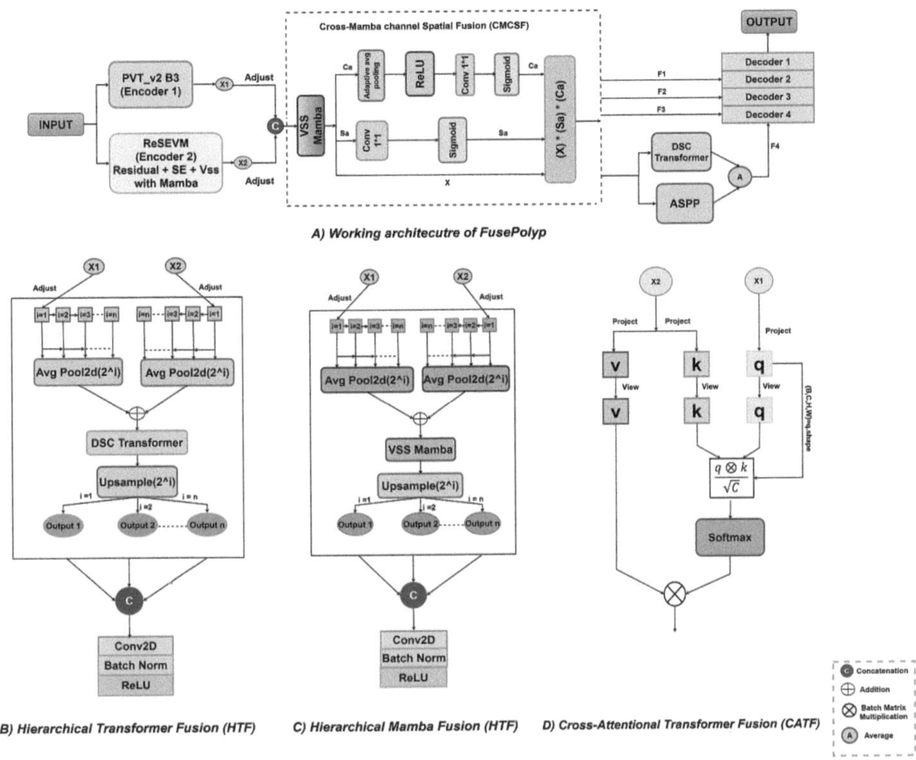

Fig. 1. Overall Architecture of FusePolyp

3.1 Dual Encoder Design: Integrating Global Semantics with Local Detail

Our framework adopts a dual encoder strategy to jointly leverage global contextual understanding and fine-grained spatial details–both of which are critical for accurate and robust polyp segmentation. The first encoder branch is instantiated using the Pyramid Vision Transformer v2 (PVTv2-B3), a hierarchical transformer backbone pretrained on ImageNet. This branch outputs a set of multi-scale feature maps $[f_1^T, f_2^T, f_3^T, f_4^T]$, where each stage employs spatial-reduction multi-head self-attention to model long-range dependencies while preserving computational efficiency. Through its progressive abstraction mechanism and global receptive field, PVTv2-B3 captures high-level semantics and structural continuity across the image–attributes essential for identifying polyps that vary significantly in shape, size, and texture under diverse endoscopic conditions.

Complementing this transformer-based encoder, the second branch–ReSEVM (Residual-SE-VSS Mamba)–is a custom convolutional encoder designed to encode localized discriminative patterns with strong spatial consistency. Each stage of ReSEVM consists of three sequential components: (1) a ResidualBlock, which enhances gradient flow and preserves low-level details via identity shortcuts; (2) a Squeeze-and-Excitation (SE) block, which dynamically recalibrates channel-wise responses based on global context; and (3) a VSS Mamba block, a visual state-space module implemented via depthwise gated convolutions, which enables efficient modeling of long-range spatial dependencies without the computational burden of traditional attention. This design produces a complementary set of feature maps $[f_1^C, f_2^C, f_3^C, f_4^C]$ that enrich the representation with texture-level cues, boundary sharpness, and local contrast variations–traits that are often underrepresented in transformer outputs. By performing cross-scale fusion of transformer and convolutional features (f_i^T, f_i^C) at each level, our model synergistically integrates semantic richness with spatial precision, ultimately enhancing its ability to delineate polyps with high fidelity and generalize effectively across challenging clinical datasets.

3.2   Design and Evaluation of Cross-Encoder Fusion Modules

To effectively leverage the complementary strengths of the dual encoders–PVTv2-B3 and ReSEVM–we explore four distinct fusion strategies aimed at integrating their multiscale feature maps. Each strategy is designed to balance global contextual awareness from the transformer branch with the fine-grained, local representations captured by the state-space convolutional branch.

Cross-Mamba Channel-Spatial Fusion (CMCSF) augments the fused features with a Mamba2D block to model spatial dependencies, while incorporating both spatial and channel attention to modulate the output dynamically. This design facilitates localized enhancement of semantically rich regions. Hierarchical Mamba Fusion (HMF) captures multiscale representations by applying Mamba blocks at various spatial resolutions through a hierarchy of downsampling and upsampling stages. This enables effective learning of deep spatial priors while maintaining resolution coherence. Hierarchical Transformer Fusion (HTF) replaces the Mamba blocks with lightweight depthwise transformer units, preserving the same hierarchical processing paradigm but focusing more on token-level interactions. Finally, Cross-Attentional Transformer Fusion (CATF) employs a transformer-style cross-attention mechanism to directly align and blend the features from both encoders using learned query-key-value projections.

Each fusion strategy was evaluated across three benchmark datasets (refer to Table 3). Among them, CMCSF consistently demonstrated superior segmentation accuracy and generalization. Its integration of channel-spatial recalibration with dynamic state-space modeling allowed it to best reconcile the semantic-global gap between transformer and convolutional representations. Consequently, CMCSF was adopted as the fusion module in our final architecture.

3.3   Bottleneck Integration and Decoder Reconstruction

Following multi-scale fusion through the cross-encoder modules, the network proceeds to a dual-branch bottleneck designed to further refine high-level semantics before decoding. This stage consists of two parallel modules: a lightweight transformer block and an Atrous Spatial Pyramid Pooling (ASPP) module. The transformer pathway captures long-range dependencies within the fused deepest feature map f_4, enriching it with contextual priors. Simultaneously, the ASPP module aggregates multi-scale spatial features via dilated convolutions with varying receptive fields, ensuring robustness to polyp size and shape variability. The outputs of these two modules are averaged to obtain a consolidated bottleneck representation $t = \frac{1}{2}(t_1 + t_2)$, which integrates both global attention and spatial granularity.

The decoder pathway follows a standard top-down structure with skip connections, progressively reconstructing the segmentation map from coarse to fine resolution. Each decoder block $\mathbf{dec}_i$ receives two inputs: the upsampled higher-level features from the previous stage and the corresponding fused encoder feature f_i. Starting from the bottleneck representation t and deepest fusion output f_3, the network successively decodes features through $\mathbf{dec}_4$, $\mathbf{dec}_3$, and $\mathbf{dec}_2$, reintroducing spatial detail and boundary information at each level. The final decoder block $\mathbf{dec}_1$ operates without a skip connection, refining the final output d_1, which is then passed through a 1×1 convolution to generate the segmentation logits. The logits are finally upsampled to match the original input resolution, ensuring dense pixel-level prediction. This bottleneck-decoder arrangement ensures a balanced decoding strategy that retains the benefits of deep semantic features while preserving edge-level accuracy, which is critical in delineating subtle and irregular polyp boundaries.

4   Experimental Results

We evaluated our framework on five benchmark datasets commonly used for polyp segmentation, encompassing diverse imaging modalities, resolutions, and annotation protocols to ensure robust generalization. A detailed summary is provided in Table 1. Kvasir-SEG [17] includes 1,000 manually annotated gastrointestinal polyp images. ETIS-LaribPolypDB [18] provides 196 high-resolution frames (966×1225) of early colorectal polyps. CVC-ClinicDB [19] contains 612 images (576×768) from 23 colonoscopy videos, each with precise polyp masks. CVC-ColonDB [20] offers 380 annotated frames (500×574). BKAI-IGH [21] comprises 1,200 high-resolution images captured under both White Light Imaging (WLI) and Flexible Imaging Color Enhancement (FICE). The model was optimized using the Adam optimizer with an initial learning rate of 1×10^{-4}, and a ReduceLROnPlateau scheduler that halves the learning rate after three consecutive epochs without validation improvement. For training stability and to enhance both pixel-level accuracy and shape-aware segmentation, we employed a hybrid loss function composed of Binary Cross-Entropy, Dice Loss, and Twerky Loss with the weights 0.3, 0.3 and 0.4 respectively. This composite loss formulation was designed to balance precision, overlap alignment, and structural sensitivity, ensuring robust performance across diverse visual and morphological presentations of polyps.

Table 1. Summary of benchmark datasets used in our experiments.

Dataset	Images	Resolution	Annotations
Kvasir-SEG [17]	1,000	Varying	Masks, bounding boxes
ETIS-LaribPolypDB [18]	196	966×1225	Polyp masks
CVC-ClinicDB [19]	612	576×768	Polyp masks
CVC-ColonDB [20]	380	500×574	Polyp masks
BKAI-IGH [21]	1,200	High-resolution	WLI, FICE masks

4.1 Performance Comparison of CNN and Transformer Backbones Within the U-Net Architecture

Table 2 presents a comparative analysis of convolutional neural network (CNN) and transformer-based backbones integrated within a U-Net framework, using the Kvasir-SEG dataset as the benchmark. Evaluation is performed using Dice Score and Intersection over Union (IoU), which are standard metrics for medical image segmentation tasks. Among the CNN-based models, EfficientNet achieved the best performance with a Dice Score of 0.8521 and an IoU of 0.7853, followed by DenseNet121 with a Dice Score of 0.8266 and an IoU of 0.7427. However, the transformer-based backbones consistently outperformed the CNN counterparts by better capturing long-range dependencies and complex spatial structures. Within the transformer group, PVTv2-B3 demonstrated the highest performance, attaining a Dice Score of 0.9015 and an IoU of 0.8206. This superior performance is attributed to its progressive shrinking pyramid architecture and spatial-reduction attention, which together enable efficient multiscale feature extraction. Owing to its strong results, PVTv2-B3 was selected as the encoder backbone for Encoder 1 in our final architecture to ensure high-quality semantic feature representations for subsequent fusion and decoding stages.

4.2 Fusion Strategy Analysis

In dual-encoder architectures, effective feature fusion is critical to reconcile complementary representations: the Global Semantic Pyramid Encoder (PVTv2-B3) provides semantically rich, large-receptive-field maps, while the

Table 2. Comparison of U-Net with CNN (left) and Transformer (right) backbones in terms of Dice Score (DSC) and IoU.

<table>
<tr><td colspan="3">(a) CNN Backbones</td><td colspan="3">(b) Transformer Backbones</td></tr>
<tr><td>Backbone</td><td>DSC</td><td>IoU</td><td>Backbone</td><td>DSC</td><td>IoU</td></tr>
<tr><td>EfficientNet [22]</td><td>0.8521</td><td>0.7853</td><td>ViT (Base) [28]</td><td>0.8453</td><td>0.7321</td></tr>
<tr><td>DenseNet121 [23]</td><td>0.8266</td><td>0.7427</td><td>PVTv2-B1 [29]</td><td>0.8836</td><td>0.7914</td></tr>
<tr><td>ResNet50 [24]</td><td>0.8209</td><td>0.7404</td><td>PVTv2-B2 [29]</td><td>0.8956</td><td>0.8110</td></tr>
<tr><td>VGG19 [25]</td><td>0.7581</td><td>0.6591</td><td>PVTv2-B3 [29]</td><td>0.9015</td><td>0.8206</td></tr>
<tr><td>MobileNetV2 [26]</td><td>0.7672</td><td>0.6692</td><td>Swin-B [30]</td><td>0.8806</td><td>0.7866</td></tr>
<tr><td>InceptionV4 [27]</td><td>0.8109</td><td>0.7304</td><td>SwinV2-B [31]</td><td>0.8723</td><td>0.7735</td></tr>
</table>

ReSEVM branch emphasizes boundaries and local spatial refinement. Our experiments with Transformer- and Mamba-based fusion strategies (Table 3) reveal that Mamba-integrated mechanisms, particularly Cross-Mamba Channel-Spatial Fusion (CMCSF), achieve the most consistent performance across diverse datasets. CMCSF attains top clinic-level overlap on CVC-ClinicDB (mIoU = 0.8816, Dice = 0.9371) and preserves high Dice on challenging ETIS frames (0.9030), while HMF, which emphasizes hierarchical multiscale aggregation, exhibits higher variance–slightly outperforming CMCSF on Kvasir (mIoU 0.8613 vs 0.8592) but dropping sharply on ETIS (mIoU 0.6860, Dice 0.8137). This pattern reflects three architectural advantages of CMCSF: selective channel recalibration aligns heterogeneous encoder statistics, spatial gating preserves boundary-salient activations while suppressing background noise, and the VSS-Mamba operator captures long-range dependencies without compromising local detail. By contrast, Transformer-only fusions like CATF provide expressive token interactions but lack per-channel refinement, and HMF's pooled aggregation can over-smooth fine structures. Collectively, these results highlight that CMCSF balances semantic coherence, edge fidelity, and cross-dataset robustness, justifying its selection as the final fusion mechanism.

Table 3. mIoU and Dice scores of four fusion variants–Cross-Attentional Transformer Fusion (CATF), Hierarchical Transformer Fusion (HTF), Hierarchical Mamba Fusion (HMF), and Cross-Mamba Channel-Spatial Fusion (CMCSF)–across five benchmark polyp segmentation datasets.

Fusion	Kvasir		CVC-ClinicDB		BKAI		ETIS		CVC-ColonDB	
	mIoU	Dice	mIoU	Dice	mIoU	Dice	mIoU	Dice	mIoU	Dice
CATF	0.835	0.910	0.833	0.909	0.869	0.930	0.797	0.887	0.829	0.907
HTF	0.858	0.923	0.870	0.931	0.862	0.926	0.785	0.879	0.823	0.903
HMF	0.861	0.926	0.872	0.932	0.846	0.916	0.686	0.814	0.791	0.883
CMCSF	0.859	0.924	0.882	0.937	0.871	0.931	0.823	0.903	0.847	0.917

4.3 Performance Analysis of FusePolyp Across Multiple Colonoscopic Imaging Datasets

Tables 4 and 5 present a comprehensive quantitative comparison of segmentation performance across five widely used datasets, namely Kvasir-SEG, CVC-ClinicDB, BKAI-IGH, ETIS, and ColonDB, evaluated using mean Intersection-over-Union (mIoU), Dice Score (DSC), Recall, Precision, and F_2 score. On the Kvasir-SEG dataset, the proposed model achieves an mIoU of 0.8592, a Dice Score of 0.9243, a Recall of 0.8960, a Precision of 0.9544, and an F_2 score of 0.9062, outperforming earlier architectures such as U-Net (mIoU 0.7472, DSC 0.8264) and ResU-Net++ (mIoU 0.5341, DSC 0.6453). On the CVC-ClinicDB dataset, the proposed model secures the highest performance with an mIoU of 0.9039, a Dice Score of 0.9495, a Recall of 0.9443, a Precision of 0.9548, and an F_2 score of 0.9464, surpassing strong baselines such as FANetv2 (mIoU 0.9039, DSC 0.9481) and G-Cascade (mIoU 0.8910, DSC 0.9374). On the BKAI-IGH dataset, the proposed model again achieves the leading results with an mIoU of 0.8928, a Dice Score of 0.9434, a Recall of 0.9249, a Precision of 0.9625, and an F_2 score of 0.9321, outperforming competitive methods such as FANetv2 (mIoU 0.8646, DSC 0.9186) and TransNetR (mIoU 0.8474, DSC 0.9107). On the ETIS dataset, the proposed model records an mIoU of 0.8552, a Dice Score of 0.9219, a Recall of 0.9379, a Precision of 0.9065, and an F_2 score of 0.9315, which markedly surpasses U-Net (mIoU 0.5482, DSC 0.6365), PraNet (mIoU 0.6838, DSC 0.7654), SANet (mIoU 0.6954, DSC 0.7746), and even recent methods such as G-CASCADE (mIoU 0.7490, DSC 0.8199) and LSSNet (mIoU 0.7754, DSC 0.8464). Similarly, on the ColonDB dataset, the proposed model delivers an mIoU of 0.8175, a Dice Score of 0.8996, a Recall of 0.8562, a Precision of 0.9476, and an F_2 score of 0.8725, outperforming U-Net (mIoU 0.6129, DSC 0.7016), PraNet (mIoU 0.6907, DSC 0.7616), SANet (mIoU 0.6876, DSC 0.7675), and even stronger competitors such as G-CASCADE (mIoU 0.7319, DSC 0.8095) and LSSNet (mIoU 0.7413, DSC 0.8203). Collectively, these results highlight the superior segmentation capability and robustness of the proposed model across diverse datasets, consistently outperforming classical U-Net-based methods as well as recent state-of-the-art architectures, including transformer-enhanced networks.

The qualitative results presented in Fig. 2 provide valuable insights into the visual reliability and generalization ability of the proposed FusePolyp across five benchmark datasets, including Kvasir-SEG, CVC-ClinicDB, BKAI-IGH, CVC-ColonDB, and ETIS. The model consistently produces accurate segmentations that closely align with the ground truth masks, effectively capturing the shape and extent of polyps under diverse imaging conditions. Even in challenging cases such as low-contrast regions, varied illumination, and the presence of overlapping mucosal structures, the predictions remain sharp and structurally coherent, demonstrating the robustness of the model in handling both local texture variations and global contextual cues. The Grad-CAM [36] visualizations further highlight that the model's attention is concentrated on clinically relevant polyp regions, confirming its ability to focus on diagnostically important structures.

Table 4. Quantitative comparison of segmentation performance on Kvasir-SEG, CVC-ClinicDB, and BKAI-IGH datasets.

Method	mIoU	DSC	Recall	Precision	F2
Kvasir-SEG					
U-Net (MICCAI 2015) [3]	0.7472	0.8264	0.8504	0.8703	0.8353
U-Net++ (DLMIA 2018) [4]	0.7420	0.8228	0.8437	0.8607	0.8295
ResU-Net++ (ISM 2019) [5]	0.5341	0.6453	0.6964	0.7080	0.6576
HarDNet-MSEG (arxiv 2021) [11]	0.7459	0.8260	0.8485	0.8652	0.8358
ColonSegNet (IEEE Acess 2021) [32]	0.6980	0.7920	0.8193	0.8432	0.7999
UACANet (ACMMM 2021) [7]	0.7692	0.8502	0.8799	0.8706	0.8626
UNeXt (MICCAI 2022) [12]	0.6284	0.7318	0.7840	0.7656	0.7507
TransNetR (MIDL 2024) [9]	0.8016	0.8706	0.8843	0.9073	0.8744
LSSNet (MICCAI 2024) [33]	0.8780	0.9261	0.9246	0.8802	0.9156
QueryNet (MICCAI 2024) [34]	0.8835	0.9328	0.8264	0.9174	0.8431
Proposed model	**0.8592**	**0.9243**	**0.8960**	**0.9544**	**0.9062**
CVC-ClinicDB					
U-Net (MICCAI 2015) [3]	0.5433	0.6336	0.6982	0.7891	0.6563
U-Net++ (DLMIA 2018) [4]	0.5475	0.6350	0.6933	0.7967	0.6556
ResU-Net++ (SM 2019) [5]	0.3585	0.4642	0.5880	0.5770	0.5084
HarDNet-MSEG (arxiv 2021) [11]	0.6059	0.6960	0.7173	0.8528	0.7010
ColonSegNet (IEEE Acess 2021) [32]	0.5090	0.6126	0.6564	0.7521	0.6246
UACANet (ACMMM 2021) [7]	0.6808	0.7659	0.7639	0.8820	0.7599
UNeXt (MICCAI 2022) [12]	0.3901	0.4915	0.6125	0.6609	0.5318
TransNetR (MIDL 2024) [9]	0.8628	0.9107	0.9044	0.9380	0.9065
G-Cascade (WACV 2024) [15]	0.8910	0.9374	0.9483	0.9349	0.9416
QueryNet (MICCAI 2024) [34]	0.8940	0.9421	0.9705	0.9705	0.9705
LSSNet (MICCAI 2024) [33]	0.9004	0.9448	0.9430	0.9200	0.9394
FANetv2 (ICASSP 2025) [10]	0.9039	0.9481	0.9514	0.9490	0.9496
Proposed model	**0.9039**	**0.9495**	**0.9443**	**0.9548**	**0.9464**
BKAI-IGH					
U-Net (MICCAI 2015) [3]	0.7599	0.8286	0.8295	0.8999	0.8264
DeepLabV3 (ECCV 2018) [6]	0.8314	0.8938	0.8870	0.9333	0.8882
PraNet (MICCAI 2021) [13]	0.8264	0.8904	0.8901	0.9247	0.8885
UACANet (ACMMM 2021) [7]	0.8275	0.8945	0.8870	0.9297	0.8882
CaraNet (MIIP 2022) [8]	0.8329	0.8962	0.8939	0.9273	0.8937
LDNet (MICCAI 2022) [16]	0.8254	0.8927	0.8867	0.9153	0.8874
TGANet (MICCAI 2022) [14]	0.8409	0.9023	0.9025	0.9208	0.9002
TransNetR (MIDL 2024) [9]	0.8474	0.9107	0.8982	0.9396	0.9018
G-Cascade (WACV 2024) [15]	0.8465	0.9096	0.8872	0.9489	0.8948
FANetv2 (ICASSP 2025) [10]	0.8646	0.9186	0.9058	0.9535	0.9096
Proposed model	**0.8928**	**0.9434**	**0.9249**	**0.9625**	**0.9321**

Table 5. Quantitative comparison of segmentation performance on ETIS and ColonDB datasets.

Method	mIoU	DSC	Recall	Precision	F_2
ETIS					
U-Net (MICCAI 2015) [3]	0.5482	0.6365	0.6000	0.5100	0.5510
PraNet (MICCAI 2021) [13]	0.6838	0.7654	0.7500	0.6520	0.6990
SANet (MICCAI 2021) [35]	0.6954	0.7746	0.7700	0.6620	0.7130
LDNet (MICCAI 2022) [16]	0.6659	0.7413	0.7400	0.6510	0.6970
G-CASCADE (WACV 2024) [15]	0.7490	0.8199	0.8200	0.7460	0.7820
LSSNet (MICCAI 2024) [33]	0.7754	0.8464	0.8500	0.7840	0.8160
Proposed model (Ours)	**0.8552**	**0.9219**	**0.9379**	**0.9065**	**0.9315**
ColonDB					
U-Net (MICCAI 2015) [3]	0.6129	0.7016	0.7000	0.6280	0.6610
PraNet (MICCAI 2021) [13]	0.6907	0.7616	0.7600	0.7230	0.7410
SANet (MICCAI 2021) [35]	0.6876	0.7675	0.7600	0.7190	0.7400
LDNet (MICCAI 2022) [16]	0.7177	0.7968	0.7800	0.7570	0.7680
G-CASCADE (WACV 2024) [15]	0.7319	0.8095	0.8000	0.7770	0.7900
LSSNet (MICCAI 2024) [33]	0.7413	0.8203	0.8200	0.7880	0.8030
Proposed model (Ours)	**0.8175**	**0.8996**	**0.8562**	**0.9476**	**0.8725**

These results collectively validate the model's strong semantic understanding, precise boundary delineation, and reliable generalization across heterogeneous colonoscopic datasets.

4.4   Ablation Study

Table 6 presents an ablation analysis of the proposed architecture across five benchmark polyp segmentation datasets. Variant A1 (PVT only, without ReSEVM) establishes a strong baseline (e.g., Dice 0.9095 on Kvasir-SEG). Adding the ReSEVM stream in A2 (without fusion) improves performance consistently, especially on challenging datasets (ETIS Dice 0.8674 vs 0.8110). Naive fusion without bottlenecking (A3) shows mixed effects: some gains on CVC-ClinicDB, but drops on Kvasir and BKAI-IGH, suggesting redundancy or misalignment in direct feature aggregation. The full model (A4), combining ReSEVM with bottlenecked fusion, achieves the best and most consistent results across all datasets (e.g., Dice 0.9243, 0.9371, 0.9309, 0.8942, 0.9219), confirming the complementary roles of semantic refinement and structured fusion.

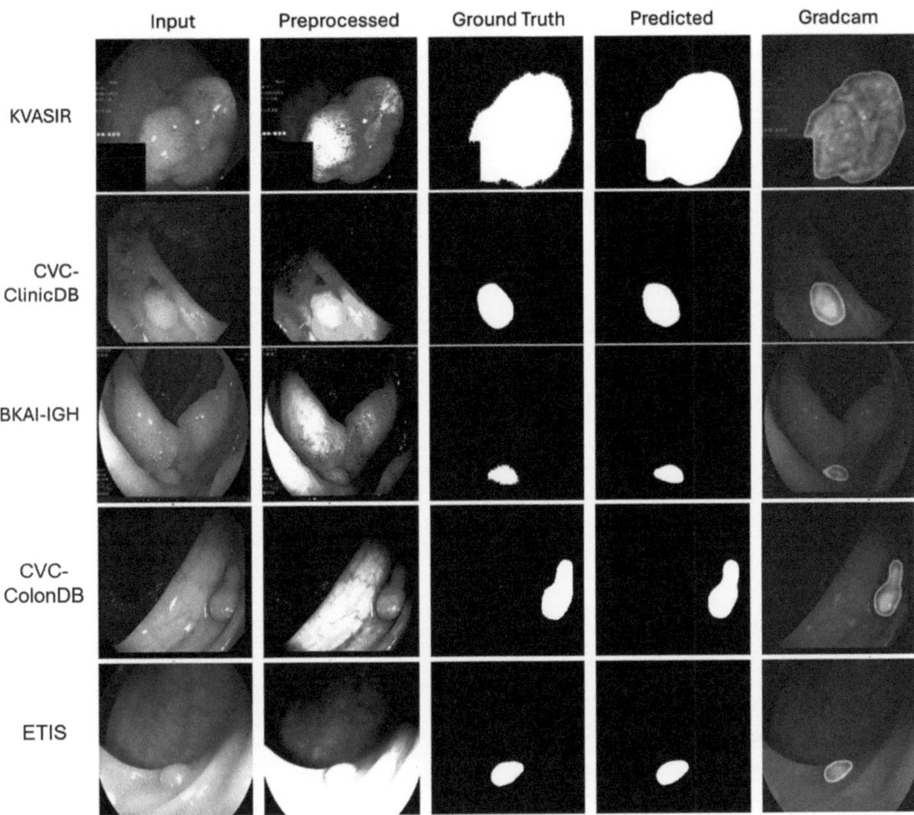

Fig. 2. Qualitative Segmentation Results and Grad-CAM [36] Visualization of Fuse-Polyp

Table 7 summarizes computational costs. Moving from A1 to A4 increases parameters (47.23 M → 66.78 M), FLOPs (10.45 G → 29.84 G), and GPU memory (1.9 GB → 3.0 GB), with modest reduction in FPS (84 → 57). Most FLOPs growth occurs when introducing ReSEVM (A2), while the bottlenecked fusion (A3→A4) adds smaller cost but yields the largest, uniform accuracy improvements, particularly on difficult datasets like ETIS. These results highlight the trade-off between efficiency and consistent performance, with A4 representing a pragmatic operating point.

Table 6. Comparison of ablation variants across five benchmark datasets using IoU and Dice. Variants: A1 (PVT only, w/o ReSEVM), A2 (ReSEVM only, w/o Fusion), A3 (ReSEVM + Fusion, w/o Bottleneck), A4 (Proposed full model).

Variant	Kvasir		CVC-ClinicDB		BKAI		CVC-ColonDB		ETIS	
	IoU	Dice	IoU	Dice	IoU	Dice	IoU	Dice	IoU	Dice
A1	0.8341	0.9095	0.8575	0.9093	0.8509	0.9194	0.7784	0.8654	0.6820	0.8110
A2	0.8364	0.9109	0.8626	0.9262	0.8394	0.9263	0.8038	0.8812	0.7658	0.8674
A3	0.8073	0.9133	0.8608	0.9292	0.8299	0.9071	0.7924	0.8886	0.7978	0.8875
A4	**0.8592**	**0.9243**	**0.8816**	**0.9371**	**0.8707**	**0.9309**	**0.8187**	**0.8942**	**0.8552**	**0.9219**

Table 7. Efficiency comparison of ablation variants in terms of parameters, FLOPs, FPS, and GPU memory.

Variant	Params (M)	FLOPs (G)	FPS	GPU Mem. (MB)
A1	47.23	10.45	83.95	1900
A2	53.48	28.72	60.83	2492
A3	55.74	29.15	61.02	2726
A4	66.78	29.84	57.37	2984

5   Conclusion

In this work, we presented FusePolyp, a dual-encoder segmentation framework that integrates global semantics from a transformer-based encoder with local spatial features from a lightweight ReSEVM encoder. A custom Cross-Mamba Channel-Spatial Fusion (CMCSF) module effectively bridges their representations, enhancing structural detail and contextual coherence. The resulting architecture yields competitive segmentation performance on challenging colonoscopic datasets while maintaining robustness and adaptability. However, the model exhibits a notable reliance on the representational strength of the PVT encoder, which may limit its scalability in resource-constrained environments or edge deployment scenarios. Despite this, the inclusion of the complementary encoder and the effective fusion module mitigates this dependency by injecting additional spatial diversity and enhancing feature richness. This work opens up several avenues for future research, including the development of more encoder-agnostic or adaptive fusion mechanisms, integration of domain adaptation techniques to improve cross-institutional generalization, exploration of lightweight or quantized variants for real-time inference, and the extension of the framework to other endoscopic modalities or multi-modal diagnostic systems. Through this effort, we aim to contribute a modular and extensible foundation for advancing clinically practical, accurate, and computationally efficient solutions in medical image segmentation.

References

1. Hossain, M.S., et al.: Colorectal cancer: a review of carcinogenesis, global epidemiology, current challenges, risk factors, preventive and treatment strategies. Cancers (Basel) **14**(7), 1732 (2022)
2. Tholoor, S.P., Tsagkournis, O., Basford, P., Bhandari, P.: Managing difficult polyps: techniques and pitfalls. Ann. Gastroenterol. **26**(2), 114–121 (2013)
3. Ronneberger, O., Fischer, P., Brox, T.: U-Net: convolutional networks for biomedical image segmentation. In: International Conference on Medical Image Computing and Computer-Assisted Intervention (MICCAI), pp. 234–241. Springer (2015)
4. Zhou, Z., Siddiquee, M.M.R., Tajbakhsh, N., Liang, J.: UNet++: a nested U-Net architecture for medical image segmentation. In: Deep Learning in Medical Image Analysis (DLMIA), pp. 3–11. Springer (2018)
5. Jha, D., et al.: ResUNet++: an advanced architecture for medical image segmentation. In: IEEE International Symposium on Multimedia (ISM), pp. 225–2255. IEEE (2019)
6. Chen, L.-C., Zhu, Y., Papandreou, G., Schroff, F., Adam, H.: Encoder-decoder with Atrous separable convolution for semantic image segmentation. In: European Conference on Computer Vision (ECCV), pp. 801–818 (2018)
7. Kim, T., Lee, H., Kim, D.: UACANet: uncertainty augmented context attention for polyp segmentation. In: Proceedings of the 29th ACM International Conference on Multimedia (MM '21), pp. 2167–2175. Association for Computing Machinery (2021). https://doi.org/10.1145/3474085.3475375
8. Lou, A., Guan, S., Ko, H.C., Loew, M.H.: CaraNet: context axial reverse attention network for segmentation of small medical objects. In: Medical Imaging 2022: Image Processing (SPIE), vol. 12032, pp. 81–92. SPIE (2022)
9. Jha, D., Tomar, N.K., Sharma, V., Bagci, U.: TransNetR: transformer-based residual network for polyp segmentation with multi-center out-of-distribution testing. In: Medical Imaging with Deep Learning (MIDL), pp. 1372–1384. PMLR (2024)
10. Tomar, N.K., Jha, D., Biswas, K., Bagci, U.: Transformer-enhanced iterative feedback mechanism for polyp segmentation. In: ICASSP 2025 - IEEE International Conference on Acoustics, Speech and Signal Processing, pp. 1–5. IEEE (2025). https://doi.org/10.1109/ICASSP49660.2025.10890567
11. Huang, C.-H., Wu, H.-Y., Lin, Y.-L.: HarDNet-MSEG: a simple encoder-decoder polyp segmentation neural network that achieves over 0.9 Mean Dice and 86 FPS (2021)
12. Valanarasu, J.M.J., Patel, V.M.: UNeXt: MLP-based rapid medical image segmentation network. In: Medical Image Computing and Computer Assisted Intervention (MICCAI), pp. 23–33. Springer (2022)
13. Fan, D.-P., et al.: PraNet: parallel reverse attention network for polyp segmentation. In: Medical Image Computing and Computer-Assisted Intervention (MICCAI). LNCS, vol. 12263, pp. 263–273. Springer (2020)
14. Tomar, N.K., Jha, D., Bagci, U., Ali, S.: TGANet: text-guided attention for improved polyp segmentation. In: Medical Image Computing and Computer-Assisted Intervention (MICCAI). LNCS, vol. 13431, pp. 151–160. Springer (2022)
15. Rahman, M.M., Marculescu, R.: G-cascade: efficient cascaded graph convolutional decoding for 2D medical image segmentation. In: IEEE/CVF Winter Conference on Applications of Computer Vision (WACV), pp. 7713–7722. IEEE Computer Society (2024). https://doi.org/10.1109/WACV57701.2024.00755

16. Zhang, R., et al.: Lesion-aware dynamic kernel for polyp segmentation. In: Medical Image Computing and Computer-Assisted Intervention (MICCAI). LNCS, vol. 13431, pp. 99–109. Springer (2022)
17. Jha, D., et al.: Kvasir-SEG: a segmented polyp dataset. In: Ro, Y.M., Hwang, S., Kim, T., Chu, W.-T., Hu, M.-C. (eds.) MultiMedia Modeling. MMM 2020. Lecture Notes in Computer Science, vol. 11962, pp. 451–462. Springer (2020). https://doi.org/10.1007/978-3-030-37734-2_37
18. Silva, J., Histace, A., Romain, O., Dray, X., Granado, B.: Toward embedded detection of polyps in WCE images for early diagnosis of colorectal cancer. Int. J. Comput. Assist. Radiol. Surg. **9**, 283–293 (2014). https://doi.org/10.1007/s11548-013-0926-3
19. Bernal, J., Sánchez, F., Fernández-Esparrach, G., Gil, D., Rodríguez, C., Vilariño, F.: WM-DOVA maps for accurate polyp highlighting in colonoscopy: Validation vs. saliency maps from physicians. Comput. Med. Imaging Graph. **43**, 99–111 (2015). https://doi.org/10.1016/j.compmedimag.2015.02.007
20. Tajbakhsh, N., Gurudu, S.R., Liang, J.: Automated polyp detection in colonoscopy videos using shape and context information. IEEE Trans. Med. Imaging **35**(2), 630–644 (2015). https://doi.org/10.1109/TMI.2015.2487997
21. Lan, P.N., et al.: NeoUNet: towards accurate colon polyp segmentation and neoplasm detection. In: Proceedings of the 16th International Symposium on Visual Computing (2021)
22. Tan, M., Le, Q.V.: EfficientNet: rethinking model scaling for convolutional neural networks. In: International Conference on Machine Learning (ICML) (2019)
23. Huang, G., Liu, Z., Van Der Maaten, L., Weinberger, K.Q.: Densely connected convolutional networks. In: IEEE Conference on Computer Vision and Pattern Recognition (CVPR) (2017)
24. He, K., Zhang, X., Ren, S., Sun, J.: Deep residual learning for image recognition. In: IEEE Conference on Computer Vision and Pattern Recognition (CVPR) (2016)
25. Simonyan, K., Zisserman, A.: Very deep convolutional networks for large-scale image recognition. In: International Conference on Learning Representations (ICLR) (2015)
26. Sandler, M., Howard, A., Zhu, M., Zhmoginov, A., Chen, L.-C.: MobileNetv2: inverted residuals and linear bottlenecks. In: IEEE Conference on Computer Vision and Pattern Recognition (CVPR) (2018)
27. Szegedy, C., Ioffe, S., Vanhoucke, V., Alemi, A.A.: Inception-v4, inception-resnet and the impact of residual connections on learning. In: AAAI Conference on Artificial Intelligence (2017)
28. Dosovitskiy, A., et al.: An image is worth 16x16 words: transformers for image recognition at scale. In: International Conference on Learning Representations (ICLR) (2020)
29. Wang, W., et al.: PVTv2: improved baselines with pyramid vision transformer. In: Computer Vision and Pattern Recognition (CVPR) Workshops (2022)
30. Liu, Z., et al.: Swin transformer: hierarchical vision transformer using shifted windows. In: IEEE International Conference on Computer Vision (ICCV) (2021)
31. Liu, Z., et al: Swin transformer V2: scaling up capacity and resolution. In: IEEE Conference on Computer Vision and Pattern Recognition (CVPR) (2022)
32. Jha, D., et al.: Real-time polyp detection, localization and segmentation in colonoscopy using deep learning pp. 40496–40510 . IEEE Access **9** (2021). https://doi.org/10.1109/ACCESS.2021.3063716

33. Wang, W., Sun, H., Wang, X.: LSSNet: a method for colon polyp segmentation based on local feature supplementation and shallow feature supplementation. In: Medical Image Computing and Computer Assisted Intervention (MICCAI). LNCS, vol. 15007, pp. 446–456. Springer (2024)
34. Chai, J., Luo, Z., Gao, J., Dai, L., Lai, Y., Li, S.: QueryNet: a unified framework for accurate polyp segmentation and detection. In: Medical Image Computing and Computer Assisted Intervention (MICCAI), pp. 544–554. Springer (2024)
35. Wei, J., Hu, Y., Zhang, R., Li, Z., Zhou, S.K., Cui, S.: Shallow attention network for polyp segmentation. In: Medical Image Computing and Computer-Assisted Intervention (MICCAI). LNCS, vol. 12901
36. Selvaraju, R.R., Cogswell, M., Das, A., Vedantam, R., Parikh, D., Batra, D.: Grad-CAM: visual explanations from deep networks via gradient-based localization. In: Proceedings of the IEEE International Conference on Computer Vision (ICCV), pp. 618–626 (2017). https://doi.org/10.1109/ICCV.2017.74

Automated RECIST 1.1 Classification in HCC-TACE Patients Using Deep Learning and 26-Connectivity

Rohit Agarwal[1(✉)], Sayoni Bhattacharyya[1], Rajib Kumar Chatterjee[1], Anup Kumar Sadhu[2], Narayan Murmu[1], and Debashis Nandi[1]

[1] National Institute of Technology Durgapur, Durgapur 713209, India
`ra.22cs1102@phd.nitdgp.ac.in`,
`{sb.25cs1105,rkchatterjee.cse,nmurmu.cse,dnandi.cse}@nitdgp.ac.in`
[2] EKO Diagnostic Center, Medical College Kolkata, Kolkata, India
`sadhujee1@gmail.com`

Abstract. Hepatocellular carcinoma (HCC) is a leading cause of cancer-related mortality, with Transarterial Chemoembolization (TACE) commonly used as a treatment for intermediate-stage patients. Accurate treatment response assessment is critical for guiding clinical decisions, where RECIST 1.1 provides standardized criteria based on changes in tumor diameters. However, manual diameter measurement is time-intensive and prone to inter-observer variability. We propose an automated pipeline for tumor segmentation, diameter extraction, and RECIST 1.1 classification using pre- and post-TACE CT scans from the HCC-TACE-SEG dataset. Nine deep learning-based segmentation models were trained from scratch to delineate tumors. Longest diameters were extracted from the axial plane using a 26-way connectivity algorithm to ensure coherent tumor representation. Based on these measurements, automated RECIST classifications, Complete Response (CR), Partial Response (PR), Stable Disease (SD), and Progressive Disease (PD), were derived. Experimental results demonstrated robust segmentation performance across models. Bland-Altman analysis confirmed high agreement between automated and expert diameter measurements for both pre- and post-treatment scans, while automated RECIST classifications achieved substantial agreement with expert labels, as quantified by Cohen's Kappa coefficient. This study demonstrates the feasibility of an objective, fully automated system for tumor response evaluation in HCC. By standardizing RECIST 1.1 assessment, the proposed framework reduces subjectivity, minimizes inter-observer variability, and supports more consistent clinical decision-making in TACE-based treatment.

Keywords: Hepatocellular carcinoma · TACE · RECIST 1.1 · Deep learning · Tumor segmentation · 26-connectivity · Automated response assessment

B. Chatterjee et al. (Eds.): ICDCIT 2026, LNCS 16420, pp. 452–464, 2026.
https://doi.org/10.1007/978-3-032-16632-6_29

1   Introduction

Hepatocellular carcinoma (HCC) represents a major global health burden, ranking among the leading causes of cancer-related deaths worldwide [18,23]. Its rising incidence, coupled with limited curative options, necessitates effective locoregional therapies and robust strategies for treatment monitoring. Transarterial Chemoembolization (TACE) is a widely adopted intervention for patients with unresectable HCC [17], yet its therapeutic efficacy is highly variable. Accurate assessment of tumor response following TACE is therefore essential for guiding clinical decision-making and improving patient outcomes.

The Response Evaluation Criteria in Solid Tumors (RECIST 1.1) provides the most widely accepted framework for response categorization, Complete Response (CR), Partial Response (PR), Stable Disease (SD), or Progressive Disease (PD), based on changes in tumor diameter measured on imaging [19]. However, the current RECIST evaluation is primarily performed manually on Computed Tomography (CT) scans [15]. This process is labor-intensive, time-consuming, and prone to inter-observer variability, posing challenges to scalability and reproducibility in both clinical and research environments.

Recent advances in deep learning have significantly improved liver and tumor segmentation, but most works remain limited to segmentation alone. A comprehensive, end-to-end solution that integrates segmentation, diameter measurement, and RECIST classification, validated on longitudinal HCC-TACE cohorts, remains underexplored.

Addressing this gap, we propose and rigorously evaluate a robust automated pipeline for HCC tumor response assessment using the HCC-TACE-SEG dataset [14]. Our approach integrates a suite of nine advanced deep learning models for tumor segmentation from pre- and post-TACE CT scans. Our key contributions are:

- **Automated Tumor Segmentation:** Utilizing a diverse suite of nine deep learning models to automatically segment tumor volumes from post-TACE CT scans.
- **Automated Diameter Extraction:** Developing a precise diameter extraction method with a validated 26-connectivity to form a single 3D object, followed by axial-plane longest diameter per RECIST 1.1.
- **Algorithmic RECIST 1.1 Classification:** Classifying treatment response into RECIST 1.1 categories (CR, PR, SD, PD) based on the algorithmic determination of tumor diameter change.
- **Rigorous Multi-level Evaluation:** Providing a comprehensive, multi-level evaluation of the pipeline's performance, including segmentation accuracy, measurement validation (Bland-Altman analysis), and final RECIST classification performance against expert-labeled ground truth.

We anticipate that this work will not only enhance diagnostic objectivity but also contribute toward reproducible and efficient imaging-based evaluation pipelines in both research and clinical workflows.

2   Related Works

2.1   Deep Learning for Medical Image Segmentation

The evolution of medical image segmentation has seen a significant shift from classical methods to advanced deep learning approaches. Early deep learning models, particularly the U-Net architecture and its 3D extensions like 3D U-Net [7] and V-Net [13], established high-performing templates for volumetric segmentation, proving foundational for numerous liver and tumor segmentation studies. Subsequent innovations have enhanced these backbones with dense connections [2,3] for improved feature fusion, multi-scale modules to handle diverse tumor characteristics, and attention mechanisms [16] to focus on salient regions. More recently, Transformer-based architectures, exemplified by Swin-Unet [5], have emerged, offering robust capabilities for capturing long-range dependencies in medical volumes.

2.2   Automated RECIST and Tumor Response Assessment

Accurate tumor response assessment, primarily via RECIST 1.1, is crucial but traditionally relies on manual diameter measurements [15], a process known for being labor-intensive and prone to inter-reader variability. This bottleneck has driven efforts toward automated and semi-automated solutions. Prior research has explored pipelines utilizing CNNs for lesion localization and segmentation, followed by algorithmic diameter extraction to derive RECIST measures [8,21]. While volumetric measurements are also gaining attention for their potential to better capture treatment effects, particularly for necrotic tumors after therapies like TACE [8,22], diameter-based RECIST 1.1 remains the established clinical standard. Benchmark datasets like LiTS [4] and 3DIRCADb [20] have spurred segmentation advancements, while the HCC-TACE-SEG collection [14] specifically offers paired pre- and post-TACE CT data with expert RECIST labels, making it highly relevant for developing automated response assessment pipelines.

2.3   Gaps and Motivation for the Present Pipeline

The current literature demonstrates mature deep learning backbones capable of accurate segmentation and growing evidence for automating parts of response assessment. However, a significant gap remains in comprehensive, end-to-end automated pipelines specifically tailored for HCC patients treated with TACE. Existing work often lacks the rigorous benchmarking of multiple segmentation architectures, a principled 3D diameter-extraction algorithm, and explicit validation of automated RECIST 1.1 classification against expert labels from paired pre-/post-TACE datasets. Our work addresses this critical gap by benchmarking nine diverse segmentation architectures, implementing a robust 26-way connectivity-based diameter extraction, and providing a multi-level validation on the HCC-TACE-SEG dataset.

Previous efforts such as Tang et al. [21] and Dahm et al. [8] have explored semi-automated RECIST measurement systems, relying on partial automation for lesion localization or 2D diameter extraction. These methods often required manual intervention or focused on specific tumor types without benchmarking multiple segmentation architectures. In contrast, our proposed framework offers a fully automated, end-to-end RECIST 1.1 pipeline integrating tumor segmentation, diameter extraction via 26-connectivity, and final classification on paired pre- and post-TACE CT scans. Moreover, the inclusion of nine state-of-the-art architectures, spanning CNNs, attention mechanisms, and Transformers, enables rigorous benchmarking that has not been reported in prior automated RECIST literature. This highlights the novelty and comprehensive nature of our contribution.

3   Methods

Our proposed pipeline for automated RECIST 1.1 classification in HCC patients treated with TACE consists of three stages: segmentation, diameter measurement, and RECIST classification. The workflow is summarized in Fig. 1.

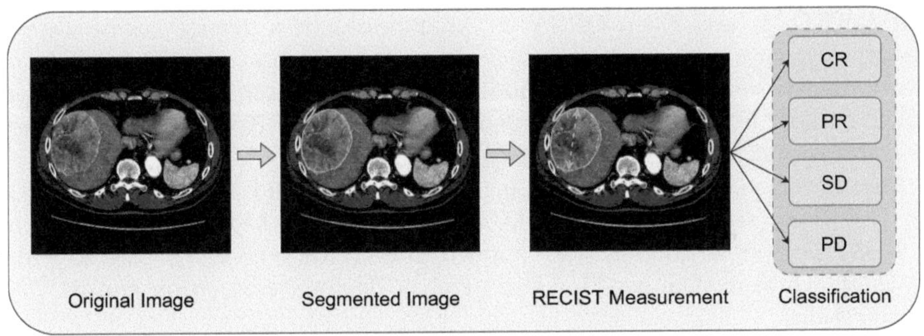

Fig. 1. The proposed end-to-end pipeline.

3.1   Dataset and Preprocessing

We used the HCC-TACE-SEG dataset [14], which provides pre- and post-TACE CT scans of 105 patients, with expert-provided ground truth tumor annotations for the pre-TACE scans and RECIST 1.1 labels for both time points.

- **Training-Testing Split:** Since ground truth annotations are available only for the pre-TACE scans, we split these into 70% training and 30% testing sets at the patient level. Segmentation models were trained on the training set and evaluated on the held-out 30%.

- **Post-TACE Segmentation:** The trained models were then applied to the post-TACE scans to obtain predicted tumor segmentations, as no manual annotations were available.
- **Preprocessing and Augmentation:** All CT volumes were clipped to [100, 300] HU to enhance soft tissue contrast and normalized to zero mean and unit variance. To address limited training data and improve model generalization, we employed a conditional GAN (cGAN)based augmentation framework, which synthesizes realistic tumor-bearing CT slices.

The dataset comprises 105 patients, which, although limited in size, is representative of the practical challenges in assembling paired pre- and post-treatment CT scans with expert RECIST labels. Such datasets remain rare in public domains, particularly for TACE-treated HCC cases, owing to the longitudinal nature of acquisition and clinical privacy constraints. This scarcity underscores the significance of publicly available datasets like HCC-TACE-SEG for advancing automated treatment assessment research.

3.2   Tumor Segmentation

We evaluated nine deep learning architectures (R2U-Net [3], RMS-UNet [11], HFRU-Net [12], Swin-Unet [5], TD-Net [9], MS-FANet [6], RMAU-Net [10], MSDA-AST [2], and Deep QRSA [1]) that represent a diverse set of state-of-the-art segmentation approaches, including convolutional, attention-based, and transformer-based networks. All models were trained from scratch on the pre-TACE dataset using a 70/30 patient-level split, where 70% of cases were used for training and 30% were held out for testing.

Segmentation results reported in Table 1 correspond to the held-out 30% pre-TACE test set. For the post-TACE scans (which lacked ground truth annotations), the trained models were applied directly to generate predicted tumor masks, which were then used for downstream diameter estimation and RECIST classification.

3.3   Diameter Measurement with 26-Connectivity

RECIST 1.1 defines treatment response based on the longest diameter of the target lesion measured on the axial plane. To automate this process, we employed a 26-way connectivity algorithm to identify and extract the tumor as a single coherent object from the segmentation mask.

- **Step 1: Tumor definition -** Connected components were extracted from the binary tumor mask using 26-connectivity, ensuring that all voxels sharing a face, edge, or corner were included in a single tumor object (Fig. 2 illustrates how 26-connectivity groups voxels into a unified structure).
- **Step 2: Diameter estimation -** Within this connected tumor region, the longest Euclidean distance between any two boundary voxels lying on the axial plane was computed. This value was taken as the tumor's longest diameter, consistent with RECIST 1.1 guidelines.

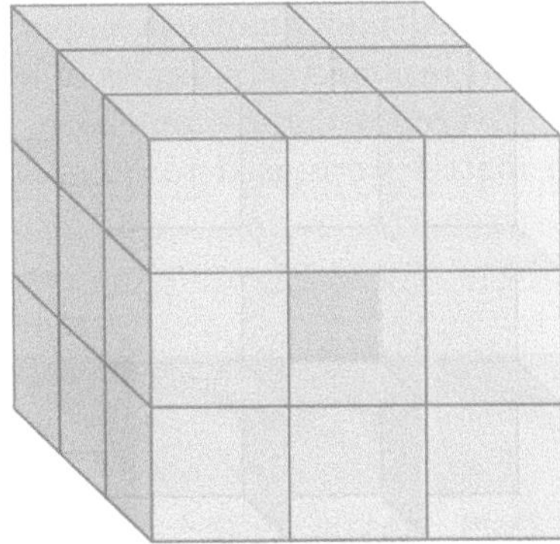

Fig. 2. Voxel 26-connectivity (faces/edges/corners) used to form a single tumor component before axial longest-diameter computation.

For pre-TACE scans, diameters were derived from the ground-truth masks. For post-TACE scans, diameters were derived from the predicted segmentation masks.

3.4   RECIST Classification and Evaluation

The baseline pre-TACE diameter D_{pre} and the follow-up post-TACE diameter D_{post} were used to compute the percentage change PC:

$$\text{Percentage Change}(PC) = \frac{D_{post} - D_{pre}}{D_{pre}} \times 100\% \tag{1}$$

Classification followed RECIST 1.1 guidelines:

- Complete Response (CR): Disappearance of the target lesion.
- Partial Response (PR): $\geq 30\%$ decrease in diameter.
- Progressive Disease (PD): $\geq 20\%$ increase in diameter.
- Stable Disease (SD): Neither PR nor PD criteria met.

3.5   Evaluation Metrics

The pipeline was evaluated at three levels:

- Segmentation performance: Dice Per Case (DPC), Dice Global (DG), Volumetric Overlap Error (VOE), Relative Volume Difference (RVD), Average Symmetric Surface Distance (ASSD), and Root Mean Square Surface Distance (RMSSD).

- Diameter agreement: BlandAltman analysis comparing automated vs. expert diameters, reporting mean bias and 95% limits of agreement.
- RECIST classification: Overall accuracy, precision, recall, F1-score, Cohen's Kappa, and confusion matrix were used to quantify agreement with expert labels.

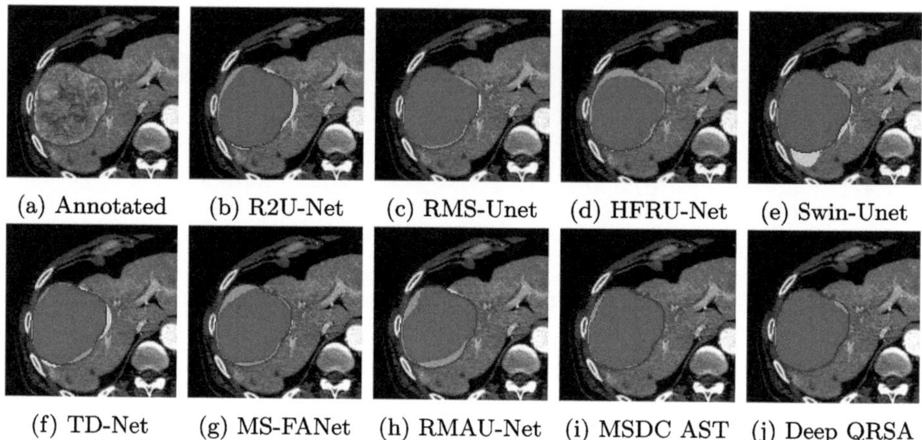

(a) Annotated   (b) R2U-Net   (c) RMS-Unet   (d) HFRU-Net   (e) Swin-Unet

(f) TD-Net   (g) MS-FANet   (h) RMAU-Net   (i) MSDC AST   (j) Deep QRSA

Fig. 3. Segmented outputs of tumors for various models. The blue boundary outlines the ground truth region. Red indicates True Positives, yellow represents False Positives, and green denotes False Negatives. (Color figure online)

Table 1. Segmentation Performance of Evaluated Models on the tumor of HCC-TACE-SEG

Model	DPC	DG	VOE	RVD	ASSD (mm)	RMSSD (mm)
R2U-Net [3]	0.776 ± 0.059	0.798	17.8 ± 5.4	3.8 ± 7.1	4.7 ± 2.4	5.4 ± 2.0
RMS-UNet [11]	0.788 ± 0.062	0.810	16.0 ± 4.3	-3.5 ± 6.5	4.0 ± 1.6	5.0 ± 2.2
HFRU-Net [12]	0.761 ± 0.068	0.784	20.3 ± 4.6	-4.9 ± 10.1	5.1 ± 2.0	6.1 ± 2.4
Swin-Unet [5]	0.695 ± 0.065	0.721	30.7 ± 6.8	-6.3 ± 11.7	6.8 ± 2.3	8.2 ± 3.0
TD-Net [9]	0.712 ± 0.070	0.738	28.6 ± 7.3	10.1 ± 13.0	6.5 ± 1.8	7.9 ± 2.8
MS-FANet [6]	0.729 ± 0.060	0.752	26.1 ± 5.1	-7.7 ± 9.8	6.0 ± 2.5	7.2 ± 2.6
RMAU-Net [10]	0.745 ± 0.063	0.768	22.5 ± 6.0	5.4 ± 8.5	5.7 ± 1.7	6.6 ± 2.1
MSDA-AST [2]	0.827 ± 0.057	0.847	13.2 ± 3.9	2.9 ± 6.7	3.3 ± 1.5	4.1 ± 1.7
Deep QRSA [1]	0.865 ± 0.050	0.886	11.6 ± 2.8	1.9 ± 5.6	2.6 ± 1.1	3.2 ± 1.5

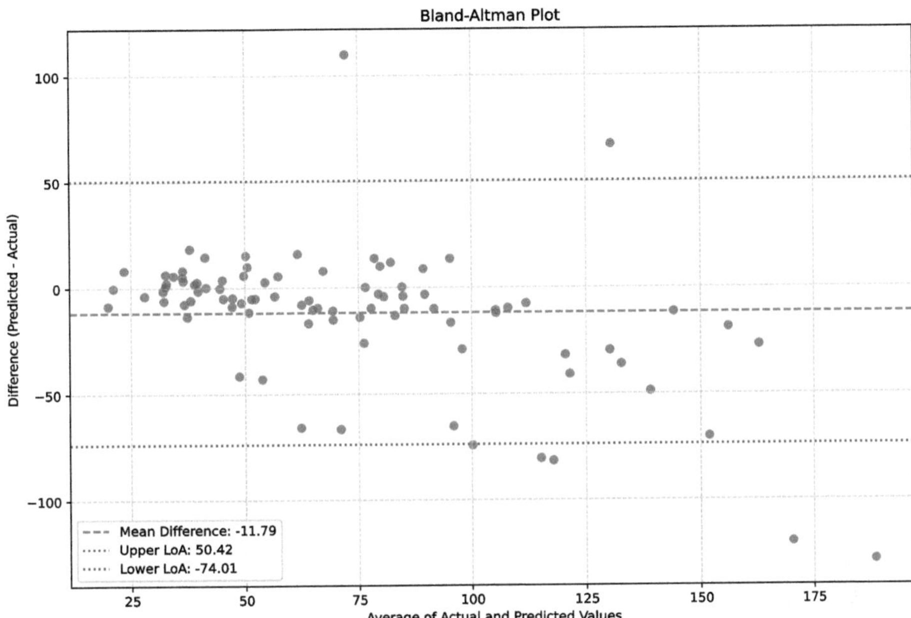

Fig. 4. BlandAltman plot comparing automated and expert diameters for pre-TACE scans.

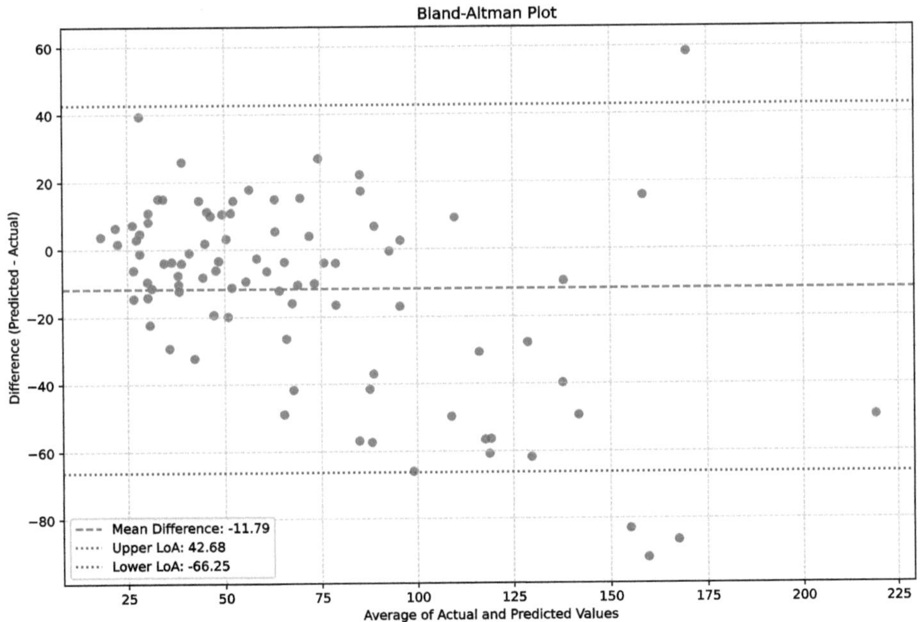

Fig. 5. BlandAltman plot comparing automated and expert diameters for post-TACE scans.

4   Results

4.1   Segmentation and Diameter Measurement

The segmentation performance of the nine deep learning models on the pre-TACE test set (30% split) is summarized in Table 1. DPC ranged between 0.70 and 0.87, with Deep QRSA achieving the highest Dice score. Volumetric metrics, including VOE and RVD, further confirmed the robustness of the models.

Representative qualitative results are shown in Fig. 3, where predicted masks closely follow expert-annotated boundaries, even for irregular tumor morphologies. Models such as MSDC AST and Deep QRSA demonstrated superior delineation of boundary regions compared to other state-of-the-art models.

Table 2. Overall RECIST 1.1 Classification Performance for All Evaluated Segmentation Models

Model	Accuracy	Precision	Recall	F1 Score	Cohen's Kappa
R2U-Net [3]	0.8111	0.8837	0.8111	0.8311	0.5712
RMS-UNet [11]	0.8556	0.9041	0.8556	0.8665	0.6603
HFRU-Net [12]	0.7556	0.8879	0.7556	0.7833	0.5135
Swin-Unet [5]	0.6222	0.8192	0.6222	0.6776	0.2946
TD-Net [9]	0.6778	0.8513	0.6778	0.7204	0.3888
MS-FANet [6]	0.7000	0.8413	0.7000	0.7471	0.3753
RMAU-Net [10]	0.7333	0.8714	0.7333	0.7660	0.4708
MSDA-AST [2]	0.8889	0.9259	0.8889	0.8978	0.7288
Deep QRSA [1]	0.9000	0.9281	0.9000	0.9077	0.7466

4.2   Diameter Measurement Agreement

To validate the proposed 26-connectivitybased diameter estimation, we compared automated measurements with expert-provided diameters on the pre-TACE scans. As the Deep QRSA model achieved the highest segmentation accuracy, its predictions are shown for this analysis. Figure 4 shows agreement between automated and expert-provided diameters for pre-TACE scans, while Fig. 5 reports the same comparison for post-TACE scans.

The automated 26-connectivitybased diameter estimation demonstrated a strong agreement with expert-provided diameters on the pre-TACE scans. As shown in the BlandAltman plots (Figs. 4 and 5), the mean bias was close to zero, with narrow 95% limits of agreement, indicating minimal systematic error.

This consistency was observed across both small and large tumors, highlighting the method's robustness. By ensuring a coherent 3D tumor object before measuring the longest axial diameter, the approach effectively reduces variability associated with manual slice selection.

4.3 RECIST 1.1 Classification

The end-to-end pipeline's RECIST classification performance is presented in Table 2. The system achieved an overall accuracy of 90.00%, with a Cohen's Kappa coefficient of 0.7466, indicating substantial agreement with expert annotations.

Class-wise performance metrics are summarized in the confusion matrix (Fig. 6). As no cases of Complete Response (CR) were reported in the dataset, the classification analysis is restricted to Partial Response (PR), Stable Disease (SD), and Progressive Disease (PD).

4.4 Inference Time and Computational Efficiency

All experimental procedures were conducted using Python and the PyTorch library, executed on a server equipped with a Tesla V100-PCIE GPU card with 32GB of RAM. The average inference time for one 3D CT volume was approximately 7.85 s for segmentation and 0.3 s for diameter extraction and classification. This demonstrates the framework's suitability for near real-time analysis, supporting potential integration into radiology workflows without significant latency.

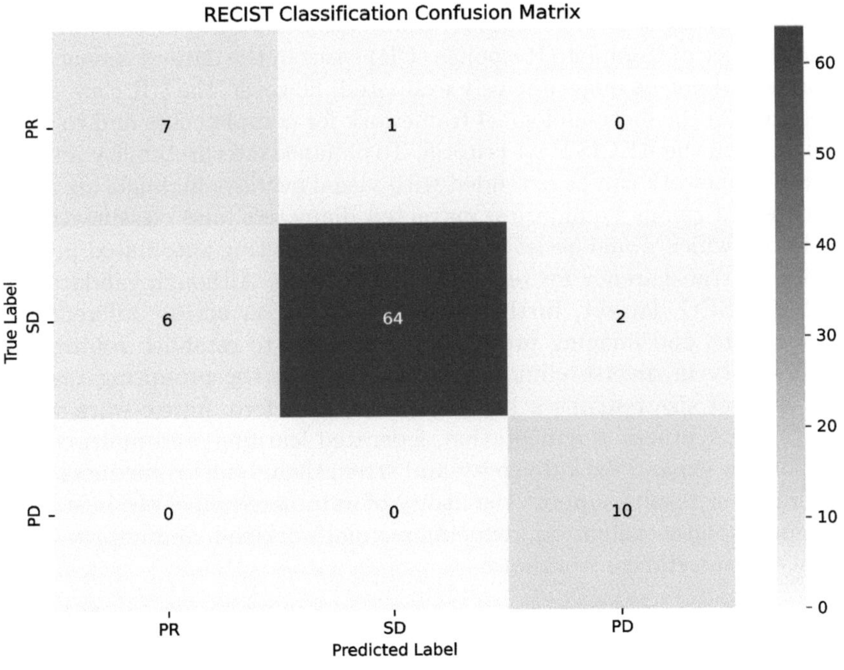

Fig. 6. Confusion Matrix for Automated RECIST 1.1 Classification (Best-Performing Model)

5   Discussion and Conclusion

This study demonstrates the feasibility of a fully automated pipeline for treatment response evaluation in HCC patients undergoing TACE, integrating tumor segmentation, diameter estimation, and RECIST 1.1 classification. By benchmarking nine state-of-the-art deep learning architectures, we showed that reliable tumor segmentation can be achieved on pre-TACE CT scans, with the Deep QRSA model yielding the best overall performance. Importantly, this segmentation capability enabled downstream tasks of automated diameter measurement and RECIST classification.

The proposed 26-connectivitybased approach for diameter estimation provided accurate and reproducible measurements, as validated by BlandAltman analysis against expert annotations for the Deep QRSA model. This highlights its ability to reduce observer dependence and ensure consistency, which is particularly valuable given the irregular morphologies of liver tumors that complicate manual RECIST measurements.

At the clinical decision-making level, the automated RECIST 1.1 classifications achieved high accuracy and substantial agreement with expert labels. Notably, most discrepancies were observed between Partial Response and Stable Disease, which aligns with clinical challenges in differentiating borderline cases. The absence of Complete Response cases in the dataset meant that this category could not be evaluated, which slightly limits the generalizability of our findings.

The absence of Complete Response (CR) cases in the dataset meant that this category could not be quantitatively evaluated; however, the CR class definition was retained in the methodological framework for completeness and to maintain alignment with the RECIST 1.1 criteria. To enhance interpretability and clinical trust, the framework can be extended with visual overlays highlighting automatically detected tumor boundaries, extracted diameters, and classification confidence levels, which would assist radiologists in validating automated predictions and improve transparency for regulatory acceptance. Although validated on the HCC-TACE-SEG dataset, further external validation across different institutions, scanners, and imaging protocols is necessary to establish robustness and generalizability in diverse clinical settings. Despite the promising results, the limited dataset size remains a key limitation; therefore, future work will focus on leveraging synthetic augmentation, federated learning, and multi-center collaborations to expand data diversity and strengthen model robustness.

Overall, our results support the utility of automated pipelines in standardizing tumor response evaluation, reducing manual workload, and improving reproducibility across clinical workflows.

References

1. Agarwal, R., et al.: Deep quasi-recurrent self-attention with dual encoder-decoder in biomedical CT image segmentation. IEEE J. Biomed. Health Inform. (2024)
2. Agarwal, R., Ghosal, P., Sadhu, A.K., Murmu, N., Nandi, D.: Multi-scale dual-channel feature embedding decoder for biomedical image segmentation. Comput. Methods Programs Biomed. **257**, 108464 (2024)
3. Alom, M.Z., Yakopcic, C., Hasan, M., Taha, T.M., Asari, V.K.: Recurrent residual U-Net for medical image segmentation. J. Med. Imag. **6**(1), 014006–014006 (2019)
4. Bilic, P., et al.: The liver tumor segmentation benchmark (LiTs). Med. Image Anal. **84**, 102680 (2023)
5. Cao, H., et al.: Swin-UNet: UNet-like pure transformer for medical image segmentation. In: European Conference on Computer Vision, pp. 205–218. Springer (2022)
6. Chen, Y., et al.: MS-FANet: multi-scale feature attention network for liver tumor segmentation. Comput. Biol. Med., 107208 (2023)
7. Çiçek, Ö., Abdulkadir, A., Lienkamp, S.S., Brox, T., Ronneberger, O.: 3D U-Net: learning dense volumetric segmentation from sparse annotation. In: International Conference on Medical Image Computing and Computer-assisted Intervention, pp. 424–432. Springer (2016)
8. Dahm, I.C., et al.: Reliability of automated RECIST 1.1 and volumetric RECIST target lesion response evaluation in follow-up CT–a multi-center, multi-observer reading study. Cancers **16**(23), 4009 (2024)
9. Di, S., Zhao, Y.Q., Liao, M., Zhang, F., Li, X.: TD-Net: a hybrid end-to-end network for automatic liver tumor segmentation from CT images. IEEE J. Biomed. Health Inform. **27**(3), 1163–1172 (2022)
10. Jiang, L., et al.: RMAU-Net: residual multi-scale attention u-net for liver and tumor segmentation in CT images. Comput. Biol. Med. **158**, 106838 (2023)
11. Khan, R.A., Luo, Y., Wu, F.X.: RMS-UNet: residual multi-scale UNet for liver and lesion segmentation. Artif. Intell. Med. **124**, 102231 (2022)
12. Kushnure, D.T., Talbar, S.N.: HFRU-Net: high-level feature fusion and recalibration UNet for automatic liver and tumor segmentation in CT images. Comput. Methods Programs Biomed. **213**, 106501 (2022)
13. Milletari, F., Navab, N., Ahmadi, S.A.: V-Net: fully convolutional neural networks for volumetric medical image segmentation. In: 2016 Fourth International Conference on 3D Vision (3DV), pp. 565–571. IEEE (2016)
14. Moawad, A.W., et al.: Multimodality annotated HCC cases with and without advanced imaging segmentation (2021). https://doi.org/10.7937/TCIA.5FNA-0924. [Data set]
15. Mohammadzadeh, S., Mohebbi, A., Abdi, A., Mohammadi, A.: Inter-reader agreement of RECIST and mRECIST criteria for assessing response to transarterial chemoembolization in hepatocellular carcinoma. BMC Med. Imaging **25**(1), 148 (2025)
16. Oktay, O., et al.: Attention U-Net: learning where to look for the pancreas. arXiv preprint: arXiv:1804.03999 (2018)
17. Raoul, J.L., Forner, A., Bolondi, L., Cheung, T.T., Kloeckner, R., de Baere, T.: Updated use of TACE for hepatocellular carcinoma treatment: how and when to use it based on clinical evidence. Cancer Treat. Rev. **72**, 28–36 (2019)
18. Rumgay, H., et al.: Global burden of primary liver cancer in 2020 and predictions to 2040. J. Hepatol. **77**(6), 1598–1606 (2022)

19. Schwartz, L.H., et al.: RECIST 1.1–standardisation and disease-specific adaptations: perspectives from the RECIST working group. Eur. J. Cancer **62**, 138–145 (2016)
20. Soler, L., et al.: 3D image reconstruction for comparison of algorithm database: a patient specific anatomical and medical image database. IRCAD, Strasbourg, France, Tech. Rep. **1**(1) (2010)
21. Tang, Y., Harrison, A.P., Bagheri, M., Xiao, J., Summers, R.M.: Semi-automatic RECIST labeling on CT scans with cascaded convolutional neural networks. In: International Conference on Medical Image Computing and Computer-Assisted Intervention, pp. 405–413. Springer (2018)
22. Wang, W., Zhao, Y., Bai, W., Han, G.: Response assessment for HCC patients treated with repeated TACE: the optimal time-point is still an open issue. J. Hepatol. **63**(6), 1530–1531 (2015)
23. Wei, J., et al.: Burden of liver cancer due to hepatitis c from 1990 to 2019 at the global, regional, and national levels. Front. Oncol. **13**, 1218901 (2023)

AI for Health and Bioinformatics

Integrating Large Language Models and Explainable AI for the Efficient Drug-Drug Interactions Prediction

Gori Sankar Borah[1], Amit Kalita[2], Debasish Saikia[1], and Selvaraman Nagamani[1,3]($\boxtimes$)

[1] Advanced Computation and Data Sciences Division, CSIR – North East Institute of Science and Technology, Jorhat, Assam, India
nagamaniselvaraman@gmail.com, nagamani@neist.res.in
[2] Computer Science and Engineering, Dibrugarh University, Dibrugarh, Assam, India
[3] Academy of Scientific and Innovative Research (AcSIR), Ghaziabad 201002, India

Abstract. Co-administration of multiple drugs is often recommended in clinical treatments to enhance therapeutic efficacy. However, inappropriate drug combinations can lead to adverse side effects and diminished treatment outcomes. Therefore, accurate prediction of drug-drug interactions (DDI) remains a critical challenge in pharmacology and patient safety. Numerous computational and machine learning approaches are available and treat DDI prediction as a binary classification task or predict specific interaction categories. However, recent advancements in large language models (LLMs) offer new opportunities, particularly in generating human-readable explanations in biomedical sciences. In this study, we propose a novel framework for generating descriptive, natural language explanations of DDIs using a sequence-to-sequence MOLT5 transformer model. Our approach leverages three variants of pre-trained MOLT5 models (i.e., small, base, and large), and uniquely integrates both the common names of drugs and their corresponding SMILES representations. This dual-modality input enables the model to capture both semantic and structural information of drug compounds. The models were trained on a curated dataset of drug pairs and their interaction descriptions from DrugBank. Among the tested variants, the large MOLT5 model achieved the best performance, with ROUGE-1: 82.92, ROUGE-2: 69.67, ROUGE-L: 78.34, and BLEU: 68.87 on the validation set. Additionally, we enhanced the model's prediction by integrating structural features from drug molecular graphs, further improving the representation and interpretability of DDI predictions. Our proposed framework demonstrates the potential of LLMs to advance the field of pharmacovigilance by generating accurate and interpretable DDI descriptions with important structural features. The model is available at https://huggingface.co/acdsd/DDI.

Keywords: DDI prediction · LLMs · Explainable AI

© The Author(s), under exclusive license to Springer Nature Switzerland AG 2026
B. Chatterjee et al. (Eds.): ICDCIT 2026, LNCS 16420, pp. 467–478, 2026.
https://doi.org/10.1007/978-3-032-16632-6_30

1 Introduction

Polypharmacy is one of the beneficial treatment methods that is commonly used to treat patients with multiple diseases. However, this leads to a negative effect in some cases due to adverse DDI. The likelihood of DDI is significantly increased as the number of approved drugs is increased to treat various medical conditions [1]. Traditional experimental approaches to studying the DDIs effect are expensive and time-consuming. Thus, various computational and machine learning approaches have gained attention [2–5]. The DDI prediction tasks can be efficiently improved by leveraging recent advancements in computer science. These methods help in developing new drug science theories and subsequently improve the understanding of drug interaction mechanisms. These methods also have significant practical values as they improve the accuracy and efficiency of DDI predictions and reduce the risk and cost of drug development, and help in advancing personalized medicine.

Most of the DDI prediction tasks involve three steps, including quantifying drug molecular formulas, extracting their features, and selecting an appropriate model to predict DDI [6]. The majority of the methods focus on the DDI prediction as a binary classification problem (i.e., is there interaction between two drugs? (yes/no)) [7]. Some studies focus on the DDI type prediction based on their categories to grasp DDI knowledge from prediction that treats the DDI prediction as a multi-class problem. Ryuet. al. (2018) applied deep learning methods and predicted the DDI using names and structural information of drug molecules [8]. The DDI prediction tasks are broadly classified into traditional machine learning based and deep learning based tasks [9]. In recent times, drug discovery scientists have been focusing on graph-based neural network methods and applying them to different biomedical domains, including DDI prediction [10–12]. These methods predict DDI by capturing the graph structures of drug molecules and analyzing biochemical feature information of drugs, including drug targets, enzymes, transporters, and proteins. However, these methods fail to capture the structural information of drugs and fail to give a human-readable underlying cause of DDI. Some studies have integrated LLMs with a biomedical knowledge graph to predict the DDI. But these models are trained with a general GPT model architecture, and thus, it limits the model's ability to fully leverage domain-specific biomedical relationships and potentially reduces prediction accuracy for drug–drug interactions [13].

In this study, we applied MolT5 [14], a self-supervised multi-model learning framework, to bridge the gap between natural language and molecular structures. This model is trained with the general natural language and SMILES strings, and thus, it can efficiently learn the relationship between SMILES strings and general sentences. We collected DDI explanations and drug SMILES structures from DrugBank [15], and the study was conducted in an inductive setting. The seq-to-seq fine-tuning method was applied along with a retrieval-based unsupervised model and an LLM-based in-context demonstration prompting model. The SMILES similarity with the DDI explanation was integrated to train the MolT5 architecture to efficiently predict the human-readable DDI prediction. Additionally, the attention score generated by the MolT5 model was integrated with the RDKit to identify the molecular features responsible for DDI.

2   Materials and Methods

2.1   Dataset and Task Formulation

We treat DDI description generation as a text-to-text sequence-to-sequence (seq2seq) task. Let X denote the set of input token sequences and Y the set of output token sequences. Each input $x \in X$ is the tokenized string containing [DRUG1], the first drug's name and SMILES, [DRUG2], and the second drug's name and SMILES. Each target $y \in Y$ is the corresponding textual description of the interaction. The model defines a conditional probability distribution $p_\theta(y \mid x)$, which is factorized autoregressively as

$$p_\theta(y \mid x) = \prod_{t=1}^{T} p_\theta(y_t \mid y_{<t}, x) \tag{1}$$

where y_t is the t-th token of y and $y_{<t}$ are previous tokens. The model is trained to maximize this conditional likelihood.

The vocabulary is augmented with the special tokens "[DRUG1]" and "[DRUG2]" to clearly mark the two drugs in the input. During preprocessing, each text pair is passed through the tokenizer to produce *input_ids* and *attention_mask*. The targets are also tokenized to produce a tensor of token IDs, and all pad tokens in the target sequence are replaced with -100 to ignore them in the loss.

2.2   Experimental Setup

All experiments were conducted on a Workstation with NVIDIA RTX A6000 49 GB GPUs. We train each MOLT5 variant (small, base, large) independently under the same conditions. All share the same data splits and hyperparameters (aside from model size). After training, test-set inference is run, and the generated descriptions for each test example are collected. Training MolT5-large (~800M parameters) presents significant computational challenges. A single Epoch consists of 1,653,915 samples with 103,370 steps per epoch. Approximately 10 h it took to complete a single epoch and the total training time is ~ 30 h (i.e. 3 epochs). The total FLOPs per training step is 3.28 x 10^{12} and the total FLOPs are 1.02 x 10^{18}. Finally, a CSV report is produced containing, for each test example, the two drug names, their SMILES strings, the reference description, and the generated description. This completes the end-to-end training and evaluation pipeline.

Optimization Procedure

We adopted several scalability and optimization strategies to train a large MolT5-large (~800M parameters) dataset. We leveraged the Accelerate library with Fully Sharded Data Parallel (FSDP) gradient sharding to efficiently distribute workloads to effectively handle this larger data set. The PyTorch DataLoader was optimized with multiple worker processes, pinned memory, and memory-efficient splits to maximize throughput and minimize CPU-GPU bottlenecks. Algorithmic optimizations such as gradient clipping stabilized training, while a linear warmup learning rate scheduler prevented destabilizing updates in early epochs. Continuous profiling with steps-per-second metrics (~2.88 steps/sec) facilitated real-time identification of compute, memory, and I/O bottlenecks.

2.3 Data Processing

The DDI data is collected from the DrugBank including drug_name, interacting_drug_name, SMILES of these drugs and description of the DDI. Each example is formed by concatenating the first drug's name and SMILES string with the second drug's name and SMILES string into a single input sequence, using special markers as depicted below,

x = "[DRUG1]" + drug1_name +" SMILES" + SMILES1 +" [DRUG2]" + drug2_name +" SMILES" + SMILES2.

The target sequence y is the interaction description (df['target_text'] = df['description']).

A total of 2442870 sentences were collected from DrugBank, and 2362736 sentences were retained after pre-processing. The pre-processing steps include the removal of redundant data sets and irregular or no SMILES representation of the drugs. The dataset is then split into training, test, and validation subsets with fixed random seeds. We first reserve 20% of examples as the external validation, and split the remaining 80% into train/test with a 12.5% test fraction (i.e., the final split is 70% train, 10% test, 20% validation). All text examples are tokenized with the T5 tokenizer and truncated to a maximum length of 128 tokens. In the tokenized labels, pad-token positions are masked by setting their label to -100 so that they are ignored in the loss computation.

2.4 Model Architecture

We fine-tune three variants of the "MOLT5" models, including MOLT5-small, MOLT5-base, and MOLT5-large. Each variant is an encoder-decoder transformer that maps a text input to a text output. The pretrained weights for each variant are loaded *via* Hugging Face transformers, and the tokenizer is similarly initialized. We then extend the tokenizer's vocabulary with the special tokens "[DRUG1]" and "[DRUG2]" and resize the model's token embedding to accommodate them. During fine-tuning, the encoder consumes the input token sequence x, and the decoder generates the output sequence token-by-token. The model is trained to maximize the log probability of the target sequence given the input. In the formula, for the target $y = y_1 \ldots y_T$ we maximize $\sum_{t=1}^{T} \log p_\theta(y_t \mid y_{<t}, x)$. The fully-connected output layer produces a distribution over the extended vocabulary at each step. The basic model architecture is represented in Fig. 1.

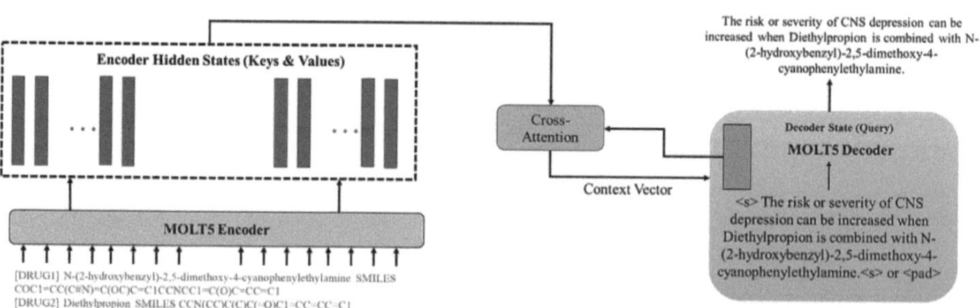

Fig. 1. The basic model architecture is implemented in this study.

2.5 Training Procedure

Each model is fine-tuned independently on the training set. We train for a fixed number of epochs (default is 3) with mini batch stochastic optimization using AdamW optimizer. The learning rate is set to 3×10^{-5} (configurable via –learning_rate), and weight decay and betas follow standard AdamW settings. A linear learning rate scheduler is employed, with 500 warm-up steps and the total number of training steps equal to num_epochs $\times$ |train_loader|.

Formally, for one sequence, the loss is calculated as,

$$\mathcal{L}(\theta) = -\sum_{t=1}^{T} 1_{[y_t \neq -100]} \log p_\theta (y_t \mid y_{<t}, x) \tag{2}$$

where the indicator $1_{[y_t \neq -100]}$ excludes padding positions (which were labeled with -100 during data prep).

After computing the loss, we use *accelerator.backward(loss)* to perform backpropagation. Gradients are clipped to a maximum norm of 1.0 to stabilize training. Then we step the optimizer and scheduler, and zero the gradients for the next batch. This is repeated over all training batches and epochs. The average training loss per epoch is logged for monitoring. At the end of training, *accelerator.unwrap_model()* is used to retrieve the underlying model, and *save_pretrained* is called to save the fine-tuned weights and tokenizer to the output directory.

2.6 Evaluation

After training, the model is evaluated on the validation and test sets. The saved model checkpoint and tokenizer are loaded, and the model is put in evaluation mode on a GPU. For each split, we iterate over batches of input examples and generate output text. Generation uses beam search with beam width B = 4 and a maximum output length of 128 tokens, terminating beams early when an end-of-sequence is generated. Concretely, the code calls *model.generate(input_ids, attention_mask =..., max_length = 128, num_beams = 4, early_stopping = True)* to produce predicted token sequences.

The generated token sequences are then decoded to strings (removing special tokens). The reference target strings are also decoded (with -100 replaced back to pad token ID before decoding). We evaluate the quality of the generated descriptions using standard NLP metrics, *viz.* ROUGE and BLEU. ROUGE-1, ROUGE-2, and ROUGE-L. These are computed by comparing overlapping n-grams and longest common sub-sequences between the generated and reference texts. BLEU is calculated as the geometric mean of n-gram precisions with a brevity penalty.

2.7 Explainable AI (XAI) Implementation for Model Interpretability

Additionally, a robust XAI framework was integrated with the model architecture to validate the model's effectiveness in learning chemically and pharmacologically relevant patterns. The core of the transformer architecture is the attention mechanism. In our sequence-to-sequence model, the decoder generates the output text token by token. At each step, a cross-attention mechanism weighs the importance of every token in the input sequence (which includes both drug names and their detailed SMILES strings). These attention weights were extracted and visualized to identify which part of the input (i.e. SMILES stings and word) is focused by the model to produce the specific output in the sentence prediction. We highlight that specific SMILES string to RDKit [16] and show the 2D representation of the molecule with the highlighted functional group.

3   Results and Discussion

We evaluated the performance of three MolT5 model variants *viz.* MolT5-base, MolT5-small, and MolT5-large on the DDI prediction task and the results are depicted in Table 1. Models were fine-tuned from their respective pretrained checkpoints and assessed on the training, validation, and test sets using ROUGE-1, ROUGE-2, ROUGE-L, and BLEU metrics. These metrics quantify lexical overlap and sequence-level similarity between model-generated interaction descriptions and reference annotations. Across all datasets, MolT5-large achieved the highest performance, with ROUGE-1, ROUGE-2, ROUGE-L, and BLEU scores of 82.93, 69.75, 78.38, and 68.95, respectively. The performance gains over MolT5-base were substantial, with improvements of approximately + 10 BLEU points and + 11 ROUGE-2 points, highlighting the advantage of increased model capacity for capturing complex interaction patterns between drugs.

Table 1. The evaluation metrics for the different models.

Base model	Dataset	ROUGE-1	ROUGE-2	ROUGE-L	BLEU
Molt5-small	Training set	78.99	64.05	74.14	64.41
	Test set	79.00	64.04	74.14	64.37
	Validation set	78.98	63.95	74.10	64.28
Molt5-base	Training set	72.64	51.67	65.77	51.04
	Test set	72.62	51.63	65.73	51.00
	Validation set	72.63	51.62	65.78	51.01
Molt5-large	**Training set**	**83.02**	**69.89**	**78.50**	**69.12**
	Test set	**82.93**	**69.75**	**78.38**	**68.95**
	Validation set	**82.92**	**69.67**	**78.34**	**68.87**

MolT5-small demonstrated intermediate performance, outperforming MolT5-base by a notable margin (+13 BLEU points on average) while maintaining computational efficiency. Importantly, all models exhibited minimal variance across training, validation, and test splits, indicating strong generalization ability and the absence of significant overfitting. These results suggest a clear positive correlation between model size and predictive accuracy for sequence-based DDI prediction, with the large variant offering the best trade-off when accuracy is the primary objective.

The results demonstrate that the capacity of the MolT5 architecture has a direct and substantial impact on performance in the DDI prediction task. The observed performance metrics MolT5-large > MolT5-small > MolT5-base exhibit that larger transformer-based models possess a greater ability to capture the subtle semantic and structural relationships underlying DDI. The performance consistency across training, validation, and test sets suggests that the models effectively leveraged the pretrained molecular and textual representations without succumbing to overfitting, a common challenge in biomedical NLP tasks. Notably, the MolT5-large variant achieved a BLEU score close to 69 on the test set, substantially surpassing both the base and small models, indicating its superior capability in generating precise and contextually coherent interaction descriptions.

While prior approaches to DDI prediction have often relied on handcrafted molecular descriptors or graph-based embeddings, the strong performance of MolT5 across multiple evaluation metrics underscores the potential of LLMs to unify molecular and textual knowledge within a single framework. However, the computational overhead of MolT5-large may limit its adoption in resource-constrained environments, where MolT5-small provides a more efficient alternative with competitive performance.

We compared model-generated descriptions with ground-truth annotations for selected drug pairs to further assess the qualitative performance of the MolT5 models in DDI prediction (Table 2). We randomly selected five different pairs that illustrate varying degrees of semantic alignment between the generated and reference outputs. In several cases, the model reproduced the interaction type and mechanistic direction with high fidelity. For instance, in the *Bunaftine–Nalidixic acid, Molsidomine–Benazepril*, and *Tofogliflozin–Clozapine* pairs, the generated descriptions were identical / near-identical to the originals, accurately capturing pharmacodynamic effects such as QTc prolongation or hypotensive activity enhancement, as well as pharmacokinetic alterations in therapeutic efficacy.

Table 2. Comparison between the original and the generated description from our model.

drug1_name	drug2_name	Original description	Generated description
Bunaftine	Nalidixic acid	The risk or severity of QTc prolongation can be increased when Nalidixic acid is combined with Bunaftine	The risk or severity of **QTc prolongation** can be increased when Nalidixic acid is combined with Bunaftine
Molsidomine	Benazepril	Molsidomine may increase the hypotensive activities of Benazepril	Molsidomine may **increase** the hypotensive activities of Benazepril
Tofogliflozin	Clozapine	The therapeutic efficacy of Tofogliflozin can be decreased when used in combination with Clozapine	The therapeutic efficacy of Tofogliflozin can be **decreased** when used in combination with Clozapine
Theobromine	Phentermine	The risk or severity of adverse effects can be increased when Phentermine is combined with Theobromine	Phentermine may **decrease** the excretion rate of Theobromine which could result in a higher serum level

(continued)

Table 2. (*continued*)

drug1_name	drug2_name	Original description	Generated description
25CN-NBOH	Diethylpropion	The risk or severity of CNS depression can be increased when Diethylpropion is combined with 25CN-NBOH	The risk or severity of adverse effects can be **increased** when Diethylpropion is combined with 25CN-NBOH

* The original descriptions are retrieved from DrugBank DDI information.

The accurate reproducibility demonstrate that MolT5 can capture complex pharmacodynamic interactions (e.g., potentiation of hypotensive or CNS effects) and pharmacokinetic processes (e.g., modulation of metabolism or excretion) when these relationships are strongly represented in the training data. This suggests the model has internalized meaningful chemical–biological associations between molecular structures and interaction mechanisms.

However, in some cases the model's performance is questionable. In the *Theobromine–Phentermine* example, the model may generate mechanistically plausible but unverified explanations. While the predicted change in Theobromine excretion rate is chemically coherent given its renal clearance pathway, it deviates from the reference's focus on generalized adverse effect risk. This suggests that MolT5 may sometimes extrapolate beyond the reference data, potentially introducing speculative but scientifically reasonable hypotheses. In early drug discovery, such outputs could be valuable for hypothesis generation, but in clinical settings, they may risk misinformation if unverified.

3.1 Explainable DDI Features

A key feature of our approach is the extraction and visualization of decoder cross-attention weights, which provide insights into how the model learns to associate specific molecular substructures with interaction-related textual outputs. By mapping these attention weights back onto the input SMILES strings and subsequently visualizing the corresponding functional groups using RDKit, we were able to interpret the decision-making process of the model at the chemical substructure level. Figure 2 shows the highlighted features with the selected drug pairs. The dark-colored regions in the RDKit visualizations reflect strong correlations between specific substructures and the predicted interaction sentences.

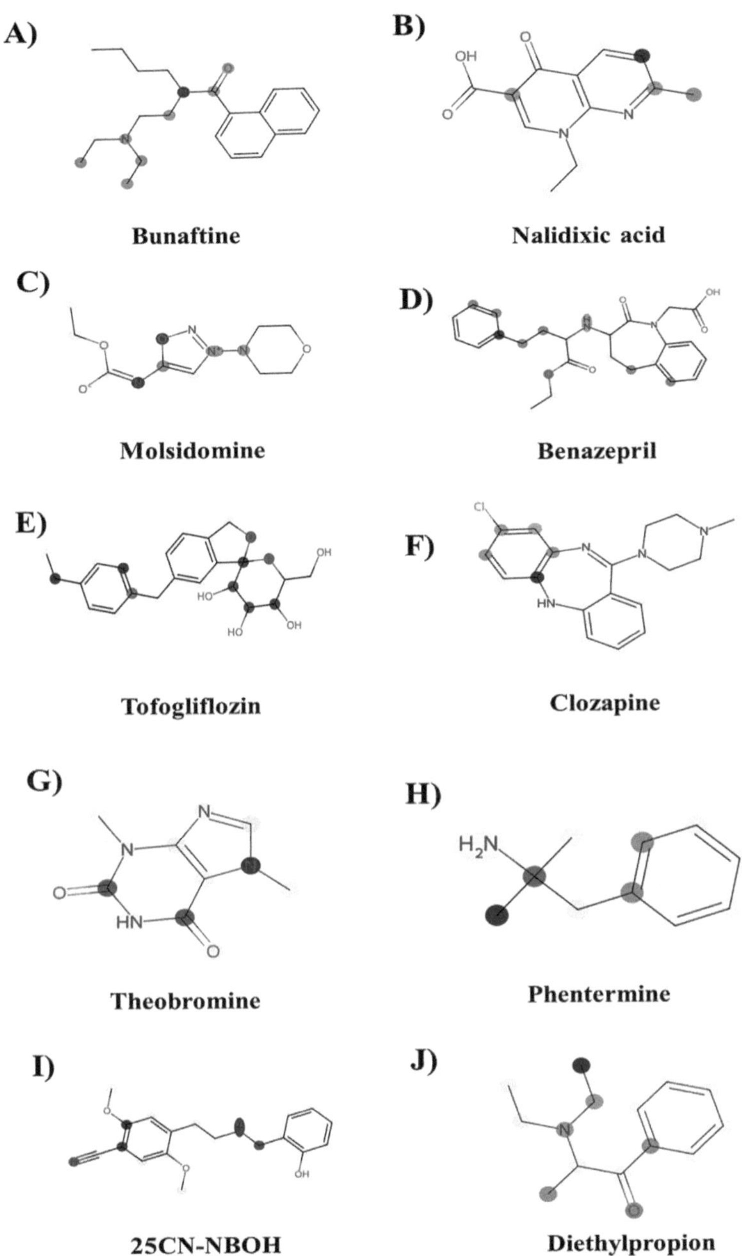

Fig. 2. The figure illustrates the substructures or functional groups identified by the model as contributing most significantly to DDI prediction. The color code represents the attention weight assigned to each token, where darker shades indicate higher attention and lighter shades indicate lower attention. The highlighted words shown in Table 2 correspond to the specific tokens considered in each drug pair.

The results demonstrate that the model does not treat the molecular input uniformly; instead, it assigns stronger attention weights to particular substructures that are chemically and pharmacologically relevant for drug–drug interactions. For example, in drug pairs **A–B**, the model highlighted aromatic rings and heteroatoms (e.g., nitrogen and oxygen-containing groups) that are well-known to influence binding affinity, metabolic stability, and CYP450 enzyme recognition. Similarly, in **C–D**, strong attention was directed towards ester and amide linkages, which are often key determinants of drug metabolism and hydrolytic stability [17]. This suggests that the model has implicitly learned to prioritize functional groups associated with metabolic transformations or binding specificity when predicting potential interactions.

Interestingly, in the case of **E–F**, sugar moieties and heteroaromatic systems were highlighted, consistent with their roles in solubility, transport, and receptor recognition [18]. For **G–H**, the attention distribution emphasized keto groups and amino substituents, structural motifs frequently involved in hydrogen bonding and enzymatic modification [19]. Finally, for the pair **I–J**, attention was concentrated on carboxyl and imidazole functional groups, both of which play critical roles in pKa modulation and drug–protein binding [20]. Collectively, these observations reinforce the chemical plausibility of the model's learned representations and demonstrate that MolT5 leverages chemically meaningful cues in generating DDI-related text. This attention-based visualization framework provides a novel bridge between black-box language models and chemical domain knowledge. Traditional DDI prediction models often rely on molecular fingerprints or graph embeddings, which, although effective, provide limited interpretability. In contrast, our approach highlights substructures in a chemically intuitive manner, thereby offering a potential explanation for why a particular drug pair is predicted to interact. This can enhance trust in AI-driven predictions, facilitate hypothesis generation for experimental validation, and potentially guide medicinal chemists in anticipating or mitigating drug interactions during drug design.

3.2 Error Analysis

Though the proposed model demonstrates promising performance in DDI interaction prediction, we could observe a few errors in actual vs. predicted interaction (Table 2). This exhibits the limitations of the model from semantic inconsistencies, mechanistic hallucinations and attention misalignment between molecular and textual representations. In certain cases, while the generated text preserves grammatical and structural fluency, it lacks intended pharmacological meaning. For example, in the pair (Theobromine, Phentermine), the generated description shifts from *"The risk or severity of adverse effects can be increased when Phentermine is combined with Theobromine"* to *"Phentermine may decrease the excretion rate of Theobromine which could result in a higher serum level."* Both sentences have unsupported mechanistic explanation involving altered excretions. This represents a form of *semantic hallucination*, where the model fabricates a mechanism not grounded in known pharmacological evidence. The model occasionally generalizes specific mechanisms with vague or unrelated sentences. For instance, in the pair (25CN-NBOH, Diethylpropion), the original description refers to *"CNS depression,"* while the generated version generalizes it to *"adverse effects."* This reflects the model's reliance on frequent DDI templates rather than context-specific reasoning. The model can be further improved by addressing these errors and strengthening model's mechanistic grounding and improving its predictive ability. In future, we will improve the model by integrating pharmacological ontologies (e.g., DrugBank, CTD) to provide mechanism-level supervision and applying attention regularization techniques to encourage the model to focus on interaction-relevant molecular substructures along with conducting quantitative error classification using semantic similarity metrics and expert validation to complement qualitative analysis.

3.3 Conclusions

In summary, our findings highlight the dual advantage of MolT5: (i) accurate sequence-to-sequence DDI prediction and (ii) interpretable visualization of substructural contributions via cross-attention analysis. The MolT5 based model is comparably better than other baseline models such as BioBERT, PubMedBERT, and ClinicalBERT etc. These baseline models excel at information extraction within biomedical or clinical text and ChemBERT is best for molecular property prediction from SMILES data. However, MolT5 is transcends all by integrating text and chemical modalities into a generative and multimodal language model, enabling bidirectional molecule–language translation, de novo chemical design, and unified scientific reasoning across life-science domains. This approach paves the way for interpretable AI in cheminformatics, providing both predictive power and chemical insight, which are indispensable for translational applications in drug safety assessment and rational drug development. We further plan to expand the work by exploring knowledge distillation or model compression techniques to balance accuracy with efficiency, as well as integrating additional domain-specific corpora to further enhance generalization to rare or novel drug interactions.

Acknowledgments. DBT is thanked for the financial support in the form of the Centre of Excellence in Advanced Computation and Data Sciences (Ref. No: BT/PR40188/BTIS/137/27/2021) and National Networking Project (NNP) (Ref. No: BT/PR40233/BTIS/137/74/2023). Manuscript reference No. CSIR-NEIST/PUB/2025/153.

Disclosure of Interests. The Authors declare no competing interests.

References

1. Jia, J., Zhu, F., Ma, X., Cao, Z.W., Li, Y.X., Chen, Y.Z.: Mechanisms of drug combinations: interaction and network perspectives. Nat. Rev. Drug Discov. **8**(2), 111–128 (2009)
2. Choi, J., Madari, S., Huang, F.: Utilising endogenous biomarkers in drug development to streamline the assessment of drug–drug interactions mediated by renal transporters: a pharmaceutical industry perspective. Clin. Pharmacokinet. **63**(6), 735–749 (2024)
3. Klopotowska, J.E., et al.: Adverse drug events caused by three high-risk drug–drug interactions in patients admitted to intensive care units: a multicentre retrospective observational study. Br. J. Clin. Pharmacol. **90**(1), 164–175 (2024)
4. Su, X., et al.: Biomedical knowledge graph embedding with capsule network for multi-label drug–drug interaction prediction. IEEE Trans. Knowl. Data Eng. **35**(6), 5640–5651 (2023)

5. Chen, Y., Ma, T., Yang, X., Wang, J., Song, B., Zeng, X.: MUFFIN: multi-scale feature fusion for drug–drug interaction prediction. Bioinformatics **37**(17), 2651–2658 (2021)

6. Nyamabo, A.K., Yu, H., Shi, J.-Y.: SSI-DDI: substructure–substructure interactions for drug–drug interaction prediction. Brief. Bioinform. **22**(6), bbab133 (2021)

7. Zhang, Y., Deng, Z., Xu, X., Feng, Y., Sun, J.: Application of artificial intelligence in drug–drug interactions prediction: a review. J. Chem. Inf. Model. **64**(7), 2158–2173 (2024)

8. Ryu, J.Y., Kim, H.U., Lee, S.Y.: Deep learning improves prediction of drug–drug and drug–food interactions. Proc. Natl. Acad. Sci. U.S.A. **115**(18), E4304–E4311 (2018)

9. Ren, Y., Shi, Y., Zhang, K., Wang, X., Chen, Z., Li, H.: A drug recommendation model based on message propagation and DDI gating mechanism. IEEE J. Biomed. Health Inform. **26**(7), 3478–3485 (2022)

10. Chen, S., et al.: An effective framework for predicting drug–drug interactions based on molecular substructures and knowledge graph neural network. Comput. Biol. Med. **169**, 107900 (2024)

11. Wu, D., Sun, W., He, Y., Chen, Z., Luo, X.: MKG-FENN: a multimodal knowledge graph fused end-to-end neural network for accurate drug–drug interaction prediction. Proc. AAAI Conf. Artif. Intell. **38**(9), 10216–10224 (2024)

12. Chen, Q., Li, X., Geng, K., Wang, M.: Context-aware safe medication recommendations with molecular graph and DDI graph embedding. Proc. AAAI Conf. Artif. Intell. **37**(6), 7053–7060 (2023)

13. De Vito, G., Ferrucci, F., Angelakis, A.: LLMs for drug–drug interaction prediction: a comprehensive comparison (2025). arXiv:2502.06890

14. Edwards, C., Lai, T., Ros, K., Honke, G., Cho, K., Ji, H.: Translation between molecules and natural language. In: Goldberg, Y., Kozareva, Z., Zhang, Y. (eds.) Proceedings of the 2022 Conference on Empirical Methods in Natural Language Processing, Abu Dhabi, United Arab Emirates, December 2022. Association for Computational Linguistics, pp. 375–413 (2022)

15. Knox, C., et al.: DrugBank 6.0: the DrugBank knowledgebase for 2024. Nucleic Acids Res. **52**(D1), D1265–D1275 (2024)

16. RDKit: Open-Source Cheminformatics Software. https://www.rdkit.org. Accessed 07 Aug 2025

17. Lai, Y., et al.: Recent advances in the translation of drug metabolism and pharmacokinetics science for drug discovery and development. Acta Pharm Sin B. **12**(6), 2751–2777 (2022)

18. Pastucch-Gawolek, G., Szreder, J., Dominska, M., Pielok, M., Cichy, P., Grymel, M.: A small sugar molecule with huge potential in targeted cancer therapy. Pharmaceutics. **15**(3), 913 (2023)

19. Robello, M., Barresi, E., Baglini, E., Salerno, S., Taliani, S., Settimo, F.D.: The alpha ketoamide moiety as a privileged motif in medicinal chemistry: Current insights and emerging opportunities. J. Med. Chem. **64**(7), 3508–3545 (2021)

Multi-agent Decision Support Framework for Bed Allocation and Patient Flow Optimization in Hospitals

Trishna Paul[1]([✉]) [iD], Tufan Paul[2] [iD], and Arindam Kolay[3] [iD]

[1] Pandit Deendayal Energy University, Knowledge Corridor, Raisan Village, PDPU Rd, Gandhinagar 382007, Gujarat, India
Trishna.Paul@sot.pdpu.ac.in
[2] KPI Partners, Koramangala, Bengaluru 560034, Karnataka, India
[3] NIMS Institute of Pharmacy, NIMS University, Jaipur, Rajasthan, India

Abstract. Efficient bed allocation and smooth patient flow are critical for maintaining high-quality hospital operations, especially under fluctuating patient demand and resource constraints. Traditional centralized decision-making systems often lack the adaptability, interpretability, and scalability required to address these challenges in real time. Our work presents a conceptual Multi-Agent System (MAS) framework designed specifically for hospital bed allocation and patient flow optimization. The framework incorporates specialized agents, such as Bed Availability Agents, Patient Prioritization Agents, Transfer Coordination Agents, and Resource Forecasting Agents that work collaboratively via standardized communication protocols. First, we present the system architecture, coordination strategies, and decision-making workflows that facilitate decentralized yet synchronized operations, ensuring patient safety, adherence to medical protocols, and transparent hospital management. The approach emphasizes modularity and explainability, enabling integration of diverse predictive models, real-time hospital data, and clinical guidelines into a unified decision-support environment. Then we demonstrate the framework's applicability through simulated hospital scenarios, showcasing its potential to improve occupancy rates, reduce patient wait times, and support surge capacity management. Our work provides a foundation for developing adaptive, trustworthy, and scalable AI-based hospital resource management systems.

Keywords: Multi-Agent Systems · Bed Allocation · Patient Flow Optimization · Hospital Resource Management · Healthcare AI · Decision Support · Explainable AI

1 Introduction

Modern healthcare systems operate in an increasingly complex environment characterized by growing patient demand, limited resource availability, and heightened expectations for service quality [1, 2]. Hospitals are constantly challenged to maintain optimal

B. Chatterjee et al. (Eds.): ICDCIT 2026, LNCS 16420, pp. 479–494, 2026.
https://doi.org/10.1007/978-3-032-16632-6_31

patient care while managing constraints such as finite bed capacity, fluctuating staff availability, and unpredictable surges in patient inflow [2–4]. The COVID-19 pandemic vividly demonstrated how quickly patient volumes can exceed hospital capacity, creating bottlenecks in emergency departments, delaying admissions from outpatient or transfer facilities, and straining critical care resources [5, 6]. Even outside of pandemic conditions, seasonal variations in illnesses, demographic changes, and rising rates of chronic diseases contribute to persistent pressures on hospital infrastructure [2, 4]. At the core of these operational challenges lies the bed allocation problem, the process of assigning available beds to incoming patients in a manner that balances clinical urgency, operational efficiency, and equitable access to care [7, 8]. Inefficient bed allocation can lead to increased patient wait times, prolonged boarding in emergency departments, delayed surgical schedules, and, ultimately, compromised patient outcomes [5, 9]. Furthermore, the interconnected nature of hospital operations means that bottlenecks in bed allocation cascade into broader issues of patient flow, affecting departments such as radiology, laboratory services, and intensive care [10, 11]. Traditional approaches to hospital resource management often rely on centralized decision-making processes, where a small team or a single centralized system aggregates data and makes allocation decisions [2, 12, 13]. While this model can ensure uniform policy enforcement, it often lacks the agility to respond to rapidly evolving conditions in real time [14, 15]. Decision-making may be hindered by communication delays, incomplete information, and a limited capacity to incorporate diverse operational perspectives [7, 8]. In high-pressure environments, this can result in suboptimal or delayed actions, undermining hospital efficiency and patient satisfaction [5, 9]. A key emerging requirement for modern hospital management is adaptability, the ability to adjust decision-making processes dynamically as conditions change [16, 17]. Additionally, there is an increasing demand for transparency and explainability in operational decisions, driven by regulatory compliance requirements, medico-legal accountability, and the ethical imperative to ensure fair and consistent patient treatment [18–21]. Decision-support systems that can meet these demands while operating in real time represent a critical need in the healthcare domain [22, 23]. While numerous computational models and decision-support algorithms have been proposed for hospital bed management, most existing systems are monolithic and tightly coupled to specific hospital workflows [10, 24]. Such designs limit scalability and make it difficult to integrate emerging predictive analytics tools or adapt to institutional variations in policy [25]. Furthermore, many algorithmic approaches, especially those driven purely by optimization or machine learning, function as "black boxes," producing decisions without clear explanations. This lack of explainability hinders adoption by hospital administrators and clinical staff, who must be able to justify resource allocation decisions to stakeholders and patients. Another gap lies in the integration of bed allocation with overall patient flow optimization. Many existing tools address bed management in isolation, without considering upstream and downstream operational processes such as emergency triage, intra-hospital transfers, and discharge planning. Without an integrated approach, localized optimizations may inadvertently create bottlenecks elsewhere in the system [10, 11].

Multi-Agent Systems (MAS) offer a promising paradigm to address these gaps. MAS architectures consist of autonomous yet cooperative software agents, each specialized for particular tasks, capable of real-time communication and coordination [26]. While MAS approaches have been explored in domains such as logistics, traffic control, and supply chain management, their application to holistic hospital resource management, particularly in integrating bed allocation with patient flow, remains limited in both research and practice [25, 27] (Fig. 1).

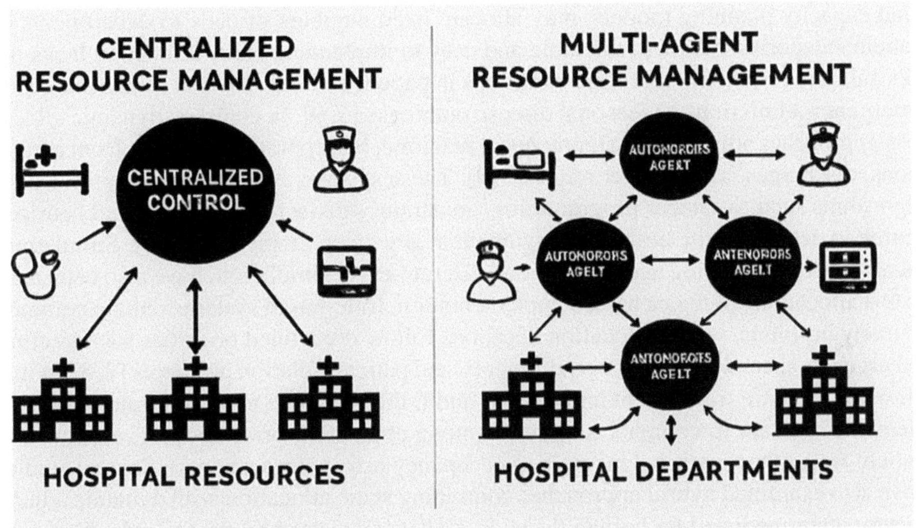

Fig. 1. Comparison of Centralized vs. Multi-Agent Resource Management in Hospitals

This work seeks to bridge the above gaps by conceptualizing a Multi-Agent System framework for decentralized hospital resource management, with a focus on bed allocation and patient flow optimization. The objectives of the study are to:

a. **Design a theoretical MAS architecture** specifically tailored for hospital operations, incorporating modular, explainable, and interoperable components.
b. **Enable real-time coordination** among heterogeneous agents representing different operational roles—such as bed availability tracking, patient prioritization, transfer coordination, and resource forecasting.
c. **Illustrate example decision workflows** that demonstrate how such a system could function in simulated hospital scenarios, emphasizing adaptability, transparency, and compliance with clinical protocols.

2 Literature Review

We explore a comprehensive range of prior research across various areas relevant to healthcare optimization. The studies examined are categorized into several key subsections, each of which contributes to a broader understanding of how to improve healthcare services. The following subsections summarize the key findings from existing literature:

2.1 Hospital Bed Allocation Strategies

Hospital bed allocation is a critical operational challenge in healthcare management, with direct implications for patient safety, service quality, and operational efficiency. Broadly, allocation strategies can be classified into static and dynamic approaches.

In static allocation, bed assignments are planned based on historical averages of admissions, discharges, and transfers [2, 3, 7]. Such approaches, often embedded in hospital capacity planning models, may allocate fixed numbers of beds to departments or patient categories. While predictable and easy to implement, static allocation lacks the flexibility to respond to real-time variations in patient demand, such as sudden surges in emergency admissions or seasonal disease outbreaks [5, 9]. In contrast, dynamic allocation approaches adjust bed assignments in real time, incorporating live data from admissions, discharges, and transfer requests [9]. These systems often leverage optimization algorithms such as integer programming, constraint satisfaction methods, and heuristic search to determine the best bed assignment at any given moment [10, 24]. Simulation-based models, including agent-based and discrete-event simulation, have also been used to test allocation strategies before implementation. Rule-based systems remain common in many hospitals, where allocation decisions follow predefined priorities such as clinical urgency, specialty-specific requirements, and patient isolation protocols [7, 8]. While these systems are transparent and easy to audit, they struggle to incorporate predictive elements or adapt to complex trade-offs among competing priorities (e.g., minimizing patient wait time versus balancing bed occupancy across departments). Several studies have also examined hybrid approaches combining static allocation with dynamic adjustments, often mediated by human decision-makers supported by dashboards. However, these models are prone to decision bottlenecks and human error under high-pressure conditions, particularly during pandemic-driven surges [6, 9].

Overall, while current approaches have advanced hospital efficiency, they tend to focus on isolated allocation problems rather than integrated, system-wide resource management that adapts in real time and supports transparent, explainable decision-making.

2.2 Patient Flow Optimization

Patient flow refers to the movement of patients through various stages of hospital care—from admission to treatment, transfer, and eventual discharge [1, 5]. Efficient flow is vital to minimizing emergency department overcrowding, reducing length of stay, and improving overall patient outcomes. Queueing theory has long been applied to model patient arrivals, waiting times, and service rates in healthcare contexts [1]. By modelling departments as service nodes and patients as customers, queueing theory can identify bottlenecks and predict performance metrics under different operational scenarios. However, classical queueing models often assume stationary arrival and service rates, which do not capture the stochastic and time-varying nature of hospital operations. Discrete-event simulation (DES) has been widely used to capture the dynamic, stochastic nature of patient flow [5, 9]. DES allows healthcare managers to test the effects of interventions, such as adding more ICU beds or streamlining discharge processes, without disrupting real-world operations. For example, DES models have been used to examine how ED triage policies impact inpatient occupancy levels. Despite their utility, these models are typically offline tools and are not integrated into live decision-support environments. Recent advancements in predictive analytics have enabled hospitals to forecast admission and discharge patterns using machine learning methods [16, 17]. Features such as patient demographics, medical history, and clinical indicators are combined with real-time data to predict bed demand in specific departments. Forecasting models can inform pre-emptive actions, such as scheduling elective admissions based on anticipated discharge volumes [22, 23]. Nevertheless, predictive models are often implemented in isolation from operational decision-making processes, limiting their potential impact. A key gap remains while patient flow optimization research addresses throughput and resource utilization, few approaches offer adaptive, decentralized decision-making that integrates bed allocation, transfer coordination, and forecasting into a cohesive framework.

2.3 Multi-agent Systems in Healthcare

Multi-Agent Systems (MAS) consist of autonomous, interactive agents that perceive their environment, make decisions, and collaborate to achieve shared or individual goals [25, 26]. Agents in MAS environments possess autonomy (independent decision-making), reactivity (responding to environmental changes), proactivity (goal-directed behavior), and social ability (communication with other agents via standardized protocols).

In healthcare, MAS have been applied to diverse problem domains, including:

- **Telemedicine**: Agents act as intermediaries between patients and providers, managing scheduling, consultations, and follow-up tasks.
- **Clinical decision support**: Diagnostic agents collaborate to suggest treatment options based on patient data and evidence-based guidelines.
- **Healthcare supply chain management**: Agents coordinate inventory and distribution of medicines, equipment, and consumables across hospitals.

These applications demonstrate MAS' potential for distributed decision-making and real-time coordination, yet their use in integrated bed allocation and patient flow optimization remains limited. Existing MAS solutions in hospital contexts often focus on single operational domains (e.g., scheduling surgeries or managing ICU occupancy) rather than enabling a holistic view of patient flow from entry to discharge [27, 28].

Furthermore, the design of MAS for healthcare faces unique challenges, including compliance with clinical safety regulations, interoperability with hospital information systems, and ensuring that decisions are explainable to human stakeholders. This underscores the need for tailored MAS architectures that address both operational efficiency and regulatory compliance.

2.4 Explainable AI in Decision Support

In healthcare, explainability is not a luxury, it is a necessity. Decisions affecting patient care must be transparent, interpretable [4, 18] by clinical staff, and justifiable in the context of medical guidelines and ethical considerations. Black-box AI models, while often accurate, risk undermining trust among clinicians and patients if their reasoning cannot be understood.

Explainable AI (XAI) techniques aim to bridge this gap by making decision-making processes transparent and interpretable. Common approaches include:

- **Rule extraction**: Converting complex models into human-readable decision rules.
- **Feature attribution**: Highlighting which input factors most influenced a decision (e.g., SHAP, LIME).
- **Visual explanation tools**: Providing graphical insights into model behaviour or agent interactions.

In the context of MAS, explainability becomes even more critical because decisions emerge from interactions among multiple autonomous agents. Transparent communication protocols, auditable decision logs, and human-in-the-loop verification mechanisms can enhance trust and accountability [20, 21].

Despite the growing body of XAI research, integration into live, operational healthcare MAS environments remains underexplored. Most XAI applications in healthcare focus on diagnosis and risk prediction, rather than operational decision support tasks like bed allocation and patient flow management [4, 18, 20, 21].

3 Methodology

A comprehensive literature review was conducted targeting publications related to hospital bed allocation, patient flow optimization, and Multi-Agent Systems (MAS) applications in healthcare. The primary databases used were PubMed, Scopus, and IEEE Xplore. Relevant search terms included "multi-agent hospital systems," "bed allocation optimization," "patient flow AI," "explainable AI in healthcare," as well as related operational and architectural topics. The review focused on works published up to the year 2025 to capture the latest developments in the field.

From the selected studies, data were systematically extracted covering system design, agent functionalities, evaluation outcomes such as efficiency, safety, and equity, practical challenges, technological integration aspects, and identified future research directions. Narrative synthesis was then performed, categorizing the findings according to major themes: MAS architectural frameworks, real-time operational capabilities, ethical and practical implementation challenges, and technological integration opportunities.

4 Problem Definition and System Requirements

4.1 Problem Statement

Hospitals are complex environments comprising multiple units such as emergency departments, intensive care units, surgical wards, and general inpatient wards. The efficient allocation of beds and the optimization of patient flow within such multifaceted systems are critical challenges that significantly impact healthcare delivery outcomes [2, 3, 5]. The coordination required among various hospital units to allocate beds to incoming patients involves intricate interdependencies. Each unit operates under different constraints, patient acuity levels, and care protocols, often resulting in competing demands for limited resources.

One of the core difficulties in this context is the need for real-time decision-making in an environment characterized by uncertainty and rapidly changing conditions. Patient arrivals can be unpredictable, and the length of stay varies based on individual clinical progress. This dynamic scenario necessitates decision support systems that can rapidly assimilate and analyze diverse data inputs to support timely and informed decisions. Without real-time insights, bed allocation decisions risk being suboptimal, leading to prolonged patient wait times, overcrowded wards, and inefficient use of hospital resources.

Moreover, any allocation framework must balance operational efficiency with patient-centered care principles such as safety and fairness [7, 8]. Efficiency entails maximizing bed utilization and minimizing patient delays, while safety requires ensuring that patients are placed in suitable care environments matching their clinical needs. Fairness demands transparent and equitable prioritization mechanisms to avoid biases or unintended discrimination in access to care. Achieving this balance is complicated by conflicting objectives and the heterogeneous nature of patient needs, making manual coordination both error-prone and resource-intensive.

The multi-agent decision support framework proposed in this paper aims to address these challenges by modelling hospital units as autonomous agents capable of collaborative decision-making. Such a framework facilitates decentralized yet coordinated management of bed allocation and patient transfers, enabling responsiveness to real-time conditions and strategic anticipation of future resource demands. The framework's design explicitly accounts for the stochastic and dynamic nature of hospital operations, supporting optimized resource distribution while adhering to clinical and ethical standards.

4.2 System Requirements

To effectively support bed allocation and patient flow optimization, the decision support system must meet a comprehensive set of functional and non-functional requirements that reflect the operational realities and regulatory constraints of modern hospitals (Table 1).

Functional Requirements

1. **Real-Time Bed Availability Tracking**: The system must continuously monitor and update the status of all hospital beds across different units, including occupancy, cleaning status, and readiness for new patients. This real-time visibility is crucial to enable prompt allocation decisions and minimize patient wait times.
2. **Automated Patient Prioritization**: Given limited bed availability, the system should automatically prioritize patients based on clinical urgency, anticipated length of stay, and other relevant criteria. This prioritization ensures that critical cases receive timely access to necessary care environments, while also optimizing overall patient throughput.
3. **Inter-Department Transfer Coordination**: Coordination of patient transfers between departments is a complex task that requires synchronization of bed availability, staff readiness, and patient clinical status. The system must facilitate smooth and timely transfers to avoid bottlenecks and reduce delays in care transitions.

4. **Predictive Resource Forecasting**: To proactively manage capacity, the system should incorporate predictive analytics to forecast bed demand and resource needs based on historical data, current patient flow trends, and external factors (e.g., seasonal illness outbreaks). This foresight enables strategic planning and mitigates risks of overcrowding.

Non-functional Requirements

1. **Scalability**: The system must scale efficiently to accommodate hospitals of varying sizes and complexities, from small community hospitals to large tertiary care centres with hundreds of beds. Scalability also involves handling increases in data volume and the number of interacting agents without degradation of performance.
2. **Interoperability with Existing Hospital IT Systems**: Hospitals employ diverse information systems such as Electronic Health Records (EHR)[22, 23], admission-discharge-transfer (ADT) systems, and laboratory information systems. The decision support framework must seamlessly integrate with these existing systems through standardized interfaces and protocols to enable accurate data exchange and avoid workflow disruptions.
3. **Data Privacy and Compliance**: Patient data handled by the system is highly sensitive and subject to stringent regulations such as the Health Insurance Portability and Accountability Act (HIPAA) in the United States and the General Data Protection Regulation (GDPR) in the European Union. The system must enforce robust data security measures, including encryption, access controls, and audit trails, to protect patient privacy and ensure regulatory compliance [2, 17].

Table 1. Presents a comparison between the centralized bed management system and the multi-agent bed management system.

Feature	Centralized Bed Management System	Multi-Agent Bed Management System
Decision Making	Single central controller makes all allocation decisions	Multiple autonomous agents collaborate in decision making
Adaptability	Limited; slower to respond to sudden changes	High; agents react locally and coordinate dynamically
Scalability	Challenging; single point limits performance with scale	Easily scalable by adding more agents
Transparency and Explainability	Often opaque "black box" decisions	Enhanced explainability via traceable agent interactions
Integration with Hospital Units	Central hub aggregates data from all units	Agents represent specific units, enabling fine-grained control
Fault Tolerance	Low; single failure can disrupt the system	High; distributed agents provide robustness

(continued)

Table 1. (*continued*)

Feature	Centralized Bed Management System	Multi-Agent Bed Management System
Resource Utilization	Less efficient due to limited flexibility	Optimizes resource use via coordinated negotiation
Complexity of Implementation	Generally simpler to deploy initially	More complex; requires agent communication infrastructure
Real-time Response	Limited by central processing and communication delays	Real-time local decision making with synchronized coordination
Support for Emergency Scenarios	Limited adaptive capacity	Designed for dynamic surge and emergency response

5 Multi-agent Framework

5.1 Agent Types and Interactions

The framework is composed of several specialized agent types, each responsible for distinct aspects of hospital bed management and patient flow:

- **Bed Availability Agents:** These agents continuously track the real-time status of hospital beds across all units, monitoring conditions such as occupancy, availability, cleaning status, and reservation. Their role is critical in maintaining an accurate and up-to-date overview of resource capacity.
- **Patient Prioritization Agents:** Tasked with evaluating incoming and current patients, these agents apply predictive models and scoring mechanisms to assess patient urgency, likely outcomes, and fairness considerations. They ensure that critical cases are prioritized appropriately in accordance with clinical guidelines and ethical standards.
- **Transfer Coordination Agents:** These agents handle the complex logistics of intra- and inter-unit patient transfers. They manage workflow triggers, coordinate with relevant hospital departments, and optimize timing and resource allocation to minimize delays and avoid bottlenecks.
- **Resource Forecasting Agents:** Utilizing historical data and real-time inputs, these agents predict future admissions, discharges, and occupancy trends. They dynamically adjust allocation policies and prepare the system for anticipated changes in demand, enhancing responsiveness and capacity planning.

5.2 Standardized Communication

To ensure seamless interoperability and coordinated operation among diverse agents, the framework adopts widely accepted healthcare communication protocols, notably FHIR (Fast Healthcare Interoperability Resources) and HL7 (Health Level Seven) [2, 3]. Each agent operates with a defined specialization yet shares pertinent data continuously with other agents, enabling synchronized and adaptive system-wide behavior. This standardized communication fosters flexibility and integration with existing hospital information systems.

5.3   Explainability and Auditability

Transparency is a cornerstone of the framework's design. All agents maintain comprehensive logs of their recommendations and decisions, using explainable AI techniques such as SHAP (SHapley Additive exPlanations) and LIME (Local Interpretable Model-agnostic Explanations) to attribute scores and rationales behind prioritizations [18, 20, 21]. This approach not only aids clinical staff in understanding and trusting automated decisions but also ensures that decision trails are human-readable and fully auditable for compliance, accountability, and continuous improvement (Fig. 2).

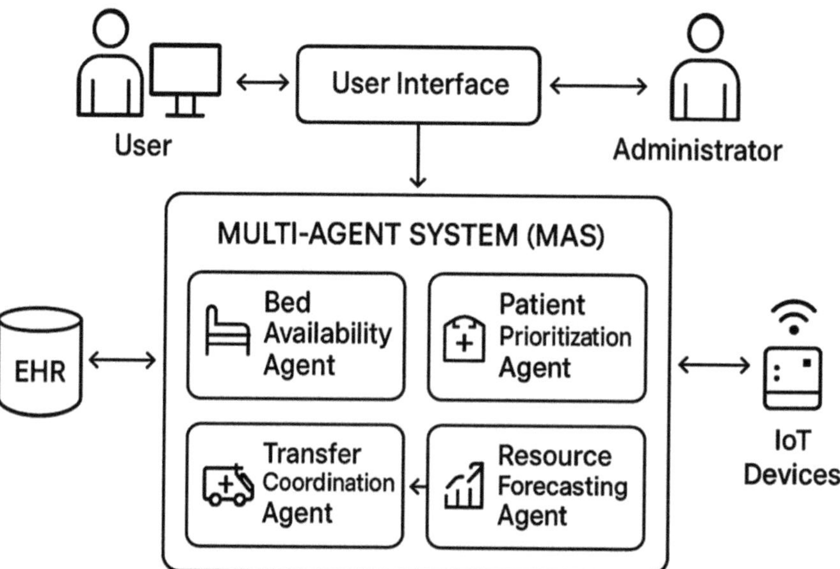

Fig. 2. Architecture of Multi-Agent System in Hospital Management

6   Framework Operation Scenarios

The proposed multi-agent decision support framework is designed to function effectively under a variety of operational scenarios common to hospital environments. These scenarios range from routine day-to-day operations to extraordinary events such as pandemics or mass casualty incidents, as well as collaborative resource sharing among hospitals. This section describes the key operation scenarios to illustrate how the framework dynamically adapts and supports hospital decision-making processes under varying conditions.

6.1 Normal Operation

Under normal conditions, the hospital manages patient admissions, transfers, and discharges routinely. The system's agents constantly track bed availability and quickly process new admission requests by matching patients' needs and urgency with suitable beds. The agents work together to allocate beds efficiently, avoid bottlenecks, and keep bed turnover smooth by predicting discharge times and sharing this information. They also coordinate patient transfers within the hospital, ensuring timely and seamless moves without causing overcrowding. Throughout, the system stays updated with hospital IT data, so staff have accurate, real-time information to support their decisions [2, 3, 5].

6.2 Surge Scenario (e.g., Pandemic Wave)

During surge events like a pandemic, hospitals face patient numbers beyond their usual capacity. This system adapts by adjusting how beds are allocated, and which patients get priority. When beds run short, agents follow triage protocols to admit the most severe cases first. They also identify less critical patients who can be transferred or discharged early to free up space for those needing urgent care [6]. The system helps expand capacity by turning non-traditional areas into temporary care zones, coordinating closely with hospital management. Using real-time predictions, it forecasts patient arrivals and resource needs, allowing hospitals to prepare staff and supplies ahead of time. The agents keep hospital units informed of changing conditions, enabling quick, coordinated responses that prevent overcrowding and maintain care quality. Additionally, the system can run simulations to test different surge plans, supporting decisions like postponing elective treatments or reallocating beds for critical patients [16, 17].

6.3 Inter-hospital Coordination

The framework helps hospitals work together during busy times by sharing real-time info on bed availability, staff, and special resources. If one hospital is full, patient admissions can be redirected to nearby hospitals with space, balancing the load [22]. This teamwork uses standard communication systems to connect different hospital IT networks smoothly. It also coordinates patient transfers between hospitals, managing transport, bed bookings, and medical records to speed up care and keep it continuous [23]. This cooperation strengthens the healthcare system, making care fairer and resources used more efficiently across the region in both daily operations and emergencies [25].

6.4 Other Emergency Situations

The framework is designed to handle emergencies beyond pandemics, like mass casualty events, natural disasters, or major accidents that cause sudden patient surges. In these critical situations, quick triage and prioritization are essential despite limited resources and infrastructure challenges [2]. The system uses smart decision-making that can override normal procedures to focus on urgent needs. Agents gather data on patient counts, injury severity, and available resources to quickly allocate beds following disaster triage rules. It also helps hospitals reorganize by setting up special trauma or isolation areas in coordination with management and clinical staff. The system connects with external emergency response teams and public health agencies to share real-time hospital capacity information. It also communicates with EMS to help direct ambulances to the best hospitals based on availability and patient needs [5, 10]. This full coordination improves patient care by reducing treatment delays during crises. Overall, the system offers flexible, reliable support for hospital operations, from everyday care to major emergencies, ensuring efficient bed use and smooth patient flow in all situations.

7   Result and Discussion

The multi-agent decision support framework developed for bed allocation and patient flow optimization demonstrates several notable strengths that position it as a promising solution for contemporary hospital management challenges. However, as with any complex system implementation, certain challenges and ethical considerations must be addressed to ensure its effective and responsible deployment.

Strengths of the Proposed Approach The framework is highly adaptable, which is one of its biggest strengths. Its modular design means it can work well in different hospital settings, from small clinics to large, specialized centers. Each agent acts independently but works together with others, so the system can quickly adjust to changes like fluctuating patient numbers, available resources, and shifting clinical priorities. This team-like, decentralized approach helps prevent bottlenecks and makes the system more resilient during unexpected events like pandemics or emergencies.

Another important benefit is that the system is easy to understand and transparent i.e. explainability. Unlike traditional "black box" systems, this multi-agent setup lets staff see how and why bed allocation and patient prioritization decisions are made. Each agent's actions can be tracked and reviewed, which builds trust among healthcare workers and managers, especially since these decisions affect patient care and must follow regulations.

Finally, because the system is modular, hospitals can adopt it step-by-step. They might start with basic tools like real-time bed tracking and gradually add more advanced features such as predictive analytics or coordination with other hospitals. This flexibility lowers barriers to getting started and makes it easier to tailor the system to fit each hospital's unique workflows and technologies.

Challenges While the framework has many strengths, there are some real-world challenges to consider. Integrating it with existing hospital IT systems can be costly and complex, especially since many hospitals use older technology that varies widely. This upfront investment might be tough for hospitals with limited resources. Training staff is also important because the new system changes workflows and requires everyone, from doctors to administrative teams, to learn new tools. Good training and ongoing support are key to help staff adjust smoothly and avoid mistakes. Lastly, the system needs reliable, up-to-date data to work well. Inaccurate or delayed information about bed status or patient details can cause poor decisions, so strong data management and real-time updates are crucial but can be technically challenging to implement.

Ethical Considerations In addition to operational challenges, important ethical issues are also need careful attention. One major concern is bias, if the system's patient prioritization is based on past data that reflects inequalities or missing information about certain groups, it could unintentionally worsen unfair access to care. To prevent this, the system's algorithms should be regularly checked and designed to promote fairness. Transparency is key too; the system should clearly explain decisions so that healthcare workers and patients understand and, if needed, question them. This openness builds trust and respects patients' rights. Lastly, keeping patient data safe and private is essential. The system must follow laws like HIPAA and GDPR to ensure sensitive health information is protected and only shared properly, preserving patient confidentiality and dignity [3, 29].

8 Related Technologies and Integration Potential

The successful implementation of a multi-agent decision support framework for bed allocation and patient flow optimization hinges significantly on its seamless integration with existing healthcare technologies and leveraging emerging tools [29, 30]. This section discusses the relevant technologies that complement the framework and explores their integration potential to enhance hospital operations.

Integration with Hospital EMR/EHR Systems Electronic Medical Records (EMR) and Electronic Health Records (EHR) are central to hospital data management, storing patient information, diagnoses, and treatment details digitally. Connecting the multi-agent system to these records is vital so agents can access real-time, accurate patient data needed for smart bed allocation and prioritization. This requires using common healthcare data standards like Health Level Seven (HL7), Fast Healthcare Interoperability Resources (FHIR), and Digital Imaging and Communications in Medicine (DICOM) to ensure smooth data sharing across different hospital systems [27, 28]. The system not only reads patient information but can also update bed status and admission records directly, keeping everything current and consistent. This integration helps hospitals follow regulations by tracking data access and changes while reducing manual work and errors, leading to better, more reliable decisions.

Use of IoT for Real-Time Bed and Patient Tracking The Internet of Things (IoT) is changing healthcare by enabling real-time monitoring using smart devices and sensors. In hospitals, IoT devices track bed occupancy, patient locations, and environmental conditions with high accuracy. Sensors in beds detect if they're occupied or ready for new patients, updating records automatically without manual input. Wearable devices and RFID tags help follow patients as they move through the hospital, giving the system real-time location data. This information helps coordinate transfers, predict discharge times, and manage bed availability more efficiently [16, 27].

Integrating IoT data improves the system's awareness and responsiveness, especially during emergencies or sudden surges. Alerts from IoT devices notify staff of important events like patient distress or unauthorized movements, boosting safety and care quality. While challenges exist, such as ensuring devices work together, handling large data flows, and protecting privacy, the advantages of automated, real-time data make IoT a key part of enhancing hospital operations [9].

AI-Based Forecasting Models Embedded in Agents Artificial Intelligence (AI), especially machine learning and predictive analytics, boosts the smartness of the multi-agent system [16]. AI models inside the agents analyse past patient data, seasonal patterns, and resource use to predict future bed needs and how long patients might stay. This helps the system plan instead of just reacting, like suggesting delaying elective procedures or activate extra capacity when a surge is expected. AI also personalizes patient prioritization by considering individual risks and health progress, making decisions fairer and more effective. These models learn and improve over time as hospital conditions change. To work well, AI predictions must be accurate, easy to understand, and integrated smoothly with clinical workflows. Clear communication of predictions and regular updates with new data keep the system reliable and useful [31] (Table 2).

Table 2. Outlines several integration challenges and presents solutions through the adaptation of multi-agent systems.

Integration Challenge	Solution and MAS Adaptation
Algorithmic Transparency and Explainability	Embed explainability modules in agents for auditability and clinical trust
Data Quality and Reliability	Integrate agents monitoring data validity and alerting for anomalies
Data Silos and Fragmentation	Use agent-based data brokers to federate and harmonize data across systems
Infrastructure and Network Latency	Optimize agent communication protocols with asynchronous messaging and fallback
Legacy Systems Compatibility	Develop middleware adapters and standardized interfaces (e.g., HL7, FHIR, DICOM)
Real-Time Data Synchronization	Employ IoT sensor integration with event-driven agent updates
Scalability to Large Hospital Networks	Deploy federated MAS architecture supporting inter-hospital coordination
Security and Privacy Compliance	Implement encryption, access controls, and audit trails within agent communications
User Acceptance and Workflow Integration	Design user-friendly dashboards reflecting agent decisions and recommendations

9 Conclusion and Future Work

This paper proposed a conceptual multi-agent system (MAS) framework to improve hospital bed allocation and patient flow management. By representing hospital units and services as autonomous yet cooperative agents, the framework supports decentralized, real-time decision-making. This approach offers key benefits such as flexibility, transparency, and the ability to adapt to changing hospital conditions, whether in routine operations or emergency situations.

The MAS framework is designed to integrate with existing hospital systems, IoT devices for real-time monitoring, and AI-based predictive models, making it a forward-thinking solution aligned with healthcare's ongoing digital transformation. Its potential to reduce patient wait times, improve bed utilization, and support equitable, patient-centered care makes it a promising tool for enhancing hospital efficiency and resilience.

Looking ahead, the next steps involve building and testing working prototypes in real hospital environments. These pilot implementations will help refine agent behaviors and address integration challenges. Incorporating machine learning—such as predictive models for patient length of stay or readmission—will enable smarter, proactive decisions. Reinforcement learning will further enhance the system by allowing agents to learn and improve strategies over time.

Expanding the system to connect multiple hospitals is another key goal, enabling better coordination of resources, especially during regional crises. Ensuring data privacy and secure communication will be central to this effort. Additionally, user-friendly interfaces will be developed to ensure the system integrates smoothly into clinical workflows and builds trust among healthcare staff.

Finally, ethical and regulatory considerations will remain a priority. Future work will focus on ensuring fairness in patient prioritization, protecting patient privacy, and developing clear guidelines for the responsible and compliant use of the system as it evolves.

References

1. Green, L.V.: Queueing analysis in healthcare. In: Patient Flow: Reducing Delay in Healthcare Delivery, pp. 281–307 (2006)
2. Hulshof, P.J., Kortbeek, N., Boucherie, R.J., Hans, E.W., Bakker, P.J.: Taxonomic classification of planning decisions in health care: a structured review of the state of the art in OR/MS. Health Syst. 1(2), 129–175 (2012)
3. Harper, P.R., Shahani, A.K.: Modelling for the planning and management of bed capacities in hospitals. J. Oper. Res. Soc. 53(1), 11–18 (2002)
4. Holzinger, A., Biemann, C., Pattichis, C.S., Kell, D.B.: What do we need to build explainable AI systems for the medical domain? arXiv preprint: arXiv:1712.09923 (2017)
5. Zhu, Z., Hen, B.H., Teow, K.L.: Estimating ICU bed capacity using discrete event simulation. Int. J. Health Care Qual. Assur. 25(2), 134–144 (2012)
6. Sargent, R., et al.: Use of a novel patient-flow model to optimize hospital capacity. Med. Decis. Making (2025)
7. Mould, G., Bowers, J., Ghattas, M.: The evolution of the pathway and its role in improving patient care. Qual. Saf. Health Care 19(5), e14 (2010)
8. Rodriguez, M., Santos, G., Pinto, A.: Agent-based hospital simulation models: a systematic review. Simul Healthc. 16(4), 234–251 (2021)
9. Kalpanapriya D, et al. Optimizing hospital length of stay and bed allocation using integrated models. Comput Ind Eng. 2025
10. Chen, L., Wang, X., Zhang, Y.: Multi-agent based surgical scheduling optimization. Oper Res Health Care. 25, 100–115 (2020)

11. Isern, D., Moreno, A.: Computer-based execution of clinical guidelines: a review. Int. J. Med. Inform. **77**(12), 787–808 (2008)
12. Porada, S., et al.: Optimization of hospital bed usage: restructuring and efficiency improvements. Health Syst. Rev. **7** (2022)
13. Balaji, R.: Hospital bed management optimization. Infosys White Paper (2024)
14. Sukrut, S., et al.: AI-driven patient flow management in hospitals: reducing wait times and enhancing care. J. Neonat. Surg. **14**(1), 1–12 (2025)
15. Al, H.S.: Streamlining patient flow and enhancing operational efficiency in hospitals. Healthc. Manag. Rev. **12**, 45–58 (2024)
16. Maleki Varnosfaderani, S., Forouzanfar, M.: The role of AI in hospitals and clinics: transforming healthcare in the 21st century. Bioengineering (Basel) **11**(4), 337 (2024)
17. Mizan, T., Taghipour, S.: Medical resource allocation planning by integrating machine learning and optimization models. Artif. Intell. Med. **134**, 102430 (2022)
18. Adadi, A., Berrada, M.: Peeking inside the black-box: a survey on explainable artificial intelligence (XAI). IEEE Access **6**, 52138–52160 (2018)
19. Moreno-Sánchez, P.A., Aalto, M., van Gils, M.: Prediction of patient flow in the emergency department using explainable artificial intelligence. SAGE Digit Health **10**, 1–15 (2024)
20. Amann, J., et al.: To explain or not to explain? –Artificial intelligence explainability in clinical decision support systems. PLOS Digit Health **1**(2), e0000016 (2022)
21. Hosteins, G., et al.: Artificial intelligence explainability in clinical decision support systems: a socio-technical perspective. Comput. Electr. Eng. (2023)
22. Jin, Y., et al.: Optimizing emergency department patient flow through bed allocation strategies: a discrete-event simulation study. Inquiry J. Healthc. Organ Provision Financ. (2024)
23. Yue H, et al. Use of a Novel Patient-Flow Model to Optimize Hospital Bed Capacity. Health Syst. 2023
24. Oliveira, B.R.P., de Vasconcelos, J.A., Almeida, J.F.F., Pinto, L.R.: A simulation-optimization approach for hospital beds allocation. Comput. Ind. Eng. **149**, 106814 (2020)
25. Gan, L., et al.: A multi-agent system for dynamic bed allocation in hospitals. J. Healthc. Eng. (2023)
26. Thakur, C.: Multi agent system applied in healthcare: a review. SSRN (2023)
27. Borkowski, A.A., Ben-Ari, A.: Multiagent AI systems in health care: envisioning next-generation intelligence. Veterans Aff. Healthc. Netw. (2025)
28. Engelmann, D., Cezar, L., Panisson, A., Bordini, R.: A conversational agent to support hospital bed allocation. In: Proc. Int. Conf. Pract. Appl. Agents Multi-Agent Syst. (2021)
29. Hosteins, G., et al.: A data-driven decision support tool to improve hospital bed cleaning logistics and availability. J. Healthc. Eng. (2023)
30. Schneider, A.J.T., van de Vrugt, N.M.: Applications of hospital bed optimization. In: Handbook of Healthcare Logistics. Springer (2021)
31. Akira AI. Innovative Agentic Workflows Redefining Hospital Resource Optimization. Akira AI Blog (2024)

Genomic Language Model Embeddings for Metabolic State Prediction from Mitochondrial Genome Sequences

Dibyendu Kishore Majumder, Sharvari Shet, Nithya Ramakrishnan, Rajalakshmi Srinivasan$^{(\boxtimes)}$, and Shyam Sundar Rajagopalan$^{(\boxtimes)}$

Institute of Bioinformatics and Applied Biotechnology, Bengaluru, India
{nithya,rajalakshmi,shyam}@ibab.ac.in

Abstract. Rapid in-silico identification of Crabtree-positive and Crabtree-negative yeasts from mitochondrial genomes is essential for guiding experimental design when annotations are missing or conserved motifs are unknown. In this study, we analyzed mitochondrial sequences from 64 yeast species (34 Crabtree-positive and 30 Crabtree-negative) and obtained new, informative representations of these DNA sequences by probing and fine-tuning the genomic foundation model HyenaDNA. To address the limitations of conventional aggregation methods such as max or mean pooling, which risk loss of contextual information, and to better capture long-range dependencies inherent in genomic sequences, we introduced a novel similarity-based embedding aggregation method, "Sim Pooling." Using this approach, fixed-length embeddings were generated and subsequently applied in downstream prediction tasks. Five classical machine learning classifiers—logistic regression, support vector classifier (SVC), random forest, eXtreme Gradient Boosting (XGBoost), and K-Nearest Neighbor—were trained and evaluated using metrics including accuracy, F1-score, AUROC, specificity, and sensitivity. Logistic regression trained on fine-tuned HyenaDNA embeddings with Sim Pooling achieved the best performance, yielding a mean F1-score of 0.79 ± 0.04 across 5-fold cross-validation, outperforming both traditional k-mer – based and probing-based models. These results demonstrate that fine-tuned genomic language models, combined with innovative embedding aggregation strategies such as Sim Pooling, can reliably predict the metabolic fate of yeast strains from raw mitochondrial sequences. With modest refinements and expansion to larger datasets, this framework can be extended to identify motifs or features driving metabolic states, reducing dependence on wet-lab validation or classical bioinformatics screening.

Keywords: Machine Learning · Genome Language Models · HyenaDNA · Crabtree Dataset · Yeast

© The Author(s), under exclusive license to Springer Nature Switzerland AG 2026
B. Chatterjee et al. (Eds.): ICDCIT 2026, LNCS 16420, pp. 495–509, 2026.
https://doi.org/10.1007/978-3-032-16632-6_32

1 Introduction

Yeasts represent a diverse group of eukaryotic microorganisms that exhibit distinct metabolic strategies depending on their evolutionary lineage. One of the most striking distinctions among them lies in their response to glucose abundance in the presence of oxygen, often referred to as the Crabtree effect. Crabtree-positive yeasts, such as *Saccharomyces cerevisiae*, preferentially adopt fermentative metabolism even under aerobic conditions, producing ethanol despite sufficient oxygen availability [11]. In contrast, Crabtree-negative yeasts rely on respiratory metabolism and switch to fermentation only upon oxygen depletion [11]. While this dichotomy in metabolic behavior is well recognized, the molecular basis underlying the divergence between Crabtree-positive and Crabtree-negative yeast species remains only partially understood. Elucidating this phenomenon at the genomic and regulatory level is of considerable importance, as it provides insights into evolutionary adaptations, energy efficiency, and industrial applications of yeasts. Because of their central role in energy metabolism, mitochondria seem to be interesting subjects for investigating this metabolic divergence. Mitochondria house the electron transport chain and are essential for respiration, making the mitochondrial genome a potential source of discriminative information [1]. A key question is whether mitochondrial DNA encodes any sequence patterns that could allow detection of Crabtree-positive or Crabtree-negative characteristics directly from mitochondrial DNA sequences. Traditional approaches to such analysis often rely on wet-lab experimentation or genome annotation – dependent comparative genomics, both of which are time-intensive and may fall short when handling unannotated sequences or newly discovered strains.

Consequently, there is growing interest in leveraging machine learning techniques, especially neural network – based models, to identify subtle sequence features in a fully data-driven manner. Neural networks have emerged as powerful tools in genomics, enabling the extraction of abstract, high-dimensional patterns from raw nucleotide sequences. Recent advances have given rise to genomic language models (GLMs) inspired by natural language processing [5]. In these frameworks, DNA is treated analogously to text, allowing models such as DNABERT [7] and Nucleotide Transformer [6] to learn sequence representations through self-supervised objectives similar to those used in linguistic domains. These approaches have demonstrated utility in various predictive tasks, including promoter recognition and enhancer activity prediction [6,7]. However, their reliance on standard Transformer architectures constrains their applicability to relatively short sequences due to the quadratic computational cost of self-attention mechanisms [2]. This limitation is particularly restrictive when studying genomic elements that span long distances, where interactions across thousands to millions of base pairs may encode critical biological functions. To address these challenges, newer architectures have sought to extend context length while reducing computational complexity. Among them, HyenaDNA [8] represents a notable advancement. Unlike Transformer-based GLMs, HyenaDNA employs the "Hyena operator," which leverages Fast Fourier Transform (FFT) – based convolutions to efficiently capture long-range dependencies. This innovation allows the model to achieve global context modeling in sub-quadratic time, making it substantially more scalable compared to attention-driven models [8].

As a result, HyenaDNA is capable of processing sequences of up to one million nucleotides [8], thereby enabling comprehensive analysis of large genomic regions that are inaccessible to conventional Transformer frameworks. This property makes it particularly well-suited for mitochondrial genomics, where associations between local motifs and distal regulatory elements may be critical in defining functional outcomes. In the present study, we sought to explore whether HyenaDNA can be employed to differentiate between Crabtree-positive and Crabtree-negative yeast strains using only mitochondrial genome sequences. Our approach involved extracting raw prediction values generated by the model and subjecting them to downstream unsupervised and supervised analyses, including clustering and classification. Through this strategy, we aim to uncover biologically meaningful patterns embedded in mitochondrial DNA, circumventing the limitations of classical bioinformatics pipelines while enabling prediction of metabolic phenotype in novel or incomplete genomic data. This integration of deep learning with comparative mitochondrial genomics provides a scalable and potentially generalizable framework for resolving complex biological phenomena without reliance on exhaustive experimental pipelines.

Recent studies have demonstrated that expression levels of some nuclear genes, such as PGl1 (Phosphoglucose isomerase), PDC1/5/6 (Pyruvate Decarboxylase), and NDE1/2 (NADH dehydrogenase) are responsible for the Crabtree effect [12]. Nevertheless, the potential contribution of the mitochondrial genome to this phenomenon remains unexplored and represents a significant gap in our current understanding. Although numerous wet-lab and classical bioinformatics approaches have been undertaken to elucidate the molecular basis of the Crabtree effect, to the best of our knowledge, no prior study has employed machine learning or deep learning methodologies for this specific predictive task.

2   Methods

2.1   Data Extraction and Pre-processing

Mitochondrial genome sequences were collected for 64 yeast strains from NCBI [3]. This dataset consisted of 34 Crabtree-positive and 30 Crabtree-negative representative sequences in FASTA format.

The NCBI ID's corresponding to Crabtree positive samples are:

NC_001224.1, NC_001326.1, NC_003920.1, NC_005253.2, NC_005789.1, NC_006626.1, NC_006971.1, NC_006972.1, NC_009638.1, NC_011133.1, NC_012145.1, NC_013147.1, NC_013830.1, NC_014693.1, NC_016756.1, NC_018044.1, NC_018046.1, NC_018056.1, NC_022162.1, NC_022172.1, NC_022174.1, NC_027458.1, NC_031185.1, NC_031511.1, NC_031512.1, NC_031513.1, NC_031514.1, NC_031515.1, NC_036375.1, NC_036377.1, NC_036378.1, NW_017264706.1, NW_023500906.1, NW_024066106.1

The NCBI ID's corresponding to Crabtree negative samples are:

NC_004918.1, NC_006077.1, NC_010166.1, NC_012619.1, NC_012620.1, NC_012621.1, NC_013145.2, NC_015814.1, NC_022151.1, NC_022152.1, NC_022153.1, NC_022158.1, NC_022160.1, NC_022161.1, NC_022165.1, NC_022170.1, NC_022173.1, NC_022176.1, NC_022434.1, NC_022435.1, NC_025331.1, NC_027433.1, NC_027457.1, NC_029458.1, NC_031184.1, NC_036376.1, NC_036379.1, NC_036380.1, NC_037730.1, NC_063596.1

2.2   Model Development and Prediction

Three distinct experiments were designed to investigate whether Machine learning models could be trained to distinguish between Crabtree-positive and Crabtree-negative yeast strains using their mitochondrial genomes.

1. Classical ML models using k-mers : Sequences were broken into k-mers, followed by the generation of a count matrix that could be passed directly to classification models.
2. Probing with the HyenaDNA model: Pre-trained HyenaDNA model was used directly to obtain embeddings that could be used for classification after a series of downstream processes.
3. Fine-tuning with the HyenaDNA model : The HyenaDNA model architecture was fine-tuned on the yeast dataset to adapt it specifically for binary classification.

Experiment 1: Classical ML Models Using k-Mers. As a preliminary experiment, we explored whether the frequency distribution of short DNA segments (k-mers) within mitochondrial sequences could provide predictive features for Crabtree phenotype classification. Each DNA sequence was segmented into overlapping 6-mers, ensuring that every possible short motif was represented in the dataset. We applied bag-of-words approach to obtain the representation vector for each sequence. The CountVectorizer function present in the scikit-learn [10] library is used for this purpose. The representation, capturing the unique compositional fingerprint of each mitochondrial genome, was provided as input to five machine learning algorithms : logistic regression, support vector classifier, random forest classifier, XGBoost, k-nearest neighbors. The ML models were trained using the 5-fold cross-validation technique to ensure model generalizability. This experiment aimed to determine whether classical machine learning models could distinguish Crabtree phenotypes based exclusively on motif frequency distributions, shedding light on the extent to which local sequence features contribute to the metabolic fate of yeast. The entire workflow of Experiment 1 has been summarised in Fig. 1.

Experiment 2 : Probing with the HyenaDNA Model. For the second approach, the HyenaDNA architecture was set up by defining the Hyena operator and a multi-layer perceptron (MLP) layer, which were then combined into

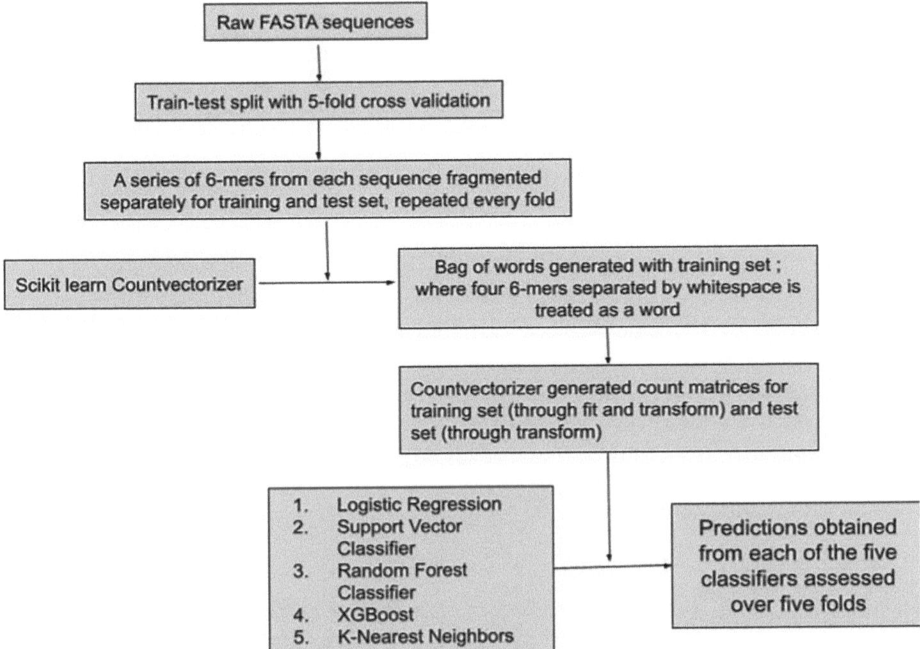

Fig. 1. Experiment 1 - Classical ML models using k-mers: The proposed model development workflow for mitochondrial genome prediction using k-mers.

repeated blocks forming the model backbone. The longest mitochondrial genome length observed in the dataset was 107,123 base pairs. In order to ensure that no genomic information was lost due to length restrictions or trimming, a HyenaDNA variant capable of handling longer input size "hyenadna-medium-160k-seqlen" was selected, allowing sequence lengths up to 160 kilobases to be processed without loss of context. Each genome was then prepared for model input through tokenization at single nucleotide resolution. The HyenaDNA built-in tokenizer was used with the padding parameter set to "right", thereby ensuring consistent input lengths for model consumption. Sequences were tokenized into the canonical nucleotides (A, T, G, C) and subsequently converted to tensors using PyTorch [9] version 2.8.0. This pre-processing pipeline resulted in tensors that could be used as direct input to the HyenaDNA model. The model outputs consisted of context-aware, 256-dimensional vector embeddings for each nucleotide position. Importantly, these embeddings capture not only the local identity of nucleotides but also their positional and relational context with respect to other nucleotides in the sequence, meaning that nucleotides situated in analogous motifs across different sequences tended to exhibit similar embedding representations. Such embeddings offered a biologically meaningful representation space suitable for classification and pattern-prediction tasks. Using this configuration, model outputs were obtained as 256-dimensional embeddings for every nucleotide across all 64 genomes. The two most commonly used methods to handle such higher dimensional data structures are index-wise Mean Pooling and Max Pooling. Both these techniques carry a high risk of causing loss of contextual significance. To cope with this problem and capture long range dependencies, we introduced a similarity based embedding vector aggregation technique. The idea behind this technique we refer to as "Sim Pooling" (similarity based pooling) is :

1. To cluster the embeddings into a certain number of structurally and functionally diverse groups.
2. To compare individual nucleotides of all sequences with the representative vectors of each of these groups and find out which of the groups does that nucleotide belong to.
3. To generate a "count-matrix" such that the rows represent individual sequences, columns represent clusters and the value at $m \times n$ position represents the number of nucleotides in the mth sequence that belong to the nth cluster in chronological order.
4. This helps us keep track of the distribution of nucleotides and their respective contribution in prediction while preserving full contextual information.

To achieve this, K-Means Clustering was used and 256 potentially analogous groups were obtained. The algorithm was set to perform 10 independent runs each with 300 iterations in order to enhance convergence stability. Cluster centroids from this process were interpreted as representative encoding vectors for the 256 distinct groups of functionally diverse nucleotides. Each nucleotide was then assigned to its nearest centroid via Euclidean distance, enabling the construction of a count matrix in which rows represented sequences and columns represented cluster centroids. This matrix effectively captured the distribution of nucleotides across functional embedding groups and was jointly considered with strain labels as input features for predictive modeling. Five classical machine learning models were developed—logistic regression, support vector classifier, random forest classifier, XGBoost and k-nearest neighbors. Cross-validation with five folds was employed to evaluate predictive robustness (Algorithm 1). A flowchart of the probing process has been illustrated in Fig. 2.

Experiment 3 : Fine-Tuning the HyenaDNA Model. In the third approach, the model was re-trained to adapt to our yeast mitochondrial genome dataset. The dataset was partitioned such that 50% of sequences served as the training set, 15% of the remaining as validation, and 85% as the test set. Sequences were tokenized as before but additionally padded according to the maximum sequence length within each set, again avoiding trimming to preserve positional information. For binary classification, a new head was created on top of the HyenaDNA backbone. The backbone itself was unfrozen, enabling full fine-tuning of its parameters. Training was performed using the Adam optimizer with a learning rate of 1×10^{-5}. The model was trained for 10 epochs with batches of size 3, and performance was measured over both training and validation sets using accuracy and cross-entropy loss. Fine-tuning allowed embeddings

---

Algorithm 1 Probing with the HyenaDNA model

Require: $S = \{s_1, \ldots, s_N\}$ (DNA sequences), $Y = \{y_1, \ldots, y_N\}$ (labels $\in \{0,1\}$)
Ensure: Classification metrics $\mu \pm \sigma$ for each model
1: **Define:** L = sequence length, N = number of sequences, T = number of tokens across all sequences, V = HyenaDNA backbone size, E = embedding vectors, C = cluster centroids, C' = number of centroids, X = count matrix, i = sequence index, j = token index per sequence, k = centroid index
2: **Embedding Extraction:**
3: **for** each $s \in S$ **do**
4:     tokens $\leftarrow$ Tokenize(s)
5:     $E \leftarrow$ HyenaDNA(tokens) // $E \in \mathbb{R}^{L \times V}$
6: **end for**
7: **Sim Pooling:**
8: $E_{\text{pool}} \leftarrow$ Concatenate($E_1, E_2, \ldots, E_N$) // $\mathbb{R}^{T \times V}$
9: $C \leftarrow$ KMeans($E_{\text{pool}}, \text{n\_clusters} = V, \text{n\_init} = 10, \text{max\_iter} = 300$) // $C \in \mathbb{R}^{C' \times V}$
10: $X_{ik} = 0$ // $X \in \mathbb{R}^{N \times C'}$
11: **for** $i = 1$ to N **do**
12:     **for** $j = 1$ to L_i **do**
13:         $k \leftarrow \arg\min_k \|E_{ij} - C_k\|^2$
14:         $X_{ik} + = 1$
15:     **end for**
16: **end for**
17: **Model Evaluation:**
18: **for** model $\in \{\text{LR}, \text{SVC}, \text{RF}, \text{XGB}, \text{KNN}\}$ **do**
19:     $scores \leftarrow [\,]$
20:     **for** fold $= 1$ to 5 **do**
21:         $(X_{\text{train}}, X_{\text{test}}, Y_{\text{train}}, Y_{\text{test}}) \leftarrow$ Split(X, Y)
22:         model.train($X_{\text{train}}, Y_{\text{train}}$)
23:         $Y_{\text{pred}} \leftarrow$ model.predict(X_{test})
24:         $scores$.append(score($Y_{\text{test}}, Y_{\text{pred}}$))
25:     **end for**
26:     Output: model, mean($scores$) $\pm$ std($scores$)
27: **end for**

---

to become explicitly aligned with the target task of distinguishing Crabtree-positive from Crabtree-negative strains. After training, embeddings were again extracted, subjected to Sim Pooling and a count matrix was obtained as output. The same five classifiers were employed as above and assessed via five-fold cross-validation (Algorithm 2).

Figure 3 explains the entire series of processes involved in model fine-tuning and prediction.

2.3 Model Evaluation

The predictive results from all three experiments were systematically compared. Primary evaluation was conducted by measuring the mean F1-score and standard deviation across 5-fold cross-validation. This ensured robust estimation

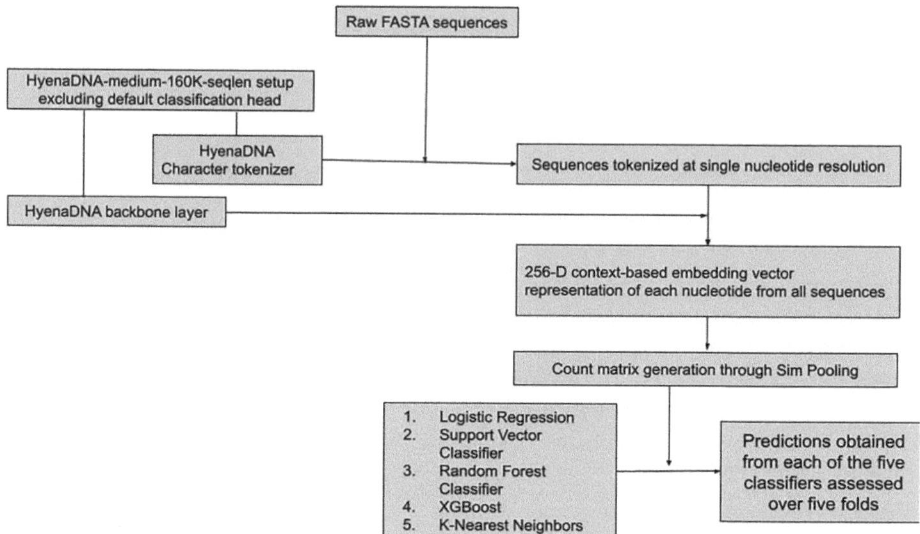

Fig. 2. Experiment 2 - Probing with the HyenaDNA model: the workflow illustrating the proposed prediction model. The representation vectors obtained from the pre-trained HyenaDNA model were used for the downstream prediction model development.

of model performance and variability across different data splits. For the best performing model from each approach, sensitivity, specificity and support was recorded. A bar graph was plotted to compare the performance of the three best classification models (the best performing model from each experiment in terms of highest and most consistent F1-score) in terms of accuracy, F1-score, AUC score, sensitivity, specificity from the best predicted folds. This visualization enabled a direct comparison between the three strategies. By comparing models across these diverse measures, we sought to determine whether fine-tuning offered meaningful gains over embeddings derived solely from the pre-trained model and to identify which classifier best exploited the embedding space for robust phenotype prediction. This comprehensive evaluation framework not only enabled assessment of methodological validity but also highlighted the potential of long-context neural representations for uncovering biologically meaningful distinctive features in mitochondrial genomes.

3   Results

The predictive performances of the three approaches were compared across five classification algorithms. Differences in mean F1-scores and their standard deviations highlight the limitations of the kmer-based count-matrix, base embeddings and the improvements gained after fine-tuning.

Algorithm 2 Fine-tuning the HyenaDNA model

Require: $S = \{s_1, \ldots, s_N\}$ (DNA sequences), $Y = \{y_1, \ldots, y_N\}$ (labels $\in \{0,1\}$)
Ensure: Classification metrics $\mu \pm \sigma$ for each model
1: **Define:** L = sequence length, N = number of sequences, T = number of tokens across all sequences, V = HyenaDNA backbone size, E = embedding vectors, C = cluster centroids, C' = number of centroids, X = count matrix, i = sequence index, j = token index per sequence, k = centroid index
2: **Fine-tuning:**
3:    $\text{Model}_{FT} \leftarrow \text{HyenaDNA}() + \text{CustomClassificationHead}()$
4:    $S_{\text{train}}, S_{\text{val}}, S_{\text{test}} \leftarrow \text{Split}(S)$
5:    **for** epoch = 1 to 10 **do**
6:        Train Model_{FT} on S_{train} using CrossEntropy loss
7:    **end for**
8: **Embedding & Sim Pooling:**
9:    $E_{\text{test}} \leftarrow \text{Model}_{FT}(S_{\text{test}})$ // $E_{\text{test}} \in \mathbb{R}^{L \times V}$
10:   $E_{\text{pool}} \leftarrow \text{Concatenate}(E_{\text{test}})$ // $\mathbb{R}^{T \times V}$
11:   $C \leftarrow \text{KMeans}(E_{\text{pool}}, \text{n\_clusters} = V, \text{n\_init} = 10, \text{max\_iter} = 300)$ // $C \in \mathbb{R}^{C' \times V}$
12:   $X_{ik} = 0$ // $X \in \mathbb{R}^{N \times C'}$
13:   **for** $i = 1$ to N **do**
14:       **for** $j = 1$ to L_i **do**
15:           $k \leftarrow \arg\min_k \|E_{ij} - C_k\|^2$
16:           $X_{ik} += 1$
17:       **end for**
18:   **end for**
19: **Model Evaluation:**
20:   **for** model $\in \{\text{LR}, \text{SVC}, \text{RF}, \text{XGB}, \text{KNN}\}$ **do**
21:       $scores \leftarrow [\,]$
22:       **for** fold = 1 to 5 **do**
23:           $(X_{\text{train}}, X_{\text{test}}, Y_{\text{train}}, Y_{\text{test}}) \leftarrow \text{Split}(X, Y)$
24:           $\text{model.train}(X_{\text{train}}, Y_{\text{train}})$
25:           $Y_{\text{pred}} \leftarrow \text{model.predict}(X_{\text{test}})$
26:           $scores.\text{append}(\text{score}(Y_{\text{test}}, Y_{\text{pred}}))$
27:       **end for**
28:       Output: model, $\text{mean}(scores) \pm \text{std}(scores)$
29:   **end for**

3.1   Experiment 1 : Classical ML Models Using k-Mers

The k-mer count matrix was used to predict Crabtree phenotype for yeast strains. Of the five classifiers tested, logistic regression was selected as the best-performing model for its consistently high F1-score across folds. Logistic regression achieved a mean F1-score of 0.71 (± 0.04), indicating moderate performance in capturing predictive signals from motif distributions. Other models—support vector classifier, random forest, XGBoost, and k-nearest neighbors—yielded mean F1-scores of 0.58 (± 0.12), 0.70 (± 0.06), 0.63 (± 0.12), and 0.65 (± 0.10), respectively. Logistic regression on the best fold showed sensitivity of 0.71 and specificity of 0.8 reflecting moderate discriminative power regarding

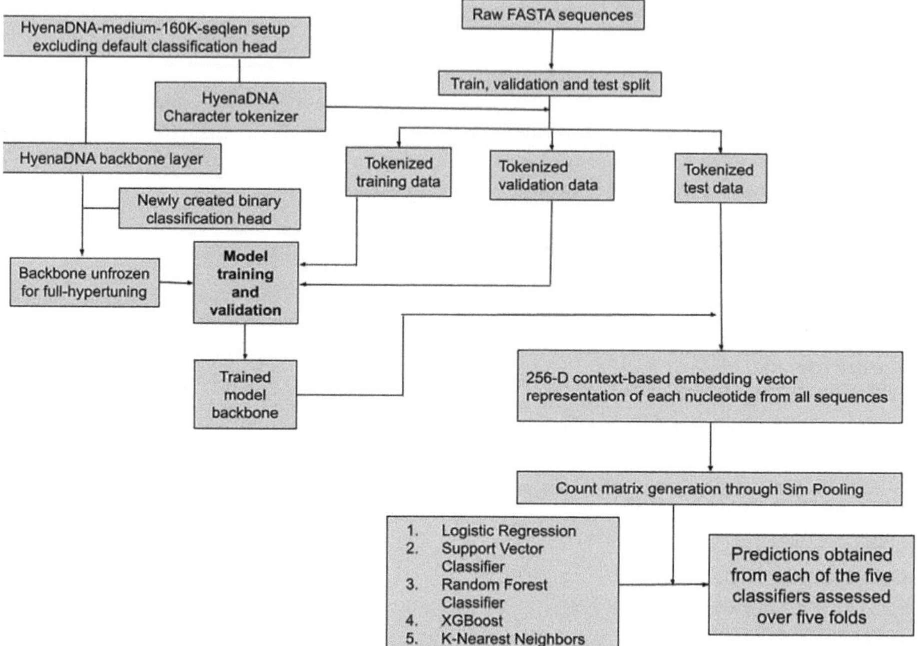

Fig. 3. Experiment 3 - Fine-tuning the HyenaDNA model: The workflow illustrating prediction model development by fine-tuning the HyenaDNA model. The representation vectors obtained from the fine-tuned HyenaDNA model were used for the downstream prediction model development.

class boundaries. The class-specific metrics reveal support of 5 for the negative class (class 0), while positive class predictions (class 1) support of 7. These results suggest that the model is sensitive to even minor class imbalances in the dataset, with classifiers heavily favoring the more prevalent class during prediction.

3.2   Experiment 2 : Probing with the HyenaDNA

Nucleotide-level embeddings from the pre-trained HyenaDNA model formed the basis of prediction. The Support Vector Classifier was chosen for its relatively high F1-score and consistency across cross-validation schemes. Here, SVC achieved a mean F1-score of 0.69 ($\pm$0.05), matching the best results from the k-mer approach. Logistic regression scored 0.56 ($\pm$0.06), random forest 0.68 ($\pm$0.17), XGBoost 0.69 ($\pm$0.05), and k-nearest neighbors 0.69 ($\pm$0.18). For the best predicted fold of SVC, sensitivity remained at 1 and specificity at 0. Detailed class-wise comparison for SVC revealed support of 5 and 8 for the negative and positive classes respectively. Inability to identify negative classes has been a persistent problem for both k-mer based and probing based approaches.

3.3   Experiment 3 : Fine-Tuning the HyenaDNA Model

Fine-tuning the HyenaDNA model substantially improved performance across classifiers. Logistic regression reached a mean F1-score of 0.79 (±0.04), showing that even simple linear models could now separate classes more effectively. Random Forest and KNN produced mean F1-scores of 0.72 (±0.15) and 0.68 (±0.10) respectively, while XGBoost yielded 0.68 (±0.19). SVC achieved the highest mean F1-score of 0.81 (±0.11), but logistic regression was considered the most reliable due to its consistency across folds. For the best predicted fold, logistic regression achieved precision 1.0, recall 0.67, F1-score 0.8 (support=3) for Crabtree-negative predictions, and precision 0.75, recall 1.0, F1-score 0.86 (support=3) for Crabtree-positive predictions. Unlike the base model, both classes were correctly identified with comparable accuracy. The AUROC increased to 1.0, specificity improved to 0.75 with a sensitivity of 1.0 and accuracy rose to 0.83. The confusion matrix showed reduced misclassification, particularly for Crabtree-negative strains, indicating that fine-tuning allowed the model to handle class imbalance and achieve balanced discrimination between positive and negative cases. Table 1 captures the difference in performance of the five classifiers used in Experiment 3. The comparison results of all the three experiments and all the metrics are shown in Fig. 4.

Table 1. The classical machine learning models performance in distinguishing Crabtree-positive and Crabtree-negative employing fine-tuned HyenaDNA embeddings. The values reported are mean and standard deviation across 5-folds.

Model	Precision	Recall	F1 score	Accuracy	AUROC
Logistic Regression	0.72 (±0.17)	0.93 (±0.13)	0.79 (±0.04)	0.73 (±0.11)	0.90 (±0.13)
SVM	0.87 (±0.17)	0.83 (±0.21)	0.81 (±0.11)	0.81 (±0.13)	0.84 (±0.11)
Random Forest	0.70 (±0.19)	0.77 (±0.20)	0.72 (±0.15)	0.70 (±0.16)	0.68 (±0.19)
XGBoost	0.77 (±0.24)	0.70 (±0.27)	0.68 (±0.19)	0.71 (±0.13)	0.83 (±0.11)
K-Nearest Neighbor	0.53 (±0.10)	1.00 (±0.00)	0.68 (±0.10)	0.53 (±0.10)	0.73 (±0.20)

The relative performance of all five classifiers from Experiment 3 is shown in Fig. 5.

4   Discussion

This study demonstrates that large-scale genomic language models such as HyenaDNA can encode biologically meaningful signals in the mitochondrial genome that enable computational prediction of the Crabtree phenotype in yeast. Our results reveal both the potential and limitations of using pre-trained representations and highlight the necessity of task-specific fine-tuning to achieve robust predictive performance. A comparative analysis across the three experiments

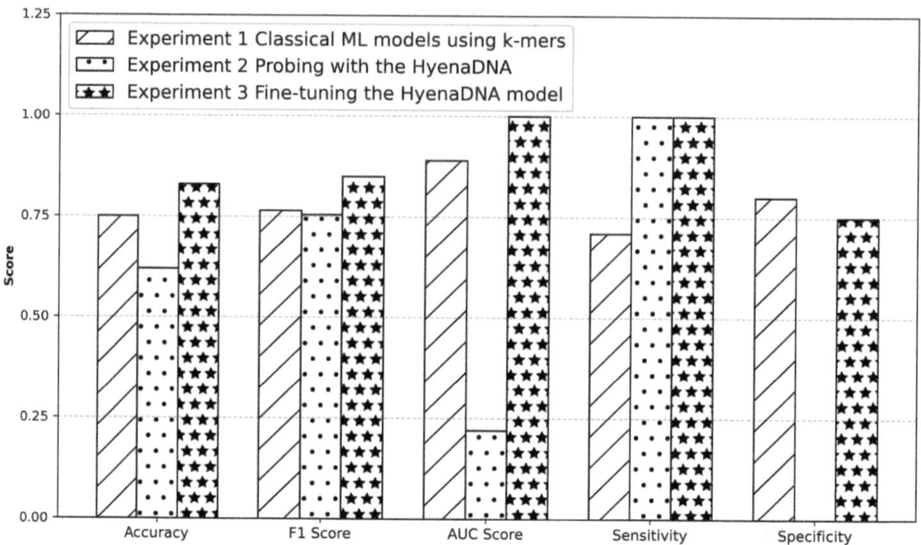

Fig. 4. Comparison of evaluation metrics across three different experiments for the best performing model in 5-folds. The Experiment 3 - Fine-tuning the HyenaDNA model performed consistently better on all metrics.

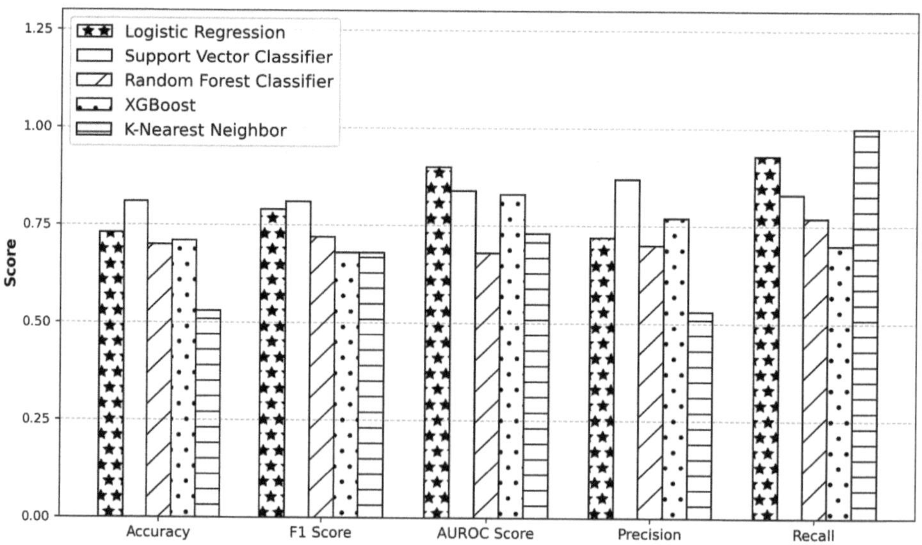

Fig. 5. The performance comparison of five ML models from Experiment 3 across all the evaluation metrics. Among all the ML models, the Logistic Regression's F1-score performance was more robust across all 5-folds.

shows that both k-mer-based features and pre-trained HyenaDNA embeddings did not contain sufficient discriminatory power between the Crabtree-positive and Crabtree-negative classes. In the case of the classical ML approach utilizing k-mers, the representation was not rich enough to discriminate between two classes. Both approaches struggled with class imbalance with the former approach predicting more false negative results and the later consistently failing to identify Crabtree-negative strains. The misclassification of the positive class in Experiments 1 and negative class in Experiment 2 underscores the limitation of relying solely on base k-mer distributions or static embeddings.

In contrast, Experiment 3 demonstrates that fine-tuning the pre-trained model with our task specific dataset allowed the model to learn robust representations leading to better performance. Figure 5 reveals that the KNN algorithm still faces challenges in negative-class prediction and although SVC seems to perform better than the rest, the results are not consistent across the folds. Predictions from logistic regression improved significantly after fine-tuning, achieving stable performance across folds and reliably identifying both classes. Unlike the pre-trained embeddings, the fine-tuned model reached the highest mean F1-score (0.79) and, importantly, delivered balanced discrimination between positive and negative classes, with sensitivity of 1.0 and specificity of 0.75. These findings indicate that while pre-trained genomic language models provide a strong foundation, task-specific adaptation is critical for phenotype-level classification. The fine-tuned HyenaDNA model illustrates how targeted optimization can transform general-purpose genomic representations into highly dependable predictive tools for mitochondrial sequence analysis. This improvement can be understood by noting that although conserved mitochondrial motifs exist across eukaryotes, some human-specific genomic patterns are not directly relevant to yeast metabolism and can act as a source of representational "noise." By retraining on yeast-specific data, the model suppressed these irrelevant features, thereby sharpening the representations toward motifs and relationships specifically predictive of yeast metabolic phenotypes.

A key challenge in this work lies in the relatively small dataset. Only 64 strains were analyzed, in contrast to the estimated >3,500 yeast species [4] currently described (and many more predicted to exist). Nevertheless, our findings indicate that mitochondrial sequences contain hidden patterns strongly associated with the Crabtree effect. This observation strengthens the argument that the mitochondrial genome holds considerable explanatory power regarding the metabolic strategy of yeast. Whether these patterns are sufficient as a stand-alone predictor of phenotype remains debatable. However, the consistently strong classification performance, particularly with fine-tuned models, suggests that mitochondrial sequence composition exerts a significant influence on the selection of fermentative or respiratory metabolic pathways. Importantly, these findings raise the immediate question of what exact features within mitochondrial DNA might influence the observed distinctions. Elucidating these genomic features will require explainability-driven methods capable of backtracing through the clustering and count-matrix generation processes to find out the distribution of nucleotides that could possibly be mutations, SNPs (Single Nucleotide Polymorphisms) or parts of functional domains causing the variation in metabolic fate of yeasts. Developing interpretability pipelines to link embeddings back to exact genomic loci will be an essential future step and could potentially uncover molecular patterns previously inaccessible through classical wet-lab or annotation-based bioinformatics approaches.

Despite these limitations, our approach introduces a computational paradigm with clear advantages. Compared to traditional experimental analyses, which are time-consuming, resource-intensive, and not easily scalable, this deep learning framework offers a faster, cost-effective alternative capable of generalizing across unannotated and novel sequences. The technological advancements in Genomic Language Models, such as HyenaDNA, opens up the possibility of building deep learning models using fine-tuning approach to alleviate the challenges of smaller datasets. This is validated from our study. Moreover, beyond predictive classification, the possibility of unveiling genomic determinants of the Crabtree effect carries significant scientific, social, and economic impacts. Rapid computational assessment of Crabtree status would facilitate strain selection and engineering strategies across diverse biotechnological processes, including biofuel production, pharmaceutical synthesis, and food fermentation industries.

5 Conclusion

Our study demonstrates that the mitochondrial genome of yeast harbors characteristic sequence patterns strongly associated with the Crabtree effect. While these features were not easily discernible through classical methods, the use of a genomic language model enabled their detection and effective use in phenotype prediction. Even within a data-limited setting of 64 strains, our fine-tuned HyenaDNA model achieved significant accuracy, specificity, and sensitivity, demonstrating that mitochondrial genomic sequences are powerful predictors of metabolic strategy. These findings suggest that mitochondrial sequence composition plays a direct role in guiding the fermentative or respiratory pathways of yeast. Although the precise sequence features responsible for this distinction remain to be elucidated, our results highlight the feasibility of using deep learning frameworks not only for cost-efficient and rapid phenotype prediction but also for uncovering previously hidden genomic determinants of complex cellular behaviors. With further interpretability-focused work, this approach has the potential to pinpoint the molecular signatures that underlie the Crabtree effect. Ultimately, such discoveries could advance both fundamental understanding of eukaryotic metabolism and industrial applications of yeast, offering wide-reaching benefits to science, society, and industry alike.

Acknowledgements. The authors gratefully acknowledge the support received from the DST-INSPIRE Faculty Fellowship (RS) and the DST-ANRF Core Research Grant (RS). We also thank the Institute of Bioinformatics and Applied Biotechnology (IBAB) and the Department of IT-BT, Government of Karnataka, for their institutional and infrastructural support (RS, SSR, NR).

References

1. Ahmad, M., Wolberg, A., Kahwaji, C.I.: Biochemistry, electron transport chain. In: StatPearls [Internet]. Treasure Island (FL): StatPearls Publishing (2025). https://www.ncbi.nlm.nih.gov/books/NBK526105/
2. Benegas, G., Ye, C., Albors, C., Li, J.C., Song, Y.S.: Genomic language models: opportunities and challenges. Trends Genet. **41**(4), 286–302 (2025). https://doi.org/10.1016/j.tig.2024.11.013
3. Benson, D.A., Karsch-Mizrachi, I., Lipman, D.J., Ostell, J., Sayers, E.W.: Genbank. Nucleic acids research **38(Database issue)**, D46–D51 (2010). https://doi.org/10.1093/nar/gkp1024
4. Boekhout, T., et al.: Trends in yeast diversity discovery. Fungal Diversity , 1–47 (2021). https://doi.org/10.1007/s13225-021-00494-6
5. Consens, M.E., et al.: Transformers and genome language models. Nat. Mach. Intell. **7**, 346–362 (2025). https://doi.org/10.1038/s42256-025-01007-9
6. Dalla-Torre, H., et al.: Nucleotide transformer: building and evaluating robust foundation models for human genomics. Nat. Methods **22**, 287–297 (2025). https://doi.org/10.1038/s41592-024-02523-z
7. Ji, Y., Zhou, Z., Liu, H., Davuluri, R.V.: Dnabert: pre-trained bidirectional encoder representations from transformers model for DNA-language in genome. Bioinformatics **37**(15), 2112–2120 (2021). https://doi.org/10.1093/bioinformatics/btab083
8. Nguyen, E., et al.: Hyenadna: long-range genomic sequence modeling at single nucleotide resolution. In: Proceedings of the 37th International Conference on Neural Information Processing Systems (NeurIPS). NIPS '23, vol. 1872, pp. 43177–43201. Curran Associates Inc. (2023)
9. Paszke, A., et al.: Pytorch: an imperative style, high-performance deep learning library. In: Proceedings of the 33rd International Conference on Neural Information Processing Systems (NeurIPS). NIPS '19, vol. 721, pp. 8026–8037. Curran Associates Inc. (2019)
10. Pedregosa, F., et al.: Scikit-learn: Machine learning in python. J. Mach. Learn. Res. **12**(85), 2825–2830 (2011). http://jmlr.org/papers/v12/pedregosa11a.html
11. RH, D.D.: The crabtree effect: a regulatory system in yeast. J. Gen. Microbiol. **44**(2), 149–156 (1966). https://doi.org/10.1099/00221287-44-2-149
12. Xiao, Z., et al.: Sucrose-driven carbon redox rebalancing eliminates the crabtree effect and boosts energy metabolism in yeast. Nat. Commun. **16**(5211) (2025). https://doi.org/10.1038/s41467-025-60578-8

Fusing Personality Profiles and Social Media Insights for Stress Detection

Rajendra Kumar Roul[1(✉)], Aarpit Kumar Roul[1], and Navpreet[2]

[1] Thapar Institute of Engineering and Technology, Patiala, Punjab, India
{raj.roul,aroul_be24}@thapar.edu
[2] Chitkara University Institute of Engineering and Technology, Chitkara University, Rajpura, Punjab, India
navpreet.4003@chitkara.edu.in

Abstract. Stress is the reality of ordinary day-to-day existence. Everyone experiences stress at some point of time in life. A limited amount of stress can help you increase your physical performance, motivation, and environmental reaction time, but stress can become a severe problem if left unchecked. Studies have shown that stress increases the likelihood of developing health problems like heart disease, anxiety disorders, depression, gastrointestinal issues, etc., and endangers human life. More and more people are stressed due to the fast-paced nature of modern society, and some are even willing to commit suicide. With the adverse effects of stress in mind and a lack of resources for early detection, the proposed approach is to create a model for stress detection using social media posts. The reason for using social media is that people post about their recent happenings on social media platforms, which can be used to represent their current and contemporary situation. Stress is inferred through a two-step process: personality traits are first estimated from a user's social media activity, after which these traits are integrated with linguistic cues to assess stress levels. Evaluation conducted on two widely adopted datasets demonstrates that the proposed method maintains strong reliability and outperforms comparable techniques. By fusing linguistic cues with personality-related attributes, the framework achieves notably improved stress identification across heterogeneous users and varying data conditions.

Keywords: Deep Learning · Machine Learning · Personality Detection · Social Media · Stress Detection

1 Introduction

Stress occurs when individuals perceive that their internal resources are insufficient to meet situational demands [1]. It reflects a coordinated physiological and psychological response to everyday pressures and has become a major concern, with nearly 74% of people reporting difficulty coping in the past year [2]. The factors that provoke this imbalance are termed *stressors* [3]. Research consistently links sustained stress to elevated health risks [4]. Estimates suggest that up to 90% of diseases may be influenced by stress[1], and prolonged exposure contributes to allostatic load [5], impairing

---

[1] Stress Management Resource: NASD Online.

B. Chatterjee et al. (Eds.): ICDCIT 2026, LNCS 16420, pp. 510–525, 2026.
https://doi.org/10.1007/978-3-032-16632-6_33

cardiovascular, immune, neuroendocrine, and metabolic systems. Stress has long been recognized as a widespread public health issue[2], and suicide frequently associated with chronic stress remains a leading cause of death in several age groups [6]. Globally, almost 800,000 people die by suicide each year[3].

Machine Learning (ML) and Deep Learning (DL) have become central to many areas of Artificial Intelligence [7] [8], and their growing ability to recognize subtle patterns has made them especially useful for identifying signs of stress from user data. Several works have attempted to detect mental health conditions using digital data. While William et al. [9] used BERT-based text representations to identify stress patterns, Li et al. [10] investigated how changes in Reddit postings reflect changes in users' mental states. Keystroke rhythms [11] and temporal microblogging patterns [12] are two behavioral signals linked to stress that have been studied by other researchers.

Despite increasing public attention to mental health, detecting stress at an early stage remains a complex task [13]. Physiological indicators such as hormonal changes, cardiovascular responses [14], eye-movement patterns, and skin conductance [15] provide reliable information [16], yet they typically rely on dedicated sensors or controlled laboratory settings. These practical constraints emphasize the need for computational methods capable of identifying stress from natural, real-time data streams without requiring specialized instrumentation [17]. Early stress detection is still a challenging task despite growing public awareness of mental health [13]. Although they usually rely on specialized sensors or controlled laboratory settings, physiological indicators like hormonal changes, cardiovascular responses [14], eye-movement patterns, and skin conductance [15] offer trustworthy information [16]. These real-world limitations highlight the need for computational techniques that can detect stress from natural, real-time data streams without the need for specialized equipment [12, 17], emphasizing that stress frequently leaves subtle indicators in routine digital activity. Even though personality is a major factor in how people express and manage stress, current computer models that primarily concentrate on language or auditory inputs frequently ignore personality.

The current study suggests a strategy that uses regular social media activity to identify stress in order to close this gap. People regularly post their everyday emotions, worries, and experiences online, creating a dynamic record of their mental health. The system seeks to detect early indicators of stress and enable prompt intervention by fusing linguistic features of posts with personality qualities deduced from long-term writing behavior.

1.1   Motivation

Many of the current social media-based stress prediction systems pay little attention to underlying psychological dispositions and instead depend heavily on text statistics and language cues. Ignoring these distinctions could lower model accuracy because personality influences both coping mechanisms and emotional expression. Instead of assuming

---

[2] http://www.stress.org/americas-1-health-problem/.
[3] https://ourworldindata.org/suicide.

consistent behavior across users, the suggested method combines deep brain text representations with personality assessments from the Myers-Briggs Type Indicator (MBTI) to enable the system to evaluate language cues in the context of stable psychological tendencies.

Furthermore, the model improves user-level prediction by substituting a discretized, mode-based aggregation mechanism for the straightforward average of post-wise probabilities. The approach reduces the impact of extreme values and produces more reliable user-level forecasts by transforming continuous probability into fixed ranges and determining the most common category. This combination of personality-aware modelling and improved aggregation contributes to stronger overall performance.

1.2   Contributions

The principal contributions of this work include:

- A single framework for detecting stress is proposed that combines linguistic characteristics from social media posts with psychological attributes.
- Short-term emotional and cognitive swings are captured by a context-sensitive assessment system that examines users' recent online material.
- An early stress recognition strategy that supports preventive intervention and reduces possible long-term psychological or physiological impacts is achieved by the proposed approach.
- Extensive experiments on two widely used datasets confirm the reliability and strong performance of the framework, showing consistent advantages over leading contemporary techniques.

1.3   Structure of the Paper

The structure of the paper is as follows: Sect. 2 presents the proposed methodology. Section 3 describes the experimental work and corresponding results. Finally, Sect. 4 provides the conclusion of the study with future enhancements.

2   Methodology

2.1   System Overview

The proposed system detects stress from social media posts by first aggregating a user's posts to predict MBTI-based personality features. In parallel, each preprocessed post is encoded using Global Vectors for Word Representation (GloVe) embeddings[4] and processed through an LSTM to extract textual features. GloVe embeddings is a widely used unsupervised learning algorithm designed to generate dense vector representations of words, also known as word embeddings, whereas Word2Vec embeddings are trained on large datasets and are effective at capturing nuanced semantic relationships. The personality and textual features are concatenated to form a unified representation, which

---

[4] https://cs-114.org/wp-content/uploads/2024/02/word2vec-glove.pdf.

is fed into a stress prediction model to estimate post-level stress probabilities. These probabilities are discretized into fixed-width buckets, mapped to bucket midpoints, and aggregated via a mode-based approach to derive a robust user-level stress probability. Algorithm 1 discuss the implementation detail of the proposed methodology.

2.2 Datasets Used in the Proposed Approach

The proposed model is validated on two datasets. Dataset-I, Myers-Briggs Type Indicator(MBTI) Personality Types 500 Dataset[5] was used for Personality prediction. Dataset-II, Suicide and Depression Detection (SDD)[6] was used for Stress prediction.

Justification for Using Two Distinct Datasets. In this work, Dataset-I (MBTI Personality Types 500) and Dataset-II (Reddit SuicideWatch and Depression Subreddits) serve complementary but distinct roles within the proposed pipeline. Dataset-I is exclusively used to train a personality prediction model that learns a mapping from free-form user text to MBTI type labels. The resulting personality encoder is then applied to Dataset-II to infer personality embeddings for users whose posts are labeled for stress-related content. These inferred embeddings are fused with textual features extracted directly from Dataset-II to enhance stress detection performance. Importantly, the two datasets do not contain overlapping participants, and no direct record-level linkage is assumed or required. This approach follows a transfer learning paradigm, where knowledge acquired from a source task (personality prediction) is leveraged to improve performance on a target task (stress detection) in a different domain. Such separation of data sources is widely adopted in NLP research, provided that the feature transfer occurs at the model level and domain adaptation considerations are addressed. Empirical evaluation in Sect. 3 compares models with and without personality embeddings to quantify the benefit of this cross-dataset transfer. A detailed discussion of these two datasets is in the following Sect. 2.3.

2.3 Datasets Description

We conducted experiments using two distinct datasets to evaluate the proposed methodology. These datasets were employed for personality prediction and text-based stress detection, respectively.

I. **MBTI Personality Types 500 Dataset:** The first dataset contains data for developing the personality identification model, which forms a crucial component of the overall stress detection framework described in the methodology. The dataset is based on the MBTI, an introspective self-report questionnaire designed to identify psychological preferences (cognitive functions) in how individuals perceive the world and make decisions. It comprises approximately 106,000 records organized into two columns: the MBTI personality type and the corresponding user-generated text.

---

[5] https://www.kaggle.com/datasets/zeyadkhalid/mbti-personality-types-500-dataset.

[6] https://www.kaggle.com/datasets/nikhileswarkomati/suicide-watch.

II. **Reddit SuicideWatch and Depression Subreddits Dataset:** The second dataset consists of posts collected from the *SuicideWatch* and *Depression* subreddits on the Reddit platform. Data was gathered using the Pushshift API, covering all posts submitted to *SuicideWatch* from its inception on December 16, 2008, to January 2, 2021, and posts to the *Depression* subreddit from January 1, 2009, to January 2, 2021. This dataset was used to train and evaluate the text-based stress detection model.

2.4 Preprocessing of Data

Each collected post from the dataset is preprocessed by removing stopwords and hyperlinks, and then the text of the post is set to lowercase letters. Finally, the numerical representation of the text is created using TF-IDF. Equation 1 shows a set of posts, P. Now, after preprocessing, each post has a numerical representation as shown in Table 1 where $P_i, i \in [1, n]$ represents the post made by the user on social media and $t_j, j \in [1, m]$ represents a word of the respective post.

$$P = P_1 \ P_2 \ , \cdots , \ P_n \tag{1}$$

where P_1 is the most recent posts, P_n is the oldest post made by the user.

Table 1. Term-post matrix of P

	P_1	P_2	P_3	$\cdots$	P_n
t_1	t_{11}	t_{12}	t_{13}	$\cdots$	t_{1n}
t_2	t_{21}	t_{22}	t_{23}	$\cdots$	t_{2n}
t_3	t_{31}	t_{32}	t_{33}	$\cdots$	t_{3n}
$\vdots$	$\vdots$	$\vdots$	$\vdots$	$\ddots$	$\vdots$
t_m	t_{m1}	t_{m2}	t_{m3}	$\cdots$	t_{mn}

2.5 Personality Types Extraction

The primary objective is to estimate the probability that the user is stressed, given $\mathcal{P}$, which is illustrated in Eq. 2.

$$s_u = \text{StressModel}(\mathcal{P}) \tag{2}$$

where $s_u \in [0, 1]$ is the predicted stress probability. Since personality traits significantly influence stress responses, we integrate personality features into the pipeline. The MBTI-based *Personality Model*, trained on a labeled personality dataset, predicts the MBTI type for each user. Instead of applying the model to each post separately, which may yield inconsistent results, it is concatenated all posts into a single aggregated text as shown in Eq. 3:

$$c_u = \text{concatenatePosts}(\mathcal{P}) \tag{3}$$

This aggregated text c_u is passed to the personality prediction model as shown in Eq. 4:

$$m_u = \text{PersonalityModel}(c_u) \tag{4}$$

where $m_u \in \mathbb{M}$ is the predicted MBTI type, and $\mathbb{M}$ is the set of 15 categories available in Dataset-I:

$$\mathbb{M} = \{\text{ISTJ}, \text{ISFJ}, \dots, \text{ENTP}, \text{ENTJ}\}.$$

Encoding MBTI Personality Into Feature Space: The MBTI label m_u is transformed into a dense numerical representation:

$$\mathbf{f}_{\text{pers}} = \phi(m_u) \tag{5}$$

where $\phi : \mathbb{M} \to \mathbb{R}^d$ maps each MBTI type to a d-dimensional vector. A learned embedding strategy is adopted to capture semantic relationships between MBTI categories, enabling better integration with textual features.

2.6   Text Feature Extraction

Textual features are derived directly from the preprocessed posts:

$$\mathcal{P}_{\text{clean}} = \{\mathbf{x}_1, \mathbf{x}_2, \dots, \mathbf{x}_n\}$$

where each $\mathbf{x}_i$ is a vector representation (using GloVe) of the ith post. These are passed to a GloVe embedding layer followed by an LSTM network to capture semantic and contextual dependencies:

$$\mathbf{f}_{\text{text}} = \text{TextFeaturesExtractor}(\mathcal{P}_{\text{clean}}) \tag{6}$$

where $\mathbf{f}_{\text{text}} \in \mathbb{R}^k$ encodes linguistic and syntactic cues.

2.7   Feature Fusion and Stress Prediction:

The extracted personality vector $\mathbf{f}_{\text{pers}}$ from Eq. 5 and the text vector $\mathbf{f}_{\text{text}}$ from Eq. 6 are concatenated to generate Eq. 7:

$$\mathbf{f}_{\text{combined}} = [\,\mathbf{f}_{\text{text}} \parallel \mathbf{f}_{\text{pers}}\,] \tag{7}$$

where '$\parallel$' denotes vector concatenation.

The combined feature vector $\mathbf{f}_{\text{combined}}$ is then fed into the stress prediction model ((MLP with sigmoid activation is for this purpose) as shown in Eq. 8.

$$s_u = \text{StressPrediction}(\mathbf{f}_{\text{combined}}) \tag{8}$$

producing the final probability $s_u \in [0, 1]$ that the user is experiencing stress, which is later used in the bucketing and mode aggregation step (Sect. 2.8) to compute the user-level stress probability. This integrated approach allows for a richer representation by fusing personality and linguistic cues, enabling more accurate stress detection compared to text-only or personality-only models.

2.8   Aggregation to Compute User-Level Stress Probability

After calculating the stress probability for each individual post made by a user, we need to aggregate these values to obtain a *user-level stress probability*. Instead of using the mean as our measure of central tendency, which is sensitive to outliers and can skew results, we use the mode, which focuses on the most frequently occurring value and is thus more robust against extreme values.Since the stress scores lie on a continuous scale between $[0, 1]$, they are first grouped into a set of uniform probability intervals (buckets). Each bucket represents a predefined subrange of probability values, and any probability that falls within that range is substituted with the corresponding bucket mean. This process converts the original continuous probabilities into a set of discrete intervals, allowing the values to be examined through a mode-based frequency analysis.

The final user-level probability is obtained by selecting the interval whose representative mean appears most frequently across all posts. This dominant bucket mean is used as the user's overall stress estimate, providing a stable summary of the user's stress pattern while reducing the impact of isolated or extreme values. The detailed computational steps are outlined in the following section.

i. Probability Bucketing for Mode Calculation:
   To derive a stable and meaningful user-level stress estimate from several post-wise probability scores, a *probability discretization* process is performed before computing the mode. In this approach, each continuous probability value $p_i \in [0, 1]$ is mapped to one of a set of predefined intervals, converting the raw numeric values into discrete categories that are better suited for a mode-based aggregation. This transformation also diminishes the influence of atypical or extreme probability values. The bucket generation process is defined using Eq. 9:

$$\mathcal{B} = \text{formBuckets}(p_{\min}, p_{\max}, \Delta p) \tag{9}$$

   where:
   - $p_{\min}$: Lower bound of the probability range (typically 0)
   - $p_{\max}$: Upper bound of the probability range (typically 1)
   - Δp : Width of each probability bucket
   - $\mathcal{B}$: Set of bucket start points

   Explicitly, the set of bucket start points is given by Eq. 10.

$$\mathcal{B} = \{b_k \mid b_k = p_{\min} + (k - 1)\Delta p, \ k = 1, 2, \ldots, n_b\} \tag{10}$$

   where $n_b = \frac{p_{\max} - p_{\min}}{\Delta p}$ is the total number of buckets.
   Each post-level probability p_i is mapped to the bucket whose range it falls into. The representative value for each bucket, $\bar{b}_k$, is taken as the midpoint of the interval as shown in Eq. 11:

$$\bar{b}_k = b_k + \frac{\Delta p}{2} \tag{11}$$

   Finally, the user-level stress probability, P_u, is computed as the mode of the bucket means assigned to the user's posts (Eq. 12):

$$P_u = \text{mode}\left(\{\bar{b}_{k(i)} \mid i = 1, 2, \ldots, M_u\}\right) \tag{12}$$

where M_u is the total number of posts made by the user, and $k(i)$ is the index of the bucket containing p_i.

ii. Computing Mean Stress Probability:

The *Mean Stress Probability (MSP)* is obtained by mapping each continuous stress probability value to the midpoint of the bucket to which it belongs. Given an initial list of stress probabilities, $\mathbf{p} = [p_1, p_2, \ldots, p_n]$, where $p_i \in [0, 1]$ represents the stress probability for the ith post, each p_i is replaced by the corresponding bucket mean $\bar{b}_{k(i)}$, yielding a discretized list of probabilities. This process is formally expressed by Eq. 13:

$$MSP = \text{mapToBucketMeans}(\mathbf{p}, \mathcal{B}) \tag{13}$$

Here:

- $\mathbf{p} = [p_1, p_2, \ldots, p_n]$: Original list of post-level stress probabilities
- $\mathcal{B}$: Set of bucket start points as defined in Eq. 10
- $\bar{b}_{k(i)}$: Midpoint of the bucket containing p_i, computed from Eq. 11
- $MSP = [\bar{b}_{k(1)}, \bar{b}_{k(2)}, \ldots, \bar{b}_{k(n)}]$: Discretized stress probability list.

The replacement operation in Eq. 13 ensures that:

$$\forall\, p_i \in \mathbf{p}, \quad p_i \in [b_{k(i)}, b_{k(i)} + \Delta p) \implies MSP_i = \bar{b}_{k(i)} \tag{14}$$

This transformation (shown in Eq. 14) converts the continuous-valued probability vector $\mathbf{p}$.

iii. Computation of User-Level Stress Probability:

Let the discretized post-level stress probability vector be denoted as

$$MSP = [MSP_1, MSP_2, \ldots, MSP_{M_u}],$$

where M_u is the number of posts made by the user and each MSP_i corresponds to the midpoint $\bar{b}_{k(i)}$ of the probability bucket into which the ith post-level stress probability p_i falls. The *user-level stress probability* P_u is determined (shown in Eq. 15) as the statistical mode of the vector *MSP*:

$$P_u = \text{mode}(MSP) \tag{15}$$

where:

- P_u : represents the user-level stress probability computed as the mode of the *precomputed* discretized probability vector *MSP*, in contrast to Eq. 12 where P_u is obtained directly from bucket midpoints $\bar{b}_{k(i)}$ without explicitly storing the intermediate vector.
- *MSP* : discretized post-level stress probability vector as defined in Eq. 13.

Equivalently, the mode can be expressed in frequency maximization form as shown in Eq. 16.

$$P_u = \underset{x \in MSP}{\arg\max}\ \text{freq}(x) \tag{16}$$

where $\text{freq}(x)$ denotes the number of occurrences of the value x in the discretized Mean Stress Probability vector *MSP*. The resulting P_u serves as a robust and interpretable summary of the user's overall stress tendency, reducing the influence of isolated extreme values and emphasizing the most dominant probability level observed across all posts. Finally, the aggregated result can be presented to the end user as shown in Eq. 17.

$$\text{display}(P_u) \tag{17}$$

which outputs the computed user-level stress probability in a form suitable for visualization or reporting.

2.9 Binary Classification Using Machine Learning Models

While the aggregated user-level stress probability $P_u \in [0, 1]$ provides a calibrated measure of the likelihood that a user is experiencing stress, certain applications require a binary decision (*stress* or *no stress*). For this purpose, a decision threshold $\tau \in [0, 1]$ is applied to P_u as shown in Eq. 18.

$$\hat{y}_u = \begin{cases} 1, & \text{if } P_u \geq \tau \\ 0, & \text{otherwise} \end{cases} \tag{18}$$

where $\hat{y}_u \in \{0, 1\}$ denotes the binary stress classification output. The threshold τ is decided as 0.5 (i.e. $\tau \mathbin{\text{¿}} 0.5$ means stress else no stress) experimentally.

For binary classification, the feature vector for each user can be constructed using Eq. 19.

$$\tilde{\mathbf{f}}_{\text{user}} = \left[\mathbf{f}_{\text{pers}} \parallel \mathbf{f}_{\text{text}} \parallel P_u \right], \tag{19}$$

where $\mathbf{f}_{\text{pers}}$ is the MBTI personality embedding (Eq. 5), $\mathbf{f}_{\text{text}}$ is the aggregated textual feature vector (Eq. 6), and P_u is the aggregated user-level stress probability (Eq. 15). The binary classification is done using different ML classifiers.

3 Results and Discussion

3.1 Experimental Setup

The experimental setup for this study was entirely software-driven. All prediction tasks, including personality prediction and text-based stress detection, were implemented using deep learning methodologies. The experiments were carried out on the Kaggle platform within a Jupyter Notebook environment, with Python serving as the primary programming language. For result visualization and comparative performance analysis, the Seaborn library was used, while confusion matrices were generated to support model evaluation and selection. A total of five models were trained and tested in the datasets. Among them, the SVM consistently outperformed the others, achieving the highest F1-score and accuracy, thereby emerging as the best-performing model within our experimental framework.

Algorithm 1 Personality-Aware Stress Detection with Bucketed-Mode User Aggregation

---

Input: Dataset-I (MBTI) for personality; Dataset-II (SDD) for stress; bucket width Δp; personality encoder $\phi : \mathbb{M} \to \mathbb{R}^d$; text encoder $\text{TextFeaturesExtractor}(\cdot)$ (e.g., GloVe+LSTM); stress classifier $\text{StressPrediction}(\cdot)$

Output: User-level stress probability $P_u \in [0, 1]$ for each user u

 1: **// Train Personality Model (once on Dataset-I)**
 2: Train PersonalityModel using aggregated user documents (MBTI labels)
 3: **//Preprocess and Encode Posts (Dataset-II)**
 4: **for** each user u **do**
 5:     Obtain ordered posts $\mathcal{P} = \{p_1, \ldots, p_n\}$ ▷ Eq. 1
 6:     Clean each p_i (lowercase, remove stopwords/URLs); build $\mathcal{P}_{\text{clean}}$
 7:     $c_u \leftarrow \text{concatenatePosts}(\mathcal{P}_{\text{clean}})$ ▷ Eq. 3
 8:     $m_u \leftarrow \text{PersonalityModel}(c_u)$ ▷ Eq. 4
 9:     $\mathbf{f}_{\text{pers}} \leftarrow \phi(m_u) \in \mathbb{R}^d$ ▷ Eq. 5
10: **end for**
11: **// Per-Post Features and Stress Scores**
12: **for** each user u **do**
13:     **for** each post $p_i \in \mathcal{P}_{\text{clean}}$ **do**
14:         $\mathbf{f}_{\text{text},i} \leftarrow \text{TextFeaturesExtractor}(p_i)$ ▷ Eq. 6
15:         $\mathbf{f}_{\text{combined},i} \leftarrow [\,\mathbf{f}_{\text{text},i} \,\|\, \mathbf{f}_{\text{pers}}\,]$ ▷ Fusion, Eq. 7
16:         $p_i \leftarrow \text{StressPrediction}(\mathbf{f}_{\text{combined},i}) \in [0, 1]$ ▷ Post-level prob., Eq. 8
17:     **end for**
18: **end for**
19: **//Probability Discretization (Buckets over** $[0, 1]$**)**
20: Define bucket starts $\mathcal{B} = \{b_k\}$ with width Δp ▷ Eqs. 9, 10
21: **for** each user u **do**
22:     Map each p_i to its bucket midpoint $\bar{b}_{k(i)} = b_{k(i)} + \frac{\Delta p}{2}$ ▷ Eqs. 11, 14
23:     $\mathbf{MSP} \leftarrow [\bar{b}_{k(1)}, \ldots, \bar{b}_{k(n)}]$ ▷ Mapped Stress Probabilities, Eq. 13
24: **end for**
25: **//User-Level Aggregation by Mode**
26: **for** each user u **do**
27:     $P_u \leftarrow \text{mode}(\mathbf{MSP})$ ▷ Eq. 15
28:     **(//optional tie-break)** If multiple modes, set $P_u \leftarrow \arg\min_{x \in \mathcal{M}} |x - 0.5|$ where $\mathcal{M}$ is set of
         modes   ▷ Pick central mode; or choose median of modes
29: **end for**
30: **return** P_u for each user

Performance Evaluation for Dataset-I:

- Figure 1 illustrates the confusion matrix for Dataset I, while Table 2 presents the accuracy obtained by different machine learning classifiers. Furthermore, Fig. 2 depicts the performance metrics of the proposed stress prediction Model.

- Table 3 summarizes the classification performance of the proposed model in predicting the 16 MBTI personality types, reported in terms of Precision, Recall, F1-score, and Support (number of samples per class). Precision denotes the proportion of correct predictions among all predicted instances for a class, Recall represents the proportion of actual instances correctly identified, and the F1-score is the harmonic mean of Precision and Recall. Support refers to the number of samples belonging to each class in the dataset. The results reveal that **ESTP** achieved the highest performance, with Precision, Recall, and F1-score all equal to 0.93, indicating consistent and accurate predictions. Similarly, **ESTJ** attained a Precision of 0.97 and an F1-score of 0.91, reflecting very few false positives. The **ESFJ** category demonstrated notably high effectiveness, obtaining both a Recall and F1-score of 0.89. On the other hand, **INFJ** showed the weakest Precision (0.37) along with a moderate Recall of 0.53, leading to an F1-score of 0.61 and indicating that this type is often misidentified. Personality groups such as **ENFP**, **ENTP**, and **INTJ** achieved steady yet moderate results, with their F1-scores clustering near 0.70.

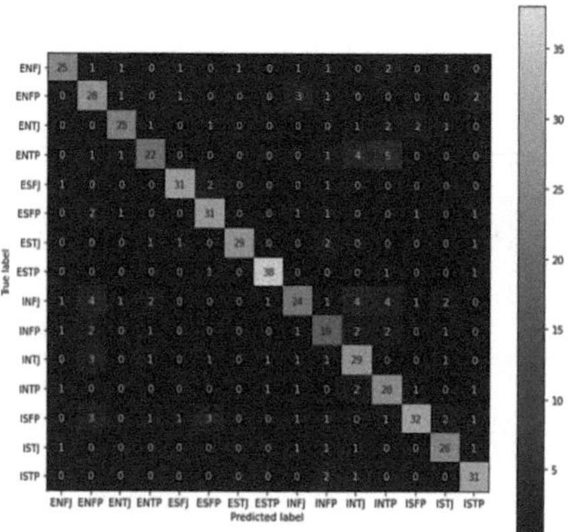

Fig. 1. Confusion Matrix (Dataset-I).

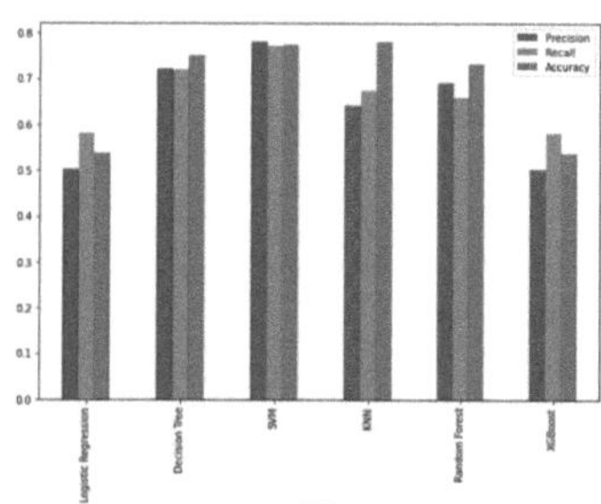

Fig. 2. Performance results(Dataset-I).

Table 2. Performance metric of different classifiers for Dataset-I

Classifier	Precision	Recall	Accuracy
Logistic Regression	0.5034	0.5797	0.5377
Decision Tree	0.7203	0.7187	0.7508
SVM	**0.7823**	**0.7732**	**0.7745**
KNN	0.6402	0.6727	0.7823
Random Forest	0.6903	0.6592	0.7312
XGBoost	0.5025	0.5797	0.5377

- Overall, the classifier obtained an accuracy of 0.77, correctly identifying 77% of the samples. The macro-level Precision, Recall, and F1-score were 0.78, 0.77, and 0.77, respectively, reflecting equal consideration of each class. The weighted averages were likewise 0.78, 0.77, and 0.77, showing that the model performed consistently without strong bias toward more frequent categories. These results indicate that the system excels in recognizing several extroverted MBTI groups, whereas introverted categories such as INFJ and INFP may need additional optimization, possibly due to overlapping linguistic patterns or limited training examples.

Table 3. Performance Matrix for different personality type

Personality Type	Precision	Recall	F1-Score	support
ENFJ	0.83	0.74	0.78	34
ENFP	0.64	0.78	0.70	36
ENTJ	0.83	0.76	0.79	33
ENTP	0.76	0.65	0.70	34
ESFJ	0.389	0.89	0.89	35
ESFP	0.79	0.82	0.81	38
ESTJ	0.97	0.85	0.91	34
ESTP	0.93	0.93	0.93	41
INFJ	0.371	0.53	0.61	45
INFP	0.59	0.66	0.62	29
INTJ	0.66	0.76	0.71	38
INTP	0.62	0.80	0.70	35
ISFP	0.86	0.70	0.77	46
ISTJ	0.76	0.84	0.80	31
ISTP	0.79	0.91	0.85	34
accuracy	-	-	0.77	543
macro avg	0.78	0.77	0.77	543
weighted avg	0.78	0.77	0.77	543

Performance Evaluation for Dataset-II: Fig. 3 illustrates the confusion matrix for Dataset-II, showing how the model distributes correct and incorrect predictions across the classes. Table 4, along with its corresponding visual representation in Fig. 4, compares the accuracy achieved by various machine learning classifiers, providing complementary numerical and graphical insights. Additionally, the ROC curve for Dataset-II, displayed in Fig. 5, portrays the balance between the true positive rate and the false positive rate.

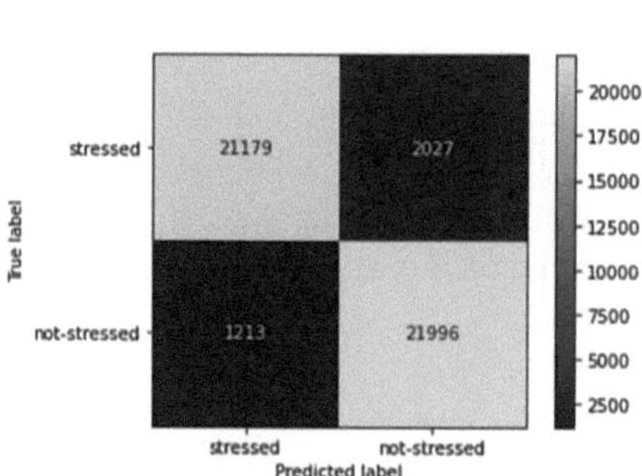

Fig. 3. Confusion Matrix (Dataset-II).

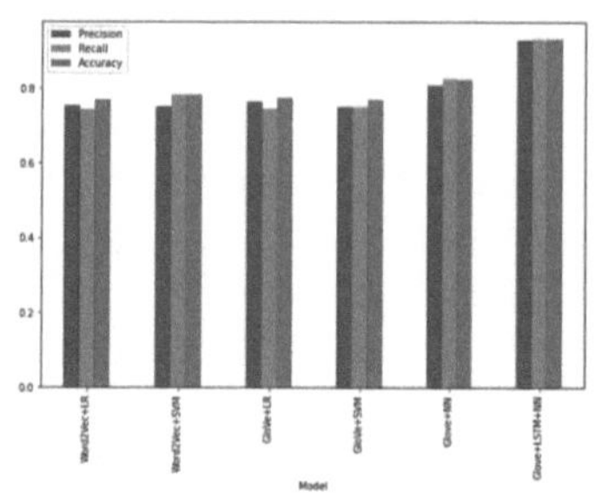

Fig. 4. Performance results(Dataset-II).

Table 4. Accuracy Comparison of different classifiers for Dataset-II

Classifier	Precision	Recall	Accuracy
Word2Vec+LR	0.7542	0.7442	0.7713
Word2Vec+SVM	0.7521	0.7831	0.7820
GloVe+LR	0.7638	0.7442	0.7756
GloVe+SVM	0.7485	0.7505	0.7692
Glove+NN	0.8088	0.8268	0.8241
Glove+LSTM	0.9302	0.9320	0.9334

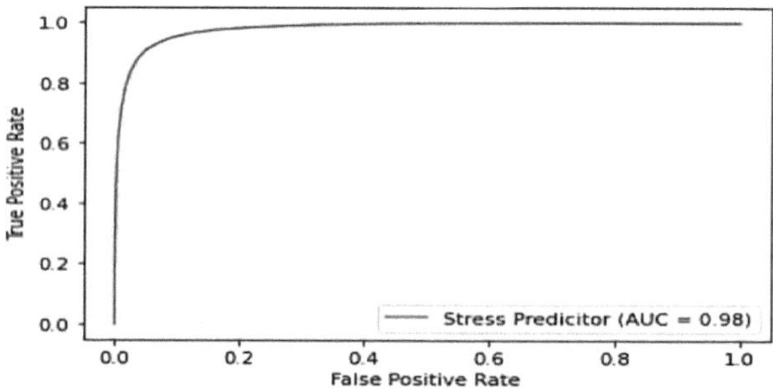

Fig. 5. ROC Curve for Stress Prediction Model (Dataset-II).

3.2 Inferences Drawn

The experimental findings provide a number of insightful observations regarding the effectiveness of the suggested two-stage stress detection paradigm. One obvious result is that, as compared to methods that just rely on text-based data, combining inferred personality traits with linguistic parameters significantly improves classification accuracy. The comparative analysis in Table 5 demonstrates that the method's performance is comparable to, and frequently superior to, well-established methodologies documented in previous work. The framework's capacity to combine short-term linguistic patterns with long-term personality tendencies is one of its main advantages, enabling a more customized and context-sensitive assessment of stress. For early, dependable, and precise detection across various user types, this combination design is very helpful.

3.3 Discussion

The empirical results demonstrate that the accuracy of stress prediction is significantly increased when personality assessments and linguistic characteristics from social media posts are combined. The SVM classifier consistently outperformed the other models on Dataset–I, which is intended to evaluate personality, achieving an accuracy of 77.45%. The model appears to treat the various MBTI categories pretty equally, as evidenced by the close match between the macro and weighted precision, recall, and F1-scores, each of which is close to 0.78. Extroverted types like ESTP, ESTJ, and ESFJ typically obtain the best precision and recall, according to a closer examination of the individual class results. This is probably because their writing style is more consistent and predictable. However, introverted personality types like INFJ and INFP exhibit somewhat poorer precision, which could be related to fewer training samples and similar linguistic patterns.

Using pretrained GloVe embeddings in conjunction with an LSTM network produced the greatest results for Dataset–II, which focuses particularly on stress identification. With an accuracy of 93.34% and strong precision and recall for both stressed and neutral categories, our model shows that it can handle many types of text with reliability. The suggested framework performs on par with, and frequently better than the previous studies. Its benefit is that it allows the system to interpret stress in a more context-sensitive and individualized manner by fusing long-term personality traits with short-term language cues. This is particularly helpful for precisely and promptly identifying stress in a variety of users.

Overall, the findings demonstrate the two-stage approach's efficacy and uniqueness. Its consistent performance and wide range of adaptation indicate that it can provide a solid basis for future research in behavioral understanding and individualized mental health analysis using social media data.

4 Conclusion and Future Work

In conclusion, the two-stage stress detection methodology presented in this work demonstrates great promise by fusing short-term linguistic patterns with personality qualities deduced from long-term posting behavior. Using an SVM classifier, the personality prediction stage achieves a balanced accuracy of 77.45%, showing that introverted types are still more difficult to identify because of their more subtle writing traits, while extroverted kinds are identified with a respectable degree of consistency. The stability and generalizability of the entire method are demonstrated by the second stage, which uses an LSTM model based on GloVe-based text representations and achieves an accuracy of 93.34% while maintaining high precision and recall for both stressed and non-stressed categories. Overall, the findings indicate that the system is

Table 5. Comparison of proposed model with existing machine learning techniques

Studies	Approach / Techniques Used	Dataset Used	Metric Type	Best Performance
Antoine et al. [18]	AdaBoost, SVM, KNN, Random Forest, Logistic Model Tree	eRisk2017 dataset	F1-Score / Precision	0.53 (F1), 0.64 (Precision)
Yaoyiran et al. [10]	SVM, Logistic Regression, Neural Network, LIWC features	Mental health-related subreddit data	Accuracy	86.14% (LIWC + NN)
Huijie et al. [19]	SVM, Random Forest, Naive Bayes, Deep Neural Network	Twitter posts	Accuracy / F1-Score	74% (Accuracy), 84.4% (F1)
Hong et al. [20]	Gaussian Mixture Models, Hidden Markov Models, LSTM	Manually labeled stress data	Accuracy / Precision / Recall	83% (Accuracy), 0.90 (Precision), 0.84 (Recall)
Vaikole S. et al. [21]	CNN, DNN, GMM + SVM	RAVDESS dataset	Accuracy	93%
Proposed Method	SVM for Personality Prediction + GloVe Embeddings + LSTM for Stress Detection	MBTI-500 + Reddit SuicideWatch / Depression	Accuracy / Precision / Recall / F1-Score	77.45% (Personality), 93.34% (Stress Detection)

well-positioned for early, dependable, and scalable stress monitoring with the potential to support prompt preventive treatments and enhance mental health. In the future, the framework might be strengthened by adding more modalities, including speech traits, facial expressions, or physiological markers, to increase robustness. Examining more sophisticated model designs, such as transformer-based architectures, might also improve the system's capacity to recognize semantic and contextual details found in user-generated text.

Competing Interests. The authors report that they have no conflicts of interest associated with the material presented in this manuscript.

References

1. Ferrarotti, A., Baldoni, S., Carli, M., Battisti, F.: Stress assessment for augmented reality applications based on head movement features. IEEE Trans. Visual Comput. Graphics **30**(10), 6970–6983 (2024)
2. Vos, G., Trinh, K., Sarnyai, Z., Azghadi, M.R.: Generalizable machine learning for stress monitoring from wearable devices: a systematic literature review, Int. J. Med. Inform. 105026 (2023)
3. Naeem, M., Fawzi, S.A., Anwar, H., Malek, A.S.: Wearable ECG systems for accurate mental stress detection: a scoping review. J. Public Health **33**(6), 1181–1197 (2025)
4. Li, Y., Li, K., Chen, J., Wang, S., Lu, H., Wen, D.: Pilot stress detection through physiological signals using a transformer-based deep learning model, IEEE Sens. J. (2023)
5. Edes, A.N., Crews, D.E.: Allostatic load and biological anthropology. Am. J. Phys. Anthropol. **162**, 44–70 (2017)
6. Naegelin, M., et al.: An interpretable machine learning approach to multimodal stress detection in a simulated office environment. J. Biomed. Inform. **139**, 104299 (2023)

7. Roul, R.K.: Topic modeling combined with classification technique for extractive multi-document text summarization., Soft Computing-A Fusion of Foundations, Methodologies & Applications, vol. 25, no. 2 (2021)

8. Roul, R.K., Asthana, S.R., Kumar, G.: Study on suitability and importance of multilayer extreme learning machine for classification of text data. Soft. Comput. **21**(15), 4239–4256 (2017)

9. William, D., Suhartono, D.: Text-based depression detection on social media posts: a systematic literature review. Proc. Comput. Sci. **179**, 582–589 (2021)

10. Li, Y., Mihalcea, R., Wilson, S.R.: Text-based detection and understanding of changes in mental health. In: Staab, S., Koltsova, O., Ignatov, D.I. (eds.) SocInfo 2018. LNCS, vol. 11186, pp. 176–188. Springer, Cham (2018). https://doi.org/10.1007/978-3-030-01159-8_17

11. Vizer, L.M., Zhou, L., Sears, A.: Automated stress detection using keystroke and linguistic features: an exploratory study. Int. J. Hum Comput Stud. **67**(10), 870–886 (2009)

12. Cao, L., Zhang, H., Li, N., Wang, X., Ri, W., Feng, L.: Category-aware chronic stress detection on microblogs. IEEE J. Biomed. Health Inform. **26**(2), 852–864 (2021)

13. Selye, H.: What is stress. Metabolism **5**(5), 525–530 (1956)

14. Cohen, S., Kessler, R.C., Gordon, L.U.: Measuring stress: a guide for health and social scientists. Oxford University Press on Demand (1997)

15. Goldberger, L., Breznitz, S.: Handbook of stress. Simon and Schuster (2010)

16. Mou, L., et al.: Driver stress detection via multimodal fusion using attention-based CNN-LSTM. Expert Syst. Appl. **173**, 114693 (2021)

17. Aguado, G., Julian, V., Garcia-Fornes, A., Espinosa, A.: A CBR for integrating sentiment and stress analysis for guiding users on social network sites. Expert Syst. Appl. **208**, 118103 (2022)

18. Briand, A., Almeida, H., Meurs, M.-J.: Analysis of social media posts for early detection of mental health conditions, In: Advances in Artificial Intelligence: 31st Canadian Conference on Artificial Intelligence, Canadian AI 2018, Toronto, ON, Canada, May 8–11, 2018, Proceedings 31, pp. 133–143, Springer (2018)

19. Lin, H., et al.: User-level psychological stress detection from social media using deep neural network, In: Proceedings of the 22nd ACM international conference on Multimedia, pp. 507–516 (2014)

20. Lu, H., et al.: Stresssense: Detecting stress in unconstrained acoustic environments using smartphones, In: Proceedings of the 2012 ACM Conference on Ubiquitous Computing, pp. 351–360 (2012)

21. Vaikole, S., Mulajkar, S., More, A., Jayaswal, P., Dhas, S.: Stress detection through speech analysis using machine learning, Int. J. Creat. Res. Thoughts (IJCRT), **8**(5) (2020)

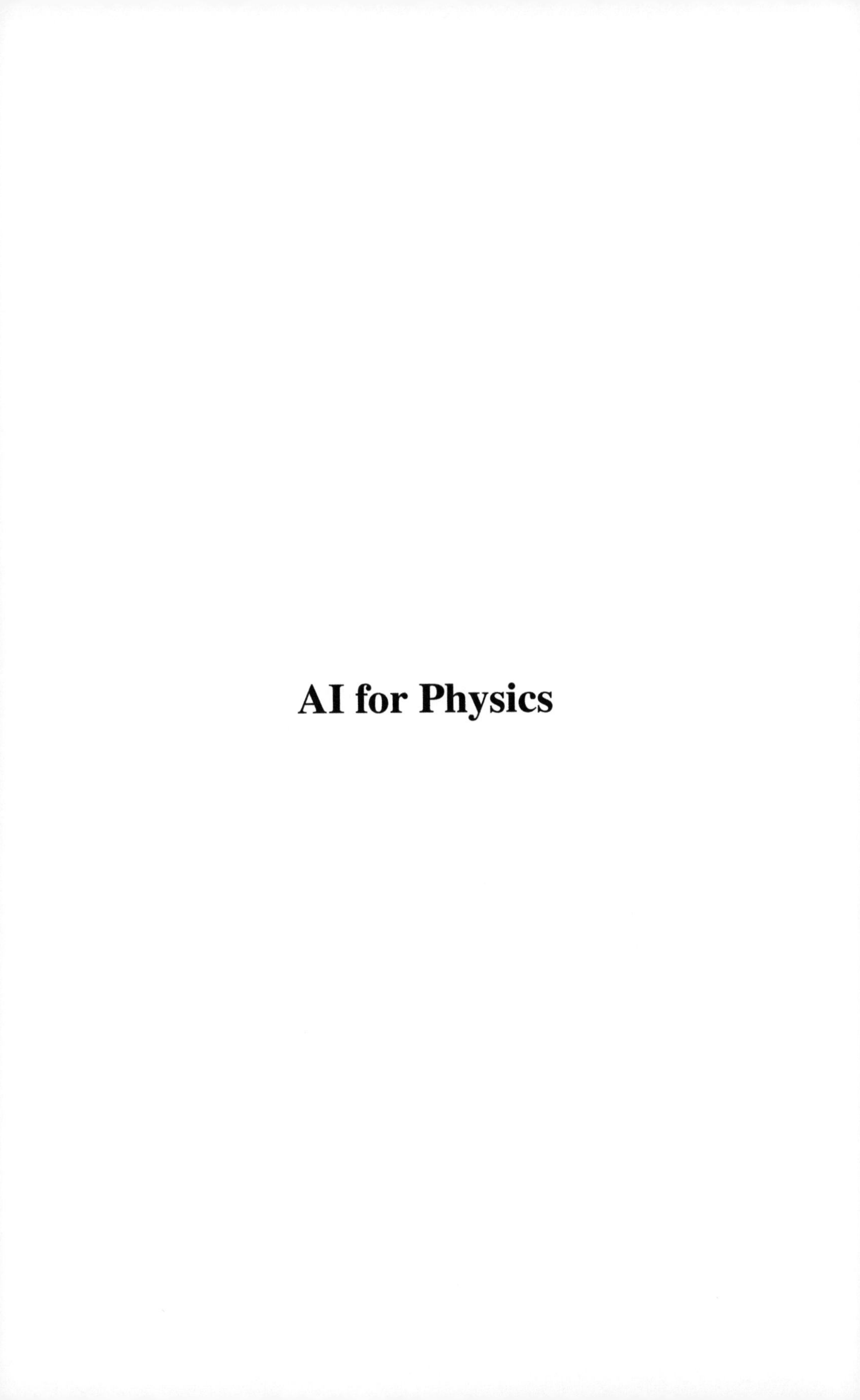

AI for Physics

Earthquake Severity and Probability Prediction Using Spatiotemporal Learning

Nikhil Dwivedi[✉], Bhumika, and Debasis Das

Department of Computer Science and Engineering, Indian Institute of Technology Jodhpur, Jodhpur, Rajasthan, India
dwivedi.10@alumni.iitj.ac.in, {bhumika.1,debasis}@iitj.ac.in

Abstract. Earthquake is one of the most destructive natural disasters, with catastrophic results such as landslides, tsunamis, fires, and fault ruptures. Therefore, anticipating earthquakes ahead of time has economic and societal benefits. However, earthquake prediction is not a trivial task, since earthquakes can occur in a variety of magnitudes and frequencies and can exhibit different types of behavior depending on the location, time, and geological setting. This variability makes it challenging to develop a single model that can accurately predict earthquakes across different regions and timescales. In light of this, we predict the probability, severity level (class 0–4) and location of the earthquakes with an end-to-end framework named *Shock-Alert* by exploiting spatial-temporal correlation. The framework is comprised of parallel probability prediction and classification blocks, comprised of transformer and convolution networks, respectively, as the transformer will capture the temporal features due to the self-attention mechanism and the convolution network will capture the spatial features. To assess the effectiveness of the proposed framework extensive experiments are performed on the California dataset, and F1-score of 94.4% and 93.2% are obtained for severity level prediction, respectively; outperform baseline and state-of-the-art models.

Keywords: Spatio-temporal learning · Earthquake Prediction · Transformer · Convolution Neural Network

1 Introduction

An earthquake is a natural phenomenon that occurs when two blocks of the Earth's crust suddenly shift relative to each other. This shift releases energy in the form of seismic waves that propagate through the Earth's crust, causing the ground to shake or vibrate. Earthquakes can range in size from small tremors to large, devastating events that can cause severe injuries and fatalities, as well as wreak havoc on buildings and infrastructure, resulting in substantial economic losses. Recently, on March 20, 2025, a 7.7 magnitude earthquake struck Myanmar, resulting in more than 1600 fatalities, thousands of injuries,

B. Chatterjee et al. (Eds.): ICDCIT 2026, LNCS 16420, pp. 529–544, 2026.
https://doi.org/10.1007/978-3-032-16632-6_34

and affecting 17 million people, triggering one of Myanmar's deadliest crises. World Bank GRADE assessment estimated USD 10.97 billion in direct damages, which is 14% of Myanmar's GDP[1]. The nations that are situated along the RING OF FIRE region such as Japan, Indonesia, Chile and United States experience higher seismic and volcanic activities resulting in large-magnitude earthquakes and associated socio-economic impacts compared to the nations which are outside this region. For the purpose of this study we will confine our scope to California region which is also the part of RING OF FIRE region. The region wise earthquakes are depicted in Fig. 1 with magnitude threshold greater than 2.5, where the intensity of the color and the radius of the circle increase with the magnitude of the earthquake. We observe from Fig. 1, the southern part of California, which is home to nearly 60% of the state's population, is particularly vulnerable to earthquakes. Consequently, the occurrence of large seismic events in this region can have severe implications, including substantial economic losses, declines in average income, and significant infrastructural damage. Therefore, earthquake prediction is vital to the safety of our civilization, since it seeks to use known seismic data to specify three factors, namely the time, location, and severity of the next earthquake.

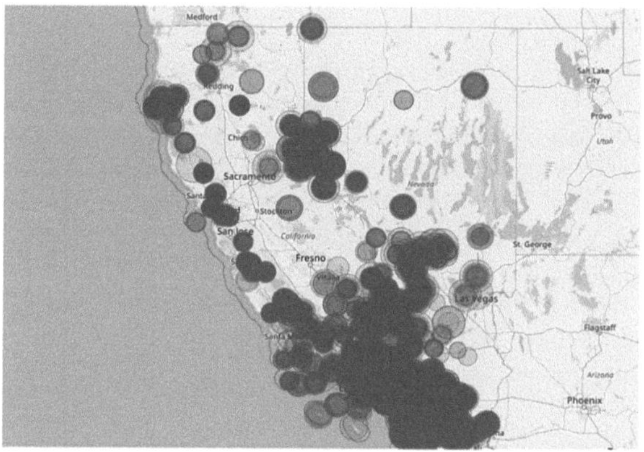

Fig. 1. Map of earthquake locations in California: Circle size and color intensity reflect earthquake magnitude, with larger and darker circles indicates higher magnitudes.

There has been a rise in academic research and interest in predicting seismic events, and the majority of works fall into four groups methodologically: 1) mathematical analysis, 2) precursor signal investigation, 3) machine learning algorithms and 4) deep learning. Although relatively few of them can effectively predict future seismic events accurately as earthquake occurrences have complex nonlinear relationships, therefore, mathematical, statistical, and machine learn-

---

[1] https://documents1.worldbank.org/curated/en/099050525010539325/pdf/P507337-f483c42a-89b3-42c3-939e-d7e93126d55b.pdf.

ing tools cannot be used effectively. However, in recent decades, the seismological community has amassed huge amounts of data, allowing for the prediction of future dynamics based on past events. Hence, we choose solutions based on deep learning to capture complex nonlinear relationships.

Most of the existing work in deep learning based earthquake prediction considered temporal scale (time series) only, whereas earthquakes are spatially and temporally correlated because of the crust movement [11]. In this line, deep learning techniques have become a popular and efficient method for a wide variety of spatio-temporal prediction tasks [5,15]. Drawing inspiration from these approaches, we also use spatial-temporal deep learning. Unfortunately, spatial-temproal prediction is not a trivial task because of the challenges: 1) Dimension (high dimension characteristics of time series sequences), 2) Sparsity (earthquake occurrence is rare) 3) Dynamic (earthquake effect changes with time and location) 4) Autocorrelation (recent earthquake can cause aftershocks and epicenter surrounding regions are more effected).

In our work, we try to tackle above challenges and propose a end-to-end framework named *Shock-Alert* to predict the likelihood of future earthquakes in a region along with severity level. In the framework, we first divide the whole region into grid cells of 10×10 Km to extract the spatial correlation and input pre-processed seismic signals. Next, two parallel blocks of transformer and convolution network is utilize to extract to predict probability and severity level. In summary, our main contribution are following:

- We propose spatio-temporal multi-output framework named *Shock-Alert*, that predicts earthquake probability (0–1) and severity (class 0–4) for the dynamic time window for that specific region. This is the first work, to our knowledge that predicts probability and severity with a single end-to-end framework.
- Utilize transformer for extracting temporal pattern for probability prediction and convolution neural network for spatial pattern classifying the severity of an earthquake for the specific region.
- Extensive experiments on the California earthquake dataset shows the effectiveness of the proposed model on different metrics such as precision, recall, and F-measure, showing improvement of around 15% on precision, 7% on recall and 11.3% on F1-score over the baseline model.
- We also compare the model performance with different state-of-the-art models on the Bangladesh earthquake dataset where Shock-Alert outperforms existing models with improvement of 14.89% in accuracy and 4% in F1-score.

The paper is structured as follows: Sect. 2 reviews related work and highlights key differences from prior studies. Section 3 presents the problem formulation. Section 4 details the datasets, preprocessing, and proposed prediction models. Section 5 covers performance evaluation, comparisons, hyperparameter tuning, and ablation study. Section 6 concludes the paper with future directions.

2   Related Work

Classical methods rely on statistical and mathematical modeling, such as probabilistic approaches for estimating earthquake timing and magnitude [7], which are effective for long-term forecasting but less accurate for short to mid term predictions. Machine learning methods are data-driven and non-parametric, requiring fewer assumptions [21]. However, ML models often struggle with capturing complex nonlinear relationships and rely heavily on manual feature engineering.

In contrast, deep learning models, with their deeper architectures and higher representational capacity, have shown greater success in earthquake prediction. LSTM networks have been used to model spatio-temporal correlations [23], while CNNs have leveraged both explicit and implicit seismic features from image data [12]. Few studies have used LSTM to capture long term temporal dependencies and RNN for short term temporal dependencies [9]. Transformers have also been explored for capturing long-range dependencies in seismic data [22]. Despite their advantages, DL models often require complex architectures, are difficult to tune, and struggle with modeling long-term spatio-temporal dependencies effectively.

Spatio-temporal approaches are essential for capturing the correlation between earthquake occurrences, time, and location. Traditional deep learning models like stacked RNNs and 3D CNNs have been used for this purpose but are often complex and require extensive tuning. Several studies have addressed this challenge: [15] used CNN-BiLSTM for magnitude prediction in California, [8] employed BiLSTM-AM with seismic indices in Bangladesh, and [17] utilized CNN-LSTM with geographic imagery in Chile. However, many existing methods overlook either spatial or temporal aspects, limiting their ability to uncover latent patterns. Given the time-series nature of earthquake data, jointly modeling past and future information enhances prediction accuracy. Existing models often excel in either prediction or classification, but rarely both. Some predict earthquakes over long time spans without precise location, while others offer binary forecasts without severity levels, limiting their practical utility.

3   Problem Formulation

Earthquake forecasting is comprised of three tasks: first, predict when the next seismic event will occur, and the second task is to determine a particular location. The third task is to predict the severity of incoming seismic events in order to prepare for large shocks. We are using multi-output model and have two tasks:

Task 1: Prediction This task focuses on predicting the probability of an earthquake occurring within a specified magnitude range at a particular location and future time frame.

$$P_{r(i,j)}^{t+\Delta t}(M_{min}, M_{max}) = f_P(X_{r(i,j)}^0, X_{r(i,j)}^1, \ldots, X_{r(i,j)}^{t-1}) \qquad (1)$$

Here, The function f_P models this probability based on historical observations: $X_{r(i,j)}^t$ represents a vector of relevant input features collected at grid cell $r(i,j)$

at time t. The grid cell $r(i,j)$ is defined by its ith row and j^{th} column. The model utilizes data from time 0 up to the current time $t-1$ to make its prediction for the subsequent time frame. $P_{r(i,j)}^{t+\Delta t}(M_{min}, M_{max})$ denotes the predicted probability of an earthquake with a magnitude M between M_{min} and M_{max} (e.g., $3.5 \leq M \leq 4.5$) occurring within the grid cell $r(i,j)$ during the future time interval $(t, t + \Delta t]$.

Task 2: Classification

In this, we classify severity level of earthquake magnitude, represented by following equation:

$$Z_{r(i,j)}^{t+\Delta t} = f_C(X_{r(i,j)}^0, X_{r(i,j)}^1, \ldots, X_{r(i,j)}^{t-1}, P_{r(i,j)}^{t+\Delta t}(M_{min}, M_{max})) \tag{2}$$

Here, $Z_{r(i,j)}^{t+\Delta t}$ represents the classified severity level of an earthquake for grid cell $r(i,j)$ during the time interval $(t, t + \Delta t]$. The function f_C performs this classification and its inputs include the same historical feature sequence $X_{r(i,j)}^\tau$ and it also incorporates the predicted probability $P_{r(i,j)}^{t+\Delta t}(M_{min}, M_{max})$ obtained from Task 1.

4   Methodology

Our goal is to predict earthquake activity for the next month (short-term prediction) in the California region. We utilize a multi-output architecture, as depicted in Fig. 2, designed to address two distinct but related tasks: **Prediction** and **Classification**. The California region is discretized into a 120×120 grid of 10km $\times$ 10km cells. For each grid cell $r(i,j)$ at time t, we prepare a feature vector $X_{r(i,j)}^t$, comprising relevant historical observations and static geological characteristics. The model processes a sequence of these spatio-temporal inputs,

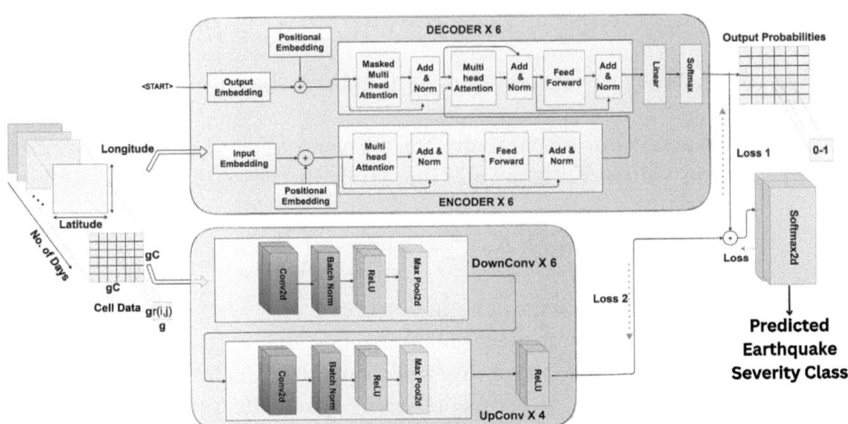

Fig. 2. Shock-Alert: Architecture for earthquake severity and location prediction

from time 0 up to $t-1$, to make predictions for the subsequent time interval $(t, t + \Delta t]$. The input is processed through two parallel pathways within our architecture:

- **Spatial Feature Extraction:** Each grid snapshot X^t from the input sequence is fed into the `DownConv` component. This component acts as a spatial feature extractor, responsible for identifying localized patterns and reducing the dimensionality of the grid data while preserving crucial spatial correlations.
- **Temporal Sequence Preparation:** The `Input Embedding` layer prepares the sequence of processed feature vectors for the Transformer encoder. Specifically, the 120×120 grid at each time step is flattened into a vector, which then passes through the `Input Embedding` layer to form the tokens for the Transformer's input sequence.

4.1   Prediction Model

The Prediction Model is primarily driven by a Transformer architecture, which excels at capturing long-range temporal dependencies in sequential data. This model corresponds to **Task 1** as defined in our problem formulation, predicting the probability of earthquake occurrence.

Transformer Encoder. The Transformer Encoder receives a sequence of input embeddings. Let E_t denote the embedded and positionally encoded representation of the flattened grid snapshot at time t. The input to the first encoder layer is the sequence $(E_0, E_1, \ldots, E_{T-1})$, where T is the sequence length.

Within each encoder layer l, the process begins with the Multi-Head Self-Attention mechanism. Let $H_t^{(l-1)}$ denote the input representation for time step t from the $(l-1)$-th layer. Query (Q_t), Key (K_t), and Value (V_t) matrices are computed for each time step t:

$$Q_t = H_t^{(l-1)} W_Q, \quad K_t = H_t^{(l-1)} W_K, \quad V_t = H_t^{(l-1)} W_V \tag{3}$$

where W_Q, W_K, W_V are learned weight matrices shared across all time steps within the layer.

The core self-attention mechanism, for a given query Q (from a specific time step), keys K and values V (from all time steps in the sequence), is defined as:

$$\text{Attention}(Q, K, V) = \text{softmax}\left(\frac{QK^T}{\sqrt{d_k}}\right) V \tag{4}$$

where d_k is the dimensionality of the key vectors.

The Multi-Head Attention mechanism applies this attention function multiple times in parallel and concatenates their outputs. For an input $H^{(l-1)}$ (representing the full sequence of representations from the previous layer) to the Multi-Head Attention sub-layer:

$$\text{MultiHead}(H^{(l-1)}) = \text{Concat}(\text{head}_1, \text{head}_2, \ldots, \text{head}_h) W_O \tag{5}$$

where each $\text{head}_i = \text{Attention}(H^{(l-1)}W_{Q_i}, H^{(l-1)}W_{K_i}, H^{(l-1)}W_{V_i})$ for specific head weights, and W_O is a learned output weight matrix.

Following the Multi-Head Attention, a residual connection and layer normalization are applied. Let $H^{(l)}_{\text{MHA\_norm}}$ be the output after this step:

$$H^{(l)}_{\text{MHA\_norm}} = \text{LayerNorm}(H^{(l-1)} + \text{MultiHead}(H^{(l-1)})) \qquad (6)$$

Next, this normalized output passes through a Feed-Forward Network (FFN):

$$\text{FFN}(H^{(l)}_{\text{MHA\_norm}}) = \text{ReLU}(H^{(l)}_{\text{MHA\_norm}}W_1 + b_1)W_2 + b_2 \qquad (7)$$

where W_1, b_1, W_2, b_2 are learned weights and biases.

Finally, another residual connection and layer normalization are applied to the output of the FFN, yielding the output of the l-th encoder layer $H^{(l)}$:

$$H^{(l)} = \text{LayerNorm}(H^{(l)}_{\text{MHA\_norm}} + \text{FFN}(H^{(l)}_{\text{MHA\_norm}})) \qquad (8)$$

These operations are repeated across 6 encoder layers.

Transformer Decoder. The Transformer Decoder takes the output from the encoder and, using masked multi-head attention, generates the output sequence. In our architecture, the decoder is designed to produce the probability of earthquake occurrence for each grid cell in the next time frame, corresponding to the $P^{t+\Delta t}_{r(i,j)}(M_{min}, M_{max})$ in Task 1. The Transformer Decoder is tasked with generating the probability map for the next time step. Its input sequence is initialized with a special [START] token embedding, which is then combined with positional encoding. This initial token serves as the starting context for the decoder's generation process. The Masked Multi-head Attention mechanism within the decoder processes this initial token, and subsequent (if any) generated content, ensuring that predictions are only based on preceding information. Concurrently, the Multi-head Attention (cross-attention) layer allows the decoder to query the full output sequence from the Transformer Encoder, thereby conditioning its probability map generation on the comprehensive spatio-temporal context learned from historical data. The final output of the decoder passes through a Linear layer and a Softmax activation function to yield the predicted probabilities. The output of this branch is a tensor of shape $[1, 120, 120]$, where each value represents the probability (between 0 and 1) of an earthquake occurring in that specific 10km $\times$ 10km grid cell for the next month, given a defined minimum magnitude threshold M_{min}.

4.2 Classification Model

The Classification Model, primarily built with Convolutional Neural Networks, is responsible for determining the severity level (magnitude range) of an earthquake for each grid cell. This directly addresses **Task 2** from our problem formulation, classifying the severity level $Z^{t+\Delta t}_{r(i,j)}$.

DownConv. The `DownConv` component processes the initial `celled` data (X^t of shape $3 \times 120 \times 120$). It consists of 6 sequential blocks, each comprising:

- **Convolutional Layer:** Extracts features that capture both spatial and temporal correlations within the grid. The convolution operation is defined as:

$$\mathbf{Y}_{i,j,k} = \sum_{m=1}^{M} \sum_{n=1}^{N} \sum_{c=1}^{C} \mathbf{X}_{i+m-1,j+n-1,c} \cdot \mathbf{W}_{m,n,c,k} + \mathbf{b}_k \tag{9}$$

  where $\mathbf{X}$ is the input data, $\mathbf{W}$ is the weight tensor (kernel), and $\mathbf{b}$ is the bias vector.
- **Batch Normalization Layer:** Normalizes the output of the convolutional layer to stabilize training and improve generalization. For an output $\mathbf{y}_{i,j}$ from a channel, the normalized output $\hat{y}_{i,j}$ is:

$$\hat{y}_{i,j} = \frac{y_{i,j} - \mu_j}{\sqrt{\sigma_j^2 + \varepsilon}} \tag{10}$$

  where μ_j and σ_j^2 are the mean and variance for channel j.

The `DownConv` effectively compresses the spatial information into a lower-dimensional feature space, analogous to the encoder part of an autoencoder.

UpConv. The `UpConv` component consists of 4 blocks. Each block is a sequence of a `Convolutional layer`, `Batch Normalization layer`, `ReLU layer`, and an `Upsampling` layer. This component aims to progressively raise the feature space back to the desired grid shape, mimicking the decoder part of an autoencoder.

Feature Fusion and Final Classification. The output from the `UpConv` branch, representing the spatially refined features for classification, is then concatenated with the output probabilities obtained from the Transformer's Prediction Model. This concatenation aims to integrate the temporal prediction of earthquake occurrence probability with the spatially extracted features for severity classification.

Finally, these concatenated matrices are fed through a Softmax2d layer. This layer performs a per-pixel classification across the 120×120 Cartesian coordinates, assigning each grid cell to one of the predetermined severity classes (magnitude ranges). This directly models $Z_{r(i,j)}^{t+\Delta t}$.

5   Experiments

5.1   Dataset and Preprocessing

The dataset for this study was derived from the Stanford Earthquake Dataset (STEAD) as well as the US Geological Survey's earthquake catalog (USGS).[2]

---

[2] https://earthquake.usgs.gov/earthquakes/search/.

Table 1. Dataset Description

Dataset	California
Longitude	-124.4~-114.13
Latitude	32.5~42
Time Span	1/1/2013 - 31/06/2022
Time Interval	1 day
Grid map Size	120 X 120
Cell area	10km X 10km

Table 2. Magnitude range

Magnitude Range	Class
0-2.5	0
2.5-3.5	1
3.5-4.5	2
4.5–6	3
Above 6	4

Earthquakes that occurred between January 2013 and June 2022 are listed in the raw data, with duplicate rows addressed and removed. The dataset consists of 22 columns out of which we have considered 5 columns in our work as given in Table 1 i.e. latitude, longitude, time, and type and magnitude to get the unique entries. The severity of the earthquake mapped to different classes according to the magnitude given in Table 2 according to the USGS[3], for example, magnitude of 0–2.5 earthquakes are mapped to class 0, 2.5-3.5 to class 1 and so on. UTC earthquake catalog timestamps were converted to year, month, day, hour, minute, and second components. We then calculated the day difference from a base earthquake; missing days implied no seismic activity. Next, To produce the cell data, we made a 10km km grid and divide California into these grids to run the forecaster.

5.2 Experiment Setup

The model was trained on GTX 1080 for 1000z epochs with pytorch version 1.13.1. The learning rate was set to 0.001 and Adam optimizer is used. The earthquake threshold M_{min} is 2.5 for prediction, as after this magnitude the human can feel the earthquake. There is a class bias problem because the higher magnitude earthquakes have fewer records than the lower magnitude earthquakes, so to solve this problem, we assigned the weights [0.01,0.261,0.570,0.878,0.999] to different classes so that it can give higher priority to the higher magnitude in classifying the severity of an earthquake. Aside from that, loss values of prediction ($\lambda 1$) and classification ($\lambda 2$) multiplied by constant that is 0.4 and 1 respectively.

5.3 Effectiveness Study

Comparison with Baseline. We have evaluated different baseline models such as RNN [4], LSTM [3], BiLSTM [10], and UNet [13], as well as the proposed model transformer. The results have been presented in Table 3 and observe that the proposed architecture outperforms the baseline models in terms of both mean loss and F1 score which clearly indicates that our proposed architecture

---

[3] https://www.usgs.gov/programs/earthquake-hazards/magnitude-types.

Table 3. Comparison with Prediction and Severity Classification Baseline Models

Task	Model	Loss	Precision	Recall	F1 Score
Prediction	RNN [4]	0.553	0.22	**0.99**	0.364
	UNet [13]	0.545	0.38	0.98	0.551
	LSTM [3]	0.531	0.66	0.95	0.783
	BiLSTM [10]	0.478	0.74	0.93	0.831
	GRU [6]	0.509	0.69	0.94	0.795
	Transformer [19]	**0.184**	**0.91**	0.97	**0.944**
Classification	MLP	0.813	0.778	0.879	0.815
	UpDown-Conv	**0.931**	**0.927**	**0.937**	**0.932**

predicts earthquakes with better accuracy. Attention in transformer allow to focus on the most relevant information at each time step. This makes them more effective at modeling long-term dependencies than RNN, LSTM, and BiLSTM which have difficulty with long sequences due to the vanishing gradient problem. We utilise MLP [14] or CNN [10] to capture spatial-properties, and our proposed architecture as a whole can capture spatial-temporal features whose results are shown in Table 3.

Comparison with State of the Art Models. In this subsection, we provide a comparison of the proposed model wrt. State-of-the-art models on, as shown in Fig 3. The authors of [1] used the Bangladesh dataset; however, in our paper, we worked with the California earthquake dataset. Therefore, for comparison, we have downloaded the Bangladesh dataset (same as the authors [1]) from the earthquake catalogue from the United States geological survey (USGS) with the same features of duration. The authors [1] have already compared their proposed model with all other models [2, 16, 18, 20] and we have taken the results from the same instead of implementing each. In our case, the input is Bangladesh dataset to our proposed model (classification task) and achieved the performance of in terms of accuracy (89.65 %) and F-1 score (0.8327), which is better than all the above mentioned methods.

5.4   Ablation Study

We performed ablation study to understand the effect of individual components on the overall performance. For the ablation study, we kept the earthquake threshold at 2.5, the future days to forecast at 30, and the days before the earthquake at 3000. Table 4 shows the results of different encoder-decoder pairs while keeping the number of each identical to ensure symmetry. Here, CA: classification accuracy, PA: prediction accuracy, CL: classification loss, PL: prediction loss, and F1 score is the overall score. In standard transformer [19], total of 6 blocks are used inside the encoder and decoder, and we check our model performance with 4 and 2 blocks. As we increase the number of encoders and decoders

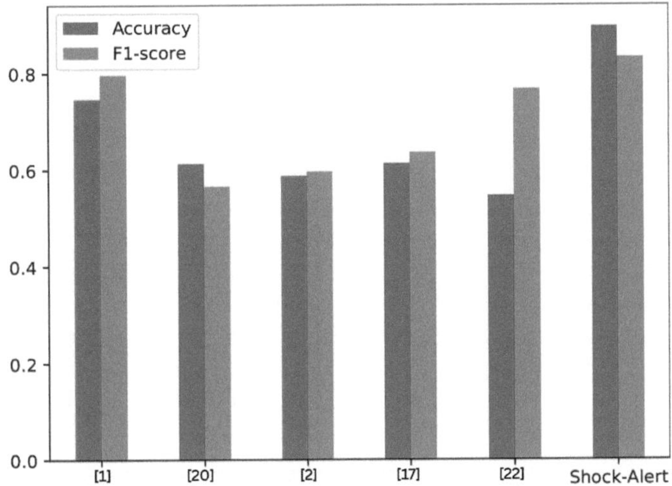

Fig. 3. Comparison of Shock-Alert with state-of-the-art.

Table 4. Ablation study with Encoder-Decoder blocks

Encoder	Decoder	CA	PA	CL	PL	F1 Score
2	2	0.782	0.815	0.69	0.312	0.805
4	4	0.892	0.889	0.62	0.264	0.891
6	6	0.941	0.953	0.525	0.193	0.944

Table 5. Ablation study with UpDown-Conv Blocks

UpConv	DownConv	CA	PA	CL	PL	F1 Score
2	2	0.902	0.909	0.554	0.222	0.926
2	4	0.914	0.928	0.545	0.213	0.937
4	6	0.941	0.953	0.525	0.193	0.944

in the prediction model from 2, 4, and 6, the overall classification loss decreased. and the results have been shown in Table 4. We find that increasing the number to 6 yielded the best outcomes; however, increasing the number further yielded stagnant results and did not improve performance significantly.

We changed the number of updown-conv blocks to show the effect on overall performance, the results are given in Table 5. We started with fewer UpConv and DownConv blocks because we thought it would be enough to handle the earthquake data, but as we increased the number of blocks, the results improved further. It may be because increasing the number helps to extract more features and get the relevant information. However, after 4 upconv and 6 downconv blocks, the performance became stagnant.

5.5   Hyperparameter Setting

Determining hyperparameter settings is an essential aspect of model development, we checked for different forecasting horizon, lag, threshold, class and loss weights.

Forecasting Horizon, Lag, and Threshold. To evaluate the performance of our proposed architecture, we used different seismic thresholds [2.5,3.5,4.5]. The other parameters we have tuned are the days before the earthquake and the days to anticipate the earthquake, which are [100,1000,2000,3000] and [15,30,60] correspondingly along with the parameters that we have fixed and explained in the previous section for which the results have been shown in Table 6. The reported results for 30 days are marked with a star (*) in Table 6, and the best results are bold which are obtained under 60 days forecasting horizon. However, most of the existing work uses 30 days horizon for prediction, thus we use the same. The second-best results are highlighted with underlining.

Class and Loss Weights. At last, the weights applied to the loss are another hyperparameter. Actually, we have two tasks and when the loss is backtracked, we can't simply sum the loss from the prediction model and the classification model since they don't have the same weightage. Therefore, we acquire the results given in Table 7 by altering the weights of both losses. Table 7 highlights the highest value with bold and the second highest with underline. We observe that classification accuracy at class weights [1,1,1,1,1] is maximum however the F1-score is the lowest. For all other cases the class weights [0.01, 0.261, 0.570,0.878, 0.999] provide best performance; therefore we used these weights in our final model.

Fig. 4. Earthquake occurrence probability: 9.38%.

Table 6. Performance comparison with different lags (Days Before), forecasting horizon (Days) and Threshold

Days Before	Days	Threshold	CA	PA	CL	PL	F1
100	15	2.5	0.08	0.29	0.665	0.748	0.24
1000	15	2.5	0.639	0.756	0.567	0.451	0.713
2000	15	2.5	0.891	0.867	0.551	0.275	0.868
3000	15	2.5	0.921	0.922	0.532	0.201	0.912
100	30	2.5	0.12	0.32	0.643	0.723	0.27
1000	30	2.5	0.687	0.772	0.558	0.436	0.746
2000	30	2.5	0.934	0.889	0.537	0.268	0.894
3000	30	2.5	0.941*	<u>0.953*</u>	0.525*	0.193*	0.944*
100	60	2.5	0.18	0.37	0.617	0.709	0.3
1000	60	2.5	0.747	0.818	0.594	0.427	0.787
2000	60	2.5	<u>0.978</u>	0.9062	0.5187	0.259	<u>0.981</u>
3000	60	2.5	**0.988**	**0.968**	<u>0.491</u>	0.189	**0.99**
100	15	3.5	0.106	0.273	0.62	0.713	0.19
1000	15	3.5	0.652	0.721	0.555	0.426	0.733
2000	15	3.5	0.831	0.842	0.5173	0.258	0.871
3000	15	3.5	0.867	0.895	0.495	0.183	0.89
100	30	3.5	0.23	0.28	0.613	0.713	0.37
1000	30	3.5	0.732	0.74	0.56	0.427	0.751
2000	30	3.5	0.912	0.867	0.526	0.258	0.867
3000	30	3.5	0.928	0.912	0.5018	**0.177**	0.922
100	60	3.5	0.26	0.356	0.62	0.7113	0.38
1000	60	3.5	0.741	0.808	0.584	0.427	0.758
2000	60	3.5	0.901	0.889	0.538	0.265	0.851
3000	60	3.5	0.912	0.931	**0.489**	0.178	0.918
100	15	4.5	0.08	0.213	0.631	0.713	0.16
1000	15	4.5	0.561	0.674	0.594	0.426	0.71
2000	15	4.5	0.782	0.798	0.567	0.258	0.824
3000	15	4.5	0.817	0.821	0.523	0.183	0.841
100	30	4.5	0.35	0.22	0.598	0.738	0.45
1000	30	4.5	0.754	0.65	0.574	0.498	0.759
2000	30	4.5	0.901	0.812	0.524	0.289	0.851
3000	30	4.5	0.931	0.87	0.512	0.222	0.926
100	60	4.5	0.239	0.321	0.639	0.7113	0.38
1000	60	4.5	0.712	0.769	0.603	0.427	0.758
2000	60	4.5	0.831	0.853	0.561	0.265	0.851
3000	60	4.5	0.858	0.891	0.501	<u>0.178</u>	0.918

Table 7. Effect of different class weights

Class Weights	PA Weight	CL Weight	CA	PA	F1 Score
[0.01,0.261,0.570,0.878,0.999]	0.4	1	<u>0.941</u>	**0.953**	**0.944**
[0.01,0.261,0.570,0.878,0.999]	1	1	0.856	0.879	0.822
[0.01,0.261,0.570,0.878,0.999]	9	6	0.782	0.795	0.714
[0.5,0.5,1,1,1]	0.4	1	0.927	0.945	0.561
[0.1,0.3,0.5,0.7,0.9]	0.4	1	0.922	0.917	<u>0.886</u>
[1,1,1,1,1]	0.4	1	**0.953**	<u>0.938</u>	0.328

5.6 Case Study

This case study on earthquake prediction aims to explore the effectiveness of the proposed model in forecasting earthquakes. We select California city for our case study with both the northern and southern parts. We have taken the forecasting horizon of 30 days, a lag of 3000 days and 2.5 as the prediction threshold. The result is shown in use-case Fig. 4, where we can observe that model predicts an earthquake of 3.5 to 4.5 magnitude in the given regions with the prediction probability of 9.381% (Higher means more chances of earthquake occurrence). It has been also observed that, the earthquake occurrence probability for the northern region is much lower than the southern region. It may be due to the frequent occurrence of earthquakes in the southern part of California.

The few drawbacks of our study are that earthquakes depend on a variety of dynamic characteristics that cannot be fit to the model; therefore there is plenty of room to research and add new features to improve the model's prediction. The same thing we will strive to incorporate more features in our future work so that the model's reliance on the dynamic parameters becomes more significant.

6 Conclusion

Earthquakes destroy infrastructure and kill millions. There are no warning signs for earthquakes, and researchers are unable to identify precursors. As a result, an earthquake prediction technique has emerged as a critical need. In this work, *Shock-Alert*, an end-to-end framework is proposed to predict earthquakes for the future month with the specified location and severity. We leverage a multi-output parallel block to forecast and classify earthquakes, respectively, utilizing a transformer and a convolution network to extract spatio-temporal correlations. The proposed architecture is been compared with the state-of-the-art model and achieved an improvement of 14.89% in accuracy and 4% in F1-score. Our proposed architecture investigates the spatial-temporal features of earthquake data, the same design can be applied to other applications where spatial-temporal features must be extracted, such as traffic prediction, weather forecasting, and early-stage pandemic analysis.

References

1. Al Banna, M.H., et al.: Attention-based bi-directional long-short term memory network for earthquake prediction. IEEE Access **9**, 56589–56603 (2021)

2. Aslam, B., Zafar, A., Qureshi, U.A., Khalil, U.: Seismic investigation of the northern part of Pakistan using the statistical and neural network algorithms. Envir. Earth Sci. **80**, 1–18 (2021)

3. Berhich, A., Belouadha, F.Z., Kabbaj, M.I.: Lstm-based earthquake prediction: enhanced time feature and data representation. Int. J. High Perform. Syst. Archit. **10**(1), 1–11 (2021)

4. Berhich, A., Belouadha, F.Z., Kabbaj, M.I.: A location-dependent earthquake prediction using recurrent neural network algorithms. Soil Dyn. Earthq. Eng. **161**, 107389 (2022)

5. Bhumika, Das, D.: Deep learning based urban anomaly prediction from spatiotemporal data. In: Joint European Conference on Machine Learning and Knowledge Discovery in Databases, pp. 242–257. Springer (2022)

6. Cho, K., et al.: Learning phrase representations using RNN encoder-decoder for statistical machine translation. arXiv preprint arXiv:1406.1078 (2014)

7. Dehghani, H., Fadaee, M.J.: Probabilistic prediction of earthquake by bivariate distribution. Asian J. Civil Eng. **21**(6), 977–983 (2020). https://doi.org/10.1007/s42107-020-00254-y

8. Hasan Al Banna, M., Ghosh, T., Taher, K.A., Kaiser, M.S., Mahmud, M.: An earthquake prediction system for Bangladesh using deep long short-term memory architecture. In: Intelligent Systems: Proceedings of ICMIB 2020, pp. 465–476. Springer (2021)

9. Kaushal, A., Gupta, A.K., Sehgal, V.K.: Earthquake prediction optimization using deep learning hybrid RNN-LSTM model for seismicity analysis. Soil Dyn. Earthq. Eng. **195**, 109432 (2025)

10. Kavianpour, P., Kavianpour, M., Jahani, E., Ramezani, A.: A CNN-BILSTM model with attention mechanism for earthquake prediction. arXiv preprint arXiv:2112.13444 (2021)

11. Laurenti, L., Tinti, E., Galasso, F., Franco, L., Marone, C.: Deep learning for laboratory earthquake prediction and autoregressive forecasting of fault zone stress. Earth Planet. Sci. Lett. **598**, 117825 (2022)

12. Li, R., Lu, X., Li, S., Yang, H., Qiu, J., Zhang, L.: Dlep: A deep learning model for earthquake prediction. In: 2020 International Joint Conference on Neural Networks (IJCNN), pp. 1–8. IEEE (2020)

13. Li, W., et al.: Epick: Attention-based multi-scale UNET for earthquake detection and seismic phase picking. Front. Earth Sci. **10**, 2075 (2022)

14. Mahmoudi, J., Arjomand, M.A., Rezaei, M., Mohammadi, M.H.: Predicting the earthquake magnitude using the multilayer perceptron neural network with two hidden layers. Civil Eng. J. **2**(1), 1–12 (2016)

15. Mousavi, S.M., Ellsworth, W.L., Zhu, W., Chuang, L.Y., Beroza, G.C.: Earthquake transformer–an attentive deep-learning model for simultaneous earthquake detection and phase picking. Nat. Commun. **11**(1), 3952 (2020)

16. Narayanakumar, S., Raja, K.: A bp artificial neural network model for earthquake magnitude prediction in Himalayas, India. Circuits Syst. **7**(11), 3456–3468 (2016)

17. Nicolis, O., Plaza, F., Salas, R.: Prediction of intensity and location of seismic events using deep learning. Spatial Stat. **42**, 100442 (2021)

18. Vardaan, K., Bhandarkar, T., Satish, N., Sridhar, S., Sivakumar, R., Ghosh, S.: Earthquake trend prediction using long short-term memory RNN. Int. J. Electr. Comput. Eng. **9**(2), 1304–1312 (2019)
19. Vaswani, A., et al.: Attention is all you need. Adv. Neural Inf. Process. Syst. **30** (2017)
20. Wang, Q., Guo, Y., Yu, L., Li, P.: Earthquake prediction based on SPATIO-temporal data mining: an LSTM network approach. IEEE Trans. Emerg. Top. Comput. **8**(1), 148–158 (2017)
21. Yavas, C.E., Chen, L., Kadlec, C., Ji, Y.: Improving earthquake prediction accuracy in Los Angeles with machine learning. Sci. Rep. **14**(1), 24440 (2024)
22. Zhang, B., Hu, Z., Wu, P., Huang, H., Xiang, J.: Ept: A data-driven transformer model for earthquake prediction. Eng. Appl. Artif. Intell. **123**, 106176 (2023)
23. Zhang, J., Sun, H., Yuan, W., Yang, C., Xue, Y.: Post-stack impedance inversion based on SPATIO-temporal neural network. IEEE Geosci. Remote Sens. Lett. **19**, 1–5 (2022)

Author Index